Letters and Diaries of
Kathleen Ferrier

Kathleen Ferrier, photographed by Norman Parkinson for *Vogue* magazine, 20th September 1950

Letters and Diaries of Kathleen Ferrier

Kleuer Kaff

REVISED EDITION

EDITED BY
Christopher Fifield

THE BOYDELL PRESS

First published 2003
The Boydell Press, Woodbridge
Revised edition 2011

ISBN 978 1 84383 091 7

The Boydell Press is an imprint of Boydell & Brewer Ltd
PO Box 9, Woodbridge, Suffolk IP12 3DF, UK
and of Boydell & Brewer Inc.
668 Mount Hope Ave, Rochester, NY 14620, USA
website: www.boydellandbrewer.com

A catalogue record for this book is available
from the British Library

The publisher has no responsibility for the continued existence or accuracy of
URLs for external or third-party internet websites referred to in this book,
and does not guarantee that any content on such websites is,
or will remain, accurate or appropriate.

Papers used by Boydell & Brewer Ltd are natural, recyclable products
made from wood grown in sustainable forests

Printed in Great Britain by
CPI Group (UK) Ltd, Croydon, CR0 4YY

'She should be remembered in a major key' – Bruno Walter

For Anna, Robin and Elodie

Contents

Illustrations

(Plates 1–16 are between pages 268 and 269)

Preface and Acknowledgements

Writing the history of a music agency (*Ibbs and Tillett. The Rise and Fall of a Musical Empire*, 2005), I came across correspondence between the firm and one of its sole artists, the singer Kathleen Ferrier, much of it hitherto unpublished. The letters peel away the layers of a musician's life and career in England during the Second World War and its immediate aftermath. What might appear on the surface to be nothing more than the mundane workings of such a firm (including negotiations, bookings, programmes, contracts, availability and fees), in fact reveal not only efficiency but also the far-sightedness, sensitivity, tact and business acumen required in the three-way flow between agent, artist and client. In the artistic world where tempers can easily fray, Kathleen's temperament and sense of humour produced plenty of light-hearted moments. Her personality was a mixture of extreme modesty and self-determined ambition, and of selflessness and stubbornness. On the one hand she could not believe her luck to have come so far so soon, 'from Carlisle to Covent Garden in five years', on the other she knew exactly where she stood in the music profession both nationally and internationally, and would not be deflected into musical territory in which she knew her voice and her persona would neither fit nor stand scrutiny. Her life was brief, far too brief, and the end was cruelly tragic, but it was only in the last year that she began to lose heart when others had given up hope long before. She must have been fun to know and, from these surviving letters and diaries, what emerges is a sunny picture in a gloomy landscape. It is hard to describe her voice, for 'a voice is a person' according to tenor Peter Pears, and how right he was. Nevertheless some images do come near to describing her voice, the touch of plush velvet, the colour of a rich claret, or the unbroken column of milk poured into the corner of a bar of well-known chocolate seen on advertising hoardings – a creamy picture depicting a creamy sound.

For the first four decades of the 20th century, the typical contralto voice was that of Clara Butt, Ernestine Schumann-Heink, Edna Thornton, Sigrid Onégin, Muriel Foster, Louise Kirkby Lunn and Marian Anderson. Even today their names evoke a regal image and a statuesque presence, but Kathleen Ferrier seemed to change all that. In her own day she joined the ranks of Astra Desmond, Muriel Brunskill, Margaret Balfour and Gladys Ripley, while after her came Constance Shacklock, Norma Procter and Helen Watts before the contralto was replaced by the mezzo-soprano in the 1970s. The contralto sound became and remains unfashionable because of a desire to 'feminise' the voice, getting away from either the trouser roles (Cherubino or Octavian) or the character roles (grandmothers, soothsayers, fortune tellers, witches and so on) in opera. Singers and their teachers push the voice up and we now have hybrid sopranos, focusing more on the brighter sound of the higher *tessitura* than the rich textures of the middle and lower ranges. It is true that initially Kathleen Ferrier had problems with the uppermost notes of her voice. She was the first to admit as much, and we know how at first she lacked the courage to tackle the climactic top A in the rape scene in Britten's *Rape of Lucretia* or the Angel's dramatic 'Alleluia' towards the end of Elgar's *Dream of Gerontius*. It was Sir John Barbirolli who helped her to extend the voice upwards. He urged her to sing French music by Chausson, and then those critically necessary notes above the stave (F to A) came more easily. Once the problems were solved, the voice was free to roam over a two-octave-plus range.

One of the many who have helped me in my task of gathering material for this book is Kathleen Ferrier's god-daughter, Kathleen Hopcroft. Born Kathleen Mary Vincent, she bears both the Christian names of her godmother. She is the daughter of Harry Vincent, a shoemaker from the Potteries who not only became a close friend of the singer, but provided many opportunities for her to sing there through the wartime concerts he organised for the Council for the Encouragement of Music and the Arts. CEMA existed for ten years, from 1942 until 1952, after which it became the Arts Council. Its Regional Director Tom Harrison described Vincent, who died in 1957, as "a remarkable man with a great enthusiasm and knowledge of music". Kathleen Ferrier made regular appearances in this North Staffordshire area, remaining grateful and loyal to Vincent and his Etruscan Choral Society. She performed in recitals and oratorio concerts in the Municipal Hall in Newcastle-under-Lyme, the Victoria Hall in Hanley (concerts by the Ceramic Choir), and the Etruscan Philharmonic Hall. This last building, seating 130, was opened on 23rd March 1945 and in 1955, two years after her death, it was renamed the Kathleen Ferrier Memorial Hall. The first recital in the rededicated hall was appropriately given by two of the singer's friends, the soprano Ena Mitchell and Kathleen's long-serving accompanist Phyllis Spurr. It was demolished in 1973 to make way for road development.

The main topic of the small number of the surviving letters and cards to Harry Vincent and his family is her god-daughter, 'my poppet' who was one of many children upon whom Kathleen lavished affection. Another was Christopher, son of Alison Milne, second violinist in Ruth Pearl's String Quartet. In the absence of any children of her own, Kathleen doted on those of her close friends. The silver propelling pencil mentioned in her letter (10th April 1950) is still owned by Kathleen Hopcroft, while the anticipated present mentioned three months later (22nd July 1950) became a christening mug. Kathleen tended to meet her god-daughter when she was singing in the area, though there was one trip made by the Vincent family to London which included tea at 2 Frognal Mansions, on 29th December 1951. Though barely 2½ years of age, Kathleen remembers to this day how she sat on the floor underneath the grand piano while her godmother sang to the family.

Some today may consider Kathleen Ferrier's voice an acquired taste, but in the music to which it was ideally suited, particularly that of Brahms, Elgar, Mahler and in folksongs, it remains unique. No contralto before or since can stand comparison. Until now Kathleen Ferrier has been a voice, but through these pages of letters and diaries we get to know the person.

My thanks go to Bruce Phillips for proposing publication of the book, and to Caroline Palmer and Michael Middeke, my editors of the respective editions. I thank Paul Strang and the Tillett Trust for allowing publication of letters from Kathleen to Ibbs and Tillett. Without the help and patient response from key figures in the town of Blackburn, writing this book would not have been possible. I gratefully acknowledge permission received from the Director of the Museum and Art Gallery to plunder the archive for its letters, photographs and diaries. To the Museum's Archivist Rebecca Hill and her successor Vinai Solanki, both of whom dealt with me in the most efficient manner, I offer thanks for endlessly running errands on my behalf. The Kathleen Ferrier Society is also based in Blackburn, and its joint Chairman, Sylvia Alexander, was an invaluable source of help. The two executors of the Ferrier estate, Richard Robinson and David Heather, kindly gave essential permission for the project, while David, a relative of Kathleen Ferrier, also took it upon himself to track down my favourite photograph of her which adorns the cover and frontispiece. As to sources of letters held elsewhere, I am grateful to the following institutions for allowing me to reproduce them in full: British Library Music Collections (Add 52364 Folios 89–91B – to Rutland Boughton), Arts Council of Great Britain at the Victoria and Albert Museum (ACGB/50/203 – to Steuart Wilson), City of London, London Metropolitan Archives (CLA/059/01/001/11 – to Maurice Cole), National Library of Canada (to John Newmark), Music Division and Reprography Services, Music Division of New York Public Library (to Bruno Walter) with special mention of Erik Ryding for steering me there and Dan Franklin Smith for copying them for me, to Julia Aries, Archivist at Glyndebourne Festival Opera, whose indefatigable efforts produced remarkable results, and to Kenneth Dunn, who supplied the letter to Isobel Dunlop with the permission of the Trustees of the National Library of Scotland. I also offer grateful thanks to the Britten-Pears Library, Aldeburgh for supplying Kathleen's letters to Benjamin Britten and Peter Pears, while the BBC Written Archives Centre at Caversham generously gave permission to quote the two audition reports (file reference RCONT 1 Kathleen Ferrier File 1 1942–1946) and, in this new edition, the extant correspondence between the singer and the Corporation 1941–1953. I also thank Peter Land (letters to Maurice Jacobson and Edward Isaacs), while Roger Gross, a New York dealer in music ephemera, and Richard Davie of International Autograph Auctions kindly supplied either photographs or letters.

Many others have helped; the late Moran Caplat and Laura Cooper recounted their memories of Kathleen, Esmerelda Martin supplied letters to Marius Flothuis, while Paula Johnson and her father Michael guided me through Kathleen's friendship with John Francis. I am grateful to fellow authors Maurice Leonard and Michael Kennedy for permission to plunder their biographies of Kathleen and Barbirolli respectively. I refer readers to Paul Campion's updated discography of the singer, which remains a classic of its genre. Simon Bainbridge identified song titles for the index, while errors have been corrected thanks to Charles Corp's encyclopaedic knowledge of singers and singing, not forgetting the material he supplied from Isobel Baillie's unpublished diaries. June Butcher, former clinical haematologist at University College Hospital, who regularly took Kathleen's blood between 1951 and 1953, identified her various medical colleagues of the day, and Clare Terrell helpfully identified the various diary references to her parents, whether Doctor Gwen or Doctor Reginald Hilton.

This revised edition of the *Letters and Diaries of Kathleen Ferrier* is larger than the original publication in 2003 by more than seventy letters. Among those newly-discovered, some came from Graham Lloyd and Ian Venables (letter to Leslie Walters), Shirley Tipping (letter to Henry Z. Steinway), Penny Robinson (who found letters to F.A. Kenmir at Spennymoor in a copy of Winifred Ferrier's biography of her sister), while David Tidboald and the late Catherine, Lady Henderson very kindly sent me copies of personal letters they had received from Kathleen. I am grateful to Elizabeth Dunlop and Susan Parmenter for their research on my behalf in Scotland. At least ten letters came up at Sotheby's for auction at the end of 2009. They were part of the late Peter Diamand's estate and, in a fast-moving operation, some members of the Kathleen Ferrier Society put together a sum which, together with a generous matching amount from the Blackburn Museum and Art Gallery, secured their purchase and safe deposition in the Ferrier Archive located there. They are all included in this edition.

Kathleen's own report to the magazine of her *alma mater*, Blackburn High School in 1948 covering September 1947 to February 1948 is reproduced for the convenience of those who have not read Winifred's 1955 biography. I have also included Kathleen's contract with Glyndebourne for *Rape of Lucretia* in 1946, which gives an insight into the demands placed upon singers, particularly those at the start of their careers, and opens further windows on music-making in the immediate aftermath of the Second World War.

Anthony Shuttleworth's immense knowledge of Kathleen's repertoire and his own scrupulous research into her performances helped substantially to put the letters and diaries into context. Finally my sincere thanks go to my friend from Manchester University days, Harry Watkins. As my unofficial sub-editor he has spent countless hours reading drafts of the book, refining details and making suggestions. We have spent hours on the telephone and exchanging emails, trying to solve many mysteries and conundrums including those caused by Kathleen's handwriting.

I may be too young to have known Kathleen Ferrier (I was eight when she died) but, having heard that unique voice, somehow life for me was never the same again, and so it should be for all of us forever, or better still as she sang it, 'Ewig...ewig...ewig'.

Editorial Conventions

No attempt has been made to censor Kathleen Ferrier's letters or diaries, and the reader should bear in mind that they contain words which, in the late 1940s and early 1950s, did not necessarily mean or imply what they may today. Some small changes have been made in order to produce consistency in spelling of names, or to correct grammar or factual errors, all to avoid breaking the flow of her writing with the intrusive use of the editorial *sic*. Any need for clarification is indicated between square brackets [ ]. Bold type is used in the draft of a letter to her American manager to indicate words or phrases scored through. Some letters are no longer extant and have had to be reconstructed from books, her only known letter to her teacher Roy Henderson being the most complex example, but apart from editorial linking text added between [ ], words in Roman are Kathleen's. None of the enclosures referred to in some of the letters (particularly those sent to her agents Ibbs and Tillett), has survived. Those items appear to have been newspaper reviews collected during her American tours, or letters enquiring after her services from British music clubs and choral societies.

As far as the diaries are concerned, some omissions have been made where there is no entry for that day, and where entries or parts of entries are just financial outgoings. Money has been left in its pre-decimalisation form of pounds, shillings and pence, but for the benefit of those unfamiliar with such sums the following illustrations may help:

> sixpence (6d) = 2½p, a shilling (1/-) = 5p, half a crown or two shillings and sixpence (2/6d) = 12½p, ten shillings (10/-) = 50p, twelve and sixpence (12/6d) = 62½p; for example £35 15s 6d = £35.77½p

In the diaries, bold type is used for engagements cancelled as a result of a serious bout of pneumonia in 1943 and those affected by her final illness, diagnosed in March 1951. Entries appear in normal type where she herself has written the word 'cancelled'. At the back of the diary for 1943 there is a list of Kathleen's repertoire as it was in that year, and this possibly formed the basis for the one in Winifred's biography of her sister. Kathleen's 1943 list has been placed in this book at the end of the Index of Works. Blank pages at the beginning and end of this 1943 diary are filled with 'things to do', such as 'Elgar returned, 2 stockings collected. Rations. P.O. money out. Bag to station. Enquire st[atio]n to Lldno [Llandudno]. Enquire re Chester concert', as well as some names and addresses of accommodation in the various towns and cities where she sang, such as Cardiff, Exeter, Darlington and Swansea. There is also the curious instruction 'shoot out right cuff and pass left hand through hair'.

Strange as it may seem in the middle of the Second World War, the 1942 diary reveals that Kathleen was receiving German tuition in Carlisle. As far as one can tell, her German Lieder repertoire was sung in English during the war years but, after she met Bruno Walter on 4th November 1946 and her German (domiciled Canadian) accompanist John Newmark in America in 1949, Kathleen began to sing in German and use the original titles. These songs have therefore been indexed using both English and German versions.

The contents of the diaries have been expanded in this edition to include train times and hotel names. Kathleen usually placed the latter in the lower right-hand corner of the date square, and to avoid confusion that they might be part of her diary commentary, they appear here in italics. Their inclusion also gives a much clearer picture of the strains and stresses of wartime travel and her piti-less schedule. It is no wonder that she opted for the life of 'a lone she-wolf' after she and her husband parted. There was no time for domesticity and, judging by her itineraries, it would have been the Buffet Room on Crewe station where she would have had to meet her husband or lover for a *Brief Encounter*.

The Letters

Introduction: The Letters

On 8th October 1953 the greatest lyric contralto Britain has ever produced died of cancer after a career which lasted barely ten years. She was Kathleen Ferrier and her name was known to millions. As a young boy in the early 1950s, I can remember listening to the radio on days off school and hearing her sing 'What is Life?', 'Blow the Wind Southerly' or 'The Keel Row' on the Light Programme in the morning, while that same evening she might well have been heard on the more serious Third Programme singing *Messiah* or *Dream of Gerontius* from the Albert Hall, or giving a song recital from Broadcasting House on the Home Service. So, if the breadth of her repertoire might be described as limited compared to a soprano (rather than by any reluctance on her part to learn new works), the range of its appeal was widespread. Nearly six decades after her premature death, her name lives on, but it means different things to different generations. My illustrated talk, 'The Life and Voice of Kathleen Ferrier', has been given 160 times over the past eight years, but it is requested by those now in retirement; to a younger generation, even of musicians, Kathleen Ferrier is associated with the International Singing Competition bearing her name since it began in 1956, and which regrettably is rarely entered or won by a contralto.

This book is not a biography. There have been three since her death as well as a *Memoir* to which her closest artistic friends contributed, among them conductors Sir John Barbirolli and Bruno Walter, critic Neville Cardus and composer Benjamin Britten. Nor does this book list her recordings as these have been well documented in recent years. It is simply a collection of letters, most of which Kathleen Ferrier wrote between 1940 and 1953, to close friends, relatives, agents, managers, organisers, musicians and fans both at home and abroad; her surviving diaries (1942–1953); letters to and from the BBC; and some final tributes. Once each year is introduced there is no need for further comment, as her bluntly honest, open-hearted Northern character speaks for itself.

In the year of her centenary, 2012, and with the main players removed from life's stage (her sister Winifred died in 1995), there remain many unanswered questions including missing letters and possibly at least one diary (1941). There was definitely a correspondence between Kathleen and Barbirolli and also with her last singing teacher, Roy Henderson. Some letters from Kathleen are quoted in part or in full in other books, or mentioned in the collection of remembrances edited by Neville Cardus, but unfortunately none of these appears to have survived despite repeated efforts to track them down. In Winifred Ferrier's biography of Kathleen there are quotations from letters, as well as complete ones, but again many others are nowhere to be found. Perhaps she destroyed them in the forty years following the writing of her biography. These have been included here as they appear in her book, as have those written by Kathleen to Barbirolli which he quotes in his contribution to the *Memoir*, or which Michael Kennedy quotes in his biography of the conductor.

Winifred tended to edit her sister's letters, cutting out some of the parts she evidently considered too outspoken or risqué. These excisions have been restored, while her unreliable dating of letters, either in her book or on the original letters where they are undated, has been corrected as accurately as possible after much sleuthing using Kathleen's diaries and other letters. As to the way Kathleen signed many of the letters: it was a three-year-old boy called Peter, the son of Kathleen's friend Wyn Hetherington (who went on to marry Kathleen's former husband Bert Wilson), who cried out 'Clever Kaff' after she had sewn a button back on to his father's coat during a picnic. She changed the spelling to 'Klever Kaff', abbreviated it further to 'K.K.' (and used it to sign her paintings), and the name stuck. Although her family and close friends (such as Benjamin Britten and Peter Pears) called her 'Kath', Barbirolli always called her 'Katie' (and she came to use for him the name by which he was known to his family, 'Tita').

Although by 1939 she had a busy singing career in the north of England, she needed to come to London and turn professional. On Sir Malcolm Sargent's recommendation she was auditioned by John Tillett, General Manager of the agents Ibbs and Tillett, at the Wigmore Hall on 9th July 1942. Once accepted, she was promoted first in Britain, then in Europe as soon as musical activities were restarted after the war in 1945 (she became particularly popular in Holland and France), and in America from 1948. After John Tillett's death in July 1948, his widow Emmie took over Ferrier's career for the remaining five years of the singer's brief life. In one letter Kathleen described Mrs Tillett as her 'manager', a word which would have been anathema to the formidable Emmie. In carrying on her late husband's business practice, she eschewed the personal management of artists in favour of a booking agency service to clients, Britain's flourishing amateur-run music clubs and choral societies, as well as the professional festivals and orchestras, radio, recording and opera. Because both Emmie and Kathleen were living in London and communicated by telephone, letters were only sent when Kathleen was abroad. This was also the case with those to Winifred, her father William (Pop) cared for by her secretary Paddy Jewett, and those to her accompanist John Newmark when he was back in Canada rather than touring with her in the United States. She made friends on tour, and Benita and Bill Cress of La Crosse, Wisconsin became particular favourites to the end, so letters to them have survived ('La X' was her abbreviation for their home town). One particular fan among many was another American woman, Laura Cooper, to whom Kathleen wrote between 1949 and 1953. They met just once at the 1952 Edinburgh Festival, Kathleen's last. Half a century later, during the period November 2002 and April 2004, Miss Cooper wrote to me more than once about their encounter.

> From 1948 to 1951 I lived in New York City, and at the time of Kathleen's debut with Bruno Walter and the New York Philharmonic I was working for Columbia Artists Management, her American agents. In 1947 I heard a radio broadcast of Pergolesi's *Stabat Mater*, and was amazed by the voice and artistry of the contralto soloist. I immediately began collecting Kathleen's records, and when I heard that she was to sing *Das Lied von der Erde* with the Philharmonic in January 1948, I was utterly thrilled.

Since I worked for her agents, I was able to obtain the name and address of the hotel where she was staying, and I sent her some flowers and a note welcoming her to the US, and my best wishes for her success. I subsequently attended all six of her New York concerts and each time I wrote her a letter expressing my deep appreciation of her work. At first I was captivated by a disembodied voice, but later when I saw her in person, by the warmth and magnetism of her personality. She invited me to the Green Room to meet her, but I was too shy and overawed.

In 1951 I moved to California for a job as a high school teacher. I had heard about her illness, and I decided to save as much money as possible so that I could go to Europe in the summer of 1952. I made several telephone calls to Kathleen both in London and in Edinburgh, but we did not finally meet until the Festival was over and we were both scheduled to depart.

I had learned of the exact nature of her illness in a record shop in Basle, Switzerland. I was purchasing records of both Kathleen and Maria Cebotari, who had died of breast cancer a couple of years earlier. The sales clerk commented, 'Isn't it sad that Ferrier has the same illness?', and this gave an added urgency to the meeting. We had an appointment to meet at the *George* Hotel early in the Festival [there were several attempts at a meeting, see diary entries for 29th, 30th August and 1st September 1952], but a last minute rehearsal of the *Liebeslieder Walzer* caused Kathleen to cancel. Originally I planned to return home after that concert, but I decided to stay on and luckily was able to obtain last-minute tickets for both the *Dream of Gerontius* and the *Messiah*. I am eternally grateful for that.

We met in front of the *George* Hotel and subsequently had a drink and visited for about half an hour in the lobby [see diary entry for 7th September 1952]. She spoke of Thomas Scherman and the Little Orchestra Society and his keen desire for her to return to New York. She also spoke very enthusiastically about Irmgard Seefried. Kathleen had bought a newspaper upon entering the hotel, but did not have the exact change to pay for it. When we left, she said, 'I must remember to pay the man his sixpence'. She was so thoughtful and down-to-earth.

When I saw her, she looked pale and exhausted after the Festival, and I noticed some blemishes on her face, as she was wearing no makeup. I said 'Goodbye' to her outside the hotel, but I knew that it was a final farewell. I managed to remain smiling and cheerful until I turned my back and then the tears started flowing down my cheeks. I have never felt more desolate. I think she knew that I truly loved her, and I hope that my flowers and letters were able to bolster her spirits.

Not only do the letters and diaries give a vivid picture of wartime Britain, they go on to describe the immediate post-war days with their acute shortages, drab greyness and strictly controlled regulations. They also highlight the marked difference in lifestyle, which Kathleen experienced in the autumn of 1946 on a tour to Holland (her first-ever trip abroad) with Britten's *Rape of Lucretia*. Similarly once the RMS *Queen Elizabeth* or *Queen Mary* were barely offshore from Southampton with Kathleen aboard for her annual visit to America (she made three trips between 1948 and 1950), the stark contrast between the luxurious opulence on board these palatial ships and the austerity of the land she had just left is vividly described in her letters home. Such was her *naïveté* that it never occurred to her that the family she left behind might have been not only salivating at the menus she listed, but also harbouring resentment at her new circumstances. In fact this was not the case, for all who knew her and loved her could not help but rejoice in her happiness and celebrate in her triumph. Parcels sent from friends in America containing food, nylons and other gifts were received like manna from heaven at Christmas, including the last one she celebrated in 1952. When she herself was abroad, Kathleen sent back parcels to her family, and when she could send cash it was preceded by a coded message one letter ahead. This would contain the euphemistic instruction to look out for 'photographs' in the next envelope. Her letters are filled to the brim with a sense of joy and childish pleasure at the hospitality and luxurious gifts with which she was showered as her fame quickly grew. This was, however, after an appallingly grim first tour of urban and rural America when she had to establish herself with gritty determination in her dealings with management, drawing on her Lancashire background to get her through.

Listening to the one surviving interview she gave (Canadian Broadcasting Company, 10th March 1950) and the broadcast she made of her impressions of the Edinburgh Festival (BBC, 11th September 1949), it is clear from the delivery in her deep, resonant voice that she had taken elocution lessons. Her inflexions recall those black and white films made at Pinewood or Shepperton Studios, in which the girls are 'heppy' and the streets are 'gay'. She has those clipped, stilted mannerisms and a flat-sounding voice which were the style of the day in news-reels or at the BBC, and indeed her voice has an air of nervous tension before the microphone. Her enunciation of the text in her singing was always of the highest, impeccable standard, whether in Italian, French, German or her native English. When Barbirolli insisted that she learn Chausson's *Poème de l'amour et de la mer* to expand her French repertoire and extend the upper range of her voice, she reluctantly agreed. 'Accept Chausson,' she cabled her agent Emmie Tillett. 'Tell Sir John to play loudly to cover my Lancashire accent.' While this accent was virtually eradicated in her singing, nothing could stop her personality shining through in her letters. Neither do they show any sign of inhibition or restraint. Her irrepressible Rabelaisian humour, much of it lavatorial and derived from bodily functions, is given full rein. Barbirolli asked if she was in any discomfort following one of her operations. 'I'm fine,' she replied. 'Farting freely!' She had a ribald, raunchy sense of fun. At a post-recording dinner for Decca she rose and gave an impromptu toast: 'Here's to the young girl on the hill. If she won't, her sister will. Here's to her sister!' Then there was this little favourite:

> Here's to love.
> Ain't love grand?
> Just got a divorce
> From my old man
>
> Ain't stopped laughing
> Since Judge's decision.

'Cos he's got the kids,
And the kids ain't his'n!

In her letters she loved to include Spoonerisms such as 'ruddy blush', 'pickled tink' or 'woody blunders' and she would indulge in wordplay such as 'cupeliar' for 'peculiar'. In music the song 'Mad Bess' becomes 'Bad Mess', Mendelssohn's aria from *Elijah* 'O rest in the Lord' is 'O rust in the lard', Brahms' Alto Rhapsody is 'Brahms' Raspberry' while 'Land of Soap and Water' requires no further explanation. On a spare page of her 1944 diary she wrote (for further use no doubt), 'Pray silence for His Goose the Drake of Portland', and (parodying Delius' orchestral work) 'On cooking the first hero in Spring'. One 'bollocks' and several 'bloodys' notwithstanding, she tends to temper her swear words by modifying the spelling such as 'barstewards' or 'bluidy', and has a delightful tendency to explode her enthusiasms with the prefix 'Whatta-', 'Gee whiz' (always one z, never two) or the ubiquitous 'Whoopee!' She loved food, drink, and parties. What her letters lack in commas (and the shortage of them is as acute as that of butter or meat in post-war Britain) she more than makes up for in dashes and exclamation marks. Her vocabulary, which includes the occasional Latin phrase such as *Deo Volente* (or 'God willing', abbreviated to D.V.), has dated charm and she uses words such as a 'limb' (a mischievous imp when describing a child), 'giddy' or 'gay', in this last instance literally meaning 'happy' with none of today's implications.

She tended to have the odd day on tour or at home when she could catch up with letter-writing, so there is an inevitable degree of repetition as she reports her latest success or new experience to her correspondents, but even so she expresses them in different ways to different people so they bear repetition. There are no letters before 1940 and the balance of the numbers which have survived over the next thirteen years is far from even. The more she toured abroad, the more she wrote back home but, considering that her financial outgoings recorded a substantial expense for 'Stamps', one can only conclude that many more letters have not survived than have. After the initial chapter covering the eight years 1940–1947, each year then has its own chapter, starting with a résumé of her musical activities. The final year includes a handful of letters written by two close friends because Kathleen was too ill to write. Bernadine (Bernie) Hammond had been taken on as a secretary in a career change from nursing, but ironically it was all too soon before her former skills were called upon once again. Yvonne Hamilton, wife of the publisher Hamish (Jamie) Hamilton and who lived opposite Kathleen for the few weeks she resided at 40 Hamilton Terrace in the summer of 1953, was a close friend of Bruno Walter, to whom she had reported the first news of their mutual friend's illness two year's earlier.

Kathleen Ferrier apparently lived in fear of the disease which killed her. In an interview with Maurice Leonard, Winifred said that, as a child, Kathleen was distressed by a woman dying painfully of cancer in their street (Lynwood Road) in Blackburn, and some ten years before her death Kathleen mentioned to Winifred an accidental blow to her left breast (the primary seat of her cancer) which she had received from her husband's elbow shortly after their marriage. In the 1950s cancer was a disease which attracted social opprobrium, and was rarely, if ever, discussed in public. As far as her professional plans were concerned, it must have been hard to judge how far ahead she should commit herself, and to whom and to what extent her illness should be revealed, even though it appears in retrospect that the music profession was aware of what was going on as soon as she had undergone her first operation in the spring of 1951. Tours were generally planned about a year in advance so the years 1951, 1952 and 1953 became increasingly prone to cancellations as the disease worsened. Inevitably gossip and rumour fuelled leaks to managements, music societies and the press, particularly in America despite attempts by Kathleen, her managers and trusted friends to stop, or at least control them.

She maintained a doggedly positive outlook, despite what she must have inwardly suspected and dreaded each time she was called back to hospital for further treatment – only once does her diary cry out in despair 'so depressed'. Her consultant physician Reginald Hilton (himself an amateur violinist and owner of a Stradivarius) refused to allow her to travel beyond his medical orbit, so America became off-limits from March 1951. With the diagnosis confirmed her letters seem to convey relief to be at home, safe from inclement weather (she was prone to the effects of draughts and the cold), the rigours of train travel and the constant touring which she had undertaken from as far back as her days with CEMA (Council for the Encouragement of Music and the Arts). She accepted Hilton's treatment unreservedly. Her constant tiredness (which went back to 1948) worsened once radiotherapy began in the spring of 1951 following the drastic surgery about which she wrote openly to her closest friends. She brushed this weariness aside, dismissing it self-deprecatingly as an inclination to inherent laziness, but this was untrue.

As suspicions or knowledge of her illness grew among her friends and acquaintances, so the support she was given was always solid and genuinely solicitous; everyone rallied to her side. In the world of music, death among those called too soon was becoming too frequent and too unwelcome a caller. The 1940s had already claimed the conductor Leslie Heward and singer Maria Cebotari. In the 1950s there were victims of an airplane crash (violinist Ginette Neveu), a car accident (horn player Dennis Brain), by suicide (pianist Noel Mewton-Wood) and from cancer, Gladys Ripley, who was another contralto with a glorious voice but overshadowed by Kathleen Ferrier. Yet somehow Kathleen's death touched the hearts of all from royalty, who knew her, to those listeners of 'Housewives' Choice', who felt they knew her. Ten years after her death Winifred received a letter from someone in Colombo, Ceylon, addressed simply 'To Somebody who knew Kathleen Ferrier, England'. The impact of Kathleen's death had a poignancy all of its own and it lay not only in her persona but also in the voice itself, which was suffused with a glow and burnished warmth. She was determined to use her voice to bring happiness to millions, and possessed an indefinable other-worldliness which not only transfigured her but also transported all those who heard her.

Shortly before the first edition of this book was published in 2003, the Barbirolli Society together with the BBC released a hitherto unknown recording of her singing Elgar's 'Land of Hope and Glory' at the re-opening of Manchester's restored Free Trade Hall in November 1951. Soon after the start, through the hiss and crackle of the damaged disc, emerges the glorious sound of <u>that</u> voice, not the sound of Clara Butt (Barbirolli would not have been interested in Kathleen if her voice was an 'oratorio contralto – that queer and almost bovine monstrosity so beloved of our grandfathers') but a silky, even voice which comes from the very soul of her being. After the introduction she eases effortlessly into the famous song, and the way she produces the initial consonant 'L' of the word 'Land' is done in a manner which would surely have pleased Elgar himself. Above all he would have appreciated the sheer musicality of her performance. The French baritone Pierre Bernac in his reply (11th May 1955) to a letter from Winifred, who was gathering memories of Kathleen for her book, marvelled at 'the care and the scruple with which she approached each phrase, each word, each note'. Unlike German and Italian, in which she had already been coached for some years, French was not Kathleen's strongest suit when it came to foreign languages, so after Barbirolli persuaded her to learn Chausson's *Poème de l'amour et de la mer*, it was with Bernac that she worked, as he described further to Winifred:

> I still remember going through it in Edinburgh during the Festival of 1951 on the piano of the Insititut Français. Poulenc was playing. How thrilling it was for me to hear gradually the music and the poem being magnified by this glorious voice and this incomparable musicianship.

Among musicians, Kathleen had closest contact either with her regular accompanists (Gerald Moore, Phyllis Spurr and John Newmark) or her conductors. Of the latter, Sir John Barbirolli (whom she met for the first time on 8th December 1944) and Bruno Walter (on 4th November 1946) were her favourites, but she also worked with many others including Ernest Ansermet, Eduard van Beinum, Sir Adrian Boult, Basil Cameron, Meredith Davies, Charles Groves, Herbert von Karajan, Otto Klemperer (her least favourite), Clemens Krauss, Josef Krips, Rafael Kubelik, Pierre Monteux, Clarence Raybould, Fritz Reiner, Sir Malcolm Sargent, Fritz Stiedry and George Szell. A notable absentee from this list was Sir Thomas Beecham, for whom she did not care very much and with whom she was to work just once. This was at the Leeds Festival on 3rd October 1950 when she sang in Dvořák's *Stabat Mater* (see Introduction to the Diaries). Beecham was scheduled to conduct *Carmen* at John and Audrey Christie's Glyndebourne Festival in 1946, but when Kathleen was under consideration for the title role, he was very dismissive, implying that she was 'embryonic material', as this extract from a letter to Audrey from Beecham shows. It was written in his wife Betty Humby's name and is dated 3rd November 1945.

> Upon a communication from Mr [Rudolf] Bing that a conference was proposed to consider Miss Kathleen Ferrier as a likely interpreter of the principal role, my husband pointed out 1) that all the great Carmens of the world from 1875 to the present year have been sopranos, 2) that only two mezzo-sopranos have ever sung the role with a fair measure of success, 3) that no contralto has ever succeeded in doing anything with the role but make a complete ass of herself.

Needless to say Beecham fell out with John Christie, though his name recurs in 1949 when a revival of *Orfeo* was discussed. Finally, in 1950 there was a somewhat bizarre offer (which Kathleen refused) of the role of Niklaus in Michael Powell and Emeric Pressburger's film of Offenbach's *Tales of Hoffman*, which Beecham conducted.

Composers Arthur Bliss and Benjamin Britten wrote works for her. Bliss composed a *scena* called *The Enchantress* for her (see page 171), whilst Britten wrote his *Spring* Symphony, the Canticle *Abraham and Isaac* and his opera *The Rape of Lucretia*, in which she shared the title role with Nancy Evans. Apart from an early concert performance of *Carmen* and a later one of Vaughan Williams' *Riders to the Sea*, Kathleen sang in only two staged operas, Britten's *Rape of Lucretia* and Gluck's *Orfeo*. After she did so at Glyndebourne in the consecutive years 1946 and 1947, the Christies tried to tempt her with the role of Ulrica in Verdi's *Un ballo in maschera* at the 1949 Edinburgh Festival, but she politely declined. Strongly influenced by Roy Henderson's view, she recognised for herself that a weightier voice than hers was required for Verdi. Yet she did make occasional concessions, such as taking the contralto part of Maddalena in the Quartet from *Rigoletto*, a popular choice for piano-accompanied Miscellaneous Concerts such as one at Burnley on 24th October 1944. For Blackpool on 27th February 1945 she offered the duet 'Ai nostri monti' from the last act of *Il Trovatore* (with Francis Russell singing Manrico), but either Russell or those in Blackpool settled for the safer option of 'It is the merry month of May' from Edward German's *Merrie England*.

Glyndebourne proposed a new production of Gluck's *Orfeo* for her during the Festival of 1950, as Moran Caplat (Rudolf Bing's successor as General Manager) wrote on 8th July 1949.

> Mr and Mrs Christie were thrilled with your performance of *Orfeo* in Holland, and I understand that they did vaguely mention to you that we were hoping to do *Orfeo* at Glyndebourne next year, and of course could not think of doing it without you. Plans are not yet quite definite, but it looks very likely indeed, rather more likely in fact then anything has seemed for some time.
>
> Can you be free to do about seven or eight performances between the middle of June and the end of the first week in July? We should rehearse for about three weeks before this but I do not think that Professor Ebert would feel that you need come to the early rehearsals. Sir Thomas Beecham has agreed to conduct, and we are of course planning to put right those things in the production which were not quite happy two years ago. Without you the thing would be unthinkable, so please have a look at your engagements and do your best to make it possible.

The offer came too late, for she was already booked for the 1950 Vienna Festival, but in a postscript to her reply (see her letter of 24th July 1949) she clearly encouraged Caplat to consider the possibility of 1951. Regrettably, and despite her availability, that too foundered, as Caplat wrote on 3rd October 1950.

> Just a line to tell you that we have failed again in our attempt to get together all the forces we need to do *Orfeo* in Edinburgh in 1951.

[Choreographer Kurt] Jooss is definitely not available until 1952 and we have not found a ballet group anywhere with which we are willing to risk it. As far as I am concerned (and a lot of other people too), if you are singing, the ballet is a very secondary matter, but I am sure you will agree that when we do *Orfeo* again it must be a really outstanding production in all respects, so let us keep our fingers crossed for 1952.

Another invitation politely declined came from Walter Legge in 1951, when, on Herbert von Karajan's instructions, he implored her to sing Brangäne in Wagner's *Tristan und Isolde* at the 1952 Bayreuth Festival. The two operas which she did make her own, *Lucretia* and *Orfeo*, were relatively static but became immediate successes with the public. As she herself wrote in a letter to Winifred from Holland, dated 12th July 1949 (not included in this edition because only one sentence has survived, taken from Winifred's biography): 'Last *Orfeo* tonight. I think I am very good now in it!' Opera, as she herself readily admitted, was not a medium in which she felt instinctively comfortable, not just because, in her own words, of her 'big feet' and arms which move like a 'broken down windmill', but because she felt intimidated by its conventions. Far from being attracted to the freedom of moving around a stage and the wide-ranging possibilities of physical expression with face and limbs, she preferred the more restricting alternatives of oratorio singing and the song recital. Somehow, being compelled to stand still on a stage for a song recital galvanised all the vocal emotion and facial expression she required to bond with her audience. She had no need of the operatic necessities such as costumes, make-up, lighting, scenery and props, despite the fact that performance had not always come easily to her.

Roy Henderson had already noted immaturity in her platform manner after he was asked by John Tillett to report on her performance, which he did after they had shared the stage together in Runcorn singing *Elijah* on 23rd December 1942. He found her presentation awkward, her deportment gauche and she had a tendency to bury her head in her score, so he took her in hand. She had been well-prepared by Dr John Hutchinson of Newcastle, to whom she went for lessons before and during the early years of the war, and Henderson commented on the excellence of her breathing technique and on the naturalness of the back of her mouth as a vocal cavity (the open throat down which he could have lobbed a small apple from across the room, as he told me in 1998 two years before his death at the age of 100). She had no academic background or music college training, and a career that had started at the age of thirty, which was about five years later than usual. Deprived of an education beyond the age of fourteen, Kathleen spent most of her short life either self-taught or playing catch-up thanks to the help from friends and colleagues. Nevertheless she had all the necessary equipment and, in Henderson's view, what she needed to do was to free herself from the copy and communicate with her public when she took the stage. It was not long before she had mastered it all.

1   *Letters: 1940–1947*

Kathleen Ferrier was born on 22nd April 1912 in a small village called Higher Walton, between Preston and Blackburn, Lancashire. When she was eighteen months old her family (parents and older siblings George and Winifred) moved to Blackburn, where Kathleen grew up. Because family resources had dwindled after educating Winifred and George, Kathleen had to leave school at fourteen and take her first job at the local telephone exchange as a telegram runner within the building. Her interest in music had already begun to show, so she took piano lessons from an early age and sang in local choirs together with members of her family. She participated in competitive music festivals as a pianist and did well, particularly at one in Manchester in November 1928 where she was awarded the first prize, an upright piano. By winning this regional round she was then sent to London to the finals held at the Wigmore Hall. She got nowhere, was totally overawed, and felt intimidated by her first encounter with a Steinway grand piano. The following year she was awarded her ARCM diploma, but did not get very far in the Blackpool Music Competition where she appeared in two classes but was not placed.

Blackpool Music Festival 1929
Test piece: Preludio e Toccata by Riccardo-Pick Mangiagalli (1882–1949)
Kathleen M. Ferrier, Blackburn [she was No.2 of 34 competitors]
Class 49 Pianoforte Solo (Open) at 9am in the Grand Foyer of the Opera House
Open to boys and girls over 16 and under 18 years of age.
Adjudicator: John Ireland
First Prize One Guinea and a Gold Medal presented by Messrs. Sharples Pianos Ltd.

Class 50 Pianoforte Sight Test (Open) at 2.30pm
Open to boys and girls over 16 and under 18 years of age.
Kathleen M. Ferrier, Blackburn [she was No.16 of 18 competitors]

Despite these ups and downs she went on to accompany many local musicians, began to win top prizes at local music festivals, gave a short recital on the BBC in 1930, and in 1931 gained her LRAM diploma. It was during the course of this year that she began to take tentative steps in singing and elocution but, as she had at no time received any formal musical education at a college of music, she never considered the possibility of a career in music. Her sister Winifred recalls in her biography:

> She also joined the James Street Congregational Church Choir to which Tom and Annie [Annie Chadwick, Kathleen's first singing teacher] belonged.... Kathleen sang in the choir in many performances of oratorio

and in 1931, in a performance of *Elijah* conducted by Harold Marsden, was chosen to sing in the trio 'Lift thine eyes'. 'Imagine me singing this,' she said, 'I shall never be a singer!' Before their entry, the girl sitting next to Kathleen whispered, 'Are your knees knocking?' 'Knocking,' said Kathleen, 'they're playing 'God save the King!'

In 1933 she met Bert Wilson, a bank clerk from a solid middle-class family living in Withnell Fold near Chorley. When he was transferred to the Lytham branch of his bank, Kathleen took advantage of a vacancy at the Blackpool telephone exchange and moved to lodgings in Bispham in 1934 to be near him. The following year she failed the voice trial for the new telephone service TIM, the speaking clock, which was surely a case of the Post Office shooting itself in the foot. How wonderful it would be to hear those Ferrierian tones enunciating that memorable introductory phrase 'At the third stroke it will be ...'

In October 1935 she entered the music competition at Blackpool for the first time as a singer and got nowhere, not even achieving a mention by the adjudicator Sir Richard Terry. There were two songs in the Tudor Class – by Dowland and Byrd – hence the marks being out of 200. According to the local newspaper Kathleen obtained 158 marks to the winner's 178. She also appeared in the Sight Reading Accompaniment Class, in which competitors had to sight-read the piano accompaniment for a soloist, in this case a violinist. Here she trailed the winner by only five marks, 87 *vis à vis* 92. She also entered the Open Piano Class, the test piece being Beethoven's *Moonlight* Sonata. This class was held over two sessions and Kathleen was the 40th of the 56 renditions heard by poor Frederick Dawson. The winner scored 88 marks, second 86 and third 85, all three from Huddersfield, whereas Kathleen scored 74. She managed to be in both the Tudor and the Sight Reading Classes; although they both began at 2 pm, she was 3rd to attempt the sight reading and 21st the Tudor, and the Opera House is only a couple of minutes walk from the Spanish Hall in the Winter Gardens complex. Note the calibre of adjudicators at these events.

Blackpool Music Festival 1935 October 21–26 1935 Winter Gardens
Monday October 21st in the Opera House at 2pm
Adjudicator Sir R[ichard] R. Terry
Class 4 Vocal Solo (Tudor period) (Open) Female voices. First prize £1
Ayre a) 'Go, crystal tears' by John Dowland
Ayre b) 'Though amaryllis dance in green' by William Byrd
Kathleen Ferrier, Blackpool No.21 of 24

Monday October 21st in the Spanish Hall
Class 10 Sight reading (Pianoforte accompaniment) at 2pm
Open to competitors of 18 years and over
Adjudicator Herbert Howells; solo violin James Shirley
Kathleen Ferrier, Blackpool No.3 of 26
First prize £1 (she came 8th with a mark of 87)

Wednesday October 23rd in the Grand Foyer, Opera House [2nd session] at 2pm
Adjudicator Frederick Dawson

Class 36 Pianoforte Solo (Open) Ashworth Cup
Piano sonata Op.27 No.2 *Moonlight* Beethoven
Competitors must be over 18 years of age. First prize £3
Kathleen Ferrier, Blackpool (No.40 of 56)

A month later, on 19th November 1935 at the age of 23, she married Bert Wilson at Hillside Methodist Church in the village of Brinscall in the West Pennine Moors. In 1936 Bert was promoted to manage the bank's branch at Silloth in Cumbria, to where the newly-weds moved. In keeping with the practice of the day, Kathleen had been forced to resign her job on marriage, and now busied herself giving piano lessons, accompanying the local choral society, and gradually developing her own voice. In March 1937 she entered the Carlisle Festival not only as a pianist but also as a singer, largely because her husband had dared her with the inducement of a bet of one shilling (5p). She walked off with first prize in the piano class, but not without encountering some displeasure from other candidates and their parents because, with her LRAM diploma, they considered her to be a professional competing in a distinctly amateur event. This complaint, however justified, could not be levelled against her when she also won the vocal class and the competition's silver rose bowl. When she won the Gold Medal at the 1938 Millom (Cumbria) Festival, the adjudicator's appraisal included the memorable words, 'her voice makes me imagine I am being stroked!' After Kathleen's death Neville Cardus' *Memoir* was published and Maurice Jacobson, who was one of the two adjudicators at the 1937 Carlisle Music Festival, felt it necessary to put the record straight when he wrote to Gordon Thorne, a music producer at the BBC in Manchester.

> 9th March 1955   re Cardus errors
> The famous 1937 Carlisle Rose Bowl is attributed to Dr Staton. In point of fact he wasn't there at all, and the remarks Cardus quotes relate to Workington Festival nearly two years later! I awarded Kathleen that particular Rose Bowl and was the first to launch her in many ways.
>   I coached her very much in those earlier years, made her sing in German, did her first *Frauenliebe und Leben* cycle at a Dover Music Club with shells screaming outside, did her first National Gallery etc. etc. – indeed umpteen important matters that appear nowhere in Cardus's book.

Kathleen's success began to lead to professional engagements in the north-west of England and she continued to participate in music festivals. Above all, though, she was beginning to be noticed by adjudicators, music producers for the radio, locally based conductors of choral societies, and administrators of music clubs, all of whom were now taking a hand in the next stages of what was beginning to look like a burgeoning career. In 1939 she began taking singing lessons with John Ernest Hutchinson, or 'Hutchy' as she invariably called him, an eminent teacher and adjudicator, who had awarded her the Gold Cup at the Workington Festival in 1938 when she sang 'Silent Noon' by Vaughan Williams. With the outbreak of war in September 1939, Hutchinson had to travel each week to Keswick. The Newcastle school at which he taught music had been evacuated here, and so it became a more practical proposition for Kathleen to make the short journey from Silloth to Carlisle (where Hutchinson stayed overnight) to receive her lessons. Hutchinson recognised the quality of the instrument she possessed, its range somewhat restricted at the time to two octaves (from G below the stave to G above) and with a break at the chest register which needed to be smoothed out.

When Bert was conscripted in 1941 the bank required Kathleen to vacate the house. Strains and stresses had begun to appear in their marriage, which had remained unconsummated from the start, and the relationship fell apart when he went off to war. It was dissolved without fuss in March 1947. From 1940 Kathleen was living at 23 Windermere Road, Carlisle with her father William ('Pop' or 'Pappy') and sister Winifred ('Win', 'Win'fred' or 'Toots'), now a school teacher. In 1941 she auditioned successfully for the North Western Counties division of CEMA (Council for the Encouragement of Music and the Arts), and began the rounds of factories, office canteens and army camps as a singer among the troupes of entertainers, who (like those working for ENSA) were sent to sustain the morale among civilians and soldiers alike. In December 1941 she appeared with soprano Isobel Baillie in Handel's *Messiah* with the Hallé Orchestra conducted by its former leader Alfred Barker in Chester-le-Street, an encounter which not only forged a friendship between the two singers, but which also made a deep impression upon the players and conductor alike. Barker at once intimated to Kathleen that she would have to move to London as soon as possible if she was interested in developing her professional career, a view which was also held by the conductor Malcolm Sargent when she sang to him in Manchester in May 1942. Sargent then got in touch with the agent John Tillett, who agreed to hear her sing at an audition which took place at the Wigmore Hall in London on 9th July 1942. It was almost fourteen years since she was last there, for this was where she had failed in the national competition as a pianist. The omens looked inauspicious.

Ibbs and Tillett was founded in 1906 and was soon predominant in the world of music-making in the British Isles. From the outset, its activities were largely centered on singers as the principal marketable commodity for recitals and concerts given by music clubs and choral societies, although over the years they also gathered many top calibre instrumentalists to their books. Aspiring singers had to be heard in audition and afterwards either of the two Directors of the firm, Robert Leigh Ibbs or John Tillett, would record their observations in a book devised expressly for that purpose. By July 1942 Ibbs had retired (he died three months later) and the firm was led by John Tillett and his wife Emmie. Three audition books survive, spanning the years 1906–1943, called 'Manager's and Conductor's Register, Vocalists and Instrumentalists', and at the top of each page is space to enter the name, address, class, age and height of the auditionee. The middle of the page is divided between singers (the entries for which are designated for 'voice, compass, quality, experience, introduced by and appearance') and instrumentalists ('compass' and 'quality' replaced by 'technique' and 'style'). A few lines are then provided for 'General Remarks' and, at the bottom, the page is signed ('examined by') and dated.

Kathleen's appearance was described as 'attractive'. She sang 'Hark the echoing air' from Purcell's *Fairy Queen*, 'Then shall the eyes' and 'Come unto Him' (i.e. 'He shall feed His flock' until the soprano takes over midway at 'Come unto Him') from Handel's *Messiah*, and a song by Hugo Wolf. She had 'an excellent voice, even throughout, very good head register, warm and vibrant, good diction'. The compass of the voice was described as 'extensive'. Her accompanist that afternoon was Daphne Ibbott. In his biography of the violinist Alfredo Campoli (*The Bel Canto Violin*, 1999) for whom Ibbott also played, David Tunley writes that Ibbott was 'asked one day whether she would play for a singer who was coming down from Carlisle to audition for Ibbs and Tillett, [and] found herself playing for Kathleen Ferrier. The rehearsal was the beginning of an association that took them on a number of tours together throughout Britain, the warm-hearted Lancastrian taking it upon herself to look after her 'Little Daf' with motherly care'. Ibbott's obituary in the *Times* (11th October 2002 – she died that August aged 84) adds that she played at Kathleen's audition with Britten for the role of Lucretia.

Having been accepted on to the books by John Tillett, Kathleen was immediately offered engagements through the agency, and for the rest of her life was never without work at the highest level. Emmie Tillett became a close friend, professionally and socially, and both were part of a small, closely knit circle of amateur painters.

Her first engagement from Ibbs and Tillett was to sing in *Elijah*, in which, as mentioned in the introduction, the title role was sung by the well-established baritone, conductor and teacher Roy Henderson. He was asked by John Tillett for a report on Ferrier's performance and thought she had 'a good voice, but it was too dark, and she kept her nose buried in the score the whole time, terrified to look up. I told her she should learn her words and throw away the book'. He subsequently became a close friend, as well as her teacher and mentor until 1950, and it was with affection that she nicknamed him 'Prof'. She was also given a National Gallery concert, her only appearance in the series run by Myra Hess. It took place on 28th December 1942 and she was accompanied by Maurice Jacobson. Before and after she sang to the audience numbering 428 (British Library Cup.404.c.1 to 1/11), Maria Donska played solo piano items by Schubert and Beethoven respectively (see Ferrier's diary entry for 28th December 1942 for her selection of songs). Lennox Berkeley attended as a scout for the BBC and less than a month later she was turned down at her Promenade Concert audition (for their respective reports see the chapter 'Kathleen Ferrier and the BBC').

Fortunately the agency and its advisers had more faith in her than the BBC and, as a result of a meeting with John Tillett on Wednesday 12th May 1943, she became a sole artist with Ibbs and Tillett. On Christmas Eve 1942 she, together with Win and their father, moved to London and rented a flat, No.2 Frognal Mansions, 97 Frognal, in Hampstead, although ironically she now became increasingly busier for CEMA in the north of England. On Boxing Day she went to hear Handel's *Messiah* at the Royal Albert Hall, her first visit to the venue with which she would, before long, become extremely familiar and make her own. As far as London was concerned, a whole new world of opera, theatre and cinema was there for the taking and she soaked up the heady atmosphere of her new surroundings. As well as travels to the far north on behalf of CEMA, she also ventured south to Sussex where she sang for the first time with the doyen of accompanists at the time, Gerald Moore (at Lewes on 13th March 1943) but, just as she was embarking on a tour of Scotland, she succumbed to an attack of pneumonia and was rushed to a nursing home in Aberdeen. She was forever prey to wartime overheated trains, underheated hotels and concert halls, and even at this stage her health proved fragile. All the letters in this chapter are written from within Great Britain, and most are to the agency, whether to John Tillett, his wife Emmie (née Bass), Sadie Lereculey, who ran the music club department, or to Audrey Hurst, who dealt with BBC matters.

During the years 1940 to 1947, covered in this chapter, Kathleen Ferrier moved quickly and purposefully up the career ladder in Britain. She started with the prestigious annual Bach Choir *Messiah* in Westminster Abbey on 17th May 1943, conducted by the influential Dr Reginald Jacques with Isobel Baillie and another relative newcomer, the tenor Peter Pears, as fellow soloists. The composer Benjamin Britten was in the audience on that occasion. Three years later, at Glyndebourne in July 1946, the significance of his presence became evident when (double cast with Nancy Evans) Kathleen sang the title role in the premiere of his new chamber opera *The Rape of Lucretia*. This is her contract for the opera dated 20th March 1946 signed by Glyndebourne's General Manager Rudolf Bing.

Dear Miss Ferrier

<u>Benjamin Britten's *Rape of Lucretia*</u>

We have pleasure in engaging you to play the part of 'Lucretia' in the above production on the following terms and conditions:-

1   Rehearsals of the production will commence on or about 10th June 1946 at Glyndebourne and will continue for approximately six weeks. You will be expected to know your part by the time of your arrival at Glyndebourne.

2 (a)   For the period of rehearsals the Management will provide you with board and lodgings at Glyndebourne Opera House, or at the Management's discretion, within a radius of five miles of Glyndebourne. In the latter case the Management will be responsible for your transport to and from rehearsals and performances. The Management will do the best it can in present conditions to provide you with reasonable food and lodgings, and you will accept these arrangements for the whole period of rehearsals and performances scheduled to take place at Glyndebourne.

   (b)   Over and above board and lodging you will be paid a flat rate of £6.0.0. per week for every week of rehearsal or at the rate of one pound per day for any incomplete week.

3 (a)   Your engagement shall be for the period of rehearsals and for a playing period of 10 weeks with an option on the side of the Management to continue the engagement on the same terms for a further period of up to 5 weeks: such option to be exercised on or before 1st September 1946.

   (b)   During the playing period it is contemplated that performances will take place at Glyndebourne, on a provincial tour in the British Isles, in London and possibly on the Continent of Europe.

(c) Within the time limit stated in the above paragraph (3a) your engagement covers all those performances as booked and played.

4 The opening performance of the production is scheduled to take place on or about July 12th 1946.

5 (a) Your salary for every playing week or part of a week in which 6 or 7 public performances shall be given (whether you are required to perform or not) shall be £40. Normally you will not be required to perform more than 3 or 4 times per week, but if the Management shall call upon you to carry out more than 4 performances in such a week, you will do so, and will receive in addition to the said salary of £40 a sum equal to 1/7th thereof for every performance by you above 4.

(b) It is to be understood that the Management may play broken weeks, in particular the first week at Glyndebourne and of the contemplated London Season and possibly also on the Continent of Europe. For every week or part of a week in which less than 6 performances are played your salary shall be £5.15.0 per performance, whether you are required to perform or not.

(c) If you should without written permission of the Management fail to be at the disposal of the Management on any day or days during the period of this engagement (whether or not you are required to perform on such a day or days), then a reduction of £5.15.0 in your salary shall be made in respect of each such day and the Management reserves the right to terminate this contract.

(d) If in consequence of illness or for any other reason, for which the Management shall not be responsible you should not perform at any public performance at which you have been required so to do, a reduction of £5.15.0 shall be made in your salary in respect of each such performance so missed.

6 On tour the Management will provide you with rail tickets, but the provision of free board and lodging applies only to the period of rehearsals and performances at Glyndebourne, and otherwise you will be responsible for discharging the expense of your board and lodging.

7 It is understood that the parts of this opera will be double cast; it is at the discretion of the Management to decide whether you or your co-performer will do an equal amount of weekly performances or not, and it is entirely at the discretion of the Management to decide whether you or your co-performer will appear at the opening night or at any other particular night at any particular place.

8 The form of publicity in the way of posters, press announcements etc. is entirely at the discretion of the Management, but the Management undertakes to make every effort to prevent any 'starring' of any member or members of the Company to the disadvantage of any other member or members of the Company. It is agreed that you yourself will not undertake any personal publicity and that you will strictly abide by the terms as agreed in this contract letter.

9 You will attend punctually at all rehearsals (if necessary Sundays and days of performances included) at all places and at the exact time notified. You will be responsible for finding out the times of your rehearsals and performances, the Management being under no obligation to give any indication of the same, other than by announcements on the notice board of the theatre.

10   You will accept and strictly follow such arrangements for transportation to and from rehearsals and performances as shall be made by the Management, otherwise to be responsible for your own transport. You will take care and be responsible for all music provided by the Management, and to wear and use such costumes, wigs, properties etc. provided by the Management and no other costumes, wigs and properties, and to return such music, costumes, wigs and properties to the Management on demand in good order. You will conform strictly to the rules of any theatre at which the Company is scheduled to perform, and carry out the instructions of the Management.

11   You will not perform in public or in private anywhere during the duration of this engagement, except at the theatre or theatres appointed by the Management, without written permission of an authorised agent of the Management.

12   The Management has the right to broadcast any performance or part of a performance under the terms of this agreement and to receive any payment for so doing, and you declare your willingness to take part in gramophone recording if asked to do so on reasonable terms to be negotiated.

13   Whether or not the public shall be admitted to rehearsals or dress rehearsals is at the discretion of the Management.

14   The Management is entitled to cancel this agreement partly or wholly in case you shall break any term hereof, or be unable or unwilling to perform your obligations hereunder (without prejudice to any other right of action) or in the event of fire epidemic war riot strike public mourning public calamity or force majeure.

15   The Management is entitled to assign this contract to a new Company to be formed, but this will in no way affect or alter your or the Management's obligations or rights.

Yours faithfully
Rudolf Bing
Director and General Manager

Will you please sign and return the enclosed copy of this letter to signify your agreement with the terms and conditions of your engagement as set out in this letter.

Kathleen Ferrier [signed]

Miss Kathleen Ferrier
3 [*sic*] Frognal Mansions
NW3

Kathleen made such a favourable impression at the Sussex opera house by her unquestioning willingness to strive for and achieve the highest musical standards it demanded, that an opera was found for her return there the following year, Gluck's *Orfeo*. Just four years earlier she had been a housewife married to a bank manager in Silloth, yet on 18th July 1946 (when Nancy Evans was singing but Ferrier was present) she received this note at Glyndebourne from Rudolf Bing.

By command of Her Majesty, Mr Christie will wish to present you to Queen Mary after the performance. Will you please, as soon as possible after the end of the performance, present yourself, in dinner gown, in the Organ Room.

After the Glyndebourne summer of 1946 she toured with *Lucretia* around the country to poorly attended houses, and at the start of October went with the company to Holland, her first taste of life in a foreign country. Gluck's opera *Orfeo* at Glyndebourne next year was followed by her first Edinburgh Festival, the inaugural one in September 1947, where she performed with Bruno Walter for the first time and sang Mahler's *Das Lied von der Erde*. Just as with Sir John Barbirolli, with whom she sang for the first time on 8th December 1944, Walter had auditioned her reluctantly, but then fell in love with the voice and became one of her musical mentors, particularly in the music of Mahler. Walter, once Mahler's assistant, was a fervent advocate of his music and to that end Kathleen Ferrier, soon equally enthusiastic, played a hugely important role by singing his music in Britain, America and Europe. Both Walter and Ferrier paved the way for Otto Klemperer to carry this exploration further in the 1960s after their deaths.

At the start of October *The Rape of Lucretia* was revived for another national tour, starting in Newcastle, and which went on to include her debut at Covent Garden for two performances on 14th and 17th October (one scheduled for the 8th was cancelled). If she had not marvelled at her meteoric rise which included that introduction to Queen Mary a year earlier, she did now with unrestrained pleasure to her sister, 'From Carlisle to Covent Garden in five years! Lucky Kaff!'

These may have been the moments to savour, but her grindingly laborious schedule which made up the rest of her career makes astonishing reading, such as the annual round of Christmas performances of Handel's *Messiah*. Between 23rd November 1943 and 2nd January 1944 she sang it a dozen times including two (afternoon and evening) on one day in Bournemouth. A year later there were seventeen performances between 2nd December 1944 and 9th January 1945, while the number peaked at a daunting twenty during the corresponding period a year later, before reducing to sixteen in 1946–1947. She was also having to refine or learn her repertoire fast, Bach's *St Matthew Passion*, Mass in B minor, *Christmas Oratorio* and some Cantatas, Elgar's *The Kingdom*, *Dream of Gerontius* and *The Apostles*, Mendelssohn's *Elijah*, Handel's *Samson* and *Judas Maccabeus*, Brahms' Alto Rhapsody and Dvorak's *Stabat Mater* are scattered amongst a myriad of song recitals and Miscellaneous Concerts. These last-named had programmes which were generally of a lighter nature, accompanied by smaller chamber or orchestral groups for which she often had to supply parts or even make her own arrangements. It was small wonder then that she pleaded with John Tillett for days off to learn new music and insisted on reserving for herself an annual holiday. This exchange of telegrams makes the point.

27th March 1947 Telegram Kathleen Ferrier 11 Oxford Drive, Waterloo, Liverpool
Lincoln transferred to April twenty-five stop. Would you sing Wakefield April twenty-three stop
Please phone urgent Organol Wesdo London

28th March 1947 Telegram 9.15am Stoke-on-Trent to Organol Wesdo
London
Lincoln OK 25th but please leave 23rd free if humanly possible Kathleen

In the summer of 1947 (having signed up as a Decca recording artist in 1946) she recorded Bach's *St Matthew Passion* with Reginald Jacques on 4th July, followed on 11th September by her first collaboration with Bruno Walter at Edinburgh. From now on her career at home and abroad was on an ever upward trajectory.

There are several points worth noting which arise from the letters over the course of this period 1940–1947. It is interesting to see how her relationship with John Tillett gradually thaws and how her letters become almost as familiar as those to her sister and father (she implores him in May 1947 to come and see *Orfeo* 'if only to see me singing my way thro' Hell fire wiv me 'arp in mi 'and!!'). What emerges about financial and other matters placed upon singers at this time is also revealing, for they not only had to pay their own travel and accommodation costs, but also those of any accompanist they took with them, as well as his or her fee (which generally prevails to this day in America). There were ways to get around both burdens if the artists played their cards right. If they were lucky enough to be invited back (not a problem in Kathleen's case), there was the probability of an offer of hospitality from a local music club official or member of the choir, and singers could take a chance on the local accompanist, but this was rarely a successful solution. Also surprising is the obligation commonly made of a singer to provide the orchestral parts for repertoire which might not be part of mainstream programming, so unsurprisingly Kathleen built up a fair collection of handwritten manuscript parts over the years.

Identifying the recipients of her letters is not always straightforward due to the absence of envelopes, date of writing, lack of surnames and having to cope with the popularity of Christian names, in particular John, Phyllis or even Kathleen! Two letters have emerged which were not included in the first edition of this book. They were written in 1946 to a Mr Giddy. Kathleen was apparently asked for her 'life story' and she implies in her letters that Giddy was involved in writing a book in which she was to be included. Some sleuthing and a basic consultation of the Swiss telephone directory led me to Reginald Giddy's widow. In 1946 he was a cellist working in Beecham's Royal Philharmonic Orchestra, but he also had hopes of writing a book of interviews with musicians of the day. His career then took him to Geneva where he joined the Suisse Romande Orchestra. Meanwhile the book project failed and the original manuscript (whether complete or not) has not survived. At one point I thought he might be an unacknowledged researcher on behalf of Donald Brook, whose series of books consisting of biographical sketches of musicians (including *Singers of Today*) began to appear from 1947. The singers' biographies (1949) appear alphabetically and (more or less) so do their photographs, except for Kathleen's which, already by 1948, takes pride of place as the book's frontispiece, so popular had she become. The strongest evidence for my supposition that Giddy may have been acting for Brook is her diary entry for 24th October 1947 '2.30. Donald Brook (Life story)', so they clearly met a year and a half after the letters to Giddy and at a time when Brook was certainly putting together his *Singers of Today* in 1948. It is also worth noting that Isobel Baillie's unpublished diaries include entries for 7th July 1947, 'Send photo to Mr Giddy' and 29th October 1947, 'Mr Donald Brook 11am re biography', so it transpires that both singers were contributing to both books, the one which was published and the one which failed to appear. Donald Brook is selective. He never acknowledges Kathleen's marriage to Bert, whose 1937 challenge is described as 'a friend bet her a shilling', though to be fair, and bearing in mind attitudes of the day, he probably wanted to avoid tainting her with the stigma of divorce. At least her encounter with the mad Yorkshire female railway porter, given to Giddy but which did not appear in Brook's book, can now raise a laugh within these pages.

Kathleen Ferrier had immense talent, captivating charisma and a sublime voice. Despite the impression gained from reading her engagement diaries that she was saddled with a lot of routine, repetitive concerts and recitals, she loved her work and was immensely faithful to towns, choral societies, music clubs and individuals who gave her the opportunity to sing because they believed in her. She would repeatedly return to the Civic Hall in Croydon and Alan Kirby's Croydon Philharmonic Society because of its deservedly excellent reputation for performances of Elgar's oratorios. She would go back to Bromley County Boys' School, and she would return to her roots for the annual Boxing Day *Messiah* in Blackburn's King George's Hall, or go to Newcastle to sing for Dr Hutchinson, or travel to Bournemouth or Nottingham for Roy Henderson, often having just sung at top venues such as the Albert Hall, Covent Garden or for the BBC. Such performances are a tribute to her loyalty.

As well as favourite places, there were also key players in her life story, many of whose names appear in her diaries or in her letters. One was Maurice Jacobson, composer, accompanist and chairman of the music publisher Curwen, who went on to play for her and become a close friend. He had spotted her at the 1937 Carlisle Festival, the first turning point in her career. Alfred Barker led her to Malcolm Sargent and then steered her to Barbirolli. Meanwhile Sargent recommended her to agent John Tillett, who took her on and sent her to, among other venues, the Three Choirs Festival. Peter Pears urged Britten to recognise that he had found his Lucretia when he heard her sing *Messiah* in Westminster Abbey. That led to Glyndebourne, and in turn to Edinburgh where Peter Diamand and Rudolf Bing had recommended her to Bruno Walter, and he opened the door to America, while the Dutchman Diamand had already done the same for her in Europe. Kathleen seemed to have incredible luck in her musical contacts, each of whom passed her on to another like the chain between uprights in a chain-link fence. Meanwhile she still went back to Hetton le Hole and Merthyr Tydfil, Knottingley and Bideford, Wimbledon and Milngavie for her recitals and Miscellaneous Concerts. She was truly unique.

No.1 [Letter to Eileen Saul, at whose house Kathleen was having singing lessons with Dr Hutchinson]

Monday 2nd [December 1940]   District Bank House, Silloth

My dear Eileen

Hello luv! This is your singing lodger at this end. How are you now? Annie said you were much better last week and had even been up for a few minutes. We are all so glad you are on the road to recovery, and do hope you will keep on improving and getting stronger. Your head can't have been as hard as you thought, luv, to knock you out so completely!

Dr Hutchy enquires after his 'little hostess' every week and has been most concerned for you, and sends his kindest regards and best wishes for a speedy recovery – his very words!

We are still taking advantage of your piano and lounge and hope we are not causing too much inconvenience. Just give instructions for us to be kicked out when you feel like it, and we will disappear into the blackout.

You have missed the first Carlisle bomb with being in Edinburgh, Eileen, and I don't suppose you mind that very much. It seems to have done very little damage, praise be.

Winnie (my sister) has got a school in Carlisle and is looking forward to starting after the New Year. Dad, especially, will feel happier now she is nearer to us. We shall be doing a little flat hunting from now on. She came up a fort-night ago and her train being late (and her expenses being paid!) we did amuse ourselves royally and stayed at the *Central*, and filled the night in by seeing *Pinocchio*, which is lovely. The next day I goose-stepped up and down English St[reet] whilst she interviewed Directors, Headmistresses, Committees etc., and had her pulse taken and ribs counted by a lady doctor.

We had ages to wait for the train eventually, so from sheer desperation we explored Tullie House and the reading room, and by chance saw that the Sadlers Wells opera company were at Keswick that week, and what an opportunity! I have never seen a real, live opera, have you? So we brooded and we counted our petrol coupons and decided we'd risk it and coast down the hills and push John Thomas [her car with its registration number JT 9376] up the hills. Anything to see the *Marriage of Figaro*. We were lucky in getting the two last seats on the fourth row (returned ones they were) and they were well worth our five bobs! though the singing wasn't too marvellous, I didn't think, but it was a matinée and Joan Cross, the first soprano wasn't on. It was beautifully finished and acted out and we fair enjoyed ourselves!

Have been singing practically every weekend somewhere and am making my debut under Hutchy a week on Sunday as Kathleen Ferrier in *Messiah*. Shivers and shivers! I shall need a lot of pennies that day!

Well, this apology for a letter is all about me and mine and I hope you will forgive it. The Hetherington family are fit and Wyn comes each Thursday to our knitting bee. Mollie and Jim Richardson enquire after you after each visit to Carlisle and you are often in our thoughts, I can tell you. Pop has been worried stiff for you, and says once each day, 'I wonder how Eileen is – poor little lass!', so you see we are always thinking of you and Gunner Low! We all send our love to you and Ronnie and are looking forward to a reunion not very far distant, we hope.

Meanwhile, chin up and all the very best to you and a speedy recovery. Heaps of love from all

Kath

No.2 [Letter to Annie (née Chadwick) and Tom Barker]

16.5.41   District Bank House, Silloth, Nr Carlisle

Dear Annie and Tom

I was in Blackburn the other day and was enquiring after you from Mr Haworth (Richard) and he gave me your address, so here I am just dropping a line to you to wish you all well for old time's sake.

Bert has been having his holiday early this year so as to get it in before he is called up. He has been reserved up to now, but will probably be in kilts or some such e'er long, much to his delight. We went to Withnell F[old] of course to see his people and I had a pleasant change from cooking and sleeping in the cellar, though the latter is not a regular habit, praise be!

I was only in Blackburn an hour or two but I ran into quite a few people I knew, including Mrs Whiteley and Isabel, Auntie Maud and Uncle George, and we went to see Margaret and Tom Duerden and their two bairns Celia and Adrien. R. Howarth is as bonny as ever, and makes me feel a real heathen as he always did, but he's more lined and crinkly than he was, isn't he? He told me about your singing at Clitheroe and Muriel's baby. You'll be glad that event is safely over these blitzy days!

Pop is with us here and very fit, bless him, and a grand wiper to my washing up! He is 74 this year!

Winnie stood the Blitz in London until Christmas and then got a job in Carlisle at a school there, so that she comes here each weekend and we have some rare 'do's'. I have singing lessons with Dr Hutchinson of Newcastle – he has me in Carlisle – so that we always have a day out together once a week and go on the spree.

I have 9 pupils here, but hardly do any playing except to accompany myself, but I have been very busy singing.

I was singing with Trefor Jones at Workington Opera House just before Xmas, and made my 'debut' as a pupil of Hutchy in the *Messiah* in the City Hall at Newcastle. I don't think there was a single muscle, tissue or bone that didn't dither within me, but it was grand when it was safely over.

Next week I'm with Laurence Holmes, baritone, at Aspatria and we're singing (if it works) the Singing Lesson. I should know it shouldn't I? I've played it often enough.

There is a possibility that I may get with CEMA in the autumn touring in the north east. I do hope it comes off – it would be grand experience.

We may have to leave here if Bert is called up, so Pop, Winnie and I would share a house somewhere, but everything is so indefinite and to be done in such a hurry when the time comes, that we are just waiting and seeing, and not troubling trouble.

I could do with a change from this old barn with its four flights of stairs and dusty floors and 37 steps for the coal! It's making me old before my time! Sez me! We still manage a round of golf now and again, and I managed a 98 – everything in – the other night. Not bad for a 'larner', eh Tom?

It's 10 past 11 and time to lay me down to rest, so here's hoping you are all fit, and keeping your chin up in these troublesome times.

All the very best to you.

With best wishes

from

Kath Ferrier

P.S. Heard Elsie Suddaby, Eric Greene, Astra Desmond and Keith Falkner in the *Messiah* in Kendal last Saturday. The latter two disappointing though. K.F. was flat nearly all the way through but the choruses and the trumpeter were grand.

No.3 [Letter to Miss Hillidge of Runcorn, where Kathleen sang *Elijah* on 23rd December 1942]

7th Dec [19]42   Scarborough, as from 23 Windermere Rd, Carlisle

Dear Miss Hillidge

Thank you for your letter – I only read it on Saturday as I am touring. I have made a note of the rehearsal at 3.30, and I should be grateful if you could arrange for me to stay in Runcorn after the concert.

I will let you know what time I expect to arrive in Runcorn nearer the time – I don't know train times yet.

If you have to write again, would you write to 23 Windermere Rd, Carlisle, as I am not being in London again until after your *Elijah*. My sister will forward any correspondence on from Carlisle – it will save time.

Yours sincerely

Kathleen Ferrier

No.4 [Letter to Eleanor and Bill Coyd, friends in Silloth, Cumbria]

[9th January 1943]   [2 Frognal Mansions, London NW3]

My dear Eleanor and Bill

Having a sit-down – it seems to be the first for many weeks – I am taking the opportunity of writing to you. I wish I could have seen you all before we removed – simply couldn't manage it. We are more or less settled in – have been in a terrible mess, with painters, electricians, joiners and plumbers. But we're looking posh now!

I made my London debut a week last Monday at the National Gallery and oh boy! did my knees knock! But I got through without running off in the middle or swallowing in the wrong place. Myra Hess, the boss of the concerts – was very nice and encouraging. There was a huge crowd there and it was a bit of a facer, so I was glad when it was safely over.

I'm going up to Edinburgh on Monday for two concerts, then on to Thirsk and Newcastle-upon-Tyne and Colne in Lancs and home again next Monday. Work is rolling in and I'm pretty well booked up to the end of April, which is just as well with the price of rents! I'm going on a week's tour in Kent, another round Birmingham, and a 3-weeker in Scotland, so I'm going to be busy.

Do you remember Phyllis Simpson, music teacher at the Carlisle High School?

She turned up here the day before the National Gallery concert – she'd come specially to hear it all the way from Cockermouth!

Win and I went to see *Blithe Spirit* the other day – it was grand. We saw John Clements in the audience. Yesterday I went to the opening exhibition of Modern Art – and Jessie Matthews and [C.B.] Cochran were there. Seeing the celebrities, begorra!

Pop and Win send their love to you all and lots of luck for 1943. Bert is at Bury at the moment, and has been made a sergeant and is to stay on there as instructor, so he's near his home and should enjoy life better now.

Lots of love and luck to you all and all at Maryport – Mollie when you see her, and Frances and Tony and all our good pals. I'll be seeing you, and you've got our address and 'phone number if you're in London, so you've no excuse!

Look after yourselves and let's hear from you when you've a spare minute.

Heaps of love.

Kath

No.5 [Letter to Pop and Win]

[April 1943]   Northern Nursing Home, 5 Albyn Place, Aberdeen

Hello Loves

Aren't I a twerp? I was feeling right as rain when I rang up, then went to have some dinner and after that started to shiver and ache in every bone, so had a hot bath and went to bed.

Had a most uncomfortable night – sick etc. – then Kathleen M[oorhouse] insisted on having a doctor, and he said I'd a bad influenza cold with high temp[erature], and 'twas a jolly good job she'd called him in.

Well, I was going to stay in the hotel but Kathleen wouldn't hear of it as she had to move on the next day. So she rang up the Dr and asked his advice and he suggested here.

I came in an ambulance, all posh! – they'd a job to lift me!! Then was left in the care of the nurses here, perfect gems, and the Dr's been twice each day. My temp's normal again now through taking M & B [May & Baker] tablets [a sulpha-nilamide compound] that Churchill had, and I'm being washed more than I've ever been washed in my life before! I've even negotiated the bedpan and haven't done anything over the edge!

Can't say when I'll be home yet, but will let you know.

Loads of love

Kath

No.6 [Letter to John Tillett]

[undated 1944]   *Thorn* Hotel, Burnley

Dear Mr Tillett

Could you answer the enclosed for me? I would rather like to do the Pergolesi, though I know you will think the fee small. I don't know Miss Jaco, only that she is a friend of Maurice Jacobson, who will have told her about me probably. So I will leave it to you to do as you think best. Mr Lingard wants me back at Hebden Bridge, but I was engaged for the date they wanted in Feb. but you will probably be hearing from them for a date in Oct. I warned them that my fee had rocketed skywards!

Re Cradley Heath 29th Oct., I shall be most happy to have hospitality, only thought if it were possible to get back to Birmingham 'twould be more convenient, especially if the others were going. Hope it will be with Miss Lawley of Sunnyside as formerly.

Here are two programmes.

Newcastle-under-Lyme Nov. 15th
1   With string orchestra (I will provide the parts for this first group)
     a. Where'er you walk – Handel b. Cradle song – Wm Byrd c. The Arch
     Denial – Arne
2   With piano accomp.
     a. Love is a bable – Parry
     b. Sweet chance that led my steps abroad – M. Head
     c. Come, let's be merry – [Lane] Wilson
Yours sincerely
Kathleen Ferrier

No.7 [Letter to Maurice Jacobson]
1st May [1944]   2 Frognal Mansions, London NW3
Dearest Maurice

Thank you for your lovely letter. It gave me the <u>warmest</u> pleasure to read your praise, bless you! I <u>do</u> love this cycle [*Frauenliebe und Leben* by Schumann] – sentimental or no – and it is lovely to know that you were moved by the broadcast [Tuesday 18th April].

I had been thinking so much about you just before I received your letter – there must have been a bit of thought transference – but then I always think of Dover [28th November 1943] and how I must have put you and the audience through it on that particular night! But you broke the back, for me, of all my German songs and I am eternally grateful to you, because I love to sing them.

I tried to ring you on Saturday at the office, but I guess you do a five-day week!!!! But perhaps we can lunch or summat together when you get back?? Here's a naughty limerick, just to cheer up Liverpool.

> There was a young lady of Nantes
> Tres chic, jolie et elegante,
> But her hole was so small
> She was no good at all
> Except for la plume de ma tante!!

I don't improve, thank God!

In a rush as usual – look after yourself, and thank you again with all my heart for writing.
God bless – much love
Kaff

No.8 [Poem to Win]
In a field, all by myself, Tuesday midday [An American army camp, Lechlade,
Gloucestershire. 30th May 1944]

Hello Chum
I'm on mi tum
(Don't confuse with bum)
To pen this letter
To my elder & better
(It makes you fink –
This field don't arf stink –
It's full of verdure
And horses manure)
Thanks for your letter
Mi elder & better
It's time you were writin'
Mi old streak o' lightnin'!
It shows how much time I've got
That I can sit here & plot
Out a letter to my elder & better
One concert a day
With these Yanks is OK.
We're taken by jeeps
In a series of leaps
From one camp to another
And listen here, brother,
Fed on chicken & fruit
(I ain't 'alf a brute)
My singing is horribull
I'm always far too full
But they just laugh & say
There's more on the way!
Then we're jeeped home again
(No buses – nor train)
To the *New Inn* at Lechlade
On the pleasant green Thames-sade (posh for side!)
We're told off for being late
At this pub, mi old mate
But we say 'Oh be damned!'
For our bellies are crammed
With the good things of life
In the midst of this strife.
Then we stagger to room
(I'm in with Tess Bloom)
And drown any sorrow
In sleep till the morrow.
But food in the tum
Does away with the glum

Longfaced crayture called Katie
And makes her all matey
And life's a fair pleasure
Mi darlin', mi treasure
So T.T.F.N. [Ta Ta For Now]
I'll be writin' again
From your pal mi' ol' Katie
The cheeky old pratie!

No.9 [Letter to John Tillett]
[undated but 1944]   2 Frognal Mansions Hampstead NW3
Dear Mr Tillett

I received a contract from you today for Pontardulais on December 30th, but I have to be in Bournemouth that night for a rehearsal in the morning and two performances of the *Messiah* on the 31st. The man from Pontardulais asked me if I could do it when I was in S.Wales last week and I said quite impossible and explained in detail about the Bournemouth concerts.

Would you be so kind as to keep the 22nd-25th Dec. incl. free so that I shall be in good form for the broadcast from Manchester on the 27th Dec. Must do that well.

Kind greetings and best wishes
Yours sincerely
Kathleen Ferrier

P.S. For the Hereford concert on 26th Oct. I shall be leaving Crewe that morning on the 10.38, arriving Hereford 1.18. For Merthyr Tydfil on Nov. 2nd I cannot get in at the guest house, and the *New Inn* there is dire! Could the promoters be asked if it's possible to get to Pontypridd after the concert, if so can they book me a room there?
Yours sincerely
Kathleen Ferrier

No.10 [Letter to John Tillett]
29th Nov. [1944]   2 Frognal Mansions Hampstead NW3
Dear Mr Tillett

I enclose a letter from Warrington which arrived yesterday, and here are two programmes you are wanting.

Shaw – Jan. 27th 1945 Ref. K[athleen] C[heselden].

1	What is life to me without thee? (*Orfeo*)	Gluck
2a	Love song	Brahms
b	Why go barefoot my pretty one?	Brahms
3a	Sweet chance that led my steps abroad	Michael Head
b	The bold unbiddable child	Stanford

Duet suggestions with Mr Lloyd [baritone Roderick Lloyd]

It was a lover	Walthew

I don't know any other 4tettes and will fall in (!) with the others, but I should have thought one quartette was enough – it means six appearances otherwise

– a continual shooting on and off stage. It is going to be endless if we all do as many.

<u>Witney 7th March 1945</u>

1a	What is life to me without thee? (*Orfeo*)	Gluck
b	Pack clouds away	Handel
c	The Erl King	Schubert
2a	Love song	Brahms
b	A May night	Brahms
c	Why go barefoot my pretty one?	Brahms
3a	Sweet chance that led my steps abroad	Michael Head
b	A Piper	Michael Head
c	Down by the Salley Gardens	Gurney
d	Pretty ring time	Peter Warlock

(Four songs in last group)

I think that is all – I hope you can read it – I am in a train.

Yours sincerely

Kathleen Ferrier

No.11 [Letter to John Tillett]

Friday [? December 1944]   In train

Dear Mr Tillett

Looking through my contracts again just before I came away, I noticed that the rehearsal for the *St Matthew Passion* for Dr Jacques on the 16th March starts at 10am. I have signed a contract for Pontypridd the day before (15th) and, even if I get up for the first train, cannot be in London before about 12.15. I don't want to miss any of the rehearsal as I am not so well acquainted with this work. I have also been told by one or two people that I am doing the Southwark *Passion* on 17th March, but I haven't had a contract as yet for it. If this is so I would be grateful if I didn't have to go to Pontypridd, and if you could keep the 14th and 15th March free, as there is a lot of exacting singing for me and I want to make a good job of it. Could you possibly?

Mr Nicholson of B'pool wants me again the day I am doing the Manchester Midday, 27th Feb. for a Miscellaneous Concert. He wants me to do some operatic and old ballads (e.g. *Angus Macdonald* and *Promise of Life* etc.!!) with orchestra <u>without</u> rehearsal, but I said I would only do it with pianist and <u>my</u> choice of songs, as I have so much to learn and very little time for learning, and I think I told him my fee had gone up too! He is a very persistent Lancastrian, but then so am I, and I couldn't possibly go straight on to sing with an amateur orchestra without rehearsal, could I? Thank you very much for the Bradford contract – that's lovely.

Yours sincerely

Kathleen Ferrier

No.12 [Letter to John Tillett]

[1945]   [2 Frognal Mansions, London NW3]

Dear Mr Tillett

Enclosed please find some contracts and also a letter from Nelson. Would you

be good enough to answer it for me. I shan't be able to do it as I am in the Albert Hall the day before singing in *Gerontius*. Definite dates for CEMA now are 4th – 8th June (Stoke area) and 30th May (Crane Hall, Liverpool, lunch hour).
Yours sincerely
Kathleen Ferrier

No.13 [Letter to John Tillett]
[January 1945]   In train
Dear Mr Tillett

Enclosed please find contract for Reading. Also returned cheque for Ferry Hill [Ferryhill] as I was paid on the night of the concert by cheque and was given Miss Baillie's cheque too to give to her the following morning on the train. (I won't refuse it if they think I was worth double!)

I wonder if you could tell me who the other principals are for Glasgow, Beethoven Mass on Feb. 3rd, because if they are willing I should be so grateful if they would rehearse <u>before</u> going to Glasgow. Would you keep the 28th Jan. – 3rd Feb. free, as this is the only time I have to really get down to learning it.

My sister and I are trying to arrange a holiday at Whitsun and in the summer, so would you also keep free 15th – 24th May and 25th July – 11th August. We hope to go to Fleetwood the latter period, during which I shall be singing there.

For the Huddersfield broadcast on Dec. 27th I received £14.7.4. which was 10gns and expenses. Should I get 25% for public performance? I am told I should by various people, so thought I would ask you.
With sincere good wishes for 1945 to you all.
Most sincerely
Kathleen Ferrier

No.14 [Letter to John Tillett]
[January 1945]   2 Frognal Mansions Hampstead NW3
Dear Mr Tillett

I enclose 5 contracts and a cheque for £76. 6. 3., also my programme for Blackpool on Feb. 27th. I hear Mr Nicholson at B'pool is hurt because I won't sing with his orchestra, but I explained when I saw him that I wouldn't be able to rehearse because of the Manchester Midday concert, and therefore would prefer piano accompaniments. I am away from home at the moment, but I don't think I have had a contract for this concert.

Here are my suggestions with alternative items:

1	What is life to me without thee (*Orfeo*)	Gluck
or	Joan of Arc Farewell	Tschaikowsky
2	Art thou troubled?	Handel
or	Verdant meadows	Handel
3	Sigh no more	Aikin
or	How lovely are thy dwellings	Liddle?
4a	Ca' the yowes	(Bevins) Scots folksong arr. Maurice Jacobson
b	The Spanish lady (Irish)	H[er]b[er]t Hughes
or 4a	Water boy	(Negro) arr. Robinson

b The stuttering lovers   arr. Hughes
Duet with Mr Francis Russell
   It is the merry month of May (*Merrie England*) German
or   Home to our mountains   (*Il Trovatore*)   Verdi
I enclose a letter from Miss Cullen of Leith Hill Festival Choirs <u>which I have</u>
<u>answered</u>, as it had been delayed a bit thro' being forwarded, and I saw that I
was already engaged.

   In reference to your letter of the 26th inst. re Bargoed – I would be grateful
if I could have those days free 13th, 14th, 15th. I also mentioned to Mr Walter
Legge that I was free on the 13th and 14th if he wanted me for recording, as he
had asked for free dates.

   I also enclose a letter from Devizes which I have <u>not</u> answered, as I thought
you would deal with the fee problem, but I shouldn't be able to do it as I am in
the Liverpool area. Hope you can make this muddle out.
Yours sincerely
Kathleen Ferrier

No.15 [Letter to John Tillett]
[received by Ibbs and Tillett on 28th February 1945]   2 Frognal Mansions,
                                                            Hampstead NW3
Dear Mr Tillett
   I enclose a letter from Bishop Auckland and would be grateful if you would
deal with it. I shan't be able to do it as I am in Swansea the day before (Landore).

   Will it be alright for me to sing for Harry Vincent at the opening of a new hall
in which they hope to do recitals in the future? It is in Etruria I think. It is in the
nature of an opening ceremony – Maurice Jacobson is going – and the date is
Friday 23rd March. He only wants a couple of songs and I would like very much
to oblige him. Do hope this is alright.
With best wishes
Yours sincerely
Kathleen Ferrier

No.16 [Letter to John Tillett]
[received 29th February 1945]   *Midland* Hotel, Manchester Friday
Dear Mr Tillett
   I saw Mr Hutchinson (Newcastle), my old teacher, yesterday and he wants me
to do the Bach Mass for him in March next year, but unfortunately can't give a
date just yet as the secretary is ill. Would you let me know if you pencil anything
in for any Sunday in March 1946 so that I can let him know? He will get in touch
with you as soon as ever it is possible, but would be grateful if you would keep
him a Sunday meanwhile.

   I would be grateful too if you wouldn't book anything else in July and August
as arranged, unless it were a broadcast or a London job, or something extra
special. I do need some time off for learning all the things I don't know! I enclose
three signed contracts.
With best wishes
Yours sincerely
Kathleen Ferrier

No.17 [Letter to John Tillett]
March 22nd 1945   In train
Dear Mr Tillett

Would you please answer the Haltwhistle letter for me. I had a card from Dr Hutchinson asking me to fix Sunday 31st March 1946 for the B minor Mass at Newcastle (YMCA). Do hope this is alright. I will ask him to write to you.
Best wishes
Yours sincerely
Kathleen Ferrier

No.18 [Letter to John Tillett, received 27th March 1945]
[?26th March 1945]   Liverpool
Dear Mr Tillett

Enclosed pse. find several contracts.

You mention Aug. 15th for Haltwhistle, but that is the date I was asked to keep for Wells Cathedral for Dr Rickett of Sherborne. Do you remember?

Please don't book me anything else in July and August – I must learn the *Apostles* sometime!
Kind greetings
Sincerely
Kathleen Ferrier

No.19 [Letter to John Tillett]
[undated but 1945]   In train
Dear Mr Tillett

I would be grateful if you would answer the enclosed letters for me, from Batley and Chelmsford respectively. Would you not engage me anywhere before the Birmingham *Gerontius* concerts (Oct 7th and 8th) so that I can have a day off before them please? Also 29th, 30th, 31st Oct if possible so that I can recover!
Yours sincerely
Kathleen Ferrier

No.20 [Letter to John Tillett]
June 14th [1945]   2 Frognal Mansions, Hampstead NW3
Dear Mr Tillett

I enclose the letter I spoke to you about from Leicester, also contract for Oxford. Please would you ask Miss Bass not to book any more engagements for me in July or August unless they are 'home' ones. I am staying in Sherborne for Wells Cathedral on Aug 15th and had said I would stay on for a little rest, and it will be rather an awkward journey, Sherborne to Oxford, but will do it now it is all arranged, and with my 'Prof'!

I should like to do the Leicester *St Matthew* [*Passion*] if it is at all possible – it's such a lovely performance.
Yours sincerely
Kathleen Ferrier

No.21 [Letter to John Tillett]

Aug. 6th [1945]   [2 Frognal Mansions, London NW3]

Dear Mr Tillett

Would you be so good as to reply to the two enclosed letters for me? I am unable to do either of them.

Yours sincerely

Kathleen Ferrier

P.S. I am very sorry I had mixed up two dates. I've got it right now I think – 23rd Jan. Witney, 24th Derby. I enclose the contract for Derby and Aldenham. I have sent the programme for the latter to Mr Maurice Miles.

No.22 [Letter to John Tillett]

Aug. 17th [1945]   [2 Frognal Mansions, London NW3]

Dear Mr Tillett

Would you reply to the enclosed for me please? I have received a contract for Blackpool on March 8th 1946.

I am in Crookhill, Co. Durham on the 9th, and can say only arrive in Newcastle (if I catch all connections) at ¼ to 4pm. Is this soon enough for rehearsal and shall I be met in Newcastle by car? Otherwise it is going to be an awful struggle to get there in time.

In haste

Yours sincerely

Kathleen Ferrier

No.23 [incomplete letter to John Tillett]

Sep. 12th [1945]   [2 Frognal Mansions, London NW3]

Dear Mr Tillett

I am so very sorry to have caused an upheaval, and to have had to cancel two concerts. I tried all Sunday morning to get a deputy, but was unsuccessful, but by having my throat painted I managed to do 3 groups of 2 songs (instead of the printed 5) and the rest as printed. I wonder if I ought to offer some rebate of fee as they didn't get the full programme? Actually they said it was much too long for the Sunday afternoon. They were all most kind and understanding.

Stroud March 28th 1946 Quite willing to do the children's programme in the afternoon.

South Shields Oct. 24th and 25th

Wed:

1	What is life to me without thee? (*Orfeo*)	Gluck
2a	Fairest Isle	Purcell
b	Hark the echoing air	Purcell
3a	Have you seen but a whyte lily grow?	anon arr. Grew
b	Come, let's be merry	[Lane] Wilson

No.24 [Letter to Rutland Boughton]

Sat 20th Oct. [19]45   2 Frognal Mansions, London NW3

Dear Mr Boughton

I have been thinking very carefully of all we discussed yesterday, and all things considered, have decided that I must reluctantly forego the pleasure of undertaking the part in your work.

Apart from anything else, my agents have plans for me next season, which will take me all my time to fulfil. I am writing this now so that you will be able to make other arrangements as soon as possible. Have you thought of Nancy Evans for the part? – her voice is a little higher than mine, and she has had much stage experience.

It was a great pleasure to meet you, and I am most honoured that you should have asked me. I wish you every success.

Yours very sincerely

Kathleen Ferrier

No.25 [Letter to Rutland Boughton]
13th Nov. [1945]   2 Frognal Mansions, London NW3
Dear Mr Boughton

Thank you for your letter and also for the two songs which look lovely – I have only just returned home from my travels, so have only been through them once, but am looking forward to studying them very much.

I'm afraid I don't know Nancy Evans' home address but c/o Messrs Ibbs and Tillett, 124 Wigmore Street, W1, would be forwarded to her.

I am so sorry to disappoint you, and it wasn't 'business considerations' that made me decide, but a surfeit of work for which I am already booked, and which is still to be learnt. I just felt I couldn't take any more on for the next twelve months, otherwise I should have bitten off more than I could chew! I am most honoured that you should have asked me.

Yours most sincerely

Kathleen Ferrier

No.26 [Letter to Rutland Boughton]
[undated]   2 Frognal Mansions, London NW3
Dear Mr Boughton

I have just sent on your manuscripts to Miss Dorothy D'Oisay, The Wilderness, Buckhurst Hill, Essex by registered post. They look lovely and I am so sorry not to be able to do them at Gloucester, but I am so inundated with works to learn at the moment. I didn't want to risk doing them badly. I do hope, if you can spare me the copies again sometime, you will send them to me – life will not be quite so full after May.

With best wishes

Yours sincerely

Kathleen Ferrier

No.27 [Letter to John Tillett]
28th Dec. [1945]   In train
Dear Mr Tillett

I should have mentioned on the telephone the other night that Maurice Johnstone had asked me to do a broadcast with Northern Orchestra on March 11th

(Monday) and I said I thought I was free. Would you pencil it until you hear from him please?

I'm sorry about the reversed charges on phone call, but it was callbox and I couldn't get change. Will settle my debts when I see you!

Best wishes for the New Year

Very sincerely

Kathleen Ferrier

No.28 [Letter to Mr Giddy]

[early 1946]   as from 2 Frognal Mansions, Hampstead NW3

Dear Mr Giddy

I am so sorry – I've <u>searched</u> the flat to try and find your address, but without success – I know it was written down on something, but it eludes me. I'm very sorry to have been a long time. Here is everything I can think of that is neither libellous nor unprintable!

Worked in the Civil Service by day and studied piano and accompanied and played solos at concerts in and around Lancashire at night. ARCM at 16, LRAM at 18. Also won piano in National Competition run by *Daily Express* in which many, now famous, pianists also entered and won.

Entered Musical Festival at Carlisle for wager, and won Contralto Solo and Rose Bowl for best singer of Festival & first prize piano, when adjudicator was Maurice Jacobson, with whom I have since toured on CEMA concerts and who gave and has given invaluable help and encouragement.

Had my first singing lesson in 1940 from Dr J.E. Hutchinson of Newcastle-on-Tyne and under his conductorship sang first big *Messiah* performance at the City Hall, N'castle. The next year Dr Malcolm Sargent heard me sing and recommended me to Mr Tillett of Ibbs and Tillett [from which date I have sung with all leading choral societys [*sic*] and music clubs – [these 14 words are deleted]].

In 1942 (Xmas) removed to London and studied (and still studying) with Mr Roy Henderson, who has helped me more than I can say, and from this date, I have sung with all leading choral societys [*sic*] and music clubs, and am supposed to have had meteoric rise! (fingers crossed!). Most exciting dates include two Xmas *Messiah* broadcasts (1944 and 1945) and the last Prom performance (1945) in the R. Albert Hall. The latter rather wearing as the parts for my aria were in the wrong key – 3rd too high – and the right ones only arrived at 1pm making very hurried rehearsal. Never forget the sight of the R.A.H. crammed to suffocation.

One silly story which I will leave to your discretion as to whether to print. One of many *Messiahs* last winter was in a small Yorks. village – my train was late – connection missed, luggage almost lost by sleepy porter, and discovered there were two stations for this small village and hadn't been told where to alight, so that I could be collected by host. Pitch black and train stops before I can find out where I am. A girl porter pushed large face with jaunty cap perched on top through window and shouted for all Yorks. to hear 'Are you t' Messiah? Where've you been – there's a chap here been waiting for you for <u>hours</u>!' No respecter of persons obviously!

Hope you can make something out of this – this summer am having first shot at Opera in Benj. Britten's new work *The Rape of Lucretia* in title role – but 't would be better to see how it turns out e'er mentioning it p'raps! (I'm a cautious Lancastrian!)

So sorry to have kept you waiting – hope you may have terrific success with your book, and I am very honoured that you should have asked me.

Yours very sincerely
Kathleen Ferrier

No.29 [Letter to Mrs Leigh, Croftdown, Witney, Oxon.]
30th Jan. '46   2 Frognal Mansions, London NW3
Dear Mrs Leigh

Once more may I say thank you so very much for all your kindness. It was lovely to be with you again and to be so spoiled. I'm only sorry the arrangements were mixed and your dinners rushed as a result. Thank you so very much too for the ½ doz. eggs which arrived home all intact. I <u>was</u> popular!

I had a most peaceful journey to Derby and a lovely concert, and have since been to Liverpool, Morecambe and Glasgow, so I hope you will forgive me for not writing sooner, but I seem to have been either singing, packing or journeying since I left you.

Once again thank you so very much for all your kindness and generosity – I am so very grateful to you and your husband.

With best wishes and my most sincere thanks
Kathleen Ferrier

No.30 [Letter to Rudolf Bing]
5.2.46   2 Frognal Mansions, Hampstead, London NW3
Dear Mr Bing

Thank you very much for your letter. I shall be very pleased to sign a contract on the lines you suggest in your letter – that is, to alternate the part of Lucretia for period covering June 10th to 2nd November at a weekly fee of £40 and £6 per week and free board and lodging for the rehearsal period.

With best wishes
Yours sincerely
Kathleen Ferrier

No.31 [Letter to Rudolf Bing]
11th Feb[ruary 1946]   2 Frognal Mansions, London NW3
Dear Mr Bing

Thank you for your letter. It will mean cancelling one or two jobs that are already booked, but I think I can manage to give backword.

I would be very grateful if you could advise me as to whether I might fulfil a contract that I have had booked for almost a year, to sing in the Albert Hall on Thursday June 20th. I should very much like to do it if I can be spared for the whole day. I have cancelled all my other bookings, so would not want to run away again!

With best wishes
Yours very sincerely
Kathleen Ferrier

No.32 [Letter to F.A. Kenmir ref: programme on 3rd April 1946 at Spennymoor]

19th Feb [1946]   2 Frognal Mansions, Hampstead NW3

Dear Mr Kenmir

Thank you for your letter. Here are my suggestions for programme – I'm afraid I don't sing 'O Don Fatale' as it is high mezzo-soprano.

1.	Joan of Arc Farewell aria	Tschaikowsky
2.	Art thou troubled	Handel
	Spring is coming	Handel
3.	Silent Noon	Vaughan Williams
	The bold unbiddable child	Stanford
4.	Come, let's be merry	arr. Lane Wilson
	Bobby Shaftoe	arr. Whitaker

I would much prefer not to sing a duet as there is never time to practise them properly, and they are very rare for our voices. Your programme is very long too, but if you insist, I suggest 'Sound the Trumpet' – Purcell.

I hope my items are what you want – and that the concert is a great success. I shall be staying in Darlington after the concert, and be coming on the day of the concert from Leeds so should be there in good time.

Best wishes

Yours sincerely

Kathleen Ferrier

No.33 [Letter to Mr Pickup]

8.3.[19]46   2 Frognal Mansions, Hampstead, NW3

Dear Mr Pickup

Thank you very much for your letter – I am afraid I am fully booked for all this year. Another time I should be delighted, and if you would contact Messrs Ibbs and Tillett, 124 Wigmore St, London W1, who are my sole agents, they would advise you as to free dates and fees.

With best wishes for a successful Festival

Yours sincerely

Kathleen Ferrier

No.34 [Letter to John Tillett]

13th March [1946]   [2 Frognal Mansions, London NW3]

Dear Mr Tillett

Enclosed please find signed contracts.

Would you be good enough to reply to the enquiry here enclosed. Also Mr Edward Isaacs wants to know if I will keep March 11th 1947 for him, as it will not be such a busy month as December. I would like to do this for him – it always means an enlargement of repertoire for me, and is good for me!

Yours sincerely

Kathleen Ferrier

No.35 [Letter to F.A. Kenmir ref: programme on 3rd April 1946 at Spennymoor]

14th March [1946]   2 Frognal Mansions, Hampstead NW3

Dear Mr Kenmir

Thank you for your letter.

Herewith confirmation of my items:

Joan of Arc
Art thou troubled
Spring
What is life
Silent Noon
Come let's be merry

I have tried to contact David Lloyd, but he is ill at the moment, so would you put down 'Sound the Trumpet' for the duet, as I am sure it will be all right.

In haste

Yours sincerely

Kathleen Ferrier

No.36 [Letter to John Tillett]

29th March 1946   [2 Frognal Mansions, London NW3]

Dear Mr Tillett

Re Liverpool May 1st – here is suggested programme:

Dearest consort	Handel
Come to me soothing sleep	Handel
Ombra mai fu	Handel
Pack, clouds, away	Handel
The Blacksmith	Brahms
Roses three	Brahms
The swallow	Brahms
Why go barefoot, my pretty one?	arr. Brahms

I enclose several contracts. Would you please in future cut out all church weekends and the like? I am getting more work than I can cope with, and I would be grateful if you would only book me for large towns, choral societies, and music clubs. The large fees only go in Income Tax, and in your case in excess profits! And the smaller places book up so far in advance, that worthwhile jobs are crowded out.

I should be grateful, too, if my broadcasting fee were to be put up to 25 gns. if you are agreeable.

Yours sincerely

Kathleen Ferrier

No.37 [Postcard to F.A. Kenmir]

[postmarked 30th March 1946]

Sat.   [2 Frognal Mansions, Hampstead NW3]

Dear Mr Kenmir

Thank you for your letter.

I shall be coming by car from Leeds to Darlington and probably bus to

Spennymoor after lunch. So will come to [your house – [scored through]] the hall and wait to be picked up – better than house I think, as I shall be rather heavily laden, and I don't know where the house is.

Am sending the more difficult music to you for Miss [Jessie] Armstrong. Can you let her have it, please.

Sincerely

Kathleen Ferrier

No.38 [Letter to John Tillett]

8th April [1946]   [2 Frognal Mansions, London NW3]

Dear Mr Tillett

Enclosed please find signed contract and enquiry from Ossett – would you be good enough to reply to this for me? Just to confirm my fortnight off – Jan. 4th to Jan. 18th inclusive 1947! Seems kinda long way away!

Yours sincerely

Kathleen Ferrier

No.39 [Letter to Audrey Christie]

8th April [1946]   2 Frognal Mansions, Hampstead NW3

[Tel] Ham.2108

Dear Mrs Christie

Thank you so very much for your kind letter – I should be delighted to stay with you if I won't be too much trouble – I'm a very good washer-upper!

I am so thrilled to have been asked to take part in a Glyndebourne production, and to have the chance to work in such surroundings – may I say Thank you too for all your kindness and encouragement at the various auditions – it did just make all the difference.

Shall look forward so much to seeing you again.

Yours very sincerely

Kathleen Ferrier

No.40 [Letter to Mr Giddy]

7th May [1946]   2 Frognal Mansions, Hampstead NW3

Dear Mr Giddy

Thank you very much for my 'life story' – it sounds almost interesting the way you have written it! I <u>do</u> think you have done it well.

Am I flattering myself, or should it be on the last line of all – 'distinguishes the great artist from the competent singer'?

The only other thing is that I could play piano – self-taught from a Small-woods! – and pleaded to learn, so that the liking was there long before I started, but I don't think that matters much.

Thank you so much for the trouble you have taken, and the nice things you say – I hope your book may be a huge success.

Yours very sincerely

Kathleen Ferrier

No.41 [Letter to John Tillett]
13th May [1946]   [2 Frognal Mansions, London NW3]
Dear Mr Tillett

Can you keep May and June 1947 and the summer months free for the moment, until I see how I am fixed for the holidays? There is plenty of time to book yet for that period, and I don't want to find myself without any free period.
Yours very sincerely
Kathleen Ferrier

No.42 [Letter to Rudolf Bing]
13th May [1946]   2 Frognal Mansions, London NW3
Dear Mr Bing

Thank you very much for the first act of *Lucretia* – hope the 2nd and worst half isn't long following.

Could you relieve my worries by telling me if, as Peter Pears told me, two seats are kept for me for the opening night, 12th July? Should be much relieved to have this confirmed, as I have already promised them to sister and friend!

So sorry to worry you, and with best wishes
Yours very sincerely
Kathleen Ferrier

No.43 [Letter to John Tillett]
17th May 1946   [2 Frognal Mansions, London NW3]
Dear Mr Tillett

Thank you very much for cheque for £68. 5. od from Cambridge duly received. Re Reading May 29th – I am in Oxford the next day. So would be grateful if accommodation could be arranged for me in Reading. Re Harry Vincent March 27th 1947. This concert is in the Victoria Hall, Hanley, so will be a proper fee as far as I know. I haven't overlooked May 3rd and May 24th 1947, but would like the summer months kept free at the moment.

Mr Sumsion of Gloucester has written mentioning Three Choirs in Sept next year, and Leeds want me for their Festival in Oct – 1st week or thereabouts. Thought I would mention it, and perhaps you will keep it in mind if they don't write immediately.
Yours sincerely
Kathleen Ferrier

No.44 [Letter to John Tillett, first page(s) missing]
[?June 1946]   [2 Frognal Mansions, London NW3]

… It's quite all right about the Liverpool cancellation. I would prefer not to take another job on that day. Please would you ask me before booking any more engagements in March next year, and I'll do the same!, as I think I have as much as I can do well now. Also if possible I would like to have Easter, April 2nd – 9th at home, as I shall be in Croydon and Wimbledon on the 2nd and 4th, would accept a London engagement, but would be glad to be free of travelling.

And would you also keep from the 10th Feb. to the end of that month free of any more work, unless it is the Dublin recital after Belfast that Miss Bass mentioned might materialise. My address from Monday [10 June] onwards until about July 22nd will be: Glyndebourne, nr Lewes, Sussex.

With best wishes

Yours sincerely

Kathleen Ferrier

No.45 [Letter to Moran Caplat]

3.6.46   2 Frognal Mansions, London NW3

Dear Mr Caplat

Thank you for your letter. I will arrange to catch the train at Victoria at 10.45 on Monday, June 10th. I shall be coming from Cambridge that morning, but unless I am held up by 'victory' crowds, should be able to catch the train easily.

Yours sincerely

Kathleen Ferrier

No.46 [Letter to Kathleen Jamieson]

26th June [1946]   Glyndebourne Opera House, Lewes, Sussex

Dear Jammie

Thank you again for lovely letter and snap. You are a wonderfully handsome lot!

I'm glad you enjoyed the Mass. It's a wonderful work – the choruses are so magnificent, a soloist feels absolutely minute after them. I was very miserable because I was just starting a laryngitical (!) cold, and sang with a fiery, tickling throat all night – I hoped it wasn't noticeable in my voice. I have been quite voiceless since, and only today feel life is worth living again! I know of nothing worse than wanting to sing and not being able to, not to mention holding up rehearsals here.

I often think of Miss Rofe, but have never seen her for years – she was such a lovely person. And Miss Cruikshank too – I should love to see her again.

Maurice Jacobson is a special 'buddy' of mine, – and helped me enormously on a CEMA tour when I was just starting – we're enormous pals. I think he's the finest adjudicator in the country.

I am down here for rehearsals for Benjamin Britten's new opera *The Rape of Lucretia*. It is wonderful to sing, but as I'm Lucretia I seem to be in for a pretty hectic time! This is my first venture in opera, and I am loving it so far. It is working under ideal conditions – no travelling, no bag carrying – early nights and nine o'clock breakfasts. I am fast becoming unbearably spoiled! We live in the house as guests and in our free time can sunbathe, play table tennis and enjoy complete relaxation.

We will find Manchester, L'pool, Edinburgh and Glasgow a very great change from the Sussex downs!

Kind greetings and best wishes to you and your nice staff, and thank you again for writing.

Very sincerely

Kathleen (Ferrier)

No.47 [Letter to John Tillett]
2nd July [1946]   Glyndebourne, Lewes, Sussex
Dear Mr Tillett

Re Leeds University recital, I should be willing to sing for them on Feb. 7th for a fee of 30 gns to include accompanist's fee. Apart from any other Irish dates at the end of the month, would you not book any more dates now in February – also all March and Easter week in April. I inadvertently signed the Bournemouth contract for Easter Saturday, but already dread the journey at that time!

I shall be quite willing to sing the *St Matthew Passion* in Newcastle for 25 gns on March 9th. We have all been approached here re next season, and I have mentioned already to Mr Bing that the Three Choirs Festival will be in September. He can let us know something definite in a month's time. Meanwhile I have neither promised nor signed anything!

Shall you be able to come to Glyndebourne? I <u>do</u> hope you can. I am doing the first night here with Joan Cross and Peter Pears, so Nancy Evans will be doing the London first night. Am enjoying it tremendously and I should think it's the most marvellous part one could possibly have. Joan Cross has helped me very much and we're a very happy band so far! Touching wood!
With best wishes
Sincerely
Kathleen Ferrier

No.48 [Letter to John Tillett]
11th July [1946]   Glyndebourne, Lewes
Dear Mr Tillett

Sat Jan. 25th will be all right for Cambridge – and also Jan. 29th for Mr Sumsion – Gloucester – at the fee you mention. I think that must be all for January now, as they are all heavy recitals.
In haste
Yours sincerely
Kathleen Ferrier

P.S. Re broadcast on 23rd Jan., that is the date I promised Nicholas Choveaux (St Bartholomew's) and it is at 6.15. What a nuisance – I'm so sorry.

No.49 [Letter to John Tillett]
Tuesday [July 23rd 1946]   Glyndebourne, Lewes
Dear Mr Tillett

Thank you for your letter. I would rather not accept the engagements you mention, March 24th and May 30th. Three concerts in a row are too much when the first two are *St Matthew Passions*, and May 30th is Whit week, and I would prefer to leave it free at the moment. It's old age creeping on, I fear!
Herewith programme for Leeds Feb. 7th 1947:

How changed the vision	Handel
Lascia ch'io pianga	Handel
Have you seen but a whyte lily grow?	Anon arr. Grew
Willow song	Anon arr. Jacobson
Flocks are sporting	Carey

Four Serious Songs	Brahms

Love is a bable	Parry
The fairy lough	Stanford
The bold unbiddable child	Stanford
Down by the Salley Gardens	arr. Hughes
The Spanish lady	arr. Hughes

Hope all is well with you and your holiday materialises.

Yours sincerely

Kathleen Ferrier

No.50 [Letter to Audrey Christie]

1st Aug[ust 19]46   2 Frognal Mansions, London NW3

My dear Audrey

Just a few words to say Thank you so very much for the most wonderful time I have ever had – to thank you for your kindness and generosity and unfailing interest and encouragement. I can't ever adequately thank you enough for, to me at any rate, the most exciting experience in my short career under the most perfect conditions.

I shall always count myself fortunate that my first opera should be a Glyndebourne one, and I am so grateful to you and Mr Christie for your faith in entrusting such a big part to me.

Thank you so very sincerely for all your kindness, and with my best wishes to Mr Christie, Professor and Mrs Ebert and 'Morny' [Miss Morgan, the Christie family governess].

With love

Kathleen

No.51 [Letter to John Tillett]

[Undated but early August 1946]   All next week c/o 11 Oxford Drive,
                                                                              Waterloo, Liverpool 22

Dear Mr Tillett

I could do the Aberystwyth concerts Apr. 15, 16, 17, but I believe John Francis has asked Miss Bass for Apr. 15 for either a Wigmore Hall or Chelsea Town Hall recital, and I believe it is the only date we could fix. I will be seeing him today and will ask what he has done about it.

Would you definitely not book Gloucester (Sept 1947) for the moment until we see how the Edinburgh Festival fits in. I would like to do Gloucester, but don't want to spoil a season for one date.

Am still enjoying being raped three and four times a week! Only Holland as far as we know is materialising for the European tour, with a possibility of Denmark, but I shall be going to Denmark in any case after Holland for a fortnight's holiday with Mr & Mrs Aksel Schiøtz. Peter Diamand, Amsterdam, wants me to do a broadcast while I'm in Holland. Is this all right to you?

Best wishes

Sincerely

Kathleen Ferrier

No.52 [Letter to Winifred and William Ferrier]
Tuesday [1st October 1946]   *American* Hotel, Amsterdam
Dearest Both

Arrived all in one piece, and enjoyed every minute. The boat lurched a bit – trying to avoid fog I understand – but was as smooth as a millpond – no casualties – and we were on time all the way. We had been huddled all together in a dormitory cabin – about 12 of us – but Joan, Nancy and I asked for and achieved cabins, which was much better. Peter Diamand – Dutch agent – met us at the Hook and we went by train from there through Rotterdam, Harlem and to Amsterdam.

The cleanest houses and windows you ever did see, and flowers in the fields all the way. Ben, Peter and Eric met us at Amsterdam with a bouquet of roses for all the girls – mine are 20 yellow ones – absolutely gorgeous – and we had a hilarious journey in a bus to this hotel, which is <u>very</u> nice. I have a room on first floor with <u>balcony</u> with chairs and table outside! We had a magnificent lunch of beefsteak – real undercut – peas and fried potatoes and gateaux and red wine – then I slept for a bit and had walk with the gang round Amsterdam. It's a most lovely city with beautiful canals down every side street and lovely, big-windowed, tall houses. We had tea in a little café and had fun pointing out which cake we wanted and Ben couldn't reckon up his change at all – guilders and cents! Peter's good at mime and was a riot with the waitress. Now we're all going out for some dinner – then I'm going straight to bed to recover from only about 3 hours sleep last night.

The traffic is terrific here and people ride on the outside lamps of tramcars, they are so packed – literally! All the tram wires had been taken I believe, and they're only just getting back.

The customs was easy – I was asked if I'd any inner tubes or bicycle tyres, so I said 'No, only a spare tyre round me waist!' What a to-do!

Peter has a sore throat but expect he'll be all right on the night! Everything absolutely grand and my eyes are popping out with excitement!

Wish you were here too, loves! Mabel [soprano Margaret Ritchie] was pleased to inform us that she only used her 'receptacle' for hair grips and nothing else!

If anything urgent – *American* Hotel, Amsterdam will find me or the address I gave you of the theatre. Shall be home Wed – the boat doesn't sail until the Tuesday.
Loads of love – I hope all is all right with you.
Look after yourselves loves.
Kath

No.53 [Letter to John Tillett, undated and first page(s) missing but probably early autumn 1946]
...work I have been doing, I just cannot learn new things.

Can I ask you again to try and keep the number of concerts down to ten a month, and to restrict these to recitals, oratorios and orchestral concerts, and to cut out all Miscellaneous Concerts? I will do the same and not promise to do them in a weak moment!

Also will you keep May, June, July and August completely clear at the moment

– (excepting the ones I have already signed in for May) and not book anything definite after that time. I have heard vague rumours of a possible first performance of a new work in America next autumn (very confidential) and if it materialises would not like to miss it, or have to ask you again to get me out of a hole!

Mr [Roy] Henderson will be sending the Elland programme [11 April 1947] in as it is a joint one.

With best wishes and many regrets for putting you to extra trouble.

Yours sincerely

Kathleen Ferrier

P.S. I am sorry to have to go to Huddersfield in a rush in November [26th 1946] and feel that as they hadn't confirmed it, it is their own lookout, but as you are so keen that I should do it, I will of course.

No.54 [Postcard to Peter Pears and Benjamin Britten, 3 Oxford Square, London W2, England]

[postmarked 23rd October 1946]   [from Denmark]

Just been with Gerd [Schiøtz] to Sweden and my eyes haven't yet popped back into sockets! Having a wonderful rest and being very spoiled.

Loads of love.

Kathleen.

We would have loved you both coming along with us! It was a wonderful experience to me to meet you and to enjoy *Lucretia.*

Gerd [Schiøtz]

No.55 [Letter to Emmie Bass]

28th October 1946   [2 Frognal Mansions, London NW3]

Dear Miss Bass

Thank you for your letter. I would prefer not to sing at Saddleworth on April 13th or 20th if you don't mind.

Re Chester on Nov 20th, they ask me to sing 'The fairy lough' which I have already put down in the programme, also a song by Elizabeth Hughes, which they say I have sung many times. It is a new one to me, and I haven't ever sung it, but if I can learn it in time with all the other things to do, I will sing it as an encore (if I get one!) and the programme can stand as it is.

I had a press cutting today which says I am singing in the Albert Hall on Nov 20th in the *Messiah* with Dr Sargent, but this is a mistake isn't it? Thought I would mention it to avoid any misunderstandings. If I can keep my engagements down to about ten a month, then without being completely worn out, I shall still be able to do a few broadcasts and enjoy it all, but otherwise I don't give my money's worth as [my] voice is tired and I go about in a dirty state because I haven't time to wash my smalls!!

Hope you are getting a little more time off now, and that you had a good holiday.

With best wishes

Yours sincerely

Kathleen Ferrier

No.56 [Letter to John Tillett]
31st October [1946]   2 Frognal Mansions, NW3
Dear Mr Tillett

Enclosed please find cheque for stationery account. Also I believe Anthony Lewis wants me to do some Bach Cantatas with John Francis on 17th March and 28th April on the Third Programme. Could you pencil in these dates for me please? I haven't been asked for programme for Brecon on the 8th Nov and as it is getting near here are some items:

1	Art thou troubled?	Handel
	Pack clouds away	Handel
2	Have you seen but a whyte lily grow?	arr. Grew
	Willow song	arr. Jacobson
	Come let's be merry	arr. Lane Wilson
3	Sigh no more	Aikin
	Star candles	Michael Head
	The bold unbiddable child	Stanford

Hope this will be in time for Brecon
Sincerely
Kathleen Ferrier

No.57 [Letter to Emmie Bass]
14th November 1946   [2 Frognal Mansions, London NW3]
Dear Miss Bass

Re New Concerts Assoc: Edinburgh – I am unable to accept any other engagement in May just yet, as I don't know what is happening about Glyndebourne. I probably shall do in a fortnight or so, and will let you know immediately.
Yours sincerely
Kathleen Ferrier

P.S. Herewith programme for Glasgow Jan. 1st evening – nearly forgot!

1	How changed the vision	Handel
	Watts Cradle song	Sumsion
	Hark the ech'ing air	Purcell

(the first and last orch parts obtainable from Novellos, have my own parts of the Sumsion)

2 (with piano)	A New Year Carol	Helen Pyke
	Star candles	Michael Head
	A piper	Michael Head
	Pretty ring time	Peter Warlock

Hope those are all right.

No.58 [Letter to Peter Diamand]
21.11.46   2 Frognal Mansions, London NW3
My dear Peter

'Scuse pencil – have come a-touring without pen! I think the best plan for Sat. would be if you could meet me at Waterloo at 5.15 – my train is 6.30 – and we could have a wishy-washy cup of tea in the buffet! What a prospect, but it would give more time than eating in the West End and struggling for taxi. I have to go home on arrival at Euston at 2pm for different case and evening frock – so have arranged for a taxi from home at 5 – so should be at Waterloo at 5.15. If this is quite hopeless for you I shall be at home – HAM 2108 – wildly packing – from about 2.30 or 3pm until 5pm.

Am so pleased Bruno Walter remembered me – I was very thrilled to meet him.

Thank you so much for your letter – it was great fun. So looking forward to seeing you.

Love

Kathleen

P.S. (Waterloo – outside entrance to buffet – 5.15 – Saturday and if I lose you, I shall sing 'Che faro senz' Peter Diamand' on the loud speaker!)

No.59 [Letter to John Tillett]

16th December 1946   [2 Frognal Mansions, London NW3]

Dear Mr Tillett

Thank you for your letter. I'm sorry but I would rather you kept July free as well as June and August for the present anyhow. I don't think I'm a very good 'Sea Pictures-ite' and have been wondering if for Brighton – May 10th – they would let me off with the middle three – 'In Haven', 'Where corals lie', and 'Sabbath morning' – and let me push in something else in which I'm happier! ('Che faro' or any of the Handel arias or Purcell)

I think I would like to give Liverpool a rest as I have been so much and have run out of a change of frock! (not to mention repertoire!) I would like to do *Gerontius* in Manchester Cathedral. I'll leave the fee to you.

'How changed the vision'. I think it is from *Admeto* by Handel – parts procurable in D major at either Novellos or Goodwin & Tabbs.

Re Glasgow and Milngavie. Travelling by sleeper 31st Dec. from Liverpool – staying *Central* Hotel 1st and 2nd and sleeper back to London on the 3rd (10.35pm).

I'm very sorry but I shall have to return this contract for Twickenham. I can't possibly do five recitals running, especially with the Third Programme at the end of the five with eight new songs which I haven't seen yet! Please, please ask me before booking any more dates. Having just done seven concerts in six days in six different towns, am feeling more than usually weary, not having recovered from travelling from Stoke to Bradford in five different trains, starting at 9.26am, catching all the right connections and arriving late for rehearsal with Dr Sargent (¼ to 3) and still lunch-less! It isn't possible to sing well at this rate.

I hear (not officially) that *Orfeo* is not materialising, I wonder if you have heard?

I wonder too if, at my own expense, Cambridge would mind if I took my own accompanist on Jan. 25th. I will write to Mr Bimrose myself to plead, but one has to rehearse so much with him, voice is a mere croon by 4.15!!

Sorry to be a nuisance. If you think I should write, could you let me have his address please

Best wishes

Sincerely

Kathleen Ferrier

No.60 [Letter to Charles D. Rigg]

26th Dec. '46   2 Frognal Mansions, London NW3

Dear Mr Rigg

Thank you so much for your kind letter – I should be delighted to join you for dinner again, as I remember last year with such pleasure.

I have had a pathetic letter from a friend in Ayrshire, saying how impossible it is to get seats for the *Messiah*. If by any lucky chance there were two seats going a-begging, could you let me have them, do you think? They are coming up in the hope of being able to stand perhaps, or get their noses in somewhere, and I know would be very grateful if they are lucky.

If it is hopeless or a worry, please don't go to any trouble, as I know the struggle for seats on these occasions!

My very kind greetings to your wife and daughter, and best wishes

Yours sincerely

Kathleen Ferrier

P.S. I am travelling overnight from L'pool – due about 8.30am on 1st, but if any sign of fog, will come earlier in the day and commandeer a couch at the *Central*!

No.61 [Letter to Leslie Boosey]

15th Jan. [19]47   2 Frognal Mansions, London NW3

Dear Mr Boosey

I want to thank you so very much for making it possible for my sister and me to go to *Carmen*. I never dreamed, when I had the audacity to ring you, that it would result in one of the most memorable evenings ever – and would have been content and grateful for a seat in the back row of the topmost gallery!

It was the most exciting evening either of us have known, and every minute of it was a delight. I do thank you and your wife for making it possible, and for being so kind.

My best wishes to you both, and, again, my most grateful thanks.

Yours very sincerely

Kathleen Ferrier

No.62 [Letter to Moran Caplat]

27th Feb[ruary 1947]   2 Frognal Mansions, London NW3

Dear Moran

Thank you very much for your letter – I was very thrilled to receive it, and would be delighted to go to New York for Bruno Walter in January next year. I have asked my agents not to book me for any engagements in this country for Jan. 1948 until I hear further news.

I am very anxious to know more about *Orfeo* – language, edition etc., so that I can get on with the learning of it. Would you let me know all details as early as possible, as I have so little time at my disposal.

I am so sorry Rudi [Rudolf Bing] is ill, and send him all good wishes for a very speedy recovery.

With kind greetings

Yours sincerely

Kathleen Ferrier

No.63 [Letter to John Tillett]
2nd April 1947   [2 Frognal Mansions, London NW3]
Dear Mr Tillett

Re Manchester April 12th – I have applied for a sleeper to get back to town, so will be unable to accept Mr Gregson's hospitality.

I have altered the date on my Lincoln contract to Friday 25th April. I enclose the signed contract.

Re Elland April 11th – I shall be arriving about 3.30 in Huddersfield from Stoke-on-Trent, staying at *Queen's* Hotel, Huddersfield. I don't know Mr Henderson's items, but mine are as follows:

How changed the vision	Handel
Come to me soothing sleep	Handel
Sweet rose and lily	Handel
Silent Noon	Vaughan Williams
A piper	Michael Head
Sleep	Peter Warlock
Pretty ring time	Peter Warlock

And a joint group with Mr Henderson

Let us wander	duet	Purcell
Fairest Isle	K.F.	"
Hark the ech'ing air	K.F.	"
Music for a while	R.H.	"
The knotting song	R.H.	"
Sound the trumpet	duet	"

Re Bournemouth 5th April – we are travelling on the 12.30, arriving Central 2.35 and hope to catch the 7.25 back to town. Would you corroborate the <u>Elland</u> programme with Mr Henderson to see that we agree!?
With best wishes
Yours sincerely
Kathleen Ferrier

No.64 [Letter to Emmie Bass]
3rd April 1947   [2 Frognal Mansions, London NW3]
Dear Miss Bass

Herewith the madrigals which you asked me to return to you – with grateful thanks for intervening (is that the right word?) on my behalf!

Might I remind you again of Romford on the 24th May? Now that Brighton has been cancelled on the 10th, do you think Romford might be transferred to that date, so as not to interfere with Glyndebourne rehearsals? I have been released for broadcast of the *St Matthew Passion* on the 22nd and don't like to ask for the 24th as well.
With best wishes and many thanks for all your kindness
Kathleen Ferrier

No.65 [Letter to Annie (née Chadwick) and Tom Barker]
Apr[il] 23rd [1947]   2 Frognal Mansions, London NW3
My dear Nan and Tom

Just to say a most sincere thank you for a <u>lovely</u> stay with you on Monday. It was gorgeous to see you again, and I shall look forward to seeing you at Glyndebourne. If you have any difficulties with tickets let me know. I can probably wangle those, but can't do much about accommodation, so I hope they can take you at either the *White Hart* or *Shelley's*, Lewes.

I had a most peaceful journey and learnt a lot more *Orfeo*, so I'm coming on now.

The photies hadn't come – 'twas just a large one for posters, but I'll let you have one when the others arrive.

I hope you weren't both worn out through looking after absent minded 'low' singer! Will let you know next time!
Loads of love, not forgetting Dorothy.
Very many thanks
Kath

Pop and Win send their love to you all

No.66 [Letter to Rudolf Bing]
23rd April [1947]   2 Frognal Mansions, London NW3
Dear Mr Bing

Thank you very much for your letter. I should be very willing to have *Vogue* take my photograph – so far they have not approached me, but perhaps will do so in the next few days.

Decca recording company have asked me to record the *St Matthew Passion* and the date they suggest is 4th July. Do you think you could allow me to do this, as I am not appearing in *Orfeo* that night?

I have asked for a date after *Orfeo* is finished, but Decca are unable to arrange for the orchestra and conductor on that date, so I hope you will agree, as I am very anxious to take part in this.
With best wishes
Yours sincerely
Kathleen Ferrier

I promise you I won't want time off for <u>anything</u> else!

No.67 [Letter to Rudolf Bing]
29th April [1947]   2 Frognal Mansions, London NW3
Dear Rudi

Thank you very much for your letter. I am doing my utmost to arrange another day on which to record the *St Matthew* – it is the difficulty of fitting in with the Jacques orchestra and the other principals, but I am meeting the Decca representative this week, and will try and make better plans. It is the one recording I don't want to miss. They are also planning for me to record parts of *Orfeo*, which will be nice? (I hope).

Eric [Crozier] has asked me to do two performances of *Lucretia* – 7th and

11th July – and I have said I would like to, as I remembered gratefully that you had said I was free to if I wished.

I have been measured today for a silver laurel wreath, and the measurer was appalled at the size of my head, but I think when I see myself in green tights, the size will be considerably reduced!!

With best wishes

Yours sincerely

Kathleen

No.68 [Letter to Audrey Christie]

May 4th [1947]   2 Frognal Mansions, London NW3

My dear Audrey

How lovely to hear from you – I can't tell you how I'm yearning to come to Glyndebourne again! I <u>loved</u> my room, and couldn't wish for a happier one, so, if I may, I would love to be there again. We live in such noisy flats here, I should be lonely without a little noise going on!

I am staggering through *Orfeo* – the memorising of the Italian was a struggle at first with all the other work I had to do – but I have been going to an Italian, Mr Gibilaro, who has helped me terrifically, and now I feel I'm getting the upper hand. (Fingers crossed!) The music, I think, is wonderful – and oh dear, I <u>do</u> hope I can do justice to it, and to the standard that Glyndebourne is famed for. I'm ready to work like a Trojan for you all!

Thank you again for your lovely letter.

Love to you both

Kathleen

No.69 [incomplete letter to Frances Bragg]

[May 1947]   [Glyndebourne]

... Until Tuesday morning I hadn't had a single free minute – I'd been cleaning my teeth with soap for days because I hadn't had time to go into Lewes for some toothpaste. I am doing *Orfeo* here with an American Euridice, a Greek God of Love, a German producer and conductor and an Italian coach. Talk about the Tower of Babel! It is all in Italian and you can guess the job I'm having to learn the words from memory. I was so pleased with myself because I'd memorised two acts whilst travelling, but when I arrived here, much of it was changed. I've cried for three days! ...

No.70 [Letter to Pop and Win]

Fri[day, May 1947]   Glyndebourne

Dearest Both

Just to let you know I'm still in one piece, and hope you are too.

The stage manager has brought me a lovely lyre of heavy plywood to get used to carrying, and it's going to make a lovely weapon when Stiedry tries me too far. One of these days he won't know what's hit him! He still shrugs his shoulders in despair, calls me an oratorio singer, and shouts himself hoarse. He was vaccinated yesterday, so Heaven help me in a day or two when his temp. goes up!

I wish I didn't cry so easily 'cos <u>I</u> can shout too. The Italian [Renato Cellini, a member of the music staff] is a poppet and has helped me very much – we've had a good laugh or two 'cos he gets mixed up in 'bitch' and 'beach'! The Christies are pets, the food very good and the weather lovely.

I've been to bed each night after dinner to alter my score – stick bits in and take bits out and have been doing about 14 hours a day, but last night I went to the local with the stage manager and had a dirty big pint. Did me a lot of good! Ayars, the American, is a love I think – she hasn't had Stiedry yet, but I should say she's pretty tough.

I took my film in yesterday and it will be ready on Tues. Whoopee!
Loads of love
Kath
Thank you for letter, Pappy. Look after yourselves

No.71 [Letter to John Tillett]
[end of May 1947]   Glyndebourne, Lewes
Dear Mr Tillett

Thank you for your letter. I had hardly a minute when I was in town for [*St Matthew*] *Passion* with rehearsal and long performance. I am probably up this weekend for orchestral rehearsals, and will come in to see you if I may. You can always throw me out if you are too busy.

Eric Crozier wants me to do some *Lucretias* in Oct. Here are the dates: 1st Bournemouth, 4th Bournemouth (matinee), 8th, 14th, 16th Covent Garden, 21st and 23rd Newcastle, 29th and 31st Oxford. The last one I can't do because of Darlington on the 1st Nov. This would rule out BBC pencilling on 29th Oct but I could do 17th Nov. Would you be good enough to pass this on to Miss Hurst.

All fairly serene here. Please, please, please will you do your very best to come? Will arrange seats and everything if you will. Shall be cut to the quick if you miss it. If only to see me singing my way thro' Hell fire wiv me 'arp in mi 'and!! Please try.
Yrs.
Kathleen F.

No.72 [Letter to John Tillett]
[end of May 1947]   Glyndebourne, Lewes
Dear Mr Tillett

I couldn't get in to see you on Sat as the rehearsal was from 10–1 and 2–5, and now it doesn't look as though I shall be up in town again before the first night. All *Orfeo* is being recorded by Decca and also the *St Matthew Passion*. Isn't that lovely! Both in June and July.

I have at last managed to get a copy of the Mozart aria for my Prom and it is completely hopeless for me. Tessitura is round about Es and Fs and finishes on top A. It is a soprano aria and says so in the score. I am looking out some Italian arias here from Mr Christie's library and will let you know if I find a suitable one.

I shall be able to sing in Romford on Nov 15th 1947. My *Lucretia* dates have been altered to fit my plans better. Here they are: Oct 1st & 4th Bournemouth, 8th, 14th, 17th Covent Garden, 21st & 23rd Newcastle, 28th & 30th Oxford.

Dr Stiedry, our conductor here, tells me he has had some enquiries about me from the New York Metropolitan, but they seem to want me to do Amneris in *Aida*, and I think it's much too much of a scream. I am very willing to let Columbia Concerts, New York, have an option on my services.

With best wishes
Sincerely
Kathleen Ferrier

No.73 [Letter to Audrey Hurst, BBC department of Ibbs and Tillett]
11th July 1947   [2 Frognal Mansions, London NW3]
Dear Miss Hurst

This is a joint letter to all and sundry about many matters to which I have not had time to reply.

BBC Tuesday 5th August: shall be sunbathing (ever hopeful) in Devonshire! I shall be on holiday from Monday 14th inst to about the 12th August.

Leonard Isaacs: BBC overseas has asked for a recital. I think it is the 27th September but am not very sure. Would you corroborate (?) this date with him and let me know? This is for Rubbra songs, so perhaps I could do the same programme for Basil Douglas on the 28th.

London Phil[harmonic]: Nov 14th repeat concert of Bruckner *Te Deum*. OK

Romford Nov 15th: Please may I take my own accompanist as I am so busy round that time. I shall need to save my voice – Phyllis Spurr would go for 10 gns and I will lower mine if necessary. What about 35gns for the whole lot?

Woking: I would rather not accept any more engagements this year and September 29th I shall be rehearsing *Lucretia*.

Bath May 29th 1948: There is a suggestion that *Orfeo* will be done next year at Glyndebourne, and if so I shall be busy in May. I will try to find out as soon as possible, but would rather you did not accept at the moment.

Archway Choral Society: As far as I know I could sing for Mr Crellin on Sat 14th Feb.

Farnham Music Club want me sometime and I have suggested Sat 21st Feb. with Phyllis Spurr as accompanist. Could you do something about this for me please?

Would somebody reply to the enclosed for me please, and all accept my apologies for having kept you waiting for my replies!
Yours sincerely
Kathleen Ferrier

No.74 [Letter to Audrey Christie]
16.7.47   Port Stewart, N. Ireland
Dearest Audrey

I don't know how to start to thank you for all you have done for me and been to me these past two months.

It has been absolutely wonderful for me and a unique experience, and one I shall remember always.

Any success I achieved – the applause, reports, attention – was exciting and gratifying, but to be a guest in your house and be spoiled as you have spoiled, remains more memorable. For all your understanding, hospitality and encouragement, Audrey very dear, I do thank you most sincerely.

Would you say to Mr Christie also, my most grateful thanks for his belief in me, for giving me the chance to do the one part I have always dreamed of doing, and for all his kindness at all times.

I am sorry I missed you on Saturday to say thank you in person, but I look forward to seeing you all in Edinburgh, and until then, look after yourself for you must be very weary.

With all my love and gratitude

Yours

Kathleen

No.75 [Letter to John Tillett]

26th August [1947]   2 Frognal Mansions, London NW3

Dear Mr Tillett

Enclosed please find cuttings, photographs and repertoire for America. I leave the biography to you as we arranged. I will just corroborate the dates for Miss Anne Wood: Oct 1st & 4th Newcastle, 8th, 14th & 17th Covent Garden, 21st & 22nd Bournemouth, 28th & 30th Oxford with a possibility of one of the Covent Garden dates being altered from the 8th to the 7th.

Yours sincerely

Kathleen Ferrier

No.76 [Letter to John Tillett]

4th September [1947]   [2 Frognal Mansions, London NW3]

Dear Mr Tillett

Could you please reply to the enclosed letter from Whitehaven for me? My sister tells me she's booked for my carol concert on December 19th in the Albert Hall – but my contract says Central Hall, and I'm wondering if there is an alteration in arrangements?

With best wishes

Yours sincerely

Kathleen Ferrier

No.77 [Letter to John Tillett]

16th September [1947]   [2 Frognal Mansions, London NW3]

Dear Mr Tillett

I enclose a contract for Cardiff. With reference to piano rehearsal at Norwich on the 22nd inst. I am sorry I shall be unable to be there as I have a rehearsal in London in the morning (*Lucretia!*)

I have noted the piano rehearsals with Dr Bruno Walter and will wait instructions as to where they are to be held. There were not very many press cuttings for the Mahler but I enclose all I have. Looking forward very much to seeing you in Norwich.

Yours sincerely

Kathleen Ferrier

No.78 [Letter to John Tillett]

[?October 1947]   [2 Frognal Mansions, London NW3]

Dear Mr Tillett

Would you please reply to the enclosed for me?

I have to tell you from Dr Hutchinson (N'castle) that he has a pupil (baritone) who is going to be a world shatterer! And is there any chance of your hearing him?

Leon Goossens has asked me to sing for him at Lewes for the Musicians' Benevolent Fund on November 28th and I have said I would. There will be Carter String Trio, Leon G and myself – all giving services. OK?

Have a lovely photograph of you at Norwich – am getting it enlarged and will send it to you.

Yours sincerely

Kathleen Ferrier

Enclosed cheque for Mr Hawkes for 6 tickets for November 13th Albert Hall

No.79 [Letter to Emmie Bass]

[Undated but probably November or December 1947]   [2 Frognal Mansions, London NW3]

Dear Miss Bass

Thank you very much for my sailing ticket. I enclose here the cheque for the remaining amount.

Mr Tillett mentioned a possibility of some *Lucretias* in New York whilst I am there. I mentioned it to Bruno Walter and he says I must be very careful as it may be some inferior opera group, and it would only do me harm. I thought I would mention it as I was keen to do it when Mr Tillett told me of the possibility.

With best wishes

Yours sincerely

Kathleen Ferrier

No.80 [Letter to Charles D. Rigg]

Boxing Day [1947]   In train!

Dear Mr Rigg

Thank you so much for your kind letter – I cannot tell you how grateful I am to you and Mr Barnes and your committee for their generous attitude to my cancelled contract. I can only promise to do all in my power to make up in the future for this disappointment – this I do with great sincerity.

I shall miss my New Year's day festivities badly, especially if there's a gale blowing! – but I shall be thinking of you and wishing you well.

My visit is only to last six weeks so have no fears! I am singing for Bruno Walter in *Das Lied* – three times in New York – and about six recitals between there and Chicago. Mr Tillett is going with me to see I behave and don't sign on the wrong dotted line, and we are both looking forward to it very much.

My bank manager says I am a valuable export, and worth about two crates of SPAM!

It was good to see Margot in Swansea – I hope you will have a lovely time at Xmas and the New Year, and send my best wishes and grateful thanks.
Yours very sincerely
Kathleen Ferrier

2   Letters: 1948

On New Year's Day 1948 Kathleen Ferrier set sail from Southampton for America, the first of three annual trips she would make, but on this one she was accompanied by John Tillett. This was an honour he was unaccustomed to bestowing upon his artists though there had been a precedent when his partner Robert Leigh Ibbs went with another contralto, Clara Butt, and her husband, baritone Kennerley Rumford on a tour of Australia and New Zealand back in the very early days of the agency in 1907. On that occasion, however, Butt was already a star and the crowds turned out to hear her, sometimes just to watch her train steam through their town even though it may not have been part of her itinerary to give a concert there. Ferrier, on the other hand, was an unknown and had a mountain to climb to make a name for herself with American audiences and particularly the critics. She was away until the middle of February and found it difficult to make ends meet on the tour for there were many unexpected expenses and the cost of living in luxurious hotels was high. She was not helped by John Tillett's indifferent health, and, being nearly forty years his junior, she was neither patient nor understanding about his ailments. He appeared 'liverish', was slow and often confused, and prone to dietary complaints. She could not know that he was suffering from terminal cancer and would die six months later. However, the highlight of the tour was her collaboration with Bruno Walter in Mahler's *Das Lied von der Erde* and the New York Philharmonic Orchestra in Carnegie Hall soon after she arrived in the country. After working with Kathleen the previous autumn in Edinburgh, Walter had been a prime mover in getting her to come to America, despite the upheaval it caused at Ibbs and Tillett to cancel or reschedule engagements back in Britain for this period, and at the end of her tour she received private coaching from him in the Lieder repertoire. Her experiences covering the period September 1947 to February 1948, from Edinburgh to America were written down for publication in the school magazine of her *alma mater*.

Blackburn Girls' High School Magazine and Old Girls' Newsletter Vol.1 No.8 1948
Article on pages 45–48 entitled 'Six Months of Music, September 1947 to February 1948'.
    As a result of my being heard by Professor Bruno Walter, this season was to prove the most exciting that I have known so far. After a holiday in Devonshire, where I had memorized the work, I had to sing for the now famous, first Edinburgh Festival (*Das Lied von der Erde* – Gustav Mahler), I arrived home again in Hampstead.
    In the midst of my unpacking the telephone rang, and to my amazement it was Professor Walter who had flown from America the previous day, and who, without waiting to catch up on lost sleep, was proposing to come up to my flat to start rehearsals! I was alarmed at the thought of the steps he would

have to climb – he is now 72 years old – and even more alarmed at his possible reactions to my piano, which is an upright, one which I won in a piano-playing competition when I was 16, and now no longer all that might be desired! I felt sure that my memorized German words, which I had learned so painfully would desert me, but a taxi from the West End to Hampstead does not take long enough to allow of too many anxious thoughts, and I was greeting the great man on the doorstep almost before I had found my score in the chaos of my packing.

After this first rehearsal, Peter Pears, the tenor soloist and I had about fifteen hours intensive study with piano of this particular work with Professor Walter. It was quite memorable for me. Professor Walter had been friend, student and confidant of Mahler, and he lived and loved every note of the score, playing and conducting the whole work from memory. My greatest difficulty was to restrain my sobs in the last lovely heartbreaking 'Abschied', and at the second rehearsal I was unsuccessful and held up work for about half-an-hour while I blew my nose, mopped my streaming eyes and tried to apologise for being a nuisance, all at one time! The intensity of this work and the emotion of Professor Walter had caught me unawares, but I was patted on the back and told – 'it's all right, my child, they all do!' But at all piano and, later, orchestral rehearsals I could never sing the last song without a lump in my throat, and it was only at the first performance in Edinburgh that I felt I could enjoy it and now make others weep instead of myself! I had not suffered so much since playing the part of Orfeo at Glyndebourne Opera the previous spring, when I lost my beautiful Euridice after defying Hades and Elysium to find her!!

The Edinburgh Festival was unforgettable. The sun shone, the station was decked with flags, the streets were gay with flowers, and music, plays, ballet by the finest artists were being performed, literally morning, noon and night, and hospitality was showered upon guests and visitors by the so-called 'dour' Scots! What a misnomer!

It was all so different from previous experiences of concerts. My almost daily routine had been mostly the same so far – travelling during the morning, rehearsing in the afternoon, performing at night, usually on an unchanging diet of sandwiches, and catching an early train the next morning either home or to another engagement. To be able to unpack for a week and come to a concert fresh and thoroughly rehearsed was novel and refreshing.

After Edinburgh came a series of concerts and recitals, the Norwich and Leeds Festivals; during October several performances of the title part of Benjamin Britten's *The Rape of Lucretia*, including two at Covent Garden Opera House; and in December many *Messiah* performances all over England and Scotland.

On January 1st 1948, I sailed with my manager to New York to repeat the Edinburgh performances of *Das Lied von der Erde* with Bruno Walter, but this time with the New York Philharmonic, instead of the Vienna Philharmonic Orchestra, in Carnegie Hall on three different dates. This was something I had never believed possible in my wildest dreams and I was excited to say the least of it! I had had one day to pack, having been singing to the last moment, but it was encouraging to think that I shouldn't need coupons for anything I had left behind!

Our journey seemed as though it might never start, for, when we arrived at Southampton there was a stevedores' strike; eventually, however, we were gliding away from Southampton, and every minute of the next five days was an experience and a delight. The ship was the *Mauretania*, newly painted and decorated after her war service and a joy to behold and inhabit. I will not make mouths water by my descriptions of the food and the comfort, but it was overwhelming after eight years of austerity.

The first sight of New York has to be seen to be believed, and with snow, sunshine and a high, blue, clear sky, it was more than impressive. We were through the customs and in a cab in record time, despite several photographers and newspaper men all asking questions and taking photographs at the same time. Our hotel was very central, exceedingly comfortable and unbearably hot. The first persons we saw were Mr and Mrs Benno Moiseiwitsch, who were also making it their home for a little while, so there were rejoicings all round and much chatter! From then on, every minute was occupied – shop gazing – museum visiting – meeting the American manager – seeing Broadway illuminated by a million lights – rehearsing with pianist for some recitals I had to do in and about Chicago – more piano rehearsals with Bruno Walter – and coping with the well known American hospitality! Ruth Draper, the famous *diseuse*, whom I had met only once in London, welcomed me with flowers, invited me to dinner and tea, left a box at my disposal for myself and my friends at the theatre where she was playing, and generally spoiled me like an only child!

As my first concert in Carnegie Hall drew near, I ceased all merrymaking and concentrated only on rehearsals, not talking too much and going to bed early. I had developed a cold due to the extremes of temperature, and I was being very careful. If I were indisposed and couldn't sing, I should not be able to pay my hotel bill – a frightening thought! But all was well and the three performances were given without a hitch – and included in the applause were asides from the orchestra such as 'Bravo Beautiful' – very American – but balm to a singer's soul, when such praise comes sincerely from an instrumental player!

The last performance was broadcast all over America, and the manager of the orchestra told me that there were between 15 and 20 million listeners! One letter, as a result of this relay, came from the famous conductor Stokowski, and was a glowing tribute – one which I treasure highly.

Immediately after this last concert, my accompanist, manager and I caught one of the famous diesel trains to Chicago. They are very quiet and comfortable and I think the dinner we had on this train surpassed any meal I had ever had – it was wonderful – and served by negro waiters with ear to ear grins of shining white teeth. My accompanist would whisper to a waiter that I was English and therefore starved, also a singer who needed fattening up, and there would appear more butter than even I could manage!! He was a great tease, but a terrific help on our travels, and in the delicate matter of tipping, saved us much thought and embarrassment.

I was a little worried about my first recital concert – I had made up a programme of Handel, Gluck in Italian, Schubert in German, the Brahms 'Serious Songs' and English folksongs. My first concert was in Ottawa, Illinois, about two hours away from Chicago, and I had travelled from 4.30 the previous day and, not having slept very much, was feeling a little jaded by the time we arrived – about noon. The town looked small and the houses were mostly wooden and I wondered where our audience would come from, and oh dear! <u>why</u> had I put down the Brahms Serious Songs? I dressed for the concert, feeling slightly sick, and was taken down to the hall. My manager, who had no rouge to hide his pallor, was looking as I felt, and even my voluble pianist was quiet!

The concert was in a lovely school hall holding about a thousand people, and it was crammed full! I never knew where they all came from, but from the first to the last notes of the piano there was a breathless silence, and then such an ovation after my first group as to dispel all doubts as to suitability of programme.

After that first concert the next three recitals went well and in each case the hall was filled to capacity. One of the things I remember learning at school were the names of the great lakes, and I had to pinch myself to realize I could look out from my room window in Chicago immediately on to Lake Michigan, stretching – cold and frozen – as far as the eye could see!

And now back to New York again for a week's holiday before boarding the *Queen Mary* on February 4th. There were no concerts looming in the near future to worry me – I had money to pay my hotel bill – I could relax or hustle as the mood took me. The bracing cold of New York seemed to produce energy in me, and I went from one excitement to another. Lunches and dinners with Mr and Mrs Schnabel, with Bruno Walter and his daughter, with Elisabeth Schumann, with Ruth Draper, and many American friends – shopping and endless window gazing – days in the Metropolitan and Frick Museums – a visit to the 76th floor of the Empire State Building to pay my income tax (!) and many memorable hours of enjoyment.

The journey home was uneventful, though the ship dipped her elbows in the sea all the way, due to a 'confused swell'! The glasses and cutlery chased each other across the tables in the dining room, and we had to pour water on the tablecloths to make them a little less mobile. We were several hours late arriving at Southampton and I was home by 5.30pm on the 10th February – only just in time for a performance of the *Dream of Gerontius* in the Albert Hall the next day.

I shall always be grateful to the manager of the Glyndebourne Opera, who introduced me to Bruno Walter and brought about these experiences – they were wonderful and unforgettable.

KATHLEEN FERRIER

Apart from visits to Holland in April (twice) and again in July, and a later trip to Denmark in September, her schedule kept her in Britain with oratorio and recital engagements. She was becoming an especial favourite in Holland not only because of the broadcasts she made there or were received from the BBC, but also due to the organisational talents of impresario and Festival Director Peter Diamand. While there she worked with new conductors such as Willem van Otterloo and Georg Szell in music by Mahler. She appeared at the Promenade Concerts during August (Alto Rhapsody with Sargent) followed by the Edinburgh Festival at the end of the month. She then went to Worcester for her debut at the Three Choirs Festival in early September (*St Matthew Passion, Messiah, Dream of Gerontius*, and Debussy's *Blessed Damozel*), and sang Mahler's *Kinder-totenlieder* under Josef Krips at the Royal Albert Hall in December.

No.81 [Letter to Pop and Paddy]
Sunday [4th January 1948]   Cunard White Star RMS *Mauretania*
Dearest Pop and Paddy

Well aren't I a lucky lass? (fingers crossed!) Fourth day at sea and I've eaten every meal, and am still intact despite 'heavy swell' – clever Kaff!

I am enjoying every minute of this and feeling wonderful for the rest. We started off with a strike at S'hampton, but managed to get on board after about 1¼ hrs without having luggage examined! It's an ill wind –!

We saw the *Queens Mary* and *Eliz* in dock – they look wonderful.

I have a lovely cabin to myself and there were lovely flowers waiting for me from Phyllis Spurr and about 8 telegrams, so my head swelled another inch and I felt prima donna written all o'er me. I have my own shower, basin and lav and everything is sheer luxury. The meals are beyond description and the service wonderful.

I start the day off with a tray brought in by a stewardess. A colossal grapefruit, toast and a week's butter ration, marmalade and tea. She also brings the ship's newspaper and events of the day. I get up slowly and have shower, then meet Mr Tillett on the SUN deck and believe it or not, we had quite a few hours of sunshine yesterday. Then we pace round and round till we've done a couple of miles – then down to the Promenade deck to our chairs, where a steward wraps us up in blankets and brings us chicken soup and a biscuit! Whattalife!

A rest for a bit, then a cocktail and some Smith's Crisps in a lovely bar and lunch – Oh my! Won't make you jealous, loves, but I'll bring some menus home.

Then back to our deck chairs with a book and sure enough a snooze and lo and behold it's teatime, and there's our nice steward with a tray of tea and a choice of Persil-white bread and butter – delicious cakes and chocolate biscuits. Then there's a gram[ophone] recital and a flick – we've seen *I wonder who's kissing her now* and *While I live*. I have missed *Sabu* today because I've seen it. Then twice round the deck and dress for dinner. Last night we were invited to the chief Purser's for cocktails – tonight to the Captain's, so we're getting around.

A special dinner has been ordered for us tonight on the orders of the Purser, so we're having caviar, sole, fillet steak, straw potatoes, salad, special ice with gorgeous little iced biscuits and coffee!! Oh dear, I keep thinking about you struggling along to make the joint spin out, but I'll send some parcels when I arrive – then you both have a good tuck in.

Mr Tillett's a bit liverish today, but if he will have two eggs for breakfast he's asking for it, isn't he? He's grand really and hasn't been ill either – there are very few people that haven't, but thanks to Dr Morton's pills, which I have taken in small doses, I have been fine.

Last night there was horse-racing on deck – wooden ones that move up as the dice is thrown. I borrowed 5/- from Mr T. and won 17/6 with backing No.4!!!

Yesterday, when the sun shone, we were north of the Azores – now as we get nearer Newfoundland, the skies are stormy and there are white horses, but I hear a lot of the snow has cleared in New York.

Ernest Ansermet (who conducted *Lucretia* at Glyndebourne) is on this boat with his wife – we picked them up at Cherbourg – 's small world, isn't it? I nearly forgot to tell you we share our table with an Australian lady and James Mason's mother-in-law, Mrs [Helen} Ostrer!! Fame, begorra! Viscountess Rothermere's on board too! Will cable when I arrive – meanwhile loads of love to you both, and look after each other.

God bless.

Kath

P.S. <u>Paddy</u>. Will you pick out a <u>large</u> photie of me by Fayer (middle drawer). Preferably the one looking sideways down, and send it with little note to Terence Gibbs Esq., 87 Heath St, Hampstead. Say in the rush I forgot, but when I see him in New York I will sign it. You could push it through his door – it's the one below Wallers antique shop. Sorry to trouble you, but don't want to disappoint him.

No.82 [Letter to Win]

Tuesday 6th Jan [19]48   Cunard White Star RMS *Mauretania*

Dearest Win

Hello love! Here I am, propped up in bed, having had a gorgeous breakfast and feeling the complete diva!

Heavens! I never expected to enjoy this trip so much. We've had sunshine, gales and heavy swells and I've never turned a hair – even when I've seen other folk in distress! Bless Dr Morton for his littul pills.

I don't know where to start, but our main conversation is the food! I have never ever seen such dishes, and we are being very spoiled by the chief steward who thinks up meals for us, so that we start with tomato juice, caviar with all the trimmings, soup, fish, lobster or salmon, beef, steaks, joints of all descriptions, and the most amazing sweets ever. Baked ice cream – that is ice cream on cake with meringue all round, or ice cream with cherries in brandy and the brandy lit with a match till there are blue flames all over it. Mr Tillett has a liver, but if he <u>will</u> have two eggs for breakfast! – True he only asked for one, but they always double the order!

I have a cabin to myself with my own shower and lav, and everything is sheer luxury. We have deck chairs on the Promenade deck, and as soon as we arrive in the morning our feet are tucked up in warm rugs and we get chicken soup and a dry biscuit!

We share a dining table with James Mason's mother-in-law, and an Australian lady – Mrs Stilwell, whom I always have to arrive at her name by steps – such as 'Quite good', 'Getting better', and 'Very well'!! Also on ship are Zoltan Korda (film man who made *Sanders of the River*), Viscountess Rothermere, and Ernest Ansermet and wife! But otherwise nobody startling. We have been invited to cocktails with the Chief Steward and the Captain, and altogether have had a wonderful time and a grand rest. I won 10/- on the horse racing and lost it all the next night!!

There are people on board who haven't had more than a couple of meals the whole trip, they have been so ill, so I'm feeling elated at my sea-worthiness! Mr Tillett's a good sailor – it's just his liver wot gets him down! He's grand and good company, and very anxious as to my welfare, and we're getting on fine.

Have seen about four films and the time has just <u>flown</u>! My earrings are lovely and I'm taking great care of them – will write again after we arrive tomorrow. Loads of love to you both, and I hope all's well with you.

Clever Kaff!

No.83 [Letter to Pop and Paddy]

Friday 9th Jan [1948]   Hotel *Weylin*, Madison Avenue, 54th Street,
                                                                New York 22, NY.

Dearest Pop and Paddy

Here I am in New York and taking it in my stride. What a city – it is just a fairyland of good things and wonderful buildings, and all the time I am wishing you could both be here to share these excitements and pleasures.

The voyage was wonderful and sheer luxury and I felt very prima donna, when I was interviewed on the boat on arrival, and pictures taken of me leaning over the starboard side!! One reporter wanted to know who this gorgeous beauty was! I could have hit him but only grinned and they were very nice and didn't hustle me as I had been warned.

We were through the customs without any trouble and in our hotel, where we both have nice rooms with bath, shower and lav. It's all exorbitantly expensive, but I expect we'll manage. I shall have to go canny with my purchases, or I shan't be able to pay my bill.

Euridice [Ann Ayars] and her pal were here almost before I'd unpacked, and there were great goings on. We're going shopping and out to dinner together tomorrow.

I've had flowers from Hans Schneider and a lovely plant from Ruth Draper, lunch with Terence's aunt, dinner with American manager and wife, hair done at Lizzie Arden's, a coffee in a drugstore, and walked the sole (literally) off my shoe. All in one day, and I've loved every minute of it.

Mr T. is bearing up, despite a liver from eating too much (don't say I said so!) and despite being bewildered by dollars, dimes and quarters, not to mention the traffic which 'honks' furiously all night!

It is all a wonderful experience but home will be lovely too. I just hope all is well with you both, and that the beastly leaks leak no longer, and that you're getting plenty to eat. Think of me on the 15th and keep your fingers crossed – it's going to be a terrific strain, but I reckon I'll survive somehow!

Look after yourselves, you two poppets – shall be with you on the 9th Feb at the latest. Whoopee!

Loads of love

Klever Kaff

No.84 [Postcard to Win]

9th January 1948   [postmarked New York Grand Central Station]

Hello love

Here I am, thrilled to bits every minute of the day. It was a wonderful voyage – sheer luxury, and NY is just unbelievable. The shops are like fairyland and the buildings superb. WISH you could be here to enjoy it too. Have had flowers from Hans and Ruth Draper – seen Euridice and Dottie, both ravishing and send their love – dinner with American manager and wife, and all's very well.

Hope all is well with you – <u>loads</u> of love to you both.

Kaff

No.85 [Letter to Pop and Paddy]
Monday [12th January 1948]   Hotel *Weylin*, Madison Avenue, 54th Street,
New York 22, NY.

Dearest Pop and Paddy

I hear the pipes and tank are all in one piece again. Three rousing cheers – wonders'll never cease! I <u>do</u> hope everything else is well with you too, and that you are getting plenty to eat.

All is well here except I've got a runny cold. The rooms are so hot and the streets so icy, the change of atmosphere has been too much to cope with. Yesterday I had no voice at all, but today my nose is running like a tap, so all is well – it'll soon be right now!

I have had two rehearsals with Bruno Walter and he is very pleased, but I keep my fingers crossed all the time. There seems to be a lot of publicity about this concert and Alma Mahler (Mahler's wife) is going to be there – my photie was in the *New York Times* yesterday – not a bad one – but there haven't been any from the reporters on the boat.

Did I tell you Ruth Draper sent me a lovely azalea (bright red). If my cold is better tomorrow, I'm having dinner with her – what a thrill! Today I had flowers, fruit and chocs from Mr Mertens, the New York manager, because he'd heard I had a cold. Clever 'im!

I bought some lovely boots, Paddy – pony skin and warm and lovely – I'm thrilled to bits with them and so glad of them as it is so cold. I haven't bought anything else except a pair of shoes and some soap and hankies. I have to watch my money as it is so expensive here. My three-course dinner tonight was over £1!! (But it was jolly good!)

Euridice (Ann) and Dottie send their love to Pop – I had a lovely day with them on Sat when they helped me find my boots. Cellini rang up today too, and is going to pay me my £10 back, he says, so that's a help.

I am in the throes of signing a contract for next year, but as there seems to be more paying out than receiving, I'm not thrilled – but expect it will work out all right.

Look after yourselves loves. Will write again after Thurs and let you know what the results of concert are.

Loads of love and keep <u>your</u> fingers crossed.

Tarawell

Kath

No.86 [Letter to Win]
[12th January 1948]   Hotel *Weylin*, Madison Avenue, 54th Street, New York

Dearest Win

Thank you very much for letter, love, with all the enclosures. <u>Four shillings</u> did it cost you? My! my! I'll pay you back when I get home. Isn't Ena a pet – she sounded disappointed on the phone, when I hadn't received her present, so now I know why. I am so glad the pipes and tank are fixed now – whaattarelief. Thanks ever so for keeping an eye on No.2, that's a relief too, not 'arf!

I long for you to be here all the time to see the sights. Mr T. and I went to see Broadway lit up the other night, but it was so cold and Mr T's a bit slow, it's given me a rotten cold. The rooms are so hot as to be unbearable and it's icy outside with a howling wind. I woke up voiceless yesterday and this morning but now voice is back, and my nose is running, so that's fine! I've 3 days still to go before Thurs[day].

I had my first piano rehearsal with B. Walter yesterday and my voice had come back by that time, so it's not laryngitis, thank Heaven! Have cancelled all lunches and dinners etc. and am just staying in and coddling myself.

I am rung up about every ¼ hour by friends of friends, who want to help or entertain etc. etc., and they're all very kind. Dottie, Ann and I had a day's shopping on Sat[urday], then a dinner with two of their boy friends at the latter's apartment. It was a lovely day – I bought some beautiful ponyskin boots and a pair of shoes and two woolly pants, a banana (!), some Lux, soap, face cloth and blackcurrant and glycerine sweets all mitout coupons.

We're going to be hard up for money as hotel, food, and everything else is very dear so I'm not shopping much till I see how I stand – but the boots and shoes were an urgent necessity I reckon!

Our rooms were on the 1st floor and <u>so</u> noisy as we're opposite two night clubs, and they were let loose about 3.30 each morning, and all the cars here drive with their hands on their horns (don't get me wrong!) and golly, what a noise! So yesterday we swapped to the 12th floor and I've had my first real good sleep.

I have to coddle Mr T. a bit. He's feeling his age a bit, I think, and it takes him hours to decide whether he ought to wear a jersey, or if he's enough dimes for a stamp, or whether his underwear will go down on the laundry list as combinations or shorts, and as for choosing a meal – well!! (Our father's positively <u>lively</u> in comparison!) I try to curb my impatience as I know I do everything quickly if slapdashly – but I could punch him sometimes! How he ever gets any work done, I can't think.

My hair is amazing. I went to Lizzie Arden's to have it done by André, Hans' pal, and it was lovely, but there's so much electricity in the air with the dryness, that it comes out to meet my comb and won't stay down. I look proper daft. 'Course I'm due for the curse on Thursday!!!!! so won't dare have it done again.

My photie was in the *New York Times* looking quite good – one of the better Edinburgh ones – and there seems to be terrific excitement about this concert and all three booked out, so I <u>must</u> do my stuff.

My accompanist is very good – Sandor a Hungarian – but I'll have to wear my barbed wire drawers – golly is he forthcoming! But I can cope, toots, he's much too effusive to make any impression!

Letters will be more difficult now, as I shall be very busy now for a fortnight, so I'll just send snippets now and again and you'll understand, eh?

Hope school went down well after Xmas, love, and that all is well with you. Much love to you and Jane [Bradfield], and keep your fingers crossed!
Loads of love
Kath
P.S. The broadcast is Sunday afternoon (18th) 3pm <u>this</u> time, but I don't know what wavelength.
P.P.S. I had a wire from Mr Cope. Wasn't that nice?

No.87 [Letter to Win]

Friday 16th Jan [1948]   Hotel *Weylin*, Madison Avenue, 54th Street,
New York 22, NY.

Dearest Win

Just a short scribble, 'cos I know you'll be wondering how I got on. Thank you love very much for wire and will you thank Paddy and Pop for theirs and Bo and Roy (PR 3144) if you've 2d to spear [erased] spare(!)

Well Bruno W. was thrilled – I've never known him to open out so – he said I was making musical history (honest).

Some of the critics are enthusiastic, others unimpressed. I'll quote from some:

New York Telegram. Miss F ought to make a permanent addition to the vocal wing of New York music. The voice is warm and vibrant, easily produced and capable of rich applications of colour. Phrasing and diction both showed a sure grasp of style and content.

New York Sun. The high hopes held for K.F. the English <u>mezzo</u> (!) were not fulfilled. Miss F. has a clear, clean and clinging voice and she is a musicianly artist. But her voice had neither the breadth nor depth to convey all of what Mahler meant, and she sounded to be more <u>soprano</u> than mezzo. One did not feel either the poise or the authority for so heavy a burden. Her uncertain pronunciation of the German text was also disturbing.

New York Times. Miss F. had but recently emerged from a bad cold. Her voice became freer as she went on. She could not, however, give full significance to her text and music. Some time before the end was reached, *Das Lied* was becoming langweilig [boring], lachrymose, old-fashioned.

I've shown you the two bad ones – there are two more ecstatic ones in the *New York Tribune* and something else. It is very disappointing. I had been in bed 3 days with the worst cold I'd ever had, but I had Ruth Draper's doctor and he worked miracles – he douched my nose and painted my throat, and quite honestly, what with all the good food and rest, I have myself never felt in such good trim. My soft top notes came as I've never known them. I was a bit nervous, but did it all from memory except for a few words which I hid behind my programme, and Bruno W. told me today my German was pure and classic and he's thrilled, so I don't really mind – only I wanted to come home sort of top of the class!

The audience was lousy – when I and the tenor and B. Walter walked on – in that order – there was a handful of clapping – I was stunned – I thought I must have dropped my pants!

Mr T. has cheered up tonight, but he had a face as long and as yellow as a bloody banana this morning!

This afternoon the performance was even better – (I thought the tenor [Set Svanholm] was excellent, but he's hardly had a kind word!) Mr T. said someone next to him said 'What a small voice' (the place holds 3500). But if they knew the score, I have to start *pp* and stay there more or less until orch[estra] gets noisy – then I do too.

The American agents have rung up wanting me to do a recital in New York whilst I am here, but I'm not going to do until I've done some Lieder with B. Walter! YES! He's going to give me some lessons when I get back from Chicago.

What an opportunity! He is truly thrilled with me and my German and interpretation, and is already seeing to my dates for next year, so I don't mind so much now. I suppose it's good for one not to hit the headlines all the time, but I <u>did</u> want to on this occasion.

My room is <u>crammed</u> with flowers. I have at least 60 pink and red carnations – 30 gladioli, white and yellow something or other, tulips and irises, dozen red roses, and a gorgeous bouquet from Rick, bless him, of gladioli, snapdragons and 14 carnations all tied in wide pink ribbon. I had a corsage of two wonderful orchids from Dottie and Ann which I wore.

I had the curse at 10am on the morning of my first concert – would you believe it! But it didn't worry me – I'd too much to think about!!

We've been to Edward Isaac's cousin's for tea after concert today in a wonderful apartment, and Bruno Walter, Frau Mahler and many distinguished people were there. Mahler's daughter was there – very amused 'cos someone wanted to know if I were her daughter!! She took it in good part – she's only about 43 – but she might have been furious!

Well love, that's about all. It hasn't ended in a blaze of glory but it's all experience.

Mr T. still grouses either about his liver, or a stiff back, or a bad taste in his mouth, or too little food or too much food etc. etc., but I get it in first now and he's stopping it a bit. He's always boasting about his inferiority complex or his shyness until I don't believe him any longer.

Hey dear! Loads of love to you from

Not so clever Kaff!

No.88 [Letter to Laura Cooper] [either the day or the date is incorrect as Sunday was the 18th]

Sunday 17th January 1948　　　　　　Hotel *Weylin*, Madison Avenue, 54th Street,
New York 22, N.Y.

Dear Laura Cooper

I cannot thank you enough for your kind welcoming letter and the wonderful gladioli. It was most generous of you to write and send me these superb flowers, and I do thank you most sincerely for your kind thought.

It has been a great experience to me to come to America, and I have loved every minute of it, and hope I shall have the chance of coming again next year.

Thank you again from the bottom of my heart, for your enthusiasm, welcome and kindness. I appreciate it more than I can say.

With kind greetings and good wishes

Yours very sincerely

Kathleen Ferrier

No.89 [Letter to Win]

Friday 23rd Jan. 1948　　　　　　The *Blackstone* [Hotel], Michigan Ave, Chicago

Dearest Win

I wonder where I left you? We left New York on Monday last – Terence's aunt came to see us off – and were given roomettes on the train – all right, but frightfully draughty! I slept in everything I had including my new woollie breeks, which start at my knees and don't finish till mi armpits! But I didn't sleep much, tho' the trains are very smooth, the beds are sprung so, I bounced up and down all night like a rubber ball. But before we went to bed, Mr T., Sandor, and I – we went down train to diner and sat at table and had the most delicious meal yet – orange juice, a wonderful steak and baked apple! Half way thru, a man joined our table and we went on talking, and suddenly he butted in saying he heard we were musical and obviously English and he had the rights of *Peter Grimes*, and he knew of <u>me</u> well! He was a most famous producer called Eddie Dowling, and was so delighted to see us he paid for all our meals! And we sat and talked to him for ages and he was really delightful. Small world did I hear you say? (Am writing small to get a lot on).

Well, we arrived in Chicago, had breakfast on station and caught train immediately for Ottawa – two hours away. I slept most of the way – but talk about a one-horse town – all wooden houses, no meals of <u>any</u> sort at the hotel, not even breakfast, and no one to meet us at the train. But it wasn't as bad as it sounds – the sponsors had met the wrong train – I had a comfortable room and there was a drugstore across the way that did us very well – I even had my hair done and very well too! I was terrified of the concert in such a place – Italian, German words, Brahms Serious Songs – my! my! it was asking for trouble, but there were about 900 there and there wasn't a whisper, and they were thrilled to bits. Wasn't that good? Sandor played very well for me and it was a real success. There was a reception for us afterwards and everybody was beaming. Even Mr T. was pleased and said something to me about vintage wine, which was meant as a compliment. It's the first time he's <u>ever</u> heard me do a recital!!!

The next day we came to Chicago to this sumpchuss hotel (I'll <u>never</u> be able to pay mi bill!). I was met by 4 women reporters and 3 photographers and thoroughly enjoyed miself. You'll see one of the pictures enclosed – isn't it good? They stayed two hours when I was wanting to go to bed – and I was photographed with music, combing my hair, singing with piano, all sorts of ways.

Then we had car to Park Ridge (Des Plaines), a sumpchuss car, and when I asked who was paying for it, Mr T. said, '<u>You are!</u>' so it's quite definite I shan't be able to pay mi bill – it was 20 miles and the man waited and brought us back at 11.30pm!

That concert went well too, tho' it was in a cinema and very dead, and I had spotlights and couldn't see a thing, but as you will see from cutting, it can't have been so bad. Cassidy is the most notable critic outside N.Y. – for all the Middle West – and is noted for her cruelty, so I'm pleased. I didn't know she was there and finished off with the 'Stuttering Lovers', and had 'em all in fits, so p'raps that put her in a good humour!

Again another reception and a bouquet of 24 red, red roses – they're here in my room looking perfectly gorgeous. Then home in our sumpchuss car and more photies to be taken when I arrive back! Bed at last and what a bed – this is the loveliest room I've ever had, with most beautiful lampshades, and a lavatory it seems almost indelicate to use – it's in the form of a wicker chair and lift the seat and there you are. I apologise every time I use it – I expect it to blush!

My big recital is tonight in this hotel in the ballroom – it's snowing horizontally across my window, so I shall be staying in and catching up on letters. I've just had my breakfast, again with a kettle bubbling on a spirit stove, and my bacon and egg keeping hot on a hot plate! I went last night to a wonderful apartment on Lake Shore Drive to the man who produced *Lucretia* in Chicago – it was a wonderful evening and I was taken there by a friend of red-haired Dottie's, who is the opposition to Columbia Concerts! He's another Richard, and nearly as nice! Dottie has a big position with National Concerts Organisation, and I can't help wishing I were with them 'cos I should get the low-down from her. But I'm coping very well so far with Columbia, but I don't think they should send me to a one-horse town after [a] Bruno Walter concert, do you?

The manager of this hotel has just sent a bell-boy up with a silver bowl with an apple, orange, pear, banana and a bunch of grapes, not to mention a fig leaf! I'LL NEVER PAY MI BILL!!!! Will you read all this out to Paddy and Pop when you see them? It makes mi arm ache so to write it twice.

Loads of love – Hope all's well.

KAFF

This is the loveliest city yet – walked along the shores of Lake Michigan yesterday – all frozen – and stretching as far as eye could see. It was 7° below zero last night!! Loving every minute now!

No.90 [Letter to Rita Berman]
18th March [1948]   2 Frognal Mansions, London NW3
Dear Mrs Berman

Thank you so much for your lovely letter – I am so glad the tulips arrived safely. They were sent with my love and profound gratitude for all you had done and been to me while I was in New York.

I was thrilled the other day to know that I am possibly to sing with Tom Scherman and his orchestra next season. I look forward to it with intense pleasure, and hope it may be a huge success. I shall do all in my power to make it so. His manager suggested I should send some records of a new work I am broadcasting by Lennox Berkeley next month with small orchestra – so I have arranged to have the broadcast recorded. It won't be as good as the real thing, but it will give an idea of the songs and if they would be suitable – on second thoughts they may be unsuitable for such a large hall, as they are rather low, but there will be no harm in sending them [*Four Poems of St Teresa of Avila*].

On April 6th I am singing for your cousin Edward [Isaacs] at Manchester and it is also being broadcast. I shall look forward to seeing him again. The audiences there are wonderful – they sit as quiet as mice and just lap it up!

I have been terribly busy since I arrived home, and have never caught up on my letters, so I hope you will excuse me for not having written sooner. I am doing the *St Matthew Passion* in Birmingham tomorrow, the *Dream of Gerontius* in Manchester the day after – one day off, then the Passion again in Birmingham, and the next day the B minor Mass in Nottingham – so I have a busy weekend! I was very thrilled last week, when singing in the Albert Hall [*St Matthew Passion*, 14th March 1948] to be introduced to the Princesses Elizabeth and Margaret and Prince Philip, who were at the concert. We had champagne too, which was a very risky thing to have in the interval, but all the bubbles went down the right way in my case! Princess Margaret admired my frock, so it was a pleasant meeting – she made me feel a 1,000,000 dollars with her interest and appreciation! Little things, but one remembers them.

I do hope all is well with you and Mr and Mrs Scherman and family. Will you give them my love and say how much I am looking forward to seeing them again. With my love and best wishes
Kathleen

No.91 [Postcard to Win]
Sunday [11th April 1948]   [Amsterdam]
Dearest Win

Arrived safely and complete! And have had a good rest since. First concert tonight. Blue skies, sparkling water and millions of flowers – wish you could see it. Shall be here at *American* Hotel, Amsterdam until Apr 23rd. Am thoroughly enjoying my book [*The Impresario*]. Loads of love
Kath

No.92 [incomplete letter to Win]
[Saturday 17th April 1948]   [Amsterdam]
... It's simply lovely here and I'm having such an easy time though an average of a concert every other day. Peter Diamand takes me everywhere by car and is so business-like and musical, it's a joy. He has been to every concert and broadcast.

The pianist [Isja Rossican] is a Russian-cum-Dutch and a poppet. We converse in pidgin German and original deaf and dumb and get on very well. I've had a real rest and feel I'm not singing so badly, and have ravishing notices. Last night I was in Rotterdam. I get bouquets at every performance – three at the Hague! – and am being ruined! Today some people are taking me to see the bulb fields, and from the few I saw in the train from the Hook, it should be a wonderful sight. Otokar Kraus turned up yesterday – he's doing some shows at the opera – so we're meeting for a good talk this morning.

I loved *Impresario* and couldn't stop reading until I'd finished it – now I'm reading *Huckleberry Finn* – Mark Twain – and finding it delicious.

The food is not so meaty as it was – I haven't <u>seen</u> a steak – but there is lots to eat – eggs and fish mainly, but all delicious. But I never get a salad anywhere like yours and Paddy's.

All clothes are on points so there's nothing to buy, but it <u>is</u> a pleasure to walk round Amsterdam with its canals and trees and lovely houses. ...

No.93 [Postcard to Pop and Paddy]
Thursday [29th April 1948]   [Amsterdam]
Had a grand journey and very quick, and a successful *Das Lied* at Utrecht last night. Klever Kaff! (Fingers crossed!) It's raining today, so am trying to catch up on letters – hope all is well with you both. Shall not be home until about 4.30 on May 3rd. Won't be long – whoopee!
Loads of love.
Kath

No.94 [Postcard to Win]
Thursday [29th April 1948]   [Amsterdam]

Had a grand journey, though my stomach dropped a yard when we took off!
Had lunch served and magazines, and sat back and enjoyed and pretended not
to feel white about the gills!! Was in Amsterdam by 12 noon – isn't it amazing!
Das Lied went very well considering not too wonderful an orch. at Utrecht last
night. Everybody seemed pleased. 3 more bouquets – beginning to expect 'em.
Love to Jane and loads as usual.
Kaff

No.95 [Letter to Sadie Lereculey]
2nd June [1948]   2 Frognal Mansions, London NW3
Dear Miss Lereculey

I should be very glad to rehearse with Mr Szell for the Amsterdam performance of the Mahler and here is a list of my free times: Sunday 13th anytime
until 3.30, Monday 14th 10am-11.30 or 2pm-4.30 Tuesday 15th anytime morning,
Monday 21st afternoon or evening, though I am recording on the 22nd and
would rather not sing too much on this day. I shall be free to record on the
evening of June 10th for Decca. Here are some suggestions for Denmark for
items with orchestra.

Che faro (*Orfeo*)	Gluck (my own parts)
Deh placatevi con me	ditto
Cara Sposa (*Rinaldo*)	Handel E minor
Ombra mai fu (*Xerxes*)	Handel
Schlage doch Contralto cantata	Bach 6 mins
Prepare thyself Zion *Xmas Oratorio*	Bach
Watts Cradle song	Herbert Sumsion (my own parts)
Evening hymn	Purcell E major
Hark the ech'ing air (*Fairie Queen*)	Purcell G major
Songs with double string quartet accomp. (I have my own parts for the following)	
Cradle song	Wm Byrd
Art thou troubled (*Rodelinda*)	Handel
My boy Willie	folksong
I have a bonnet trimmed with blue	folksong

You say in your letter this concert in Copenhagen is November 20th but I take
it you mean September!?
Here are the words to Rahoon.

Rain on Rahoon falls softly, softly falling where my dark lover lies
Sad is his voice that calls me, sadly calling at grey moon rise.
Love, hear thou how soft, how sad his voice is ever calling
Ever unanswered and the dark rain falling, then as now.
Dark too our hearts O love, shall lie, and cold as his sad heart has lain
Under the moon-grey nettles, the black mould and muttering rain.

If the programme for Edinburgh has not been printed could you ask for the order of the last group to be altered? I would like it to be: Parry, Stanford, two Moerans and the Warlock last. I found this worked better in Holland!

Yours sincerely

Kathleen Ferrier

No.96 [Letter to Rudolph Bing]

22nd Oct [1948]   In train! [to Bradford]

My dear Rudi

Your letter arrived this morning. Thank you very much for asking me to sing Ulrica. I went immediately and borrowed a score, and studied it carefully yesterday – after our telephone conversation.

I don't mind a bit appearing as an elderly witch (!), but I feel that the *tessitura* is high, and that I should be inclined to tie myself in knots. Roy H. won't let me do the Verdi Requiem for the same reason. (He also says there is a lack of heat in the blood for such things!! This I am determined to prove him wrong one day!)

Another thing is that I am singing in Amsterdam Ben Britten's new Symphony on July 15th, and it would mean that I should have no holiday, and this, I am sure, is essential.

I would like, if I may, to concentrate entirely on the one recital, and be really fresh for it. It is going to mean much work and memorising, and I want it to be the best thing I have ever done. It has been the greatest compliment I have ever received to be asked to sing at Edinburgh with Bruno Walter, and I want to be worthy of it.

You will not mind if I accept the Salzburg offer for 23rd and 24th August, as if Bruno Walter is there, then I shall not be needed either? As it is *Das Lied von der Erde*, it will entail extra study.

Please excuse my writing – this train is more than usually buoyant!

With best wishes

Yours very sincerely

Kathleen

No.97 [Letter to F.A. Kenmir]

3rd Dec. [?1948]   2 Frognal Mansions, Hampstead NW3

Dear Mr Kenmir

Thank you very much for your letter – I have been away – hence the delay in my reply.

I am afraid I am completely booked up until next autumn, and am so sorry to disappoint you.

With the amount of work which has been coming in for me, I have had to cut a lot out, and this has meant concentrating alone on oratorio, music clubs and orchestral concerts, and refusing the miscellaneous ones. I wish I could quarter myself and not have to disappoint people, but I have had to come to this decision.

Thank you for your good wishes, which I heartily reciprocate, and hope your concerts may continue to be the successes you have made them.

Yours sincerely

Kathleen Ferrier

No.98 [Letter to Mr Williams]
8th Dec. '48   In train!
Dear Mr Williams

Thank you very much for your kind and enthusiastic letter. I am so glad you enjoyed the recital the other night and most grateful to you for writing to tell me so.

With all good wishes
Yours sincerely
Katheen Ferrier

No.99 [Letter to Yvonne Dunlop]
31st Dec [19]48   2 Frognal Mansions, London NW3
Dear Miss Dunlop

Thank you so very much for sending me your song. I am only sorry I haven't written earlier but my only chance of trying it was to take it home during the Christmas holiday.

I am sending it back to you now, because I am just going to Holland, America and Switzerland, and I feel it is very unfair to keep your copy, when for the next nine months I shall not have a chance of doing it, and also, I am so behindhand with a terrific amount of work that I must do, I couldn't promise to give it my whole attention. I am so sorry to disappoint you and hope you will understand.

With my grateful thanks for all your kindness to me, and with every good wish for the New Year.
Yours very sincerely
Kathleen Ferrier

The year 1949 began with the usual rounds of recitals and oratorios, a trip to Holland in the second half of January, a brief one to Ireland at the beginning of February and a performance of Dvorak's *Stabat Mater* with Rafael Kubelik at the Royal Albert Hall followed by a BBC recording and other studio recordings in the middle of the month. Then it was back to America on a trip which would last for more than three months before she arrived back in Britain at the end of May. This time she was on her own, although she would be renewing acquaintances and friendships struck up a year earlier as well as making new ones. On 14th February she collected the orchestral parts for *Orfeo*, which she took with her to New York four days later, an unheard of obligation on any solo artist today. The voyage took a day and a half longer than the scheduled week due to poor weather, and so she had to go straight into rehearsal of *Orfeo* at New York's Town Hall. Familiar complaints arose as she began to tour to relative backwaters such as Granville, Ohio. These often involved long overnight train journeys which left her exhausted. She was not helped by Arpad Sandor, her accompanist of the previous year, who was suffering a nervous breakdown, though Kathleen was unaware of this at the time. And so the tour progressed with mixed fortunes in terms of weather, hotels and audience behaviour. Her spirits revived when she was rapturously received at her New York recital (28th March), which consisted of a typical Ferrier programme starting with the Baroque era, and proceeding via Schubert and Brahms' Four Serious Songs, to a group of lighter British folksongs and arrangements. After the energising success of New York it was back to earth with a bump, a slow train journey to Ottawa, Canada, and increasing worries about her accompanist. Another journey, this time to Highland Park, Illinois for a concert on 1st April, incurred a four-hour delay, which only made her even more 'bad-tempered.' If this was someone's idea of an April Fool, Kathleen was not amused. On 4th April she was in La Crosse, Wisconsin, where she was wonderfully received by new friends Benita and Bill Cress, so it was not all bad – at least not until Easter in Battle Creek, Michigan where the nightmare resumed due to poor arrangements by the administration of the town's music society. The same thing occurred in Flint, Michigan, and she probably did the best thing by going to the cinema while matters were sorted out. At least one other serious problem was now resolved when Arpad Sandor finally acknowledged his mental state and withdrew from the tour to be replaced by John Newmark, a fine accompanist recommended by Aksel Schiøtz and Szymon Goldberg. Kathleen was lucky that the bass George London released Newmark from his accompanist's duties on a tour they were undertaking (at the time they were on Prince Edward Island). They met each other in mid-April 1949 and immediately began to work. Thus began a fruitful musical partnership on that side of the Atlantic comparable to the one she had with Gerald Moore back in Britain.

She included Cuba on this tour and from there returned to New York via Miami. When she got there on 17th May, it was to find a backlog of some two months' correspondence, which Columbia Artists had neglected to send on to her at various pre-arranged locations on her tour. Unsurprisingly when she met Andre Mertens for lunch the next day, she did some straight talking. This was no longer the timid, inexperienced ingénue of a year ago protected by her agent John Tillett, but the blunt Northern lass who knew her worth and how she should be treated. If it now meant acting the role of prima donna (p.d. in her letters and diaries), she was fully prepared to do so.

Resuming her travels, on 22nd May she flew to Louisville, Kentucky, through a tornado, but a week later she was returning home to Britain on the *Queen Elizabeth* in the pleasant company of other artists such as Moiseiwitsch and Heifetz with their spouses. She had about a week at home before flying to the Holland Festival and a busy schedule for June and July. There were recitals to give, choral concerts of Bach, performances of *Orfeo* under Pierre Monteux, and the premiere of Benjamin Britten's *Spring* Symphony at the Concertgebouw on 14th July under Eduard van Beinum. After two London engagements at the end of the month, Kathleen and her sister went to Switzerland for a holiday and to recuperate from this gruelling schedule, which, for the first time, had begun to take its toll on her health. She then sang Mahler's music for Bruno Walter at three different venues. During late August there were two performances of *Das Lied von der Erde* in Salzburg. At the Edinburgh Festival in September she sang *Kindertotenlieder*, while at the beginning of October she was a soloist in the *Resurrection* Symphony (No.2) and for *Kindertotenlieder* again but this time at London's Royal Albert Hall. The rest of the month was spent working in Norway and Denmark, with November and December given to UK appearances, apart from one brief foray to Paris. On 21st December she sailed for her third and last trip to America, arriving in New York on Boxing Day 1949.

No.100 [Letter to Margaret Gardner]
23rd Jan [19]49   as from 2 Frognal Mansions, London NW3
                                   [she was actually in Amsterdam]
Dear Miss Gardner

It was with great pleasure I received your card, signed with all the names of the people who meant so much to me in my youth! How <u>very</u> kind of you to write – I do thank you all very sincerely.

I am sorry I have not replied sooner, but I have been in Holland for the past week, and my letters have only just been forwarded to me. This is a wonderful country to visit, and though I have a recital every other day, the living is so luxurious and easy, it does not seem like hard work.

I think of Blackburn and my schooldays with deep pleasure, and my great regret is that I had to leave so early. In my particular work, how grateful I should have been for fluent French, German and Italian. The bit of Latin I did has stood me in good stead, but I have spent many painful hours trying to memorise German and Italian without any knowledge of their meaning!

I am so glad you enjoyed the Brahms Serious Songs. They are one of my favourite cycles, but it was strange to sing them with orchestra, as ordinarily they are accompanied, as originally intended, by a piano. But I think they are such wonderful and moving words to sing, and I always love doing them.

I send sincere and affectionate greetings to you all, and thank you again for your great kindness and thought.

With all good wishes
Very sincerely
Kathleen Ferrier

No.101 [Letter to Rita Berman]
9th Feb [1949]   2 Frognal Mansions, London NW3
Dear Mrs Berman

Thank you so much for your letter. I am looking forward with great pleasure to seeing you and all my friends again, and to working with your Tommy! [Scherman]

I leave here on the 18th on the *Queen Mary* and shall be staying, whilst in New York, at the *Weylin* Hotel again.

For the past month I have been in Holland and Ireland, and am just now trying to catch up on all my correspondence, which has almost defeated me!

March 16th I am in Pittsburgh. I am sad to miss the Boston Symphony concert, but perhaps may have the good fortune to hear them another time.

I hope you are keeping well, and I can't tell you how I am looking forward to coming again. I remember my day in the Metropolitan and Frick Museums with the greatest pleasure.

With best wishes
Affectionately
Kathleen

No.102 [Letter to Win]
23rd February [1949]   RMS *Queen Mary*
Dearest Win

I've just written a long letter to Pop and Paddy with all the chatter in, and I've arranged to send the chatty letters alternately to them and you – then you can swap. Okeydoke?

Everything is marvellous. I've never had such fun or so much to do, and I feel a new woman for the rest – the extra hour put on every night – and the good food and exercise – pingpong, shuffleboard and deck golf etc.

I'm at the Staff Purser's table – a L'pool lad – so I'm all right!, with 2 American girls and 3 other males, and they're all fun. The chief steward has kept me supplied with fruit in my cabin – peaches, apricots, apples, oranges and black grapes, and altogether it's just unbelievable luxury. I've taken to oysters too and like them, and had corn-on-the-cob which tickled my ears and filled them with melted butter! Scrumpchuss!

It's been rough and we shall be a day late in New York, but I wouldn't have minded if it had been a week! Good old Kwells. I've never turned a hair – well, not more than two or three, and have enjoyed every meal. Lucky Kaff! I hope I can justify, with my singing, this luxurious living!

Will write a long letter on arrival love, and meanwhile look after yourself –
I'm longing to hear news of Alison – and thanks for everything.
Love to Jane and buckets for yourself.
Klever Kaff

No.103 [Letter to Henry Z. Steinway]
[This was possibly written in response to a request from Steinway pianos to
endorse their products. The tone would imply a polite refusal, yet the original
has editorial brackets and small additions in coloured ink, suggesting that they
could not resist what she wrote, so perhaps they persuaded her. The phrase 'to
me [it] is the most perfect instrument and in a world by itself' was lifted from
the first paragraph of this letter and therefore may have been used in an adver-
tisement for Steinway pianos]
26th Feb.'49   Hotel *Weylin*, Madison Avenue, Fifty-fourth Street,
                                                         New York 22, N.Y.

Dear Mr Steinway
    Thank you for your letter. This is a little difficult for me as I haven't had the
luck to own a Steinway, which, – and this is not for a quotation, but my sincere
opinion – to me, is the most perfect instrument and in a world by itself.
    As a young girl, I used to accompany and play solo at many concerts in the
north of England, and when I was sixteen won an English upright piano in a
competition – which I still have.
    Steinway pianos are most rare and precious in England, because so many of
them were bombed, but it is my ambition to own a 'grand' in the not too far
future, and I shall not have achieved this ambition unless its name is Steinway!
Thank you for your good wishes
Yours sincerely
Kathleen Ferrier

No.104 [Letter to Pop and Paddy]
9th March [1949]   c/o Columbia Concerts, 113 W 57th Street,
                                                         New York City

Dearest Pop and Paddy
    I'm just back in New York from my first recital in Granville, Ohio, and have
spent two nights and most of today in the train! I go off in a few hours for
another overnight journey to Montreal, and would have been glad of a bed for
a change!
    We had wonderful hospitality yesterday at a very modern farm – bulls,
Guernsey cows and lovely hunters (eleven), and I had a few hours in the sunshine
watching the latter being trained to jump. The concert was about ¼ filled and
some of the audience were knitting!! I could have spat on them – they seemed
to enjoy it as something to be suffered, and quite a few were enthusiastic at the
end, but my gosh, I'd to work hard!
    Thank you, love, for the three letters in envelope. I think you'll have to get
stronger envelopes, love, – they are arriving in ribbons. And I think you ought
to send them airmail even if you only send them once a fortnight. (I know it's
expensive, but they take so long to catch up with me here).

I can't cope with prices here. The food is exorbitant – and the simplest toast and coffee is at least 5/- and a steak!! I had just a steak before my *Orfeo* concert, and the bill was $4.45 – that's £1–2-6d!! I could have had potatoes and veg but didn't want them! Drugstores for me in future!

I have started off this tour hundreds of dollars in debt due to advertising and Sandor, this abominable accompanist, has put his fee up 25 dollars (£6.5.0d) a concert and an extra 25 shillings when we stay in an hotel! And he plays very badly – he's sacked already for next year – I hate his guts!! Mr Mertens has written to Gerald Moore to see if he'll come – then 'twould be wonderful. So I've to be a bit careful with my money, but I'll send you some tins as soon as I've a bit of spare cash.

Paddy love, could you look up Mr Anderson's address for me? It will be on the outside of an envelope, in one of the holes of the lefthand side of my desk. I must get in touch with him to tell him when I'm in Chicago. I know it's Suite 1122 but I forget the street. (The man who sends the parcels!)

I'm talking prices tonight, but do you know how much my room was at the Weylin with no food? Nine dollars a night (£2.5s!) It's staggeringly expensive.

Am just going to have a bath and leave a tidemark just to get mi money-sworth, then I'm off to Montreal!

Hope all is well with you two loves – much love to you both and Win, when you see her. I'll write again soon. Let me know when you're short of money – I've plenty in the Westminster, God be praised! Let me know <u>before</u> you're short! Look after each other and love and a dribble to 'Closet' [the cat].
God Bless
Kaff

No.105 [Letter to Marius Flothuis]
Wednesday, I think! 9th March [1949]   c/o Columbia Concerts, 113 W 57th
                                                Street, New York City
My dear Flot!
    I now owe you two letters, and can only apologise for not answering your first and hope you will forgive me. Thank you for 'Love and Strife' and the *Lamento* which has just this moment reached me. I am in New York waiting in between trains and you have found me out in a bad temper, as I have been travelling for two nights and most of today and must go off again at 10.30pm tonight for a 'lower berth' on the sleeper to Montreal for a concert tomorrow <u>afternoon</u>! Not content with that I must travel again overnight after the concert and most of the following day to reach Indianapolis in time to sing two groups of songs, and the most feeble, trite, anaemic, wishy-washy song with male chorus called the *Angelus*.

    I have a temperamental accompanist called Sandor, who I could kick in the pants (forgive me!) if I hadn't been brought up to control myself, and I am continually borrowing money, which to me is a nightmare, having started the tour hundreds of <u>dollars</u> in debt due to advertising. So I'm unhappy at the moment and you would probably say it was good for my art – but if this is art, then I hate it – I hated the audience last night – quite a few of the people were knitting! – I hate music, I hate my own voice, I hate people and I hate America!

There!! I'm sorry – it's just tiredness and you wouldn't think from this that *Orfeo* at the Town Hall was a riotous success, if critics here are anything to go by! But to me that was discouraging because the conductor was inefficient, the strings were so harsh they made one jump, and, if I had been a critic, I should have said it was amateur in the extreme. But the newspapers were all unanimous in their praise, so the management's happy!

Thank you for your sweet letters – of course I'm not angry. You are quite right in all you say. I have already asked Mrs Tillett not to book me anything from May to August inclusive for 1950. But I am already booked here for 2½ months from Jan 1st and am completely booked up for Nov and Dec '49. I have asked for Gerald Moore here next year, which should make all the difference, and I am already booked for Montreal, Chicago Symphony and the New Friends of Music in New York, so I will give it another try and see what happens.

I had 2 hours with Bruno Walter the other day and we went over the programme for Edinburgh and it was wonderful to work with him.

After this week it is easier here, so don't be too alarmed – you have just hit on a bad day. I shall be full of cheer and dry-eyed by the weekend.

Thank you again for all your great kindness. Will you let Peter [Diamand] know that the music for *Orfeo* has been despatched and I will write him when I'm good-tempered? And thank him for his letter and postcard.

With best wishes and apologies for my outburst

Sincerely

Your friend

Kathleen

No.106 [Letter to Win]

Thursday March 11th [1949]   In train, just somewhere past Toronto

Dearest Win'fred

Well, all goes fairly well here still. My one humbug is money, because each concert is paid by cheque which goes straight to Columbia, and I have to borrow from them all the time to pay hotel and Sandor. So it just disappears like water down a drain, as a room in an hotel, even if I only use it in the daytime, is 9 dollars (45/-) and no food! It's just exorbitant!

This is my fourth consecutive night on a train, and I'm on another tonight, and if anybody had warned me, I wouldn't have come, but surprisingly enough, I'm perky as old Nick and have just had breakfast. Orange juice, Kellogg's and <u>cream</u>, bacon and 2 eggs, coffee and marmalade, and I slept like a top last night from 11.30 until 9. Klever Kaff!

After Granville, Ohio, which I spoke about in letter to Pop, we had long journey back to New York arriving about 4.15pm, and then another train to Montreal at 11.15pm. We arrived there in a snowstorm and I went straight to bed and slept till 1.10pm. Imagine! the concert was 3 in the afternoon after 4 nights in train!! Well, I arose slowly, had a bath and left a tidemark (just to get mi moneysworth!) and donned a face and mi white satin, and surprisingly felt fine. The hall was packed – it was one of the most important concerts – and from the first they purred – so different from Ohio where half the audience were knitting! It was well worth the long journey, and they have booked me again for next year.

We went out for dinner with the President, and it was all really lovely. We went for train at eleven and now we're somewhere north of Lake Erie on our way to Detroit. There's thick snow everywhere – we are just stopped for the moment at London, Ontario! Sandor (pianist) is a bit of a trial. I think he plays very badly – he plays Schubert arranged Sandor! Leaves out notes and puts notes in. He's put his fee up 25 dollars (£6.5s) a concert, and 5 extra dollars a night when we stay in an hotel. He's temperamental, and is in a brown study most of the time because his wife is ill – which is hard luck – but he should have refused the jobs.

Anyhow he's sacked already for next year, and Mr Mertens has already written to Gerald to see if he would come. Wouldn't it be wonderful?! I <u>do</u> hope he will.

I've grumbled to Mr Mertens about these 5 nights in the train and he's apologised, but didn't want me to miss Montreal, and I'm glad I didn't. But after this, the journeys are all much nearer together and there should be no difficulty.

In Montreal a relation came and claimed me. Some cousin of Mr Taylor? of Azalea Rd, Blackburn. She was so thrilled to meet me and brought me a lovely white silk scarf. She is almost blind and teaches in the blind school in Montreal. Do you know who Helen Medved is? She wrote welcoming me – Dear Kathleen – in New York and said what a pity Anne and David [Ferrier] couldn't be there, so I've a feeling it's Anne's sister? I tried unenthusiastically to get her on the phone and luckily was unsuccessful! But I'd like to know who she is. Have just been talking to a man and his wife on the train and he came from Oldham!

Well, love, I hope all's well with you and the two bairns at Hampstead. Much love to you and I'll write again soon.
T.T.F.N.
Kaff

No.107 [Letter to Marius Flothuis]
March 12th Sat [1949]   Hotel *Lincoln*, Indianapolis
My dear Flot

In my self-centred, wailing letter the other day, I was so busy grumbling I forgot to thank you for the most lovely job of my *Orpheus* copy. I didn't recognise it when it came back – thank you so very much.

I'm sorry I let off steam to you, and I have calmed down considerably now! My pianist is a bit temperamental, and we've both just had five consecutive nights in the train, and youngsters knitting in the audience – I had just come to the pitch of wondering why I bothered! But two days ago in Montreal was simply wonderful – with a most receptive and cultured audience – and I came away from there much happier, and took my 'lower berth' on the train in my stride.

I should have waited to write to you, and I'm sorry I was so miserable. (Excuse my writing – I have hiccups and my pen keeps taking off!)

Thank you again for the most lovely copies of the *Lamento* and your dedication on your work – I only hope I may do great justice to it, for I am very proud of it.

Am just off for a concert here – the famous *Angelus* with male choir and two groups, then I have three clear days before a recital in Pittsburgh.
Thank you again for all your help and kindness always.
Very sincerely
Kathleen

No.108 [Letter to Win, incomplete typewritten transcript, probably made for her biography]

March 17th 1949   Hotel *Weylin*, Madison Avenue, 54th Street, New York

Dearest Win

Your airmail written on the 6th March has only just reached me this morning.

I am so very relieved to hear Alison's baby has arrived. I have sent off a cable – whattarelief and a joy for them. Klever, klever Alison. I want to know <u>all</u> details when you write again!

I'm so thrilled with the camera. I had 3 more films back yesterday and the girl at the shop asked me what camera I was using, she was so impressed!! I've even got a squirrel in Central Park.

I'm fit as a flea – walking a lot when I have an opportunity – drinking <u>milk</u> (Gott in Himmel!) and haven't had a cigarette since I left the boat – in fact I'm too bloody good to live (only I hope no-one's listening, 'cos I like it just the same!) ...

Letter No.109 [Letter to Pop and Paddy]

Sunday 20th March 1949   Hotel *Weylin*, Madison Avenue, 54th Street, New York

Dearest Pop and Paddy

The batch of letters arrived yesterday, so I am just clearing them up. Thank you, both of you, for your letters – two from Paddy and one from Pop, when I got back here on Thursday from Pittsburgh – not to mention the regular ones from Paddy before – clever loves! It's wonderful to get them and know you are all right.

I now have six concerts off mi chest, and they have all gone very well, Pittsburgh was a huge success, thank goodness!

Sandor continues to annoy me almost more than I can bear – he played so softly in the 'Ash Grove' the other night, I could hardly hear him, and I had to say "LOUDER" out of the corner of my mouth in between verses, but of course he didn't hear me! He's the only thing that makes me nervous for my recital here – I never know what he'll do next. At Pittsburgh we did 'Haiden Röslein' as an encore, unrehearsed and he put in trills where there weren't any – I stood with my mouth open – the audience would think it was peculiar interpretation!! Twice he's put in a major chord where there's only an octave in the 'Erlkönig', and when I asked him to play it and 'Röslein' again at a rehearsal the other day, he played them both just as written!! I think he'll go ga-ga one day very soon!

I think mi pitcher's good in the *Evening News* – it flatters me. I can hardly wear that hat now 'cos Ann chopped mi hair off the other day and now I'm like this – 's rather flattering!! Yesterday I bought myself a girdle for mi spare tyre – it's a beauty and comes right above mi waist line. Instead of oozing at mi waistline, I just ooze top and bottom – it's beautiful! I also got a brassiere-top petticoat – no bra needed – in nylon and 3 pairs of pants – all needing <u>no ironing</u>!! And it works too, 'cos I've washed a pair of pants to make sure! I think even John [?Turner] would be proud of mi waist now.

Bruno Walter is going to play for me in a New York recital next year as well as Edinburgh and London (Sep 28th). Isn't that marvellous? He's given me 8 new songs to learn, but I do it gladly for him! We've also (Ann and I) been booked for two repeats of *Orfeo* in N.Y. Klever Us! Will write again soon. At this address until the 29th.

Loads of love to you all, not forgetting Closet.

Kaff

Let Roy and Bo see this if they would like to, love, and I'll write them after my recital here. Loads of love to them all, and Emmie and Momma.

Letter No. 109

No.110 [Letter to Win]
Sunday 29th March 1949   Hotel *Weylin*, Madison Avenue, 54th Street,
                                                                                New York

Dearest Win

Well, that's over thank goodness! It was a complete sell-out with about 100 people sitting on the platform!!

I've never known such applause – I couldn't start for about 5 mins! Must have been mi red frock! Sandor behaved himself too – Bruno Walter and Eliz Schumann were in the audience! – and the clapping almost became a nuisance. I was a bit dry about my throat, and so wet about the torso, I had to keep my frock from sticking to my legs by holding it out in front of me when I walked.

People shouted and stamped, but the critics this morning are only lukewarm. I can't get away with the budders here, but it's the audience that are the final judges, and they couldn't have been more marvellous. Whattastrain!

I'm just in the throes of packing and it's some job! Have sent you a meat parcel – do hope it's all right. Should be there in about 2 weeks. Will write later when I've seen the other afternoon papers.

Bruno Walter rang me up – he said the loveliest things and that he was really proud of me. The afternoon papers are better. I hear the strangest things! I hear that if my gown had been made by Mr Bohm's <u>boy</u>friend, I would have had a wonderful notice!!! (*Tribune*) But I'm told these are the most wonderful notices, and that I've had the greatest success ever, and quite honestly, I'm past caring. They were the most lovely audience and they're the ones who've paid for their seats. Incidentally I've raked in about 500 dollars from last night – over £100 – so I'm going to have a spend on the strength of it!!

Will you let Paddy, Pop, Roy and Emmie Tillett see the notices, love? They're the only ones I have.

Am just dashing to catch train to Canada and am in the midst of packing. Eeee! If mi mother could see me now!! Sandor's wife told me last night that he has been a <u>mentally sick</u> man for 12 months!!! I wondered what the heck was wrong. What a blinking nerve to palm him on to me – he weeps and is permanently miserable, and if I have any bother, I'm going to pack him home. Oh! for dear Phyllis! Mr Mertens didn't know and was staggered when I told him.

Well, poppet mine, look after yourself – love to Pop and Paddy. I haven't time to write anymore, so ring them up will you, love, and tell them all's well.
Will write again soon
Loads of love
Klever Question Mark Kaff!

No.111 [Letter to Win]
30th March [19]49   Chateau Laurier, Ottawa, Ontario, Canada
Dearest Win

Am sending you and Paddy a photograph envelope with a nice filling in the middle. I'm just hoping they'll make it, but if, by any chance, it's opened, you've no idea who it's from. Okeydoke? Tell Paddy too, love, will you? It's ordinary post, special photographic rate, so 'twill take a little time! Mm! Mm!

Off on travels again and have just come overnight from New York via Montreal.

Was grey with tiredness after recital, but have been to bed this afternoon and hope I can murmur something tonight! I do wonder why I do it sometimes but wouldn't miss it! I was furious today because when we arrived at noon they said there wouldn't be a room ready until late afternoon, and I enjoyed myself for 5 mins telling them what I thought of them, and they had one ready for 1.30! Very nice too. I've wiped mi face on every towel, and opened four pieces of soap!

Will send another 'photograph' from US just to pair up with the other. Here's an idea where you can get me direct allowing a week's post: 9th to 17th and 21st to 23rd April, *Bismarck* Hotel, Chicago, 28th to 30th April, *Colonial* Hotel, Florence, South Carolina, 8th to 20th May, *Coronado* Hotel, Miami Beach, Florida!

I think the forwarding from Columbia is a bit erratic, so if you'll allow a good week to the <u>first</u> date mentioned, I should hear from you, and, oh boy, that'll be a red-letter day. You have been a poppet to write so much.

Arpad Sandor is behaving so far, though now and again I find him with his eyes brimming with tears! He's been under psychriticicicick treatment for 12 months and they've never told Mr Mertens – I'm sorry for him, more for his wife, but infuriated just the same.

Must go and put mi Tampax in!! T.T.F.N.

Look after yourself, love. Much love to Jane and I'll be dying to hear if the photographs arrive.

Loads of love to everybody.

Kaff

Did I tell you Bruno Walter rang me up yesterday morning and told me how proud he was of me, and asked me to sing in London with him playing, for a charity concert? Klever Kaff and Klever 'Im, the poppet.

No.112 [To Roy Henderson, reconstructed as far as possible from extracts in books by Peter Lethbridge and Maurice Leonard. Some editorial links are added within [ ]. The letter, written on Canadian Pacific Railway notepaper, is evidently no longer extant, missing parts are denoted by ...]

31st March [19]49   Somewhere between Ottawa and Toronto

Dearest most beloved Prof

I have been waiting to write until my recital was over so that I should have lots to tell you, so here goes. I expect Paddy has kept you 'primed' with snippets of news and sent you all my love on several occasions.

I'll start at the beginning with the voyage which was a riot from beginning to end, and I was delighted we were nearly two days late to prolong the fun. An hour extra each day too because of going westwards – it was just heavenly!

I ping-ponged and danced and shuffle-boarded and even played golf shots into a net! I was so stiff I couldn't move for two days!

Then *Orfeo* with Ann Ayars and Tommy Scherman conducting ... with the audience going mad and the critics too ... [but she thought the production was 'scratchy and amateurish'- Leonard p.121]. Then I had a few days in New York to rehearse with [my] pianist and see about Income Tax and other dull jobs, and had two hours with Bruno Walter re Edinburgh. He altered my programme quite a bit, and now I have six new Brahms to learn and two Schubert, but he's such a love I don't mind, except that I wish I had a chance to try them out before Edinburgh. Phew!

[Kathleen now gives a list of her amended programme – Lethbridge p.97, followed by]

Okey-doke, love?

[Kathleen then describes how she has discovered the true nature of Arpad Sandor's condition from his wife, who has paid her a visit – Leonard p.126]

Kinda cheering when we're going off together for six months. I thought there was something most peculiar. Well, now at least I know what it is.

[and then describes the rehearsals with him for her New York recital – Leonard p.126]

[After telling him] 'Please don't rush, play lightly and in correct time – don't go quicker in between verses – don't put trills in 'Heidenröslein' where it's only a turn – play all the notes in the Brahms – play what's written – let me hear the diddle diddles in the right hand of the 'Junge Nonne', etc etc'. It was much better, but oh! dear!

[She then goes on to describe her concert on 8th March in Granville, Ohio – Lethbridge p.97].

The concert was in a church which held about 2,500 people and some of the audience never saw me all night 'cos they were knitting! Oh my, I was depressed....

So from there we had to catch a train at 2am for Montreal via New York. In to N.Y. at 4pm, the next day, and another night on the train (the 3rd) to Montreal. Wakened at 7.15am by customs, and in the hotel, looking like death mashed, at about 8.30 with an important recital at 3 in the afternoon.... This concert just saved me from getting the next boat home, because it was packed with ardent music lovers – a nice room holding about 800 – and they just went mad. An official tea followed, and then dinner with six of the nicest pets ever, and I was feeling a lot better....

Then off again for <u>another</u> night train – via Toronto and Detroit (two nights travelling making the 5th!), then another whole day to Pittsburgh – only this time the train broke down four times and instead of arriving at 10.25pm, it was 2.15AM!

Well, that was my first week on the road.... Then I had two days to recover before the Pittsburgh recital and I was ready for it.... The concerts have all gone very well, some quite thrilling as regards audience reaction, and others ordinarily enthusiastic. But here (Canada) the halls are very well filled. Last night there were 2,500 again in Ottawa!

Then back in New York with four days off before my town hall recital. It was good to have tried the hall out in *Orfeo* – I felt at home there. I had four more hours with Bruno Walter which were wonderful.

[On a visit to the office of Columbia Artists, she was advised by an employee on stage make-up – Leonard p.124]

She also told me what to wear on my nails, my ears, my arms and neck in the way of jewellery, and I was in trouble for not having taken my make-up down to try it out and also my frock. I felt about fourteen, until I started to laugh and told her I'd done a few recitals before. What a silly witch!

I wore my new red dark satin and no jewellery whatsoever except my ring – the witch hasn't spoken to me since!!

People were standing and there were 100 sitting on the stage! It hasn't happened before for years, I was told. I cheered up at this news because, at least, for all my pains, I would now be in pocket, which is also, except for Maggie Teyte and [Lotte] Lehmann, unheard of! (At least, there'll be hell to pay if I wasn't). And, true enough, I've made over 500 dollars – well over £100.

I walked on, and mi pals must have been there, because the clapping went on for five minutes before I could start. That was touching and encouraging, and I put my all into it, and the audience just shouted and stamped. It was lovely, Prof dear, and I think you'd have been happy if you'd been there.

Bruno Walter rang me up the next morning to ask to be excused for not coming round, but there was such a crowd. He said some of the loveliest things I could ever have dreamed of hearing, and he said two or three times that he was very proud of me. I said, 'What about the Brahms?' because he said I shouldn't do them. He says he thinks that, musically, they can never live up to the words and only a Bach or Beethoven could have done so, and he's still of the opinion, I think, that they are unsuitable. His only two criticisms [of her singing of Lieder by Schubert] were that the 'Junge Nonne' could be a little wilder and that I must watch the top notes in 'Du bist die Ruh'. I think I spread them a bit in my effort to make a stunning crescendo!! Because he approved them mightily when we rehearsed. But I'm watching them!

Well, the papers the next day were mixed. They all criticised something. One said I could have been better gowned! One said I was breathy – another said I wasn't intense enough – another very intense – another it was a pity that, like Marian Anderson, I couldn't sing the bottom F sharp in 'Tod und das Mädchen'. Of course it's a D, and a third lower if he had the sense to know, which makes quite a difference! But in a grudging way they said I was worth watching.... Well, well, I can't cope with the New York critics – it seems to be the biggest political racket ever, and what Bruno Walter said to me just blots out their silly ravings and I honestly haven't lost a wink of sleep. I think the audiences are often the judges in the long run, and they were wonderful.

Your adoring 'pupe'

Klever Kaff

No.113 [Letter to Pop and Paddy]
Sunday 3rd April [19]49   Chicago
Dearest Pop and Paddy

Have just had two days off in Chicago and was ready for them. Mr Anderson met me at the hotel and we had a lovely lunch together, and I'll be seeing him again next week. He had loved Pop's letter, and was thrilled to bits with it.

I have written to Mr Mertens for a new accompanist because Sandor is very ill I think. He's almost St Vitus Dance and weeps when he talks to me, and is in a very bad way. I'm sorry for him, but he's ruining my trip, so I hope by next week I shall have someone else. Tonight he's just rung me to say his friends say he shouldn't give up the trip, but I'm not having any – he's so expensive and I ought to be paid for being a wet nurse, so my mind is made up. I bet anything he improves from tomorrow, because it's a mental illness – we shall see. His wife told me he'd been ill for 12 months!

We're off tomorrow morning at 8am to La Crosse, Wisconsin. Sandor went out with friends, thank Gawd, and I've had a wonderful day snooping round Chicago with mi camera and walking for miles along Lake Michigan. It's been a beautiful day with never a cloud, cold but sunny. I've taken a pitcher of a Red Injun for our father but he's only a statue I'm afraid! Then this afternoon I slept solidly for two hours and tonight I went walking again and, passing by a flick, went in and saw Loretta Young in *Mother is a Freshman.* There was a stage show too and I sat next to the blackest negro you ever saw, who roared loudly at everything. I enjoyed him more than the show. Loretta Y. is quite beautiful – it was very amusing and lovely colour, so see it if you get a chance. Then I came out, went in a favourite drugstore and had a sandwich about 2" thick, and a lovely ice cream with pineapple juice and cream, so I'm fat and full.

Look out for either photograph envelope or *Vogue* magazine, I'm not sure which yet – I'm dying to hear if the last arrived.

Have written so many letters, my store of news seems stale, but all is very well. I'm looking really fit and feeling fine, because I've been doing a lot of walking and the air is wonderful here. Hope you two loves are all right too. Here's where you can write to, and it's just wonderful to hear from you. You've been pets to write so often.

April 14 – 18 *Bismarck* Hotel, Chicago, Illinois
    21 – 24   "   "   "   "
    28 – 30 *Colonial* Hotel, Florence, South Carolina
May 8 – 19 *Coronado* Hotel, Miami Beach, Florida

Allow at least a full week to the last date for Florence and Miami, 'cos I'd hate to miss your letters. T.T.F.N. loves, I'll write again soon. Look after yourselves and get lots to eat.
Buckets of love
Kaff

No.114 [Postcard to Mr and Mrs Tom Barker]   [postmarked Saint Paul,
                                        Minnesota, 7th April 1949]
How are you loves? Could just do with you here – have a pianist with acute melancholia and am yearning for a good laugh! Otherwise it's a wonderful tour. At the moment I'm in Minnesota on the banks of the Mississippi!! Will shortly go to the South, and Florida, and Cuba – with new pianist – praise be! Aren't I a lucky twerp? This is a wonderful country – and oh! the food!
Hope all is well with you all
Much love and God bless
Kath Ferrier

No.115 [Letter to Win]
Monday 11th April [1949]   [Chicago]
Dearest Win'fred

All goes well here – concerts are consistently a success and Arpad Sandor goes this week! Whattarelief! On the advice of a woman in Montreal, in whom

I have great faith, I have managed to get a man called John Newmark. Aksel Schiøtz and Simon Goldberg have both had him and been thrilled – the latter is taking him to S. Africa – but if he has a sense of humour I can bear almost anything!

I haven't heard from you for a bit 'cos of travelling and I wonder how you got on at your Ritz luncheon – I hope the Maitlands didn't go specially for Maria's recital to find it not taking place.

Peter [Diamand] wrote me a snotty letter about Emmie T[illett] the other day, so I wrote back and pointed out that it was all true what she had said. He'd asked for me in 1946 for recitals and she said I wasn't suitable – well! I certainly wasn't for Holland – I knew 3 German songs and that was all. My 4th ('Erlkönig') I learnt coming to America last year and all the rest I've learnt since. (Klever me when I come to think about it!) And she'd said I was booked up in April 1950 – well so I am at my request – I don't want to miss the *St Matthew Passion* again – he'd said Lucerne couldn't get me – well, you know how she's tried for that – even tried to alter dates in Lucerne and Salzburg – so he's talking thro' his hat, and I told him so. I've sung more in Holland than anywhere, and every song I know, so I have personally told Emmie Autumn 1950 at the earliest, as I can't keep it up.

Then he wrote for me to learn two Bach cantatas – brutes – and Flothius wrote wanting me to do his cantata and I've to do Ben's [*Spring*] Symphony, which I haven't seen yet, and on top of all this, *Orpheus*. And he's the one who talks about not working me too hard – bollocks! He also, after I'd arranged the sending of the *Orpheus* orch. material to Holland, said I must help him find the scores for the chorus as he couldn't get them back from Novello's – so I'd just had a bad overnight journey and I said I was in the bleeding Rockies and they'd never heard of *Orpheus* there. I'm humbugged to death on this trip – yesterday Mr Mertens wrote saying there will be papers to sign for taxation when I'm leaving and "I do not see how you can leave by boat or train without permitting yourself at least one day in N.Y." He's the silly bugger that's booked me in Wisconsin on the 26th, when the boat leaves on the 28th – and despite all my curves, I can't stop the *Queen Eliz.* sailing until I've paid mi Income Tax! Really!

I wanted you to know about Peter though, because if he talked to you about it, he was only stating one side of the case – and I won't have a word said against Emmie – not unless I say it. I've only six weeks in England this year, so she isn't exactly preventing me going abroad is she?

Well that's that, and I feel better. If I just had to sing, and no visas, taxes, mad pianists and jealous impresarios to think about, I shouldn't know what to do with myself – but I'd probably sing better!!

I had a wonderful time at Carleton College, Northfield, Minnesota – the head was Professor Gould, who was second-in-command of the Commander Byrd expedition to the South Pole, and one of the nicest pets you ever did see – both he and his wife – incidentally great friends of Ailie Cullen in Glasgow. The audience were students – mostly voice and they all clammered around afterwards asking me how I did this and that – I felt about 90 – and most of the things I didn't know I'd done! Next morning they took me all round their campus – to the farm, the river and island, and all the different buildings. They're nice, friendly, intelligent creatures, these young Americans. At night I went – solo – to dinner with the Goulds and we ate marvellously, and laughed as I hadn't laughed for ages, and I felt a new woman. They saw us on our sleeper and I felt I was leaving my oldest friends.

I've seen Mr Anderson, who sends us parcels – he's a bit worried 'cos his wife is ill, so I haven't seen as much as I otherwise would have. I'm staggered at the number of people I meet here, who send parcels to Britain, and not to friends either, just to names they've got from the local 'aid-bureau'. Mr Anderson and his daughter-in-law are coming to hear me on Wednesday, so I must sing good that night.

Must pack once more, love – am off in about 2 hours. Hope all is well with you – and your tonsil spot no longer visible. Soon be time for <u>us</u> to gallivant – whoopee!

Loads of love to you and Jane.

Kaff

I didn't tell you – the new pianist is 25 dollars a concert cheaper too than Sandor! So I'll be sending some more photographs if the first two arrived safely?

No.116 [Letter to John Newmark]

14th April [1949]   *Bismarck* Hotel, Chicago

Dear Mr Newmark

I am so very sorry not to be able to meet and welcome you. For some unknown reason I had got it into my head that you were travelling overnight tonight and arriving early morning.

I have been invited to a luncheon and a tea – the latter to meet the manager of the orchestra here with whom I am singing next year, but I will be back at the *Bismarck* as near 2.30pm as possible, and I hope you will excuse my elusiveness!

I have heard such lovely things about you from Mrs Langdon and Mrs Russell-Smith, and I am looking forward with great pleasure to working with you, and I hope with all sincerity that this may be the happiest of tours for you. The 'reception' have altered the names of the booking, and it should be all in order when you arrive.

Very sincerely,

Kathleen Ferrier

No.117 [Letter to Win]

15th April [19]49   *Bismarck* Hotel, Chicago

Dearest Win'fred

I've just had the time of mi life – I've been telling the Chicago manager what I think of him and the whole management set-up here, and what's more I didn't cry! Klever, klever Kaff! I'm so proud, I could bust! Mind you, it won't make any difference, but at least I've got it of mi chest!!

I've really been miserable until now – what with Sandor being an acute melancholic and a lousy pianist into the bargain, and my money disappearing down a drain of advertising and managers' pockets!

Well, Sandor went yesterday – and I didn't cry <u>then</u> either. John Newmark has come today and thank God he looks bright and hasn't a drugged look about the eyes! We rehearse tomorrow but I've a feeling he's all right.

I saw Mr Wisner here tonight, and his secretary, and I said I wanted to know where – if the Community Concerts were non-profit making – the money went. I have an average of 3000 in the audience, which means at least 3000 dollars, and they pay me 800 out of which I pay an accompanist 105 – 20% managers – rail travel for two (which is a colossal amount here), hotel, taxis, porters, tips, and income tax. I told him I was the highest paid artist (singer) in England and was wanted in every country on the Continent – that I hated the halls here – they were too big for recitals – and if I was going to suffer and not enjoy my work, I wanted well paying for it – not go home penniless. Klever Kaff, don't you think? Otherwise I would cut down my visits here to the minimum, and sing in England where they'd been waiting to get me for 3 yrs! I also said I came to this country as an established artist, and didn't want to be treated like a bloody beginner – and I told how one of the girls at Col[umbia] in N.Y. at my rehearsal had told me what nail polish to wear, what hair style, how much eye shadow, and the colour of lipstick, and I said I didn't want to outshine Hollywood and remove all signs of character.

I said a lot more – for a whole hour and a half – and I feel wonderful. I did say that if American artists came to England, we didn't tell them how to dress, nor did we send them to Knuzden and Great Harwood to sing for two hours, and then be out of pocket! I think I've made him think. He agreed with most of what I said! He's a nice man and a business man, and I'm learning to talk straight here – but am becoming hard-boiled in the process. I had a good dinner out of him too and we're firm friends now! But isn't it hard work!

Well! Some more news. At the concert last Mon[day] near here, a woman and little boy were waiting for me before the concert and it was Anne and David!! She had taken her 3 weeks holiday and came to friends in Chicago so that she could hear me. She was lucky 'cos they've had a terrific earthquake right in Olympia! I've only seen her in company so far, but she seems a very nice girl – placid and kind eyes – and David's bright and a noisy limb. I hope it's *joie de vivre* and not hereditariness!! He's the image of George, there's no doubt about his parentage! I'm eating with her tomorrow so will know more then. ODTAA! [One Damn Thing After Another].

Well your little camera's taking beautiful pictures, and it's been my main source of enjoyment.

Oh! I feel 10 years younger now I've got rid of Sandor! Phew!

I had a grand letter from Paddy today, when she said you'd been helping her to cut out and also they'd been to lunch with you and to Kew. That's lovely. Tell them always to have a car – I've a big credit a/c – when Pop's going along – never hesitate.

Listen buddy – how do I lose weight? I'm 12 stone 1lb!!! I got the shock of my life! That's been creeping on for 12 months, so I must do sump'n about it.

I've made some wonderful friends here – all women o'course. I've had women following me from one concert to the next, 200 miles apart – and they are the nicest pets and the most generous I could ever wish to meet – so, with proper fees it can be wonderful.

Well toots, must go to bed. Will write soon again. Loads of love to you all
Klever Kaff!!

No.118 [Letter to Win]
April 20th 1949   Chicago
Dearest Win'fred

Thank you, love, for two airmails and a cable – I hope you recd. my reply
safely – I'll repeat number just in case: 637927.

I haven't had any forwarded letters from Columbia for quite a bit – and hope
I haven't missed them anywhere – I have written asking them to look into it.

John Newmark continues splendidly and we've even had 3 hours extra good
work at my Edinburgh programme on the new Brahms songs – he's German and
an excellent coach, so is invaluable. It's such a relief – I've learnt 6 new Brahms
songs in the last month and I feel so righteous, I'm unbearable.

I saw Anne for dinner one evening and went up to her relations the next day
for lunch. I think she's a really nice person, and I thought she coped wonderfully
with David. There was a young nephew there and the two kids were showing
off as they always will, and I thought she was splendid. She's calm, placid, and
could cope beautifully without bullying. I took off my hat to her. David's a good
looking, healthy boy and has every chance to be normal and nice with her, I
think.

She told me George had been getting a big wage and could retire in two years
time on a good pension! She said they couldn't hit it off very well, and they had
more or less parted, but when she asked him to come and see her to try again,
he didn't turn up. They had a bought a house in California, as it was the only way
they could get a roof, 'cos of housing difficulties – it was about £2000, which was
cheap in comparison with most prices and they were paying it off like rent – but
she said she thought it may have been a millstone feeling for him. He was away a
lot on army ships, and with his army papers and identification he never had any
difficulty in cashing cheques, and evidently he'd found it so easy, he'd gone on
to the tune of about £2000 (8000 dollars). He'd pleaded guilty and was likely to
be in prison one year before being sent to England – but she didn't know more
details than that. I asked if he drank or gambled, but she said he couldn't drink
much – he couldn't hold it – but he gambled a bit and was extravagant with
money – no idea of value. He'd told them 'our father' was a Lieutenant General
in a Chinese (?) war, and that he and you were twins, and born on the West
Coast. Why twins, for God's sake?

Well, that's about all that, as far as I can remember now. She said he'd a
splendid record in the army. She even said that she couldn't help hoping that one
day they might get together again. She said it was a hurried wartime wedding,
that they hardly knew each other, but she believed every word he said, and was
very much in love when they married. What a to-do! Don't worry too much –
we'll meet any trouble when it comes!

I'm glad you've had a lovely Easter. It snowed here in Chicago and was very
cold, but now it's sunny, nice but windy. This certainly is a windy city!

Some kind people have lent me their apartment complete with cook and
maid, on the Lake Shore Drive (frightfully grand!) and I've had a grand three

days – that's why I've been able to practise. She also left me 4 prs. of nylons for my birthday!! The people really are amazingly generous and energetic!

We're off tonight to Cape Girardeau in Missouri. I have sent my fur coat home to save carrying and also some old undies – as I only need <u>one</u> of every-thing in nylon. I just wash my nightie out – and the dirt just falls out – and it's dry and not needing ironing – in 2 hours! It just makes travelling a joy. I've sent old ones home, so that'll have room to bring some for you and Paddy. <u>Do</u> hope your stockings arrive.

Loads of love and look after yourself.

Klever Kaff

No.119 [Letter to Emmie Tillett]

27th April [1949]   The *Gilcher* Hotel, Danville, Kentucky

Dearest Emmie

I have a feeling you may have written me, but my letters don't get forwarded, or have missed me, so I thought I would write and let you know where I am in case you need me in a hurry.

Florence, South Carolina (Hotel *Colonial*)	April 28th, 29th
Macon, Georgia (Hotel *Dempsey*)	April 30th, May 1st & 2nd and probably 3rd
Havana, Cuba (I don't know where!)	May 4th – 7th
Miami Beach, Florida (*Coronado* Hotel)	May 8th – about 20th

All goes fairly well. Sandor (accompanist) turned out to have been mentally ill for 12 months. I didn't find out for some time until his wife told me after the New York recital!, and a fortnight ago I asked for a new accomp. – one John Newmark from Montreal. He's played for Simon Goldberg and Aksel Schiøtz and he's <u>excellent</u>, so life has taken on a rosier hue! Sandor had acute melan-cholia and nearly drove <u>me</u> nuts too, and his playing to me was unbearable as well, so the change to someone normal, who plays beautifully too is just heaven!

I believe I am completely booked up for next year here too, at slightly increased fees. I have been so hard up and have been eating in drugstores (very nice too!) and taking the cheapest rooms etc, and to me this seems crackers! The fees seem good – 600, 700 and 800 dollars – but I had to pay Sandor 105 and all his travelling, 20% to Mr Mertens, my own travelling and expenses, all cabs and tips, income tax, and accountant's fees, and learned on arrival that I was hundreds of dollars in debt despite the 800 dollars I left last year for advertising!

I have no money except what I earn so I borrow in advance all the time. It's a miserable feeling and I loathe it.

I have been singing to audience of 2500 and 3000 regularly at these Commu-nity Concerts, and I couldn't help wondering where the rest of the money went, they are supposed to be non-profit making.

I tackled Mr Wisner (Columbia – Chicago) and for 1½ hours told him how good I was (I'm getting very American!) I even managed not to cry, which is a triumph for me! – but his only answer was that Chicago was a young city. I don't get it!

Two ladies from one of the Concerts who are on their committee, travelled 200 miles to hear me again, and to tell me that I ought to have a lawyer, and that

I was being exploited, which just capped all I was thinking in my own suspicious way. In a way these committees have, they discussed fees and I am getting just about the lowest fee paid.

I am rambling on like this, Emmie dear, because if Mr Mertens writes you for 1951 my fees must be at least doubled or I don't want to go. I told Mr Wisner I hated singing in such bad conditions, huge halls and bad acoustics and oh! this travelling, and that if I were not enjoying the job I wanted a <u>lot</u> of money recompense. I can't talk to Mr Mertens, <u>he</u> talks all the time and his phone rings constantly on which he has longer talks than to me.

I seem to be 'sold' to places by glib-mouthed salesmen like a bloody vacuum cleaner, and I arrive in some of the queerest places you ever did see. <u>This</u> is not what I want of foreign appearances – I only want to go where I'm wanted. I suppose it's different here in such a big country and I'm not known, but I'd rather sing less at a bigger fee where I'm wanted. I know Toronto have tried to get me two or three times <u>this</u> trip, but I was booked up. The concerts have gone very well and I've met some <u>lovely</u> people, but I don't think my programmes are right for the sort of concerts I'm doing.

Forgive this long screed, love, but I did want you to know something of conditions before Mr Mertens wrote you. I had to sign a contract before I started on the tour and it is for two years and a year's option (this year and next – and then a year's option I suppose – I'm not very clear). I haven't written to Mr Mertens because I want to see how much money I have left at the end of it all! I hate myself for counting every nickel, but I just have to.

I hope all is well with you, love, and your sweet Momma – my fondest love to you both, and again apologies for this grouse! Look after yourself! – if I can't get nylon tricot, would you like me to get you either night-gown, pants or pettis, because I'm told there isn't much sold by the yard? I've bought a nightie and it's marvellous. Wash it in the morning, it's dry for mi afternoon nap! (No ironing!)

Shall have lots of time to shop in Miami – let me know love.
Fondest love
Kathleen

No.120 [The draft of a letter from Kathleen to Andre Mertens, but it is not clear if it was ever sent. Words or sentences in bold type were originally scored through]
Thursday 28th April 1949   *Colonial* Hotel in Florence, South Carolina
My dear Andre

Thank you for your letter. It seems hardly worth going out of the USA in the middle of a tour, with all the bother of Income Tax clearances etc. I will ask for Mr Meyer's letter at Macon (I have already sent him all my accounts to date) and do as he says.

Mr Newmark is absolutely first rate, the difference to my own performance is unbelievable, and he also helps enormously with the travelling, tipping and general looking after. I should like to have him for next year, and would be glad of a list of engagements – with fees – so that I know how I stand and what I can afford to pay him.

I spoke to Mr Wisner because it is never very possible with you in the office with numerous telephones ringing and interruptions, and I hadn't had much experience of touring when I last saw you. I told him I was disappointed and amazed that I should come here as an established European artist and receive the lowest possible fees. Committees told me of this in good time, though I didn't need to be told, as I have been eating in drugstores and taking the cheapest rooms in hotels to save money, and I didn't think this was usual unless one was a local beginner.

The halls are terrifyingly large for recital – oh I can fill them – but only by bawling all night, so that they have been a worry and an effort instead of a great pleasure. The Evanston concert particularly was miserable. The piano was shocking, the stage was unlit and it was in a high school gymnasium where the people at the back couldn't see me at all, and yet they were receptive. For work like this I should receive a double fee and some recompense for wear and tear!

I am becoming very American and speaking straight out, but there won't be time after the tour. I am completely ignorant of this commercial way of using artists and of all other business regarding visas, income tax etc., and that is why I have you to guide me.

I told you about the customs form when I was in your office one day. They told me you were responsible for my appearance here and would have to claim an extra week. It's nothing, just a formality, and considering I'm supposed to be a musician I think my organisation is surprisingly good!

I tried to get the Income Tax clearance for Cuba from Mr Meyer, but it was only possible to get the two Canadian ones, as I couldn't let them know what my expenses were a month or two ahead. I think the organisation has been lacking at your end, Andre, not mine. I am trying to cope with you, Holland, Salzburg, London, Edinburgh, Scandinavia, and so far have managed it as well as coping with these long journeys and singing at the end of them.

I want to sing only if I am wanted. I have only a short time to spare here and I want to sing not more than twice a week if there are long journeys and get a top-rate fee. I have turned down lovely work in Europe at the highest fees to people who have been trying to get me for three years – this is the honest truth. My war work was singing to village and factory audiences and now I must pick and choose. If I have any money left out of this tour, it will be because I have scrimped and saved, and that for 3½ months work is just plain silly. **There is so much work in Europe that I am not interested in coming here unless I can make a lot of money.**

I am getting this off my chest, what with Sandor and everything else, I have been **going about in a** most harassed **state**, and I want you to know, because after all your endeavours on my behalf, **and not just say to you** I don't want to disappoint you at the end of my two year contract by saying "Sorry, I've had enough". I want you too to advertise as little as possible. I can not afford 480 dollars for *Musical America* and 500 dollars a time for leaflets. I need that money to pay my rent in England.

I am very tired after three nights and a whole day in the train **including a bilious attack**, and am also recovering from **succumbing to** a bad bilious attack, and your letter saying I needed better organisation was just too much for me, so I hope you will forgive me for talking straight out to you in this fashion. ...

No.121 [Postcard to Win]
May 3rd [1949]   [Miami, Florida, USA]
  Sitting in a 4-engined Constellation high up above the clouds on this your
birthday. Wish I could just pop down and say 'Bung-ho cock!!' Arrive in Miami
in about ¼ hour and fly to Cuba tomorrow. Weather is unbelievably beautiful.
Oranges 2/6 a sackfull!
Loads of love
Kaff

No.122 [Postcard to Win]
May 5th [1949]   [Cuba]
  Arrived here safely yesterday after 4 air journeys in 2 days. Really feel in a
foreign country now – architecture Spanish and palm trees all over. Weather
only just fine and not too hot. Would you believe it! Going back to New Y. on
17th for business talks!! Writing.
Love
Kaff

No.123 [Postcard to Benjamin Britten]
May 5th [1949]   [Cuba]
  Wish you were here to see these strange sights – but looking forward enormously to Holland! Getting worried though about seeing my notes and getting
used to the augmented 19ths I know await me!! Hope I don't let you down, mi
darlin'! Will try awful hard not to! This has been such a tour – could write a
book! Have never been 'sold' so often for so little before! I sound like Winston!!
Loads of love to you both
Kathleen

No.124 [Letter to Win]
Monday 10th May [1949]   *Coronado* Hotel, Miami Beach
Dearest Win'fred
  Here I am at last, ensconced safely after flying from Cuba yesterday – I'm
almost beginning to enjoy it – and yesterday was quite rough, and we had to
fasten our belts. Klever Kaff! There were a lot of letters waiting for me including
your most amazing translation!! Ta ever so ducks – it did make me laugh. I'm so
sorry about Jane's boil – poor love, I bet it was painful.
  John Newmark has gone back to Montreal for 10 days, and I'm on my own
(Miami is with orchestra). He does play beautifully – does all the dirty work like
enquiring for trains and planes, and seeing the piano and stage is all right etc –
he bosses me completely which is quite a new feeling for me! – and has a typical
Jewish energy, terrific concentration, and absorbs everything he sees and hears
and never forgets it again, – how I envy him his memory.
  The tall darkie in the picture is called Roosevelt Williams, and is a friend of
his, and came to Flint to hear the concert. He was a poppet and a professor in
Detroit University for speech defect training.
  Columbia Concerts do some amazing things – no letters have been forwarded
for a month and they've put me in this hotel almost 20 mins bus ride from

Miami Beach, and about 20 miles from the concert! I <u>ask</u> you! There isn't a shop for a cupplamiles, but there's a delectable beach, and I've been in the water this afternoon, and it was like a warm bath – it was gorgeous. I am pink in some amazing places, but feel self-conscious with my lily-white legs here, with everybody else <u>dark</u> mahogany! Just now it's lightning and thundering and pouring with rain!!

Havana was amazing and really tropical and oh! so luxurious and oozing rich, fat women, but we had a good time and the concert went well. The British Ambassador went, and last Sunday we went to his home for dinner. It was very nice and his home was a palace!

I <u>was</u> pleased with Ena Jacobson's article – kinda unsolicited and enthusiastic. Goody, goody. Quite right too!! I'm <u>so</u> glad the stockings arrived – I'll call again!

They paid me in cash in Cuba, so I've been having fun – I bought two sundresses, two pure silk and a bathing costume – none of the frocks more than £4.10s each! I had only one thin one with me and I can't wear anything more than one layer here and a pair of pants!

I leave here on the 17th very early and fly to New York to talk business with Mr Mertens. He's paying my fare!! I'm mad at leaving here, but it's best I think. Shall be at the [Hotel] *Weylin* 17th-22nd, *Brown* Hotel, Louisville, Kentucky 22nd-25th, then leave midnight 27th. Whoopee!
Loads of love
Kaff

No.125 [Letter to John Newmark]
Wednesday [12th May 1949]   *Coronado* Hotel, Miami Beach
My dear Johnny,

I hope your journey was pleasant and uneventful – mine was, except there was no reservation for me! But I was pushed in after a cafuffle – heigh ho! Here are your pitchers including three to pass on to Roosevelt – they're good, aren't they?

I am a bright puce lobster colour and must have a temperature of at least 205°, but have been in the water twice, and it's just heavenly. This hotel is about 20 miles away from the University, and I have a 25-minute bus ride even to get into Miami Beach!! You were expected to come here with me to play the encores, but I'm sure the audience will have had enough by the time I've splashed my way through the *Sea Pictures*. I have a horrible feeling I shall go under four times and only come up three – Whattalife!

My great sorrow is that the masterpiece I took of you at the Yacht Club [in Havana] has intermingled itself with the Hotel *National* swimming pool! So I am two snaps missing, but the others are rather good, especially one I took of a sunset that I never expected to turn out. Klever Kaff!

Look after yourself – I look forward already to Louisville, and hearing your superb accompaniments again. The straight sales programme has been accepted at Neenah Menasha [Wisconsin] but they wanted to know where to put your solos. I said you didn't usually do them, as the programme was long – is that right, or did you want to do them? It is not too late to alter it if you do.
God bless

Love
Kathleen
Fingers crossed – but I haven't lost my watch yet!

No.126 [Letter to Emmie Tillett]
17th May 1949   Hotel *Weylin*, New York City
Dearest Emmie

I have just returned from Miami to talk business with Andre Mertens, and found waiting for me here 56 letters from 28th March onwards!! Some ass at Columbia hadn't bothered to look up my itinerary, and had just sent everything here – and I've been enquiring for 2 months where all my letters were! So I have a whole batch from you, love, requiring answers, and I'm terribly sorry to have kept you waiting. I'll try and work 'em out! chronologically. (What lovely contracts!)

In reply to 25th March. BBC Proms. I would like to do the 4 Serious Songs the week 23rd–30th July. OK?

31st March: letter. I have had a letter from Decca saying they won't release me to Columbia unless Columbia loan them Bruno Walter, and as Columbia won't do this, things are at a deadlock I'm afraid. They say they have lent artists before and never can they get one out of HMV or Columbia. But the flying can still remain the morning of the rehearsal in Copenhagen, just in case it works out with Columbia.

I thought the 13th was a good date for Edward Isaacs as I am already in Manchester, that is why I agreed so readily, but abide by your final decision. I always love to sing there.

I do hope Central Hall [Westminster, 28th September 1949] is all right with Bruno Walter – don't like the sound of the *Dorchester*. But shall see!

11th April: I refused Knokke as I must be at home sometime, and will do the Prom instead. Poor Peter [Diamand], I'm refusing everything!

I am booked in Chicago March 23rd/24th. Oh dear! I hadn't known Passion Sunday was on the 26th – I am sorry about that. I would have loved to have done it, but I'm even advertised already. I couldn't do it now if I flew. Tell Dr Jacques I'm terribly sorry, will you love?

14th April letter : I think to do the *Passion* in Holland is too complicated as we can't know how the boats sail, and I don't want to fly, 'cos I'll be ready for a rest. I'll write to P.D. [Peter Diamand] and explain.

Oh! good! I see in this letter the Central Hall is straightening out. Hurrah! I don't know anything about broadcasting rights, but will do what you suggest.

I note I fly now to Denmark on Oct 5th O.K.?

I'm sorry about Gerald as he has probably kept this time free, and if I wouldn't be completely out of pocket by taking him, will gladly pay something out of my fees.

22nd April letter: I think the 8th Nov is impossible for the Central Hall, especially as I shall have already been there, and the thickness of my bookings just then. Will you refuse firmly but kindly for me, love? Ta ever so!

I could do the 13th in Edinburgh but not the 11th. Think I'd be better not doing either as I've been there so much a few weeks previously?

2nd May: Well I lunched with Mr Mertens today and dined with him and the big white chief Ward French. They tell me a sob story of managers going broke here because of a depression (he took me to the *Waldorf Astoria*!), and that I would never get any work if my fee were put up. I pointed out the success I'd had and that my fees, if anything for 1950 were down, not up, and he immediately put my lowest fee up from [$]700 to 750, which is better than a kick in mi new nylon pants!

They were very nice and I've got things off my chest that have been smouldering there for 2 months, and didn't wrap it up, and they seemed to like me for it. My contract, which I have only read today, tho' I signed it before I left on the tour, is for 1949 and 1950 with an option for '51, but Mr Mertens says if I'm unhappy he wouldn't bind me.

There's so much to tell you, I'll save it up for a great fat dinner (on me!) when I get home, if you'll do me the honour, love?

Miami and Havana were wonderful, and I'm peeling off in large chunks all in mi exposed parts! I was sick at having to come back to New York, but feel, after today, that it was worth it! If you have written me again in Miami it will be forwarded to me at the *Brown* Hotel, Louisville, Kentucky (22nd – 25th) as I left a forwarding address.

Much love to you, dear Emmie, and a 1000 apologies for not replying – but it <u>really</u> wasn't me this time.

See you soon – whoopee!

Love

Kathleen

No.127 [Letter to Win]

18th May [19]49   Hotel *Weylin*, Madison Avenue, 54th Street, New York

Dearest Win'fred

Back 'home' again and they were all thrilled to see me at this ole pub. Also all my letters were here from March 28th!!! 56 of them! I played hell in Columbia this morning! I'm just beginning to enjoy playing hell – I had lunch with Mr Mertens and dinner with he and the big white chief – Ward French – and I never stopped! I didn't cry either, Klever Kaff, and think I've made 'em think. I pointed out they hadn't put up my fee for next year, and got it put up on the instant! My! but isn't it hard work! Only 50 dollars a concert but better than nowt. Actually I wouldn't have missed this tour for anything, especially Miami and Cuba, but I don't like being put on!

To give me courage I bought a new hat, bag, shoes, stockings and summer nylon pantie girdle, and could have coped with a whole blinking board of directors. I have only sagged a little now, having discovered that the tab on my dress had been sticking out at the back of my neck all the time. I thought people were looking at me, but I thought it was admiration!!! That'll larn me!

I bought a navy blue and white spotted pure silk dress for £4 in Miami, so I bought a little white hat, blue and white shoes, white bag and gloves and felt real dandy. The white hat has a navy blue veil – fair pretty. I gave my black one to a negro porter in a rushed moment when I hadn't a hand free!

Thank you for all your letters, love – you <u>would</u> think I wasn't appreciative of them – but I'd just not had them, the twerps!

I'm so glad you had a good weekend when Rick was down – he'd be thrilled to bits to take two bonny lasses out, the old sheik!

Of course I've just got the form for Switzerland, but it's not necessary now is it? Ta ever so, love, for doing all the donkey work. Yes, the flimsy letters come all right – I always marvel that they do. Oooooh! I'd love a black paint box for mi burfday – yes please!

Will get on with the other 54 letters now! Ta ta for now love. Shall be at *Brown Hotel*, Louisville, Kentucky 22–25. Leave N.Y. 27th midnight. Whoopee!
Loads of love to you and Jane
Kaff

Have kept the Swiss form in case I still need it.

[The following is a PS to Winifred which has become separated from the letter to which it was attached, but the contents would indicate mid-May 1949]
Just realised I never answered the questions in your other letter!
1. I don't know about certificate but I don't see it will make much difference, they can easily get one, and <u>we</u> are the easiest people to trace, speshully me!
2. Didn't receive form for Swiss currency. I <u>did</u> write to the bank two months ago about it and haven't heard.
3. B. Walter – Central Hall – Sept. 28th. It won't be publicised until <u>after</u> Edinburgh because it's being put on by Glyndebourne, and they don't want to detract from Edinburgh. But three weeks will be plenty of time.
4. Tentative bookings for Holland June 24th (Friday) First night *Orfeo*, 27th The Hague, 28th Amsterdam.

The Maitlands are <u>flying</u> on the 24th so as not to miss the first night!! Aren't they poppets? Clever our Winnie – you'll be a ruddy MP before we know where we are – but then politics goes mit painting, don't it? Tarawell!

No.128 [Letter to Harry Sarton; probably a draft, judging by its untidy signature]
19th May [19]49   [Hotel *Weylin*, Madison Avenue, 54th Street, New York]
Dear Mr Sarton

I have only just received Mr Olof's two letters as all my mail had been forwarded to a wrong address, and I see that by this time Mr Olof will be Festival-ing on the Continent.

I can't tell you how disappointed I am that you have decided not to release me for this recording with Bruno Walter. I rang Mr [Goddard] Lieberson up this morning and agreed with him when he said it was too uneven an exchange of artists – Bruno Walter for me! I told him you had lent artists before and had no one in exchange and that it was too one-sided, and he said he was willing to exchange any pianist, singer or other executant, in this case, as B.W. had asked for me personally.

He had started recording Mahler with him against opposition from the firm, and must carry on this series under a Columbia label.

If you don't release me to do this, they will have an American singer – of whom there are many – to do it.

Can't you see, that with all this competition, what an honour it is, for you as well as for me, to be singled out – to have to borrow an artist? When I came to Decca at first, it was with the promise of a recording of the *Messiah* – which never materialised. This same recording is the biggest hit in America and one of the largest money-makers.

I never expect to make money with a recording of the *Kindertotenlieder* – but the honour of appearing on a label with Bruno Walter would put me in the top flight of artists both here and in Europe, and would compensate completely for my disappointment over the *Messiah* recording.

Please reconsider your decision. Professor Walter is an old man, and such a chance would probably never come my way again.

My records – when they are purchasable – are going like wildfire here, but there are just not enough to go round in this huge country.

I hope you are pleased with my latest recordings of folk songs. I have been singing them from Canada to the Middle West, Florida, and Cuba, so send a lot – they'll sell too!

I shall be home on June 2nd for four days and hope to hear from you then.
Yrs sincerely
KF

No.129 [Letter to Laura Cooper]
20th May [1949]   [Hotel *Weylin*, Madison Avenue, 54th Street, New York]
Dear Miss Cooper

My letters for the past two months that have been addressed to my manager, have only just arrived due to a mistake in their office, and I am so sorry to have kept you waiting so long for a reply to your lovely letter.

Thank you once more so very much for your great kindness – I am so happy you enjoyed *Orfeo*, and hope you will be able to go next year, when we repeat the performance.

I cannot express in words how much I appreciated receiving your letter, and do thank you with all my heart.
Very sincerely
Kathleen Ferrier

No.130 [Letter to Paddy and Pop]
Monday 23rd May [19]49   The *Brown* Hotel, Broadway at Fourth Avenue,
Louisville, Kentucky

Dearest Paddy and Pop

Thank you, love, so much for all your letters – I can't tell you what a joy it has been to receive them, and to know how well you are doing. I only don't want you to tire yourself out cleaning paint etc., tho' it'll be gorgeous to see it all sparkling! But I want to see you sparkling too!!

I'm terribly sorry about your Auntie – it sounds too awful for anyone to have to bear, and rather hope, like you, for your own and your mother's sake that she has not to suffer too long. Poor love! I think it's dreadful.

My coat's nice, isn't it? It is the colour (or was) of my 'Lady Margaret' wedding dress, and is the most comfortable I have ever known. It's not particularly rainproof, but it is gabardine. Klever Paddy! They are fairly expensive, but I bought one or two little silk frocks that wouldn't squash, for £4 in Miami, so I reckoned that what I lost on the roundabout I made up on the swings sort of!

I thought if I didn't spend a bit – as I'd been so careful – the management would say I'd made a lot of money, so I've enjoyed miself this last fortnight! I was telling Win in her letter – my earnings were $17,500 (£4375) and when I've paid my fare ($1000) and left something here for advertising ($1500) I shall have just about $1500 out of 17,500 (£375)!! Better than a kick in mi nylon pants, but still! – I haven't arf worked hard! I have told them to stop all advertising so the $1500 should be there to go back to, which will be better than starting in debt.

Well, I never expected to reach Louisville. We started off from New York in a downpour of rain – splashed thro' a lake of water to get to our places and came through a <u>tornado</u> in West Virginia. It rained, it lightened, it leapt up and down, it nearly turned ruddy somersaults, and we were 3 hours late, and 'twas a good job we'd had no lunch or I'd have lost it!! There were 37 people killed in the tornado and much damage, but the old airplane came down eventually, safely, if lopsidedly in the wind! Talk about being glad to be on terra cotta!!

Then this morning I couldn't raise my head! – it was draughty in the plane and getting wet was very uncomfortable. I've a concert tonight and tomorrow, and I've been to an osteopath, but I don't think she's a bit of good. I still can't do mi hair or scratch mi back!!

But otherwise I'm fine – I've got everything off my chest to Mr Mertens – I've written telling Decca off – I've paid my Income Tax ($3500!!) I've got my extension as an alien, and I've got mi sticky labels marked 'Cunard White Star to Europe' and in 4 days I'll be sticking 'em on and look out Hampstead, here comes Kaff. Of course have your few days off – I should be home the latest the 1st June, and 'twould be lovely to have you there, but if you want another day or two, have it. You're a Klever Paddy! Buckets of love and see you awfu' soon – WHOOPEE!
Kaff

No.131 [Letter to Benita Cress]
Whit Monday [June 6th 1949]   2 Frognal Mansions, London NW3
Benita love

How good to have your letter this morning, and thank you, love, for all your efforts on my behalf – a letter like yours should work wonders with the bigwigs in Rockefeller Center. Even if nothing comes of it, if they hear my name again, it may ring a bell on their old telephone!! Thank you, love, very much.

I made the boat as you will gather! I had about three hours in NY – just time to have a meal and a bath – then when I arrived on the boat I had to go on television – I must have looked a mess because the bags under my eyes were bulging just like the rest of my luggage!!

The next morning my telephone rang and it was Moiseiwitsch's wife asking me to share their table with Heifetz and his wife and accompanist [Emanuel Bay], so I had a wonderful voyage and some unexpected debauchery!! It did me good!

All was well at home – my pappy beaming and the house sparkling – and a suitcase full of bills and letters, so I am just getting down to them now!

Our last concert couldn't have been lovelier with its celebrations afterwards and we both loved every minute of it. My glove ring has been so much admired, and when I arrived at Southampton, photographers there made me hold it so that it could be seen in the 'pitcher', so I have sent for some copies and will send you one when they arrive. It is lovely – bless you both – and so very useful. I just love it!

Now I am trying to get down and learn a new symphony by Benj. Britten – two Bach cantatas and *Orfeo* before Thursday when I fly to Holland – and it is nearly driving me daffy – but 'spect I'll get through somehow. [She actually flew to Holland on Friday 10th June]

Thank you again for everything, you two sweet poppets – it was a lucky day that sent me to La Crosse!

Here's a rough programme:

9th June – 15th July	*American* Hotel, Amsterdam
16th July to 31st	2 Frognal Mans. N.W.3
1st – 15th August	Hotel *Alpenrose*, WENGEN, Berner Oberland, Switzerland
1st – 11th September	c/o 6 Heriot Row, Edinburgh
12th – 30th September	2 Frognal Mans.

Much love to you both and to Stella when you see her, and thank you again for everything.

Kathleen

No.132 [Letter to Rita Berman]　　　　[Notepaper from RMS *Queen Elizabeth*, Cunard White Star]

6th June 1949　　　　　　　　　　[2 Frognal Mansions, London NW3]

Dear Mrs Berman

Thank you so much for your kind letter awaiting me at the *Weylin*. Unfortunately I only had two hours from the plane to the boat, in which to collect the rest of my luggage and have a word with my manager, and I just hadn't time to do any ringing up. I am so sorry. I was in Neenah-Menasha (Wisconsin) the night before sailing and travelled all night by train and then from Chicago by plane and just made the boat! What a rush!

I was so sorry not to have let you know about the concert, but as you see, I was rushing until the last minute and then was on the high seas by the 28th.

I am so fond of my lovely Chinese brooch, and it goes with so many things that I wear, and I think of you very often as I wear it.

Thank you so very much for all your great kindness – I am looking forward so much to seeing you and Tommy and his family next year. Meanwhile, God bless, and much love to you.

Very sincerely

Kathleen

No.133 [Letter to Win]

[?mid-June 1949]   [*American* Hotel, Amsterdam, Holland]

Now look 'ere our Winnie!

Peter Diamand's going to be disappointed, cross and put out if you don't come to Amsterdam for *Orfeo*, specially as he is arranging a Saturday and Sunday performance for your benefit.

Now here's an idea! And be honest and tell me if you don't like it – catch morning plane Friday [24th June], lunch in Amsterdam – stay three nights – fly back Monday morning. You could be in school by 2pm. The journey and hotel expenses would be my birthday present to you with my love. Howzat? Go on, be a devil!

It's just grand here – I'm full of steaks, eggs, sole fried in butter, salads, Bols and Chianti and surrounded with flowers. I've had a running cold but it's only improved my resonators!

Look after yourself.

Loads of love

Kaff

No.134 [Letter to Sadie Lereculey]

16th June [1949]   [*American* Hotel, Amsterdam, Holland]

Dear Miss Lereculey

Herewith my programme for Hull Nov 16 and York Nov 17

Spring	(*Ottone*)	Handel
Like as the lovelorn turtle	(*Atalanta*)	Handel
Hark the ech'ing air	(*Fairy Queen*)	Purcell
Mad Bess		Purcell arr. Britten
Gretchen am Spinnrade		Schubert
Tod und das Mädchen		Schubert
Heidenröslein		Schubert
Erlkönig		Schubert
Wir wandelten		Brahms
Botschaft		Brahms
Sonntag		Brahms
Von ewiger Liebe		Brahms
The ash grove		Welsh folksong arr. Britten
Ca' the yowes		Scottish arr. Jacobson
Spanish lady		Irish arr. Hughes
Shenandoah		American
Bobby Shaftoe		English arr. Whittaker

Here also is my Scandinavian programme for recitals: No! As you were! If you don't think it is too late, I'll send it after July 16th when I can see my last year's diary! OK? Will send other programmes soon.

Best wishes

Kathleen Ferrier

No.135 [Letter to Benita Cress]

Friday 17th June [1949]   In bed [*American* Hotel, Amsterdam, Holland]

Benita dear

Well! Well!! WELL!!! My! somebody's going to have a headache at Columbia, begorra! Thank you very much for sending the article, for two letters and insertions. You are a poppet! Poor little Cape Girardeau – I can't believe or imagine how awful it must have been in the tornado.

It is freezing cold in Holland, and as a result I awoke voiceless this morning! Fortunately my first night is next Friday (phew! I shall have tummy ache that night with fright!) so have a week to recover. I'm taking my iron pills, Vick in every exposed spot (!) and a hot rum tonight, so mi old vocal chords should be just ashamed of themselves if they're not functioning soon.

I have recovered from the rush I had, and am doing a Garbo act here in that I just go to rehearsals, come back, eat, wash mi smalls and go to bed. But yesterday I was on the stage from 11–1, 4–6 and 8–11.15pm, so I'm working quite hard, but need every minute of it, as I think I'm lousy on the stage. Can cope with expressing sorrow, happiness and fright on mi old dial, but oh! my large extremities! I fall upstairs, down stairs, over my own feet and wave my arms like a broken down windmill! There is a nice pet of a producer who is very patient and long-suffering and it'll p'raps be all right on the night! I hope so! – my sister and three friends are all flying over speshully – I wish you all could too!

Re Columbia – For straight sales I pay 20% commission and for Community 15%. But for the latter, if the fee I get is $800, Columbia quote me as $1000 artist, and they get the 200 and then I pay the 15% on the 800. So it means that on one concert they get $320 of my fee! But this next year they have quoted me for 700, until I made a fuss and they put it up to 750! But whether they still quote me at 1000, I don't know. I'm terribly glad to read the article. Somebody certainly has courage to be so outspoken with such a powerful organisation.

Out of my 700 or 750 I pay accompanist – $90 or 100 (Sandor was 105, the barskit!) 15%; all travelling and tips for both of us, and when I finished up $3500 Income Tax!! Don't spread this abroad, love – but out of a gross $17,500, I had $2500 left and had worked harder than I've ever worked in my life! However, one lives and learns and gee whiz! I'm learning fast. Mrs Tillett, my manager in London, is coping with it now and I shall send her your article, so she knows the racket.

I know Rudi Bing well and I think if anyone can cope with the Metropolitan – he can. He's done a wonderful job of the Edinburgh Festival and everybody in London is so amused – because our own Sadlers Wells Opera and the great London 1951 Festival have both turned him down – so they will feel idiots now!

'Scuse writing, love; I'm half lying down writing on the 'phone book and mi nose keeps running and I'm sneezing fit to bust, so it's all rather difficult.

Hope you like the 'photies' – you will have a complete rogues gallery soon!

Much love to you all and

God Bless

Affectionately

Kathleen

No.136 [Postcard to Winifred Ferrier]
Sat[urday 18th June 1949]   [postmarked 20th June 1949, Amsterdam]
It's freezing cold, ducks, so bring something warm. Could you bring me 2 tins of
Meggezones and a bottle of VICK. I can't get them here. Have got a snotty cold,
but fine otherwise. OH BOY! I think you're going to enjoy yourself! If only the
sun would shine! See you soon – whoopee!
Loads
Kaff

No.137 [incomplete letter to Win]
[20th-22nd June 1949]   [*American* Hotel, Amsterdam, Holland]
... All goes well here – haven't rehearsed with [Pierre] Monteux yet, but he
should be lovely to work with. Had my first night out last night and went to
Manon – it was excellent.

If you could get any cigs, would you bring some, love? The manager is pining
for some English ones.

I may not be able to meet you because of rehearsals, but the bus will bring
you from the airport, almost next door to the hotel – I'm yearning to take you
to a Dutch meal! Don't forget your camera and there are some films in my ward-
robe....

No.138 [Letter to Emmie Tillett]
Tuesday [June 28th 1949]   *American* Hotel, Amsterdam
My dear Emmie
Thank you for your letter re Denmark. I do not want to do another concert
either 25th or 27th as it will be strenuous enough, and the 2nd Copenhagen
recital is too important. I'm sorry about Gerald – I only hope there is time to
rehearse, but will leave the choice to Mr Gylling.

All goes wonderfully well here, and *Orfeo* has been a great success and I'm
surrounded by Dutch flowers and roses as I write! I'm very spoiled! An American
friend sent me the enclosed article [not extant], and as it is very true I thought
you would be interested to read it before you write to Mr Mertens.

Hope all is well with you, Emmie dear, and love to your Momma.

Just off to Hades and Elysium again with mi flamin' 'arp! Quel vie! Mr Monteux
is a poppet, and so is the producer, so life is most pleasant. The Maitlands are
here, absolutely adoring it all – Win too for the weekend.
See you soon, love, I hope.
Much love
Kathleen

No.139 [Letter to Harry Vincent]
28.6.49   *American* Hotel, Amsterdam
My dear Harry
Just had your letter – it having been forwarded here. Can't <u>tell</u> you how
excited I am for you both, and please, do drop me a note here – I'm here until
the 16th July. Have my fingers crossed until I hear from you!

Here for opera – *Orfeo* – and Ben Britten's new [*Spring*] Symphony and a

Bach concert. *Orfeo* first night over and a great 'wow', so everybody happy! (Oh gosh! how I hope it's another Kathleen!!)

Am away in Salzburg, Edinburgh and Scandinavia, which leaves only Nov and Dec and I'm inundated love – but if I can find a minute, I will always come for you.

Just off to *Orfeo* and in a rush – but please write soon.

Much love

Kathleen

Alison [Milne] has a boy – Christopher – and is thrilled to bits.

No.140 [incomplete letter to Win]

[3rd July 1949]   [*American* Hotel, Amsterdam, Holland]

... WELL! Life gets <u>more</u> hectic, but I couldn't miss the opportunity of hearing the Vienna Opera each night! *Il Seraglio* was wonderful (Krips conducting) but *Rosenkavalier* last night – Phew! – it goes on for hours and though the production was wonderful, I'm completely unimpressed, unmoved and rather bored.

The Monteuxs went yesterday – he weeping I'm told – because the orchestra and chorus came to the hotel and played *Carmen*, 'For he's a jolly good fellow' and many more things. It was like a scene in a film, with crowds standing all round and police guarding them! Dear, sweet Holland! Have to rehearse *Orfeo*, still learn mi Bach – not to mention B.B. [Benjamin Britten], which I still haven't started on! The Maitlands go tomorrow – the Christies arrived yesterday – it's all much too social to work, but awful nice....

No.141 [Letter to John Newmark]

5th July [19]49   *American* Hotel, Amsterdam

Johnny dear!

How lovely to hear from you – thank you very much for your letter. You must be sweltering in the heat just now, whilst here I am wearing a woolly frock! I'm so sorry your asthma is worrying you again, and do hope it disappears soon.

Did you by any chance read the article in June 4th Colliers – 'Geniuses have it tough too'? All about Community Concerts and what a racket it is. I am told NCAA are suing them for $1,000,000! I'm surprised it isn't Columbia, because it was mostly about them. My spies in La Crosse tell me my Community fee is $1100, but I get 750 – originally 700 until I pleaded poverty! Phew!!

<u>Wish</u> you were here, love! This is a lovely festival. *Orfeo* has gone well – 4 performances already with Pierre Monteux, and all sold out. Everybody ruining me, and I'm surrounded by Dutch flowers and overwhelming kindness. I am just going to a final rehearsal for the Bach [Cantata No.169 and *Magnificat*] (tomorrow), also a Purcell *Te Deum*, which I hadn't been told about – but which is very short and straightforward. The Bach 169 is gorgeous – with organ *obb*[*ligato*]: and oh! the *Magnificat* – I am in my element in this sort of music! I still haven't really started on the Britten [*Spring* Symphony], but have been so tired and so hardworked, I could only tackle one job at a time – and I had many cuts to learn in *Orfeo*. But after tomorrow I must really get down to it! It's on the 14th and 15th.

I have also seen many things. The Dutch Opera in *Manon* – v. good – Monte

Carlo ballet – Vienna Opera in *Entführung, Rosenkavalier, Don Giovanni*. The Mozarts were wonderful – Krips conducting beautifully – and I suppose *Rosen-kavalier* was good too, but I was hearing it for the first time, and was slightly embarrassed in the first act, it hurt my ears in the 2nd, and I'm afraid I was bored and had corns on mi sit-upon by the 3rd. (No likey!) But then I'm no Wagner fan and I suppose it's the same school – but oh! the Mozart!! Weylitsch was singing Donna Anna, but she was sharp and shrill – disappointing after Edinburgh last year – and she spoiled the sextet and concerted things, but the music is overwhelming isn't it! Must dash now – will finish this when the Bach concert is over, and let you know if <u>you</u> did your work well!

Wednesday, no Thursday morning 2.20am!
    Just home after supper, and in bed after trying to dispose of <u>ten</u> bouquets in a small single room!- TEN! Honest! It <u>is</u> time I went home – I'm ruined here! All went smoothly Johnny love, even the Purcell – learnt in 5 days! But this is such a wonderful hall [Concertgebouw] in which to sing – it makes anything sound beautiful. The 169 Cantata is gorgeous but another 6 performances in public and I shall be less tense!
    And now for Ben and his beastly augmented 9ths!! And then home on the 16th and Switzerland on the 30th. Whoopee! Gerald Moore is not going with me to Scandinavia after all – because of fee. I am not well enough known there to ask a big one, so I must have [a] local [accompanist]. <u>HOW</u> I wish you could come with me, though I know I should lose you at intervals, and probably find you playing 4tets of Mozart with some blonde Norwegians on an ice-floe!!
    I hope your tour with Simon Goldberg is an absolutely wonderful one – I know you will both have infinite pleasure in each other's music – I wish I were coming with you to make a trio!
Look after yourself – God bless and
Love from
Kaff

No.142 [incomplete letter to Benita Cress]
8th July [19]49   *American* Hotel, Amsterdam
Benita dear
    Thank you so very much for all your goodies – and another letter this morning. The cold is completely cleared up and I'm as fit as a flea! What wouldn't I give for some of your weather – I'm still wearing woollies here! The throat lozenges seemed to work wonders, 'cos I had a 'pimp' on mi tonsil, but I sucked the sweets, 'cos they tasted good anyway, and it's completely gone! Klever you, love!
    Did you know that NCAC (Civic) are suing Colliers for $1,000,000? The *Time* magazine man has been here and told me! Whew! I'm surprised it isn't …
    I'm getting a corporation. I'm getting so fat, people are thinking of pouring me into my tights. [This is quoted in Leonard p.144 as having been written to Benita Cress. It is missing, but nevertheless may be part of the rest of this letter].

No.143 [Telegram to Harry Vincent]

11th July 1949   Amsterdam

   Delayed [?delighted] to have your wonderful news. Very happy and honoured
to be godmother.

Love Kathleen

No.144 [Postcard to Win]

[12th July 1949]   [Holland]

Ta ever so for music and letter. Have been asked to stay for grand finale of Sat
and I think I should, so flying first thing Sunday [17th July] – home D.V. for
lunch. Working like a nigger at the Britten – not thrilled with <u>my</u> bits and I can
get my 'oo' but I'm buddered if I can get mi 'cuck'! Poor Kaff! I'm a shadow! Oh
yeah! Last *Orfeo* tonight. I think I'm very good now in it! Ben and Peter here –
both poppets!

Much love

Kaff

No.145 [Letter to Peter and Maria Diamand]

18th July [1949]   2 Frognal Mansions, London NW3

Dear sweet poppets!

   I don't know where to start! First an apology to have to worry you about my
coat. The fair page boy in the hotel brought it down for me and I don't think it
went with us to the airport did it? Klever Kaff – I don't think!

   And now to the nice things. Oh my poppets! the <u>butter</u> and the <u>eggs</u> and the
<u>chocolate</u> and the <u>cream</u> – oh boy!! oh boy!! as we Americans say! Bless you very
much for such a wonderful case full of good things. It is absolutely gorgeous.

   Before I forget Peter love, can you pay Maria Austria for her nice pictures –
I'll put in her bill – they only came the day before I left and I never saw her again.

   Thank you loves with all my heart for everything – for your great care of me
– for all the spoilings – for all the lovely seats at the performances – for all your
encouragement for a thousand and one things that you all did for me – bless you
very much – I am <u>very</u> indebted to you! And especially for all the lovely flowers
that you showered upon me, that gives me so much pleasure – thank you again.

   I am looking forward to seeing you next week Peter love, and only wish your
sweet Maria were coming too – but perhaps Edinburgh who knows?

   I was home at 1 o['clo]ck safely and soundly – and everything was sparkling.
Paddy has gone off today, and I am trying to cope with many things – but 'our
father which art in Hampstead' is a great help with the shopping and occasional
washing up and we're doing foine!

   Look after yourselves loves one and all – and all my love till our next meeting
– well not quite all – just a little bit for nrs [Nos.] 2 and 3!! Whattalassie!

God bless darlings and thank you again for everything.

Jars, bottles and buckets of love

From

(Not so) Klever Kaff!

No.146 [Letter to Moran Caplat]

24th July [1949]   2 Frognal Mansions, London NW3

My dear Moran

Thank you so much for your letter. The idea of *Orfeo* at Glyndebourne is a wonderful one, and I do thank you all for thinking of me for it again.

I am already booked for the festival in Vienna for the 4th, 8th and 15th June, which would mean, with rehearsals, my leaving the end of May and coming home about the 16th June. This cuts right into the middle of the period you suggest! This is the only engagement I have accepted, because I did want more time off next year to study – and also to have a rest – and it was arranged before I went to Holland. I suppose it wouldn't be possible to do *Orfeo* at Edinburgh instead, when I would have had the chance of a complete rest?! Oh dear! The year's too short for all the lovely things!

I have refused Holland again next year and also Italy, to be able to have an extra rest, because in 1951 there will be the big London festival which spreads itself from May to September.

I am terribly sorry to be unhelpful, Moran, especially for Glyndebourne, who set me on a long, exciting road of musical experiences, and I do hope I can come there another time.

Kind greetings to you and your wife and I look forward to seeing you in Edinburgh.

Very sincerely

Kathleen

P.S. The 1951 Festival only means single engagements here and there – <u>not</u> the whole period hopeless.

No.147 [incomplete letter to Emmie Tillett]

25th July [1949]   [2 Frognal Mansions, London NW3]

My dear Emmie

I am enclosing a letter from Mr Mertens [of June 21st but not extant], which I received some time ago, and also my itinerary so far for next year. It is not so busy as I thought it was because two of the orchestral concerts have been cancelled. I don't know a Welsh Choir for the Bible Belt, do you duckie? I could sing many praises miself about mi Nylon Belt!

I talked to my Prof on Saturday, as I always do when puzzled, and he says I must have first a rest and then some study on my vocal chords, which are showing signs of wear and tear, so I have decided, apart from Vienna, not to accept anything after May 15th next year, and have refused both Holland and Glyndebourne. It seems an awful shame to miss them and to miss Italy too, but I think it is only sense, especially if the 1951 Festival is going to spread over the summer months of the following year. The Brighton contract for May 14th 1950 I thought was going to be for *Das Lied von der Erde*. The *Lieder eines fahrenden Gesellen* are too high for me. I have written to Sir J.B. [Sir John Barbirolli] about them too, and we have changed them to the Lennox Berkeley *Poems of St Teresa*. Do you think the Brighton one can be changed too? I could do the *Kindertoten-lieder* if he particularly wants Mahler.

I enclose a cheque for 12/- for Prom tickets – thank you very much indeed....

No.148 [Letter to Emmie Tillett]

[early August 1949]　　　　　Hotel *Alpenrose*, Wengen, Nr Interlaken [Switzerland]

My dear Emmie

Here is my Reading programme [29th November 1949] but I think I sent it in already as I have it all marked down in my diary – but perhaps I am mistaken:

Spring (*Ottone*)	Handel
Come to me soothing sleep (*Ottone*)	Handel
Hark the ech'ing air (*Fairie Queen*)	Purcell
Mad Bess	Purcell arr. Britten
Die junge Nonne	Schubert
Du bist die Ruh	Schubert
Romance from *Rosamunde*	Schubert
Der Musensohn	Schubert
Wir wandelten	Brahms
Botschaft	Brahms
Am Sonntag Morgen	Brahms
Von ewiger Liebe	Brahms
The ash grove	Welsh folksong arr. Britten
Ca' the yowes	Scottish arr. Jacobson
Spanish lady	Irish arr. Hughes
Shenandoah	American
Bobby Shaftoe	English arr. Whittaker

Do you want to buy any masterpieces in oils, love? Win and I have been painting madly and she has one, supposed to be of a hillside that is the perfect reproduction of stewed tired lettuce! And I have some pine trees that look like Holland bulb fields in flower!! So speak quickly 'cos I know there'll be great bargaining for them! It <u>so</u> lovely here and the weather has been perfect – we're both bright puce, sore and itching, but it's worth it! We have to watch our pennies 'cos everything's <u>very</u> expensive but think we will just last out until Salzburg.

If you have any news from Salzburg of where we are staying or who we can rustle for a little ready cash, 'twould be a great help. We leave here for Zurich on the 16th, arr. Salzburg 17th. Hope you are well, mi darlint – <u>wish</u> you were having a holiday. I feel re-born for the rest and the good air.

Much love and God Bless you and your Momma!

Kathleen

No.149 [Postcard to Kathleen Vincent]

22nd August [1949]　　　　　　　　　　　　　　　　　　　　Salzburg

How's my little God-child! Flourishing I hope! Tell your Daddy I've been singing here with Bruno Walter and they <u>liked</u> me – fancy that! Alison Milne was thrilled to hear of your safe arrival and wants you to meet her Christopher sometime. Hope to see you very soon!

Much love

Kathleen

No.150 [Postcard to Emmie Tillett]

22.8.1949   Salzburg

Furtwängler enquiring about my services for 29th Sept for Brahms' Alto Rhapsody in London. Original date 28th but have told him impossible, but if 29th then should be very happy to do it. So you will know what it's all about when you hear! Am willing to do Norwegian radio date if possible at all. Have already sent programmes to Mr Gylling. Will send prog for Worcester tomorrow. First perf[ormance] here just over and a colossal success. Whoopee.

Luv.

Kathleen.

No.151 [Letter undated and incomplete, probably to Emmie Tillett]

... Re Wimbledon April 25th. Phew! That's a long time ahead! Same programme as Oxford Nov 6th

    Spring

    Come to me soothing sleep

    Ech'ing air

    Mad Bess

    Suleika

    Wandrers Nachtlied

    Musensohn

    Erlkönig

    Wir wandelten

    Botschaft

    Sonntag

    Von ewiger Liebe

    Ash grove

    Ca' the yowes

    Spanish lady

    Shenandoah

    Bobby Shaftoe

also for Dorchester May 5th

I am a bit worried about Highgate, as I am in Kings Lynn the day before with two recitals – could it possibly be altered do you think? Here are the words of 'Du liebst mich nicht'. I will call in with the *Frauenliebe*.

Mein Herz ist zerrissen, du liebst mich nicht!

du liessest mich's wissen, du liebst mich nicht!

Wiewohl ich dir flehend und werbend erschien,

und Liebe beflissen, du liebst mich nicht!

Du hast es gesprochen, mit Worten gesagt

mit allzu gewissen, du liebst mich nicht!

So soll ich die Sterne, so soll ich den Mond,

Die Sonne vermissen? du liebst mich nicht!

Was blüht mir die Rose? Was blüht der Jasmin

Was blühn die Narzissen? du liebst mich nicht!

I haven't got a poetic translation, but here is a literal one: My heart is broken, you do not love me. You want me to know that, although I have implored you, you even said it in words, with complete certainty that you loved me not. Am I to miss the stars, the sun and the moon? Why do the roses, the jasmin, and the narcissi bloom for me when thou lovest me not? (She's in a bad way, poor lass!) Hope this is all right.

Love

Kathleen

No.152 [Letter to Emmie Tillett]

29th August 1949   2 Frognal Mansions. London NW3

My dear Emmie

Here's mi life story love! I thought if I painted it I should use too much scarlet!! I have used all your exaggerated sentences about mi gracious appearance etc., and just brought the other bits up to date.

I was asked by a Mr Saab in Salzburg to contact Mr Carl Schuricht, Fontanirent, Montreux, Switzerland about singing under his direction in the Bach Mass in Paris next year with the Orchestre des Concerts du Conservatoire. He thought it was probably about the 30th May and if so, it would be lovely to break my journey to Vienna – what do you think – and will you write to him for me luv? I will put in his card. Okeydoke?

What shall I do about an accompanist for Paris, and are you coming too love? I do hope so. Mr Gylling wrote saying he hadn't accomp[anist] yet and who did I want, so I have suggested taking Phyllis as our time is going to be so short for rehearsal and they are long programmes.

I shall be at Mrs Maitland's, 6 Heriot Row, Edinburgh until the 11th Sept., if you want me for anything.

I'm still thrilled with your house [11 Elm Tree Road, Hampstead, London NW3] – I think it is gorgeous, and it will be a wonderful surrounding for all your lovely furniture. Klever Emmie!

With love

Kathleen

PS I'll enclose the snap in case you can use it. The negative is away at the moment but if you need that I shall have it in two weeks time.

No.153 [Letter to Benita Cress]

29.8.49   2 Frognal Mansions. London NW3

My dear Benita

It was lovely to receive your lovely scarf – it is a beauty – and such gorgeous silk. Bless you, love – it was a lovely surprise. (Three lovelys in one sentence – my lunch is lying a bit heavy!)

I've an awful confession to make, and I can't enjoy writing until I have it off my chest! I've lost my beautiful glove ring!! I'm heartbroken and furious with myself. Win and I were walking gently round Salzburg one night, and I suddenly noticed my handle had come off my bag, just at one corner, and when I got back to the hotel, my lovely ring and gloves had both disappeared. I'm terribly sorry, love – I couldn't not tell you, and I was so proud of it and had never changed a bag without changing the ring too! It was so useful too as well as being decorative, and everybody who saw it admired it. It was terribly bad luck that it must have just been on the end of the strap that broke. We went back and searched all round, but not a sign! I have left a message with the police so it may yet turn up – but it would be rather a miracle if it did. Isn't it infuriating – it was my proudest possession! I'm terribly sorry.

Salzburg went very well and I had grand notices which was more than I expected, 'cos the Austrians are kinda swelledheaded about their music – but Bruno Walter was wonderful and very exciting to work with. On Wednesday this week I go to Edinburgh – c/o 6 Heriot Row – until the 12th September, and there I have 4 important concerts in 6 days, so I shall have to wrap myself in cotton wool to be able to cope efficiently. I have had my pianist – Phyllis – up each day, to go over things and memorise them, and I'm feeling nearly ready for owt now! But always fingers crossed!

I am so glad you received the records and that you like them. I believe they're also going to be brought out on Decca long-playing records too.

Your house and garden look lovely – gee whiz! I'd like a home like that where I could do my mee-mees without deafening the neighbours! I'm going to look round for one next year, when I have more than half an hour at home!

Will you say thank you to Stella too for her nice letter and hope that by this time her Patty is safely home again.

Much love to you and your Willie, and oh dear I am sorry to have lost your lovely present! Look after yourself.

With love

Kathleen

No.154 [Letter to Win, Pop and Paddy]
Friday morning [2nd September 1949]   6 Heriot Row, Edinburgh
Dearest Win, Pop and Paddy

Am writing this in the hope that you will all get it for Sunday. All's very well – the sleeper was grand and I slept most of the way. Was here for breakfast with many welcomings and regrets that you weren't here too. Could hardly finish breakfast without showing each other's pitchers, and we had a session immediately after. Alec is thrilled to bits with your mountain Op.1 – dark foreground – and says he'll never attempt another mountain after that! He wants to buy it from you, and I think is going to offer you 10/6d as Rosalind has sold one of hers for that price!! He is a pet – he is genuinely thrilled with it – and wants to ask your advice. He has pinched my Op.1 and hopes Pop doesn't mind too much, but he is going to start a pitcher gallery of Opuses oneses! He kept saying 'but she's a genius – she must have done it before!' Rosalind thinks my pitcher of you is a libel – and the Lady Alice thinks it's a bit of orlrite. Much divided opinion, but all impressed. Of mine they like your painting the best – and thought it was 'Kaff after Vuillard'! Theirs are amazing too – Rosalind has done one of a mountain that is simply lovely, and they have a box full of them.

We went to a morning concert with Leon Goossens – lovely and Kubelik conducting last night. The Queen and Princess Margaret were there looking absolutely ravishing – and the castle was lit up when we came out, so it was a gala day. I didn't like the Beethoven concerto much, with Serkin. He leapt about like a cat on hot bricks – American showmanship I thought! Could have done better miself at 18 yrs!! But Kubelik is a wow – I think he is the coming one of the generation!

Today I'm going to see Aksel and Gerd Schiøtz and Ailie Cullen – and a concert tonight – I don't know what yet – and *Balla Maschera* [Verdi's opera *Un Ballo in maschera*] on Monday. The sun's shining and it's crisp and lovely and I've slept like a top, so am feeling reborn!

Hope all is well with you loves – have a gorgeous time on the river – and look after yourselves. Much love to you all and Jane of course, and I hope school goes down with a bang on the first day our Winnie!

Buckets of lerv, and keep all your fingers crossed even if it hurts!

T.T.F.N. and God bless

Kaff

I nearly forgot! My negligee is absolutely lovely – a real wow! It is a success, duckie – comfortable, glamorous and hardly a crease in packing. I'm thrilled to bits with it, and feel a real p.d. in it! Ta ever so – it will be such a pleasure to me and I promise not to paint in it!

No.155 [Letter to Emmie Tillett]
11th September [1949]   [6 Heriot Row, Edinburgh]
My dear Emmie

I think it is too much of a rush from Bideford to Manchester and Birmingham. They are all recitals and a bit too strenuous I think, to do all well! I'm very sorry for Edward [Isaacs] – it is just bad luck, but I'll go another time.

Am enquiring about the orchestral material for the Lennox Berkeley and will send on a score when I get home. Herewith Cambridge programme November 27th:

Spring	Handel
Come to me soothing sleep	Handel
Ech'ing air	Purcell
Mad Bess	Purcell arr. Britten
Die junge Nonne	Schubert
Suleika	Schubert
Musensohn	Schubert
Romance (*Rosamunde*)	Schubert
Erlkönig	Schubert
Wir wandelten	Brahms
Botschaft	Brahms
Am Sonntag Morgen	Brahms
Von ewiger Liebe	Brahms
Sleep	Peter Warlock
Pretty ring time	Peter Warlock
Rahoon	Moeran
Merry green wood	Moeran
Ash grove	arr. Britten
Oliver Cromwell	arr. Britten

I have had a strong week with both Holland and Glyndebourne chasing me for next year, but you will be surprised and pleased to know that I was firm – just for once! Klever Kaff!

Wish you had been here – I missed you because I felt the recital with Bruno Walter was a peak to which I had been groping for the last three years! He was pleased and so were the critics, so everybody's happy. I hope you enjoyed your change at Hereford and feel refreshed for it – am home tomorrow – in fact, I'm just rushing for my train now! See you soon I hope.

Yours

Kathleen

No.156 [Letter to Benita Cress]

11th September [1949]   [as from] 2 Frognal Mansions, London NW3

My dear Benita

Oh my goodness! I only told you about the loss of my glove ring because I had such a bad conscience – not because I wanted another !!! But it is lovely to have it, and now I see that my bag handle is firm before I put it on! Once bitten etc. Thank you a thousand times for your generosity – it was my pride and joy, and I was absolutely miserable to lose it.

Well, after a week of stomach ache, Edinburgh is over – and oh so success-fully! Bruno Walter was pleased with me – it was broadcast to I don't know how many places, and everybody seems to have been pleased – even including the critics!! I have had four concerts in five – no six – days, three of them with him, so it has been kinda alarming. But it is a nice feeling now it is all safely over. I have a rest now for ten days before repeating it all in London! (More tummy ache!)

I was very pleased to see the gram. record criticisms! and it is lovely if the broadcasting people put them on – it's wonderful publicity. That's fine – clever Benita!

Am just running for my train in about an hour's time, and must finish my packing, so excuse a short note this time.

Thank you again for my lovely glove ring – thank you for everything and much love to you all.

Am so glad your holiday was lovely – it looked a wonderful place.

Much love

Kaff

No.157 [Letter to Emmie Tillett]

27th September [1949]   [2 Frognal Mansions, London NW3]

Dear Emmie

I am sorry Decca worried you with details of rehearsals and recording sessions, because usually they contact me direct. I am not happy about the fee on your contract, as I should be paid in royalties (for my old age!), and I have spoken to Mr Sarton and this is going to be arranged.

Hoped you liked the photies of your Momma, but I shall be seeing you tomorrow?? I have the negatives if you would like them. Herewith programme for Ministry of Supply Nov.30th:

Spring	Handel
Come to me soothing sleep	Handel
Hark the ech'ing air	Purcell
Mad Bess	Purcell arr. Britten
Have you seen but a whyte lily grow?	arr. Grew
Willow, willow	Eliz[abethan]: arr. Warlock
Pur dicesti	Lotti
Che faro (*Orfeo*)	Gluck
Gretchen am Spinnrade	Schubert
Romance (*Rosamunde*)	Schubert
Der Musensohn	Schubert
Wir wandelten	Brahms
Botschaft	Brahms
The ash grove	arr. Britten
The Spanish lady	arr. Hughes
Ca' the yowes	arr. Jacobson
Bobby Shaftoe	arr. Whittaker

Keep your fingers crossed for me love!
Yours sincerely
Kathleen Ferrier

No.158 [Letter to Emmie Tillett]
7th October [1949]   [Copenhagen]
My dear Emmie

I'm sorry I didn't get in to see you before I left – I was recording with Bruno Walter until the last minute, and had a ruddy blush, love!

I enclose the Paris contract. What am I to do about an accompanist? I think I'd better have a French one because the fee won't cover expenses and fees for two.

I think it would be a good idea to do a similar programme to Edinburgh – all Lieder – with a slight change in the Schubert:

Die junge Nonne/Suleika/Romance (*Rosamunde*)/Musensohn/Tod und das Mädchen/Du bist die Ruh [Schubert]

Frauenliebe und Leben	Schumann
Six songs (as Edinburgh)	Brahms

Re Oxford: Nov 6th Brahms Serious Songs OK and English Songs. I haven't my last year's diary with me, so don't know what I sang but here are two alternative groups:

Silent Noon	Vaughan Williams
Merry green wood	Moeran
Rahoon	Moeran
A soft day	Stanford
The bold unbiddable child	Stanford
or	
Love is a bable	Parry
The fairy Lough	Stanford

Sleep   Warlock
Pretty ring time   Warlock

I could have done the Rubbra Psalms, but they won't go with the Brahms Serious Songs – much too much gloom!

Our plane was an hour late leaving! You should have seen us skid through the Customs and the traffic to the Radio for immediate rehearsal! Being very well looked after – but nearly dead! Fly to Stockholm today. Hope all is well with you. Love to you and your Momma.

Kathleen

P.S. I hate being called Katleen! (see contract!)

No.159 [Letter to John Newmark]
8th Oct[ober][19]49   Hotel *Stockholm*
Johnny dear,

Bless you for postcard! I did larf! – I bust my guts etc! – All the same I hope your second half turned out much better and that this finds you at home safely and happily dug in once more with your sweet puss.

I'm looking forward enormously to 1. seeing you and 2. having you play for me again. I wish you were here to play these all-Lieder recitals I'm doing in Copenhagen, Stockholm and Oslo. They are going very well and I had a full hall last night here for a first concert in Sweden, which was a nice surprise – thank Goodness for records – they do help.

I keep having argie-bargies with Andre Mertens, and so far I haven't been sacked, but who knows?

['Some of these days']

I think he purposely misunderstood when I said I would come in Oct. Nov. Dec. instead of Jan. etc, and expected me 1950 instead of 1951! Now he says I ought to go Jan. 1951 instead of the autumn as the public soon forgets – however I've stuck out, as I must have a rest and learn a repertoire.

It has been wonderful working with Bruno Walter. The two recitals in Edinburgh and London were a wow, and he seemed very pleased. He altered very little in your Brahms – only 'Botschaft' slower – but apart from that he couldn't find anything to say! Klever Johnny. They're lovely songs – I adore singing them. Here's my programme for Montreal, hope you like it.

How changed the vision	Handel
Like as the lovelorn turtle	Handel
Hark the ech'ing air	Purcell
Mad Bess	Purcell
Frauenliebe und Leben	Schumann
Immer leiser	Brahms
Sonntag Morgen	Brahms
Botschaft	Brahms
Wir wandelten	Brahms
Von ewiger Liebe	Brahms
Silent Noon	Vaughan Williams
Merry green wood	E. J. Moeran
Rahoon	E. J. Moeran

A soft day   Stanford
Bold unbiddable child   Stanford

Am very thrilled that Decca let me record for Columbia – *Kindertotenlieder* with the Vienna Phil. and Bruno Walter. What a lucky twerp I am! Only hope they are all right. We heard the playbacks and he was thrilled to bits, so I hope the finished article is all right.

Am sailing Dec 21st on the *Lizzie* and will be at the *Weylin* Hotel, New York. Whoopee! Hope all is well with you and that your asthma is no longer troublesome.

God bless
Love
Kathleen

No.160 [Letter to Benita Cress]
10th Oct[ober 19]49   Hotel *Stockholm*, Stockholm, Sweden
Benita dear,

Just a rushed note – I'm off to Oslo in an hour or two – to let you know that La Crosse is on! Whoopee! Ain't that fine! 21st Jan 1950 as ever was! How the divil do I get to New Mexico after that? – but never mind, it'll work itself out!

I didn't see Stella's brother – I only managed to speak to him on the telephone and he'll remember me for ever 'cos I woke him up!! It was only 10.15pm but I bet he could have killed me! Just before coming here on the 5th, I had the busiest time I've ever known – recital with Bruno Walter – Wednesday. Royal wedding and first night of new British Opera – Thursday [see diary for details]. Rehearsals all day with B.W. – Friday. Rehearsal and concert Albert Hall – Saturday. Broadcast repeat and reception Austrian minister – Sunday. Two interviews and a dress-fitting – Monday. Recording all afternoon – Tuesday with Bruno Walter, and first plane Wednesday – so that was my week!

I was nearly a corpse when I arrived but have perked up since! It's lovely to have any cuttings, especially record reviews, as I never see those, and records on radio are grand advance publicity. Klever, kind you! Home on the 29th – D.V. – then a mad rush round Britain before leaving on the 21st December – whoopee!

'Twill soon be here. Give my love and apologies to Stella for waking up her brother, and I'm so sorry I didn't see him. Look after yourselves and love to you all.
Kathleen

No.161 [Postcard to Win]
Sat.   [postmarked Sunday 16th October 1949 Oslo, Norway]

All still well with us – hope it is with you *aussi*. Concerts have gone well so far and crits wonderful. K.K.! Am singing a song ['Altar' by Ludvig Jensen] in Norwegian tomorrow – I'm a bluidy marvel! Leave tomorrow for Stockholm and home on 29th – whoopee! Love from littul Phyll[is Spurr] – she's spoiling me to death.
Much love to you both
Kaff

No.162 [Postcard to Win]
[c.19th October]   [postmarked 23rd October 1949, Copenhagen]
  Just on ferry – coming back from Sweden. Can't believe it's other name isn't Fairyland! Just had a very rude search at customs too!! See you Sunday, both of you. Whoopee!
Loads of love
Kath
and from Gerd [Schiøtz]. We will miss her terribly!

No.163 [incomplete letter to Win]
[22nd October 1949]   [Aarlborg]
  ... We've just rolled off the boat from Copenhagen and are about to go to bed for the day! It's raining hard and rather miserable, so a book and bed seem the answer. No concert until tomorrow night!
  This seems to have been our first pause in the rush, but it's been wonderful everywhere with sold-out halls and superlative criticisms. K.K.! There were no fur coats in Oslo, but I've got two lovely blue foxes for – well, I'll let you guess when you've seen them. Phyllis [Spurr] had hers made into a cape and it's lovely, and I've got two tiny minks for decoration on a coat – lovely dark brown.
  We flew back from Stockholm to Copenhagen in the oldest Czecho-Slovak 'plane you ever saw – but we made it – but the next morning I woke up and couldn't lift my head again – there'd been a hellofadraft – so I've been having beautiful massage – they come to the house (I was staying with the manager in Copenhagen) and pommel one for an hour for seven shillings!! The reason for my fat right arm is rheumatic, the man says, and he says I ought to have massage weekly. So I'm going to try to find someone to come to the flat now and again – it's a wonderful excuse to have massage. At the concert in Copenhagen the other night I could bend down but could hardly get back, so they had to be content with superior nods of the cranium! They went mad, and I couldn't go on till we repeated 'Botschaft'. I've never had that happen before. Phyllis has been fine – she's spoiled me and looked after me and she's played well. She's thrilled with her cape.
  The British Ambassador gave a reception for me yesterday in his gorgeous home and I went dolled up in my grey frock and furs and felt wonderful. My last concert's Friday [28th October] in Copenhagen and we'll be home Saturday – 4.30–5pm. D.V....

No.164 [Letter to Emmie Tillett]
30th Oct[ober] 1949   [2 Frognal Mansions, London NW3]
My dear Emmie
  I would love to sing the Alto Rhapsody on Aug 31st or Sept 1st 1950 at Edinburgh – than please can I have the rest of the ten days off to hear the other concerts there? I've heard so little in my time and it is such a wonderful opportunity. I would prefer not to sing at the morning concerts this time, but just do the one appearance and really do it well.
  How wonderful if 1951 with Bruno Walter comes off!! (Fingers crossed!).
Haslingden: Shall be happy to accept same hospitality.

Herewith Chelsea:

How changed the vision	Handel
Like as the lovelorn turtle	Handel
Hark the ech'ing air	Purcell
There's not a swain on the plain	Purcell
Mad Bess	Purcell
Frauenliebe und Leben	Schumann
Immer leiser wird mein Schlummer	Brahms
Wir wandelten	Brahms
Am Sonntag Morgen	Brahms
Botschaft	Brahms
Von ewiger Liebe	Brahms

Will speak to you tomorrow about Worcester and Oxford. Hope your home is looking beautiful, I'm sure it is.

Affectionately

Kathleen

No.165 [Letter to Benita Cress]

31 Oct[ober 19]49   2 Frognal Mansions, London NW3

My dear Benita

There were two lovely letters waiting for me when I arrived home yesterday – I am so glad you are happy about the concert – my gosh I hope I don't let you down!

It will be <u>lovely</u> to stay with you – please can I go to bed in the afternoon? – just so's I don't talk too much, and clear mi old brain with a bit of sleep. I wonder how long it will take to get to New Mexico – Santa Fe – by train? I don't want to fly in January – I hate it any time. Have just been staggered by the death of Ginette Neveu in a plane crash to the USA – she was one of the finest fiddlers in the world and just 30! Just can't think why that should have had to happen – also her brother killed at the same time – <u>isn't</u> it a waste!

Well, love, the Scandinavian trip was fine – I was spoiled wherever I went, but I did have to work hard – eleven concerts in 3 weeks in 3 different countries – but it was very rewarding and my managers are thrilled to bits and have done me proud, so we're <u>all</u> happy. Now I'm off at a rush again – recording tomorrow, Albert Hall *Messiah* (1000 in the choir!), Paris, Scotland and all over the place until I leave on 21st Dec. Then I can have a rest on the boat and I'm looking forward to it already.

I'm terribly sorry to hear Mr Trane was ill – he sounded <u>very</u> hoarse when I rang him – I <u>do</u> hope he's all right now. I'm fine but just a bit worn out and if you saw my letters to be answered, I think even <u>you</u> would faint!! So 'scuse this brevity, love, and much love to you both and to Stella when you see her. Bless you, love, we're fine for everything – we've managed at last to get a 2nd-hand ice-box, so life's a lot easier, and our nylons will last until I get to America again – we don't have them here at all but I stocked up well last trip!!

Much love

Kathleen

No.166 [Letter to Mrs Kellond]
1st Nov. [19]49   2 Frognal Mansions, London NW3
Dear Mrs Kellond

I am terribly sorry I have kept you waiting so long – I have been in Scandinavia since the 5th Oct and I am afraid my letters have just remained unanswered owing to a very hard tour.

I am also very sorry to disappoint you, but I have turned down a lot of work including Glyndebourne, Holland and Florence Festivals for the next summer months as this year has left me with only a fortnight off. It has been such a strain to work at this speed, that I feel if I don't give my voice a rest next year, I shall be singing very badly. I have therefore instructed Mrs Tillett not to accept any more work, as I must have the 3 months off for rest and study – so she is only carrying out my instructions!

Having refused so much already, I cannot go back on my word and make exceptions, and I do hope you will understand.

I do hope, too, that it may be my pleasure to sing for you e'er long and I hope you will ask me again.

Thank you for your most kind letter – I <u>do</u> appreciate all the lovely things you say in it.
With best wishes
Very sincerely
Kathleen Ferrier

No.167 [Postcard to John Newmark]
8th November 1949   Paris
Just here for two days – concert tonight. <u>WISH</u> you were playing for me! Thank you for sweet letter – sail on 21st so should arrive D.V. 26th. I don't know when we leave for Tenn: but Jan 1st should be all right, but would love to see you whenever you can make it. Have sent lovely Community programme – Handel, Purcell, Italian, Elizabethan, Schubert, Brahms and folksongs! <u>We'll</u> enjoy it if nobody else does! Whoopee! Shall be at Hotel *Weylin*, 54th Madison from 26th. Love to Jicky [Newmark's Siamese cat]. Hope her morning sickness has passed!
Love
K.K.

No.168 [Postcard to Win]
9 November 1949   Paris
Fancy K.K. in gay Paree! The bits I've seen are lovely, but have been busy rehearsing and sleeping! Concert tonight – pianist tries hard, but is no Gerald or Bruno! But he kisses mi hand so life has its bright side! And oh! the food – mm! mm! Home before you receive this but shoot off to Scotland Thursday night. Quel vie! Abyssinia! [I'll be seeing you!]
Much love
Kaff

No.169 [Letter to Benita Cress]

29.11.[19]49   2 Frognal Mansions, London NW3

Benita dear

Just a short note – in a rush as usual – to say thank you for your lovely letters and always the enclosures – which are always interesting and amusing.

I'm enclosing a photie this time – taken in Switzerland with a bevy of boys from Berne admiring (?) my artistic efforts! Thought 'twould amuse you.

I have a date in New York for the New Year, love. With 'Euridice' and her buddies (Ann Ayars of City Center) and I shall be sacked for ever if I don't keep to it – but I'll be seeing you – never fear!

Don't tell everybody I'm too wonderful – I'll never be able to live up to it! Gee whiz! I mustn't let you down!

Yes, Hotel *Weylin*, 54th and Madison until just about the 1st Jan. Bless you for offers of dough, love. I left some with Mr Mertens and there should be some left – but he'll always advance me some.

Just shooting off to a recital and my little housekeeper's shooting off to sing in the *Messiah*, so my Pop is left in charge! We are a cupeliar household!

Much love to you both and God bless

Kathleen

No.170 [Letter to Peter Diamand]

Friday 2nd Dec. [1949]   In train! [postmarked London NW3]

My dear Peter

I am a rude witch for not replying to your lovely telegram but as soon as my concert was over in Paris I caught the boat train home and went straight to Edinburgh for *Gerontius* and I have never stopped since. It has been a terrible month because of being out of the country all the rest of the year, and I have staggered through it with a revolting cold, so all my letters have been neglected and I have just gone to bed in between concerts. I have stopped writing in trains – a) because they are unreadable and b) because it makes me sick!, but your letter sounded so worried, I had to reply immediately.

WHY ON EARTH you should think I'm mad, I can't think! I left messages for you all over Scandinavia because you said you might be there, but I didn't write to anybody as I had 11 concerts in 3 weeks in 3 different countrys [sic], and arrived home to start immediately on the November rush. Paddy has also been away twice and Pop wasn't well – he's quite recovered now – so I've been busy!

You of all people, Peter my love, should know better than to wonder if you've done anything! Being a thorough Lancastrian, I should tell you if you had, but I feel nothing but deep affection and respect for you and Maria – except when you write damn silly letters!! If I don't write it's – no news is good news – and if I've been neglectful, then it has been unconscious on my part – but after my recital I was surrounded by friends and was taken off to supper afterwards, and tried to say Hello and Thank you to everybody. After the wedding I had to leave for the opera and I can't think of another occasion so help me God!

About the only other letter I have written is to Mr Mertens to tell him to cancel the New Friends of Music concert in N.Y. They have been so awkward about programme and I feel I can't do the one they want well, so I have lost all interest, and if he won't cancel it, I shall just have to go sick.

I am still refusing everything for next year and have turned down Australia, Africa, Portugal, Italy, Strasbourg, Glyndebourne – so you're not the only one love! I am looking forward to Nov[ember] next year after a rest – I would be grateful if you would be happy with <u>one</u> recital programme – and I'll make it a real good one!

Nearly at Kings X – so must stop. Much love to Maria and I <u>do</u> hope she is really better very soon. Love too to your Mutti and Werner and his wife. Look after yourselves – oh! I nearly forgot – I haven't my diary with me so don't know my dates but ring when you're in London and Paddy will look after you and tell you where I am. <u>Hope</u> I'm at home.
God bless and much love
Not so Klever Kaff!

No.171 [Letter to Leslie Walters]
17.12.49   2 Frognal Mansions, London NW3
Dear Mr Walters

Thank you very much for your letter and songs. I know how difficult it is to get new ones performed.

Unfortunately I am going to America on Tuesday until April and my programmes are all set, and I am sending them back to you because you will probably want to send them to another singer, rather than wait many months.

I am so sorry to be unsatisfactory, and send my best wishes for Christmas and the New Year.
Sincerely
Kathleen Ferrier

No.172 [Letter to Win]
29.12.49   [Hotel *Weylin*, Madison Avenue, 54th Street, New York]
Dearest Win'fred

I hope you've had a lovely Xmas and get back to find all safe and sound at home. Here are some photies Victor Olof sent for you with <u>much</u> love, and I forgot to give them to you at Waterloo – aren't they fun?

The journey was grand again, and – Klever Kaff – didn't miss a meal.

Arrived to find a note from Columbia to say John Newmark, being Canadian, had been refused permission to work in the US!! So got to work – contacted lawyers, British Embassy and Canadian Embassy, and this morning I've had news that the original decision may be cancelled, and that – fingers crossed – he may be allowed to play for me. I shall know definitely tonight or tomorrow! Hardly dare breathe – because all the best accomp[anist]s are booked up now!

Mr Mertens can't do enough for me and I still have $1500 to my credit, so life's bright.

Had my hair done yesterday and was advised to have my backside permed – and did – and it should be a help on tour – it looked like Claudette Colbert's bang! Am going to have some photies taken this morning for publicity – Edinburgh want some etc.

I have been to Ruth Draper's and she spoils me to death. I was round at Ann and Dottie's almost before I'd arrived and they <u>are</u> poppets. I've been out to lunch and dinner each day, and can hardly catch up on my smalls and letters etc.

There is bright sunshine here today and not too cold a wind and it's just perfect. I love New York, and the few shops I've seen so far are breathtaking.

Must rush for mi photies now, so tarawell and buckets of love.

Shall be back here for a couple of days on Jan 7th and c/o Mrs Cress, 2005 King St, La Crosse, Wisconsin, Jan 20th, 21st, and 22nd; c/o Dr Walter 608 North Bedford Drive, Beverley Hills, Calif. Jan 31–Feb 7th – so that'll do to be going on mit, eh? (Allow a full week airmail for Calif!)

Much love to you and family and Jane, and thanks for taking Our Father for holiday.

God bless

Love

Kaff

4   *Letters: 1950*

For Kathleen Ferrier, much of the year 1950 was spent away from Britain. Her third trip to America took up a quarter of the year, from the third week of December 1949 until the end of March 1950. In April and May she worked in her native land apart from a three-day trip to Holland. The second half of May brought the blessed relief of a holiday in Scotland. During June and the first few days of July she was in Austria, Switzerland and Italy, and at the end of August she went to Edinburgh. From September to mid-November her diary was filled with recitals and concerts in Britain, and then it was back to Holland for three weeks. There were no *Messiahs* after the one at the Royal Albert Hall on 25th October.

One would have thought that by the third visit to the United States arrangements would have gone smoothly, but she had been there barely hours when news came through that John Newmark had been refused a work permit when attempting to cross into the USA from Canada. On the first page of her 1949 diary she drafted a telegram to the Board of Immigration:

> Please do everything possible to obtain admission to USA. Stop.
> Indispensable to me on concert tour. Stop. Have contacted my
> ambassador in Washington already. Stop.

It took the power of her reputation and a lot of telephone calls to cut through the bureaucratic nonsense which was preventing his joining her, but in the end she was successful. The train rides were as arduous as before (missed or delayed connections meant much longer Greyhound Bus rides instead), and her adventures were as varied and stimulating as ever. She was lucky to have ten days free at the beginning of February, during which time Bruno Walter made his Beverly Hills home available to her, complete with manservant, maid, swimming pool and cars, while he and his wife were away in New York. This was a luxurious respite for which she was very grateful. She met up with Monteux again in San Francisco for *Orfeo*, and appeared happier than ever as she progressed through the states of Oregon and Washington, back to Chicago and on to New York for what was to prove to be the last time. Her tiredness was put down to long journeys, late night parties and dinners after concerts, but occasionally there were signs which, with the benefit of hindsight, might have been more serious than appeared at the time.

Back in London she was guest of honour at a luncheon, after which she gave a speech. Winifred and Leonard describe this as the 'shocking red-faced speech' which is mentioned in Kathleen's diary, but this is entered on 22nd February 1951, and she gave it at Imperial College. In the spring of 1950 Kathleen had been asked to describe her recent American tour and at one point says 'My three months this year', placing the luncheon after her return on 4th April 1950. It was more likely, therefore, to be the one she attended on 9th May 1950 at the Forum Club, Hyde Park Corner. This is what she said:

I would like to say 'Thank you' to you all for the great honour you have paid me today. I must warn you that I am making my debut as an after-luncheon speaker and am more nervous than when I had my first broadcast many years ago in Newcastle singing 'The End of a Perfect Day'. We are coming to the end of a perfect luncheon and the obvious thing to say would be that I am too full for words, but I do thank my friends here who have proposed and seconded my health, and said so many complimentary things.

I have been asked if I would say a word or two about my American tour and to start with I must say the thing that gives me so much pleasure is the voyage, which after a hectically busy time in this country and in Europe, is five days of sheer luxury. Five days of no telephone or letters, and every excuse to stay in bed, especially if the ship rolls!

My three months this year have taken my pianist and me to many lovely places – New York for three concerts, Pennsylvania, Tennessee, New Mexico, Arizona, Los Angeles, San Francisco, Chicago, Toronto, Montreal, and many other smaller places. I can honestly say I haven't a single bad memory – we caught all the right trains – the halls on the whole were quite good – some of them superb, like the San Francisco Opera House and the Chicago Orchestra Hall – one uncomfortable moment was Santa Fe, where we were 7000 feet above sea level and when, for the first half of the programme at any rate, I had the greatest difficulty in breathing, because of the rarified atmosphere. The audiences were most receptive and were delighted if I explained some of the German songs because of my English-cum-Lancashire accent!

One always reads of Americans coming here and saying 'Aren't your policemen wonderful?' I feel I should say to them – 'Isn't your plumbing wonderful?' because wherever I went, in the smallest hotels, I always had a room with a bath and a cupboard or closet long enough to hold my evening dresses. The train travel on the main lines is superb with the best meals one could possibly hope for.

This time too, I had a superb accompanist, who not only played beautifully, but did all the organising and train chequing [*sic*] and tipping, and looking after our numerous bags, so all I had to do was to get to a place and sing as well as I knew how. This organising just made all the difference to my peace of mind and was the main cause of the pleasure of the whole trip.

We did about 32 concerts in the three months and made lovely programmes of Bach, Handel and Purcell, Schubert, Schumann, Brahms and Mahler, Elizabethan songs, some contemporary English and folksongs, and I managed to do a little studying as well – usually in the trains.

I had two weeks holiday in Beverly Hills and was a guest in Bruno Walter's house. This was just superb – the sun shone, and I was taken round to see the coast and the old missions of California, the orange and lemon groves, and also to Edward G. Robinson's house (the film gangster man), who has one of the most superb collections of French paintings.

We came back from California, over the Rockies to Chicago and then Canada – now back into winter woollies after sunbathing in January in Arizona and California. We were taken to see the Niagara Falls, which is certainly a wonderful sight – but rather spoiled by factories and ugly buildings.

Our last concert was in Toronto and I had just time to catch a night train, pay a large amount of Income Tax in New York, hastily buy a few nylons and catch the boat back. I even had a ~~sizable~~ cheque in my packet of dollars for Britain – I don't suppose there will be many left when the tax has been taken off it at this end too, but it made my bank manager smile. He said what a grand job I was doing, bringing dollars into the country, but I think he should have said, what a lucky person you are to be so spoiled to see so many wonderful places and be <u>paid</u> for doing it!

On to the *Queen Elizabeth* again – five lovely days – and home to a green England with the blossom looking more lovely than I've ever seen it, and despite the plumbing, the steaks and the nylons, and leaving behind many wonderful friends, it was good to be home.

No.173 [Letter to Win]

7.1.50   Hotel *Weylin*, 54th Street, New York

Hello toots!

How are you? I kept thinking about you at Xmas and the New Year and wondering how you were getting on – which driver you had – and if Pop bolted the door before piddling etc. I <u>do</u> hope it all worked out well, and was not too troublesome. I've had 3 good letters from Paddy and she seems to have settled down again – she said you'd been over to tea.

My troublesome concert is tomorrow – the Bach and Brahms – and I shall be exceeding glad when it's over. Ralph Hawkes (of Boosey etc) is giving a party for me afterwards, and we leave finally until March, on Tuesday. John Newmark got here finally – it's cost me £11 in telephone calls and him $500 for lawyers – but he's playing <u>quite</u> beautifully and I wish you could hear him.

We're going to work in California – 'cos if I pay him for an hour's work each morning, it will be grand for me and pay his hotel! He's still bossy and a bit self-satisfied and has halitosis, but his playing is superb and that's all that matters. Our first concert went beautifully and the second miserably – just the difference in small things of hall, organisers and thoughtfulness – so pr'aps if it goes alternately, tomorrow's won't be so bad after all!

Ruth Draper has been a peach – and had a lovely party for me on New Year's Day, when I sang and Johnny played – we tried most of our programmes out on the few guests there – so haven't much left to rehearse now! She's a charmer and we're fast buddies.

I forgot what I told you in my last letter – I write so many – to Pop and Paddy, and Peter D. and Mrs Tillett and Rick and John T[urner]. I get mixed up.

But I've had my back fringe permed and it's a treat – haven't had a curly bob in all week. Even if it's all a frizz, it keeps all the other hair up. I've had mi photie taken again, and some of them aren't bad.

The Columbia people are being so careful with me – I can do no wrong – Klever Kaff! Will write again soon, love, and would love to hear from you. Buckets of love and look after yourself.
Kaff

No.174 [Letter to Benita Cress]
7.1.50   Hotel *Weylin*, 54th Street, New York
My dear Benita

Back here once more, and my first five minutes to write to you. (Three nights out of four on the train, so have been sleeping when I haven't been singing and eating!)

We were terribly sorry you couldn't make the trip to Nashville – I kept wishing you could have been there – the concert went with a bang and Johnny played absolutely beautifully. Never mind, love, I'll have a day to go really gay in, after the La X concert, and we'll both talk and giggle our heads off, eh?
Here's my itin[erary] just arrived:

Leave Chicago 20th 3.30 arrive La X 7.28pm
Leave La X 23rd 12.02 (A.M.?) arrive Chicago 6.20 a.m. (phew!)
Leave Chicago 1.30pm arrive Santa Fe 1.40 on the 24th

If I leave LA at midnight 23rd, that's <u>two</u> days with you! Can you bear it? I'm a good washerupper and bedmaker, and I can toss a pancake in more pieces than anyone else I know!

Just dashing for rehearsal now with Johnny for tomorrow's New York concert – and I <u>shall</u> be glad when it's over. I've had a bit of a fuss about programme and I'm afraid the atmosphere will be somewhat cool. However I know I can be sure of anything but a cool welcome at La X and number 2005 in particular – and bless you both for asking me to come. I'm looking forward to it more than I can say.
Love to you both and look after yourselves.
Kathleen

No.175 [Letter to Emmie Tillett]
15th January 1950   Hotel *Phillips* 12th and Baltimore,
                                           Kansas City-6-Missouri USA
Dearest Emmie

I am a diva of the deepest dye for not writing e'er this, and I'm very sorry. All is very well now, but I was met with the news that my pianist, John Newmark, being Canadian, would not be allowed to enter the US to play for me, so I had to contact Canadian and British Embassies and a Washington lawyer, and, finally, at the 11th hour he was allowed to come! Quel greeting! But it was worth all the cafuffle, because he is superb. But it did make me neglect all else meanwhile.

Our concerts have gone well, and I've got the New Friends of Music off my chest, which was worrying me frightfully because of the fuss I had had over programme. I thought I dithered my way through like an un-set jelly, but the critics were good. Paddy has the *Tribune* and *Times*, and I will enclose the afternoon papers.

I <u>do</u> hope your back is really better now, love, and that Momma is blooming as usual, bless her.

John N and I went to dinner with Andre Mertens the other night and the next day, when I was starting off for the rest of the tour, he rang me to say that if I didn't sing in the US until Oct '51, my year's option would be out of date, as the contract ends in May '51. It would mean signing another one, and he wasn't allowed to get jobs for me without a signed and sealed contract and, as it was just like the last, he'd put it in post and would I sign it? So I said I had promised you I wouldn't sign anything, and that these matters were beyond me and distasteful to me (!), and that I would either have to send it to you or take it to a lawyer. Strangely enough, two nights before I had been with the Simon Goldbergs and he is with Schang of Columbia, and was urging me to take any contract to <u>his</u> lawyer, as he says they know exactly what fees one should get and will fight for orchestral dates and straight sales and keep the Community down etc; and keep an eye all the time to see that one isn't overworked. So I thought I would put this all down and see what you think? Andre flared up for a minute when I said I needed a lawyer, and asked if I had had such bad treatment under his care? All frightfully difficult, having just had a smashing great dinner!

Otherwise I am enjoying every minute, and am looking forward to some hot sun in Santa Fe and Phoenix, Arizona in a fortnight's time and then a fortnight's holiday in Beverly Hills. Lucky me! What'll you say if I get signed up with Bing Crosby for a musical? Would be able to afford <u>two</u> bags of white flour then!

I had some money to my credit when I arrived, so all's very well this time. Prices are exorbitant of course at the new devaluation, but <u>I</u> still divide by 4, and it's much less startling! Shall be coming back on 30th March with Mr and Mrs Benno M[oiseiwitsch], also the Goldbergs, so have a stretcher ready love!

If you would write me direct, I shall be at *La Fonda* Hotel, Santa Fe, New Mexico on the 24th Jan and c/o Dr Walter, 608 North Bedford Drive, Beverley Hills, California from 31st Jan to 6th Feb. But my letters seem to be arriving also thro' Columbia this year. <u>Do</u> hope you're <u>really</u> better – much love to you and Momma and all my buddies in the office and your two German girls.
God bless
Love
Kathleen

<u>Today's funny story</u>

After the New Friends Concert where I sang Bach in German and Brahms in English, a German came up to someone and said – of course I was German, because my German pronunciation was perfect and I sang in English with a marked accent. (It's true, honest!) I didn't know my Lancashire came thro' quite so strongly!

No.176 [Letter to Pop and Paddy]
[Tuesday about 23rd Jan? 1950]   In train from Chicago to Santa Fe,
                                                                              New Mexico

Dearest loves

I don't seem to have had a minute this last week except to send off two long envelopes – ordinary post – with <u>one</u> in each! (So mind when you open them!) K.K! Last week we were in Nebraska when it was I don't know how many below zero, and now we're just steaming thro' New Mexico, where the sun is so hot I've to keep the blind down in my 'roomette'! We've been going for hours through desert, with just occasionally a horse or a few cows and an awful lot of dust. Johnny and I have just had breakfast on the train – orange juice, delicious coffee, chopped ham and scrambled eggs, toast and marmalade! – and after a jolly good sleep last night – 10 hours – I'm feeling very well, thank you! Hope you both are too!

I was at La Crosse on Saturday last and was just ruined. I did the Brahms *Alto* and Pergolesi *Stabat Mater* with their choir, and offered to do another group, as they were paying me a lot and brought Johnny from Chicago speshull – so they were all thrilled and pleased with me and pleased with themselves for tackling such nice works, so all was very well. I had a bouquet of red and yellow roses from a millionaire (dollars – no good!) admirer, and one of lovely pink ones from the choir, so I was a real p.d. I stayed with Mrs Cress – (I suppose her stockings never arrived?) and her eyes just popped all weekend with excitement.

We have been on this train since 1pm yesterday and it's nearly noon today, but it's so comfortable and the food is so good, that I am loath to get out – and that's a change!

Our concerts are going beautifully – and the reviews we've seen so far have been fine, so all's well and we're as happy as larks. Johnny's playing gets better, which I didn't think was possible, and we get on very well. I have an extra broadcast in San Francisco on Feb 5th, but shall probably be coming back to Los Angeles, so my letter addresses will still stand. If you have any doubts, send to Columbia Concerts, 113 W 57th St, New York City, as they seem to be getting through this trip.

I will enclose a cheque for £10, just so's you won't be short, and don't skimp <u>anything</u> on either paint distemper, food or drink. I'm delighted with anything you do, so don't worry about any expense – think what it would cost if we'd to get Mr Enigma Variations! [This is the sisters' nickname for Mr Elgar, a local painter and decorator they had used]. I think it's lovely of you and your Momma and Auntie to go to all the trouble, and I'm thrilled to bits, so just get the best every time when you're putting all that work into it, and I'll send you a cheque any time – gee whiz! I'm looking forward to seeing it all – not to mention you two poppets. Hope John's [John Turner] doing all right – I had a short note to say he was in hospital – why not go and see him and take him some flowers from Kaff, eh? He's in the London Clinic off Marylebone Rd. You could ring up and see if he's still there or at home. Would you like to? (A real posh bouquet). Loads, buckets and barrels of love from Kaff

No.177 [Letter to Bill and Benita Cress]

25.1.50   La Fonda, Santa Fe, New Mexico

Two sweet poppets!

I don't know where to start to thank you for all you did for me this last weekend. It was all so lovely, and will be for ever memorable. I only hope I haven't worn you both to shreds and eaten you completely out of house and home!

My robe is just lovely – I've sewn on the button and moved the 'popper', and quite took Johnny's breath away when he came upon me suddenly yesterday wearing same.

I do hope the reports from your buddies have been good of the concert. I did so want it to be the best ever for your sake.

Our journey was grand – tho' I was wakened at 5.50 getting into Chicago – (could have willingly strangled the porter!) – and had checked in my luggage at Dearborn by 6.35am. Johnny's case was put out by mistake at Kansas City and we were worried stiff as it was not labelled. But have just heard that it has been discovered and should be here this afternoon.

We have had run round here this morning by nice secretary of concerts in thick snow and brilliant sunshine, and it is quite lovely and very Mexican and foreign looking. It's very high here and I'm awful short of breath, so if you hear of me singing in Santa Fe in short pants, you'll know what it's all about!

I still have no official itinerary, but from 29th to 31st Jan will be c/o Mrs Tete, 13756 Chandler Boulevard, Van Nerys, Calif., and 31st to 3rd Feb c/o Dr Walter, 608 North Bedford Drive, Beverley Hills, Calif., and I'll let you know after that.

Am just going to catch up on a batch of letters a month old, but wanted to write to you first. I've been spoiled before, but I didn't really know what it was until I came to 2005 King St, bless you both! Will you say 'thank you with all my heart' too to Stella for her lovely presents and delicious dinner and her kindness and bonny smile at all times – and, if and when you see Mr Hood, a very sincere thank you for the lovely roses.

Thank you, loves, for everything – I can't start to enumerate all my gratitude for all you have done for me – only thank you both with deep sincerity and much love – and a hug and lots of good wishes to the Doc too – I hope 1950 may hold much more happiness than he could ever dream.

Look after yourselves and thank you again for everything.

With love

Kathleen

No. 178 [Postcard to Win]

26.1.50   [Santa Fe]

Isn't this a lovely place to be staying? We're 7000 feet high and mi breath's coming in short pants, but it's lovely. Hot sun, blue sky and today, snow. Everything Mexican and Indian and very interesting. Go tomorrow to Arizona and stay in a ranch house!! Then on to Calif to stay with Ann's and Dottie's parents and Bruno Walter. Lucky old twerp, ain't I? Concerts going well and enjoying it all. Thank you for two letters – it's grand to hear from you.

Much love to you and Jane

Kaff

No.179 [Letter to Laura Cooper]

26.1.50   La Fonda, Santa Fe, New Mexico

Dear Miss Cooper

Thank you so much for your letter – it is so gratifying to know you have enjoyed my work – and I <u>do</u> hope *Orfeo* and the recital will give you pleasure too.

It would be nice if you would come round after one of the concerts, so that I could thank you in person for all your kind interest.

Yours sincerely

Kathleen Ferrier

No.180 [Letter to Win]

[3rd February 1950]   [c/o Dr Walter, 608 Bedford Drive, Beverley Hills]

All is simply <u>perfect</u> here. I have started my ten days off now and shall be here until the 13th at Bruno Walter's.

He has a lovely house with swimming pool and man and wife to look after me – all the Walters are in New York – but Lotte rang me this morning to see if I was alright – 3000 miles! Each room has its own bathroom with the most wonderful plumbing! Adolf, the man, takes me anywhere I like in either a superb Cadillac or an open Oldsmobile!! It's fantastic! This afternoon Johnny and I have been all round Bel Air and to the top of the mountain in the open car to see the wonderful homes and views – also to the Hollywood Bowl that holds 20,000 people. The sun is glorious and the oranges are on the trees and it all just makes my mouth water.

Last night we performed in a lovely hall of a University – and all Ann's and Dottie's buddies and families went. They (the audience) stood and shouted at the end, and it really did go well. Unfortunately Rodzinski was conducting the same time, so there isn't a single criticism – I could spit – but the audience loved it, so what the hell!! Ann's Momma gave a party for me afterwards and it was all lovely. I stayed there last weekend and they met me off the train from Phoenix at 7.25am!! They're real poppets and their new home is lovely.

Tomorrow Dottie's people are coming for me and I'm going there for a long weekend – they look absolute sweetie pies too. The people are so [hitherto handwritten, the letter is typewritten from here] kind, it's almost overwhelming. Fanny, the wife here, has just brought me Bruno's tzpewriter to use – so I should get on better now. I have a stack of letters waiting to be answered – so this should help. There is no exclamation mark tho', and I'm lost without one for all my adventures. By the way, I had a letter from Paddz bz the same post as yours, so all is known.

I gave John and Leon [Fontaine] the new *Kindertotenlieder* records for their Xmas present, as I had promised them, and he said he would ask zou in to hear them – but with going into hospital he couldn't make it, so if zou have a minute to go and see him he'd be verz thrilled, and zou could hear them. Thez only came the day before I left – I hope zou like them, tho' the first record is not the one to be published as I run out of breath in one phrase. Gee – I'm getting mi zzzzs mixed up, ain't I? I do hope zou like the records – I was rather pleased with them myself, for once, but will probablz change my mind when I hear them again. I will look out for some brushes – I want some myself for my next masterpieces. Would be grateful if you would write to Miss Singular [Beryl] Ball – ta ever so.

Johnny is fine – his playing gets better and better – I think he must be one of the finest in the world, and he enjoys it so. He disappears most of the time – says he plays chamber music with his buddies, and I think it's probablz true – but is a joy to be with because he knows, does and thinks everything, and I leave all the messes to him and all the travelling onuses – it couldn't be better, and this tour is unbelievable compared with last year. And oh, he <u>does</u> play beautifully.

Well, love, this is all for now – look after yourself and I do hope the weather cheers up – I wish you could share some of this sun – p'raps one of these days – who knows??

Much love to you and Jane, and I'm glad you like your photies.
God bless
Buckets
Kaff

No.181 [Letter to Emmie Tillett]
3rd February 1950   c/o Dr Walter, 608 North Bedford Drive,
                                             Beverley Hills, California

My dear Emmie

Thank you so much for your letters love, but I have only had two of them – 24th and 30th January. What a nuisance, and I thought they were coming through well this time, but perhaps they have been forwarded too late somewhere. I am so sorry to cause you extra work. Anyhow I will answer the questions you ask in these two letters, and write to Columbia to check up on them.

I am so glad your back is better again, and your Momma well – much love to her, and I am looking forward to seeing her when I get back. I heard Dame Myra is ill and has cancelled her tour here. I <u>do</u> hope it isn't serious.

Oooooooooo, boy....*Orpheus* with Dr Bruno?????? YES PLEASE---would forgo all my holiday for that.

The Hallé and *Orpheus*? I think as it was my suggestion that they do it, I must do the Sheffield date, tho' I feel rather badly about the *Passion* if Dr Jacques has asked for me – but I couldn't travel overnight to do it, as you say.

I have no arrangement with Peter Diamand over fees, but have always been well in pocket from previous visits. What <u>shall</u> I do about an accompanist there? I wish I could take John Newmark – he's absolutely superb, but he'd be out of pocket to come to Europe, even if I paid his fare..ach well, we'll see.

Gee whiz//// all this work// aren't I a lucky ole twerp/ (I have no exclam. marks on this machine – it does limit me).

Yes, I can do the *Apostles* for Hanley – it is the *Music Makers* that gets me doon. Lovely to do *Gerontius* for the Royal Choral on May 24th – whooppee.

All is going so well here. The concerts have been a great success – we've been to some lovely places – and now I am installed here, and have the house to myself with man and wife to look after me. It is just wonderful. Dr Bruno and his daughter and husband are in New York, so I shan't see them until March. The sun is shining – this place is just amazing – the palms and the houses and the glamour pussies, and the luxury of it all. I am being ruined here – I have the use of two superb cars at any time – my bathroom plumbing is an hourly – well nearly – delight, and oh it's so warm. I have so many dates with new found friends that it is almost embarrassing, but today I have started on my real holiday – ten days before going to North California, so I am as happy as a lark, and feel very grateful for this wonderful opportunity to see so much.

Mr Mertens has not sent on my contract yet – and I am being pressed all the time not to delay until the Autumn of '51 to come back, but of course it is all arranged. I have said I will come Oct 1st to Dec 15th 1951 and I STILL HAVEN'T SIGNED ANYTHING. Even *Musical America* wrote to me saying it was a bad policy not to return next Jan. What the heck.. it's only 6 months later.

The concerts are much better this year, smaller halls and altogether different, and I should say I have one of the best accompanists in the world..honest..so we enjoy our music making and make the most of opportunities to study new things, so it is grand for me.

Here is where I am going to be, so that you can write me direct? I'll give the day of the concert, then you can make that day the latest for letters.

Leave here Mon 13th

Feb 14th Hotel *Senator*, Sacramento, Calif.

16th, 17th, 18th, 19th Hotel *Whitcomb*, San Francisco

21st Hotel *Morek*, Aberdeen, Washington

24th, 25th c/o Mrs Cress, 2005 King St, La Crosse, Wisconsin

27th Hotel *Tivoli*, Downers Grove, Illinois

I think that is all love – I hope I have not forgotten anything. Much love to you and thank you for all your endeavours on my behalf – I am a lucky twerp – love too to Miss Lereculey and Miss Cheselden.

Look after yourself.

Love

Kathleen

No.182 [Letter to Benita Cress]

3rd Feb [1950]   c/o Dr Walter, 608 Bedford Drive, Beverley Hills

Dearest Benita

I have neglected you, but I have been waiting to get my itinerary – it has just arrived, so I can give you some dope on future travels.

I am just catching up on a stack of letters and have borrowed a typewriter, but the letters aren't all in the same places as mine, so you may have to decipher them a bit.

It is just wonderful here – I have the house to myself with a man and wife to look after me – the use of two cars – and permission to practise as much as I like – in fact, to use it as my home. Isn't that wonderful? I am a ruined ole twerp.

Today my holiday has started, and Johnny and I have been taken high up into the hills here to see the wonderful homes and views – it is just unbelievable – my, what a country! We're just drooling with admiration and envy of the things we see, and it is all a wonderful experience. Our concert went well last night – they stood and cheered, but unfortunately Rodzinski was here at the same time and there isn't a single criticism, but what odds, the people loved it and they are the ones that matter.

I had a sweet note from Bernard McGhee, and cannot reply because I have lost his address again – also from Norris Pynn – all my buddies in sweet La Crosse – and a lovely book from Mr Hudson, and of course I haven't his address either – he didn't put one in – perhaps I could thank him through you, love, or when I come again??

Here's where I am:

Leave here 13th Feb.

Feb 14th Hotel *Senator*, Sacramento

16th, 17th, 18th, 19th Hotel *Whitcomb*, San Francisco

21st Hotel *Morek*, Aberdeen, Washington

Arrive La X Fri 24th 9.35am (Milw. #16)

Leave La X Sun 26th 3.08pm (Milw. #100)

Howzat??

It is lovely to know that everybody has enjoyed the concert – it was a great privilege and thrill for me to come and to see all the hard work you had put in to it all – and it was unforgettable – so it is all round pleasure we have had, and that is the very nicest, ain't it?

Much love to you and your Bill – shall be seeing you soon, and thank you again for everything.

Kathleen

I am sitting writing in my lovely robe – it's such a joy, I wear it all the time.

No.183 [Postcard to Win]
[postmarked 13th February 1950]   [Beverly Hills]

Our last day here and it's been just perfect. Leave tomorrow for Sacramento and San Fran. Hope all is well with you both.

Buckets

Kaff

No.184 [Postcard to 'Messrs Pears and Britten']
[postmarked 13th February 1950]   [Beverly Hills]

Just had two weeks holiday in Los Angeles and been spoiled to death – it's wonderful! Yearning to see you and hope all is well with you both. John Newmark (my pianist – Montreal – wunderbar!) sends greetings.

Much love

Kath

Best regards sunbakingly

John N.

No.185 [Letter to Emmie Tillett]
3rd March 1950   c/o Columbia Concerts 113 W 57th St. N.Y.C

My dear Emmie

I am a diva of the deepest and dirtiest dye for not having written e'er this. My only excuse is that I have been a darn' industrious diva for the last two weeks, and I hope you'll forgive me. I will take your questions in turn and see what happens!

1. Me in a film? 'Pon mi soul! I don't know the part, or if it is suitable – and

could the camera man remove my curves? – but I couldn't give a definite answer just now until I know more about it. It would be interesting if it were rewarding, musically and financially!

2. If it is possible to do some Holland Festival 1951 I would like to, having missed this year. We will see what our programme looks like when I get home?

3. *Das Lied* April 23rd. I think I can stagger through the BBC if it's the only time it can be done. Wonder why they don't broadcast it from the hall?

4. <u>Gloucester</u>. I <u>would</u> like to stay on in Edinburgh. I would do Gloucester for Dr Sumsion with pleasure, but this is such a wonderful chance to hear some music, and Edinburgh and Gloucester are such miles away.

5. I don't remember promising to sing for Roy on Good Friday, but I've got a good 'forgettery'. All right Scandinavia March 27th onwards.

6. Would like to do Sagra Musicale de Perouse if it's something I can do well. Ask as big a fee as you like, and can. I'm awfully sorry Keith [Falkner] has left Italy. Whattashame!

7. <u>Zurich</u>. I wonder if they would be interested in Lennox Berkeley *4 Hymns of St Theresa*. I am awfully short of orchestral things. Am just learning Chausson *Poème de l'Amour et de la Mer*, but would rather not do a first performance there – but if you are stuck, then I could manage it. What about Brahms *Serious Songs* – they are orchestrated, but I suppose I would have to do them in German there, and that's an awfie sweat!

I think that is all your questions, love. I saw Bruno Walter in Chicago. He asked me to do a recital with him in Salzburg <u>this</u> year, but I'm afraid 'twill clash with Edinburgh – whattapity! He wasn't at all sure about *Orfeo* in 1951 – it's rather far ahead for him, but I'll keep the dates just the same, eh? All still goes well and San Francisco was a wow – everybody thrilled, and want me next year – whoopee! Mrs Monteux gave me a lovely black fox stole, a pearl ring and the manager a lovely necklace, and Mr Monteux a kiss on each cheek with his walrus mustache! Mm! Mm! Ain't I spoiled!! Just off to see Niagara Falls before going to Toronto. Shall be at Hotel *Weylin*, New York 15th, 16th, 17th, 18th, 19th, 20th and c/o Mrs Cardelli, 1130 Lake Shore Drive, Chicago 23rd, 24th, and 25th March if you need me.

Hope all is well with you and your sweet Momma.

Much love to you both

Kathleen

No.186 [Letter to Peter Diamand]

March 3rd [1950]   c/o Columbia Concerts, 113 W57th St. N.Y.C.

Dearest Peter

I wrote to Flot because he wrote to me – so there!! How are you, mi darling? It was gorgeous to have your letter yesterday, but I was so <u>very</u> sorry to hear Maria's father had died. Poor love – I <u>do</u> hope she is all right.

I have been meaning to write for two months – honestly!! – and on my two weeks holiday I wrote 32 letters – all replies to a large stack. Now the stack has grown again to even larger proportions, and I am tackling it as a low singer should, with mi voice in mi boots, at 8am on a zero morning in Canada!

This has really been a wonderful tour. Johnny Newmark has made all the difference in the world – in that he plays superbly and is so competent in train arrangements, tipping etc., that I just relax and let him do it, and know everything will be all right. His playing has spoiled me for anyone else, and I wish I could bring him to Europe. He is even coaching me in some Chausson and my French, mit Lancashire accent, is something to be heard to be believed!

San Francisco was absolutely wonderful and the three *Orfeos* went with a bang! The Monteuxs and the manager of the orch. were absolute poppets and made our stay there just memorable.

I stayed in Bruno's house in Beverly Hills and was spoiled to death – really. I've had to buy two Paris models, my head has enlarged itself so.

We are being taken this morning to see the Niagara Falls as it's only 20 minutes car drive from here – St Catherine's, Ontario – and I must put mi face on, and try not to look as though I were up until 2am this morning. What <u>would</u> I do without Elizabeth Arden?!

I'm looking forward so to seeing you and to coming to Holland – I must work hard now at new programme. Life is quite dull for Johnny – haven't had any temperaments so far – but don't think he'd enjoy them like <u>you</u> do!

Look after yourself, Peter love – hope to see you very soon.

Much love as always

from a

Klever Kaff

No.187 [Letter to Benita Cress]

7th March 1950   In train to Montreal

Dearest Benita

We've been shooting around, since you left us so hurriedly, like two proverbial scalded hens! It was wonderful to see you so unexpectedly – only wish Bill could have made it too. But loveliest of all was our two days together, which was such a lovely rest and spoiling for me. It was so wonderful, in the midst of a busy tour, to take time off to be giddy and I loved every minute of it – and gee whiz! how you can spoil, bless you both!

All goes well, though it's a ruddy blush now, but our concerts are a pleasure and we even floored a Columbia representative at Peterborough last night. He went straight back to write a letter to Columbia saying nice things – clever him!

We're in Montreal on Thursday, then the wilds of Eastern Canada – don't ask me where! – then *Weylin* Hotel, New York from the 15th to 20th and c/o Mrs Cardelli, 1130 Lake Shore Drive, Chicago 22nd, 23rd, and 24th. I saw her for lunch the other day, and she has arranged a dinner and theatre after the afternoon concert – so I shall be inundated I'm afraid. I thought she <u>would</u> have arranged something – that is why I was discouraging about a meeting with you in Chicago. Never mind, love. I've been awfully lucky to pass through La Crosse twice on my travels, and both times have been memorable and quite lovely and I can never thank you and Bill for all you have done for me.

I will get some prints of photographs made in Montreal and mail them to you, so you will have something else for your 'One-rogue gallery'! Thank you too for your lovely letter – I'll write to Norris when I have a minute. I <u>do</u> hope he's better.

Much love to you both and a goodie for Teddy. God bless.

Love

Kathleen

No.188 [Letter to Win]

11th March 1950   [*The Admiral Beatty*, Saint John,

New Brunswick, Canada]

Howdy toots! I'm sorry I haven't written for a bit, but have never stopped since San Fran[sisco]. Just come here from Montreal and have a concert in four hours' time. Came straight to bed for my afternoon siesta off the train, so haven't seen nuttin! Montreal was wonderful – notices just raving – Klever Kaff! I'm so pleased cos they are all such poppets there. Saw Terence Gibbs (late Decca) in Toronto for a minute last week and will be seeing him at my final concert there on the 27th. He's doing awfully well in the radio there – clever him! Won't be long now eh? O boy. Haven't shopped yet, but going to in N[ew] [Y]ork or Chicago. Is there anything you want especially? Shall be at *Weylin* Hotel from 15th – 20th and c/o Mrs Cardelli, 1130 Lake Shore Drive, Chicago, Illinois 22nd – 24th and Massey Hall, Toronto on 27th.

Have you ever had the whiskers in your nose freeze? Well I have – all these last few days in Montreal – it's been 10° below freezing – give me California!

All's wonderfully well – keep fingers Xd for 17th *Orfeo* – 19th recital with Bruno. Hope it is with you, toots.

Much love to you and Jane.

See you purty soon – whoopee!

Kaff

No.189 [Letter to Emmie Tillett]

12th March [1950]   *The Admiral Beatty*, Saint John,

New Brunswick, Canada

My dear Emmie

I am enclosing a few criticisms I have collected on my travels, Los Angeles, San Francisco, New York and Montreal, and I would like – if you agree – to have an insertion in the *Times* and *Telegraph* with a few quotations, just to let people know I've been working hard and not disappeared for three months! Aren't they lovely ones? I'm being very spoiled and just lapping it up!

The two poppets in Montreal – Mrs Langdon and Mrs Russell-Smith – send kind greetings to you.

Just shooting off for yet another train! but wanted you to see that I've been behaving myself! All goes well here – it's been a lovely tour – and I still haven't signed owt! Klever Kaff!

Hope you are well, darling, and your Momma too. Won't be long now until I arrive in my new hat and the white flour under mi arm! O boy! Tell Miss Lereculey my French grows apace – I'm learning some Chausson – and she'll have to look out for competition! I can say 'Darling, je vous aime beaucoup', passepartout, cul-de-sac, 'Voulez-vous coucher avec moi?' – oh no! that's the rude one!!

Heigh ho quelle vie! Ain't I a lucky ole budder!

Much love to you all
Kathleen

No.190 [Letter to Win]
24th March [1950]   1130 Lake Shore Drive, Chicago, Illinois
Dearest Win

Haven't written for an age, but have had my busiest time to date and everything important. All's gone well despite draughts in train and a stiff neck – have just finished my 2nd concert here and it's been a wow – will enclose a cutting. [Claudia] Cassidy is the most feared critic in America and can be just <u>cruel</u> to say the least – so everybody's happy and my fee's gone up a lump as a result! K.K.

Off to Toronto for last concert and then shall be on the boat on Wed. night. Oh boy!

It couldn't have been a lovelier tour and I haven't (so far, fingers Xd) had a single adverse criticism, but some of the most glowing I've ever read, so that's fine.

Have just not had enough time to see shops, but will do my best in between paying my Income Tax next Wed. in N.Y. Hope all's well – see you soon – oh boy – will let you know by cable when I expect to arrive, then perhaps you can make it?

Bruno has asked me to do a recital with him in Salzburg the middle of August if it doesn't clash with Edinburgh – so I should, shouldn't I? And sometime Paddy must have a holiday etc so I'd better say No to Jersey – tho' it sounds wonderful. I shall be away all June, you see. OK?
Much love to you both
In a horrible rush.
Hope all's well
K. Kaff
(feeling rather self-satisfied today, but I'll soon lose it!!)

No.191 [Letter to John Newmark]
31st March [19]50   RMS *Queen Elizabeth*
Johnny darling

I've just had my back pummelled and a salt bath, and a jolly good breakfast, and I wouldn't even call Mr Churchill mi uncle – cocky, that's me!

All's very well here, and I hope it is with you too. I finally finished with my Income Tax after two visits, had lunch with Andre Mertens, bought 24 pairs of nylons and some underneaths, both male and female, dined with Mrs Mundy and Dottie. Willie and Dennis took me to the boat. Quite a day, but I wasn't half so tired as last year, and have bounced back again to my lively normal after two good nights sleep. K.K.

Benno and Anita Moiseiwitsch were in my cabin when I arrived, and dragged me off to the Purser's cabin for a nightcap. Rex Harrison and his wife were there, she only to see him off, and Danny Kaye is on board!, also at our table Szigeti's son-in-law Paganoff? No! I'll have to look it up! I haven't seen Symon [Goldbergs] yet. I searched all over at the boat drill yesterday, but will find them today.

There were flowers for me and telegrams from Wisner, Stella at La Crosse, the Michigan Ave Fan Club!! and Howard Skinner, bless 'em all! Ain't I spoiled!

I'm afraid I shall have to perform this crossing as Benno is determined to play for me – heigh ho! Spoils the whole trip but perhaps they won't wait for the last night. He says I'm very foolish not to come next season, as I should cash in on the success of this season. However it's done now and I can't see that six months will make <u>so</u> much difference. I am going to Holland after all in May – Mrs Tillett has switched some concerts round so that I can fly. Pore Kaff!

Well, my very dear Johnny, I don't know where to start to thank you for making this 3 months so perfect. It would have been perfect for just your superb, lovely playing, but you have done and given so much more, and I think you know, despite all my inadequacies of speech and writing, how much I have loved and appreciated it all – and I thank you with all my heart – deeply and sincerely – for everything.

I hope we may meet in London or on the Continent – but even if it doesn't work out – there's always 1951 and I look forward to it already. Bless you love! Look after yourself and kindest greetings to Eric McLean and Paul Roussel – with grateful thanks to the former for his sweet telegrams – a kiss on the snitch for Jicky, and again my deep gratitude to you for this memorable tour.
With my love
Kaff

No.192 [Letter to Sadie Lereculey]
1st April [1950]   RMS *Queen Elizabeth*
Dear Miss Lereculey
    Herewith my suggestions for B'ham programme – May 8th.

Bist du bei mir	Bach
Like as the lovelorn turtle	Handel
Have you seen but a whyte lily grow?	arr. Grew
There's not a swain of the plain	Purcell arr. Britten
Mad Bess	Purcell arr. Britten
Frauenliebe und Leben	Schumann
Silent Noon	Vaughan Williams
Rahoon	Moeran
The merry green wood	Moeran
Flower song (*Rape of Lucretia*)	Britten
Down by the Salley Gardens	arr. Britten
Oliver Cromwell	arr. Britten

Howzat?
Here also <u>Highgate April 29th</u>.

Bist du bei mir	Bach
Turtle	Handel
Hark the ech'ing air	Purcell
Che faro senz' Euridice (*Orfeo*)	Gluck
An die Musik	Schubert
Du liebst mich nicht	Schubert
Suleika	Schubert

Der Musensohn	Schubert
Botschaft	Brahms
Wir wandelten	Brahms
Sonntag	Brahms
Von ewiger Liebe	Brahms
Down by the Salley Gardens	arr. Britten
The Spanish lady	arr. Hughes
Blow the wind southerly	arr. Whittaker
The Keel row	arr. Whittaker

'Che faro' and 'Have mercy Lord' OK for Brighton. Sorry to have kept you waiting <u>so</u> long – just haven't had a minute. See you soon – whoopee!
Affectionately
Kathleen F.

No.193 [Letter to Bill and Benita Cress]
8.4.50   Frognal Mansions, NW3
Dearest Bill and Benita

Well loves, home at last, and the spring is here to welcome me with blossom, bulbs and sticky horse-chestnut buds. It all looks green and lovely.

I had a wonderful voyage with the Moiseiwitschs, Danny Kaye and Rex Harrison – we <u>did</u> have fun and I have never had so many late nights. Benno M. won the lottery on the ship's run – £755!! – so we had to celebrate!

Win, Paddy and John Turner came to Southampton to meet me, and I could show them round the *Lizzie* before sliding innocent-eyed through the customs!

The flat looked lovely – Paddy's mother had colour-washed the walls of all the rooms and I had new curtains and carpet in my room – very swish! And everybody was well and happy, so it was a good homecoming after the most wonderful time and tour ever. Lucky Kaff!

Eggs are off the ration too and somebody brought us a pound of real farm butter this morning, so we're in clover.

I'm seeing Mr Mertens next week and if I ask him to send you a cheque for $100, could you send us a few things occasionally? Our greatest miss at the moment is sugar – not cubes – and soap – toilet and flakes – and if it were possible to pack some white flour for baking cakes I should be top of the class with [Emmie Tillett] my manager here! The grocery stores – I think – will do it all for you rather than you having the bother of finding boxes, paper and string. I <u>hope</u> this isn't asking too much of you, love. Don't trouble for <u>one</u> minute if it is.

Mr Anderson in Chicago sends us Peacock Sliced Dried Beef (Cudaly, Wisconsin) and Paddy and her mother have thought of every way of cooking, steaming, baking and grilling it – with no success. Do you know anything about it? – it comes from your part of the world. They've even tried soaking it over-night, but it still baffles.

It's been wonderful to be with you both – I have such constant reminders of you – if I needed any – my lovely housecoat and blouse and perfume – you are so generous in every way, I am at a loss to thank you enough for all you have done for me. But I do thank you with all my heart a thousand times, and shall remember this tour as one of the happiest times I ever had – bless you both for your great share in it.

I had a lovely cable on the boat from Stella and Owen, which cheered me on my way, and one from my Dr buddies in Chicago – they called themselves the Michigan Ave Fan Club – which mad me larf. Will you thank Stella when you see her and give her and Owen my love and love to all my buddies in La X.

Roll on 1951 – I'm looking forward to seeing you all again then, I hope.

Much love to you both and thank you again for all your wonderful and many kindnesses.

God bless and keep you

Yours till hell freezes

Love

Kathleen

No.194 [Letter to Sadie Lereculey]

10th April 1950   2 Frognal Mansions, NW3

Dear Miss Lereculey

Here, I hope, are the missing programmes:

<u>King's Lynn</u> [April 28th]

Bist du bei mir	Bach
Like as the lovelorn turtle	Handel
Hark the ech'ing air	Purcell
Suleika	Schubert
Wandrers Nachtlied	Schubert
Musensohn	Schubert
Sonntag	Brahms
Botschaft	Brahms
Down by the Salley Gardens	arr. Britten
The Spanish lady	arr. Hughes
Blow the wind southerly	arr. Whittaker
The Keel Row	arr. Whittaker

I will change the middle group for the children to:

Who is Sylvia?	Schubert
Heiden Roslein	Schubert
Musensohn	Schubert
Sonntag	arr. Brahms
The Vain Suit	Brahms

Howzat? I don't think Phyllis needs to suffer and play solos – I'll stagger through – but it was a kind thought, n'est pas?

<u>Dorchester and Bideford May 5th and 7th</u>

Bist du bei mir	Bach
Like as the lovelorn turtle	Handel
Hark the ech'ing air	Purcell
Che faro senz' Euridice (*Orfeo*)	Gluck
Frauenliebe und Leben	Schumann
Wir wandelten	Brahms

Sonntag	Brahms
Botschaft	Brahms
Love is a bable	Parry
A soft day	Stanford
Blow the wind southerly	arr. Whittaker
The Keel Row	arr. Whittaker

I <u>have</u> sent Birmingham haven't I? I enclose a letter from Mr [Alan] Kirby, Croydon, and if Mrs Tillett agrees, I should like to sing for him – he's a sweet poppet! And also – if you can read it! – a letter from Dr [Edgar] Cook, South-wark – I leave them both in your hands – lucky me!
Best wishes
Sincerely
Kathleen Ferrier

No.195 [Letter to Laura Cooper]
10th April [1950]   2 Frognal Mansions, NW3
Dear Laura Cooper
    Thank you so much for your kind letters. I am so happy that you could come to both my concerts in New York and that you enjoyed them. I am sorry about 'Blow the Wind Southerly', but, it being a recital of Lieder, I had to stick to them in my encores – another time, with pleasure!
    I enclose a photograph for you to hang in your rogues gallery.
With all best wishes and grateful thanks for your many kindnesses.
Very sincerely,
Kathleen Ferrier

No.196 [Letter to Harry Vincent]
10th April [1950]   2 Frognal Mansions, London NW3
My dear Harry
    What a lovely picture!! I was thrilled to receive the first picture of my god-child, and nobody could be prouder. I showed it to Alison too – she thinks she's wonderful – and so say all of us. <u>Her</u> little boy is a cherub – no hair, pink cheeks and a broad grin, and they are very thrilled with him too. You clever people!
    The little pencil was just a put-me-on until I could find something I really liked, and I haven't had much chance so far. But I'm glad you liked it just the same.
    I would rather not chatter before my concert – can't we come up afterwards, then I can really let my hair down? Gerald [Moore] has already booked for me at the pub in Newcastle [under Lyme], and I think I had better stay there as I have to be in Bournemouth the next day for a [4.30pm] rehearsal, and it will mean a very early start – but would you thank them very much indeed for their kind invitation?
All news when I see you – meanwhile much love to you all from
Kathleen

No.197 [Letter to one of the so-called Michigan Ave Ferrier Fan Club]
18th April [19]50   Newcastle-under-Lyme
Dear Dr John

Didn't I tell you? Why, I tried out my first mee-mees on the 2nd green and
by the 6th I had tuned up to:

[The Frank Crumit song 'Donald the Dub': 'Oh! the naughty little pill went
a-rolling down the hill and it rolled right into a bunker. From there to the green
I took sixteen and then, by God, I sunk her'.]

Well, well – hidden talents – British understatement and all that! But you
have left me agog to see how I came out finally!

It was wonderful to hear from you, and your cable to the boat was a wonderful
send off – thank you so very much.

The voyage was peaceful 'climatically' but fairly hectic socially as Benno
Moiseiwitsch won the pool on the ship's run and so we had to celebrate – with
Danny Kaye as the auctioneer it was very amusing. Benno had a piano on board
in a small room, so we had music until all hours – it was lovely to be able to stay
up late and not think about a concert the next day.

Now I'm back in the swing. I am writing this in bed before a concert here
tonight with Gerald Moore, and I must be up with the lark in the morning to
sing *Das Lied von der Erde* (Mahler) tomorrow in Bournemouth.

I don't know the Mahler 9th – shame on me, but it would be a good performance with George Szell I'm sure, he's very competent, caustic, and cold! I envy
your being in Florida and having much sun and bathing – have a wonderful time,
and I hope the amazing work you do doesn't take up too much of your time,
so that you may enjoy yourself. Greetings to the M[ichigan] A[venue] F[errier]
F[an] C[lub], and thank you again for all your kindness to me
Best wishes always
Kathleen

No.198 [Letter to Harry Vincent]
26th April [1950]   2 Frognal Mansions, London NW3
My dear Harry

Thank you so much for your lovely letter – both Gerald and I loved seeing
you, and talked of nothing but my God-child, bless her. She is a credit to you
both, and as bonny as they're made – but I might have known! Look at her
Momma and Poppa – bless them too!

In February next year I am going to be in France and Italy in Feb[ruary] and am booked on March 1st with the Hallé – am in Hanley on the 7th March doing *Orfeo* with them, with 'our Ena'! I'm seeing Mrs Tillett tomorrow so I will tell her I would like to do it, then you can compare dates with her – it saves time for you when I am away so much.

Thank you again for all you did to make the concert such a success and for our lovely supper and evening with you afterwards.

Bless you for everything and look after yourselves.

Much love to you all

Kathleen

No.199 [Letter to John Newmark]

28th April [19]50   2 Frognal Mansions, London NW3

Dearest Johnny

Thank you so much for your letter, which gave me great pleasure, except the bit about being so much out of pocket! Next year our tour will not be so long, and I will be able to pay you more too, because my wages will have risen (D.V.). Mrs Tillett and I are having lunch with Andre Mertens tomorrow, when things should be clinched – money matters I mean! I hate the thought of you being down for my pleasure, and don't want it to be that way at all.

Well, I had lunch today with Victor Olof – the musical adviser of Decca. He is all for you coming to make the *Frauenliebe* with me here, and doesn't think there will be difficulty about labour permit, but is finding that out in the morning. I shall hear more news tomorrow when he rings me, but so far he suggests paying your fare from Paris and your hotel room from the night before you record to the night we finish, and so much a record – I don't know yet how much, but I said it must be their top fee for accompanists. He wondered if an American contract would be better for you, then there would not be English tax, and there is another difficulty of taking money (more than five pounds) out of this country, but we shall see what happens, but it is as good as in the bag!! O BOY! He wants to do much more than *Frauenliebe* – lots of Lieder so keep your fingers crossed darlint! My only slight cloud is breaking the news to Phyllis Spurr, because she's a nice poppet, but these things have to be done and we can record other things together. Victor told me ages ago I should have someone else – if that someone can be you, then I am indeed blessed! He wasn't keen on the thought that you would already have recorded the *Frauenliebe*, but doesn't think it will hurt to do it again. Josef Krips, conductor, has asked to play it for me on records, but I want <u>you</u> to do it, and am going to stick out – Klever Kaff!

Am back in the swing again, and have done a million things since I returned, including three *Das Lieds*, *St Matthew Passion* and sundry recitals. Hampstead is looking simply superb with all the blossom and spring flowers doing their best to outshine each other – it has never looked so green and fresh, and I wish you could see it just now, but p'raps it is just as well you're not here as our flat has dry rot and fungi growing on the bricks, and the builder can't understand why I haven't floated out in the bath before now! SO, the bath is in the hall, along with the water heater and wash basin, and the lavatory is due to join them any minute!! Our timing for inner cleanliness is something of a feat, and our outer

cleanliness is reduced to washing vital parts in the kitchen!! Quelle vie! Also the electrician is here putting extra plugs in, the gas man also giving us extra heating, and we are having felt surrounds put down to keep out the draughts, so everything is being done at once – we couldn't be in a worse mess, and we couldn't <u>care</u> less, so what the hell! We're going to look quite grand one day, but it may be 1953! Win wrote a limerick for my birthday – here it is: There was a young lady called Kath, who did like to sing in the bath. When the dry rot did creep in, the bath sank so deep in, that Kath had her bath on the path! Talking of birthdays Johnny, I wish you would celebrate mine by spending your money on yourself instead of me! You have bought me so much, love, these past few months and I still have my [Easter] egg from last year! But bless you many times for remembering. Will write again as soon as I have news.
Much love
Kaff

No.200 [Letter to John Newmark]
May Day! 1950   2 Frognal Mansions, London NW3
Dearest Johnny

I'm a cautious ole budder, but I really begin to have the highest hopes for our recording! Mr Sarton, the business manager, rang me up the following day after I wrote you, and here are his suggestions: Decca will pay your fare from Paris (you are coming from there, aren't you?): they will pay you three pounds a day living expenses whilst recording and pay you ten pounds for each double-sided record – and we can make as many as we can get in – until my chords start steaming in fact. That is the highest they pay for any accompanist – they don't pay by royalties – and I am terribly pleased – I <u>do</u> hope you are. I have asked to record in the evening, as my voice has warmed up then, and they will just do anything to get some records on wax. Ain't that nice? I'm pickled tink! Please let me know at your earliest, definite times when you will be in London, and then I will reserve with them recording times – because much of their time is booked already for sessions, but fortunately not the evenings. Oh boy!

I <u>think</u> Miette Dernbach came round to see me after a broadcast the other night, – I know I'm dumb – but there were a lot of people, and it was only after I left her that I realised it was probably she, as she said she knew you. I haven't contacted her yet because I've been working ever since I came home, and now must get on with the *St Matthew Passion* in German – I have only done it in English before, and I have only one month, so my French is in the background. Except yesterday, I was going through some music and found a volume of Fauré!! Such lovely ones – which may I sing Johnny? Help please!

And last night I went to a party – a rare occasion for me, but it was to Arthur Benjamin's house, and all my buddies were there and it was great fun. Some – well one – of your buddies was there too – 'Viola' of Vic and Viola – does it convey anything to you? She was nice, and when I said you might be coming over, very excited.

My lovely necklaces, earrings etc. have a continued success and have and are giving me the greatest pleasure, bless you!

Sir Thomas Beecham's secretary has just left me – he was wanting to know if

I would record some Delius songs mit him on Columbia, but I don't think Decca will keep on lending me – but it's nice to be asked. He also told me that Ann Ayars is doing Antonia in the film of Hoffman! – it would have been fun to be there with her – but I couldn't do it anyway 'cos I'm in Wien.

I have some sad news for you. Lotte Walter wrote the other day to say 'our Fanny has passed away and Adolph would be so pleased if you would write!' I can't believe it, Johnny – she was so lively and full of fun. Would you write too love? His surname is Boden. She had been with them 16 years, and I know they will be lost without her.

That's all for now – write soon and say you are pleased too about the recording. Much love
Kaff

No.201 [Letter to Bill and Benita Cress]
May 1st [19]50   2 Frognal Mansions, London NW3
Dearest Bill and Benita

Thank you so much for your letter this morning and the record review – I haven't heard those records because they are on long-playing and won't play on my recorder. I hope they are all right – I wasn't a bit impressed with the recording session – it seemed a bit of a muddle to me. Trust ole Benita to have them!

Mr Mertens is here at the moment and my contract is being all fixed up with my manager here, so that's something I haven't to worry about. I have written to his secretary and she will be sending you a cheque for 100 dollars, and if you could send us a box of toilet soap, some soft sugar and some plain white flour, we will be eternally grateful. The flour is for my manager, who wants her German cook to bake her a white cake, but I would like some of the ready mixtures to try – but, love, I don't want you to have a lot of trouble and packing and our real need is for soap and sugar – we are fine for canned meats and butter thanks to my buddy in Chicago! Lucky us!

Well! I'm just negotiating with Decca to bring Johnny over to make some records with me, and they are all for it – so if he is happy with their terms, we shall be working till my chords steam in July – won't it be gorgeous? – I'm pickled tink! He is in Europe, so it is just asking to use him. So you should have a few more in the next months to put in your rogues' gallery.

We are in a real pickle at home – we have acute dry rot in the bathroom and lavatory – I haven't had a bath for a week and have had to time my penny spending to the nnth degree! Thank goodness it's not my property – but when they are through with the mess, we should be rather grand, and will be able to have a bath without worrying about sinking through the floor into No.1!!

Here's a naughty limerick for you:
There was a young lady of Nantes
Tres chic, jolie et elegante
Her hole was so small
She was no good at all
Except for la plume de ma tante!

I am in Amsterdam for a cuppla days next week and on the 31st July [this should be 5th June] go to Vienna – but I don't know where I'm staying yet, but will let you know. I leave Vienna on the 17th June and go to Zurick [*sic*], but I don't know where I sleep there yet either. Shall be home on the 3rd July and will be having a rest and learning new things and recording all that month and August – so there is an outline of my travels.

Hope all is well with you both – much love to you and Doc.

Kaff

No.202 [Letter to David Tidboald]

1st May 1950   2 Frognal Mansions, London NW3

Dear Mr Tidboald

Thank you for your letter. I would be very happy if you would send your songs of the Housman poems, though I shall be away next month in Vienna. I should have a chance after that to study them. I am so glad you enjoyed the broadcasts this week. It gives me enormous pleasure to know this.

With best wishes

Sincerely

Kathleen Ferrier

No.203 [Letter to Peter Diamand]

19th May 1950   [on Hotel *Stockholm* writing paper] 2 Frognal Mansions,
                                                                            London NW3

My dear Peter

First of all let me say thank you a million times for saving my life and looking after me last week – it was so lovely to see you and Maria again – and was a joy to be with you. My lilac is still with me – would you believe it – it has been lovely, bless you.

I spoke to Gerald [Moore] about coming with me in Nov. and he would love to. He can manage from the 21st (Leiden) until about the 6th Dec and I am wondering if it is possible to put Arnhem somewhere else. Could you let me know as soon as possible because he has somebody else waiting if it is quite impossible.

Re Easter *St Matthew Passions*: March 15th, 16th, 18th 1951 – I am booked in Liverpool on the 13th for a *Das Lied* so it would mean that I couldn't arrive until the late afternoon of the 14th if flying is possible (weather permitting I mean). It is going to be a fraightful rush ain't it, but if it is all right to Mr V. B. [Eduard van Beinum] I can do it – also the other two on the 20th and 21st.

I shall have to think a bit longer about Jan. for *Orfeo*, because I am getting so overloaded already with work that I must be careful. It is going to be a heavy year with this British festival – but I will let you know.

Went all prima donna yesterday and told Mr V. Beinum off – got out of bed to do a rehearsal and then was kept waiting for an hour – the third or fourth time now – so I told him about it and I think he will be more careful in future. I sang like a pig at night in the *Kindertotenlieder* and I think it is time I rushed off to Scotland – I shall be with the Maitlands until the 27th May and my address is:

Eilean Darach, Dundonnell, by Garve, Ross-shire.

Telegrams Dundonnell,
Phone   "   2 just in case you want me – and letters take a long
time to get there.

Much love to you and please let me know how much I owe you and I will
send it to Peter's account.

Thank you for everything and I hope to see you soon.

God bless you both

Love

Kaff

No.204 [Postcard to Win]
Thurs. 8th June [1950]   [*Vienna*]

Everything fine here. Karajan very pleased with me – first performance
tomorrow – <u>wish</u> you could hear it. 'Twill be broadcast – perhaps you will! Met
Gordon Smith on Zurich station – kleine Welt!! Weather simply superb and food
superber! Victor Olof here being absolute pet. Going to hear Krips recording
tonight – then on to dinner with them both.

Would have liked to have seen Vienna before the war – the buildings are
superb. Everything very cheap – Austrian shilling = 3½d now! Had some photies
taken – one in particular v.g.

Hope all's well with you and Jane

Much love

Kaff

No.205 [Letter to Emmie Tillett]
15th June [19]50   Vienna
Dearest Emmie

I have neglected you because dates were still being altered when I received
your wire. Now we're back to where we were and it's <u>two</u> concerts in Milan. Are
they willing to pay the £175 – oh boy! I don't need to leave Zurich until the 29th
and I hope I can get back in time to get a sleeper home as originally arranged.
But there isn't one booked on any special day, is there? So I'll go to Cooks in
Zurich on Saturday.

I think the last performance in Milan is the 2nd, but I'll find out tonight. It's
only 4½ hours train journey Milan to Zurich, and the easiest way home I'm told.
<u>MUST</u> be home in time for G[lynde]bourne with you and the Prof and Profess.
[Mr and Mrs Roy Henderson]

All's gone well here and my crits have been wonderful, and they want me
to do a recital here next year. Klever Kaff! Last concert tonight, so fingers still
crossed!

If Scala comes off, could you ask them to arrange hotel <u>with bath</u> (oh! the
agony here!) and that I shall be met in Milan as I shall have no money. I'll let
you know train and date.

Victor Olof (Decca) is here recording and met me in, and has been an absolute pet – otherwise it would have been 'O sole mio!' Denis [Matthews – pianist]
had good success too, so we haven't let you down, love!

Why I say 'the agony here'. The food is frrrrrightfully rich – too rich for my ole liver, and the pongy lav is a mile down the corridor – oh! the exercise I've had!

Am full of beans once more and back to my Wiener Schnitzels!

Shall be at *Dolder Grand* Hotel, Zurich until the 28th or 29th if you want me. Could you let me know who to contact for some of my earnings in Switz[erland] in advance? Am doing myself proud at the *Dolde*r – shall <u>enjoy</u> having dearmaria with me own lav!

Hope all is well darling – much love to you and your Momma.

Love

Kathleen

No.206 [Letter to Win]

15th June [19]50   Vienna

Dearest Win

Ta ever so for your letter, which Paddy forwarded – glad you had a good time in Scotland and Durham.

All's well here. Victor Olof and his three engineers have been perfect pets, and we've lunched together each day, and Victor has come for me after a concert to rescue me from the terrific crowds of autograph hunters – they're worse than in England. The Krips have been pets too and we've seen a lot of them.

My last concert is tonight – B minor Mass – the other two safely and success-fully over. The crits are marvellous – especially for here – and I've been asked back for a recital. K.K.

It's been terrifically hot – lovely for lounging, but a bit much in a crowded concert hall. It's a bit depressing here – there are still uniforms of 4 armies about and so many beggars and lame, halt and blind. I'm looking forward to being in Zurich – *Dolder Grand* Hotel – on Saturday – with its blitz-free look! My 'man without hairs' has sent me a red rose each morning and I've had one invitation to go on his motor bike, but otherwise have been unmolested!! Am going on to Milan for Bach Mass with Karajan, but otherwise will be home D.V. about the 5th July.

Hope all's well with you – more chatter in Pop's letter.

Much love

Kaff

No.207 [Postcard to Harry Vincent]

18 June 1950   Zurich

Zurich. Just come from Vienna today – been singing Bach there and had a lovely time and notices. As a result go to the Scala, Milan July 2nd and 3rd to repeat the B minor Mass, and am very happy about it. Now having 10 days holiday here before a concert, and looking forward to the rest. Hope you and Madge and my poppet are all well and happy.

Much love to you all and God bless.

Kathleen

No.208 [Letter to Peter Diamand]
18.6.50   *Dolder Grand* Hotel, Zurich
Dear Peter

I have been thinking about the Kunstkring concert next Nov. and wondering if it would be possible to perform the Flothuis work with flute, oboe, viola and cello. If this were so I could also use the flute and viola in other items – the former in a lovely cantata by Telemann and the latter in the two cradle songs by Brahms – and I am sure many other things to make a varied, interesting programme.

Would you ask whoever is responsible if they are willing to agree to this? Hope all is well with you and send my best wishes.

In haste
Sincerely
Kathleen

No.209 [Letter to Peter Diamand]
[19 June 1950]   *Dolder Grand* Hotel, Zurich
Dearest Peter

Flot wants me to write to the Kunstkring about performing his work – but as I don't know a name to write to, and can't very well write 'Dear Bricks & Mortar' I thought I would enclose a letter in this which you may think fit to pass on, eh?

How are you after the opening of the Festival? (I saw pictures in *Het Parool* here). I <u>do</u> hope it all went off well, and am sorry I wasn't there.

I have just arrived here from Vienna where the 3 concerts have gone well and the notices were a 'bit of orl rite'! Klever Kaff!

I found it very depressing. The hotel – one of two that isn't commandeered – was mucky, noisy and smelled of garlic. I have never seen so many beggars except perhaps in Havana, nor so many maimed, halt and blind, and with 4 armies there, there is an uncomfortable atmosphere. But the concerts were lovely and the audiences very enthusiastic. It was lovely to get here and see the cleanliness, and have a lovely bathroom all to myself.

My concert here is on the 27th and afterwards I am going for two days to the Scala, Milano, to repeat the B minor Mass with the Wien Orch. and Karajan – it seemed a pity to miss it when I was so near.

Shall be home on the 6th and from the 8th Johnny Newmark will be in London and we're going to record steadily for a week – all sorts of nice things – but this means that I can't get to Holland now for some part of the festival, and I am <u>very</u> sorry about that.

I <u>do</u> hope Maria is really feeling better and your Mutti too. Much, much love to you all – I would love a note from you if you have just one single minute – and I hope you haven't a single hitch for the whole festival.
God bless and love from
Kathleen

The first person I banged into here yesterday was George Szell sitting at the next table alone! – am just waiting for Rick [Davies] to turn up for a week, so we shall all be going golfing together! I wonder if George Szell knows the meaning of 'gooseberry'!

No.210 [Postcard to Win]

Wed. 21st June [1950]   *Dolder Grand* Hotel, Zurich, Switzerland

This is a delirious place and we're swimming and golfing every day. I'm sore all over – muscles and scorches! Vienna was grand – thanks to Victor and the engineers – now I'm looking forward to Milan and the Scala – oh boy! Hans Schneider will be there, so I shall have a buddy there too. Home on the 5th D.V. Hope all is well with you. Ta ever so for letter. Rick sends his love – he's full of beans and we're both feeling fine. Hope you are too.

Much love

Kaff

No.211 [incomplete letter to Win]

[27th June 1950]   [*Dolder Grand* Hotel, Zurich, Switzerland]

... My concert here is tonight and I shall be relieved when it's over because my bill is terrific – but it's worth it – it's so comfortable. I leave here on Thursday [29th June] lunchtime for Milan.

[Erich] Kleiber, whom I was rather dreading, as I had heard he was such a stickler, is a fine conductor and cancelled my final rehearsal this morning as he was so happy! Klever Kaff!! I hope he is as pleased at the concert tonight!

The impresario tells me I'm not allowed to spend so much of my fee, as a part of it <u>must</u> go back to England, and I'm only <u>just</u> going to have enough to pay my bloody bill, the barstewards! and will be counting every franc until I leave. <u>Honestlee!</u> ...

... I guess I'm meant to be a lone she-wolf. I don't mind him [Rick Davies] for a buddy for two days, then I've had enough and want to retire behind an iron curtain and not have to listen and make conversation! Fickle, that's me....

No.212 [Letter to Emmie Tillett]

10th July [19]50   2 Frognal Mansions, London NW3

Dear Mrs Tillett

Here are a few replies to your queries

<u>Rhyl programme Oct 22nd</u>.

Spring is coming	Handel
Come to me soothing sleep	Handel
Hark the ech'ing air	Purcell
Mad Bess	Purcell
An die Musik	Schubert
Lachen und Weinen	Schubert
Du liebst mich nicht	Schubert
Der Musensohn	Schubert
Wir wandelten	Brahms
Botschaft	Brahms
Sonntag	Brahms
Von ewiger Liebe	Brahms
Love is a bable	Parry
The fairy lough	Stanford
A soft day	Stanford

The bold unbiddable Child   Stanford

<u>Cambridge May 17th</u>   OK for Brahms Viola Songs

<u>Bolton 14th Nov</u>   Phyllis Spurr will accompany

<u>Highgate May 5th</u>   No to recital here as I may go to Vienna, will come in and see you about this?

<u>Bryanston May [19]51</u>   I thought I could perhaps go the weekend May 19th, but perhaps you have something booked there? I would like to go as she is an old school friend, and leave it to you to fix.

<u>Edinburgh '51</u>   Ian Hunter tells me there is still a possibility of *Orfeo*, so would you keep all the time free from July 20th onwards until we hear definitely – I shall have to ask off to go to King's Lynn if it does materialise – I <u>do</u> want it to.

<u>No Television</u>   Bitte no time and too fat!!

<u>Hindemith Requiem</u>   Still in Holland and can't do rehearsals

Will speak to Basil Douglas about concert in Wigmore Hall – want to know what he wants me to do – am I free on the 11th?

Mr Karajan wants me to sing in the Bach B minor in Munich on Easter Sunday, and I said I would ask you, but I think it is pretty hopeless don't you? 25th March '51. Gamsjäger wants me in January but I am hoping I shall go to the Scala, then for *Orfeo* – and if I don't, I want a rest – but I said I might go in May for the Beethoven 9th and two recitals 8th and 10th? But I will come and see you about all these bits and bobs. Thank you so much for booking Leeds and Bath. What fun!

Hope your back is much better now, love.

Love

Kathleen

No.213 [Letter to Harry Vincent]

22nd July [1950]   2 Frognal Mansions, London NW3

My dear Harry

Home once again and have neglected my God-child on her first birthday, which is shocking of me – I am looking round, and have been ever since the eventful day she was born, for something to keep which is worthy of her. So far I haven't found what I want, but I just wanted you to know that I am really far from forgetting her! Bless her wee heart – I hope she is blooming?

Milan was wonderful and La Scala something to remember – the President was thrilled and has asked me back to do a stage version of *Orfeo* – next Jan[uary] if it can be fitted in – How I hope it can. I only saw one notice as I left the following day – but it being the Bach Mass, there was more about the performance and Karajan the conductor, than the artists. However here is a translation from the *Corriere Lombardo*: 'Kathleen Ferrier, new to the scene, revealed a stupendous voice and an interpretation of irresistible emotion', and I will enclose two Vienna ones that were translated for me – you may be able to use one or the other of them.

I am looking forward so much to 'our' concert and am just working on programme now – will send it soon. Any ideas or requests!?

Paddy, my little housekeeper, is probably taking a job as a model and is just staying on until she gets settled and finds a room, as I haven't room for a lodger here as well as a housekeeper. Now I must think about a new housekeeper and would prefer a northern one; do you know any angels there? Someone good-tempered and honest and clean – willing to do everything in the house and shopping, and look after our father – and not be lonely when I'm away?? It's a tall order, but I thought you might just hear of somebody.

Hope all is well with you all – and looking forward to seeing you. I am at home now until the 24th Aug[ust], studying and making new programmes – but the time does fly so!

Much love to you all and God bless

Kathleen

No.214 [Letter to Win]

27th July [1950]   2 Frognal Mansions, London NW3

Dearest our Winnie

Just thinking about you and Jane going off for your holiday – and wishing I were coming too – have a lovely time, and don't go short of anything, and here's a little extra for you both for a good stuff and a gentle booze.

'Twas a lovely tea on Saturday – I <u>did</u> enjoy it and I <u>do</u> think we are lucky in our various god-children, don't you?

Would you like my Deccalian record player, because I am treating myself to a long-playing Decca-cum- short-playing-cum-radio? I spoke to an RGD man the other day and he says with our table models they have discovered that the buttons are hopeless, but they will take them back, re-do them and put in a new panel for about nine pounds – but you have to do it through an RGD agent. I think it would be worth it, don't you, because they are good speakers, and you'd get nothing in return for them.

Must go and do some mee-mees – you'll never believe it, but the Prof is pleased with me – I nearly fainted!!

John rang up this morning – says he's going to join the Navy – so I said I'd join the Wrens and now he wants to know if he can be attached to my base – or anyway, anchored! Whattaladdie! Ta-ta for now! Tell that driver to keep his hands on the handlebars!

Much love to you both

K.K.

No.215 [undated postcard to Laura Cooper, stamped Fayer, Wien 1, Elisabethstrasse 2. She was in Vienna in June 1950 but this was probably written from London from mid-July].

Thank you so much for your kind letter. It gives me the greatest pleasure to know you enjoy my work and my records. I have recorded the *Kindertotenlieder* with the Vienna Phil: and Bruno Walter – Columbia – [October 1949] – probably out in Sept. Have just done *Frauenliebe und Leben* and *Vier ernste Gesänge* on L.P. Decca – should be out in October. New Schubert 'Musensohn', 'An die Musik', Decca just out. Hope you will be able to get some of these.

With best wishes

Kathleen Ferrier

No.216 [Letter to Bill and Benita Cress]
10th Aug.[1950]   2 Frognal Mansions, London NW3
Dearest Bill and Benita

A wondrous parcel arrived yesterday, full of just all the right things!! Bless you a 1000 times – we haven't seen such salmon for 10 years, so we're going to have a feast one of these days. Thank you so very much for all your trouble. It couldn't be lovelier. Yes, love, the 2nd June box arrived safely here and in wonderful order – food seems to get here without difficulty – fingers Xd! – we are getting a good store now – but as you say, it's a jolly good idea with the world situation looking menacing! Isn't it a bluidy shame for young boys and their parents to be suffering five years after the last holocaust! Whattaworld!

Haven't you got the sack yet? Gee! They must be short-staffed!!! Klever old Benita earning a few more shekels to help Bill out with that new fridge and car – not to mention Mr Schlabach. I hope you are happy and well – that's all that matters, isn't it?

Going back to your letter. Coffee has always been easy here, because we are a tea-drinking nation – so there is no difficulty there. Paddy is still gloating over the cake mixtures! – they really are a blessing in a hurry particularly! We can get Fab here now too, and soon soap should be off the ration altogether, so we shan't need any more – it will be gorgeous to go in a shop and buy soap without coughing up a niggly bit of printed paper!

Schwarzkopf is a fine musician and she does a terrific amount of work – some things absolutely superb and others, I think, unsuitable – but all the Viennese singers work themselves to a standstill – I just dawdle in comparison! Klever me – I've been home nearly two months – having sometimes two lessons a day and a real rest from concert-giving – and I think it has done me a world of good. I've been going a bit gay too, and going to theatres and dinners. Tonight [11th] I am going to the Promenade concerts – a Beethoven night – and dining afterwards with Malcolm Sargent and a friend – M.S. is conducting. I've been spending a lot of money too – bought a fur coat – dyed Russian ermine (very unpatriotic!) but very beautiful – ordered three cupboards to fit in my room for all my odds and sods – and ordered a Beau Decca – longplaying, shortplaying and radio – so now I'm broke, but tickled pink, so what the heck!!!!

My first concert is Aug 28th at Edinburgh with the Brahms Alto Rhapsody, with Fritz Busch – and it will be lovely when that is over, because I shall be able to relax and enjoy the rest of the Festival.

Now I must get ready to go to a lesson before my night out, so thank you again for everything and God bless.
Much love to you both
Kaff

No.217 [Letter to Benita Cress]
30th August [19]50   6 Heriot Row, Edinburgh
Dearest Benita

Your lovely scarves arrived safely – thank you a 1000 times – and I have worn them with great success. You are a buddy to think of these things and they give me such pleasure, bless you. The parcels have arrived safely too and are just wonderful – we have a wonderful store of goodies now. I have been rushing a bit as usual, but now my concert here is over and I can relax and enjoy the concerts for the next 10 days. It is a lovely festival and I'm just ruined here. My 'crits' this morning are all to be desired, so all's well. I have your little pressed flowers in my diary, so tho' I don't write as often as I might, you are continually in my thoughts. And I thought the 'pitchers' were just lovely.

Have to rush to see someone called Yacamini about a programme, bother him, but will send you a p.c. of the lovely castle here.

God bless – much love to you both and I hope the new car comes up to expectations.

Yours till Hell freezes

Kathleen

No.218 [Postcard to John Newmark]

Sat. 2nd Sep [1950]   [postmarked Edinburgh, 5th September 1950]

Now, what about it? Did you ever get home, you old son of a gun? Not a word, but hope you are fit and well. Am pleased with records and hope you will be. Lunching here with George L[ondon] and pulling you to pieces!! Wish you were here to see him as Figaro and hear all the other lovely things. God bless.

Love

Kaff

Du alter Gauner, was machst Du überhaupt? I have been enjoying a wonderful lunch with the world's champion contralto. Actually we miss you and wish you were here. Yours 'til we play Antigonish [a town in Nova Scotia] again together.

Love G.L.

No.219 [Letter to Emmie Tillett]

3rd September '50   2 Frognal Mansions, London NW3

My dear Emmie

Here are a few answers to your queries luv:

Worthing: Brahms Rhapsody in English (Novello)

English group with Arthur Wayne

Love is a bable	Parry
A soft day	Stanford
The Fidgety Bairn	arr. Roberton
Ca' the Yowes	arr. Jacobson
The Spanish Lady	arr. Hughes

I could rehearse Fri or Sat 22nd or 23rd. If they want something more solid – e.g. Lieder – will change, but thought this might cheer things up!

May 28th   Elgar *Sea Pictures*

Only sheer love for you Emmie makes me acquiesce, as the Bishop said to the actress!

Bridge of Allan etc. Gerald will be playing for me. (Miss Lereculey wanted to know – and will you say 'thank you', 'bless you' to her for her postscript – it did mi heart good!)

I have already given my prog: for Perth to David Yacamini – here is the prog: for the other two:

Bridge of Allan Oct.30th Dundee Nov. 2nd

Spring	Handel
Come to me soothing sleep	Handel
Have you seen but a whyte lily grow	arr. Grew
Che faro senza Euridice	Gluck
An die Musik	Schubert
Musensohn	Schubert
Lachen und Weinen	Schubert
Erlkönig	Schubert
Wir wandelten	Brahms
Botschaft	Brahms
Sonntag	Brahms
Von ewiger Liebe	Brahms
Ca' the yowes	arr. Jacobson
The fidgety bairn	arr. Roberton
Blow the wind southerly	arr. Whittaker
The Keel row	arr. Whittaker

If only three groups are needed, will you cut out the Brahms?

I'm sorry about the Verdi Requiem. It breaks mi bloomin' heart, but it's no good, it's too high. The more I see of opera, the less I want to take part in it, except *Orfeo*. I think I'll have a rest in May. Am seeing Ben and Peter tomorrow and will let you know if any persuasions corrupt me!

Would love to take Ernest Lush with me to Scandinavia and agree to his fee, I don't want him to reduce it. [I&T's pencilling: 'Lush advised by phone']

Would prefer not to go to Aberdeen May 20th, too big a jump in between Cambridge and Peterborough.

Think that's all for the moment.

Much love

Kathleen

No.220 [Postcard to Win]

Sun[day 3rd September 1950]   [Edinburgh]

Ta ever so for letter – so glad the broadcast was all right. Must have got a chill in train, but am quite OK now. Enjoying all this enormously – home the morning of the 9th. Rosalind and Alec [Maitland] in great form, and we're all satiated with music – but have the bi-carbonate handy. Peter Diamand coming to lunch today – wish you were too.

Much love

Kaff

No.221 [Postcard to David Tidboald]

13th September 1950

Thank you so much for your kind letter, I am so glad you enjoyed the Brahms broadcast. The Pastoral arrived safely, I am so sorry I didn't acknowledge it but was just rushing away somewhere. Am only back from E'burgh but hope to study it soon.

Sincerely

Kathleen Ferrier

No.222 [Letter to Harry Vincent]

13.9.[19]50   2 Frognal Mansions, London NW3

My dear Harry

It is I who should be writing to you to thank you for all you have done for me! But it was lovely to get your letter and to know that the audience had enjoyed the concert. I am still marvelling at the crowd you brought together – they were a <u>superb</u> audience – and it will certainly be a memorable night for me. I can't thank you enough for all the work you have done and you <u>must</u> have felt tired out the next morning – <u>I</u> didn't sleep much – it was too exciting an evening and our lovely supper just topped it off! It is always the greatest pleasure to come and see you and I always will when it's possible, 'cos I know you would tell me if it were inconvenient – besides, I want to keep an eye on my namesake and see that you don't ill-treat her!!

Well, Harry love, it was a wonderful evening, and I can't thank you enough – and Madge for the lovely supper. God bless you all and see you soon.

Thank you again

With love

Kathleen Mary

No.223 [Letter to Emmie Tillett]

15th September [1950]   2 Frognal Mansions, London NW3

My dear Emmie

Re Worthing Sept. 24th. Will use the Simrock edition of the Brahms, and can rehearse with Mr Wayne at his pleasure Saturday afternoon – 23rd. Will you ask him to bring a copy with him, s'il vous plait? Shouldn't I wear gloves if it were Kirkby Lunn's copy?!

Will you tell Einer Kleine Gylling I can't do three recitals in a row. I would rather arrive on the 29th and perhaps sing on the 31st – if it's orchestral it's a different matter, but recitals are too hard work. It's no good working so hard – Chenhalls tell me I'm going to be highly taxed on my American dollars – and I just get tired into the bargain!

Haven't raped Ben and Peter yet, but shall be seeing them this week – don't really want to do *Lucretia* – would much rather have the time off – middle age crapeing on!

Hope to have a drop of fizz on the twenty-tooth with Momma!

Please can you book hotels for Bridge of Allan, Perth and Dundee for Gerald and me. Just shooting off to rehearsal.

In haste

Love

Kathleen

No.224 [incomplete letter to Hans Oppenheim]

[?20th September 1950]   [2 Frognal Mansions, London NW3]

My dear Oppi

What a lovely letter – I am so glad I didn't let you down completely – that would never do.

Actually, one run through with a pianist is impossible – and all on the day of the broadcast. Usually I manage to get him [Frederick Stone] to come up here a day or two before, but this time just couldn't get him. The first song in a broadcast is always a trial to me because I am so humbugged with my bronchial wheeziness, that it is about all I can concentrate on for the first two minutes as the mike picks up every frog. But it did my heart good to have you say this was true Lieder singing – now I am getting a better idea all the time of when I can make a fuss of the words and when I must concentrate on line more etc. Quelle vie! ...

No.225 [Letter to John Newmark]
28th Sept. [19]50   2 Frognal Mansions, London NW3
Dearest Johnny

'Our father which art' was pickled tink to have your letter and enclosures the other day – but I was just mad as a hatter! – not a word since I don't know when – you neglecter of p.[rima] d.[onna]s etc., etc., – have to ask our father if you got home safely – what the heck??!! Well, that's off mi chest and I feel a bit better.

How are you, love? I hope all is well with you and with the sweet Paul and my favourite cat! Tell Paul I'm working hard at the Chausson now, and am feeling particularly comfortable in my own brand of Lancashire French! I shall be in Paris for concerts before the Chausson takes place so shall have some polishing up there. I think I am going to enjoy it enormously – it is very singable.

Edinburgh was exciting – the outstanding things for me were the Hallé with John Barbirolli – de los Angeles' voice – Tourel's brain, intelligence, intellect – what you will – Primrose in the Bartok – Curzon in the Brahms – *Ariadne*, original version, until the opera part started and then I thought she and Bacchus would never stop – but the Zerbinetta was fine – Ilse Hollweg – and disappointing for me the Scala in the Verdi Requiem with De Sabata – but I am one of the few who think this, so it must be me! But de Sabata is so acrobatic, and the singers [used] such varying speeds of vibrato that the *a capella* bits were terrifying, I couldn't enjoy the performance as a whole – though it was very exciting, but to me never moving and you know it doesn't take much to move ole Kaff! [She was not alone in her opinion. Maurice Lindsay made the same point about the ill-mixed 'operatic' vibrato of the soloists in 'Northern Diary', *Music 1951*, p.240 (Penguin, London 1951)] But it was a wonderful busman's holiday for me, because I had two concerts a day, once my Brahms Raspberry [Alto Rhapsody] was off my chest – and it was grand to hear so much music for a change.

I saw George London several times and liked him enormously, and loved his voice. He has a nice silly sense of humour and we got on like a house on fire. He seems to be well established over here now, though Figaro is not the best part for him, I shouldn't think. He is back in Wien and going to Bayreuth, and very pleased about that – good for him! (Did you get our p.c.?)

Did a concert for the United Nations the other evening with Ben and Peter. Did 'Bad Mess' and several of his folksongs – 'Bess' rather quicker, especially in the dance rhythm parts than I had remembered – and oh he is a superb pianist. I didn't have enough rehearsal with him, and found him a little bit disconcerting, whilst still loving what he did – forgot my words several times as a result, but put in some rude German ones and the Churchills and Attlees, who were there, would be no wiser I am sure!!

Look after yourself, dear Johnny and take pity on a palpitating p.d. and post her a p.c.

Much love

Kaff

No.226 [Letter to Benita Cress]

28th Sep. [19]50   [2 Frognal Mansions, London NW3]

Dearest Benita

It's a long time since I wrote to you, but since Edinboro' work has descended upon me and I have neglected mi buddies! The old so-and-sos – I didn't get a letter at the Usher Hall – and goodness – they know me well enough – the old barstewards!

Your new car sounds just wonderful, and if it looks a million dollars, then it's just right for its inmates! – I hope it is a lucky car for you, and gives you lovely times.

Beesnees? I have been asking Paddy about our store cupboard and she says the things that are particularly wonderful are the noodle soups, the cake flour – except the spice which is not so exciting – chicken, salmon and stewing steak and spam. We wonder – for a special treat – if biscuits could be sent without breaking into a million pieces? We would adore some fancy creamy ones, if it were at all possible.

Soap is off the ration – isn't it gorgeous? To be able to pick and choose as much as you like – oh boy!

I can't <u>tell</u> you what a joy your parcels are, love, and I just hope it doesn't make too much trouble for you? Only my Pop smokes here, and he has a girl friend at the shop who gives him his 20 a day – they are dutiable too. The canned ham sounds wonderful, and if there is still enough money in the kitty, we would love to have it. I'm all right still for nylons, but if you could send a pair of 9½ for Paddy – it would just make her day – and they would come like the scarves? Gee whiz, what a fairy godmother you are!

Concerts going down well. Did one with Benjamin Britten and Peter Pears the other night for the United Nations and made a lot of money for them – only hope it works a miracle among the nations, but have mi doubts! Have a broadcast tonight and will be glad when it's over – I don't like broadcasting – always dither and get frogs! Whattalife!

Hope all's well with you both – I loved your photies. We've had the worst summer I remember and now it's cold Autumn, and we have a gas strike and electricity cuts!! What's wrong with everybody?

Looking forward already to next year – oh boy, oh boy! Thank you a 1000 times for everything.

Much love

Kaff

No.227 [incomplete letter to John Barbirolli]
9th October 1950   [2 Frognal Mansions, London NW3]
... It is always such an experience to make music with you, and I count myself
so wonderfully lucky to be able to do so. I should lay me doon and dee were I
ever to let you down.... Now I am looking forward to *Orfeo* and the Chausson,
and I hope to come back from Paris with all my 'des, les et mes' put right! ...

Much, much love to you and Evelyn – safe journeying for you in the Southern
Hemisphere....

No.228 [Letter to Mrs van Hessen-Kattenburg]
11th Oct [1950]   2 Frognal Mansions, London NW3
Dear Mrs Van Hessen

Thank you very much for your two letters and the enclosed snapshots. Your
home looks very lovely.

I have made the *Kindertotenlieder* records for Columbia with the Vienna Philharmonic and Bruno Walter. They should be coming out in the next month or
two.

My next trip to Holland is in November this year and I shall be staying in
Amsterdam, as I am so hard worked, it is the most convenient and central spot.
But I thank you most sincerely for your kind invitation to stay.

My photographs all seem to be bigger than your frame, but perhaps you may
be able to cut this one down a little to fit.

I hope you may be able to come to one of my concerts in Holland – and
perhaps – if it is not possible, then to one of them in England when you are
over here.

Meanwhile I send my best wishes and grateful thanks for your kind invitation.
Yours very sincerely
Kathleen Ferrier

No.229 [Letter to Moran Caplat]
11th Oct [1950]   2 Frognal Mansions, London NW3
My dear Moran

Thank you for your letter. It is perfectly all right and understandable that
Orfeo is not possible for this year [1951] – and it will give me the chance of a
holiday in this busy British Festival year. Bless you for trying so hard to make it
possible, and if and when it does come off, I hope I shall have done it in other
places, and make a much better job of it than in 1947 at Glyndebourne!

I could only see you in the distance last night, which is neither right nor
proper – but there <u>was</u> a riotous squash, wasn't there? I thought it was excellent,
did you? [*School for Fathers* by Wolf-Ferrari at Sadlers Wells].

Hope we may meet soon – meanwhile look after yourself and my love to you
both.
Kathleen

No.230 [Postcard to Win]
19th October 1950   [Bath]

   Hello sweetie! Having such a lovely time here, it's a <u>lovely</u> town and have had lots of time off to enjoy it. Lucky K. Home Friday and off to Rhyl lunchtime Sat. Quelle vie! But nice! Hope all's well mit du!
Much love
Kaff

No.231 [Letter to Vincent family]
Nov 10th [1950]   2 Frognal Mansions, London NW3
My dear Madge, Harry and Kathleen Mary

   My little lady is absolutely beautiful!!!!! Thank you very much indeed for such a lovely present – she goes so well with my other treasures from the Potteries, and will be a constant reminder of you all. It <u>is</u> kind of you to have thought of such a lovely gift, and I can't tell you how much I appreciate it, bless you! I loved seeing you the other night and loved my supper and home made cake. Since my 'Camilla' boyfriend [see letters 320 and 323] thinks I'm plump, I've started dieting, but somehow I don't think it will last very long – I'm not very strong-minded where food's concerned, and I know all efforts will go to the dogs when I go to Holland next week and see all the food there! What the heck! say I, but it's a nuisance when I can't climb into a nearly new frock ain't it? <u>You</u> should know Harry (oooooh! what a dirty crack!!)

   Well loves, thank you once again for everything – it is always such a pleasure to see you – look after yourselves and much love to you all.
Kathleen

No.232 [Letter to Benita Cress]
13th November [1950]   2 Frognal Mansions, London NW3
Dearest Bonnie

   I am 'all behind' mit my letters to you, but have been dashing madly round, now that the season is in full swing again.

   The records should really be out now in the States – if they're not soon, I really will get a hat pin to Decca – they said Sept[ember], the barstewards!

   The boxes you have sent sound just wonderful – all your others have been perfect, and it is nice to be a bit extravagant sometimes and not wonder if the rations will run out before the weekend! – and such lovely things too. The canned chicken was gorgeous and fell to bits with tenderness, the pore little budder! The cookies were a treat too – but they are off for me now, 'cos I'm getting too fat – so I'm cutting all starches (when I'm strong enough) and trying to get my bulges a bit less rotund. I had some new photies taken the other day, and I look like the bull at the other end of the Toreador!! – fraightful!! But otherwise all is well and we're all full of beans – and hope you are too. You are lucky still having nice weather – ours is terrible – cold and wet – am hating the thought of flying to Holland on Saturday. Shall be at the *American* Hotel, Amsterdam until the 13th December – just in case you have a minute to spare!

   Dashing off to the north tomorrow – Manchester, Bolton, Huddersfield and Grimsby.

Thank you for everything, bless you, and look after yourselves.
Much love from us all
Kaff

No.233 [Letter to Emmie Tillett]
Monday [27 November 1950]   *American* Hotel, Amsterdam
My dear Emmie

I keep wondering how your Momma is, but haven't heard a word. I hope no news is good news, love.

Enclosed two letters with which, perhaps, you will deal, eh!

All is grand here, except the fog, Gerald and I getting more rotund with every meal! Four concerts safely over, and all gone well, praise be. Home on the 14th and look forward to seeing you.
Much love
K.K.

P.S. What <u>do</u> we do with Netherwood and his intimate association with me for 20 years? I'll <u>sue</u> 'im! Don't mind doing it for him at a proper fee, but perhaps he's mistaking me for Clara Butt or Muriel Foster??

P.S.S. Would be glad if Mr Read will book an <u>inside single first mit bath</u> – what the heck! It comes off mi Income Tax. I'm glad he's interested in my passage!!

P.S.S.S. Will write to Bruno Walter myself re programme and his suggestions. OK? TTFN

No.234 [Letter to Bruno Walter]
27.11.50   [*American* Hotel, Amsterdam]
Dearest Professor

I am thrilled that we shall be making music together at the next Edinburgh Festival – I can't tell you how proud I am – and happy – that you have agreed to play for me again. It's just wonderful!

Now I am being asked about a programme, and I wanted to contact you first – though I hope I don't trouble you too much. I had thought of 1) perhaps two large groups – the first Schubert – the second Brahms, Mahler or 2) Schubert – Brahms – Pause – Wolf and Mahler. I like to include Brahms because I feel they are so 'grand' for the big Usher Hall. But if you have other suggestions I would be very happy to consider and learn them. The only Mahler songs I have done so far are: 'Wo die schönen Trompete blasen', 'Ich ging mit Lust', 'Starke Einbildungskraft', and I know you love 'Ich bin der Welt abhanden gekommen' – though I haven't actually performed it.

I don't know a "chunk" this time – other than the *Brautlieder* of Cornelius, and I have a feeling that wouldn't give you much pleasure?

I have lots of Brahms to work at including 'Scheiden und Meiden', 'In der Ferne', 'Blinde Kuh', 'Mainacht', 'Therese', but I would be terribly grateful to you for a general idea of what you would like me to do.

It will be just heavenly to see you again – I <u>do</u> hope you are well – and I send my fondest love to you and Lotte. I hope Adolph is well too, and bearing up bravely after his great loss.

The very best wishes to you all.
With my love
Kathleen

No.235 [Letter to Emmie Tillett]
[received by Emmie Tillett 4th December 1950]   *American* Hotel,
                                                                Amsterdam

Dearest Emmie
    You <u>must</u> come to Holland just once, if only to let me see your eyes light up
at the sight of the food here. Gerald and I still expand daily, but our morale is
high, so what the heck!
    I have written answering all Mr Mertens' questions, so you don't have to
worry, at least until the next batch descend!
    I tried to phone you from the airport and waited, because you were engaged,
then had to join the plane and couldn't wait any longer.
    Now to biz:
Lucretia's Rape.   Can you get me out of this, sweetie? The thought of it worries
me enormously, my big feet and all that, I don't want to go careering off to Wies-
baden when I'm only just back from Europe. I'm only going to have a few days to
rehearse and re-learn the whole bluidy thing, and I certainly don't want to work
any more in July. Can you talk me out of it, do you think? I <u>would</u> be relieved.
<u>Italy</u>.   I'll take the material (orch.) for 'Cara Sposa' and 'Ombra mai fu'.
<u>Paris</u>.   I think I'll have my little handkissing Parisian again – because I want to
study some French pronunciation with him. (Voulez-vous coucher avec moi?
and all that!!)
<u>Bournemouth.</u>   OK for Roy and *Gerontius* Sept.15th
<u>Gylling</u>.   Am in communication with Ernest Lush and have altered original
arrangements to weekly payment – my responsibility – because of time-waster
of orchestral concerts – but he has asked off from the 30th March, which means
that he would fly that day. Could he make Silkeborg – where is it I wonder?
Perhaps he could leave 29th night, depends on him entirely.
    Will think out Paris popular programme and let you know.
In a rush
Much love
Kathleen

No.236 [Letter to John Newmark]
5.12.50   *American* Hotel, Amsterdam
Dearest Johnny,
    'Twas lovely to have your letter two days ago, and your lack of 'Bs' made your
remarks about ach, eethoven, artok, and rahms very amusing – I only thought
'ritten' would have been included! You have been having a sad time with Jicky
and tumours and no Haydn series for which I am truly sorry. This international
tension I suppose is responsible, though here in Europe things are going on –
musically – as busily as ever. What a 'barsteward' it all is. It all looks enormously
serious whenever I have the courage to read the news.

Gerald Moore and I are here in Holland for three weeks – we both get fatter every day with the superb food. I was on a diet before I arrived here to reduce some too fulsome curves – but what's the good when everything's cooked in butter? I give up and thereby expand daily! Our musical diet here – Bach cantatas – two recital programmes (8 concerts) – Brahms *Alto Rhap.* with [Issay] Dobrowen (3 times) and *Das Lied von der Erde* with Klemperer (once), so it is a full programme. But everything is arranged so well and I can sleep so late, that I am as fit as a flea and enjoying it all.

Gerald plays beautifully and is a comedian into the bargain, so there is much hilarity too, and I would rather go home poor, through having passed my monies on to him, rather than the Income Tax people!!! He's <u>very</u> expensive! I will send a photograph as soon as I get home – I haven't any here with me.

I'm furious with Decca – the *Frauenliebe* should have been out two months ago – the chumps. Victor has been in Vienna again, so I guess he wasn't there to keep them up to scratch.

Do you remember rehearsing Mahler songs at Bruno Walter's and my dissolving into tears? Do you know, I haven't seen the copy since? You don't have it tucked away anywhere, do you? I can't replace it here – I've tried. Gerald bought the Brahms folksongs for me the other day in the right keys, so that's a lovely set to have. He wants me to do the *Zigeunerlieder* – would you?

Shall be sailing on Sep. 21st for New York and I am looking forward to it already and to working with you again – what fee do you want, mi darlin? Am home for Christmas, then come back here for 3 stage *Orfeos*, then Paris, Zurich, Rome, Florence, Milano, Perugia and Paris again – then Chausson and *Orfeo* with Barbirolli (Klever Kaff, I hope!), then Scandinavia for April. Then opening the Festival of Britain hall in the Beethoven 9th with Toscanini. Have more work than I can really manage, but am enjoying it.

Have new fur coat, Johnny – mm! mm! Russian ermine – phew! phew! Much too grand ever to wear!! I read the Korean news and it looked so black, I went out and blewed all my savings! Hope you are better again. Look after yourself. Much love
K.

P.S. If you want that money I owe you from Decca, I could get Mertens to send it?? <u>Do</u> say if you do.

No.237 [Letter to Emmie Tillett]
5th December 1950   *American* Hotel, Amsterdam
Dearest Emmie

Enclosed the Scandinavian contract duly signed. Good that Ernest Lush can fly on the 29th – we can go together, can't we?

<u>Edinburgh</u>. I'm happy with 200 gns and 25% for broadcasts. I haven't a lot to do in the Chausson, but I leave it to you, luv.

Wired you tonight because Peter Diamand wants me to do my 3rd *Orfeo* on the 16th Jan and I just wanted to make sure that I don't have to leave for anything before the 17th. Okeydoke? I take it my 1st engagement after that is Paris 23rd Jan?

BBC North Region. OK for broadcast with Gerald 29th December – 'spleasure.

All goes well here – lovely concerts and a day off in between. Weather unpronounceable!!

Hope your Momma is better, love.

Love from us both,

Kaff

No.238 [Letter to Bill and Benita Cress]

28th Dec. 50   2 Frognal Mansions, London NW3

Dearest Bill and Bonnie

Thank you for my lovely slippers and hanky and Christmas card – they are all delicious – except they give me such a bad conscience because I haven't done anything from this end! – and your parcels have been wonderful, love – by this time, surely the kitty must be empty and in debt – but I will be able to give it to you when I see you – oh boy!!!! You send just all the right things and we really have got a store cupboard now in case of emergencies. We are all right for medicines and soap etc., now it's just the meats particularly that we run short, and the things you send are just heaven – the ham was a riot – it lasted for ages and we licked our lips every time we opened the fridge door!!

I arrived home a few days before Xmas and Paddy went to her home in York, so my Xmas has been spent cooking and washing up, fetching coal and dusting. I enjoy it when I haven't anything else to do, but I was in such a mess with correspondence and programmes, having been away a long time, I didn't know which jobs to tackle first. I am just getting on with letters now, but am far behind in my learning – but I cooked a wizard turkey, girl! I haven't forgotten the essentials, and I said my prayers and crossed my heart, and it must have worked, because it was succulent and tender. Klever Kaff, eh?

Tonight I have a broadcast which is a nuisance 'cos I am out of practice – and on Jan 2nd I fly again to Holland to do some stage *Orfeos* – shall be at the *American* Hotel until the 17th Jan, then on to Paris, Rome, Zurich, Florence, Milan, Perugia, Paris and home about Feb 18th. Exciting places, aren't they?

Paddy will be here any minute and I know she would send her love if she knew I was writing – you make her life much less burdensome, knowing she can open a beautiful tin if all else fails, or the weather's too bad to go out – you can't imagine how we appreciate all you have done for us, bless you.

My tour for next Oct seems to be coming along, though I have no details yet – but I am looking forward to it – but I have so much to learn in between then and now, I hardly dare look ahead. But I wouldn't have it otherwise.

I hope you had a wonderful Xmas and lots to eat and drink – I hope your New Year will be more than wonderful for you both, and I thank you from us all for the wonderful things you have done for us – bless you always!

My love to you both

Kaff

No.239 [unsigned letter to Bruno Walter]

28th Dec. 50 2 Frognal Mansions, London NW3

My dear Professor

Thank you very much for your lovely and most helpful letter. Now here are my ideas, based on the ones you sent, and I hope you approve, or will correct me in any way if you think it can be improved.

Schubert:	Brahms:	Mahler:
An die Leyer	Liebestreu	Wo die schönen Trompeten blasen
Ganymed	Ruhe Süssliebchen	Ich ging mit Lust
Lachen und Weinen	Auf dem See	Ich bin der Welt abhanden gekommen
Wandrers Nachtlied	Dein blaues Auge	Ich atmet' einen Lindenduft
Suleika	Die Mainacht	Um Mitternacht
Suleikas zweiter Gesang	Heimkehr	

I have only put five Mahler Lieder down, because 'Trompeten' and 'Um Mitternacht' are long, and I feel it will be long enough. The only thing I feel is that it may be a little on the <u>very</u> serious side, and whether to put the groups in this order: Schubert-Mahler-pause-Brahms, then I could follow with encores of less serious nature?

I have sent this programme to [the] Edinburgh programme committee as they are worrying me for it, but with the proviso that you may still want it changed. Is that all right?

Much love to all and a very, very happy New Year – and thank you for everything!!

No.240 [undated postcard to Laura Cooper written after 13th December 1950].

Thank you for your kind letter. I know the record business is difficult as they are changing managements at the moment. I am just home from Holland and leave again on Jan 2nd for Holland, France, Switzerland, and Italy and Scandinavia, and am just trying to pack and un-pack all at once! Please excuse, therefore, the brevity, but with all good wishes for 1951.

5   Letters: 1951

The year 1951 was to prove a watershed in Kathleen Ferrier's life and career. In the middle of December 1950 her agent and friend, Emmie Tillett introduced her to a New Zealand nurse, Bernadine Hammond, or 'Bernie' as she came to be called. It was a fortuitous meeting. Emmie's mother, whom Bernie had been nursing, had just died, and by March 1951 'Paddy' Jewett would leave Kathleen because her charge William Ferrier (or 'Our Father who art in Hampstead' as Kathleen described him) had died and soon after she became engaged to be married. Over tea on 26th February Bernie agreed to take Paddy's place, but it soon became apparent that all thoughts she had entertained of giving up nursing for secretarial work would have to be abandoned. It was certainly true that Kathleen now needed a full-time secretary rather than the part-time arrangement she and Paddy had entered into when her workload was lighter at the start of her career, but Bernie's nursing skills would be required more than ever after Kathleen was diagnosed with breast cancer in March 1951. She also became a close friend as well as a member of the painting circle called the 'Elm Tree Road Group', consisting of Emmie (who from 1949 lived at No.11 Elm Tree Road in St John's Wood), Bernie, Winifred and Kathleen. The four may have had nicknames judging by the word 'Remanren' in the letter to Emmie dated 21st January 1951. Is this perhaps a reference to two of them, Winifred and Bernie, in a combination of the painters <u>Rem</u>brandt and <u>Ren</u>oir? Who was Rem and who was Ren is impossible to say; neither can we complete the quartet with the nicknames for either Emmie or Kathleen herself.

With no hint of impending personal tragedies, Kathleen's year began with a tour of European countries and its obligatory packed schedule. She flew off in a snowstorm on 2nd January to Amsterdam for four performances of *Orfeo*. She then went to Paris for a recital. Whilst there she studied Chausson's *Poème de l'amour et de la mer* and French with the baritone Pierre Bernac, followed by recitals and *Kindertotenlieder* in Zurich. She left for Rome on 29th January and upon her arrival the following day news came of her father's death, but she was dissuaded from returning home by her sister. The rest of the tour was mainly confined to Italy (Florence, Milan, Turin and Perugia), with recitals and a concert with Klemperer for Turin radio, but on the way home she stopped off in Paris for more lessons with Bernac and to give a concert with orchestra. Winifred and Emmie came over to meet and console her, for she felt considerable guilt at being absent from her father's bedside.

On Sunday 18th February she sang under Carl Schuricht, followed by dinner with Nadia Boulanger. Once back home in London the following day (and her diary reflects her relief), she had another dinner to attend (given by the Women's Association) followed by a speech, and she clearly hated these invitations. On 27th February Kathleen left for Manchester where she was to sing Chausson's *Poème de l'amour et de la mer* for the first time under Barbirolli (he had urged her to learn the work), followed by *Orfeo* both in the city and on a short tour of other northern centres. A series of diary entries charts the continued success of this artistic collaboration as well as the first sign that all was not well regarding her health.

She gave a recital in Cologne followed by one in Amsterdam two days later, then two performances of Bach's *St Matthew Passion*. She returned to London on Maundy Thursday (22nd March) and gave another performance of the Passion, this time at Glyndebourne on Good Friday and this was the last public appearance by Kathleen Ferrier in good health. She attended Dr Hilton's surgery at noon the next day in the middle of the Easter weekend, and noted it in her diary followed abruptly by 'All work cancelled'. Much of April should have been taken up with a Scandinavian tour. Recitals in UK towns were scheduled for May, while in London there should have been engagements with Sargent and the Royal Choral Society, and at the Royal Albert Hall, where she should have sung the *St Matthew Passion* once again on 3rd June with the London Bach Choir. There had been a recital planned for Newcastle, Elgar's *Dream of Gerontius* in York under Barbirolli, a Wigmore Hall recital, *Das Lied von der Erde* in Bournemouth, and another recital in Dorchester. In the event, her return to the concert platform was on Saturday 19th June in Bach's Mass in B minor with the Bach Choir at the Royal Albert Hall in London, followed by a trip to Holland at the beginning of July, which included a performance of Mahler's *Resurrection* Symphony under Klemperer and four stagings of *Orfeo*.

For the rest of the year the schedule picks up its relentless treadmill of travel, broadcasts, recordings and performances, but interspersed among them now are regular visits to hospital or consultations with Dr Hilton, and gloomy comments in the diary. At the beginning of October she gave the premiere of *The Enchantress*, a *scena* written by Arthur Bliss. When Winifred was gathering material for her biography in 1955 she received the following recollection from Bliss:

> It was not until 1951 that I first met Kathleen Ferrier, although I had heard her beautiful voice many times before then, both on the radio and on records. My opportunity to know her came when, in admiration of her singing, I wrote a special *scena* [*The Enchantress*] that she could sing with an orchestra at concerts.
>
> I well remember the autumn morning when I climbed to her home in Frognal to rehearse my music with her. I can vividly recall her welcoming smile and charming hospitality, the talk about pictures she was painting, her quiet music room and the first run-through at the piano.
>
> She sat beside me humming her part and occasionally striking a note on the piano. She asked me to describe her role in this dramatic *scena* and I told her she was a proud Syracusan lady, deserted by her lover and now invoking the powers of black magic to win him back. The words came from the second Idyll of Theocritus, and had been translated for me by Henry Reed.
>
> As I went through the score with her, I could not help feeling that though the solo part did some justice to the magnificent two octaves of her voice,

Kathleen herself bore no resemblance to this Medea-like heroine, needing a nobler role for <u>her</u> personality.

In October of that year, 1951, I went to Manchester to hear her give a broadcast of *The Enchantress*. We lunched together near the Art Gallery, and afterwards visited it to see an exhibition of modern English painting. She was in a gay and happy mood and I remember teasing her about her old-fashioned ideas of painting, and trying to convince her that her true leanings were towards purely abstract art.

One of the unforgettable things about Kathleen was her ability to enjoy the moment. She had a completely easy and natural manner when meeting new admirers of her gift. The balance between pride and modesty that she showed in talking about herself is found, I believe, in all great artists.

The same evening at a party after the concert, I saw another side of her, for she sang to us, almost in a rapt trance, unaccompanied folksongs. Her personality on the concert platform expressed a radiant happiness. She had a glorious gift, and she used it generously to the delight of millions.

On Friday 16th November Kathleen sang 'Land of Hope and Glory' at the end of a brief afternoon concert conducted by Barbirolli to mark the official re-opening by the Queen of the restored Free Trade Hall in Manchester. In the diary for 1951, all dates, including the proposed autumn and winter tour of the USA and Canada, which were cancelled as a result of the diagnosis of her illness are reproduced in bold type. Included among the letters for the year 1951 are a couple from Yvonne Hamilton to Bruno Walter, two of Kathleen's closest friends. They describe the unfolding tragedy at first hand.

No.241 [Letter to Emmie Tillett]

5.1.51   *American* Hotel, Amsterdam

Dearest Emmie

I don't mind the words of folk songs being printed – they like to have them when they're in another language (I'm talking about Zurich!).

I've just rung Paddy and she says 'Bernie' called round to see Pop – how terribly kind of her – I <u>do</u> appreciate it. Paddy says he's a lot better the last two days so that's a relief.

The flight was all right after the take off – though a young man in front lost all his Christmas cheer for the <u>whole</u> journey! But I'd had mi 'Quells' [Kwells – travel sickness tablets] and I tucked in – I was so glad to be up and on an even keel! You're bound to come down once you're up, as the actress said to the bishop!

Emmie love, has your accountant made a mistake with Milan commission, £17.10.0? I think he's charging me 10% and, unless I am mistaken, we arranged 5% for Europe, as most of the fee goes on accompanist, fares and hotels. It's so much more than Edinburgh, where I had a good fee and few expenses – thought I would ask before sending cheque.

All goes well here – working hard but treated with great care and all the others look as daft as I feel, so guess it's all right!

Yearning to see Op. 4, 5 and 6 – look after yourself and much love to you and Bernie.
Kaff

No.242 [Letter to Win]
11th Jan [1951]   *American* Hotel [Amsterdam]
Dearest Win

You <u>were</u> a pet today on the week of your holiday to keep an eye on number 2, and I felt so much better going away than I otherwise would have done. I'm so sorry I have missed you twice on the phone. I didn't know you were going to Mr Miller. What's up? Have you got 'spit' too, as they call it here! I hope he has done whatever he was meant to do – I could do with him here – though mine's much better today – but I still have the utmost difficulty to fasten my left suspender!

The first night [*Orfeo*] was a wow – and nothing awful happened and I quite enjoyed it. If I could act confidently, it's really much easier than a recital, but I still feel it's a lot of playacting, – where I live and love and die in a song.

Joan Cross and Hans [Schneider] are coming on Sat. – Roderick Jones tomorrow – and Otta [Otakar] Kraus is already here, so it's like home.

I told Paddy in a letter – the curse arrived the morning of the *Orfeo*, so I had to use a lot of pads in my already tight tights – but I 'spect the audience would only think I was a well-developed young man!

Am yearning to hear of your decision re M & S. I think Hans is very conscientious and reliable where his work's concerned – he has too many female relatives living on him to be otherwise! But you'll know best what to do – but it <u>would</u> be a change. I'll always bail you out, as long as I am able, if <u>everybody</u> sacks you!!

Off to the Hague tonight for *Orfeo* and have just had my hair ringletted for it – the whole dining room stares!

I leave here 12.30 train to Paris on the 17th – I shall be with the conductor Charles Bruck, so will have a guide and mentor.

Thanks ever so for two grand letters and enclosures. Am so glad Xpher is all right again – nothing must happen to <u>that</u> child, eh? Had the nicest possible cable from Webster Booth wishing me luck and thanks for flowers – also one from the faithful Rick, bless him!

Just going for a nap before the performance – much love and thanks for everything
Kaff

No.243 [Letter to Stella [?Jackson], a friend in La Crosse, Wisconsin, USA]
16.1.51   *American* Hotel, Amsterdam
Dear Stella

I am a disgusting diva for not having written sooner to thank you for your <u>wonderful</u> parcel – bless you, bless you. I can't tell you what a joy it was to have it – and all <u>just</u> the right things. Thank you so very much for your great kindness.

Now I'll try to make my excuses for not replying, and hope you will excuse me just this once! I was in Holland until a week before Xmas, and when I went home, Paddy – the girl who looks after my Pappy – went off home for a week, so I cooked a wizard turkey, and did the chores, and enjoyed it for a change, but didn't get any forrader with the pile of letters waiting – then my sweet Pappy nearly had pneumonia, so everything went by the board, and on Jan 2nd I had to come to Holland again – much against my will, though he was much better by this time – and from the plane I went straight to rehearsal for *Orfeo* on the stage and I haven't stopped since!! It is the last performance tonight and I am just sitting under the dryer in the hairdresser's, having my Grecian curls put back! That's why my writing is so bad!

I wish you and Benita could see me in my black woollen tights. They're all right when I stand up, but I bounce like a rubber ball when I try to sit down – they're so tight – and it hasn't helped having what the Dutch call 'spit' which is backache – but I hope the audience took my groans for passion!!

Tomorrow I go to Paris, then Switzerland and Italy – so I'm looking forward to it – but it will be lovely to be home too, in the middle of Feb.

How are you all, loves? I hope you had a lovely, merry Christmas, and that 1951 will be the best ever for you all – not forgetting Pat. Thank you again for everything – I look forward to seeing you sometime after Oct 1st this year – OH BOY!

Much love to you and all my buddies, God bless. Love
Kathleen

No.244 [Postcard to John Newmark]
20th January [19]51   [Paris]
Dearest Johnny.

Just received your letter today and terribly sorry to hear of your worries and ills. You must have had a miserable and alarming New Year. Will tell Decca off – they have been reviewed in England. I understand they should be out in America. I'll play HELL! Am thrilled to little peppercorns and hope you'll approve. I am in gay Paree for one concert and lessons with guess who? – Pierre Bernac. Am so thrilled and working hard at Chausson, have just about conquered the N in 'chantez', so am coming on!! Will write soon – this is just a put-you-on!
Much love
Kaff

No.245 [Letter to Emmie Tillett]
21st January 1951   Hotel *Roblin*, 6 Rue Chauveau-Lagarde, Paris 8
Dearest Emmie

I'm afraid 'Remanren' haven't got together after all, as I have just rung home, and it sounds as though Win is in bed with flu. She will be furious and disappointed. I hope you are keeping free from these so-and-so germs, the little budders are rampant, aren't they?

I rang home for all the things I might need, as the orchestral concert here isn't decided yet and I haven't had a word from [Carl] Schuricht. So Gerald will bring everything I possess, including 'Che faro' and Lennox Berkeley and *Frauenliebe* etc.

I'm THRILLED with my French lessons with Pierre B[ernac]. He roared with mirth at first – but in the nicest way! – but now he's getting quite excited, and even I, by a series of lip contortions that might prove serious if indulged in too long, can hear an improvement. I would love a lesson a day for twelve months, then I would feel I was really getting somewhere! I passed on your message and he purred with pleasure – tell Miss Lereculey to look out! I'm after her! I don't really mind losing money here, it's such a gorgeous city! Why not pop over for Feb 16–18th????? Be a devil – I shall have found all the good eating places by then!

Now here is a programme for Italy. I honestly don't know where that programme came from – and I will stick to this for <u>all</u> the recitals unless they decree otherwise. I shall have everything with me if they insist.

1.	Where'er you walk	*Semele*	Handel
	Like as the lovelorn turtle	*Atalanta*	Handel
	Hark the ech'ing air	*Fairie Queene*	Purcell
	Mad Bess		Purcell arr. Britten
2.	Pur dicesti		Lotti
	Lasciatemi morire		Monteverdi
	Che faro	*Orfeo*	Gluck
3.	Gretchen am Spinnrade		Schubert
	Lachen und Weinen		Schubert
	Der Musensohn		Schubert
	Sonntag		Brahms
	Botschaft		Brahms
4.	Love is a bable		Parry
	The fairy lough		Stanford
	Ca' the yowes		arr. Jacobson
	The Spanish lady		arr. Hughes

That should keep 'em going a bit, shouldn't it?

Realised I couldn't stay in Zurich as I have rehearsal. Hating the thought of catching a 7.30 train!! Middle of the nuit!

I think that's all for the moment, love. All going beautifully so far – wish you were here.

Much love
Kathleen

No.246 [Letter to Bruno Walter]
21.1.51   Hotel *Roblin*, 6 Rue Chauveau-Lagarde, Paris 8
My dear Professor

Your letter has just arrived here – thank you so very much. I would adore to sing *DAS LIED* for you – but March '51 is filled for me with engagements in England, Holland and Denmark – I don't see a hope even if I flew both ways, which I gladly would do for the pleasure of taking part in *DAS LIED* again with you.

I am so glad you approve of the programme – I am working hard at it on all available occasions. I am also studying French here with Pierre Bernac and very excited about it – I could wish for each hour to be doubled – there is so much to do!

Imagine – in February I shall be in Rome and Florence – my first visit – isn't it exciting?

I hope you are keeping well and happy, and I look forward to our meeting again, more than I can say.

Thank you for everything.

With my love to you and Lotte

Kathleen

No.247 [Letter to Emmie Tillett]

28th January 1951   *Dolder Grand* Hotel, Zurich

Dearest Emmie

I <u>KNEW</u> you wouldn't let me have all my own way with Pierre Bernac!!! Oh! clever Emmie! 'Twill be <u>lovely</u> to see you. Wish you could have been there for the recital – it <u>did</u> go with a wow – I think it was my new Maitland frock wot done it! – but I'll have to put my best foot forward for the 18th, so's not to let you down. OH! BOY! (Programme still not settled!!)

Oh! I've <u>kept</u> forgetting in all the excitement – it's not going to be possible for me to do Cheltenham July 3rd with Sir John. They have tried all ways to make it possible, but I'd just be worn out with rushing around madly. I <u>am</u> sorry, I've kept forgetting to tell you. Peter D[iamand] told me just before I left Holland. It will be nice in Holland in July – just *Orfeos* and oratorios and orchestral – no recitals.

Gerald played like an angel in Paris, and was a source of confidence and inspiration as ever! I could <u>murder</u> the man here in Zurich and he's not really bad – just dumb! and no soul to boot! O sole mio!

All tickets and arrangements doing fine and managed to change money, languages and trains twice from Paris to St Gallen, and still have 5 bags at the end of it. I think I'm a ruddy wizard! What I would do if everybody didn't speak English, I can't think!

I'm afraid I shall have as near-bunk-mate tomorrow to Rome Herr Klemperer!! And as he sets everything on fire by putting his cigs all over the place, anything may happen! But at least it may melt some of the avalanches!

God bless, love, and see you soon – whoopee!

Kaff

No.248 [Letter to Win]

Tues[day 30th January 1951]   *Savoia* Hotel, Rome

Dearest Win

Here is a cheque for £50, which I have made 'open' so that you can get cash.

It was wonderful to speak to you this morning, and hear you sounding so calm and managing everything so well. I feel at a loss here, and feel I'm not pulling my weight – and knowing you coped with mother too doesn't make me feel any better – I've always had that on my conscience! I <u>do</u> hope I'm doing the right thing in not coming home and that you don't feel I'm getting out of the responsibility.

I have two days off here to rehearse with new pianist, and never felt less like singing in my life.

<u>Later</u>. Have just got your second telegram, thank you, love, for sending it. Also your's and Paddy's letters this morning. Rosalind and Alec send their

fondest love – they were round here by 10am this morning to see if they could do anything. Poor old Pop! I <u>shall</u> miss him – but I think he enjoyed life, and especially being in Hampstead – don't you? I <u>do</u> hope the funeral arrangements are not too complicated or miserable – and don't hesitate to take taxis anywhere for comfort or convenience – it's paid well in advance. And ask me for any more money – I'll do all the paying there is.

How kind of Emmie to come up – bless her a thousand times – and of Paddy's Momma to come too. And how lovely that Pop had just had his best Christmas ever at Shepherd's B[ush] – and he really meant it.

Much, much love to you and bless you for everything and to Paddy and her Momma. Can Mrs Jewitt stay on a bit until I get home, or Paddy have a pal in? I don't like the thought of her there by herself. Look after yourself and I shall be thinking of you all the time.
God bless
Kath

No.249 [Letter to Win]
[3rd February 1951]   [Florence]
Dearest Win

Have been thinking of you all today and hoping that it was a lovely service (as I thought it was for Mr Tillett) – and hoping you are not too weary and miserable with all the arrangements you would have to make. I <u>am</u> grateful to you, love, for coping so marvellously, and I <u>do</u> hope things were made as smooth as possible for you. I shall be thinking of you and Emmie tomorrow, finishing your paintings. I'm glad Mrs Jewitt was a help – she's a calm person I should think in illness, she's had to deal with so much, and I do hope Uncle Bert came to give you moral support. I am grateful to whatever Gods there are for making such a peaceful ending for him, bless him. He was wonderful when you think – apart from anaemia he never had an illness in his life. It must have been abstinence and smoking too much!

Things go fairly well here – though my concert last night in Rome was only a third full to start – in a small hall (600) – I'd been told it was sold out. But it seems they're subscription tickets, and if they don't know a name, they won't come. So I told the manager, if they didn't come, they'd never know a name! However it filled up at the end, but they are the shuffliest audience I've ever known. It certainly isn't worth staggering around on my own, trying to cope with strange languages and monies, to sing to such people. I was in fairly good voice I think and they shouted 'Brava' and 'Bis'.

Then the manager came round afterwards with all the people there and asked me to change my programme for Milan – on the spot – so I let out all my inhibitions and repressions and went prima donna and waved my arms and said, 'Not bloody likely' – or words to that effect – and enjoyed myself. But when I thought about it afterwards, it was really my fault as I had mixed up the programmes – so it was temper – not temperament.

I have glowing notices and I am told I have had a *succès fou* – but I still don't like 'em. I'm told they're much worse in Florence, so anything may happen in the *Kindertotenlieder* tomorrow. Was up at six this morning to catch a train for here – no heat and enormously cold – and straight to rehearsal and no breakfast – but I'm all right.

The Maitlands have come with me and I think they will be terrified in case the audience shout or spit! They are darlings and have been absolute pets. And Alec's cousin – Catherine Henderson – has been an absolute angel, and put her car at my disposal and given me meals and been just adorable.

Rome is amazing and I'll bring you one day (D.V.) if only to see the Colosseum and the Pantheon – the latter built 2000 B.C.!! The pianist is very good, though he <u>will</u> duet with me in a hideous falsetto all the time – but he's a trier and very sensitive, so I can bear anything. I daren't leave anything about here – and I lock my fur coat up all the time – I had all my Swiss francs stolen the day I arrived, about £30, taken out of my bag, and however much you give a porter or taxi, they shout for more. This is one country I'll never retire to! But I'm getting good at shouting back and saying 'Basta, basta' – and often adding the 'rd'!

Am just going to have dinner with the Maitlands, then go straight to bed. The concert is at 5pm tomorrow of awful times. Hardly saw any snow in Switzerland – must have come another way! Look after yourself, love, and much love and bless you for everything. Do you need any money? Do say. Will write again soon.

My love
Kaff

No.250 [Postcard to Win from Florence]
Sunday [4th February 1951]   Florence

Hope you are having fun today with Emmie and painting your masterpiece of all. I thought this would appeal to you with its lovely nose and head. Alec doesn't care for it much – he's says the original is too big – but I haven't seen that. Unfortunately no time here to see much, and the real gems are here I'm told – leave for Milan tomorrow. Rosalind not <u>terribly</u> well – been in damp British Railways sheets on way up to London, and her leg <u>very</u> stiff. My back's much better – I can do up my back suspender again now! Hope you're not too exhausted.

Much love to you and Jane.
Kaff

No.251 [Postcard to Emmie Tillett]
4th February 1951   Florence

Thank you <u>so</u> much for your lovely letter, darling. Win says you have been an absolute angel and I can't thank you enough ever, bless you, bless you. Can only feel deep gratitude that it was all so peaceful for our sweet 'Pop'. Apart from his anaemia, he had never really had an illness in his life – wasn't it amazing! Just hope I did the right thing by staying and didn't leave too much responsibility to Win.

All goes fairly well here tho' I think the Rome audience were rude and fairly ignorant! Started ¼ hour late, then still a third empty but filled up by the end. Critics raving but I couldn't get over the way the people talked and wandered about. Have never used my compelling eye so much!! Am ready for anything

today with Mahler in Florence!! The Maitlands here and in Rome – absolute poppets.
Much, much love
Kaff

No.252 [Letter to Emmie Tillett]
6th February 1951   *Grand Hotel Duomo*, Milan
Dearest Emmie

Arrived safely here all by miself and still with five bags, and now know the Italian for 'porter', 'hurry up' and 'go to blazes!', so I am managing fine.

To answer some of your queries, love:

Salzburg.   No, because I will need both holiday and time to learn Edinburgh programme, so must keep August free, but thank you very much all the same ([*Lieder eines*] *fahrenden Gesellen* still too high).

Holland fee.   If you could just send it home or give it to Win, she will keep it for me. I think there is some difficulty of sending it straight to the bank.

Sir John rehearsal.   I would much prefer to leave the next day (19th); it's such a rush to get out of evening things and pack and catch a train – but if you feel I should, then of course I will. I think Win should get Monday off too. Tell her not to be so blooming conscientious!

I can rehearse all the 20th, 21st, 22nd and 23rd with JB and will travel to him if it helps.

OSLO Filharmonik programme.   This is what I could do and provide my own parts (all strings).

Where'er you walk	Handel	4 min
Cradle song	Wm Byrd	2½ min
Dearest consort	Handel	6 min
Hark the ech'ing Air	Purcell	4 min
Water boy	Negro song	3 min
I have a bonnet	Irish arr. Hughes	1½ min
My boy Willie	arr. Sharp	3 min

Otherwise the Brahms Serious Songs take 23 minutes and I haven't my own parts, or for any other Purcell.

Would you say a big and sincere thank you to Miss Lereculey for her most lovely letter. I was most moved to receive it and to know she had taken time out of her busy life to write to me. It was kind of her – thank you very much.

Mr Gylling.   I could do a radio ½hr on the 16th April if that would be any good.

Ripley Choir. (Miss Lereculey).   Would you tell her I can provide all my own parts for May 26th and that if it's all the same to Miss Whyte, I feel it would be a better programme to sing 'Where'er you walk', Cradle song and then 'Hark the ech'ing air' (Purcell), it being a lively end. But if she prefers 'Art thou troubled', it's all right because all the orchestrations are together. I will post them to her the end of April.

I think that's all, love – business at least.

The weather's just like Manchester here today – cold, raining, and terribly slushy. I hope there isn't too much sickness that you must cope with – and that you are keeping fit. Bless you again for everything and I look forward to Paris.

Much love, darling,
Kathleen
    P.S. Rome a great success – also Florence. Critics in ecstasies, so that's summut!

No.253 [Postcard to John Newmark]
8.2.51   [Turin]
Dearest Johnny.
    Keep wondering how you are and hope and pray you are much better. Wish
you were here with me to cope with these Latin races. Am travelling alone with
dollops of money like wallpaper, with no instructions, and have finished up
today in Turin too late to rehearse *Kindertotenlieder* with Klemperer. Quelle vie!
Arrived in Rome to hear that my sweet Pappy was dying, and when I telephoned
to London they were blanketed in thick yellow fog and no planes landing for
days, so my sister persuaded me to carry on here, as I would be too late to see
him anyway, so haven't felt much like singing this past week – but am grateful
that he was unconscious and only just stopped breathing. He had had flu but
was almost recovered when he had a slight stroke. My sister was there and two
nurses, so he was well looked after, but oh! I shall miss him and his good temper
and ear-to-ear grin. The concerts have gone well, but the audiences the most
uncivilised anywhere – come ¾hr late after starting 20 mins late, and get up and
walk in and out, and chatter all the time. I loathe their very guts, darling – but
p'raps it's me! Love to Paul and do hope you are really better.
Much love
Kaff

No.254 [Postcard to Win]
8.2.51   [Turin]
Have arrived in Turin for *Kindertotenlieder* tomorrow on radio. Milan concert
went well yesterday – best audience yet – but still shuffly! Go to Perugia to stay
with the Marchese with two castles and you know what, and thank God he
speaks English. Am yearning to be home and swear where I'll be understood.
Phyllis Spurr has written to say she'll stay with Paddy till I arrive. Isn't she a kind
soul? See you in Paris and am sending you a cheque in an envelope so you can
get some French francs and anything new you need. Long to see you
Much love to you and Jane.
Kaff

No. 255 [Letter to Catherine Henderson]
Sat. 10.2.51   *Grand Hotel Duomo*, Milan
Dearest Catherine
    It's 6.30am and I am just waiting for my train to start for Perugia – having just
made it – though minus a wash – as the porter called me half-an-hour late – and
I am wondering how you all are, and if Alec took up his bed and walked. I do
hope young Rosalind is better again too, and that all goes smoothly once more.
    I want to thank you with all my heart for all your many, many kindnesses –
for the lovely party you gave for me – for the many meals I had with you – for
the unforgettable sightseeing – and just for generally saving my life at least once

a day! Thank you so <u>very</u> much for everything – I just don't know what I should have done without you and Rosalind and Alec.

All is under control both here and at home – concerts in Milan and Turin went well, and now only <u>one</u> more before Paris! A nice pet called Phyllis Spurr, an accompanist, has written to say she will stay with Paddy at home until I arrive, so that's marvellous. I <u>do</u> hope Alec and Rosalind are both well now and send all my love and deep gratitude to them and good wishes for a wonderful time in Portugal, and thank you again for your great kindness to me, and send much love to you and your three poppets! Bless you, bless you, bless you! I can't ever thank you enough!!

With much love

K.Kaff

No.256 [Letter to John Newmark]

Feb 28th [19]51   Manchester

Dearest Johnny

Thank you, love, for your sweet letter. It did me much good, bless you. Mrs Tillett and Win came to meet me on my way back home in Paris, and it just made all the difference. I had a last concert with [Carl] Schuricht, rather slow and elderly, but a nice poppet – and then home again. Paddy is still with me, and in the last few days before coming here, I've sold a stack of furniture, engaged some more help, done two hours a day with Phyllis Spurr and generally have rushed around kinda lot! Talking of Phyllis, I put on our records the other night and if anyone should be jealous it is she, but she said you ought to be furious on hearing them as anything that is wrong is obviously technical. I'm furious! I spoke to Victor yesterday, and said there was a 'wow' on the Schumann but not on the Brahms, and he said it must be my copy, but I said no as it had been mentioned in the *New Statesman* – so he's going into it – because on my short playing there is no wow. Two crits that I have seen thought my Schumann was heavy, and you were insensitive and heavy – the blinking idiots – when it's obviously in the balance or the manufacture. Of course Columbia heard about our doing it, and they brought out one on the same day – E[lisabeth] Schumann and Gerald M[oore] – and they can do no wrong. But our Brahms had good crits. When we did them I thought it would be the other way about, because of the Brahms being meant for a man. Have you seen Claudia C. and *Review of Literature*? Those are stunners, so to hell with London. I'll send the *Gramophone* and *New Statesman* if you like, but don't worry, they are both a couple of dried up inhibited fairies! [Desmond] Shawe-Taylor is the one who once called me this 'goitrous' contralto and being elephantine in many ways, I don't forget!

I will bring out our folksongs, I think it would be the simplest.

Well darling, this is a great day. The first performance with Barbirolli of the Chausson. We rehearsed last night, and oh! boy! is it lush!? He's pickled tink, and I'm enjoying it – there's such support for the high bits – didn't worry me last night. *Orfeo* at the weekend – that I <u>am</u> looking forward to. Barbirolli with his Italian blood seems to me just right. But then I'm a fan, so am probably biased.

It is wonderful news that you're 99% OK. God bless all doctors – and <u>do</u> look after yourself.

Am going to Germany for the first time on the 14th – Cologne with Gerald M. – then on to Amsterdam for *St Matt. Passion.*

Have got a New Zealand girl to stay with Paddy and see to all things secretarial – she just started yesterday. Paddy is engaged to be married, so will be going in perhaps 12 months – then I hope the other one will take over – having got the secretarial chaos straightened out in the meantime.

We <u>do</u> miss our father which art.

Much love

Kaff

P.S. I think <u>my</u> first Schumann <u>is</u> heavy going, but I've heard lots worse than that.

No.257 [Postcard to Laura Cooper]

28.2.51   [Manchester]

Thank you for your exuberant letter – I am <u>so</u> glad you like the records. I am disgusted with a bad 'wow' on the long-playing *Frauenliebe* – I hope it has missed yours.

Things that might come out:

An die Musik	Schubert
Musensohn	"
Botschaft	Brahms
Sapphische Ode	"
The fidgety bairn	Scottish folk
Ca' the yowes	"

That is about all I have had time for, as I have been abroad a long time. I am still waiting for *Kindertotenlieder* to be released by Columbia – they were made a year last October!!

With best wishes

Kathleen Ferrier

P.S. Was asked to do *Orfeo* at Scala, but couldn't fit it in.

No.258 [Letter to Emmie Tillett]

2nd March [1951]   [Manchester]

Dearest Emmie

Herewith suggestion for Newcastle – June 7th. He's awful highbrow, ain't he?

The Lennox Berkeley are only for strings and not suitable with piano. I could do the Bliss if that would please him, but I've forgotten its proper title [*The Enchantress*], but Bernie would tell you. It's in a brown-backed manuscript copy with either a Novello or Boosey & Hawkes label, and it's something about frying mi lover in hot oil!

I would prefer to do that with the Brahms Serious Songs but the Rubbra would be all too much religious. Will you suggest this:

An die Leyer	Schubert
Suleika	"
Lachen und Weinen	"
Gretchen am Spinnrade	"
Wandrers Nachtlied	"

Der Musensohn	"	22 mins
[*The Enchantress*]	Bliss	18 mins
Pauze		
Four Serious Songs	Brahms	23 mins

Or if he prefers a mixed group instead of the Serious Songs I could do

Ich ging mit Lust	Mahler	
Ich atmet' einen Linden duft	Mahler	
Liebestreu	Brahms	
Dein blaues Auge	"	
Sonntag	"	
Botschaft	"	
Von ewiger Liebe	"	about 25 mins

If either of these are suitable will you send me a copy and I'll pop it, for posterity, in mi pocket book! Hope your invalids are back in good form, darlint, and that all is well with you.

It's lovely to think Bernie is at home – a strong rock! – I hope she's happy and getting enough to eat!

All well here – it's gorgeous to be with Sir John – but he's shrunk inches!

I suppose it's not possible to fly direct to Cologne on the 15th? I seem to remember it isn't. Could you be an angel and let Mr Finemann know my time of arrival wherever and whenever it may be so that I may be met?

Much love
Kaff

No.259 [Letter to Harry Vincent]
8.3.51   The *Grand* Hotel, Manchester
Dear Harry

Thank you so much for your lovely letter. I am so terribly sorry you are laid up and <u>do</u> hope you will soon be about again.

I was desolate to have you miss *Orfeo* – what <u>bad</u> luck – but here's hoping you'll hear it another time. Sir J.B.'s a wonder and it's glorious to work with him.

We miss our sweet Pop more than I can say, but I shall be eternally grateful that he just fell asleep and was in no pain. This winter has been hard for old folk – Ena [Mitchell] lost her mother at the New Year.

It was lovely to see Madge – and she looked so bonny. I'm sorry I didn't see Kathleen Mary this time, but I hope to remedy that e'er long.

Do be careful when you're up and about again, and <u>much</u> love to you all
from
Kathleen

No.260 [Letter to Audrey Hurst]
9.3.51   [Manchester]
Dear Miss Hurst

Thank you for your letter. I shall be happy to sing the *Alto Rhapsody* on the 23rd June for Mr Isaacs.

Would you please pass on this group for Mrs Tillett for the Danish broadcast.

Gretchen am Spinnrade	Schubert

Lachen und Weinen	Schubert
Sonntag	Brahms
Botschaft	"

This is with piano to go alongside 'Inflammatus' and 'O Rust in the Lard'!
In haste
Sincerely
Kathleen Ferrier

No.261 [incomplete letter to John Barbirolli]
[?14th March 1951]   [2 Frognal Mansions, London NW3]
... I can't ever forget that you put off your "appointment" with Billy Douglas [the surgeon for Barbirolli's appendix operation in March 1951] until *Orfeo* and the Chausson were over. Those ten days – working and being with you – were inexpressibly wonderful.... It is the loveliest time I ever remember and I keep on re-living it, and purr with pleasure every time I do so....

No.262 [Letter to Bruno Walter]
19th March [19]51   *American* Hotel, Amsterdam
My dear Professor
    Thank you with all my heart for your lovely letter. I have no words to tell you how I appreciate your sympathy. My father died as he had lived – simply and very peacefully – and for this I can never be grateful enough.
    I hope you are well, and that all your New York concerts are going well as they surely must. I look forward with enormous pleasure to working and learning with you in Edinburgh.
My fondest love to you and Lotte
Yours ever
Kathleen

No.263 [Letter to Benita Cress]
28.3.51   2 Frognal Mansions, London NW3
Dearest Benita
    I have neglected you I fear – but things have been happening with such rapidity, I haven't written any personal letters for ages.
    First I have got a 'jewel' to look after me and to keep Paddy company until the latter marries. She is a New Zealand girl called Bernie and a trained nurse – but wanting a job where she can be independent. She nursed my manager's mother when she died – and I knew her well, but never thought she'd consider such a mundane job. But she seems in her element, has a wonderful sense of humour and is altogether a pearl. She hasn't got out of her nursing as she thought, as I have to go into hospital any day now for a rather formidable 'op' for a 'bump on mi busto'. But having Bernie here has lightened the load enormously and I am in the finest radiologists' and surgeons' hands in the country. I have had to cancel a month's tour in Scandinavia and everything until the middle of May – but I am glad of a rest – and feel better now that everything is getting done. I should have gone earlier, but haven't been home for months. The X-ray yesterday was better than they thought.

So don't worry, love, and I'll ask Paddy to send you a line. We are fine for everything in the food line and don't want for <u>anything</u> – thanks to you. And I'm smoking with abandon being as 'ow I've not to sing for 6 weeks! I hope you and Bill are both flourishing and much, much love to you.

Yours till hell freezes

Kaff

Will you thank Stella for her lovely letter and cutting? Ta ever so!

No.264 [Letter from Yvonne Hamilton to Bruno Walter]

April 1st 1951   43 Hamilton Terrace, London NW8

Dear dearest Bruno

I meant to write to you before leaving New York to thank you for the memorable performance of *Fidelio*, which will forever remain in my thoughts – but those last five days flew by in an instant, and we were as usual swamped over, as one invariably is in New York. Now that I am back again in the peace and the difficulties of our dear but decrepit Europe, I have time and leisure to look back on those wonderful weeks in New York and all the things that I saw and heard there. First and foremost is our visit to you and our evening at *Fidelio*, which inspired, moved and thrilled me to the bottom of my soul. I cannot thank you enough for it, dear, dear friend.

Kathleen Ferrier was the first person I saw on my return and we spoke long and enthusiastically about you. I have something of the strictest confidence to tell you, and I know I can rely on you to talk it over only with Lotte and no one else in the world. Our dear Kathleen is going into hospital at the end of next week to have a very serious operation. They have discovered that she has cancer in her left breast and it has to be operated on. It is a terrible thing for such a young and beautiful woman to have to submit to, and yet I suppose it is a small price to pay for life. I need hardly tell you that she is marvellously courageous and serene about it, and she has talked it over with us as if it were an ordinary occurrence. Above all, she does not want it talked about or mentioned, and so if you are writing to her, please say that you have heard from me that she has to have an operation, but do not state that you know what it is. I am sure she will tell you about it herself one day, for it seems that this has been going on for some time and is the result of a knock on the breast ten years ago. We are terribly concerned about her, and I will let you know how the operation goes. I believe the date is April 11th [actually the 10th].

And now there is one more thing which I would like to ask you. Could Lotte occasionally send her a meat parcel? I feel she will need some good, wholesome food to recover from the shock of such a terrible ordeal, and nothing is better than meat. But please, not a word of it to Kathleen herself. The cruelty of life always shocks one afresh. Why do such things happen to those who least deserve it?

I have been looking through the programme of the music which inaugurates the Festival of Britain next month, and it strikes me as terribly unimaginative, commonplace and boring. That worthy man Malcolm Sargent is opening the Festival – one cannot say anything more.

Alastair is here for the holidays and delights me – it's really the only bright spot of our return home, as otherwise London is a desolation of rain and perishing cold. It's such a disgusting atmosphere that I wonder why on earth one survives. This is a letter full of gloomy news, but I hope to send a better one as soon as I know the result of Kathleen's operation. Meanwhile our warm, warm love to you and Lottie, and bless you ever, dear, dear Bruno.

Your affectionate

Yvonne

No.265 [Letter from Bernadine Hammond to Peter Diamand]

April 12th [1951]   University College Hospital,
                                        Private Patient Wing, London

Dear Mr Diamand

Just a note to let you know that Kathleen is making very good progress. Everyone is very pleased with her and I think that today she is feeling a little pleased with herself – "Klever Kaff" once again! Each day she will be stronger and soon in full force again, I am quite sure. She is a good, very, very good patient, and I hope that soon this will all become a distant memory and well and truly shelved.

Kath sends her love. At time of writing she is snoring and giving her vocal chords a rest, think really I prefer the latter "noise"!

My love

Bernadine Hammond

P.S. Sorry about the odd envelope, a hospital one.

No.266 [Letter from Yvonne Hamilton to Bruno Walter]

April 14th 1951   43 Hamilton Terrace, London NW8

Dearest Bruno

Only a hurried line to let you know that all is well with our dear Kathleen. The operation took place on the 10th and was <u>completely</u> successful. I'm in quarantine for chicken pox (of all the childish diseases to have at my age!) and so dare not go near her, but Jamie [Hamish Hamilton] saw her yesterday and is with her today. He says she is doing remarkably well and has been fantastically courageous throughout it all – just what one can expect from such a remarkable person. The day before she went into hospital, she came to see us and sang Schumann and Schubert Lieder for two hours. Her voice was stupendous!

Where are you? I don't know where to send you this message, but have a feeling that you will soon be in California. The spring is now struggling to come through here, and with the winds and showers of April, hope springs anew in one's heart.

Our devoted love to all three of you and many blessings.

Yvonne

P.S. It <u>is</u> September 9th that we are expecting you here is it not? Kathleen will try and be here too on that evening. I have just spoken to Kathleen on the telephone. Her spirits sound high, and she tells me she feels wonderful now that the operation and the awful crescendo of the last few weeks are behind her.

No.267 [Letter to Benita Cress]
18th April [19]51   [University College Hospital]
Dearest Bonnie

Bless you for my lovely birthday present – they arrived yesterday – and are <u>so</u> lovely – thank you very, very much.

I am writing my first letters for a bit and feeling real cocky – just waiting for the doctor to come – and being glad it isn't this time last week – when I threw up four times all down Bernie's front – poor, sweet Bernie – she's been an absolutely bluidy marvel – and I just don't know what I should have done without her.

I don't know about my itinerary yet, love – it's at home and I'm not even thinking about singing yet – but I'll let you know in a bit. I shall be in here another week or ten days yet – then have to have some rays for a few weeks – then a holiday – so I'm really enjoying a rest – and gee! I <u>was</u> ready for it. I seem to have startled all the staff here with quick recovery, and I'm being spoiled to death and thoroughly enjoying myself!!

I hope your arm is much better, love – you just be a good honey-chile now and have a good rest – and thank you again for the gorgeous present and lovely card. I am not telling any of my buddies in N.Y. about my op. as such exaggerated rumours get around – you're the only one wot knows!
Much love to you both.
Kaff

No.268 [Letter to Peter Diamand in Bernadine Hammond's hand]
April 23rd [1951]   [University College Hospital]
Sweet Pea

The most gorgeous lilac arrived on Saturday making my room look simply beautiful. Thank you so very, very much. I had an almost hysterical birthday party with Ben and Peter and Basil D[ouglas], Myra Hess, Emmie Tillett, Wyn, Bernie and Paddy, Norman Lumsden, Mr and Mrs Roy Henderson, Margaret Field-Hyde and when they had gone, the place looked debauched in the extreme. The hospital chef baked me a beautiful cake and all the nurses came in one by one, not really for their cake – but to gaze on Ben and Peter.

All goes very well and I have had my last stitches out. I go for some treatment this afternoon and will probably be home on Wednesday or Thursday. They couldn't have been nicer here, and it has all been much less terrifying than I expected and I am full of bounce and perkier than ever. I hope all is well with you and that Maria improves every day.
Much much love to you both, and hope to see you soon.
K. Kaff

No.269 [Letter to John Newmark]
1st May [19]51   2 Frognal Mansions, London NW3
Dearest Johnny

Thank you so much for yours and Paul's last letters on my birfday – it is always so grand to hear from you both – and it is lovely to know you are feeling fit again. Look after yourself now!

Things have been happening to me since I wrote to tell you about my Pop. First I have taken on a 'jewel' as secretary and eventually – everything – when Paddy leaves to be married. She is a New Zealander called Bernadine Hammond (Bernie) and a qualified nurse, but wanting a change – so she thought, having coped with fractious children, she could manage me! I was just rushing off for *Orfeos* and Chaussons with Barbirolli (merveilleux!!!) and on to Cologne and Holland – so didn't see much of her – but she had worked wonders when I came home of setting the chaos of press cuttings, photies and letters straight. Whattajoy!

Then I had to go into hospital for a rather serious operation and she insisted on coming with me – donned her nurse's uniform again – and I am sure suffered more than I did at all the jobs she had to perform and see – poor love.

I had discovered a bump on my 'busto' and after much X-raying had one breast removed just 3 weeks ago today. Now I have to have six weeks of ray treatment, which is sick-making, lazy-making and rather depressing – but so far I'm holding my own, and it's wonderful to have Bernie here to help me. Please don't broadcast what is wrong with me, because it is unnecessary, and I have wonderful camouflage! And things get so magnified in the telling. I only want you to know.

The miserable thing is that my doctor insists that I am not away so long in the USA as he must keep his eye on me – so I am having to cancel the first part of our tour, but have suggested I start in Montreal as I couldn't bear to let them down, i.e. 25th October, and that would be convenient for you, wouldn't it?

Bernie is coming with me to keep an eye on me too – I have paid so many hundreds of pounds in America and England in tax for the last trip, I might just as well spend it on her!

I am so terribly sorry if I have spoiled any other concerts for you at the beginning of October, and hope you can make up, by my telling you at this stage. I only knew on Sunday I wouldn't be coming as originally arranged.

I haven't worked since 23rd March and am off until June 19th – so at least my voice should be rested! I miss the opening of the Festival in the New Hall and *Gerontius* with Barbirolli, but am so tired, don't really mind.

My stay in hospital was the pleasantest possible time and I have just about been ruined by kindness. Mrs Tillett and Myra Hess waited all during the op. and for me to come round, and came in almost every day. My birthday was riotous with the two of them bringing champagne – the hospital chef icing a gorgeous cake – and visits from Ben and Peter, Win, Paddy, and many musical buddies, and all the sweet nurses trying to find an excuse to come and peep at Ben Britten!! Flowers from Barbirolli and Malcolm Sargent amongst others – just ruined, darling, I am!

It's lovely to have it over, because I had been worried for a bit and had been abroad all the time, and couldn't do anything there – and it's miserable to sing and feel leeousy, ain't it?

Write soon – I love to hear from you – much love to you and don't forget to thank Paul for his sweet letter and to excuse me writing just now. See you fairly soon – D.V.

God bless

Love

Kaff

No.270 [Letter from Bernadine Hammond to Bruno Walter]
May 2nd 1951   2 Frognal Mansions, London NW3
Dear Professor Walter

Kathleen has asked me to write to thank you for your sweet letter, and to tell you that she is making splendid progress. I am living with her now to help with her correspondence and to look after her. She had an operation about three weeks ago, and is at present having treatment, but all her doctors are very pleased with her, and I think she was ready for a good rest. She will be singing again about the middle of June.

Kathleen sends her best love to you and to Mrs Lindt [Walter's daughter Lotte Walter-Lindt] and is looking forward with pleasure to seeing you in Edinburgh. She will talk to Mrs Tillett and Victor Olof about dates for the recording as it is her greatest ambition to do this with you. I enclose her programme and she hopes that it meets with your approval.
Yours very sincerely
Bernadine Hammond

No.271 [Letter to Benita Cress]
17th May [19]51   2 Frognal Mansions, London NW3
Dearest Benita

Thank you so much for all your letters – I am sorry we have neglected you lately – Bernie has written but forgot and sent it ordinary post – so that will be coming one day soon.

I'm feeling better each day and my anaemia, which was rather low, is almost normal again. I have been going each morning to the hospital for rays, and should have only another two weeks to do – perhaps even less. The budder of it is, I haven't to wash mi neck, and it's about an inch deep in dust – but I suppose one of these days I'll be a clean girl again! I haven't had a bath for over six weeks! – I don't arf pong!

The doctors are enormously pleased with me – and I'm in wonderful hands – I couldn't have been better cared for – and I've loved the rest, and don't ever want to start again!! My Dr says I have to go canny for 2 yrs, that is why I have had to cancel the first month of America – but I shall be doing Chicago, so hope to see you there. Bernie is coming with me and is 'pickled tink'!

Between you and me, I'm very lop-sided at the top but am camouflaging with great taste and delicacy!! And what the heck, as long as I feel well and can sing a bit, eh?

I am so glad you saw Ann – I think she's a lovely artist – and has great character – you <u>do</u> get around. We're all right for parcels for the moment, love – and I'm not short of a single thing – I'm just spoiled to death!
Much love to you both – will write again
Kaff

No.272 [Letter to Sadie Lereculey]

21.5.51   2 Frognal Mansions, London NW3

Dear Miss Lereculey

Here is a programme – baht 'at – for Ilkley, September 12th. Phyllis Spurr is already booked for it, so that's fine.

1.	Where'er you walk	Handel
	Come to me soothing sleep	Handel
	Hark the ech'ing air	Purcell
	Mad Bess	Purcell
2.	*Frauenliebe und Leben*	Schumann
	Pauze!	
3.	Après un rêve	Fauré
	Lydia	"
	Nell	"
4.	Silent Noon	Vaughan Williams
	Go not happy day	Frank Bridge
	The little road to Bethlehem	Michael Head
	Pretty ring time	Peter Warlock

I think that will be all right for Scarborough too, don't you? Goody, goody! Oh no! Gerald [Moore] plays group [of piano solos] at Scarborough so I'll leave out the Fauré there.

No.273 [Letter to Beatrice (Trixie) Ward (née Ferrier)]

May 21st [1951]   2 Frognal Mansions, London NW3

Dear Trixie

You are a proper poppet sending such a lovely letter and for such delirious chocs. It was lovely to have them both and I do thank you very much for sending them.

I am feeling really grand again now and have only another fortnight to go to the hospital each day and then Bernie and I are going to have two weeks holiday in Sussex, and we are both looking forward very much to it. Bernie is the New Zealand girl who came to me after Pop died, and as she is a trained nurse she has looked after me all the time – my Doctor calls her Jewel so that speaks for itself.

I am terribly sorry to be missing York in June as I was looking forward to seeing you. I hope to start singing in the middle of June, but will not be allowed to then unless I am bursting with health. It has been lovely having this long rest as I was weary after dashing madly around Europe.

Your sweet Momma [Maud Ferrier] sent us some lovely biscuits the other day which we appreciated very much; grand to know that she and Uncle George are both keeping very well. I do hope that we will see you soon, meanwhile much love to you and to Frank, and grateful thanks to you for your kind thought.

Look after yourself – God bless – and much love

Kathleen

No.274 [Letter to John Newmark]

22.5.51   2 Frognal Mansions, London NW3

Dearest Johnny

It was lovely to hear from you again yesterday – two letters in a short time – gee whiz! but I'm spoiled!

All's well, sweetie! I'm still going to the hospital for rays each day, but should have finished with them in ten days. I have only been slightly queasy on a few occasions, when they seem to lay most people completely out – making them violently sick, anaemic and suicidal – so I am feeling very cocky and with the end in sight, I perk up each day. 2,000,000 volts is quite a lot of current going into one's innards isn't it? The doctors are very pleased with me – I have gained weight this last two weeks, and from wanting to sit and twiddle my thumbs all day, I have an urge to do a bit of work now – which is just as well, as I have lots to learn for Edinburgh.

Voce seems better for the rest, and oh! I <u>was</u> ready for one! I'll always approach Italy tentatively in future wot with one thing and another! Where's your Latin grammar, mi darlint? – D.V. is *Deus volat* or God willing.

I haven't thought out programme for Montreal etc yet, but have just sent in Community – here it is:

1. Where'er you walk	Handel
Willow, willow	Elizabethan arr. Warlock
Hark the ech'ing air	Purcell
Mad Bess	Purcell
2. Gretchen	Schubert
Lachen und Weinen	"
Wandrers Nachtlied	"
Erlkönig	"
3. Après un rêve	Fauré
Lydia	"
Nell	"
4. The little road to Bethlehem	Michael Head
Go not happy day	Frank Bridge
Down by the Salley Gardens	Ivor Gurney
Pretty ring time	Peter Warlock

As far as I can see, the Florida date is just orchestral, Johnny, so as you are in Canada with me on the 14th, you can be free until the 26th in Carmel, Calif. OK? Hunter recital on the 10th Nov is with you, please! Goody, goody. I don't think the Chausson is suitable with piano. I have already done it with Barbirolli and I can't imagine it other than orchestral now. Oke?

I don't need anything, love. I have lots of tins of butter and meat that Mr Anderson has sent from Chicago – the ration here is still one chop per person per week! Quel country! But really we're fine, so don't worry your ole head, honey-chile!

I will ask Peter Pears about the Janacek when I can get hold of him – he is away so much just now – but I have made a note of the title, and will see what I can do.

Much love to Paul – will you thank him again for his sweet letter – I look forward to seeing you both so very, very much. Thank you again for writing and look after yourself.

Much, much love

From a fairly Klever Kaff

No.275 [Letter to Emmie Tillett]

22nd June 1951   [2 Frognal Mansions, London NW3]

Dearest Emmie

I am so bad at saying 'thank you' in 'poisson', love, so I just wanted to write and say how your simply lovely party the other night just made my day and completed my cure! It was just right and so lovely and oh! so delicious. Thank you, dear Emmie, so <u>very</u> much – not only for this, but for our lovely weekends, for your care and concern, – and I shall never forget how you and Myra [Hess] waited for me to come round from the anaesthetic.

Bless you for everything – I only wish I could take a little of the burden of your work from your shoulders, but August <u>will</u> come and I sincerely hope you will holiday then. I know you have a fantastico 'panel' doctor who works miracles, but I don't want him to have to resort to his magic for you. That is another thing I have to thank you for (it is unending!), and that is for the most wonderful doctoring it is possible for anyone to have, and for the friendship of such rare people.

Thank you, love, for everything and look after yourself, and as Bernie said to me in a letter she wrote to Holland 'for goodness sake don't mention this or I shall fall down the lavatory in embarrassment!'

God bless, love, and much, much love

Kaff

No.276 [Postcard to Win]

[2nd July 1951]   [Amsterdam]

Here safely once more – good flight. Met by news cameras – five ordinary cameras and Peter D. armed with carnations!! Bernie very impressed! Flowers in room, and fruit from manager! Whattacountry! Going to flix as often as possible to see how photogenic I am! 4 hour rehearsal today (Mon) but feeling fine. Tomorrow in the Hague – Wed here – so going to be busy.

Hope all's well – much love.

Kaff

No.277 [Letter to Bruno Walter]

July 8, 1951   *American* Hotel, Amsterdam

Dear Professor

Thank you for your lovely letter and to Lotte for another <u>wondrous</u> parcel that arrived before I left home for Holland. How kind you all are – I can't express in mere words my deep gratitude for the lovely things that have been sent – and for your solicitude. Thank you with all my heart!

I shall be in London on August 18th and be very happy to rehearse with you anytime at your convenience. Will you come to my flat? – it's a little more comfortable now I have a lovely Steinway.

I am back at work these past three weeks – but quite gently. Singing here in *Orfeo*. But it's such a poor production it hurts!! But the meals are wonderful and I have regained all my lost poundage!!

Thank you again for everything

With my love to you both

Kathleen

No.278 [Letter to Emmie Tillett]

9th July 1951   *American* Hotel, Amsterdam

Dearest Emmie

Thank you for your letters love, and here are a few replies first. I haven't heard direct from New York about the Little Orchestra Concert. I can still do the 20th, because if I'm in N.Y. I can pay my Income Tax in advance – that's the only real rush – but if you are writing to Mr Mertens it would perhaps be a good thing to mention it. Ta ever so for booking our singles – why not come too, love? Oooo! I would have you merry on champagne cocktails, and Miami and San Fran – two of the loveliest, hottest, sunniest places. Eh? Eh?!

OK for car from Liverpool to Kings Lynn

OK Bliss October 2nd

Alternative programme for Kings Lynn.

Where'er you walk	Handel
Like as the lovelorn turtle	Handel
Dido's Lament	Purcell
Mad Bess	Purcell
Pur dicesti	Lotti
Lasciatemi morire	Monteverdi
Che faro	Gluck
Ganymed	Schubert
Ich ging mit Lust	Mahler
Dein blaues Auge	Brahms
Botschaft	Brahms
Down by the Salley Gardens	Gurney
Go not happy day	Frank Bridge
Sleep	Peter Warlock
Pretty ring time	Peter Warlock

Sorry to have caused such a cafuffle here!

I'm going on my holidays on the 30th July. I'm going to Sussex for a few days with the whole Barbirolli family! But I don't think I should be much good for John Lowe on a Monday morning after these four days!! I don't mind keeping Kings Lynn especially as I have so little to sing in the Krips concert – I leave it to you.

All well here – still hoping you might just pop over tomorrow – but it really is a pretty awful production, so p'raps it's just as well if you don't.

I spend most of my time in bed in between whiles being thoroughly lazy. It's <u>so</u> tiring here, being below sea level I suppose. Oh! <u>so</u> looking forward to coming home on Saturday – can I paint on Sunday? Is it a date, or is it awkward? Dying to see your masterpieces!

Been rehearsing with Klemperer this morning – took Bernie for safety and she hasn't yet regained her natural colour! He terrified her!!

Hope work is easing up a little bit for you now – thought and talked about you such a lot.

God bless love

Much love

Kaff

No.279 [Letter from Bernadine Hammond to Peter and Maria Diamand]

July 16th [1951]   2 Frognal Mansions, London NW3

Dear Peter and Maria

First of all, thank you for the wonderful chocolates, they all have the most fascinating birds sitting on top, that it fairly breaks my heart to eat them.

Secondly, thank you both for always being so sweet to me. I know you are used to seeing Kath on her own, but you always made me most welcome for which I am most grateful. Now that you know me a little better, I hope that you will say when you want our most "valuable dollar export" on her own, and I do not only refer to weekends in Paris!!!!!!!!!!

Thirdly, both Doctors have seen Kath and she is having a few routine checks but they seem quite satisfied with her. I know how you both love Kath and very often love goes side by side with worry, you must always feel that she has the very best treatment from two of the very best Doctors in England who will constantly watch her with the greatest of care.

Had a good flight back, not at all bumpy.

My very best love to you both

Bernadine

No.280 [Letter to John Newmark]

1st Aug [19]51   2 Frognal Mansions, London NW3

Dearest Johnny

I'm all right, are you? Only sorry I haven't written sooner, but there have been great issues at stake! I'm <u>terribly</u> sorry to tell you my doctor thinks I must cancel my whole trip this autumn. I can't tell you how worried I am on your behalf thinking of all the jobs you must have turned down, and getting this off at the first possible moment in the hope that it may not be too late to get others. Mrs Tillett asked me to wait two days so that Mr Mertens would hear first. I have money returned from excess income tax in the care of Mertens, and can easily ask him to let you have your Decca money from that – will you let me know? Holland took it out of me rather – after all it's only just over three months since the operation, and *entre-nous*, darling, I have to have more treatment on my back, which is rather uncomfortable around my sciatica [*sic*] nerve, and the doctor feels that if I needed more whilst I was away, it is such an intricate business of X-rays and how to apply them, that it can only be done by a radiotherapist, who has the complete details of the case. I am enormously disappointed and sorry, and grieved beyond measure, that I let you down. I hope I can make up to you for this very quickly and can only repeat how <u>terribly</u> sorry I am.

I have asked Peter Pears for the Janacek – he has been away on the Continent until now – and he has promised to send it to me. He is very willing to lend it to you but does not want to lose sight of it completely as it is irreplaceable. Perhaps your friend can bring it to you – he said he would ring me up again before leaving – and I know you will look after it. I hope you are feeling really well and fit again. I have a month off now before Edinburgh, and shall be glad when that is over as it is completely new programme, lots of words to remember.

Dearest Johnny, again I must say how terribly sorry I am to let you down and hope with all my heart that it is not <u>too</u> great a loss financially.
My love to you and many thoughts
Not so Klever Kaff!

No.281 [Letter to Sadie Lereculey]
2nd August 1951   2 Frognal Mansions, London NW3
Dear Miss Lereculey
    Herewith some programmes
<u>Marple</u> and <u>Southall</u>

Where'er you walk	*Semele*	Handel
Like as the lovelorn turtle	*Atalanta*	Handel
Dido's Lament		Purcell
Hark the ech'ing air	*The Fairie Queene*	Purcell
Frauenliebe und Leben		Schumann
Love is a bable		Parry
The fairy lough		Stanford
Down by the Salley Gardens		Gurney
Pretty ring time		Warlock
Ca' the Yowes		arr. Jacobson
Kitty my love		arr. Hughes

Some more following, but I know you are waiting for these. In a rush!
Sincerely
Kathleen Ferrier

No.282 [Letter to Emmie Tillett – first two paragraphs from Bernadine Hammond]
7th August [1951]   [2 Frognal Mansions, London NW3]
Dear Emmie
    Ta everso for votre grande carde de poste, prego! Hope you are having a wonderful time. I am expecting great things of your canals. At least I won't have to spend me hard earned pennies on bus fares to the Wallace Collection when I can see the Tilletts at Elm Tree Road.
    Have had conversations slightly one-sided with Mona and Erica and all is well. I had Erica laughing 'cause I rang and asked her if she was cleaning the windows when it never ceased raining yesterday. Kath spent the weekend at Seaford and had a wonderful time. Everything settled there most favourably. Will talk to you about it when you come back. She is sparking on all plugs and doing a good hour with Phyllis daily singing now, and I just cannot concentrate. The treatment isn't making her feel too poorly and everything is going along well. Your pan-doc [panel doctor] left today.

My best love
Bernie

Hello love!

Ta ever so for the Van Gogh-like pitcher – hope the weather's cheered up for you now. It's leeeousy here, pouring and hailing.

Had a lovely weekend with the whole Barbirolli family and have never seen John and Evelyn happier. Ethel B[artlett]'s talking through her bleedin' hat or I'm a Dutchman. Your pan-doc was invited to supper there before bringing me home on Sunday and it was a riot. He talked French to Mrs B., Italian to an aunt, set puzzles for two kid relatives, offered to make reeds for Evelyn and talked fiddles and *Turandot* with John. It was a riotous success.

<u>Do</u> hope you are having a gorgeous time and thinking of you so much and so relieved you really managed to get away. I'm fine – just can't touch mi toes mitout bellowing, but guess that's just old age! Bernie's a jewel, a jewel, a jewel. Bless you and much love
Kaff

No.283 [Letter to Benita Cress]
7th August [19]51   [2 Frognal Mansions, London NW3]
Dearest Bonnie

Well duckie, you <u>have</u> been neglected, but it has only been lack of time and not because we haven't thought about you! I have been dashing about a bit since Holland, and have just been hibernating on my bed in between concerts to be ready for the next one. Bernie has been doing everything!! Keeping me in control, the housework, shopping (quite a long job here with queues!) and endless letters and the cooking – and she's still bright and cheerful. You'll have to see her – she's every jewel rolled in one. Lucky Kaff!

Here it comes love! I have to cancel my American trip – not because I'm any worse – I hasten to tell you – but because Holland took it out of me a bit, and the doctor feels that so heavy a tour would be asking for trouble so soon. If I needed treatment, it can really only be given here, as it is such an intricate business that only a doctor who knows the case could cope. HELL! HELL! HELL! My tour started off with a recital every other day and travelling in between, and it just makes me tired to think of it, but I am grieved to the core to miss my buddies there and especially La Crosse, but I think it is wise, and it will be the first long rest I have had in ten years! I know you will understand and try not to be too disappointed, because by this time next year I hope to be bouncing with health. I think it is better to cancel now than to have to give up in the middle and worry everybody stiff. Poor Mr Mertens – I <u>am</u> leading him a dance. He has only just been told, love, so will you keep this to yourself until it becomes public property?

I am off until Edinburgh now – Sept 6th and 7th – and so relieved to be, as I have much learning to do. But it's gorgeous to be at home and not rushing about. I'm getting my cumbersome flat into some sort of order – I've never had time before and I <u>do</u> enjoy it. The parcels you have sent have been an absolute Godsend and we have plenty to be going on with and are short of nothing. But

I owe you money, and Mr Mertens has some returned income tax of mine, and I can ask him to send you a cheque for the amount. Would you let me know what it is, love?

I do hope you are both well and happy, and forgive me for not writing sooner – the days go so quickly!

God bless and look after yourselves and much love from

Kaff

No.284 [Letter to Sadie Lereculey]

14th August 1951 — 2 Frognal Mansions, London NW3

Dear Miss Lereculey

Here are some more programmes for you:

<u>Dorchester September 18th</u>

Where'er you walk	Handel (*Semele*)
Like as the lovelorn turtle	Handel (*Atalanta*) (by special request)
Dido's Lament	Purcell
Mad Bess	Purcell
Die junge Nonne	Schubert (by special request)
Lachen und Weinen	"
Suleika's zweiter Gesang	"
Ganymed	"
Der Musensohn	"
Silent Noon	Vaughan Williams
Pretty ring time	Peter Warlock
Down by the Salley Gardens	Ivor Gurney
Ca' the Yowes	Scottish
Kitty my love	Irish
Bobby Shaftoe	Northumbrian

It would be nice to stay with Mrs Higginson, but Bernie will probably be with me too, aussi Phyllis. If she can cope with us all that'll be fine. Will travel down the day of the concert.

<u>Skipton</u> January 27th 1952, and <u>Belfast</u> February 8th 1952

Where'er – in fact as for Dorchester.

<u>Fribourg and La Chaux de Fonds</u> February 21st and 29th

Spring	Handel (*Ottone*)
Come to me soothing sleep	Handel (*Ottone*)
Dido's Lament	Purcell
Mad Bess	Purcell
Die junge Nonne	Schubert
Lachen und Weinen	"
Suleika's zweiter Gesang	"
Ganymed	"
Der Musensohn	"
Après un rêve	Fauré
Lydia	"
Nell	"

Silent Noon	Vaughan Williams
Go not happy day	Frank Bridge
Down by the Salley Gardens	Ivor Gurney
Pretty ring time	Peter Warlock

Klever Kaff!! I'm feeling very virtuous, having got these off mi chest, but fingers slightly crossed in lieu of objections! This'll do for Zurich too I think, and will you ask Gerald if he can do these dates with me – I don't mind the expense, but I should strangle Walter Lang – and though it would be good publicity, it's not good for me blood pressure! He (Gerald) is already reserved for the German tour. T.T.F.N.

Yours sincerely
Kathleen

No.285 [Letter to John Newmark]
Aug. 14th '51   2 Frognal Mansions, London NW3
Dearest Johnny

Thank you so much for your letter. You are a pet to be so understanding.

I had word from Mrs Tillett yesterday asking me not to inform you of the cancellation of the American tour at Mr Mertens request – until Edinburgh is over. Well, it's too late anyway, and in any case I wanted you to know as soon as possible so that you could get other jobs – but if you could keep it to yourself as much as possible for the next month, it would be a help. It isn't a case of not singing – it's the exhaustion of a tour. My voice has improved I think, with the rest and a chance to practise peacefully – but I know I couldn't cope with a recital every other day and travelling as well.

Yes my back is a 'coda' from the frontispiece – for your information only please Johnny dear – and I am going three times a week to have several thousand volts through mi middle! The trouble is on a knob of the spine – one bit has cleared up beautifully, and now they are working on another bit – but my last X-rays were very encouraging. Meanwhile this treatment makes me rather queasy and very tired – and I only practise because I must – for Edinburgh. But after this week at the hospital I can have a rest for a bit and I soon chirp up!

I have written to Peter P. to remind him that he promised me the Janacek – and I have made enquiries about records. The Schumann 'Widmung' is not out because it is only on the 78s, and they are not produced here yet – only long playing – but you can have my test record. I have ordered the Scottish folk songs and Len Berger is coming up on Friday to collect them all.

I have asked Mrs Tillett to keep me completely clear for June, July and August next year – so I won't promise any recording or recitals in case I would have to let you down again – but it would be gorgeous to see you if you will be here. Oh Boy!

I am so delighted that your health is good – I'll be catching you up one of these days, and then we'll paint the town red! Meanwhile look after yourself – much love to you and Paul and Eric when you see them – and thank you again for being a poppet.

Much love
Kaff

No.286 [Letter to Sadie Lereculey]
3rd September 1951   6 Heriot Row, Edinburgh
Dear Miss Lereculey

Herewith Croydon. I haven't seen Gerald, but I'm sure he'd hate to play solos, don't you think?

Prepare thyself Zion	*Xmas Oratorio*	Bach
Like as the lovelorn turtle	*Atalanta*	Handel
Hark the ech'ing Air	*Fairie Queene*	Purcell
Frauenliebe und Leben		Schumann
She walked thro' the fair		Irish arr. Hughes
I once loved a boy		"
The Spanish Lady		"

<u>Carnforth</u> as for Croydon
<u>Carlisle</u> Have seen Gerald and I believe he has already wired you, so I will do the date that is convenient for him. Okeydoke?
Best wishes to you
Very sincerely
Kathleen Ferrier

No.287 [Letter to Trixie Ward]
5th Sep. [1951]   In bed. Edinburgh
My dear Trix

Thank you so much for your nice letter. I wish I could have come to Paddy's wedding, but I was having a holiday in Sussex. I would have loved to have seen you all. It <u>was</u> kind of you to make things for the 'feast' – I bet they were jolly good.

I am just beginning to perk up now – I have been having some extra treatment which is rather sick-making and exhausting – but now that is over and just this last week I feel fine. I shall feel even finer when these two concerts are over – they are a great strain – then I'm going to have a good rest from October onwards, and enjoy being at home.

Bernie is here keeping an eye on me and is an absolute jewel – she's loving it too, and going to all the concerts and operas, as the guest of mine host! I'm not going anywhere – just saving up for Thurs and Friday and enjoying my own company and going to bed early. Bruno Walter is angelic – though tired – he's 75 – but thrilled me by saying it was a privilege to work with me – so my cup is very full!

It's a long time since our paths crossed – I hope we may meet <u>very</u> soon. And meanwhile much love to you and Frank and to your amazing mother and father when they arrive. They are a cupplawizards, aren't they?
God bless and much love
Kath.

Win started her new job on Mon. and I've just had a letter – the first day went well and she sounds thrilled to bits. Isn't that grand! I'm sure she'll do well.

No.288 [Letter to Laura Cooper]
24th Sept. [19]51   2 Frognal Mansions, London NW3
Dear Miss Cooper

Thank you very much for your letter and the enclosure. I was most interested to read the latter, as the records are not out here yet, and I was interested in what the critic would say – though it is the ordinary listener that counts, and it gives me enormous pleasure to know you enjoy them.

I am terribly sorry to disappoint you, but my American tour has had to be cancelled as I have been rather seriously ill since April, and my doctor thinks it is too soon yet to make a strenuous tour – though I have done several jobs here – Edinburgh Festival etc. I am so very sad to have to miss it – but feel it is better to cancel now rather than in the middle of a tour, and thereby cause worse confusion.

I am having a complete rest until the New Year so that I should be bursting with health by that time.

Thank you for your loyal appreciation – I hope I may come California-wards next year.
Yours very sincerely
Kathleen Ferrier

No.289 [Letter to John Newmark]
24th Sept. [19]51   2 Frognal Mansions, London NW3
Dearest Johnny

'Twas lovely to hear from you and to know that the records had arrived safely – auch Janacek. Even lovelier to know that your check-ups are perfect – good lad. I had a final X-ray the other day, and the doctors are enormously pleased with them – no more treatment for the moment. So I am having a rest, the like of which I haven't had for ten years! I am turning everything down, and am silent until Jan[uary]. Ain't that gorgeous? I'm playing Mozart violin sonatas with the Doc – not singing a note at the moment – and just being at home and it's lovely!

Edinburgh went well – though I always find it a terrific strain as I don't get much rehearsal with Bruno, and I was doing nearly all new things. But there was a crowded house, and a very appreciative one, and I didn't forget mi words!! I did the Chausson the next night with Barbirolli and he was 'pickled tink' with my French abandon! Sang some Fauré the other night, so my repertoire grows – Klever Kaff! Will enclose Edinburgh programme – the titles are too long to take up space here!

I'm so glad you prefer Walter's interpretation – I hate to work with Klemperer. I find him gross, bullying, unmoving and conducting insecurely from memory, because – to quote his words – that snot Toscanini does! I find he shouts like a madman – not at me, not bluidy likely – just to try and impress – though why he should think it impresses I can't think. Perhaps his Mahler comes off sometimes, because he wastes no time nor sentiment – but ohh!!!! whattaman!! I had to share a train journey and many concerts with him when I was feeling proper poorly, and oh boy, I was glad to arrive in Rome and have all my Swiss francs pinched!! Brrrrr.

It is sweet of you to repeat you have not lost much by losing my tour, and it makes me feel a bit better – but I shall miss your lovely, lovely playing more than I can say – and I <u>do</u> hope to make it up to you very soon, and sing better than I ever have as well.

God bless love – look after yourself – and I hope our paths may cross sooner than we expect.

Much love to all my buddies there, and a whole heap for yourself from

Kaff

No.290 [Letter to Emmie Tillett]
24th September [1951]   2 Frognal Mansions, London NW3
My dear Emmie

I signed the enclosed cheque by mistake when it was given to me at the BBC in Edinburgh, so could I pass it on to you to cope mit, love?

<u>Belfast: 8th February 1952</u>

OH! for ever more!! I have not sung Dido before in Belfast, and if they look at their programmes they wouldn't get their facts wrong. I have sung Mad Bess – probably the first time they ever heard it, and it's worth hearing twice, otherwise there is no resemblance to the 1949 programme. Anyhow let's see if this will be Third Programme enough for them.

Die junge Nonne	Schubert
Lachen und Weinen	"
Suleika's zweiter Gesang	"
Ganymed	"
Der Musensohn	"
Poème de l'Amour et de la Mer	Chausson
Four Serious Songs	Brahms

Gerald suggested we do the Chausson sometime – it was originally piano, and it will be a lovely rest for me 'cos it's nearly <u>all</u> piano – only don't tell them!!

<u>Newcastle: January 17th</u>

Die junge Nonne	Schubert
Lachen und Weinen	"
Suleika	"
Ganymed	"
Der Musensohn	"
Frauenliebe und Leben	Schumann
Four Serious Songs	Brahms

<u>Skipton: January 27th</u>

Would you ask them if they would like *Frauenliebe und Leben* Schumann, which is eight songs. Would have to shorten the other groups or it really would go on all night!

Where'er you walk (*Semele*)	Handel
Like as the lovelorn turtle (*Atalanta*)	Handel
Dido's Lament (*Dido and Aeneas*)	Purcell
Mad Bess	Purcell
Ganymed	Schubert
Lachen und Weinen	"
Suleika's zweiter Gesang	"

Der Musensohn	Schubert
Frauenliebe und Leben	Schumann
Silent Noon	Vaughan Williams
The fairy lough	Stanford
Love is a bable	Parry
Kitty my love	arr. Hughes

Hope these several programmes straighten things out a bit.
Sincerely
Kathleen Ferrier

No.291 [Letter to Benita Cress]
24th September [19]51   2 Frognal Mansions, London NW3
Dearest Bonnie

Thank you for letters, postcards and snaps – the latter are splendid and it was grand to see you looking so fit and well. You sound to have had a wonderful holiday and it does my heart good – hope the home chores aren't going down too badly!

Edinburgh went well – Bruno was 'pickled tink' and said it was a privilege to work with me, which made music in my heart! The hall was full and sitting on the platform, and it was broadcast all over the place, so it was quite a strain – and I've never felt better since!

Had another X-ray last week and the doctor is very pleased, and I have finished my treatment at the hospital, which is a lovely thought – pets though they are! I hope it's for good. I'm putting on weight and getting so perky there's no holding me – but it's a lovely thought that I can have a complete rest until the New Year, even though it means not seeing my buddies in La Crosse. I'm even catching up on letters as you can see – have tidied my drawers – the first time in ten years!! – and have even had a bit of decorating done to cheer up the place. We're looking <u>fraight</u>fully posh now, old girl!

I had no idea the *Kindertotenlieder* were out – they aren't here – we're like the donkey's tail – always behind!!

Bernie is going everywhere with me at the moment and will go on the continent with me next year – getting so used to her, and being spoiled by her, should imagine I would go all prima donna and refuse to sing if she weren't there. I think she's an angel, but Doc Hilton calls her 'Jewel' – so you can guess how lucky I am. Will enclose a pitcher taken in hospital on my birthday – or have you had one already? Hope not.

We really are all right for things, love. I'll scream for help if we're short of anything – really. Thank you, thank you for all your offers of help. I would always turn to you if I needed it, because I know you would be faithfully there, bless you.

Much love to you and Bill and God bless, and thank you for everything.
Kathleen

No.292 [Letter to Emmie Tillett]
25th September [19]51   2 Frognal Mansions, London NW3
Dearest Emmie

Could you cope with the enclosed for me, love? And I have found a letter from Victor Olof in Vienna: quote:(!) "I have fixed the recording of *Das Lied* for May 12th-18th next year with the VPO. The Committee are delighted of the opportunity for a concert on the 18th with the general rehearsal on the 17th. Orchestral rehearsals will begin on the 12th so it will not be necessary, I don't suppose, for you to be there until the 14th. However Mr Hanyl (?) will discuss the details with Bruno in Lugano as he is going there to see him for his 75th birthday" – end quote.

Orl-rite love? Victor should be home tomorrow for just ten days, if you need to contact him.

I am up-to-date with my letters – it's the first time I ever remember it in the last ten years! It mikes yer fink!
Much love, sweetie pie!
Kaff

No.293 [incomplete letter to John Barbirolli]
4th Oct. 1951   In train [to Hanley]
... I think the old Chausson is growing a bit now, isn't it? I enjoyed it really for the first time last week and now feel I'm getting away from a *Messiah*-like sound. As for the banquet, luv!!! Well!! Words fail me. It <u>was</u> so good and so beautifully served – you're a ruddy wizard....

No.294 [Letter to Laura Cooper]
6.10.51   2 Frognal Mansions, London NW3
Dear Miss Cooper

How terribly kind of you to send me such lovely roses – they are making my room look quite beautiful.

I was away for a few days when they arrived last Mon or Tues but the care-taker of these flats had kept them and they were still very lovely dark red roses – but last night <u>another</u> bouquet was delivered from the shop, as they thought I would be disappointed to find a not so fresh bouquet!! What <u>have</u> you done to them? I've never heard of such a thing before – so now my room is more beau-tiful than ever with luscious fresh roses!

Thank you a thousand times for your great generosity and thoughtfulness. I am most touched by your kindness.

I am looking forward to a complete rest now until the New Year, and you will be glad to know that my last X-rays have pleased my d[octo]rs considerably – so what with one thing and another, I'm feeling very happy!
Thank you again for everything.
Very sincerely
Kathleen Ferrier

No.295 [Letter to Benita Cress]

27.10.51   2 Frognal Mansions, London NW3

Dearest Bonnie

Just a word in your ear of real thanks for the heavenly soap, which arrived this morning – bless you – it's a very special treat and a real luxury. You are a poppet of the first rank!

Thank you too for your letter last week with all its interesting chatter – your holiday sounded marvellous and I'm so glad you made the West Coast finally!

All's well here – I'm having a complete rest from singing and going gay a bit – to Covent Garden and theatres – first time in 10 yrs!

I hear there are all sorts of rumours about me there – originated from Edinburgh – Mr Mertens says. Between you and me, love, I think some of it comes from Ethel Bartlett – I may be wrong – but will you keep your pretty pink ears open – or perhaps just ask for news of me if given the chance – and tell me what she says? I'd like to be proved wrong, but have mi suspicions! There are malicious rumours going around – so don't let on you know me. Okeydoke? And don't believe any of the rumours – I'll let you know the truth, first thing – and at this moment I'm jes full o' beans!

God bless darlings – I'll write again soon.

Much love to you both

Kaff

No.296 [Letter to Emmie Tillett]

24th Nov. 1951   2 Frognal Mansions, London NW3

Dear Mrs Tillett

Re your letter of the 25th Oct., asking me to include another aria for Frankfurt. I could finish the group with 'Che faro senza Euridice' (*Orfeo* by Gluck), which would bring it up to the time required.

Here are some programmes.

Cleethorpes: Jan. 14th '52

Where'er you walk	*Semele*	Handel
Come to me soothing sleep	*Ottone*	Handel
Hark the ech'ing Air	*Fairie Queene*	Purcell
Mad Bess		Purcell arr. Britten
Gretchen am Spinnrade		Schubert
Heidenröslein		"
Suleika		"
Der Musensohn		"
Four Serious Songs		Brahms
Silent Noon		Vaughan Williams
The little road to Bethlehem		Michael Head
Pretty ring time		Peter Warlock
Kitty my love, will you marry me		Irish arr. Hughes

Carlisle: Jan. 19th 1952

Bist du bei mir		Bach
Like as the lovelorn turtle		Handel
Hark the ech'ing Air	*Fairie Queene*	Purcell

Mad Bess	Purcell arr. Britten
Frauenliebe und Leben	Schumann
Gretchen am Spinnrade	Schubert
Lachen und Weinen	"
Der Musensohn	"
Sonntag	Brahms
Botschaft	"
Ca' the yowes	Scottish arr. Jacobson
Blow the wind southerly	Northumbrian arr. Whittaker
The Keel row	"
Kitty my love	Irish arr. Hughes

If the Brahms Serious Songs are preferred, I can easily change the programme.

I will pass on a copy of the Chausson *Poème* today to Miss Hurst, who will be visiting us to see our offspring, one Miss Rose Ferramond! [a kitten; once again a fusion of surnames]

Sincerely

Kathleen Ferrier

No.297 [Letter to Walter Homburger]

Nov. 24th 1951   2 Frognal Mansions, London NW3

Dear Mr Homburger,

Thank you so much for your kind letter – I was so terribly sorry to let you down this year, and hope I may make up for it very soon. I am feeling heaps better, and having a real rest to give myself a chance – I must say it is a change to sit and do nothing, and my weight grows at an alarming pace!

I do hope all goes well for you, and send my very best wishes and renewed thanks for your kindness.

Yours sincerely,

Kathleen Ferrier

No.298 [Letter to Benita Cress]

24th Nov. 51   2 Frognal Mansions, London NW3

Dear Bonnie

Thank you so much for your letter with news of the Robertsons [Ethel Bartlett and Rae Robertson] – I had just wondered how much they were saying and with what detail! You're a wizard sleuth!

Thank you too for the parcel of lovely jam which arrived yesterday – one had bust, love, but three were fine except for a slight emission!!!!

We are really all right for food, duckie – meat is scarce and butter, but we have tins to carry us through, and we can always go out for a meal if we're really short. We are never hungry, and I'm gaining weight in an alarming manner – so you see!

I am just back from the frozen north, where I sang – in Manchester – at the opening of the new hall which was bombed in the war. The Queen was there to open it – looking delicious – and it was all very exciting. Sang 'Land of Hope and Glory' with orch. and choir and made 'em all cry – luvly!

After that, I met Bernie and we went to a friend's house in Yorkshire for three days. It was a good change but rather cold and it was lovely to get home again to mi little virgin couch! Not mention our sweet Rose – who was much too busy gnawing a rabbit's carcass to take much notice of us!

We are painting tomorrow – then Gerald Moore and his wife are coming up for a meal – so it should be a riotous evening – they're poppets!

It's lousy weather – gales, wet, fog and cold – so it is lovely to be in with a good fire. We have enough coal to last us quite a bit, and we are making the most of it.

Am doing some more recording next week – folk songs etc., so I'll let you know when they might be out. Must start doing some mee-mees to prepare for it! 'S'nuisance – am well content to be lazy and not sing!

Thank you again for sending such a lovely parcel – look after yourselves, love, and we'll be writing again.
Much love from us both
From
Kathleen

No.299 [incomplete letter to George Ferrier]
24th Nov. [19]51   2 Frognal Mansions, London NW3
My dear Uncle George
      Thank you so much for your long interesting letter. I'm so glad you enjoyed the broadcast – it was a great thrill to be there and a memorable occasion. The Queen looked lovely – she is a gracious lady – and clapped like billyo at the end. It is more frightening to sing just once, than to do a whole recital, and I was glad when it was safely over! Barbirolli said he was so moved he wanted to cry, and he knew it would put me off if he did so he scowled at the violas instead! He is a love and a wonderful musician.

It is grand to know that you are both so well, and that Margaret [Duerden née Ferrier] is recovered from her illness [pneumonia] – it's a miserable business – I had it in Aberdeen seven years ago.

It was grand to see Dorothy [Atkinson née Ferrier] in Nottingham a little while ago – she and George looked flourishing, and we did enjoy the pies that arrived the next morning!

Win is fine and loving her new job – she seems to have taken on a new lease of life. Bernie – my New Zealand girl – is a jewel, and spoils me to death – it's lovely!

I am having a real rest now instead of going to America – it was to be a strenuous tour so I cancelled it – and I am sitting at home for a bit, and it's gorgeous....

No.300 [incomplete letter to John Barbirolli, written after she sang 'Land of Hope and Glory' at the re-opening of the Free Trade Hall, Manchester on Friday afternoon 16th November. She then spent the weekend with the Barbirollis]
[?24th November 1951]   [2 Frognal Mansions. London NW3]
... It has been a memorable and very moving one for me, and I have never been so proud to take a small part in your concert and triumph and to see, although I know it already, the love and respect Mancunians have for you – they BETTER

HAD! ... The run round Cheshire was an eye-opener and a delight on Sunday [18th November]; and as for Sunday evening – what fun, what food, what <u>festa</u>! ... It has been a memorable and most lovely few days, and I have saved some of the heather and rose petals of my posy to keep and gloat over in my old age! ...

No.301 [incomplete letter to John Barbirolli. Kathleen withdrew for health reasons from the *Messiah* in Sheffield and sent a good luck message on the day of the performance, for this was the first time Barbirolli had conducted the oratorio].
[8th December 1951]   [2 Frognal Mansions. London NW3]
... I am thinking of you so much today and wishing you well for your first ever *Messiah*. I only wish I could be there to share in your triumph, as I know it is sure to be – I think Mr Handel will revolve in pride and peace tonight instead of whizzing round in bewilderment at the strange things done to his heart's outpouring! ...

No.302 [Letter to Benita Cress from Bernie Hammond]
29th December 1951   Hampstead
Dear Mrs Cress
    Is your second name Santa Claus? I am sure there have been extra ships to carry all those parcels, and they have been appreciated by us both, and Rosey is delighted with her cat food, and we had great fun with the gay Xmas candles. We have had a wonderful Xmas. Kath is brimming over with health and spirits, and it is grand to see her old vitality back again. As I write this, we are both in front of a large fire, having eaten a good meal. Kath is busy cracking an inexhaustible supply of nuts, and Rosey has her own chair as she says it is very draughty on the floor! We did not have any snow this Xmas, in fact it has been very mild and I expect we will "get it in the neck" very soon.
    On Xmas Eve we were out for dinner and it was Xmas Day by the time we got back, so Kath and I lit a fire and opened our presents. Thank you very, very much for the nylons and pretty Xmas card – the nylons are a great thrill and I washed them to wear on Xmas Day! We left early and went down to our friend Emmie Tillett (I nursed her darling mother for over a year and that's how I met Kath). We opened more presents around a little tree with the air filled with screams of delight and then settled down to four hours painting, and then had a large dinner at night – turkey and all the trimmings and a wonderful Xmas pudding with brandy sauce.
    Boxing night Kath had a party here, about 14 people, and as you can imagine we had quite a busy time preparing everything. Kath is an excellent cook and her mince pies and tarts were a treat, also her scones and sponge cakes. Your packets of cakes look very interesting by the way, and I am longing to try one. I had a Xmas cake sent to me from N[ew] Z[ealand], and we iced it and put some decorations on it, and put it on a table with your candles in dishes all around it. The assembled company gasped with delight and it certainly looked "proper pretty". Gerald Moore was at the party and most entertaining he was too. Kath and I staggered into bed at 1.30, but she was not at all tired the next day.

Kath sends her best love. She will be writing to you shortly.
A thousand thanks and again my best, best love
Bernie

No.303 [Letter to Benita and Bill Cress]
29th Dec 51 Saturday   2 Frognal Mansions, London NW3
Dearest Bonnie and Bill

The MARVELLOUS wallet has just this minute arrived, and I can't tell you what pleasure it has given me already. It IS beautiful and I am proud of it, and will treasure it for many years to come – thank you, thank you, thank you for all your sweet kindness and generosity. I am thrilled with it and think it is most beautifully made and arranged. I SHALL swank with it, bless you! Various wondrous parcels have arrived too, and I just have no words to thank you for all the trouble you have taken to pick out such luscious items – our store cupboard is well filled, and I am putting on weight all the time, much to everyone's delight! Thank you for everything, loves – you are 'woody blunders' – I am just wordless at your faithful, generous friendship. Thank you, thank you a thousand times.

We have had a grand Christmas. Bernie, Win (sister) and I went to Mrs Tillett's on Xmas day – opened presents and gave some – and painted a pheasant as being in the Xmas spirit! Had a light lunch and we went across to my doctor's for tea – played Lexicon with them and the daughter and friends and the first word I achieved was 'urine'! Klever Kaff!! Couldn't miss putting that down however polite the company! Back to our painting and a dinner of turkey and plum pudd! – a bit of orl rite!

Bernie and I had a few friends in the next night – including Gerald Moore and his wife, and my teacher – Roy Henderson – Norman Allin, a wonderful bass singer – now 60 something and a darling – and we opened some tins of meat and salad and I made some wizard mince pies and sponge cakes and we had a 'right good do' helped along with a drop of champagne! One of the best Xmas[es] I remember, and the end of this year in sight too.

I start again on Jan 7th with the Four Serious Songs in the Albert Hall with Malcolm Sargent conducting – and from then on I am very busy. But I have had a wonderful rest and it has been heavenly to be at home for so long.

Sir John Barbirolli came up the other night and brought his cello – he was a prodigy before he started conducting – and we went through several sonatas and pieces and had a wonderful time. I adore accompanying and he loves playing, so we were very pleased with ourselves!

And now, darlings, thank you again for everything.
God bless you and so much love and luck for the New Year,
from a very grateful
KAFF

No.304 [Letter to Emmie Tillett]
31.12.51   2 Frognal Mansions, London NW3
My dear Emmie

Can you have a look at the Promotion of New Music letter for me and advise me as to reply thereto???? Ta ever so! Also this letter from Vienna is just a corroboration of the arrangements made with Bruno Walter. I haven't replied yet, as I thought you would want to see it first as no fee is mentioned, but I suppose it is all right?

Have replied to Mr Sykes saying you arrange all my work and that you will contact him. O.K.?

Yours etc.

Kathleen Ferrier

No.305 [undated incomplete letter to a member of staff at Ibbs and Tillett, probably Sadie Lereculey]

Would you pass on a message to Mrs Tillett re Berne 23rd Feb 1952. Here is programme I suggest:

Dearest consort	Handel
Hark the ech'ing air	Purcell
Che faro	Gluck
Alto Rhapsody	Brahms

I have my own parts for the first group. If they insist on two Handels instead of Handel and Purcell, I can sing 'Where'er you walk' and then 'Dearest consort' and 'Che faro', but the first is more varied.

I think that is all, isn't it? It was grand to see you all today – bless you for everything!

Love

Kathleen

6   Letters: 1952

Kathleen's Christmas 1951 was, in her own words, 'one of the best I remember' because she was at home, surrounded by her sister and her closest friends. She continued to be indomitably optimistic about her cancer throughout 1952, even describing the result of an X-ray in February as 'perfect' despite the fact that more treatment was required and she was immediately compelled to cancel all her singing engagements forthwith, including a trip to France, Switzerland and Germany. Her voice was silent, in public at least, until the end of March but, rather than feel sorry for herself, she diverted the sympathy she received from her friends to the Royal family when King George VI died in February. On the other hand, she became very depressed when she heard that her cellist friend Kathleen Moorhouse had died from breast cancer, having had the same mastectomy operation Ferrier herself had had a year before. Typically she revived her spirits by promptly taking up gardening and put in bedding plants, despite the minuscule patch of earth behind No.2 Frognal Mansions which passed for a garden. Sure enough, later in the summer, she had reason to boast to John Newmark of her achievements in horticulture.

January and the first half of February had been taken up with engagements around Britain, ending with the first London performance of Benjamin Britten's Canticle *Abraham and Isaac* at the Victoria and Albert Museum on 3rd February after its premiere a fortnight earlier on 21st January in the Albert Hall, Nottingham. The work was recorded at Maida Vale the next day, but its broadcast on 6th February had to be postponed because the King had died in his sleep during the previous night.

In her diaries Kathleen usually placed a tick against an engagement's venue implying that she had received her fee. When she sang Brahms, Gluck ('Che faro' – what else?) and Bach with the London Philharmonic Orchestra under Sir Adrian Boult at the Festival Hall on 25th March, it was after her absence of five weeks, and the tick against this entry has a defiant ring of 'I'm back!'

Unlike the *Messiah*, which she sang mostly at Christmas but also at Easter, the *St Matthew Passion* was clearly reserved for the Easter period, often, as it was in 1952, with an all-day performance on Passion Sunday (30th March). Her return to the concert platform and radio or recording studios was marked by a Brahms recital and what she described as 'two newish works', *Four Poems of St Teresa* by Lennox Berkeley and *The Enchantress* by Sir Arthur Bliss. These she premiered at the Royal Festival Hall, London, with the London Symphony Orchestra under Hugo Rignold on Palm Sunday (6th April), their first hearing having been a BBC studio broadcast from Manchester on 2nd October 1951. Then she travelled north for Hallé concerts with Barbirolli, once more in her element singing her favourites, *Dream of Gerontius*, *Messiah* and *Das Lied von der Erde*. She still considered herself to be 'Lucky Kaff'.

While in Manchester, Barbirolli expressed his concerns about her health to Bernie Hammond and Winifred. It was now a year on from her mastectomy and yet she continued to suffer chest and back pains. The question of obtaining a second opinion was discussed, though which of the three of them would broach the matter with Kathleen was uncertain. Although Barbirolli was deputed to do so when Kathleen returned north on 19th April, once back in London the 'plot' was accidentally revealed by Bernie. Kathleen was furious and had a row with Winifred (16th April) because she not only feared her doctors might refuse further treatment if she went elsewhere, but more importantly she did not wish to offend her doctor, Reginald Hilton. Her fears were allayed however when he himself encouraged her to do so. Her hospital appointments became more frequent during the last few days of April, as if to underline the concerns of those closest to her, and she consulted the surgeon Sir Stanford Cade on 7th May. The eventual outcome was to continue with doses of radiation. Cade must have been surprised to learn that after their appointment at 10 o'clock in the morning, she would be on the 11.45 train from Euston to Hanley in the Potteries for a 4 o'clock rehearsal of *Das Lied von der Erde*, followed by a performance with Barbirolli that night. A year earlier she had travelled to Liverpool straight from a third consecutive morning of radiation treatment from Dr Gwen Hilton. Whenever possible, she made absolutely no concessions to her schedule.

Similarly, despite a hospital appointment on the afternoon of 12th May, she was on a plane the following day, for what was to prove to be her last trip abroad, when she flew to Vienna to record *Das Lied von der Erde* with Bruno Walter. To put this collaboration on disc had long been their mutual wish, but contractual wrangling between their respective record companies, Decca (Ferrier) and Columbia (Walter), had always got in the way. Now at last, and not a moment too soon as it turned out, they would make what would be a legendary benchmark recording. As a filler for the fourth side of the two-record set, she recorded three of the five *Rückert Lieder* on 20th May, but this was a bad day and she was in great pain when she awoke that morning. Back in Britain she went to Newcastle to sing Chausson's *Poème* with Barbirolli on Sunday 25th May. Three days later Sargent conducted her in Britten's *Spring* symphony at the Festival Hall, then came a few recitals, the last one being for the BBC on 5th June, followed by a planned summer break from singing until the end of August, when she returned for the last time to Edinburgh. She took her holidays, first at Britten's Aldeburgh Festival, during which the composer persuaded her to sing *Abraham and Isaac* once more (19th June), and then in Cornwall with Win, Emmie and Bernie. Fortunately it was a good summer and the warm sun did her good. After her return (12th July) she spent some days at the luxurious Hertfordshire home of a friend, Burnet Pavitt, whose neighbour at St Paul's Walden Bury was David Bowes-Lyon, brother of Queen Elizabeth, who had now become the Queen Mother. At the time Kathleen was there, the new Queen happened to be visiting her uncle and so an informal soirée was organised on 19th July at which she sang.

At the end of July, Barbirolli proposed that instead of concert performances of *Orfeo*, he wanted to stage it for Kathleen at Covent Garden the following February. David Webster, General Administrator at the Royal Opera House, readily agreed and put aside four nights at the beginning of that month. Meanwhile the three of them decided collectively to write a new English translation, and Kathleen began work on it at once, collaborating with Barbirolli whenever he could visit her in London. Then, on Sunday 24th August, she went north to Edinburgh for the last time. This year there was no Bruno Walter, for on 21st May he and Kathleen had parted forever on the tarmac of Zurich airport, where they had both changed planes en route to their respective destinations after recording in Vienna. However, she did sing *Das Lied von der Erde* again, this time under Eduard van Beinum conducting the Concertgebouw Orchestra, with the tenor Julius Patzak, her co-soloist in Vienna in May, rejoining her in the Scottish capital. It was a busy Festival for her, not only *Gerontius* and *Messiah* (with Barbirolli) but also as one of the quartet of singers in Brahms' *Liebeslieder Walzer*, among whom was the young soprano Irmgard Seefried. She and her German compatriot, the baritone Dietrich Fischer-Dieskau (also in Edinburgh that year) were much admired by Kathleen as two of the up-and-coming genera-tion of new singers to look out for.

For the rest of the year Kathleen had a modest amount of concert and recital work around the country, generally in the larger towns and cities, singing Handel, Brahms, Mahler, Elgar with orchestra and some recitals accompanied by Gerald Moore. One engagement was a performance of *Dream of Gerontius*, which she gave at Hereford Cathedral on 11th September 1952. The conductor was the cathedral organist Meredith Davies who, in 1988, recalled his meeting with Kathleen in a letter to the tenor Charles Corp.

When Mrs Tillett suggested that Kathleen Ferrier might be able to sing *Gerontius* at the 1952 Three Choirs Festival, she warned me that rehearsal time would have to be limited, but of course I gladly accepted, even though I had not conducted the work before – or very much else for that matter! In the event there was no rehearsal at all, not even with a piano: Kathleen had not sung a note to me before the performance. We had met a week or so before [in fact it was a month earlier on 8th August – see her diary], over a cup of tea in Emmie Tillett's house, and she simply filled me with confidence that it was all going to be alright, and that I could manage. She was so friendly, kind and calm that it would have been churlish to have misgivings. I remember two points she made – that she would like enough time to sing 'beasts' in the phrase 'like beasts of prey' [Part 2, one bar before fig.42], and that the phrase 'cherish a wish which ought not to be wished' [Part 2, three bars before fig.20] was not the easiest to sing musically! I may have asked her about one or two other places, but certainly our conversation about the music was brief. I think she knew (as I have learned since) that discussing details of performance intentions can be dangerously misleading. Her approach was entirely right; at the performance she radiated calm assurance, and with relief I realised that so unwavering and certain was her sense of direction that I could relax and follow instinctively. From the moment she came onstage (dressed in white) she held the packed Cathedral spellbound – including me. I am sorry I can't give a more detailed account musically. I don't think we realised quite how ill she was (and certainly she concealed it), but we knew we should spare her as much as possible, so that my actual contact with her was minimal, but unforgettable.

There was a brief trip to Dublin in October with the Hallé, and early in the same month she made what was to be her last commercial recording. This was of arias by Bach and Handel with Boult conducting because Barbirolli could not get a release from EMI. The sessions lasted two days, 7th and 8th October, and the producer, John Culshaw, recalled in his autobiography that on the second day Kathleen took a telephone call from University College Hospital to get the results of more tests made a few days earlier. 'They say I'm all right, luv,' she smiled. 'They've just phoned to say I'm all right.' The date was 8th October 1952, exactly that of her death one year later. Inevitably this was a period in which, as Benjamin Britten put it 'everything she did had a more than usual significance', considering what, in retrospect, turned out to be last appearances at certain venues or singing certain works, such as *Das Lied von der Erde* at the Festival Hall on 23rd November under Josef Krips. On the other hand, that very month she made her *first* appearance at the Hall as a recitalist (with Gerald Moore) in a series promoted by the Philharmonia Concert Society. It was standard Ferrier fare, proceeding from the Baroque to English folksongs via Schumann and Brahms and all the critics were favourable but for Neville Cardus, who, in the *Manchester Guardian*, picked on what he considered to be distracting mannerisms such as smiles, hand movements and swaying of the head. Kathleen wrote him a dignified response.

Her last visit to Carlisle took place on 8th December and she stayed with her old friend, the soprano Ena Mitchell. Her last *Messiah* was on the 23rd at the BBC for a broadcast from its Maida Vale Studio. Meanwhile first rehearsals for *Orpheus* were beginning at Covent Garden. Kathleen's last Christmas was spent quietly with friends. On Christmas Day Myra Hess came to tea, while dinner was with Emmie Tillett. On Boxing Day and again on New Year's Eve, Kathleen was with Barbirolli and his wife at his mother's house in Streatham, South London. By now it was in the full knowledge that from the following day she would be Kathleen Ferrier CBE.

No.306 [Letter to John Newmark]

28.1.52   In train [from Skipton, Yorkshire to London]

Dearest Johnny

I have been an age replying, but I have just started work again – with a heavy programme – 9 recitals in two weeks – so have been concentrating on those – thereby neglecting you which is shameful. Have had some with Gerald M. and some with Ben and Peter P. – Ben wrote a new Canticle for the two of us on the Biblical story of Abraham and Isaac – the ink was still wet for the 1st performance! But it's a sweet piece – simple and very moving.

It's heaven to be going home! We have just been having a very cold spell of frost and snow, and the coal shortage is rather serious, and I haven't been warm for a week – the hotels have been nearly all unheated in the bedrooms, but I seem to have weathered it all right. Our plumbing is the worst in the world – it's much colder inside than out!!

Now to answer your questions: I have said I am having June, July and August off, and don't want to go back on that, as I have already turned so much work down, and I think it is wise to go carefully for this year. I am having Gerald exclusively now to save as much effort as possible, and it would be a bit difficult to change over – much as I would adore you to play for me. The only thing might be recording – and I will ask Victor Olof when I see him – I have several dates to record, but all orchestral at the moment.

I still have money of yours – I forget the exact amount as it is in my last year's diary – but it won't go far here – but it's waiting for you anytime you can get here. I have cancelled a trip to France, Switzerland and Germany because it was going to be too heavy (February and March) but I am perfectly all right – but my Dr wants me to stay in England as much as possible so that he can keep an eye on me. I go to Vienna in May to record *Das Lied* with Bruno Walter, but shall only be away just over a week. I am feeling fine and very perky, and am fair, fat and forty (nearly!)

I had a wonderful parcel from Ethelwyn, bless her, and I yearn to see you all. It would be <u>wonderful</u> to see you here – I just don't want to hold out hope of work and perhaps let you down <u>again</u>.

Have quite a few more masterpieces in oil – mostly 'Stilles Leben' of food and drink! Very photographic and not your style at all – but it <u>is</u> fun! Have been accompanying a lot for fun – Barbirolli on his cello – Evelyn – his wife – oboe and the Doc – fiddle – heaven!

Write again love – it's wonderful to hear from you. Much love to Paul and Eric and buckets for you – <u>do</u> hope you are well. I'M FINE!

God bless, sweetie

Love

Kaff

No.307 [Letter to Margot Rigg]

28.1.52   In the train [from Skipton, Yorkshire to London]

Dear Margot Rigg

Thank you so very much for your <u>most lovely</u> flowers – you had chosen all my first favourites! It was most kind of you to think of it, and I appreciate it more than I can say.

I am only sorry you couldn't get to the concert [Birmingham 22nd January], so that I could have thanked you in person. I took them on to Liverpool [24th January] with me, and they made my hotel room look really spring-like. Thank you again most sincerely.

I do hope you are well and happy in Birmingham, and send my best wishes to you and to your father and mother when next you write.

With kind greetings

Sincerely

Kathleen Ferrier

No.308 [incomplete letter to Benita Cress]

28th January 1952   [In train, from Skipton, Yorkshire to London]

... I have just done my first work since Edinburgh, nine recitals in two weeks, and I have weathered the storm well.

For some concerts I have been with Gerald Moore, who is an angel, and Benjamin Britten and Peter Pears for others. They've all gone well and I have been spoiled to death by them. Now I'm almost home again. Look after yourself and don't worry about those extra pounds as long as you are well – that's what matters! ...

No.309 [Letter to Peter Diamand]

1.2.52   2 Frognal Mansions, London NW3

Dearest Peter

Thank you for long letter – it's always lovely to hear from you. What a cafuffle you have been having – these people can't seem to realise that but for you, we probably wouldn't come half so often to Holland, and that other countrys [*sic*] don't get the chance or the opportunity to have us as often as they would wish. Heigh-ho! I suppose these things are always bound to happen, but they'll come round to know your value my sweet, the stupid asses!

I have been chased by the *Express* reporter once after concert – I was in bed, and it was before I received your letter – and I said nothing about it, but that I wasn't going to Holland this year. But if it comes up again, I will stick to your story. (The reporter didn't see me in bed! – I relayed the messages via Bernie – it was after a concert – 11.40 at night!!) (B's <u>such</u> a spoilsport!!!!!)

The Canticle is a pet – I think you would love it – very simple and moving – I cried all the way to Ald[e]burgh in the train learning it – but I have recovered now!

I am fine – the Doc has just been up and is very pleased mit mir – have just done ten concerts in about 18 days in different cities, and despite excruciating cold, have survived and enjoyed it.

Was playing trios last night with John and Evelyn Barbirolli – piano, cello and oboe – heaven! I <u>did</u> enjoy myself and I think they did too.

Ben and Peter are coming up to rehearse here tomorrow and we're at the Vic and Albert on Sunday – I hear it's packed out so that's nice. Wish you could be here for it!

Much, much love to you all and God bless you – come and see us soon.

Buckets, baths and oceans of love from Kaff

No.310 [Letter to Benjamin Britten]

12.2.52   2 Frognal Mansions, London NW3

Dearest Ben

It was so lovely having concerts with you and Peter, and I felt renewed and refreshed by them and not a bit weary – (as I feared I might do after such a long rest, being a lady of leisure instead of a busy 'low singer'!) Thank you so much for everything, and for spoiling me so – I <u>did</u> love it.

Bernie and I would love to come to Aldborough whilst the festival is on – and I would love to sing in the Canticle again if it would fit in to your programme.

We don't want to bother you with housing us when you are so busy, but would adore to stay at the hotel you said was so good, and be able to see you occasionally. Do you think they might have room for us – either two singles or a double-bedded one? I don't know its name – could you be an angel and send me its title, also the dates of the festival? Just a p.c. when you can find a minute to spare, then I can write and ask them to reserve a corner for us.

We would bring our paints and try to follow on and improve on the schools of Cotman and Constable!!

My heart bleeds for our royal family, doesn't yours? I think it is cruel that they should have to suffer these traditional mournings – poor sweet darlings.

I hope you are both thriving and that Rhyl was a wow, and that you weren't put in a boarding house like I was last time, with the last meal at five and a plug that wouldn't pull!

Much love to you both, and hope to see you in June if not before – whoopee!
Kaff

No.311 [Letter to Laura Cooper]

14.2.52   2 Frognal Mansions, London NW3
Dear Miss Cooper

Thank you very much for your letter. I have started working again now, and have enjoyed being busy and all the concerts seemed to go well.

Your tour here sounds as though it should be great fun, and I hope it will be a memorable one for you.

I am having three months off in the summer – June, July and August – so I am afraid you won't be able to hear me sing in person – I am so sorry – but I usually try to do this as the rest of the season is so hectic, and the money only goes to the government anyway!

I have no plans for a visit to America at the moment, but I hope it won't be too long delayed, as I enjoy it so much, and have been so spoiled there!
My best wishes to you and a very happy year.
Yours very sincerely
Kathleen Ferrier

No.312 [Letter to Benita Cress]

[begun] 19th Feb.52 [finished 2nd March]
Oh! you angel face!!!!

And that is as far as I got and now it's March 2nd – it is amazing how the tempus fugits when doing nothing! Thank you, thank you, thank you, for two most beautiful presents. They are gorgeous – so lovely and long, and don't cut my fat calves in half! They're wonderful – bless you – and such a lovely colour. I was thrilled to receive them –thank you again.

It is lovely to be at home, and I have been taking life easily and very lazily – staying in bed in a morning – napping in the afternoon, and several times going gay at night, which has been a nice change for me. Haven't sung a note for ages but have been playing chamber music with a friend of Myra Hess and with Barbirolli and his wife – they are cello and oboe respectively – and I tinkle on the joanna – and also with my doctor who scrapes along on a Stradivarius fiddle! I love accompanying but ordinarily don't have much time.

Have been dining and to the theatre (*King Lear*) with Hamish Hamilton (publisher) and his wife. They know many interesting people, so it is always fun. I generally sing when I go there, but it's always after food and much drink, so I don't mind!

Last Saturday Sir John Barbirolli and I were shown round Lincoln's Inn – the famous law buildings – and then went on to his mother's house, where she cooked us a southern fried chicken – oh boy! it melted in the mouth.

My doctor still comes regularly, but really only so that I will accompany him on his Strad, more than to examine me! I go to the hospital at intervals so that they can keep an eye on me, and apart from rheumatiz in my back, feel okey-doke.

Kathleen Mary looks divine, and must be a great joy to you! I don't know if I should, but I feel very flattered at the names she bears. They are lovely photographs, and she is the bonniest thing. Lucky Kathleen Mary! As I sit at my desk, I can just picture your sweet house, and the cardinals peeping in at the windows, and feel the new blanket on my bed, and the warmth of your welcome – these things I always remember with gratitude. Bless you for everything.

I start working again on the 25th Mar[ch], so have a little time yet to be idle. I'm very lazy at heart!

Look after yourselves and much love

Kaff

No.313 [Letter to John Newmark]

4.4.52   2 Frognal Mansions, London NW3

Dearest Johnny

What a lovely letter – and I had no idea about the French award!! Pon mi soul! I always thought we were a bit of orlrite! Well! Well! If I get a medal and you don't, I shall split it in half with mi false denture and send it at once – then when I sing flat, or you play a wrong note, each half will jingle! Heigh-ho! How <u>very</u> nice.

We had Ethelwyn up here yesterday for lunch and tea, and had much to talk about. I am so glad you have been busy – she says you are playing better than ever, though I should hardly have thought this possible, and that you are looking better too. Klever Johnny! That's the stuff.

I have had six weeks off and have been very lazy. I had to have a bit more treatment on my back, and it's ached like heck in this cold weather, but is better again now, and I feel fine in miself. Started again last week with Sir Adrian Boult in the Brahms Alto Rhap. 'Che faro' and 'Schlage doch, gewünschte Stunde', and had lovely notices – then the *St Matthew Passion* all day Sunday – a Brahms recital two nights ago on the radio, and on Sunday with the London Symphony Orchestra two newish works – *Four Hymns of St Theresa* by Lennox Berkeley and *The Enchantress* by Sir Arthur Bliss. Then Bernie and I go off to the north for lots of Hallé concerts with Barbirolli, which I always adore – *Gerontius* – the *Messiah* and *Das Lied von der Erde*. Lucky Kaff.

On April 30th I have been asked to sing at a little private party for the

Queen Mother and Princess Margaret, and am tickled pink. They are evidently, and obviously, very sad and heartbroken by the death of the King, and it was suggested by one of their ladies that they had a little 'do', and I am told they have cheered up considerably at the idea – so ain't that nice. I won't have to sing 'Oh I wish I were a fascinating bitch' or anything too sad, but guess I can hit a happy medium. I am thrilled – they're such dears.

Did I tell you Win had changed jobs from teaching to dress designing, and is having the time of her life? She is in Paris at the moment studying all the models etc. It has taken 20 years off her life, and I have never seen her look so perky. Good for her. I think it takes a lot of courage to give up a steady, pensionable job at her age, don't you? I'm so pleased it has turned out so well, and she is getting more money to learn the job than she did as a headmistress. Such is life!

Bernie is angelic! She thinks of everything, and I am ruined – oh I enjoy it.

Gerald Moore tells me that Fischer-Dieskau is a superb singer – I certainly hope you will play for him e'er long.

It is lovely to know your bank balance is looking healthier – I still have twenty-three pounds five shillings of yours. I can always let you have it through Andre Mertens if you need it.

That's all for now, sweetie. I would let you know if there were any possibility of work here, but I am not very hopeful at the moment. It would be heavenly to see you.

Meanwhile look after yourself – bless you for lovely letters – and God bless.
With love always
Kaff

No.314 [Letter to Laura Cooper]
8th April 52   2 Frognal Mansions, London NW3
Dear Miss Cooper

Thank you very much for your kind letter. I hope you may be able to get to Edinburgh as it is a lovely festival.

I shall be away June and most of July in Suffolk and Cornwall, but if you ring me – HAMpstead 2108 – towards the end of June, perhaps we may be able to arrange a meeting. I hope you have a wonderful trip.
With best wishes
Sincerely
Kathleen Ferrier

No.315 [incomplete letter to Benita Cress]
8th June 1952   [2 Frognal Mansions, London NW3]
... Now I'm free till Edinburgh, 26th August, and it feels wonderful! I'm going to Ald[e]burgh and Cornwall for a month. Whoopee!

I am feeling heaps better this month with the warmer weather and the doctor's very pleased mit mir. But for twelve months at least I shan't be leaving this country, so that if I need more treatment I shall be on the spot. It's not the singing that's wearying, it's the travelling and social side, and I'm doing so well that it seems potty to overdo, eh? So I shall work gently here and give a little less to the government! There's great excitement at No.2 – Bernie's mamma arrived from New Zealand yesterday – by air – her first flight, and came off fresh as a flea – she is just trying to catch up on sleep now – not having had much for four nights so – Bernie's cup is very full – she hasn't seen her for four and a half years. 'S'long time, ain't it?

Have just made another LP record – folksongs on one side – on the other Roger Quilter songs and arrangements of 'Drink to me only', 'Ye Banks and Braes!' etc. Hope you approve....

No.316 [Postcard to Win]
Wed.[nesday 18th June 1952]   [Aldeburgh]
Being very spoilt here – and feeling fine. Hotel is marvellous – with good food galore. Ben saved me tickets for anything – lecture or concert I like – so am fully occupied. All mi buddies here – couldn't be nicer. Even got mi nose brown! See you soon – whoopee!
Much love
Kaff

No.317 [Letter to Benjamin Britten]
Saturday [?21st June 1952]   [2 Frognal Mansions, London NW3]
Dearest Ben
This is just to say a sincere thank you to you and Peter and Barbara [Britten's sister] for the most wonderful holiday ever. Every minute was sheer joy, and I only wish words came more easily to me to say what I really feel. It was so lovely, and I can't think of one part being lovelier than another – it was all so happy. Thank you very much indeed for asking me – I feel rejuvenated! I hope your 'innards' are behaving, love – I thought they were rather leading you a dance on Friday morning.

My journey was peaceful and uneventful, and I even secured a taxi – with my records intact – by keeping my left arm straight and my head down and shouting 'Fore' at intervals!

I have just been delving into all the Purcell, and having a wonderful time!
Bless you for everything. It was just perfect.
My love to you all and deep gratitude.
Kathleen

No.318 [Letter to Mrs van Hessen-Kattenburg, Holland]
29th June '52   [*Budock Vean* Hotel, Falmouth, South Cornwall]
Dear Mrs Hessen-Kattenburg
Thank you very much for your kind letter. I was in Holland for last year's festival, but haven't toured abroad since because of illness. I am just working in this country for the next twelve months, and taking life a little easier.

I haven't recorded the Bach Mass arias yet – but have taken part in a Decca recording of the *St Matthew Passion*. I have also recorded for Columbia the *Kindertotenlieder* of Mahler with Bruno Walter – also just recently *Das Lied von der Erde* – this won't be out until about Sept and America should have it first (Decca).

There are also folk songs and Roger Quilter songs on Decca long playing, and

Vier ernste Gesänge and *Frauenliebe und Leben* – also Decca L.P. All these you should be able to get in America. I hope you have a lovely time there, and thank you again for your kind enquiries.

Yours sincerely
Kathleen Ferrier

No.319 [Letter to Brigadier H A F Crewdson, London WC2]
June 29th 1952   *Budock Vean* Hotel, Falmouth, South Cornwall
Dear Sir

Thank you very much for your kind invitation for the 8th July next.

I am so sorry I shall be unable to attend, as I shall be still here on holiday.

With renewed thanks
Yours sincerely
Kathleen Ferrier

No.320 [Letter to Harry Vincent]
21.7.52   2 Frognal Mansions, London NW3
My dear Harry

Thank you very much for your letter. I am just home from my holiday, and feeling full of beans.

You <u>are</u> going to be grand when all your decorations are finished – I think you'll find it's worth all the mess!

I do hope Kathleen Mary is feeling better now, and that she had only a temporary indisposition.

Now about this autumn and winter. I think if you don't mind, I'll have a rest from another recital just at the moment. I have a few already booked for various places, but I am asking Emmie only to book oratorio for a bit, as it is not such an exhausting business, and then I can go on just easily singing things I know without taking on too much.

I would love to do another one for you – you know how I love coming to Hanley – and if you'll ask me again next season I would love it.

I am feeling heaps better, and have a rest from the hospital for a bit now, so I'm just going canny for a bit and not tempting providence too much! I know you'll understand.

I saw Mr Harvey (?) last time I was in Hanley, and he asked me how my Camilla china was – so I admitted to some breakages. He said he could get me some more, tho' he had left the factory, but I didn't want to ask him without first mentioning it to you. But if there were a possibility of getting half a dozen cups and saucers it would be heavenly. But I want to pay for them and I don't want to get anyone in trouble. Okeydoke?

I hope Madge is well and enjoying her new fireplace and I send my fondest love to you all.

Bernie is still a jewel and her Mum is here at the moment.

Much love
Kathleen

No.321 [Letter to Mrs Heidrich]

22.7.52   2 Frognal Mansions, London NW3

Dear Mrs Heidrich

This is just a very small 'thank you' from Bernie and me for our <u>perfect</u> weekend.

We are both still up in the clouds from the loveliness of it all, and just cannot thank you enough for all you did to make it so.

Thank you with all my heart – it was a memorable weekend.

With all good wishes

Affectionately

Kathleen Ferrier

No.322 [Letter to Emmie Tillett]

22.7.52   2 Frognal Mansions, London NW3

My dear Emmie

Here are a whole lot of bad-to-decipher letters. The ones with 'write Ibbs and Tillett' on have been answered by Bernie. Could you make excuses for me on grounds of not accepting recitals at the moment or sump'n? And if you could have the Hanzl letter deciphered, that would be a help. It might contain a most interesting proposal – I should hate to miss that!!

The rest are signed contracts, and I am working on programmes at the moment and will let you have them in a day or two. Okeydoke?

Luv

KAFF

P.S. Re my relations – see United Appeal – no Mildreds in our family – only Fannys and Nancys!

No.323 [Letter to Harry Vincent]

1st August '52   2 Frognal Mansions, London NW3

My dear Harry

Out of the blue this morning came six cups and saucers from Mr Harvey! He must have looked up the name of them as I couldn't recall it when I met him, and he's had them done for me somehow, as they are not now on the market!

I thought he was waiting for me to let him know name and shape, but he evidently went ahead, and here they are – so I'm all complete once more and very thrilled. Thought I'd better let you know, as I had told you about it in my letter, and don't want you to go to any trouble for me, unnecessarily. Do hope Kathleen Mary is quite all right again now, and send much love to you all. I'm fine – fingers crossed! God bless

Love

Kathleen

No.324 [Letter to John Newmark]

August 10th '52   2 Frognal Mansions, London NW3

Dearest Johnny

You are an angel to send me such a heavenly present. Thank you very, very much. I hadn't any of the Debussy songs, and I am having a wonderful time staggering through them. Bless you love.

It has been heavenly having all this time off – the first time in my life – I have even taken to gardening on my coal shed and have one hollyhock, five marigolds and six geraniums! Fantastico! I am just warming up gently on mee-mees for Edinburgh in a fortnight's time, but have taken life very easily. Haven't been to the hospital since the middle of July, and it's been lovely to have a rest from it, and to feel well again – fingers crossed!

Bruno Walter was thrilled with the recording of *Das Lied* in Vienna – tenor, Patzak – fine! Shall be singing with him again in Edinburgh – *Das Lied* (Concertgebouw, van Beinum) – *Liebeslieder Waltzes* – <u>wish</u> you were playing in those – and *Gerontius* and *Messiah* with Barbirolli – so I'm looking forward to it.

It will be heavenly if you are over here next year – so far I am taking the summer months off again, tho' I have been asked to do Erda at Bayreuth – but I think it is a wise policy and I pay the government less tax! Tommy Schermann wrote asking me to do two concerts in New York, but it seems a bit daft to go such a long way, much as I would love to.

The folksongs were made this spring – I thought 'Waly-Waly' was awful, especially when I did it later with Ben in recital. No, last year they were recorded, not this. I'm relieved that you don't mind it.

Bernie's Mum is over from N. Zealand, so she's busy showing her round, but still angelic.

We were invited for a weekend to a friend's house three weeks ago, and the young Queen was staying next door – and we were asked in to sing for her – mine host [Burnet Pavitt] plays very well – sang for about half an hour – then chatted with her for another on all subjects – sweet poppet, she is. Wasn't that a lucky chance, eh?

Much love to you and thank you again for remembering me – bless you love.
Kaff

No.325 [Letter to Trixie Ward]
22.8.52   2 Frognal Mansions, London NW3
Dearest Trix

Thank you so much for your sweet letter. It is always lovely to hear from you.

Enclosed a glamour-puss pitcher as requested taken in Vienna in a heat wave – that's why it looks as tho' I'm wilting!

Win is just home from a fortnight in Paris – tickled pink – and eyes shining – I don't know what she's been up to! but it seems to suit her.

I am off to Edinburgh on Sunday night – am feeling very well, but just keep my fingers crossed! It's been lovely having three months off. I've just turned down Bayreuth, Scala, Germany for a new Stravinsky work and two concerts of anything I like in New York – all this last week! But am just taking things easy for a bit, and seeing a bit of England for a change. Am coming to York on March 12th so hope to see you then if not before.

Bernie is still angelic – her Mum's here at the moment and we're being decorated, so it'll be peaceful to get to Edinburgh!

Must stop now – in a hellovarush.

Much love to you both,
Kath
    Funny rumours get about! Have no intention of leaving here.

No.326 [incomplete letter to Benita Cress]
[26th August 1952]   [Edinburgh]
... I am having a peaceful evening while the family are out at *The Magic Flute*. It gives me a chance to practise and to catch up on some letters. It's a lousy day and it's good to have the curtains drawn against the stormy weather. Our holiday was very good ... it was rather nice to get home to the slopes of Hampstead again. Since then I have just lazed, and gardened quite a bit on our eight square yards on top of the coal bins!, seen a lot of my buddies, made several Yorkshire puddings with great success and, in fact, just thoroughly enjoyed being a *Hausfrau*. ... Arrived here yesterday and my first concert, *Das Lied*, is on 28th, *Liebeslieder Waltzes* 2nd Sept., *Gerontius* 5th and *Messiah* 6th, so I have plenty to think about. Am just concentrating on work and not going to any concerts or parties. Good girl, eh? Now I am fairly busy till December and must take an interest in singing again. It <u>does</u> interfere with my gardening! Had a week of invitations last week – funny how everything comes at once. Bayreuth, Scala, New York and now Stravinsky in Germany, turned them all down – <u>must</u> get my bulbs in!!!! ...

No.327 [Letter to Emmie Tillett]
14th Oct 1952   [2 Frognal Mansions, London NW3]
Dearest Emmie
    Herewith some programmes
<u>Highgate November 15th</u>

Where'er you walk	Handel
Come to me soothing sleep	Handel
Hark the ech'ing air	Purcell
Mad Bess	Purcell
Frauenliebe und Leben	Schumann
Après un rêve	Fauré
Lydia	"
Nell	"
Love is a bable	Parry
October Valley	Michael Head
Go not happy day	Frank Bridge
Pretty ring time	Peter Warlock

<u>Carlisle December 11th</u>

Prepare thyself Zion (*Xmas Oratorio*)	Bach
Come to me soothing sleep	Handel
Pur dicesti	Lotti
Che faro (*Orfeo*)	Gluck
An die Musik	Schubert
Die junge Nonne	Schubert
Wandrers Nachtlied	Schubert

Erlkönig	Schubert
Four Serious Songs	Brahms
Love is a bable	Parry
Go not happy day	Frank Bridge
The Little Road to Bethlehem	Michael Head
Pretty ring time	Peter Warlock

Leigh November 30th

Bist du bei mir	Bach
Like as the lovelorn turtle	Handel
Hark the ech'ing Air	Purcell
Pur dicesti	Lotti
Che faro (*Orfeo*)	Gluck
Frauenliebe und Leben	Schumann
or	
Four Serious Songs	Brahms
or	
Love is a bable	Parry
October Valley	Michael Head
Go not happy day	Frank Bridge
The fairy lough	Stanford
Pretty ring time	Peter Warlock

Now that's a good job done, ain't it, except that I haven't mentioned any duets – perhaps Richard [?Lewis – tenor] has some ideas?

Could you answer the enclosed for me please?

Did we tell you that Hilda Gélis-Didot died a few days ago? We had a letter from a friend. She had a heart attack and a stroke. Won't she be missed? I think she was the loveliest, warmest person.

Much love, sweetie

Kaff

No.328 [Letter to John Newmark]

21st Oct.'52   2 Frognal Mansions, London NW3

Dearest Johnny

How are you, love? I had a letter the other day from Paul Frankfurther asking if I had news of you, as he had written several times and had no reply. I didn't say perhaps you didn't <u>feel</u> like replying, but that I would write miself, and see if that had any effect! I <u>do</u> hope you are all right, sweetie, and would love a note to that effect. He is at 1D Belsize Park Gardens, London NW3, just in case you want to drop the old burghter, Frankfurther, a line. Okeydoke?

I am still on mi two feet, and apart from the rheumatiz, doing very well. Singing here and there, not too much – paying much less income tax! and enjoying a bit of gardening in mi spare time. Old age creeping on, eh? I am off to Dublin on Thursday to sing in the *Dream of Gerontius* with the Hallé and my favourite conductor – not Klemperer, but Barbirolli! It's the 100th anniversary of Cardinal Newman who wrote the poem, and according to the priest, after the performance is over successfully, we're going to have 'hoi jinks'!

Then on to Manchester to sing Four Serious Songs with the Hallé again – Sargent orchestration – then a recital in the new Festival Hall on Nov 4th with Gerald – *Frauenliebe* and all sorts and sizes of things. Then *Kindertotenlieder* with Clemens Krauss – should have been Furtwängler but he is ill – and *Das Lied* with Krips – nice concerts, eh?

I do hope all goes well with you, and that you have lots of lovely concerts too. I still have twenty-three pounds, five shillings of yours from your recordings – I haven't forgotten – do you need it?

Much love to you and to Paul and all my buddies there – look after yourself and God bless.

Much love from

Kaff

No.329 [incomplete letter to Neville Cardus]
11th November 1952   [2 Frognal Mansions, London NW3]
My dear Neville

It was kind of you to write, and I appreciate it very much. I know I use my hands and I am trying to get out of what is an unconscious gesture – one must be told of these things, because it must be most irritating. I suppose it's hard to please everybody – for years I've been criticised for being a colourless, monotonous singer – 'this goitrous singer with the contralto hoot,' said *The New Statesman* – so I have plodded on!

I adore the *Frauenliebe*, and I can see that girl growing up from a child to a woman – and these light songs are all the highlights of joy and sorrow. If someone I adored had just proposed to me, I should be breathless with excitement and unable to keep still; and if I had a child, I should hug it till it yelled, so I can't help doing it this way, especially as I usually sing it to English audiences with little or no knowledge of German. I probably underline more than I ordinarily would the changes of mood.

But I promise you I am never aware of the audience to the extent that I do anything to impress or wake 'em up! I admit I was more nervous than usual at my first real London recital. I don't think you were 'unkind' – it's just made me to think, and that doesn't do anybody any harm....

No.330 [Letter to John Barbirolli]
1st December '52   [2 Frognal Mansions, London NW3]
Tita darling

This is just to bring you all my love in boundless measure on this your birthday, and to say that all my thoughts and dearest wishes are with you – now and always. I hope you are not too weary, my darling, though it would seem difficult for you to be otherwise with all the work you have done and are doing – but if unceasing and loving thought can speed through the air and reach you in gloomy Sheffield, then, perhaps, a little of the burden of your work may be lightened. You have helped me so unbelievably these last 18 months that I feel sure that such thoughts <u>can</u> aid and heal and bless, and with each meeting we have added more treasures to our store of memories, both grave and gay, haven't we, love?

Look after yourself, beloved Tita – many, many happy returns – you have all my love.

God bless you,

from Katie

No.331 [Letter to Bill and Benita Cress]

16th December 1952   2 Frognal Mansions, London NW3

Dearest Bill and Bonnie

WELL! of all the angelic souls! Your two heavenly parcels and the marvellous photographs have all arrived safely, and I'm terribly sorry, but we just couldn't wait to open them. You are angels to take all this trouble to send such wondrous things, and I can't tell you what joy they have, and will, give us. Thank you, thank you, thank you with all my heart for being so generous and thoughtful. I have never seen such parcels! We will bless you with every mouthful of food, with every drip on the bathmat, with every wipe of our washed faces, and with every avoided snag in the heavenly long stockings, due to wearing the sweet gloves! I shouldn't be surprised if Bernie might not give me a whiff of her beautiful soap tooo! Thank you for all these heavenly things – just to gaze on them has made our Christmas.

I haven't started to do anything about the festive season yet, the weather is icy with sloshy cold snow and rain, so I am forbidden to go out except when I really must. I am still rheumaticky from the neck down – makes me feel my age, ducks!! – so am staying quietly by the fire, and going to bed in the afternoons like an old lady! But I'm happy as a lark, especially as two weeks ago – can you keep a dead secret until New Year's Day? – I had a letter from the Prime Minister asking if I would be willing to receive the honour – Commander of the British Empire – if the Queen sanctioned it? Can a duck swim? I can't believe it can be true, because these honours usually come after 90 years singing or some such, so perhaps it won't come off – but won't it be exciting looking in the honours list on New Year's morning, eh? Private and confidential, darling!!

I haven't much work until I do *Orfeo* at Covent Gdn in Feb – have specially kept these bad travelling months free, and it's gorgeous to be at home. Have one or two broadcasts and the Christmas broadcast *Messiah*, but that's all. Bernie is still angelic, and ruins me considerably, though she has had difficulty in doing her chores recently as she caught her thumb in a car door, and nearly took the end off – but it's looking a little less angry now, and I hope will soon be all right.

And now, thank you again for your wonderful kindness – a merry, merry Christmas to you both, and a splendid New Year, and God bless you both.

With much love from

Kathleen

7   Letters: 1953

Kathleen had her own New Year party on 1st January 1953, a dozen guests in all: the Barbirollis, Gerald Moores, Norman Allins, Ormerods, Win, Bernie and herself. As ever, and in all modesty, she considered herself 'very spoiled' whenever she was the centre of attention, whether because of her failing health or because she was now receiving 'hundreds of messages' congratulating her on the CBE award. Rehearsals for *Orpheus*, more plentiful and necessary in this work because of the inclusion of a ballet, began in earnest on 2nd January. At the end of the first week of the new year she caught a cold, which forced her to cancel recording sessions of music by Brahms (the Four Serious Songs and the Alto Rhapsody), but the visits to hospital, the X-rays and the increasing pain continued. Her cold cleared up in time for her broadcast recital with Ernest Lush on 12th January of music by three living British composers, Howard Ferguson, Edmund Rubbra and William Wordsworth, though it was not transmitted until 4th April and proved to be her last recording. The song recital planned for Scarborough's Central Hall with Gerald Moore accompanying on 14th January was cancelled and she never left London again. Her last appearance outside the capital had been a month earlier, on 11th December 1952 for a recital accompanied by Moore. The wheel had come full circle, for it took place appropriately enough at Central Hall in the city of Carlisle, from where she had moved south to start her career ten years earlier almost to the day. This time, no longer having a home at 23 Windermere Road, she stayed at the *Red Lion* Hotel.

There were ten visits to hospital throughout the month of January, interspersed with rehearsals for *Orpheus*, which opened on 3rd February to rapturous acclaim. Barbirolli, Win, Bernie and her doctors continued to marvel at her determination to keep going despite the daily negotiation of the staircases leading from her Frognal flat down to the road, the treacherously icy pavements she had to negotiate to and from taxis, the flights of stairs to and from rehearsal rooms or the stage at Covent Garden, all of which placed an extra burden on her increasingly weak condition. Kathleen herself felt a huge sense of foreboding, however, when she awoke on the morning of the second performance three days later. She somehow knew that she would not get through, and sure enough during the second act a bone in her left thigh disintegrated and the leg gave way. In the pit Barbirolli knew something was wrong. So too did Adele Leigh on stage singing Amor, but she was helpless to do anything because she was placed on a platform suspended above the stage. As Euridice, Veronica Dunne, and also the chorus and dancers adapted all their moves and came to Kathleen, who sang leaning motionless against the scenery. Not able to withstand the pain any longer and supported by Veronica Dunne, she limped into the wings where she vomited. Somehow she managed to return to sing the rest of the opera, after which she was given a pain-killing injection which enabled her to come back onstage to receive her applause from the enthusiastic audience.

Kathleen Ferrier had made her last public appearance. She was stretchered home and a portable X-ray machine brought to the Frognal Mansions flat next day. The X-rays revealed that her femur had partially disintegrated and a fragment of bone had actually broken away, producing the agonising pain onstage the night before. She was taken to University College Hospital, where by now she had many friends among the nursing staff and the team of doctors who attended her. She remained there until 4th April, after which she went to live in a maisonette at 40 Hamilton Terrace in St John's Wood, opposite the house of her long-standing friends Hamish and Yvonne Hamilton. This had been found for her to avoid negotiating those awkward steps at Frognal Mansions, and she was given dispensation by the hospital to have a look at it in advance of the move (which took place on 20th March in her absence). She enjoyed her new home (half an old house with a bedroom and bathroom downstairs) for just seven weeks, delighting in the visits of friends, the fine weather and the new experience of a decent sized garden. She even went to one of her beloved parties, across the road at the Hamiltons on 30th April, where Princess Margaret was among the guests. It proved too much for her, and she became unwell and was taken home. There were happier days, none more so than her last (41st) birthday on 22nd April. The weather was lovely and the birthday 'gorgeous', one of the last occasions when she had cause to use this favourite word of hers in the letters and diaries. She was inundated with messages of goodwill, so much so that answering them had to be limited to a printed card sent to all as a round robin which read:

> The number of kind messages I have received these last few days, make it impossible for me to personally answer all, as I would wish, but please accept this little card as a token of my deep appreciation and pleasure.

For some she managed a handwritten postscript, such as 'Grateful thanks and kind greetings to you all, Kathleen', on the card she sent to Glyndebourne. She was forced to return to hospital on 26th May and her ovaries were removed. Her condition then deteriorated for a while but she rallied once again later in June. Earlier that month, and at Emmie Tillett's instigation, she was awarded the prestigious Gold Medal by the Royal Philharmonic Society, the first female singer to receive it since Muriel Foster in 1914. Towards the end of July she was transferred to the Westminster Hospital for a bilateral adrenalectomy performed by Sir Stanford Cade, the surgeon at the heart of the argument between Kathleen and Win a year before. Although it reduced the intense pain that had been draining her strength, it did not stop the relentless progress of the cancer. Barbirolli visited her there and later recalled that though her body was ravaged she sang to him parts of Chausson's *Poème* which they had performed together, and though she sang quietly, her voice had lost none of its radiance. In September, at her own request, she was transferred back to the more familiar surroundings of University College Hospital. To her devoted radiologist Gwen Hilton she wrote a valedictory (undated) card which read: 'With my love and oh! such deep gratitude for so much care and kindness. Kathleen'.

In her letters for the year 1953 she writes of plans for the coming months, even declining an invitation from Pablo Casals to sing at his Prades Festival in France, because she had already committed herself to an engagement in Rhodesia. It was only during the summer that she came to terms with the gravity of her condition and realised that she would not win the battle, which she had taken on in March 1951. Others may have been more pessimistic about the prognosis from the outset, but never Kathleen, at least not until the last few weeks of her life. Barbirolli visited her on 6th October. In his letter of condolence to Winifred (see Selected Tributes) he recalled that when he took his leave, he knew it would be forever. And so it was that two days later, on the morning of 8th October 1953, she died peacefully. She had expressed a wish to her nursing Sister, 'Wouldn't it be lovely if I could just go to sleep and not wake up again?'. Mercifully that, at least, was granted to her.

On the reverse of the printed card to well-wishers who had sent congratulations on her CBE Kathleen added some personal notes.

No.332 [Card to Annie and Tom Barker]   [January 1953]
It was lovely to have your sweet letter and one from Tom at Christmas. I <u>am</u> thrilled by this Honour and it has started the New Year beautifully for me. I am sitting up in bed like a real prima donna dictating 250 replies to Bernie, hence the strange handwriting. Am feeling fine and hope you will be able to come to the Birmingham concert [5th March 1953].
Much love and God bless
Kath

No.333 [Card to Trixie Ward]   [January 1953]
Bless you for lovely letter – it was grand to hear from you. I am thrilled, love, and looking forward to going to the Palace.
Much love to you both
Kath

No.334 [Letter to George and Maud Ferrier]
4th Jan. 1953   2 Frognal Mansions, London NW3
Dear Auntie Maud and Uncle George
     Thank you so very much for sending the lovely handkerchief – it is sweet of you to remember me so faithfully, and it <u>is</u> a lovely one.
     I am so sorry I didn't even send a card at Christmas. I was stewing by the fire trying to keep the ache out of my rheumaticky bones, and only went out once to the *Messiah*. So I didn't send a single card, but you were very often in my thoughts, and Win and I were reminiscing about our Xmas's in Langham Rd and the fun we had.
     Isn't it grand about my CBE? I'm so thrilled, and had a nice letter from Dorothy congratulating me. I'm feeling fine apart from being a bit stiff in the back, and soon I'm doing *Orpheus* at Covent Garden – DV -and looking forward to it.
     Win is grand – <u>thrilled</u> with her job – and Bernie, my 'keeper' is a jewel – spoils me to death.
I <u>do</u> hope you are all well and send my fondest love to you all
from
Kath

No.335 [Letter to Emmie Tillett]

14.1.53   [2 Frognal Mansions, London NW3]

My dear Emmie

Could you answer these enclosed letters for me, please?

I have had a letter from Bernard Miles asking me to sing in the City in May, June or July, but have said I haven't a Friday in May and will be in Rhodesia in June. Okeydoke luv?

In haste

Love

Kaff

P.S. Shan't be able to go to Aldeburgh if I go to Rhodesia, eh?

No.336 [Letter to Stella [?Jackson]]

16.1.53   2 Frognal Mansions, London NW3

My dear Stella

I am utterly ashamed of myself not having written to thank you for the most lovely stockings. It was kind of you to think of sending such a lovely present and I was thrilled to receive such super long ones. Thank you very much indeed, and with all my heart.

My excuses are true and numerous!

I expect Benita has told you I was made a CBE at the New Year, and in the next week's post I had 300 letters and telegrams! Then I had to take to my bed for sundry aches and pains, only getting up to go to the hospital for treatment – and latterly for rehearsals of *Orpheus*, which I am doing at Covent Garden on Feb 3rd, and so I've neglected you!

I am so sorry and hope you will forgive me – I am writing this in bed – it being the most comfortable place! We have been having filthy weather and fogs and the slightest cold sets off my 'screwmatics' – I think I must hibernate next winter! I am praying my aches will clear up, and that I shan't have to limp through *Orpheus* – because it looks as though it should be a lovely production with the Sadlers Wells ballet – so keep your fingers crossed for me, won't you?

I do hope that you are all well and happy and I yearn for a sight of you all in La Crosse. You'll have to come here, that's the long and short of it.

My sister, uncle and I go to Buckingham Palace on Feb 17th for my decoration and we are all thrilled – hope I can manage to curtsey!!

Thank you again for your most lovely present and much love to you all from

Kathleen

No.337 [A note to John Barbirolli accompanying a gift of cufflinks and evening dress buttons in appreciation of their collaboration in *Orpheus*]

[3rd February 1953]   [Royal Opera House, Covent Garden]

For my beloved maestro! With my devoted love and oh! so many thanks for making an *Orpheus* dream come true – and for many other blessings spread over the last three years.

Katie

No.338 [Letter to John Newmark]
27th February 1953 [University College Hospital, London]
Dearest Johnny

It was lovely to hear from you, and I laughed a lot at all your CBE imaginings. It is grand to know that you have so much work, especially with such lovely people. It gives me a nice catty sense of superiority that you said 'No' to Nicolaidi [Elena Nikolaidi]. What a pal!

I have been having a wonderful time rehearsing *Orpheus* with Sir John Barbirolli and Frederick Ashton producing at Covent Garden. For the first time I really felt it had been done as I could have wished, with a most lovely ballet and fine chorus, and between you and me I wasn't so bad meeself! The first night was a wow, and a very elegant audience shouted their heads off at the end. The second night was also going fine until I snipped a bit of bone in my hip during the second act, and had to limp for the rest of the evening. It was an experience I don't ever want to have to repeat. I could not walk next day, and had to be carried down our stairs at great risk to my life (do you remember our stairs?!!) by two perspiring, hefty ambulance men. And here I am in University College Hospital once more, furious at letting Covent Garden down, furious at missing my investiture, but counting my blessings in that I am in wonderful hands with Bernie here to nurse me, Sir John's niece also here doing all my letters in shorthand for me, and being thoroughly spoiled by everyone. But isn't it a budder?

I am getting better each day, but will probably be here another four or five weeks, and now must look for another flat or house as the stairs are a bit of a trial in my old age.

Write again soon – it's always lovely to hear from you.

Much love to all my buddies and passionate, lascivious love to you.
Good luck and God bless
Kaff

No.339 [Letter to Benita Cress]
27th February 1953   [University College Hospital, London]
Dearest Benita

I am so sorry I have not written for such an age, but I have been terribly busy rehearsing *Orpheus*, and then at the second performance I snipped a bit of bone off in my leg, so here I am once again, reposing in University College Hospital! I am having treatment every day and it is already much better, but I shall probably be here for another month at least. I don't feel a bit poorly, but am not allowed as yet to stand up on my legs, but hope I'll be all right for some more performances of *Orpheus* in May.

Your wonderful, amazing, delicious, heavenly, gorgeous chocolates arrived a couple of days ago, and I haven't tasted anything like them for ages. They are so pretty too. Thank you so very much – you do spoil me terribly, and how I lap it up!!

I had to miss going to Buckingham Palace, but have heard a whisper that I may be pushed in to one of the summer Investitures. I do hope so, because I've got a new hat and coat!

The first night of *Orpheus* was absolutely thrilling, with a very distinguished audience shouting their heads off at the end. Everyone was thrilled and the notices were all splendid, which makes it all the more disappointing that I could not carry on.

I have your face towels here with me – that you sent for Christmas – so have a constant reminder of you both. Bernie is here nursing me most of the day, not that I need much, so that makes it very pleasant.

I do hope you are both full of beans and thank you again with all my heart for innumerable kindnesses.

Much love to you both and God bless.

Kathleen

No.340 [Letter to Harry Vincent]
27th February 1953   [University College Hospital, London]
My dear Harry

Bless you for your sweet letter – it was most kind of you to write.

I was terribly disappointed to miss the other performances of *Orpheus*, but just could not carry on, having snipped a bit of bone in my hip. I am here in UCH for about another month, having treatment every day and being very spoiled at the same time.

I do hope you are all well, and send my fondest love

Kathleen

No.341 [Letter to Thea Dispeker]
2nd March 1953   [University College Hospital, London]
Dear Miss Dispeker

Thank you so much for your letter of 12th February. It was good to hear from you in a letter containing such a wonderful invitation.

I would have answered you before, but I damaged my leg in the middle of a performance of *Orpheus* at Covent Garden, and am now in hospital and will probably be here for another month.

I am very much afraid I shall be unable to attend the Prades Festival, as I have already promised at that time to go to the festival in Rhodesia with the Hallé Society, and it would not be possible to manage both. I am bitterly disappointed, as I have heard such lovely accounts of the Festival from Dame Myra Hess, and can only hope that another year I may have this great privilege and pleasure.

With best wishes to you

Yours sincerely

Kathleen Ferrier

No.342 [Letter to Mrs Heidrich, The Bury Farm, St Paul's Walden Bury, Nr Hitchin Herts]
2nd March 1953   [University College Hospital, London]
Dear Mrs Heidrich

I can't thank you enough for the most heavenly treats you have sent me. The paté is divine with my evening drink, and the chicken arrived safely Friday and I had it for my dinner that night. I haven't tasted anything so delicious or so tempting since our little party with you. Sir John Barbirolli happened to be here when it arrived and had a mouthful of it and made approving gurgling noises at its deliciousness! I am so grateful to you for your great kindness and can only say that it is a wonderful treat after the adequate but dull meals here.

We will be careful with the dishes and let you have them back as soon as possible.

Thank you again. With love, in which Bernie joins,

Kathleen

No.343 [Letter to Maurice Cole]

6th March 1953   [University College Hospital, London]

My dear Maurice,

Thank you so much for your kind letter. It is grand to hear from you after this long time.

I am in hospital for the next three weeks or a month, but getting better every day and being very spoiled.

Unfortunately, I must find another flat as my leg is a bit wonky and I can't negotiate 48 steps. So I may no longer be a near neighbour, but I hope this won't stop us from meeting again very soon.

I send my best wishes to you and your wife, and thank you again for writing.

Yours very sincerely

Kathleen

No.344 [Letter to Kathleen Vincent]

11th March 1953   [University College Hospital, London]

My dear Kathleen Mary

Thank you so very much for your beautiful card and most lovely flowers that Win brought in today. It is terribly kind of you to send me such a heavenly present and they make my room look grand.

I am feeling much better and hope to be out in about three weeks, but I shall be going back to a new address, as the steps at No.2 are too difficult. So from the 20th of this month I shall be at:-

   40 Hamilton Terrace, London, NW8.

Win and Bernie are moving for me.

I do hope you are all well, and send my best love to your Mummy and Daddy. Thank you again for the lovely flowers.

With much love

Kathleen

No.345 [Letter to Laura Cooper]

27th March 1953   [University College Hospital, London]

Dear Laura Cooper

I meant to write to you some time ago in reply to your letter of the 7th February. I have been in hospital for the last six weeks and have been very lazy, but I do want to thank you most sincerely for two superb bouquets which came this week, a mass of roses about four days ago and a heavenly mixed bunch of lilac, tulips, irises and roses today. It's terribly kind and generous of you to send them, and they make my room look quite beautiful.

I am feeling much better again, and look forward to going to a new home at 40 Hamilton Terrace, NW8 next Thursday. I chipped a bit of bone off my hip while doing *Orpheus*, and so I am giving it a real chance to get better by having a complete rest until September. It's disappointing to miss so many concerts and *Orpheus* performances, but I think it's the wise thing to do.

I am so glad you have enjoyed *Das Lied*. I think I have only one more long playing record and that is Bach and Handel Arias. The Brahms Songs were never issued, and I can only remember doing one version of the *Vier ernste Gesänge*, but someone came the other day and was sure I had made an earlier version. However, unless I am losing my memory completely, I don't think I have.

Thank you again for your lovely floral tributes, and with my best wishes to you.
Very sincerely
Kathleen Ferrier

No.346 [Letter to Margaret Gardner]
30th March 1953   University College Hospital, London
Dear Miss Gardner

Thank you so very much for your kind letter. It was lovely to hear from you and your letter has given me great pleasure.

I haven't been to an investiture yet as I have been here for almost seven weeks, but I hope to go to one of the summer investitures. It made a lovely start to the New Year to receive such an award – Win was very excited too, and will go with me to the Palace.

I am feeling much better now and leave here on Thursday week – not to Hampstead as there were too many steps to climb – but to a new home at 40 Hamilton Terrace, NW8, where there is a lovely garden – to my great joy.

I broke the ligaments and a piece of bone in my hip in the middle of an *Orpheus* performance, so that is why I have stayed so long here, to give the leg a chance to get strong again. For the time being I must go round in a wheelchair, but I expect I shall soon become expert at steering a middle course and avoid scratching the paint on the doors!

It <u>was</u> lovely to hear from you, and I do hope that if by any chance you are in St John's Wood, you would call, and give me the great pleasure and privilege of welcoming you.
With all good wishes
Yours affectionately
Kathleen
(41 on April 22nd!!)

No.347 [Letter to Benita Cress]
3rd April '53   40 Hamilton Terrace, London NW8
Dearest Benita

Thank you so much for your sweet Easter card and handkerchief – it brightened my day considerably, and it's <u>such</u> a lovely hanky. I'm still in hospital, but leaving in the morning – whoopee, whoopee – and going to a new home at 40 Hamilton Terrace, which Bernie tells me is looking lovely. I should have gone three days ago but caught a bug from somewhere and a temperature and a very queasy stomach, so had to stay – I was furious! But I'm quite all right now and looking forward to the morning. My legs are much better and I can take a few steps, but not too many and for the moment will be whizzing round in a wheel chair.

We had 48 steps to my old flat and it meant that once up them and I should be a prisoner there, so Bernie and Win had to rush round and find something else. We've been very fortunate and got a maisonette (half an old house) with a bedroom and bathroom downstairs for me and a lovely garden, which is something I have always yearned for. We've had the house papered and painted (to hell with the expense!) so I can hardly wait to see it.

I am going to have a complete rest this summer and work quietly for Edinburgh. Will write again when I'm home and tell you all about it.

Much love to you both

from

Kathleen

No.348 [Letter to Peter Diamand]

9th April 1953 40 Hamilton Terrace, London NW8

Phone: CUNningham 8899

Dearest Maria and Peter

What a heavenly surprise when I came to my new home to find such a bowl full of glorious lilac. Thank you, loves, so very very much.

And also tonight we have been stuffing ourselves with superb meat which came via Ibbs and Tillett yesterday. It was absolutely scrumptious and I do thank you with all my heart for your sweet thought.

My new home is simply lovely. Win and Bernie have worked miracles, and it's heaven to be in my own bed again – virgin couch though it be!!

I can't wait for you both to see it and to hear Maria playing on my piano. Even Rosie likes it, despite opposition from a marmalade cat and a large black brute.

I do hope you are both well, and send you much love from us all and grateful thanks for your sweet thought.

Much love

Kaff

No.349 [Letter to Benjamin Britten]

10th April 1953 40 Hamilton Terrace, NW8

Phone: CUNningham 8899

My dear Ben

Thank you so much for your letter and for sending the Canticle hot from the press, and also for the sweet inscription. I do hope we are able to record it at the end of this month, even if it means sitting down to it.

I am feeling heaps better, being terribly spoiled and am home in a lovely new house with a garden. So life couldn't be sweeter.

I was terribly sorry to hear you had been flooded, and only hope you haven't lost many treasures of music or records.

You must be feeling lighter with *Gloriana* off your chest. I think you are <u>very</u> clever. That will be a night of nights at Covent Garden won't it.

Peter brought in some lovely steak back from Holland, which was absolutely grand. Would you say 'Thank you very much' to him. Hope you are both very fit. Much love.

Kathleen

No.350 [Letter to William Wordsworth]

[mid-April 1953]   40 Hamilton Terrace, London NW8

Dear Mr Wordsworth

Thank you for your postcard. I was in hospital when it arrived, and had already recorded the songs. I hope my F sharp [a misprint in the score] didn't offend your ears too much, and that my interpretation did not cause you too much agony.

I have been home for a fortnight now, and am feeling better every day.

With best wishes

Yours sincerely

Kathleen Ferrier

No.351 [Letter to Trixie Ward]

21st April 1953   [40 Hamilton Terrace, London NW8]

My dear Trix

Thank you so much, love, for your note and for sending me a heavenly box of Terry's. It was sweet of you to think of it, and I am purring with every mouthful.

It's heaven to be home and in such a lovely new one, and I am having great pleasure out of quite a large garden, and have been sitting out in the sun for the last two days.

I do hope you are both well and had a lovely time at Easter with your Ma and Pa – (they are really a remarkable pair) – and I do hope you will come and see us if you are down here.

Win is fine and is having the time of her life. Bernie is still with me, bless her. Much love to you both, and thank you again for your sweet thought.

Kathleen

No.352 [Letter to Margaret Duerdon née Ferrier]

21st April 1953   [40 Hamilton Terrace, London NW8]

My dear Margaret

Thank you so much for your sweet letter. I wish I could see you all, especially Adrien's plaits.

It is lovely to be home from hospital, and I am thrilled with my new house and especially the garden and a swinging seat therein that was bought for me by about twenty friends including Sir John Gielgud, Sir Lawrence [*sic*] Olivier, Sir John Maud, Sir Benjamin Ormerod, Sir John Barbirolli, Sir Malcolm Sargent, Ruth Draper, Gerald Moore, Freddie Ashton and a host of others. It was a surprise for me on the day I came home, and I must say I never had a greater or lovelier one. These last three days have been sunny so I have been able to stagger out and soberly swing!

I had a sweet note from Trixie and a beautiful box of chocs, also a lovely letter from your Mother a little while ago. They are a marvellous couple, aren't they?

Win is doing wonders. She has been made head of her department and in her spare time is in her element pottering in the garden and scraping out the drainpipes! Bernie is still with me and I think will grow wings any moment. She's such a love.

Much love to you all, and thank you again for writing.

Kathleen

No.353 [Letter from Bernie Hammond to Benita Cress]

29th April 1953   [40 Hamilton Terrace, London NW8]

Dear Mrs Cress

Kath sitting beside me up to her ears, eyes and nose with letters, saying will I please write to you to give you our new address and to tell you that she will be writing. The new house is one of the greatest thrills I have ever had, and now the workmen are gone and left us spotlessly clean and painted from the ceiling to the lav <u>seats</u> (N.B. we have two), It is all looking so pretty and it is heavenly to have a garden to sit in now that it is getting so much warmer and the sun is honouring us with its presence. Kath is sleeping downstairs at present, and her room opens right on to the garden – some kind friends send us their gardener, who comes twice weekly and makes a grand job of the lawns and we have so much planted now, there is not a space for a daisy to grow.

Kath has been given one of those wonderful swinging garden seats and we have the sun in one corner of the garden from 10am till 7pm, so we are both getting very brown and rosy about the cheeks. Kath has gone ahead with leaps and bounds since she came out of hospital a month ago, and is now up and dressed and getting about the garden, and in the house entirely under her own steam, has even made some very good sponge cakes. She is her usual bright cheery self and we have a steady stream of people coming, who all admit they come to be cheered up!

Kath is not doing any work till September, but has a lot of recording to do and will be starting on that shortly. She says she adores being lazy and doing nothing. She's worked dreadfully hard these last ten years and has deserved a good rest. We have got a television set now and love watching it, haven't allowed myself to fall under its spell in the daytime – but it is grand after dinner to watch for a couple of hours. Those dates you sent were a treat – they must have taken ages to do and were so beautifully packed – you are a clever girl.

Much love

Bernie

No.354 [Letter to Edward ?Isaacs]

29.4.53   40 Hamilton Terrace, NW8

My dear Edward

Thank you so much for your letter and kind enquiries at the hospital. It's heaven to be home, even tho' I was spoiled to death at UCH.

I have a garden here, which will give me endless pleasure, and the adorable

Ruth [Draper] has instructed the gardeners to make it look beautiful for me, so my cup is very full!

I'm slowly getting better – walking a bit each day, but in this cold weather, spending most of my time in bed, it being the most comfortable place!

I do hope you are both well and send best love and wishes, and thanks again for writing.

With love from

Kathleen

No.355 [Letter from Bernie Hammond to Benita Cress]

[May 1953]   [40 Hamilton Terrace, London NW8]

Dear Mrs Cress

Thought you would like this lovely picture of Kath, we are all enormously thrilled with it as it shows up Kath as something more than a 'Glamour Puss', and it is such a grand write-up too. She was thrilled with your gold slippers – put them on immediately and admired her pretty feet all day. She is doing well, and has caught the sun these last four weeks – looks really bonny, pink-cheeked and freckled. Sorry this is short but a tube of friends are arriving for tea and I must get some cakes baked.

Much love to you

Bernie

No.356 [incomplete letter to John Barbirolli]

5th May 1953   [40 Hamilton Terrace, London NW8]

… How are you my beloved adored wizaldric maestro? Working too hard, I know, but I won't bully you – I know it's no good! But you are precious to us all, my darling, and to me in particular – so just remember that, won't you love, when you are debating whether you can crowd in a morning concert in Llanelli as well as a matinée in Cork and a *Tristan* in C[ovent] G[arden] in the evening!? …

No.357 [Letter to Constance Shacklock]

15th May 1953   40 Hamilton Terrace, London NW8

My dear Constance

Thank you so very much for your sweet letter and for all your news. It was lovely to know that you enjoyed doing *Gerontius*, and I know that Sir John enjoyed it too and said what a lovely performance you gave.

I would adore more than anything to come and see you but at the moment am not walking very much, and haven't been out yet.

Bernie and I would love it if you had a minute to come and see us in our new home. We are so thrilled with it, especially the garden where I can sit out in the sun when there's any!

Thank you again very much for writing.

With love to you both

Kathleen

No.358 [Letter to George Baker]

[9th June 1953]   University College Hospital, London

Dear Mr Baker

Thank you so much for your most wonderful letter of 5th June.

Would you accept and convey to the Committee of Management my humble and deeply grateful thanks for offering me the award of the Gold Medal of the Royal Philharmonic Society. I accept with a very full heart and a real knowledge of the supreme honour you do me.

I am in hospital again and am, as yet, not allowed to see anyone – or have any knowledge of when I might be released from here. Mrs Tillett receives a regular bulletin and, as the telephone has been removed from my room, might I ask you if you could possibly contact her?

Your letter, with its unbelievable, wondrous news, has done more than anything to make me feel so much better. I have no words to describe my feelings on receiving it, but I send you all my affectionate greetings too, and renewed, sincere thanks from a very full heart.

Yours, in all sincerity

Kathleen Ferrier

No.359 [Letter from Bernadine Hammond to Bruno Walter]

June 14th [1953]   Kathleen Ferrier, 40 Hamilton Terrace, London NW8

Dear Bruno Walter

I am writing to you about Kathleen. At the moment she is unable to do any letter writing but she was very pleased to have your letter last week and wishes me to tell you so and also how sorry she is to have to miss the Edinburgh recital with you.

She has not been at all well these last few weeks and is back again in hospital, having further treatment. Everything that can possibly be done is, and will be, done for her. I am at the hospital nursing her. I need hardly tell you of her courage and great patience at all times – a wonderful, wonderful person.

Please may I just tell you that being able to hear with you and with Kath the recording of *Das Lied von der Erde* in Vienna was something I shall remember all my life.

Kathleen sends her love and blessings to you – please may I very humbly add mine also.

Bernadine Hammond

No.360 [undated letter from Bernadine Hammond to Harry Vincent]

[Summer 1953]   [40 Hamilton Terrace, London NW8]

Dear Mr Vincent

I have bought Kath a lovely cyclamen and some fruit with the money you sent. She was so very thrilled and so touched, and says to send you much, much love and blessings. She is a little better today – we just go on from day to day, some days she is just like her old self.

I don't think Kath ever feels that her real friends forget her, so don't worry that you had not written.

Thank you so much from Kath, who sends love to you all.
My love too
Bernie

No.361 [Letter from Bernie Hammond to Laura Cooper]
September 9th [1953]   [40 Hamilton Terrace, London NW8]
Dear Miss Laura Cooper
    Miss Ferrier has asked me to thank you for your card and for sending the
cutting. She has not been very well, but had a change of treatment two months
ago and has made some promising progress since.
Yours sincerely
B.M. Hammond

No.362 [Telegram postmarked 11th September 1953 sent from London to
Bruno Walter in Edinburgh]
Greetings. Professor Bruno Walter. *George* Hotel, George Street, Edinburgh.
    Sincere and loving greetings. Deepest gratitude now and always. Thanks for
your wonderful letter. All my thoughts for your birthday next week. Hoping it
may be a most happy one.
    In deep affection. Kathleen.

No.363 [Letter from Bernadine Hammond to Harry Vincent]
September 13th [1953]   [40 Hamilton Terrace, London NW8]
Dear Mr Vincent
    Kath asks me to thank you for your letter and was pleased with all your news,
astounded that Kathleen Mary has reached school-age! She has asked me to tell
you that she has had a complete change of treatment. She has been in hospital for
nearly four months now and seven weeks ago had an operation for the removal
of certain glands. It is a new operation and has been very successful in that it has
removed all pain and it is hoped that in time the bones will strengthen and she
will be able to get out of bed, and eventually – God willing – home again. I need
hardly tell you of her astounding courage and patience through these difficult
months, she is a perfect wonder and deserves the success which we all hope and
pray will be the outcome of this operation.
My love to you all
Bernie

No.364 [Letter from Bernie Hammond to Benita Cress]
[15th October 1953]   [40 Hamilton Terrace, London NW8]
Dear Mrs Cress
    I am so sorry that I did not send you a cable or let you know about Kath. It
must have been an awful shock to you – we were just snowed under with the
Press and millions of other things, and I just did not manage to do it. But I
would like you to know that Kath was perfect to the end, the last few days she
had injections and slept most of the time and just went very quietly in her sleep
as I had hoped and prayed she would.
    If this had to be in the first place, one just must accept it and make the neces-

sary adjustments. Kath would expect that of us. She had so much to bear these last few months, if she was not going to get out of bed, then it is much better thus, and I am convinced that the essential part of Kath is never very far from those who loved her – so don't grieve too much sweetie, be thankful that now nothing can hurt her or cause her pain and know that she is happy somewhere. Do keep writing to me.

All my love

Bernie

8   Kathleen Ferrier and the BBC: 1941–1953

The relationship between Kathleen Ferrier and the BBC is a fascinating one. Always keen to pigeon-hole artists for ease of programming, as far as the Corporation was concerned her career path was not so straightforward. At what point should she be considered as a singer rather than as a pianist? There is little information about her pre-War activities on the wireless, no works, no fellow performers and no surviving recordings. After her death Maurice Johnstone, Head of Music at the North Region of the BBC, listed a few of these early engagements in a letter to Winifred.

[Maurice Johnstone to Winifred Ferrier]
Ref. 38/M/MJ
24th June 1955
  By all means quote from my letter, and this one if you feel the 'info' I can supply deserves a place in your book. Since I wrote to you on 8th June, I have discovered a few more facts about Kathleen's earliest associations with the BBC. On 3rd July 1930: she took part in a Ballad Concert in the Manchester Studios as a <u>pianist</u>! As a singer she broadcast from Newcastle on 1st and 18th May, 20th June and 10th July 1939.
Yours sincerely
M.J.
Head of Programmes (Sound)

The four programmes listed by Johnstone were produced by Cecil McGivern and called:

Monday 1st May 1939	'Quick Change'
Thursday 18th May 1939	Ballad Concert
Tuesday 20th June 1939	'All the Best'
Monday 10th July 1939	'Quick Change'

By 1941 Kathleen Ferrier wanted to be regarded only as a singer and not as a pianist, but this took some time. Using her experience with CEMA was not enough, and several hoops had to be jumped through before she was accepted. Nevertheless, once she had convinced a Regional Director or a Producer of her worth, she found them loyal and supportive, some becoming firm friends as well as employers. Maurice Johnstone, himself a composer, was one.

No.365 [Letter to Maurice Johnstone, BBC Manchester]
29.9.[19]41   23 Windermere Road, Carlisle, Cumberland
Kathleen F. Wilson LRAM, ARCM, Gold Medallist, Teacher of pianoforte, theory and harmony.
Dear Sir

I have been singing under the auspices of CEMA for Miss Eve Kisch of Liverpool, the North Western Organiser, and at her request I am writing to ask if I might have an audition in the near future at your studios. I have had broadcasts from Newcastle, but only one since the war began, and I believe that the studios there are now very little used for vocal or instrumental work.

I am a Contralto and include in my repertoire solos by Bach, Handel, Purcell, Schubert, modern English, Lieder, Negro Spirituals etc, and all oratorios including *Dream of Gerontius*, *Stabat Mater* (Pergolesi), *Elijah*, *Messiah* etc. etc. Hoping I shall receive a favourable reply.
I am yours faithfully
Kathleen Ferrier (Mrs Wilson)

[From Maurice Johnstone, Music Director North Region]
14 October 1941
Dear Madam
In reply to your letter of 29th September, auditions for solo performers are not being held at present except in very special circumstances, but as you have broadcast for us a good deal in the past we would be willing to audition you as a singer. It may be some time before members of our Music Department can visit our Newcastle studios, but we will let you know when an audition there would be possible. Alternatively if you have occasion to visit Manchester, we would be very pleased to hear you here, but as we have very few opportunities for offering engagements to solo singers, I do not think it would be worth a special visit.
Yours faithfully
Maurice Johnstone
Music Director, North Region

[From Maurice Johnstone to Cecil McGivern, Newcastle]
2nd October 1941

<u>Kathleen Wilson (née Ferrier)</u>
I attach hereto a letter I have received from this lady who asks for an audition as a singer, although her letter heading suggests that she is a pianist. She refers to previous broadcasts from Newcastle, but we have no record here of her work. Will you please advise me, bearing in mind that we only hold auditions of individual performers in exceptional circumstances and with strong professional recommendations.

[From Cecil McGivern to Maurice Johnstone]
3rd October 1941
As Kathleen Wilson says, she has broadcast from Newcastle studios several times, but chiefly in variety and light entertainment programmes. She is a

trained contralto with a warm 'Clara Butt' voice. I personally like her voice very much, but I am not enough of a musician to 'place' her correctly.

When war started, we had determined to use her in straight shows, but had no opportunity to do so. I personally should recommend that she be given an audition. Her voice is of a rather unusual type and, as I said, I found it attractive.

I understand from her that she once broadcast from Manchester many years ago, but on that occasion as a pianist.

No.366 [Telegram to Maurice Johnstone]
1 Nov 1941   23 Windermere Road, Carlisle
Visiting Manchester on 18th and 19th Nov. Seeing Alfred Barker re *Messiah*. Can you arrange audition as suggested in your letter?
Kathleen Ferrier

Regrettably her diaries do not begin until 1942, but we may deduce that all went well, for before long the more sympathetic Northern Region was offering her a broadcast early on a Sunday morning. Her first surviving contract as a singer is dated New Year's Day 1942, a watershed year as far as her career was concerned, for by its end she had relocated to London.

[Contract with BBC dated 1st Jan. 1942]:
Sunday January 11th 1942
Time: 7.15–8am
Studio Manchester
Light music by Alfred Barker's Orchestra
Fee £3.3.0d plus 3rd class return voucher Carlisle-Manchester plus one night allowance @ 17/-
(an extra 5/9d if transmitted overseas, an extra guinea if given a Home Service repeat, and an extra two guineas for any other repeats).

Having won over BBC officials such as Johnstone and McGivern, Kathleen had to start all over again when she moved down to London. At the request of Arthur Wynn at the BBC, composer Lennox Berkeley was in the audience at the only National Gallery concert at which Kathleen sang. It took place on 28th December 1942. Even with the benefit of hindsight it is hard to recognize her voice as described in Berkeley's report, especially its apparent inability to move a listener.

Kathleen Ferrier

I heard the above at the National Gallery on December 28th. She has a fine and powerful voice of real contralto quality, and seemed to me an accomplished singer. Her intonation was on the whole very accurate and her diction was good. On the other hand I found her rather dull; her tone was monotonous. I cannot imagine that she could ever move one, though there is no doubt about her competence or the good quality of her voice.

Less than a month later, on 20th January 1943 she auditioned for the BBC Promenade Concerts with Handel's 'Where'er you walk' and the aria 'Softly awakes my heart' from *Samson and Delilah* by Saint Saëns. The report on her, in an unsigned memo, was even more qualified, not to say damning, and unsurprisingly she was turned down.

> Rich, clarinet-like quality voice, limited in range and technique at the moment. Good diction. A promising singer, but only suitable at present for small works such as Bach's songs from Schemelli's *Gesangbuch.* Sang the Saint Saëns completely without passion.

Once accepted, she made eight appearances at the Henry Wood Promenade Concerts, starting with the prestigious Last Night. Thereafter her repertoire was (but for an operatic aria by Tchaikovsky and a concert aria by Mozart) exclusively restricted to Brahms.

Saturday 15th September 1945	Joan of Arc's Farewell	Tchaikovsky	cond. Boult
Wednesday 27th August 1947	Alto Rhapsody	Brahms	
	Ombra felice! Io ti lascio	Mozart	cond. Cameron
Tuesday 17th August 1948	Alto Rhapsody	Brahms	cond. Cameron
Wednesday 12th January 1949	Four Serious Songs	Brahms	cond. Sargent
Thursday 28th July 1949	Four Serious Songs	Brahms	cond. Sargent
Thursday 14th September 1950	Four Serious Songs	Brahms	cond. Sargent
Monday 7th January 1952	Four Serious Songs	Brahms	cond. Sargent
Thursday 18th September 1952	Four Serious Songs	Brahms	cond. Sargent

She returned to Manchester in the summer (7th August 1943) to record (with Stanley Wootton) the Two Songs with Viola by Brahms in a lunchtime recital from 1.30–2pm, and according to a telegram sent in July from the North London office (to the future agent Basil Douglas then working for the BBC) declared herself 'Very pleased to sing Widmung and the Trout, Kathleen Ferrier'. On 8th December and broadcast from Bedford Corn Exchange on the Home Service, she sang in Dvořák's *Requiem* for a fee of ten guineas plus travel costs of 10/1d and one pound for subsistence. Thereafter work from the BBC began to flow in.

On 11th December 1943 at Huddersfield Town Hall she sang Handel's *Messiah* with the Huddersfield Choral Society conducted by Clarence Raybould, a staff conductor at the BBC. An exchange of letters between the two followed.

[From Clarence Raybould to Kathleen Ferrier c/o Ibbs and Tillett]

1 January 1944

I had intended before this to send you my thanks for your beautiful singing in the *Messiah* at Huddersfield; please accept these belated acknowledgements along with my best wishes for a happy and prosperous New Year.

Do you know the Bantock *Sappho* song cycle? If not, may I call your attention to them as they constitute, in my opinion, one of the finest cycles for a mezzo voice which have ever been written. They are magnificently scored for orchestra and I would like to have an early opportunity of broadcasting them if they appeal to you.

No.367 [Letter to Clarence Raybould]
[received 12th January 1944]

Frognal, Tuesday [11th January 1944]

Dear Mr Raybould

The *Sappho* song cycle is out of print, but I have managed to get a copy from a library. They look lovely and are right as regards range. It would be lovely to do them with you. I do hope we can.

In haste to catch post.

Yours very sincerely

Kathleen Ferrier

On 17th February 1944 for the London Home Service, she gave a nine-minute recital of English music for voice and organ (William Cole), in which she sang three songs by Maurice Greene:

The sun shall be no more thy light	3½'
I will lay me down in peace	3'
O praise the Lord	2½'

On Saturday 26th February 1944 she returned north to Stockport's Centenary Hall for a programme called 'Our Northern Choirs' on the Northern Home Service and sang the contralto solo in Debussy's *Blessed Damozel* (*La demoiselle élue*), and the brief part for Mary in the Spinning Chorus of Wagner's *Flying Dutchman*. Once again she was offered the engagement by Basil Douglas. It was with the BBC Northern Orchestra and the Maia Ladies Choir with a single rehearsal at 3pm. The soprano soloist was Joan Cross and the conductor Charles Groves. The contract is dated 22nd September 1943 and she was offered a special fee of ten guineas, her return rail fare of £1.16.6 and one night's subsistence of a pound, totalling £13.6.6. According to an account given in 2011 to the author by a participating chorister, there was a marked contrast in the standard of musical preparation by the two soloists with Kathleen impressively on top of all the details in a Debussy work, which even today is a comparative rarity in the concert hall. This was her reply written back in September 1943 accepting the engagement for five months later.

No.368 [Letter to Basil Douglas, Music Section North Region BBC]
Received 28th Sep 1943   Clearview, Silsden, Yorks
                          [2 Frognal Mansions, Hampstead, London NW3]

Dear Mr Douglas

Thank you very much for your letter. I should be very pleased to take part in the broadcast – I have passed your letter on to Ibbs and Tillett as they are sole agents for me. There isn't anything for me to sing in the Mendelssohn [*Midsummer Night's Dream*] is there? I shall look forward to doing the Debussy and the Spinning Chorus.

In haste

Yours very sincerely

Kathleen Ferrier

The following letter and postcard to Leonard G. Dennis, BBC London, concern a studio recording on 31st March 1944 of Ballad Concert No.15 for broadcast on 14th and 15th April. This concert was broadcast between 11.00–11.30pm for the North America Service, with Gethyn Wykeham-George (cello) and Stephen Manton (tenor). The song by Leoni is scored through on a BBC memo.

No.369 [Letter to L G Dennis]

[7th March 1944]   [2 Frognal Mansions, London NW3]

Dear Mr Dennis

Thank you very much for your letter – I shall look forward to doing the recording. I am sorry to have been a long time but have only been home one day in the last month.

Can I let you have the publishers' names later, as I don't remember them from memory?

I hope my suggestions are the sort of thing you want. I shall be glad to fall in with any songs you suggest that may be more suitable.

With best wishes

Yours sincerely

Kathleen Ferrier

No.370 [Postcard to L.G. Dennis]

10th March 1944   [Keighley, Yorkshire, as from Frognal]

Please excuse the postcard. It is all I possess at the moment. I here confirm the four songs for Ballad Concert No.15.

The silver ring	Chaminade
The leaves and the wind	Leoni
Irish lullaby	[Alicia] Needham
The wind	Bantock

I think they will make a nice group.

Best wishes

Yours sincerely

Kathleen Ferrier

On 18th April 1944 she gave a recital with violinist Alfredo Campoli. She sang 'Four songs of the Hill' and 'Down in the Forest' by Landon Ronald for a fee of 10 guineas inclusive. A month later, on 18th May, she sang Bach's *Ascension Day* Cantata with Peter Pears, Joan Taylor, Laurence Holmes and the BBC Northern Orchestra, once again from the Home Service in Manchester, with whom she had a busy summer beginning with a recital in June.

No.371 [Letter to L.G. Dennis]

[undated but received 25th May 1944]   [as from 2 Frognal Mansions, NW3]

Dear Mr Dennis

I am so sorry to have been a long time replying, but am away on tour and have got behind with my correspondence.

My 'Largo' (from memory) is in Eb (I will verify this when I get home). I would be most grateful if you could let me have 'Rejoice ye souls' and 'How pure a light' at the above address.

I will give you a list of songs to choose from for the 14th June programme, as you will know the most suitable items better. The timings are rough, but if either of the groups appeal to you, I will retime them when I get home.

In haste

Yours sincerely

Kathleen Ferrier

27th July 1944 Manchester, Home Service. One 12-minute group of good English songs.

> I will go with my Father a-ploughing.
> O men from the fields
> Song to the seals
> Boat song
> Merry Greenwood

On 26th August 1944 Manchester, Home Service Kathleen sang Sargent's orchestration of Brahms' Four Serious Songs and another short item lasting about 7½ minutes. This was once again with the BBC Northern Orchestra, but because Sargent's daughter Pamela had died the day before, Julius Harrison took his place on the podium.

Her acceptance at the BBC was made easier by reports such as this one from Steuart Wilson, at the time Music Director of the Overseas Service. It concerns Isobel Baillie, Heddle Nash, Henry Cummings and Kathleen herself, though the other singers fared less well.

From Steuart Wilson   15 September 1944

[Kathleen Ferrier]: I think this is a fine voice, the best singer of the four. A natural sense of interpretation, tempo, phrasing and a long flow of rhythm.

Isobel Baillie: Why do we keep on with her on top B? No good above G.

Heddle Nash: All too lachrymose at the start, you get tired of the "tear in the voice". Some very fine singing later on when grief was worn out.

Henry Cummings: Not a bass at all – low G. No good in a quartet as a bass foundation.

The year 1944 ended with her return to Huddersfield for the annual *Messiah*, this time (on 27th December 1944) conducted by Malcolm Sargent. It was broadcast at 2pm by BBC Manchester, and her fellow soloists were the soprano Joan Cross, tenor Heddle Nash and the bass George Pizzey. The year 1944 had proved something of a watershed for Kathleen and her relationship with the BBC. She could be said to have arrived.

Having already broadcast in 1944 for the North America Service, her voice would now be transmitted to Africa between 9.15 and 9.30pm with a rehearsal starting at 8. From Studio 4 at 200 Oxford Street she sang the works listed in this letter to L.G. Dennis.

No.372 [Letter to L.G. Dennis]

[7th February 1945]   [2 Frognal Mansions, London] NW3

Dear Mr Dennis

Here are my suggestions for the African broadcast on March 31st for a 12½ minutes group.

1. Prepare thyself Zion (*Xmas Oratorio*)	Bach – Novello 4¾ mins.
2. Margaret at the spinning wheel	Schubert trans. Fox Strangways and Steuart Wilson 2¾ mins.
3. Love's answer (Geheimnis)	Schubert trans. *ditto* 1¾ mins.
4. Why go barefoot my pretty one?	Folksong arr. Brahms trans. Whistler 2½ mins.
5. The Blacksmith	Brahms trans. Whistler ¾ mins.

You <u>do</u> want them all in English, don't you? Please say if you have any better ideas.

Yours sincerely

Kathleen Ferrier

On 6th May 1945 she sang Brahms' Four Serious Songs at Newcastle's City Hall with the Northern Orchestra again under Clarence Raybould. Later in the year she wrote to Basil Douglas, with the two of them on first name terms by now.

No.373 [Letter to Basil Douglas, BBC, 35 Marylebone High St, London W1]

12th Nov. [1945]   Frognal

Dear Basil

December is hopeless for me I fear – I am away all the month – but should be very grateful if there is another opportunity of hearing the recording some-time. Thank you very much for letting me know. Am just recovering my normal hearing after my ringside seat in the *Field of Kulikovo!* [which she had recorded five days earlier on 7th November].

Best wishes

Yours sincerely

Kathleen Ferrier

There are more letters from Kathleen in the year 1946, reflecting a growing willingness on the part of the Corporation to satisfy a growing popularity with the general public. She was fast becoming what half a century later would be clumsily termed a 'crossover artist', satisfying audiences across the various BBC Services.

No.374 [Letter to Eric Warr, General Overseas Service, BBC London]

14th January [1946]   2 Frognal Mansions, London NW3

Dear Mr Warr

Here are my suggestions for a 17¼ minute group. Will the ¼ minute extra matter?

6¾' Dearest Consort (*Rinaldo*) Handel – Boosey

3½' Let me, my freedom crave (Lascia ch'io pianga (*Rinaldo*) Handel –

                                                                                       Boosey

2' Pack, clouds, away – Handel – Patersons

3' The Nightingale – Henry Carey (XVIII cent. song) (Curwen)

2' Flocks are sporting – Henry Carey (Curwen)

I can cut the ending of Dearest Consort, which would make about ½ min. difference.

Hope you think these are suitable.

Yours sincerely

Kathleen Ferrier

No.375 [Letter to Maurice Johnstone, Music Director North Region, about a concert on 11th March 1946 to be conducted by Charles Groves]

Received 4th February 1946   2 Frognal Mansions, Hampstead NW3

Dear Maurice

I like your choice very much for 11th March. Here is timing for you:

> Dearest Consort 7 mins
>
> Where corals lie 2¾ mins
>
> Four Serious Songs 18 mins.

This is generous timing and Dearest Consort could be cut a bit if too long.

Yours sincerely

Kathleen Ferrier

After her performance as Lucretia at Glyndebourne, Steuart Wilson, who had moved from the BBC in 1945 to become Head of Music at the Arts Council (until 1948 when he moved back as the BBC's Director of Music), contacted her directly and received a reply.

[From Steuart Wilson to Miss Kathleen Ferrier, Glyndebourne, Nr Lewes, Sussex]

18th July 1946

Dear Miss Ferrier

I went last night to *Lucretia*, and I should like to tell you how very much I was moved by your own performance.

I know that you are not an experienced 'opera singer', but you gave no sign of lack of confidence on the stage, and the whole performance was deeply moving and satisfying. You and your two attendants are certainly the highlight of the production, and I hope that I shall see it perhaps on tour and certainly in London.

Yours very sincerely

[Steuart Wilson]

Director of Music

No.376 [Letter to Steuart Wilson]

22 July [1946]   Glyndebourne, Lewes, Sussex

Dear Mr Wilson

Thank you so very much for your letter. I can't tell you how it cheered me up! There has been so little time for acting, with two complete casts. I have been very worried by my automaton-like extremities! So your letter helped me more than I can say.

I hope if you come again, you will speak to me after the performance – it would be a great pleasure to see you again.

Thank you again very much indeed for writing.

Yours most sincerely

Kathleen Ferrier

This was her contract for the broadcast of the opera from the Camden *Hippodrome* in London later in the year.

Glyndebourne Productions   Sadler's Wells Theatre

66 Great Cumberland Place   Rosebery Avenue

W1   London EC1

16th September 1946

Dear Mr Bing,

"The Rape of Lucretia" Broadcast

(3rd Programme) Friday 11th Oct. 7.15–10.25 p.m.

with one hour's interval at approx. 8.15.

I agree to participate in my usual part in the above broadcast and to hold myself available for a full rehearsal on the same day at a time still to be decided. I agree to the fee of £20.0.0.

I further agree that the performance may be recorded by the B.B.C. subject to the following understanding:-

a) The B.B.C. shall be entitled without further payment to make a record of the rehearsal or of the performance broadcast for its private purposes and to broadcast extracts from a record in programmes of a historic or reminiscent nature and in trailer programmes;

b) In the event of the records being broadcast in the B.B.C's Overseas Services I will receive an additional fee equal to 20% of my fee for the original broadcast each time the records are broadcast in the Overseas Services, subject to a maximum of five such payments. After payment of fees for five such reproductions the B.B.C. will have the unrestricted right to broadcast the records in the Overseas Services without further payment.

Yours sincerely

Kathleen Ferrier [signed]

Another BBC staff conductor with whom she worked was Stanford Robinson.

No.377 [Letter to Stanford Robinson]

14th November [1946]   Frognal

Dear Mr Robinson

Thank you very much for your letter – I only received it two days ago as I have been on the move as usual.

I would have loved to have sung some Handel for you, but can only manage the first date, as your secretary would tell you. Whattashame! Better luck next time.

With best wishes

Yours sincerely
Kathleen Ferrier

The conductor and musicologist Anthony Lewis also worked with her in late 1946.

No.378 [Letter to Anthony Lewis]
24 November [1946]   Frognal
Dear Mr Lewis
    Thank you very much for your letter – I am looking forward very keenly to the Music Anthology.
    I haven't yet received the music, and would be so grateful to have it as soon as possible, as I am away now until the broadcast and will have very little time to learn it. I hope it hasn't gone astray as you said you were sending it with your letter [19th November].
    Is the Byrd 'Cradle song' "My sweet little darling, my comfort and joy"? I know that if it is, but the Schütz *Christmas Oratorio* is a total stranger to me! With best wishes
Yours sincerely
Kathleen Ferrier

Her Boxing Day task was to sort out some bureaucratic muddles which were clearly annoying her.

No.379 [Letter to BBC, Portland Place, W1]
26 December [1946]   Frognal
Dear Sirs
    I occasionally receive letters re-addressed by you, and many of them have been sent to a very old address at Carlisle, which I left four years ago. Could you please make a note of my present address so as to avoid much delay – 2, Frognal Mansions, Hampstead NW3.
Yours sincerely
Kathleen Ferrier

The broadcast scheduled in her diary for 17th March 1947 was postponed to 28th April due to Kathleen's indisposition (which resulted in four days of cancellations 16th to 19th March inclusive). Her diary shows that she was going to lunch with George Barnes, Head of the Third Programme on 17th March, but the name is scored through and replaced by that of her agent John Tillett. In the event that lunch was also postponed (to 20th March), while no further mention is made of George Barnes.

No.380 [Letter to George Barnes]
13th March [1947]   Frognal
Dear Mr Barnes
    Thank you very much for your letter. I am rehearsing Monday morning for the broadcast, and could lunch at 1pm if that were convenient for you – I would love it if it is.

I shall be at home tomorrow morning if you care to ring me, and to save writing another letter.

With best wishes

Yours sincerely

Kathleen Ferrier

[PS] Only received your letter this morning

No.381 [Letter to the Accountant BBC London NW3 [*sic*]]

9th April [1947]   Frognal

Dear Sir

I received a cheque from you a few days ago for a broadcast on the 17th March, and paid it into my account without noticing the date. Afterwards, when examining the counterfoil, I noticed it was for [a] date on which I had not sung owing to indisposition.

I am doing this same broadcast again (London Harpsichord Ensemble) on April 28th (Bach Cantata 170), so I am already paid in advance.

I hope this is all right, and has not caused chaos in the accounts department!

Yours faithfully

Kathleen Ferrier

Steuart Wilson's admiration for Kathleen's operatic performances knew no bounds after he heard her at Glyndebourne in the summer of 1947.

[From Steuart Wilson: Music Director, Arts Council to Miss Kathleen Ferrier, Glyndebourne, Nr Lewes, Sussex]

June 27th 1947

Dear Miss Ferrier

I came down on Tuesday to *Orfeo* and while I cannot agree with everyone, no one would expect admirers of *Orfeo* to be satisfied with anything except the imaginary production that we all have in our armchair reveries. The Elysian fields are Elysian because no one has ever seen them and we only imagine them, but your Orfeo is the nearest thing to the armchair dream that most of us will ever see.

The music is my 'Desert Island' choice. If I never heard anything else in my life I should choose the whole opera. If I were limited to twenty minutes music, I would prefer the Hades and Elysian fields and "Che puro ciel".

I am not the sort of old opera goer who can say I heard X, Y or Z. I can only say that I have known the music for approximately forty-seven years and that it is lucky that during my life time I have heard it, at any rate in some particulars, as near my dreams as I could ever want.

Yours sincerely

Steuart Wilson

Music Director

Leonard Isaacs, Music Supervisor of the BBC Overseas Service, asked her for a recital programme for broadcast from Bush House Studio 1 on 27th September 1947 between 10–10.30pm, and with a rehearsal at 8.30.

No.382 [Letter to Leonard Isaacs]
Wed. August 20th [1947]   [Frognal]
Dear Mr Isaacs

Thank you for your letter. Here is an idea for my 24½ minutes programme for Sep 27th and do please say if it offends you in any way.

The Song of Songs	Maurice Jacobson	5 mins.
Three Psalms	Edmund Rubbra	[10 mins.]
(O Lord, rebuke me not 4½ mins., The Lord is my Shepherd 4 mins., Praise ye the Lord 1½ mins.)		
Rahoon – words by Joyce	Moeran	2½ mins.
The merry greenwood	Moeran	1 min.
Three folksongs	arr. Britten	6 mins.

  The trees they grow so high – Somerset
  O can ye sew cushions? – Scottish
  Oliver Cromwell – Nursery rhyme from Suffolk

Looking forward to singing for you and being with Edmund Rubbra again.
Yours sincerely
Kathleen Ferrier

From mid-1947 it was not uncommon for Kathleen to have to send in her "life story" as she often called summaries of her career to date.

No.383 [Letter to J.C.R.Penna (Latin America Publicity BBC)]
28th Aug. [1947]   [Frognal]
Dear Mr Penna

Here is a brief history for your use.

Born at Higher Walton, nr Preston, Lancashire, and brought up in Blackburn, where I had piano lessons from the age of eleven with an excellent teacher – Miss Walker. Passed ARCM and LRAM at sixteen years of age, and also won a Cramer piano in a competition for all the British Isles. Accompanied and played solos at many concerts in the Lancs area and in my free time – for at this time I was working in the Post Office – 48 hours a week.

Went to live in Carlisle in 1937, and in that year entered the Carlisle Music Festival for a shilling wager! I was dared to enter the singing class – which I did, and won the first prize and the silver rose bowl for the best singing of the festival – also the first prize for piano as well. I was a dark horse – and not very popular. It wasn't until 1940 that I had my first singing lesson and this was with the adjudicator who had given me first prize at Carlisle – Dr Hutchinson of Newcastle. Soon after I sang in Newcastle City Hall in the *Messiah* under his baton – and in the next year started with CEMA doing concerts in factories and villages.

I have been living in London since 1942 – have sung with all the principal choral societys [sic] in Britain, at recitals and orchestral concerts, and in the last two years have been in opera at Glyndebourne – the first, the title role in the *Rape of Lucretia* – and this year as Orfeo (in Italian).

In September I go to Edinburgh to sing in *Das Lied von der Erde* with the

Vienna Philharmonic Orchestra and Bruno Walter, and also to sing it again with him in Jan next year in New York.

There was one anxious moment in 1942, when I spent most of my money on two beautiful concert gowns, and went off in high spirits on a CEMA tour to Scotland – but before I had arrived in Aberdeen for one of the concerts I was taken off to a nursing home with pneumonia – and in my more depressed moments wondered whether I should ever wear my two wonderful gowns, or even sing again!

Hope you can make something of this – I'm afraid it isn't very exciting.

Yours sincerely

Kathleen Ferrier

As she did in the wider performing world in which she moved, Kathleen Ferrier took immense care with detail when compiling programmes for the BBC. She followed timing requirements with as much precision as possible and sought to balance the content of programmes, whether short or long (and some required only two or three brief works). In so doing, she built relationships with her producers which were of paramount importance, and which relied upon mutual trust of both taste and judgement. Three letters to Arthur Spencer at the Music Section, North Region of the BBC in reply to his initial offer dated 24th October 1947 of a recital at 6.30–7pm to be broadcast from Manchester on 3rd December illustrate this. In the absence of her (at that time) usual Northern-based accompanist Albert Hardie, her partner was Beryl Dallen, whom she would have met in Stockport in February 1944 when she sang with the Maia Choir and where Beryl Dallen was accompanist. Kathleen's diary indicates that they met for a rehearsal at 5pm despite her hopes for a morning session. It was perhaps a mark of gratitude on Kathleen's part to include two songs by the Head of Music for the BBC North Region, Maurice Johnstone in this recital, for it was he who took a chance on her when she made her approach to him six years earlier in the autumn of 1941.

No.384 [Letter to Arthur Spencer]

31st Oct [1947]   Frognal

Dear Arthur Spencer

Thank you so much for your letter. I am looking forward tremendously to coming to Manchester. How is this for a suggested programme? I thought all English would be a good idea – tell me if you disagree.

Evening hymn	Purcell	Novello	E flat 4½
Like as the lovelorn turtle	Handel	OUP	E major 5½
Sleep wayward thoughts	John Dowland		E flat 2½
When Laura smiles	Philip Rosseter		F major 2½
Willow, willow	Anon		D minor 4½
Rest sweet nymphs	arr E F Fellowes	Stainer & Bell	D major 2
Sleep	Peter Warlock		F major 3
Pretty ring time	" "		D major 1½
			25½

Having written them out, I'm wondering if it is all a bit too major – let me know.

Sorry to have been so long, but have been being 'raped' twice a week in the Provinces and I find it very tiring!! Do hope you are keeping fit – all good wishes and looking forward to Dec 3rd.

Very sincerely

Kathleen

Am very willing to have string 4tette, but haven't the parts for all this programme – it would be nice.

No.385 [Letter to Arthur Spencer]

11 Nov [1947]

Dear Arthur

Thank you very much for letter – sorry I have been an age replying – have been shouting my head off in Huddersfield! How is this for programme now?

Evening hymn	Purcell
Like to the lovelorn turtle	Handel
When Laura smiles	Philip Rosseter (1601)
Rest sweet nymphs	Peter Warlock
Sleep	[Peter Warlock]
Pretty ring time	[Peter Warlock]
Two songs:	Maurice Johnstone
a. Hush	
b. At Night	
Slumber song of the Madonna	Michael Head
A piper	Michael Head

Think there is a bit of everything there! Hope it is suitable – shout if it isn't. In a fearful rush as usual.

All good wishes

Sincerely

Kathleen

No.386 [Letter to Arthur Spencer]

28th Nov [1947]   Frognal

Dear Arthur Spencer

Thank you for your letter – where's Albert Hardie? Am a bit worried about accompaniments, but expect 'twill be all right. Shall come on Tues night, so please I must have rehearsal Wed morning – it is too long a programme to do just before the broadcast. We can do a bit more at the balance test, but would be terribly grateful if you would arrange for studio and Beryl somewhere, sometime Wed morning – then I can go to bed in the aft: Sorry to be fussy, but must have it right! The Warlock songs are OUP.

Shall be at the *Midland* from 9pm onwards on Tues if any messages.

In haste

Sincerely

Kathleen

Confirmation that she had 'arrived' came when she was offered the weekly distinguished visitor's spot in 'Woman's Hour', the flagship programme of the BBC. The approach came from Anthony Derville at the Talks Department.

Ref 04/HT/ATD
31 March 1948
Dear Miss Ferrier

I wonder if you would be interested in the idea of broadcasting in our 'Woman's Hour' programme?

'Woman's Hour' is a daily programme which has achieved an audience of some five million housewives. Normally the programme consists of short, five minute talks like "How to Bottle Tomatoes" or "How to Bring Up Your Children", but once a week, every Monday, we like a visitor of distinction to come and talk on some general subject. This month our guests have been Peggy Ashcroft on "What I Like in the Theatre", Sheila Kaye-Smith on "How I Began to Write", and Celia Johnson on "Looking About You". Before that our guests have included Dame Lilian Braithwaite on "Why I Love my Profession", Ninette de Valois on "Some Aspects of the Ballet" and Dame Sybil Thorndike on "Acting and Children".

If you are at all interested in this idea, I would be so pleased if you would come and lunch with me one day, and we could discuss the matter. Will you very kindly drop me a line here or telephone me sometime? My telephone number is Welbeck 4468, Extension 131.
Yours sincerely
Anthony Derville
Home Talks Department

No.387 [Letter to Anthony Derville]
3rd April [1948]   Frognal
Dear Mr Derville

Thank you very much for your letter and inviting me to do something in 'Woman's Hour'. I am just going to Holland until the 1st May, but would be very pleased to talk to you then about it, if it is not too late.
With all good wishes
Yours sincerely
Kathleen Ferrier

More immediate upon her return from Holland, Kathleen gave a late night recital on 16th June 1948 called 'On Wings of Song' from the Manchester Home Service. The venue was Milton Hall on Deansgate for the half-hour 10.15–10.45pm with a rehearsal at 3pm and at a balance test at 9pm. Gordon Thorne, himself a pianist and composer, was her producer.

No.388 [Letter to Gordon Thorne]
19th May [1948]   Frognal
Dear Mr Thorne

Here are a few suggestions for 'On Wings of Song' on June 16th.

Sigh no more ladies	Aikin	E major 2½
Star candles	Michael Head	D minor 3
The little road to Bethlehem	Michael Head	F major 3
The bold unbiddable child	Stanford	D minor 1½
A soft day	Stanford	D flat 2½
Do not go my love	Hageman	D minor 2½
Madonna and child	Thiman	D major 2½
To daisies	Quilter	B flat 2½
Over the mountains	Quilter	G major 2

I wonder if it is possible, as they are going to be orchestrated, if I could buy the parts? They would be most useful to me, if this is allowed. If you would let me know which are suitable, I will forward copies to you. [The orchestral arrangements were made by Jack Hardy for his Little Orchestra].

Yours sincerely

Kathleen Ferrier

No.389 [Letter to Gordon Thorne]

31st May [1948]   Frognal

Dear Mr Thorne

Thank you for your letter. I sing 'Verdant Meadows' in E major – that would be a good one to sing – but the Rachmaninov ['To the children'] I am afraid I do not know, and would prefer to sing something else, as I am already loaded with new work. I think 'A soft day' and 'The bold unbiddable [child]' would go well together – the latter making a good contrast – otherwise they are going to be all rather sober! I enclose copies of the five songs and leave the final choice to you – 'The little road to Bethlehem' – 'To daisies' – 'Verdant meadows' – 'A soft day' – and 'Bold unbiddable [child]'.

I do not [sing] 'A soft day' and 'To daisies' from memory and will need the copies for the broadcast, but if they are needed in the orchestra and you let me know, I will get duplicate copies.

I note that the concert is in the Milton Hall, Deansgate and the rehearsal is at 3pm.

Yours sincerely

Kathleen Ferrier

Correspondence between Anthony Derville was resumed in July, but it was becoming increasingly hard for a date to be agreed to record 'Woman's Hour' in view of her heavy schedule. The date offered was 23rd August. Derville's letter of 12th July sought to tempt her by listing recent guests for the celebrity spot. 'Lately our guests have included Harriet Cohen, who spoke on "A Pianist's Life", Evelyn Laye on "My Idea of Beauty", Lady Megan Lloyd George on "Parliament is your Affair" and Rosamond Lehmann on "Books that last a Lifetime". Kathleen replied from Ireland.

No.390 [Letter to Anthony Derville]

15 July [19]48   as from *Rosapenna* Hotel, Co. Donegal [Eire]

Dear Mr Derville

Thank you very much for your letter. I am afraid I must disappoint you again, as I shall be in Edinburgh for the Festival from the 22nd August onwards.

I am so sorry, and hope that it may be able to be arranged at some future date. With all good wishes

Yours sincerely

Kathleen Ferrier

By now it was recognised across the whole of the BBC that Kathleen Ferrier was a 'must have' artist and that boats were in danger of being missed left, right and centre. This memo with its two annotations sums up the situation.

Third Programme   From John Lowe to MBM [Music Booking Manager]
22 September 1948

Is there a method by which, since this artist gets so much booked up, we could reserve her for say three dates per quarter – even twelve months or more in advance?

[pencilled response] OK 3 dates per qtr from June '49.
[annotation from John Lowe to Basil Douglas] Mr Douglas – as you suggested J.L. 24.IX.

Progress with 'Woman's Hour' began in the late autumn when Kathleen probably sent her draft of the talk.

No.391 [Letter to Anthony Derville]
10th Nov [1948]
Dear Mr Derville

Would you see if you can make anything of the enclosed? I do hope it isn't just what you <u>don't</u> want – it is written in rather a hurry, and has probably many grammatical errors, but you are at liberty to weild [*sic*] a large blue pencil!

Thank you so much for my luncheon the other day [*Akropolis* restaurant in Percy Street on 2nd November] – I enjoyed it very much.

Yours sincerely

Kathleen Ferrier

A few days later Basil Douglas added his plaudits to the Music Bookings Manager John Lowe.

To MBM from Basil Douglas
16th November 1948

<u>Kathleen Ferrier: *Frauenliebe und Leben*: Third [Programme] 11th Nov.</u>

I have seldom heard a more beautiful vocal performance than this – it was a model of finely controlled tone, musical phrasing and excellent German diction. As an interpretation it lacked imagination – the impeccable line of tone was untroubled with the extremes of passionate exultation and sorrow which are the life blood of this cycle. But you can't have everything – it was lovely singing. Incidentally Bruno Walter has asked her to sing 'D L v d E' [*Das Lied von der*

Erde] in Salzburg next year and is going to accompany her recital in the Edinburgh Festival.

Kathleen Ferrier's talk for 'Woman's Hour' was not her "life story" but called "My first opera". It was broadcast between 2 and 3pm on Monday 6th December 1948 on the Light Programme. Her fee was 'Ten Guineas, to include provision of script and presentation at the microphone'. She met Anthony Derville at Broadcasting House at 1.15 and the programme went out live at 2pm.

<u>My First Opera</u>

In a bus one evening going back to my hotel after a performance of the *Messiah*, I was told the story of the second opera which Benjamin Britten proposed writing – *The Rape of Lucretia*. It sounded fascinating, and at the end of the description I was asked if I would consider singing the part of Lucretia. Heavens! What thoughts raced through my mind! Could I even walk on a stage without falling over my own rather large feet, not to mention sing at the same time – that is of course, if I could ever learn the music.

It was to be at Glyndebourne – that most lovely opera house on the Sussex Downs – and in the late Spring when I wasn't busy. To be able to stay in one place for several weeks, I thought – to be able to unpack, instead of living in suitcases – to have regular meals instead of a succession of excruciatingly dull sandwiches! I would learn that music if it was the last thing I did!

The opera still had to be written, but by the end of May the first pages began to come in – and it was printed and completely legible – thank goodness – not bad manuscript which has to be deciphered before learning!

It was lovely music – the first act was peaceful and most beautiful – and as I studied it, it became simple. The second act was very different – there was terror, sorrow, hysteria and a suicide with which to cope! But with the help of my accompanist and much hard work on incessant railway journeys, I learned each portion of the work as it came through. Now too, I was being fitted for the gowns. This new experience was exciting and I never found standing for two hours or more exhausting; I was much too interested seeing the wonderful designs of John Piper emerging from paper to reality in yards of lovely material. From a gown fitting I would rush to a wig fitting and the first sight of it gave me the surprise of my life. To give the impression of a sculptured head, it was made of papier-mâché curls stitched on to a lining, and reaching to my shoulder blades. It was hard and headache-making, and I wouldn't be able to raise my eyebrows to get a top note with this on, however hard I tried!

It had been decided to have a double cast, to avoid singers becoming tired, and one day in June we all met on Lewes station and were taken in omnibuses to Glyndebourne.

After we had settled down and unpacked, notices were posted about rehearsals, and we began in earnest to really know the music and everybody else's parts by dint of many and careful rehearsals. Until this time each singer had only had their own parts, and now it was fitting together like a jigsaw puzzle. Long before we made acquaintance with the stage we all knew the music well, and I for one, was terribly anxious to get going, with what I knew would feel and look like seven-leagued feet and arms! We had much time off when we weren't rehearsing – a singer is lucky in this respect – he or she just can't work all day or the vocal chords will go on strike!

Sometimes in the evenings, we would sing madrigals in one of the lovely rooms of the house, or play table tennis or knit furiously. Bright yellow socks I remember growing apace with every hour – and on red-letter days, trips to Brighton in an open car and a browse round the old junk shops – a real holiday after months of living in trains and not always hospitable hotels.

When the work was becoming knit together, there was not so much free time – and now we were to walk the boards. I remember the first day trying to walk in a pair of heel-less shoes which flapped like a tap-dancer's as I moved or curtsied – that was a mistake I didn't repeat! This first day let me down lightly – I was sitting most of the time anyway, but I couldn't believe how difficult it was just to do the simplest arm movements without looking like a broken-down windmill. I used to practise them anywhere – on the lawn, in my room and for hours in front of a mirror, and watch other peoples' gestures when they were acting, and when they weren't, it was hard going and I was an embarrassed beginner.

I was helped enormously by the other singers – they could have been very intolerant of my inexperience and impatient of my readiness to giggle or cry – one just as easy as the other – but they gave me tips and advice and encouragement for which I can never be grateful enough. I found the second act so moving, that I went round the place with a permanent lump in my throat, and was relieved when rehearsals were over for the day and I could breathe again until the morrow.

About the only other time I had been on a stage was at school as Bottom in *A Midsummer Night's Dream*, which is rather a far cry to the chaste Lucretia. (Wait)

Of course to do the job really properly I should have had lessons in deportment, acting and make-up, but this is a branch of art which it seems has, until just recently, been neglected by opera singers – in this country at any rate. I am so glad to hear of an opera school which has been formed here in London for speech, acting, deportment and interpretation, and which I hope will thrive and produce singers who can make an opera as convincing as an actress can a play. Good luck to Miss Joan Cross, who has had the brains, courage and unselfishness to make this a tangible reality out of a dream.

The dress rehearsal came – and when – struggling to change gowns and shoes in about four minutes, I missed my entry, and when I stabbed myself and fell like a hard-baked dinner roll, I thought it was time I 'shuffled off this mortal coil' and did an Ophelia-like exit in the lake with only a belligerent swan for company! What a life! Oh for a peaceful *Messiah*!

(Pause)

I was given more instruction and help and by the time the first night came along, I was feeling a little better. Apart from the fact that my wig stuck on my shoulder pads every time I moved my head, and I had to free it by a series of jerks, nothing went very wrong for the remainder of that memorable evening!

There are no extant memos or letters between the BBC and Kathleen in 1949 and just one right at the end of 1950, when on 29th December she gave a recital accompanied by Gerald Moore broadcast from Studio 2 at Maida Vale. Her producer was Arthur Spencer.

No.392 [Letter to Arthur Spencer about a recital at Studio 2, Maida Vale on 29.12.1950 with Gerald Moore]

[?20th December 1950]   Frognal

My dear Arthur

In great haste – what about this

Handel	Where'er you walk	3½
	Like as the love-lorn turtle	3½
Schubert	Gretchen am Spinnrade	3
	Lachen und Weinen	2
	Heidenröslein	1½
	Der Musensohn	2½
Vaughan Williams	Silent Noon	4
Michael Head	The little road to Bethlehem	3
Stanford	A soft day	2½
Aikin	Sigh no more ladies	2

Hope this is all right – let me know if not.

Inahellovarush

Love

Kathleen

On 4th May 1951 Kathleen's BBC fee was raised from 50 to 80 guineas.

It is a matter of regret that so very little survives in moving pictures of Kathleen, and what does has either no sound (disembarking from the plane at Schiphol Airport, Amsterdam on 1st July 1951) or is not synchronised (the New York post-performance party in 1949). This is the more to be regretted because the burgeoning television medium was beginning to take an interest in her, but she responded in determinedly negative fashion. Despite the glimmer of a possibility of agreement at the end of her letter to Kenneth A. Wright, Assistant Head of Music at BBC TV, in fact nothing was going to change her mind.

No.393 [Letter to Kenneth A Wright]

24 September 1951   Frognal

Dear Mr Wright

Thank you very much for your letter. I have been frightened of television as I imagined close-ups showing all my teeth fillings, and making my singer's girth even more rotund than it is! And my diaphragm would pant from fright, and my hands clutch the air and be out of focus – horrible fascination for the viewers – nightmare for me!

By the way, I thought the broadcast with Bruno Walter strangely balanced. He was on top of the mike and I sounded a mile away – most peculiar, and rather disappointing as my soft – and what I foolishly thought were subtle moments – were completely lost. Don't you honestly agree?

May I ponder still on your proposal and see if, after watching myself in a mirror, I might even consider wrecking your cameras??

With best wishes
Sincerely
Kathleen

On the same day she wrote to Winifred Roberts at the Music Section, North Region to confirm arrangements for her Third Programme studio broadcast on 2nd October 1951, 7.50–8.45pm, in which she sang *The Enchantress* by Arthur Bliss with the BBC Northern Orchestra conducted by Charles Groves.

No.394 [Letter to Winifred Roberts]
24th September 1951   Frognal
Dear Miss Roberts
Thank you for your letter. I should be very happy for the extra rehearsal on the 1st Oct. I'm not sure of trains yet, but will get there as soon as possible after 2.30 (Milton Hall).
With best wishes
Sincerely
Kathleen Ferrier

According to John Lowe's memo dated 14th November 1951 to Head of Programme Contracts, the BBC wanted to record Kathleen Ferrier, Benjamin Britten and Peter Pears at Birmingham Town Hall on 22nd January 1952 at 7–9pm for transmission as 'The Monday Concert' on 11th February 1952. 'Their programme contains a group of Schubert songs, a new Cantata by Benjamin Britten [*Abraham and Isaac*], a group of folksongs and a group of English songs'.

By the end of 1952 Kathleen's health was in serious decline leading to her final public appearance on 6th February 1953 at Covent Garden. During that time a plan was taking shape for a series of autobiographical programmes 'to widen her recognition' as Kenneth Adam, Controller of the Light Programme wrote to the Controller North Region on 18th November 1952, followed by a very questionable view that 'She is, however, at present very largely a name only, if that, to the Light Programme audience'. In view of her spot on 'Woman's Hour' and the indisputable popularity (largely thanks to radio) of 'What is life?' and 'Blow the wind southerly', this is hard to understand.

Denis Mitchell of the Features Department wrote on 11th December 1952 that 'Arthur Spencer liked the idea very much and considers it would make three half-hour programmes (with say four songs in each). He says however that Miss Ferrier is a retiring sort of person and may fight shy of the idea. He will make the first approach to her. I will have something definite to report at the beginning of January'.

The ensuing exchange of letters and visits to the ailing Kathleen reflect her increasingly desperate condition.

[From Arthur Spencer to Kathleen Ferrier]
30 December 1952
[Dates suggested Tuesdays 5th, 12th, 19th and 26th May, 9.15–9.45
in the Light Programme]

I have in mind two programmes with piano, and two with our Northern Orchestra conducted by John Hopkins, each programme to contain about 15 minutes music and 15 minutes talk in which, of course, you will sing and play an autobiographical part, done conversationally with an announcer to tell the story with you.

I believe you said you were free on three of these dates, which could, therefore, be broadcast 'live', whilst the fourth, whichever it might be, could be recorded. I have spoken with Ibbs and Tillett who will be getting in touch with you

In the meantime it will be necessary for our Features Producer, Mr Denis Mitchell, and I to meet with you with regard to the script. I have in mind the weekend of the 16th-19th January, when we would be pleased to come to London.

[From Audrey Hurst at Ibbs and Tillett to Arthur Spencer]
31 Dec 1952
Kathleen Ferrier would be pleased to see you on January 17th at her address to discuss the biographical programmes in May. It looks as though at least two of these dates will be pre-recorded but perhaps we can discuss this a little later on when her arrangements are clarified.

No.395 [Letter to Arthur Spencer]
5.1.[19]53   Frognal
Dear Arthur
I am so thrilled you want to 'do' me! The weekend of 16th-19th Jan is fairly free for me apart from *Orpheus* rehearsals. Could you ring me on arrival, as I don't know yet when I am wanted and it certainly won't be all 12 hours of every day.

The only other thing is that there are probably going to be some more *Orpheus* performances in May, and I haven't been told the dates as yet – but will let you know immediately I am informed of same. Okeydoke? I will try and rush them at Covent Garden, but it's a bit like moving the Pennines!
A very happy New Year to you and best wishes
Very sincerely
Kathleen

Because of a rehearsal at Covent Garden in the early afternoon of 17th January, Ibbs and Tillett asked Arthur Spencer (Michael Wharton also attended) to meet Kathleen at 5pm at Frognal Mansions. Her diary notes 'Arthur Spencer. 3pm' on Sunday 18th January.

On 20th January 1953 more detail emerged in an unsigned memo.

'My Life of Song': Kathleen Ferrier and the BBC Northern Orchestra now proposed for Monday nights starting May 4th and 11th. Series of four programmes. [pencil annotation] Ferrier with Liv[erpool] Philharmonic on May 3rd. Mondays in May doing four performances (Coronation series) of *Orpheus* (Gluck). [Not finalised].

Reports of the meeting with Kathleen at Frognal Mansions were made and plans took a step further.

[From Denis Mitchell, Features Department to Head of North Regional Programmes]
22.1.[19]53
Michael Wharton and Arthur Spencer met Miss Ferrier last weekend. I enclose Michael Wharton's report, and I think he is right in stressing that the dramatised biographical type of feature would be quite inappropriate. Both Mr Wharton and Mr Spencer are confident that pleasant programmes will result, but do you think that these will be quite what CLP [Controller Light Programme] is hoping for?

[Memorandum written by Michael Wharton]
[c.20th January 1953]
<u>Kathleen Ferrier</u>
After a preliminary talk with Kathleen Ferrier about the proposed series of four half-hour programmes on the Light Programme in May, the following ideas emerged:

1. I do not think that Kathleen Ferrier would be effectively presented by a dramatised biographical feature treatment. The interest of the programmes would be predominantly musical, and this interest could best be brought out by using the interview method. Kathleen Ferrier would be the main speaker, but other musical personalities with whom she has been connected during her career could also be introduced. These include Bruno Walter, Sir John Barbirolli, Gerald Moore, Alfred Barker etc. The programme would thus take the form of a musical miscellany, presenting the life and career of a famous singer.

2. Kathleen Ferrier began her career as a singer of ballads. She is not primarily an operatic singer, but will shortly be appearing in *Orfeo*. She is particularly noted for her singing of Brahms and Mahler. She could not be expected to sing "popular music". The half-hour programmes would each include c.15 minutes of music in two or three groups e.g. arias from oratorio, groups of folksongs, Brahms' Alto Rhapsody.

Kathleen now began to formulate the content of the music for the four programmes. It was typed on her own notepaper, but with neither date nor address, and was possibly dictated to Bernie Hammond.

First Programme		Second Programme	
Che faro	Gluck	Homing	[Del Riego]
To daisies	Quilter	Hark the echoing air*	Purcell
Fairy lough	Stanford	Art thou troubled?*	Handel
Bold unbiddable child		If my tears are unavailing*	Bach
Keel row		Nearer my God to Thee*	arr.?
Where e'er you walk*	Handel	*Messiah* (He was despised)*	Handel

Third Programme		Fourth Programme	
Softly awakes*	Saint Saëns	To Music	Schubert
Verborgenheit	Wolf	No.4 from *Song of the Earth**	Mahler
Who is Sylvia?	Schubert	['Von der Schönheit']	
Cradle song	Brahms	Group of Lieder (in German)	

Third Programme		Fourth Programme	
Spanish Lady*	Folksong	Che faro*	Gluck
I have a bonnet	"		
Oliver Cromwell	"		
My boy Willie	"		
Cradle Song	Byrd		

* with orchestra (some commercial recordings)

From its side the BBC proposed a programme format into which her selection of music could be inserted.

Kathleen Ferrier   (programme format proposed)

I

1. Extract from *Orpheus* and description of scene. A great singer at the summit of her career. How has she got there?
2. A piano lesson in Blackburn (age 11).
3. Playing at festivals.
4. Dragged away from music to do a job in the Post Office. But music reasserts itself. The *Daily Express* competition in Manchester. Visit to London. Singing with the Blackburn Choir.
5. Oratorio (?)
6. Pianist or Singer?
7. The Carlisle Festival.
8. Songs

II

1. Learning to sing. Teachers of singing.
2. Songs.
3. First big concert, Christmas 1941 – the *Messiah* at Newcastle under Dr Hutchinson.
4. Dr Hutchinson (recording).
5. Extract from the *Messiah*?

III

1. Christmas 1942. Meeting with Sargent
2. Sargent (recording).
3. Singing for CEMA. Wartime experiences.
4. Good and bad audiences in the factories.
5. Songs.
6. Travelling conditions. The pleasures and pains of being a singer.
7. Songs.

IV

1. 1946 Meeting with Bruno Walter.
2. Walter (recording).
3. The first Edinburgh Festival 1947.
4. Songs.
5. A world reputation. Travel to European countries and America. Contrasts in audiences and in conductors.
6. Songs.

7.   Learning songs and learning languages.
8.   Barbirolli (recording)
9.   Flashback to early days, leading to
10. *Orpheus* extract.

Following the dramatic events of 6th February at Covent Garden it became clear that for the moment no further discussions should take place until Kathleen had recovered sufficiently, and even then a successful outcome for the project seemed unlikely.

[Controller Light Programme, Kenneth Adam to Head North Region Programmes] 13 February 1953
Private and confidential
Have you heard that *Orpheus* has been withdrawn from Covent Garden because of Kathleen Ferrier's illness? <u>Privately</u> I understand this is serious enough to make her appearance for us in 'My Life of Song' unlikely in the extreme.

Hopes for dates were briefly revived when two memos from Muriel L Watson dated 26th March and 2nd April 1953 and headed 'From Music Programme Routine', allotted the first two programmes to Weeks 21 and 22 in the BBC Light Programme schedule.

This is to advise you that the following period has been allotted to you for the above week.
Monday 18th May 9.00–9.30pm and Monday 25th May Whit Monday
Kathleen Ferrier??
'My Life in Song' (To be decided later)

By 8th April however all hopes were finally abandoned and an unsigned memo indicates that the final decision had been taken. 'This is to confirm that the series under the above title projected for Weeks 19–22 inclusive has been postponed indefinitely'. The following day Arthur Spencer wrote Kathleen a touchingly sensitive letter.

9 April 1953
Dear Kathleen
   I returned yesterday from 12 days leave to learn it is suggested the series 'My Life in Song' in other words the story of your life, projected for the Mondays in May, be postponed until you are quite fit and well again. I think it is a wise decision, for as it was proposed to dramatise the story, the rehearsals would perhaps have been rather complicated and very tiring for you.
   I spoke to Ibbs and Tillett this morning, who informed me that you had left hospital and gone to your new home. I hope you are liking it, that you will be happy in it, and that it will bring you complete recovery to health.

Kathleen's final surviving letter to the BBC was written on the day she received Arthur Spencer's, but it returned to the subject of television. She was no longer fending off requests for her to appear on the medium, but she still had the Ferrier fire within her to air very strong opinions on this developing technology. She still had her ha'porth to contribute, whether she was asked for it or not.

No.396 [Letter to Kenneth A Wright]
10th April 1953   40 Hamilton Terrace, London NW8
                                                                              Tel: Cunningham 8899

Dear Ken

Thank you so much for your kind letter. I was terribly disappointed to miss 'Les Sylphides'. I should have left hospital on Thursday and my television set went on ahead; then at the last minute I got a temperature from some unknown bug and had to stay in hospital two extra days. I was furious, especially as I also missed your introduction of David Buchan.

I am enjoying it all and thought the Cochran show most successful for such a big and varied subject. But the other night I was showing my set and the good programmes to a friend and had to turn off 'Joking apart', which did not amuse me at all. But of the things I have seen, that's my only grumble, except perhaps the lighting – unless I am not used yet to my set – which seems to vary enormously. 'What's my line?' is, I think, excellent, but later in the same evening on Sunday, there were the brother and sister Theuveny, and very often I found, as with other programmes of this kind, the lighting seems very flat and the faces without bones. I am mentioning these things as you suggested it might be helpful.

We would love to see you here, and after next week we should be free of painters and carpenters. So perhaps you could ring me one day.

With best wishes to you and your wife.

Yours sincerely

Kathleen

Kathleen Ferrier, photographed in 1943 or 1944

At 2 Frognal Mansions in 1949, playing the piano she won as a prize in a
competition in November 1928

Orfeo at Glyndebourne, 1947, mourning at the tomb of Euridice

On her first American tour with Hungarian accompanist Arpad Sandor.

Back from her first American tour, 10th February 1948

With boyfriend Rick Davies in July 1948

Edinburgh Festival, 7th September 1949 at the Usher Hall,
accompanied by Bruno Walter

Outward bound for the third tour of America on board
the RMS *Queen Elizabeth*, 21st December 1949

The third and last tour of America, January to March 1950,
accompanied by John Newmark

Paris, [17th] February 1951 with Emmie Tillett

Recovering from her first operation in University College Hospital,
22 April 1951, her 39th birthday

Her *joie de vivre* restored once again, June 1951,
photographed by her teacher Roy Henderson

With John Barbirolli at 2 Frognal Mansions

Rehearsing the Canticle *Abraham and Isaac* with Benjamin Britten and Peter Pears,
January 1952

Awarded the CBE on New Year's Day 1953

Kathleen Ferrier. Ewig ... ewig ... ewig

The Diaries

Introduction: The Diaries

The only surviving diaries are those from the years 1942 to 1953 inclusive, all of which are kept in the archive at the Museum and Art Gallery in Blackburn. There appears to have been one for 1941 which was still extant in 1988, according to references to events in that year in Maurice Leonard's biography, but it has since disappeared. I have omitted days, sometimes weeks, if nothing was entered, especially in the summer months out of the concert season. Apart from cancer, Kathleen Ferrier's greatest enemy was the taxman, to whom she resented paying anything more than necessary, and therefore most entries from the start of her professional career in 1943 include items of expenditure which could be offset against her earnings when it came to making her annual tax return.

Unlike some of the later diaries, those for the years 1942 and 1943 are packed with detail, particularly for 1942 when highly significant events occurred in her life. During this year one can follow the transition from her role as a housewife burdened with the drudgery of washing, ironing, knitting, sewing, mending, shopping and cooking (although these were tasks which she often insisted she enjoyed), to that of a professional singer. By the end of 1942 she had uprooted 300 miles from Carlisle south to London; war had taken away her husband and she was freed from the shackles of a loveless and unconsummated marriage. She and Bert were divorced with no fuss in 1947. Like a bird released from its cage she took full advantage of her freedom. By 1943 she had become an avid theatre-goer, having always enjoyed the cinema or 'flix'. She now had her favourite London restaurant, the *Casa Prada* at 292 Euston Road, and also enjoyed regularly going to 'Chop Suey' in London's Chinese restaurants. She became a member of the MM Club (the Mainly Musicians Club run by cellist May Mukle) in North Audley Street. Wherever she went she would have hours to while away between rehearsals and performances and would visit antique shops. It was in Liverpool that she encountered her partner of several years Rick Davies, the antique dealer who appears in the diaries between 8th February 1943 and 17th February 1952.

All her professional engagements are included in the diaries (by the end of the 1940s there were as many as four a week) with most of the entries listing what she sang. There was a logical structure to the recital programmes she devised. They would usually proceed chronologically, starting with Monteverdi, Purcell or Handel followed by some Schubert. Schumann's *Frauenliebe und Leben* or the Four Serious Songs by Brahms would often be placed at the central point of the recital, after which she would almost always 'go native' with songs by Stanford and Parry. Her recitals would invariably end with a group of traditional British folksongs in arrangements by Vaughan Williams, Britten or Quilter. Programmes would rarely be repeated without some kind of variation, for she would usually drop or add one or two songs or change the order, thus avoiding any exact repetition and thereby keeping things fresh. From 30th June 1944 (after a cancelled session on 19th May), the first recording is logged. Though this event and all the later ones are tersely noted, with the help of Paul Campion's discography it is possible to flesh out more details of these sessions.

She was not a 'Dear diary' person. They are not full of deeply philosophical thoughts, though her mood-swings, her successes and what she deemed to be her failures (she was very self-critical) are vividly described. When travelling around Britain she took care to note down what she wore at concerts, in order to avoid any repetition when she (usually) received a return invitation. Entered alongside the name of the venue would be short-hand descriptions of dresses such as 'Chinese green', 'Pink lamé', 'Black woolly', 'Olive green', 'Turquoise velvet', 'White silver' or simply 'red', 'blue' or 'flame'. Her blue/green dress with gold sequins has survived to form part of the Kathleen Ferrier collection at Blackburn. Her habit of noting which dress she wore ceased by 1949 (probably as her career moved up through the gears both nationally and internationally), but fashion often held a place in press reviews of concerts. Sometimes a newspaper (for example, the *Yorkshire Post* 4th October 1950, recording Kathleen's only performance under Beecham) would carry both a music critic's review (in this case by Ernest Bradbury) and an accompanying feature by a news reporter (here it was Joyce Mather). Rather tactlessly Joyce Mather pointed out the difference in height between the diminutive soprano, Elsie Suddaby, and the taller Kathleen Ferrier, but she did give her reader a vivid snapshot in full colour of how they both looked.

> On the platform the two women soloists presented a delightful contrast in black and gold. Miss Suddaby, small, charmingly sedate, reaching no higher than Miss Ferrier's shoulder, was dressed in black chiffon velvet, a graceful, full-skirted dress with transparent black net yoke and closely fitting sleeves. Her fair hair was parted in the centre.
>
> Standing beside her, Miss Ferrier's tall figure seemed a slender column of pure gold. Her dark hair was dressed smoothly on one side, waved gently on the other and her gleaming lamé evening dress spread about her feet when she was seated, like a golden pool. Most of the time she covered her shoulders with a square of yellow chiffon, folded *fichu*-fashion as protection perhaps against the icy draughts for which the Town Hall is noted.

Mather's article bears the title 'Special applause for the short-notice soprano'. The booked soprano was Gwen Catley, who awoke that morning with a cold. Hastily Elsie Suddaby was summoned from London and arrived in Leeds too late for the start of the afternoon rehearsal. Until she did, Kathleen sang both parts!

> The early part of the rehearsal was not held up because Miss Kathleen Ferrier, the contralto, sang both the contralto and soprano parts [of Dvorak's *Stabat Mater*] – to the evident amusement of Sir Thomas Beecham.

Fees begin to be mentioned more regularly during Kathleen's diary for 1944 and show considerable variety depending on the engagement. John Tillett, and his widow Emmie when she took over the firm in 1948, had a canny knowledge of the financial circumstances of choral societies and music clubs up and down the land and set their soloists' fees accordingly. The procedure for payment appears to have been that Kathleen was paid on the night by those who had engaged her, and she would then make monthly payments to Ibbs and Tillett of their 10% commission. Sometimes the words 'Not paid' are scored through when she had received the money, but more often a tick indicated that she had been paid on the night.

So the bulk of the diary entries concern engagements, venues, recital programmes, accompanist's name, train times, taxi and train fares, lunch and dinner engagements, or simply names of people she was scheduled to meet. There are, however, other scribblings, all part and parcel of the complex character called Kathleen Ferrier. In some of the calendars for the year she would ring her monthly period ('the curse' as she called it in her letters) to give her due warning if she was to perform that day, because she was convinced that it affected her singing. She offered a reward of ten shillings if a diary was lost and then returned to her. She includes the numbers of her National Registration book (HCZK 552), her Ration Book (NH 247033), her Post Office Savings Bank Book (559), her BSA bicycle, her London telephone number (HAMpstead 2108), and the registration number of her car, JT 9376, which, given her raunchy sense of humour, she had to christen 'John Thomas'.

Kathleen frequently declined invitations to sing the mezzo-soprano part in Verdi's Requiem, and the question of how near she came to taking part in it is tantalisingly raised at the back of the diary for 1944. It was her habit to adapt either the Memoranda or Cash Account sections to list her advance engagements for the following year and, at the bottom of the Cash Account page for January 1944, she clearly wrote 'April 28th Verdi Requiem' followed by the initials 'P.J.'. Possibly P.J. was the tenor Parry Jones to whom she was close, and perhaps he had suggested she sing it with him in a performance for which he was already engaged. A few pages earlier, however, on the last of the Memoranda section, she started a list for 1945 with this entry, 'April 28th. Royal Albert Hall Sat[urday] Aft[ernoon] 2.30, Reh[earsal] 10am, Mass in D [*Missa Solemnis*] Beethoven. Royal Choral Soc[iet]y. 12[guineas]', and for this her fellow soloists turned out to be Joan Hammond, Trefor Jones and George Pizzey. All the advance engagements she noted at the end of 1944 came to fruition in all details, except for Verdi's Requiem. Coincidentally however, just a week earlier than the speculative performance, on 21st April 1945, she went to hear Barbirolli conduct it in Sheffield, so perhaps she was still undecided on the question of whether or not this work was one for her, but see her letter of 3rd September 1950 for her final word on the matter.

There is one folksong above all others for which Kathleen Ferrier is renowned and that is 'Blow the Wind Southerly'. It is first mentioned in her diary on 23rd January 1949 when she sang it in Holland, but it would appear that she sang it in public and on the radio almost a year earlier. On 21st February 1948 Kathleen gave a recital for the Farnham and Bourne Music Club, whose secretary recalled the occasion in the programme marking the club's Diamond Jubilee in 1983.

> I think the outstanding personality must be Kathleen Ferrier, who came
> with Phyllis Spurr on a snowy February day in 1948. I asked her if she
> would give as an encore a folksong which I had heard her sing a few
> days previously on a radio programme. She replied, 'I've never sung it
> in public before luv, but I'll have a go'. I can still see that lovely presence
> singing 'Blow the wind southerly' and feel proud that we heard the first
> of what must have been hundreds of subsequent public performances.

The radio programmes 'a few days previously' consisted of a recital of music by
Stanford on 16th February and Music in Miniature on 19th February. While the
content of the Stanford recital is known, that for Music in Miniature is not, but
it was probably when she first sang 'Blow the wind southerly'. On 10th February
1949 she recorded it for Decca.

The diaries have sinister yet poignant touches, the more moving because we
know the tragic outcome to this story. From the summer of 1952 Kathleen was
hard at work with Barbirolli on a revised translation of *Orfeo* for the Covent
Garden production planned for February 1953. Whenever they could, they got
together to refine the text, and she would jot down ideas as they came to her.
Scribbled in pencil under the mundane details of ownership in the frontispiece
to the diary for 1952 are three lines in English for part of 'Che farò', from about
the twentieth bar. In the original Italian these are as follows –

> Io son pure, il tuo fedel.
> Ah! non m'avanza più soccorso,
> più speranza nè dal mondo, nè dal ciel!

For this she wrote –

> I thy love am faithful ever
> In my dread anguish no one can me comfort
> Nothing can aid me in this earth or the sky.

To work on such bleak lines at this time when her health was fast dete-
riorating must have been particularly difficult for her. Even harder to bear,
however, were the cancellations as she withdrew from public life, for she hated
letting people down. Brutally scored through in pencil, in the monthly summaries at the start of the diaries for 1951 and 1952, are the months of work she
was compelled to replace with hospital appointments or to recover from the
effects of radiotherapy. These months were April, May and half of June (during
which she worked nowhere) and October, November and December in 1951,
followed by February and two thirds of March in 1952, when visits abroad were
replaced, where possible, by work in Britain. The back of her diary for 1952 has
advance notes of engagements as far as May 1953, including her usual fare of
Bach, Handel and Elgar oratorios and Mahler's vocal music with orchestra, as
well as a scattering of recitals up and down the land. After a projected Promenade Concert at London's Royal Albert Hall with Mahler's *Kindertotenlieder*
on 1st September, the diary is eerily blank until, with almost uncanny presci-
ence, the last week of her life. This is also true of the diary for 1953, in which

there is an absence of any amendments, just the occasional 'Cancelled', but more often just a sense of weary reluctance to bother to cross out an engagement. The diary's lack of forward planning to 1954, tells its own story. There are the scheduled performances which would never take place, such as the third and fourth *Orpheus* at Covent Garden, recitals at various places, and oratorios in London's major concert halls. She never sang in public again after the second *Orpheus* on Friday 6th February, but some projected bookings continue to appear in the diary. All goes quiet after the first week of June of that year, picks up again for the Edinburgh Festival in September, and then there are four scheduled appearances within a week at the Leeds Festival on 5th, 6th, 8th and 10th October. In that week she was engaged to sing Mozart's *Coronation* Mass on Monday 5th under Josef Krips, Elgar's *Apostles* on Tuesday 6th under Malcolm Sargent and, on Thursday 8th, Delius' *Mass of Life* (a work she had not sung before) also under Sargent. As well as the Mozart Mass, her diary entry for the Monday of that week includes 'Mahler 2', but the words are scored through. It may well be, therefore, that she had decided to sing only in the Mozart, for both works were performed that night with Helen Bouvier as the substituted contralto while the other two concerts were sung by Marjorie Thomas. The diary entry for the 8th reads: 'Leeds. *Mass of Life*. Delius', but Kathleen died peacefully that morning, giving the work's title an ironic twist. As to Saturday October 10th, the words 'Leeds Festival' probably mean one of the newly-introduced morning chamber concerts at Harewood House, rather than the evening's excerpts from Handel's *Israel in Egypt* back at the Town Hall which required no contralto. This morning event included Brahms' *Liebeslieder Walzer*, which Marjorie Thomas sang in Kathleen's place. In any case, the two words 'Leeds Festival' are scored through, and the diary for the rest of 1953 is completely blank. Whatever engagements Kathleen had accepted or was considering, she chose not to enter them in her diary for reasons we shall never know. Neither will we ever know what she really suspected about her own destiny.

Diary for 1942

January:

Saturday 3rd	Letter from [brother] George. Married on Xmas Eve. What a shock. First letter for 12 months.
Monday 5th	Went to see *Jeannie*. Barbara Mullen. Lovely!
Tuesday 6th	Saw Vic Oliver in *He made a Star*. Rotten!
Wednesday 7th	Win [Ferrier] fire watching
Thursday 8th	Carlisle concert. Didn't go. Terribly cold. Pop at Silloth.
Friday 9th	St Annes. Arrived tea time. Polly met me. Stayed in.
Saturday 10th	Went to Hallé at B'pool. Introduced to Malcolm Sargent! Went to Manchester for rehearsal.
Sunday 11th	Broadcast – Manchester. Nice announcer! 7.15am! Back to St Annes to hear Bessie Collins. Alfred Barker ill.
Monday 12th	Caught ¼ to 10 home. Freezing! Rang Hutchy up.
Tuesday 13th	Had lesson. Good one. Had tea with Wyn [Hetherington] and Con. Went to *Skylark*. Constance Cummings. Grand!
Wednesday 14th	Washed a bit. Bought new musquash coat!!! 39 guineas!!!! Going quiet for a bit now begorra!
Thursday 15th	Knitting bee at Buster's. Went in bus. Had tea and supper at Wyn's. Back on later bus. Freezing!
Friday 16th	Cleaned up for a change. Did piles of shopping and ironed at night.
Saturday 17th	Shopped and saw Phil and Grace. Phil's mother ill in infirmary. Wyn and Jack called. Knitted Pop's glove.
Sunday 18th	Awful day. Knitted and had a hot pot for lunch. O boy!
Monday 19th	Snowing and sleeting. More hot pot! Out to tea and Arthur Askey in *I thank you*.
Tuesday 20th	Winter set in, snowing and blowing gale. No lesson. Hutchy couldn't get through. Finished Pop's gloves.
Wednesday 21st	Thick snow. Didn't go out. Winnie fire watching.
Thursday 22nd	Thick snow. Pipes frozen! What a to-do! Stayed in all day. Didn't go knitting.
Friday 23rd	Cleared up. Tea out and *The Devil and Miss Jones*! Quite good. Knitted and waited up for Bert. 2.45A.M! Not come yet! Thaw, thank Heaven. No bursts yet!
Saturday 24th	Bert arrived 4.5AM. Talked till 6AM. Went to Silloth – Win as well.
Sunday 25th	Stayed in bed a bit. Went to badminton match with Wyn and Jack [Hetherington].
Monday 26th	Went to Silloth. Tea at Jim's. Sing at the Golf. Grand time!
Tuesday 27th	Good lesson. Bert met Hutchy. Bert to London for interview. Win fire watching.

Wednesday 28th	Had Leslie [piano pupil]. V.G. crowd came. Bert home 8pm. No luck.
Thursday 29th	Knitting bee and dance at Wigton. Very good.
Friday 30th	Went to Silloth. Sang. Brought Laura back with us.
Saturday 31st	Played golf at Carlisle – Lovely. Went down to Ena Mitchell's. Horrible letter from A.B.

February:

Sunday 1st	*Elijah* and *Judas*. Cecil St. Went off very well. Laura still here.
Monday 2nd	Laura and Bert went back. Snowing.
Tuesday 3rd	No lesson. Hutchy snowed up. Phyllis came. Chatter chatter.
Wednesday 4th	Pupil. Ironed. Arthur Sykes came. Sewed jumper up. Nice.
Thursday 5th	Knitting bee and flicks with Wyn. Deanna [Durbin] in *It started with Eve*. Splendid. Hutchy came and I was out. Shame!
Friday 6th	Phyllis 7.30. Chatter chatter. Knitted and listened to the Brains Trust. Went to flicks. Sunny.
Saturday 7th	Rehearsal. Sykes 7.30. Had supper there. Took Bettany home. Mrs Simpson broke collar bone Friday
Sunday 8th	Troop concert – Penrith. Went in J.T. [car] Visited Mr Wiesner and Mrs Lorm in afternoon. Nice!
Monday 9th	Milder weather. Practised well. Stayed in. Knitted.
Tuesday 10th	Good lesson. Saw Wyn. All had our tea at Mr Shaw's. Went to *Kiss the Boys Goodbye*. Letter from R. Hunt.
Wednesday 11th	Rehearsal for Percy. Went very well. Took me home after.
Friday 13th	Warships Week concert for Percy. Walter Elliot M.P. on platform. Sang 'Rule Britannia' and 'Land of Soap and Water'.
Saturday 14th	Went to St Annes. 1.19 train. Tea at Chadwick's. Went to Rep players. Bed late.
Sunday 15th	St Annes concert. Went off very well. Everyone thrilled. Double encores.
Monday 16th	Home at 2pm. Bert moved to London. Went to Phyllis for practice with Mr Spears.
Tuesday 17th	Good lesson. Cold weather.
Wednesday 18th	Win fire watching. Stayed in and knitted.
Thursday 19th	Grammar School. Wore black velvet. All posh. Went off well. Everybody pleased. Mr Wiesner and Mrs Lorm there.
Friday 20th	Mr and Mrs Hayton came up. Phyllis and Papa called for sausage.
Saturday 21st	Laura and Ena came. Stayed in. Snowing again. What weather! Car won't stop. O dear!
Sunday 22nd	Mr Wiesner and Mrs Lorm to supper. V.G. time and interesting. Went at 1a.m.
Monday 23rd	Report from St Annes. V.G. Stayed in and knitted. Down town in afternoon.
Tuesday 24th	Good lesson. Went out to tea and 1st house theatre. Free tickets! Not bad.

Wednesday 25th	Good letters from [Eve] KISCH. Whoopee. Washed and ironed and practised hours. Win fire watching. Knitted and mended.
Thursday 26th	Stanwick concert. Henry Wendon soloist. 7.30. Knitting bee at Mrs Robinson's. H. Wendon didn't turn up. Parry Jones. <u>Very</u> disappointing.
Friday 27th	Out to tea and to *Lady Hamilton* – Vivien Leigh – Splendid! To Phyllis for sing. Home in J.T.
Saturday 28th	What letters. Telegram from Helen Anderson. Letter from Kisch as well. Whoopee! Didn't go out. Win bad cold.

March:

Sunday 1st	A day to be remembered! Warwick Braithwaite concert 8.15. <u>What</u> a day! Gorgeous concert. Met W.B. Sang for him at Percy's. Came up with Wiesner and Lorm for supper. Didn't go till 4.15 A.M.! Gorgeous time! Phyllis up all day too.
Monday 2nd	Shopped and visited. Tea at Eileen's. Phyllis came up – upset about political views. Had good cry! Win to drs.
Tuesday 3rd	Win stayed in bed all day – about time too! No lesson today. Had tea with WYN. Saw Eileen.
Wednesday 4th	Winnie in bed. Cough, cough, cough! Shopped and visited. Tea at Eileen's.
Thursday 5th	Had Dr to Winnie. To stay in bed till next Wed. Called round at Mr Wiesner's. Had supper and chat. Home late. No knitting bee.
Friday 6th	Cleaned up. Bettany came up. Went to see Phyllis. Alright again now. Awful wind and cold weather.
Saturday 7th	Snowing! Shopped. Knitted. Listened to wireless. Telegram from Penrith asking me to sing. Already booked. How busy I am!
Sunday 8th	Raining and milder. Stayed in and listened to W.B. and Scottish Orchestra. Had bath – wrote letters.
Monday 9th	Practised. Stayed in. Knitted.
Tuesday 10th	Good lesson. Had tea with Wyn and Jack. Bed early. Sore throat.
Wednesday 11th	Ena Mitchell's. She came up in morning. I'm feeling rotten – aching in every blinking bone. Winnie gets up. Dr puts me to bed.
Thursday 12th	Wrote to Hutchy. Throat worse. Can't go to Newcastle! Furious.
Friday 13th	Throat still lousy. Slept and drank all day. Sent telegram to Hutchy and wrote.
Saturday 14th	Dr came. NOT to get up and not to do CEMAs either. Hell's bells! Wires to Kisch, M. Head, Bootle and Millom.
Sunday 15th	<u>Elijah</u> for Hutchy. Throat better. Still in bed. Hell's bleeding bells! Biggest disappointment ever.
Monday 16th	Still in bed. Can get up tomorrow.

Tuesday 17th	Bootle. Couldn't go! Hutchy came. Never got my 3 letters and wire! Stunned!
Wednesday 18th	Millom. Couldn't go! Out first time. Round the block.
Thursday 19th	Went to Newcastle. Rehearsed with Helen Anderson. Stayed at her digs. The same as Dorothy F. used to stay at. What a coincidence.
Friday 20th	Newcastle CEMA. Went off grand, Mrs Lorm there. Had lunch and tea with Helen Anderson. Rehearsal at night.
Saturday 21st	Mr Bettany's concert. Went off very well. Packed house. Pop, Win and Eileen went.
Memo	Jimmie bad cough all week. Getting worried. Quite asthmatic, pore little thing.
Sunday 22nd	Workington Steel Works. Phyllis played for me. Had tea at Broughton. Brought P. back to Carlisle. Pleasant day.
Monday 23rd	Lovely weather. Spring at last. Crocuses out on the lawn. Down town in morning. Practised in aft.
Tuesday 24th	Jimmie poorly still. Good lesson. Tea out and flix. Sonja Henie. Rotten! Had the vet to Jimmie.
Wednesday 25th	Rehearsal with Mr Danskin 6.30. Called at Phyl's.
Thursday 26th	*Creation.* Lousy. Knitting bee in afternoon. Met Hutchy at station with sausage. Jimmie better.
Friday 27th	Shopped. Dr Simpson came. Went to flix. *Moon over Miami.* Lovely colours. Wrote Bert. Weather cold.
Saturday 28th	Went to Silloth with Pop and Win in J.T. Had few holes of golf and rejoined. Stayed at Birnie's a bit. J.T. running like a bird.
Sunday 29th	Used up Feb's petrol round Lanercost [Priory]. Lovely day. Put a lot of seeds in garden. Had bath and hair wash.
Monday 30th	Washed and ironed. Win went to WEA lecture. Listened in and knitted. Heard of possibility of house at Stanwix.
Tuesday 31st	Rutherford College. ¼ to 3. Got £1.11.6. Went off very well. Had tea with Phyl and Miss Forster. Called at Ena's. Knitted and listened to Brains Trust.

April:

Wednesday 1st	Down town in morning. Had Leslie. Stayed in. Awful weather. Pore little seeds!
Thursday 2nd	Lunch hour. R.A.F. 12 noon. Went off alright. Went to knitting bee. Saw Dr Simpson. Win went to the Lakes.
Good Friday 3rd	Cleaned up all day till 8.30. Listened in afternoon to *Dream of Gerontius.* V.G.
Saturday 4th	Shopped in queues! Practised well in aft. Wrote letters and took them to post.
Sunday 5th	Cecil St. 6[pm]. Went off OK Stayed to troop concert too. Very windy. Rotten weather.
Monday 6th	Awful weather. Blowing and raining. Got a bad cold again.
Tuesday 7th	Win came home. Can hardly speak. Went to pictures.

Wednesday 8th	Stayed in all day nursing my cold. Wyn called.
Thursday 9th	Ena's. Had practise at duets. Missed bus and had to walk home.
Friday 10th	Had hair done. Tea out with wee Phil and Papa.
Saturday 11th	Went on bus to Ansdell. What a journey! Went to Whittaker's. Played cards. Won 1/6d!
Sunday 12th	*Elijah* Lytham 2.30. Went off well. Chadwicks, Lees, Tom and Lana Goodwin there. Stayed at Whittakers. Church at night.
Monday 13th	Went to Withnell Fold. Chorley in afternoon. Stayed in and listened to *Messiah* celebration on wireless.
Tuesday 14th	Audition with Ed Isaacs after concert in Manchester. Very thrilled. Bought new coat at Kendal Milnes. Posh! Posh price too. Pictures at Brinscall.
Wednesday 15th	Went to Blackburn. Saw Uncle George. Others out. Up to Florence's at night. Got some gin and rum!
Thursday 16th	Came home on bus. Very hot weather and me in fur coat! Pop at Silloth.
Friday 17th	Cleaned up. Ena's in afternoon. Christopher Wood there. Schaffer and Wiesner came at night. Very nice.
Saturday 18th	Went to Silloth. Game of golf and new frock! Beauty. Music club meeting. Quite interesting.
Sunday 19th	Wesleyan's. Lovely day. Win to Silloth. Rehearsal in morning. Wrote letters. Sang at night. Not very well.
Monday 20th	Cecil St. Went off alright. Went to Ena's later with Lorm and Wiesner. Home ¼ to 2!
Tuesday 21st	Went after house but taken by Government. Washed. Mrs Huggan and Betty arrived for the evening. Had bike ride.
Wednesday 22nd	Y.O. Dr Garry. Very nice dinner and musical talk. Borrowed two books.
Thursday 23rd	RAF MU [RAF Maintenance Unit] cancelled. Phyllis came to tea. First opera class with Mrs Lorm. V.G. Saw Jim R.
Friday 24th	Supper at Wiesner's. Lovely time. Saw press cuttings etc. Home late. Went to see Mollie R in home.
Saturday 25th	Y.O. Meeting. Quite interesting. Walked home with Garry.
Sunday 26th	Busy day filling plant pots in preparation for tomatoes.
Monday 27th	Went to 1st German class. V.G. Wiesner and Lorm round after.
Tuesday 28th	Lovely lesson. Had cup of tea with Hutchy. Tea out and pictures. Quite good.
Wednesday 29th	Went to pictures again. Ridiculous!
Thursday 30th	Dr Wadely's *Pickwick* postponed. Had knitting bee. Sang *Orfeo* for opera class at night. To Phyl's after. Lovely. Leslie.

May:

Friday 1st	Dr Simpson called with orgy of fruit and flowers. To Kendal to hear Muriel Brunskill.

Saturday 2nd	Stayed the night at *Kendal* Hotel. Home again on bus. Pottered after tea at Shaw's.
Sunday 3rd	Lovely day. Pottered. Washed hair, bathed etc etc.
Monday 4th	CEMA Wordsworth Hall, Penrith with Maurice Jacobson and Eve. Marvellous. Phyl and Win there, Mr Chadwick too. M. Jacobson grand. Sat up late.
Tuesday 5th	Barrow. What a day! Colossal. Two concerts and most successful. Bed late. Stayed at the *Sun*, Ulverston. Played word games. Climbed Kirkstone and had to walk part of the way.
Wednesday 6th	Ulverston Grammar School. Perfectly marvellous day. Picknicked in morning. Two concerts. Saw Maurice off on 9 train. Celebrated with two gin and tonics. 'Parting is such sweet sorrow'.
Thursday 7th	Packed up. Home 5ish. Had Leslie. Opera class. The end of a perfect holiday. To Mrs Lorm's after for meeting and supper. Very tired.
Friday 8th	Cleaned up, washed and ironed. Practised. Bed elevenish. Bath and washed hair.
Saturday 9th	Music Club. Very crowded. Phyl up for tea and crowd also after. Records at club not very successful. Too quiet. Telephone call to St Annes. Bed late again.
Memo	Never forget my little first tour. Never a hitch for 3 whole days. Lovely!
Sunday 10th	Had Phyl, Ena and friend up in morning recovering lost property. Practised, darned, mended and had easy day generally. Foul weather.
Monday 11th	Stockton-on-Tees. CEMA. 8.35 train. Arrived for lunch. Met Helen, Harry Isaacs and John Francis. Went to lovely new school at Norton. Very successful concert. Home very late to Helen's digs. Wore black velvet!
Tuesday 12th	CEMA for Helen A. Annfield Plain. Again very successful. Helen didn't go – just John, Harry and me. Very cold. Home quite soon – bed quite late. Walk in Jesmond Dene in afternoon.
Wednesday 13th	CEMA Jarrow and South Shields. V.G. Had lunch out and gorgeous supper – fresh salmon mayonnaise and sherry. Went to Helen's friend after and sang for a change!! Bed late – oh dear!
Thursday 14th	Aspatria. Home on 10.20. John saw me off. Lunch at Silver Grill. Went to Aspatria. Pretty awful. Didn't sing enough ballads. Home early. Phyllis played for me. Lots of letters waiting!
Friday 15th	Had easy day. Win cleaned all up yesterday. Bath and preparations for Sunderland. Early to bed. Leslie.
Saturday 16th	Sunderland. Up at 5AM!! John met me at Newcastle. Had breakfast in station. Went to Station Hotel to pass time till lunch and train for Sunderland. Concert went off very well. Tea in *Station* Hotel all together. Home on 8.20 after salmon

mayonnaise in Eldon Grill! Walked home. Two heart-to-heart talks today! What a strain.

Sunday 17th Maryport? 7.45 *Empire* Theatre. Went to Eleanor's for tea and supper. Phyl played for me. Not very popular these days locally. Getting too highbrow. Home <u>very</u> late.

Monday 18th Slept till 10.30. Wrote John. Washed and ironed – practised hours. Card from Malcolm Sargent's secretary. Missed my German class.

Tuesday 19th Lesson. Eve K. coming. Met her from train. Had lunch at Grill. Lesson. Introduced Eve to Ena and Hutchy. Lorm and Wiesner came at night.

Wednesday 20th Up with the blooming lark! 6.30 having slept on settee. Made date with Malcolm in Manchester! Flix in afternoon. Holst in concert at night – slept in a bathroom at the *Albion*.

Thursday 21st 3pm Malcolm Sargent. O boy! Lunch with John. Saw him off on train. Had audition. Very pleased. Caught train to St Annes. Stayed at Chadwicks.

Friday 22nd St Annes (Aid to Russia) Breakfast in bed and lovely bath. Good concert. Went off well. Double encores.

Saturday 23rd Home at lunchtime. Dad met me. Shopped and had tea in town. Practised at night.

Memo 'How Changed'. 'Fishermaiden'. 'Secrecy'. 'Hark, Hark'. 'Swing Low'. 'Vigil'. 'Arch Denial', 'I Have a Bonnet'.

Sunday 24th Up latish. Blowing a gale. Practised almost all day and wrote five letters.

Monday 25th Write to Malcolm Sargent. Wrote yesterday. Should have picknicked, but poured all day. Saved petrol and practised hours!!

Tuesday 26th Parcel from John. Had good lesson. Lunch out. Practised hours. Rehearsal for *Pickwick*. Bought <u>gorgeous</u> frock! O boy!

Wednesday 27th Houseworked. Practised <u>hours</u>. Went out to tea and on to *Fantasia*. Beautiful. Bed soon. Letter from Eric Greene.

Thursday 28th Had knitting bee but all went to pictures to see *Choc Soldiers*! Not bad. Practised lots. Letter from John Francis. Leslie.

Friday 29th Music Club meeting. What a lot about nothing. Phyllis came up after. Letter from Sargent confirming agreement to write to Ibbs and Tillett.

Saturday 30th Shopped. Biked to Wetheral. Letter from I & T. Good. Washed a bit. Had bath. Wrote to Greene, Jacques, Shrewsbury, George, Uncle Bert. Bed late.

Memo Claimed £13.12.0d from N.E. tour. Got £16.15.0d!

Sunday 31st Heard John broadcasting on overseas. Went to Silloth – picnic lunch. Rained of course in afternoon, but lovely at night. Called at Wyn's on way home. Nice day.

June:

Monday 1st Rotten weather. Cleaned my room out – drawers and all!

Washed a bit, ironed a bit and made a posh vest out of skirt and pants! Nice work! Frock came. (Hell's bells!)

Tuesday 2nd   Cleaned up bedrooms. Went to Cicely Haye's for practice. Letter from John and Maurice. Wiesner and Lorm round at night – washed hair.

Wednesday 3rd   Leslie. Cleaned up. Down town. Slept in afternoon. Tea out. Got ready for tomorrow.

Thursday 4th   3pm Eric Greene's. Went off very well. There an hour. Went to flix – stayed at the *White Swan* – wrote letters. Bed soon. Very hot weather.

Friday 5th   Still gorgeously hot. Home by 3pm. Managed to get woman to clean. Hip! Hip! Letter from Maurice – wire from Helen. Whoopee! Garden looking lovely. Simpsons called.

Saturday 6th   Shopped. Sunbathed. Had tea in garden. Practised. Wrote letters. Knitted. No exciting letters today.

Sunday 7th   Blowing a gale all day. Sewed all day. New pair of cami-knickers. Nearly finished them. Baked a bit.

Monday 8th   Cicely Haye 3pm? Didn't turn up. Practised a lot. Finished cami-knickers. Posh! Letter from John. Had walk with Win at night. Still lousy weather. Very windy.

Tuesday 9th   Lesson 2.30. Good one.

Wednesday 10th   Bert coming home.

Saturday 13th   Music Club. Tom Clay went to Silloth instead. [Beethoven] 5th Symphony. *Fidelio*. Violin Sonata. Poured all day

Memo   Lost my beautiful fountain pen!

Sunday 14th   Rained all day. Practised and washed hair.

Monday 15th   Raining still. Doing the cabbages good!

Tuesday 16th   Good lesson. Ena and Billie came up. Bed late. Weather improved. Whoopee!

Wednesday 17th   Washed hair. Did odd jobs. Had Leslie.

Thursday 18th   To Liverpool! Whoopee. Auntie Annie met me. Had walk at night and rang Battens up. Bed late. Took posh new frock!

Friday 19th   Eve's ¼ to 4. Breakfast in bed! Lovely. Called at Battens. Met Stephen Wearing. Went round to Hon. Ruth Lever. Had dinner there. Party at Eve's after! Bed 1am.

Saturday 20th   Chester. Went off well but no attention from anybody. Nearly stranded in L'pool but hitch-hiked to Battens. Rena waiting up for me. Bless her!

Sunday 21st   Had breakfast and lunch at Battens. To W.F. on 5 o'clock train. Went in Higsons and gambled. Lovely time. Bert at S'port.

Monday 22nd   Came home from W.F. Good journey. NO letters waiting. Poor do.

Tuesday 23rd   Letter from John. Good lesson. Jack and Wyn came. Played pontoon. Lovely weather.

Wednesday 24th   Listen in 10.30 – European. Good. Leslie. Paid. Lovely letter from LV man re Chester. Out for lunch and tea with Flo. Bert went back. Wyn and Irene.

Thursday 25th	Washed. Went to Buster's for knitting bee in J.T. Opera class at night and ironed.
Friday 26th	Shopped. Exasperated. Stayed in – practised.
Saturday 27th	Went to Newcastle. Win to Lakes. Train packed. Stayed at Helen's digs. Had two walks in Jesmond Dene for old time's sake. Photo in N/c paper.
Sunday 28th	Eve coming up. Concerts at N/castle. Rehearsal in morning and 2 concerts. Busy day. Very nice though.
Monday 29th	Came home 10.30am. Practised all day and wrote letters. Had lovely bath.
Tuesday 30th	No lesson today. Went to see Greta Garbo. Quite good. Lovely weather. Practised hard. Cut out cami-knicks.

July:

Wednesday 1st	Leslie. Sewed and mended. Washed, ironed and practised all day. Never went out. Letter from John.
Thursday 2nd	Good letter from Eric Greene. Cleaned up (a bit). Sewed. Ena came to tea. Henry Holst concert. He was fine. Wiesner and Lorm, Ena and Billie up at night.
Friday 3rd	Finished my sewing. Went to Ena's for supper. Very nice. Bed late.
Saturday 4th	Up early. Cleaned up. Shopped. Win came home. Practised, darned, listened in. Bed late. Made jam. Lovely.
Sunday 5th	Washed, ironed and got ready for London. Whoopee!
Monday 6th	London on the 8.30. Long journey 9 hours! John met us and collected fiddle. Had tea and up to Madge's. Good dinner.
Tuesday 7th	Met John. Went to Guildford and punted! Tea in town and to *Lifeline*. Good but harrowing rather. Home on bus. Hardly any traffic.
Wednesday 8th	Ring Miss Crook. Visit Maurice – Curwen's. Lovely. He is a pet. Arranged for accompanist. Stayed in at night.
Thursday 9th	Wigmore Hall 2pm. Miss Crook 12pm. Very nice. Audition went off well. Decided to live in London. Phew! Went to ballet. Lovely.
Friday 10th	John came to Madge's to rehearse Bantock. Lovely. Stayed to lunch. Went to lunch hour concert. Had tea and up to Gottfelts. Lovely time. Home late.
Saturday 11th	1pm Maurice. Lunch with him and Kathleen Moorhouse and Miss Crook. Lovely lesson. On to Prom in Albert Hall. Grand. *Rio Grande*. Joyce Sutton, Margaret Good. John rang up from Bedford.
Sunday 12th	Travelled to Leeds. Stayed at the *Mount* Hotel. Nice. Bed soon and arranging parts for string quartet.
Monday 13th	Dewsbury at a lovely school. Concerts went off well. E. Greene and wife there. Lovely headmistress Other artists Elsie Winnale-Johnson and trumpeter.
Tuesday 14th	Came home. Lesson with Hutchy. Had heart to heart talk re

JULY 1942

5 Sun. 5th after Trinity.
Washed. Wanted l get
ready for London
weather!

Dangers despised grow greater.

6 Mon. London on the 8.30.
long journey gloves!
John met us I collected
fiddle. Had Vea I up to
Theresa's. Good wine.

To speak his thought is every free man's right.

7 Tues. Met John. Went
to Guildford and printed
deal down I to
Lifeline. Caught bus however
rather Homebus. Home first.

We may give advice, but we cannot give conduct.

8 Wed. Ring Miss Cook.
Visit Maurice tomorrow.
Lovely. He is a pet. Arranged
processcopering. Stayed in
at night.

Learn all you can, but learn from the learned.

JULY 1942

9 Thurs. Fire Insurances Expire.
Wigmore Hall 2 pm.
Crook 12 pm very nice
audition went off. Music. Plan!
Decided to live in London. Plan!
Went to Balcot. Lovely.

Calamity is man's true touchstone.

10 Fri. John came to Margie
to rehearse Bartock. Lovely.
Stayed to Lunch. Went to
luncheon concert. Have Vea
and up to Gatyfeets. Lovely.
Time Home late.

Why should we anticipate our sorrow.

11 Sat. 1.0 Maurice.
lunch with him & Kathleen
Afternoon spring Crook. Lovely
lemon. On to Prom in Albert
Hall. Grand. Ro Grande.
Foyer Supper merry evening Good.

Adversity makes a man wise, tho' not rich.

Johrucuing up Memo Redford

	London. Mrs Wilson spring-cleaned the house! Very ashamed of myself.
Wednesday 15th	Rained of course. Shopped in morning. Tea out and pictures. Washed hair. Good letter from Eve.
Thursday 16th	Listen in 2pm. Went to Wyn's, knitted, talked, round to Irene's. Had Leslie. Practised. Rotten weather. Mrs W. and Auntie Louie went back.
Friday 17th	Wrote music and practised all day. Phyllis and Papa called. The only bright spot! Lousy weather.
Saturday 18th	Shopped. Practised all day. Letter from LV. midday. Good. Having quiet time!
Monday 20th	Practised and moped. Went to Lydia Kyasht ballet. Very good except orchestra. Washed and ironed.
Tuesday 21st	No lesson. New woman. Seems very good. More ironing. Baked for a nice change.
Wednesday 22nd	Win came home. Good news re flat. Hope it comes off. Phyllis came up. Practised. Walked down with her after. Win firewatching. Leslie.
Thursday 23rd	Shopped and sewed new frock. Win firewatching. Telegram from John – rang him up re dates. Frock very good so far.
Friday 24th	Went to W. Fold on 1.19. Packed. Pouring down. Went up to Flo's at night.
Saturday 25th	Went to B'burn. Saw Margaret, Tom and Auntie Maud. Waited years for Bert and Papa to come from match. Browned off.
Sunday 26th	Walk in afternoon.
Monday 27th	Went to Flo's musical evening. Home very late.
Tuesday 28th	Went to Ferriers for tea. *Grand*. Theatre after. Norman Long, Stanelli etc. Not bad.
Wednesday 29th	Went up to Auntie Harriet's. Home very late.
Thursday 30th	Came home on early train. Overflowing! Lunch out. Finished frock. Ver goot.
Friday 31st	Supper at Wiesners. Didn't go. Went to flix and Phyllis after. Helped with circulars. Tea out.

August:	
Saturday 1st	Shopped. Went to Silloth. Full round of golf. 3 down on handicap. Whoopee! Back on crowded train.
Sunday 2nd	Up late. Practised and wrote music <u>all</u> day till ¼ to 1am. Can hardly see!
Monday 3rd	Miserable weather. Practised. Washed and ironed. Had walk at night. Letter re B'pool concert!
Tuesday 4th	Practised. Cleaned up. Wyn and Peter came to tea. Went down to station with them. Bed early. Letter from John and Bert.
Wednesday 5th	Town in morning. Met John McKenna and Norman Long! Washed hair, had bath, packed etc. Win firewatching
Thursday 6th	Burton on a punt. Went off alright but daft. Ruth Pearl quartet

and John. Red letter day! 4tet arrangements good. [Placed in a punt on the River Trent, Kathleen sang with the string quartet and flute, an idea of CEMA Midlands organiser Tom Harrison which misfired when strong currents carried them swiftly to and fro past a somewhat bemused bank-side audience].

Friday 7th   Rotherham. Stay at *Grand Hotel*, Sheffield. Went off very well. John Morel, Kenneth Skeaping, Charles Elland and me. Sargent and Moiseiwitsch staying in hotel. Posh!

Saturday 8th   Came home. Shopped. Went to Music Club. Dreadful. Phyllis' after. Home late. Very tired.

Sunday 9th   Rotten weather. Wrote letters, practised etc. Phyllis came up. Stayed all night. Bed ¼ to 2!

Monday 10th   Send songs to Barbara. Slept most of the day. Practised. Wrote letters. Foul weather. Letter from J.

Tuesday 11th   Washed and ironed. Tea out and pictures. Letter from Ed Isaacs. Bit snooty. Wrote back and to Miss Crook. Win bought me diary. Nice.

Wednesday 12th   Ena's 3pm. Send copies to Jackson Little tomorrow. Went out to tea, flix with Ena and Cynthia Farndell. Home late. No letters.

Thursday 13th   Gateshead. Miners' Welfare Hall, Whickham. Stay at Miss Cooke's. Letter from John. Rang him up. Final break. Concert not bad.

Friday 14th   Came home. Depressed. Went to flix with Mrs Simpson. Shopped. Listened in.

Saturday 15th   Shopped. Telegram from John. Rang him up. Might get Phil concert next Sat. Here's hoping. Stayed in and lazed! Bed soon.

Memo   Love Song. Lovely Cheeks. Love is a Bable or Water Boy. Swing Low. I have a Bonnet.

Sunday 16th   Cockermouth? 7.45. 'He shall feed His flock'. 'Arise O Sun' Duet. Went off well. Nice time. Stayed at *Lakes* Hotel. Ena went.

Monday 17th   Music Club meeting 6.30pm. Phyllis came for night. Dr Simpson took us to Wigton in morning. Washed and ironed and baked etc.

Tuesday 18th   Wyn and Phyllis to lunch. Flix with Wyn. Very good. Tea out. Wrote letters and practised.

Wednesday 19th   Shopped. Practised. Washed hair. Bath. Bed ¼ to 9. Good letter re Scotch tour. Whoopee!

Thursday 20th   Lancaster. 8.30 train. Eve and Steve. Good concert at Hest Bank. Bed late.

Friday 21st   Eve. Urmston. Where'er you walk. Hark the echoing air. Caro mio ben. Love is a Bable. Town Maid. Water Boy. Bonnet. Cheeks. Love Song. Pleading. Secrecy.

Saturday 22nd   L'pool Philharmonic 6.45. Rehearsal 2.30. Very successful.

	Janet and Win, Stephen and Nina, Rena and husband. Kathleen Colville there.
Sunday 23rd	Rotherham 7pm. Rehearsal 2.15. *Messiah*. Couldn't get any breakfast. Pouring down. The worst pub ever. Stayed at the *Grand*, Sheffield. Had siren. No fireworks. *Messiah* went off well.
Monday 24th	Home again 3pm. Wrote letters and manuscript. Bed early.
Tuesday 25th	Washed and ironed. Woman didn't turn up. Poured all the ruddy day. Never knew such weather!
Wednesday 26th	2 o'clock train to York. Arrived 7pm. Deluge of rain. No room at pub. Had dinner. Went to Trix's. Stayed there.
Thursday 27th	YORK. Midday concert for Rowntrees. Noisy audience but wonderful lunch, buckshee choco and free seats to theatre. Also siren! Sun shining, wonderful.
Friday 28th	YORK concert cancelled. Went to Helen's. Stayed there. Saw Rep co. in good play. Had sing. Sirens and gunfire. Slept well. Getting used to it. Boiling hot.
Saturday 29th	Lesson 10.55. Good one. Had lunch, news theatre and home on 2.10. Win met me. Woman never turned up this week. Cold weather. Curse all chars!
Sunday 30th	Stayed in all day. Poured down. Practised. Knitted and listened in. Dreadful weather.
Monday 31st	Washed. Cleaned up a bit. Practised. Wyn and Peter called on bikes. Went a short run on ours. Knitted and listened in.

September:

Tuesday 1st	Mrs T. turned up, thank Heaven. Ironed. Practised. Bath. Went to *Auld Acquaintance*. Edith Evans splendid.
Wednesday 2nd	Practised a lot. Tea out and shopped. Saw Kitty Smalley of all people. Weather nice. Strange!
Thursday 3rd	11 train to Wigton. Had day at Wyn's and knitting bee. Grand. Kitty Smalley and husband came up at night.
Friday 4th	Cleaned up. Shopped. Hair wash, bath etc. Practised. Dreadful weather.
Saturday 5th	Blackburn concert went off very well. Bert, Flo and Ma [Wilson] there, Auntie Maud and Uncle George, Miss [Frances] Walker, Wilma. Saw Lenna and Tom Barker. Audrey Brearley, Mrs Sweeting, Mrs Parmley etc. etc.
Sunday 6th	10.44 from Preston. Good journey. Good dinner. NCC came to listen to wireless. Took my case to station. Bed and bath soon.
Monday 7th	Stranraer. 7.15am train. Caught it too! Margaret Davie met me. Had lunch. Rehearsal. Yacamini came! Very pleased. Made nice speech. Concert in chapel in semi-darkness.
Tuesday 8th	Kirkcowan by bus. Wrote letters. Rehearsed. Went to country mansion for dinner before concert. Went off well. Came home in Bunty's car.

Wednesday 9th	Newton Stewart. Walk in morning. Lovely weather. Watched Horace fish. No luck. Good concert at night. Wonderful hospitality.
Thursday 10th	Wigtown. Another walk. Packed up to go to Wigtown. Good concert. Walk after. Several gin and limes. Oo-er!
Friday 11th	Whithorn. Betty's wedding. 11.50 from Dumfries, arr. Carlisle 12.33. 1.0 from Carlisle arr. Newcastle 2.45. Lovely day. Boated, brambled. Dreadful hotel.
Saturday 12th	Newcastle. *Samson.* 6.30 Brunswick Methodist. Went off very well. Very tired. Long journey. Stayed at Helen's. Fun!
Sunday 13th	Home again. Phyllis met me. Wrote letters. Practised. 3 lads in to listen to symphony concert.
Monday 14th	Washed and baked for a change. Down to earth with a wallop. No letters.
Tuesday 15th	Lesson. Good one. Ironed in morning. Thank goodness. Hutchy nice.
Wednesday 16th	Shopped. Had tea out. Mr Earnshaw came at night. Played and sang. Very nice. No letters.
Thursday 17th	Bad cold. Didn't go to knitting bee. Practised, dosed myself, and knitted. Early to bed.
Friday 18th	Cleaned up. Practised. Knitted. Still dosing myself. Didn't go out. Phyllis came up. Chatter, chatter.
Saturday 19th	Win did the shopping. Stayed in again. Cold improving. More than I deserve!
Sunday 20th	Rained all day. Practised. Knitted a lot! No visitors. Quiet day.
Monday 21st	Washed. Cold a bit better. Still not been out. Weather foul. Knitted and practised.
Tuesday 22nd	Went on 8.30 to L'pool. Shopped with Auntie Annie. Rehearsal at night with Suckling. Met Louis Cohen. Eyes and nose streaming.
Wednesday 23rd	L'pool midday. 'Night in May', 'Cheeks', 'Love Song'. 'Love is a Bable', 'Silent Noon', 'Bier Side'. Splendid day but <u>very</u> tired. Bromborough with Eve and Steve.
Thursday 24th	Came home. Phyllis came up. Parcel of songs from Jackie – Lovely. Cold still dreadful. Letter from Wyn.
Friday 25th	Bert coming home. Went to CEMA. Very few there. Saw 3 in orchestra. Drink in *County.*
Saturday 26th	Went to Silloth. Win to London – lucky B. Saw lots of folk – came home. That's all.
Sunday 27th	Went to Wyn's. Early bus. Bert and Jack off on bike. Jack and Wyn came back to 23. Bed late.
Monday 28th	All went to see *How Green was my Valley.* Wet through – cried my bloomin' eyes out. Gorgeous. Tea out. Played cards. Bert went back midnight.
Tuesday 29th	Lesson. Good one. Bless little Hutchy. Very tired. Slept, practised, wrote letters etc. Bed and bath soon.

Wednesday 30th	Cleaned up – a bit! Practised and knitted. Listened in to *Magic Flute*. Very good!

October:

Thursday 1st	Wadely? No. Went to Wyn's. Knitting bee at Buster's. Tea at Irene's. Home on 7.20. Mended. Engagement from Ibbs and Tillett. Whoopee!
Friday 2nd	Another engagement from I and T! Cleaned up. Wyn called.
Saturday 3rd	Shopped etc. Win came home. Talked and talked and knitted.
Sunday 4th	1.5 to Manchester. Absolutely crammed full. Met Eileen Ebsworth. Very nice. Bed soon.
Monday 5th	Manchester tour 3 weeks. Gas and Oil. Ashton-under-Lyne. Very good audience. Shop gazed. Bed early.
Tuesday 6th	Renold Works, Didsbury. Went to see *Midsummer Night's Dream*. Good audience at concert.
Wednesday 7th	Mirrlees, Stockport. Wonderful audience. Went to flix. *The man who came to dinner*. V.G.
Thursday 8th	Concert at Stockport. Very good audience. Bought two beautiful rugs. Bed soon. Lovely weather.
Friday 9th	Concert at Oldham. Quite good. Bit noisy at first. Good lunch. Raining cats and dogs.
Saturday 10th	No concert today. Went to Auntie Annie's. Lovely to sit in front of a fire and knit. Slept on camp bed.
Sunday 11th	Had walk with Jan, Reg and baby. Knitted, slept and talked. Nice day.
Monday 12th	Came to Manchester on 9am train. Good two concerts. Given 25" zip. Whoopee. Saw them making rubber dinghys. Wonderful. Bought new boots!!
Tuesday 13th	Another concert. Rather rushed. Read and slept in afternoon. Knitted at night in front of gas fire.
Wednesday 14th	Concert in gun factory. Enthusiasm tremendous. Shopped and knitted. Bath and bed.
Thursday 15th	Concert with Tilly at spinning mill. Terribly cold. Shopped, knitted and read.
Friday 16th	Concert at magnesium works. Very bad acoustics. Read, bathed and packed for weekend.
Saturday 17th	8.45 train to Chorley. Did 3 concerts at Euxton. Went on to W. Fold. Bert home. Poured all the time. Stayed at Flo's. Slept at No.9.
Sunday 18th	Rained all day. Came back to Manchester with Bert.
Monday 19th	Manchester Victoria 11.0 to Bolton. V.G. concert. Good lunch! 52 double decker to Wilmslow, Chapel Lane. Practised hard all night. Bed 11.30. Tired.
Tuesday 20th	Manchester Midday. Went off very well. Bit scared. Knees shook!
Wednesday 21st	Good crit in *Guardian*. Concert at Dukenfield. Embarrassing. Bed earlyish. Very tired!

Thursday 22nd	Concert at Burtons. Very nice. Beryl went instead of Tilly. Frrrrightful head! Lousy weather
Friday 23rd	Last concert at Oldham. Very nice one. Said fond farewells to Tilly, Eileen and Beryl. Home 8pm. Phyl there. Stayed up talking till 2am. Letter from Maurice.
Saturday 24th	End of tour. Made a house coat out of two rugs. Beautiful! Shopped. Saw Bettany. Letter from Jackie. Phyl went noon. Rang Wyn.
Sunday 25th	Bettany came up. Knitted. Sewed. Win baked. Busy day. Lousy weather.
Monday 26th	Washed. Foul weather. Rang Wyn up.
Tuesday 27th	Lesson. Good one. Saw Eileen Moffitt. Washed hair etc. and packed.
Wednesday 28th	Liverpool (Speke) 8.30 train. Went to midday concert – Laffite. Lunch with Tully. Good concert with Steve. Mick at Murray's.
Thursday 29th	Allerton. Ken, Reno and Evie there. Phew! Packed house. Lovely time. Home late. Very tired but couldn't sleep.
Friday 30th	Had lunch with Ken. Tea with Eve. Flick in afternoon. Up to Battens at night. Home afterwards with Ken.
Saturday 31st	Met Maurice in Manchester. Went to his 1st perf. *Lady of Shallot*. Dreadful orchestra. Went to news flick. Lovely time. Met Uncle Henry.

November:	
Sunday 1st	Leigh Parish Church with Maurice J. Went off terribly well. Gorgeous day. Maurice played on mini piano! Stayed in Leigh.
Monday 2nd	Left Maurice at Manchester. Came home.
Tuesday 3rd	Lesson. Bit bilious. Hutchy nice, bless him!
Wednesday 4th	Durham (Consett) *Samson*. 6 gns. Went off well. Forgot long frock. Borrowed one!
Thursday 5th	Washed. Ironed. Packed. And a thousand sundries!
Friday 6th	Frognal Mansions. Bert met me. Stayed to dinner at McArthurs. Lovely flat.
Saturday 7th	Wandered round. Went to stay at Winchmore Hill. Dreadful party. Charades etc! Phew!
Sunday 8th	Walk in afternoon. Pub crawl. Bed late again.
Monday 9th	Lunch Maurice. 12.30ish Curwen's. Lovely. Got new hat. Met Bert etc. went to flix. Home 10.30pm. Dinner awaiting me. Most welcome.
Tuesday 10th	Matinée. Quiet weekend. V.G. Saw Tillett. Very nice.
Wednesday 11th	Went to *Fine and Dandy*! Not thrilled.
Friday 13th	Went to *Lilac Time*. Quite good. Also lunch hour. Menges 4tet. Went to see Eileen. Good scream.
Saturday 14th	Brahms Requiem. Good. Met Jacques and saw Ruth Pearl. Went to Winchmore Hill. Had photos taken.

Sunday 15th	Had lunch at Bobbie's. Off to recital but cancelled. Went to Myra Hess and Griller concert at night. Lovely!
Monday 16th	House-hunting. Quite hopeless. Looked around Hampstead. More photos taken.
Tuesday 17th	Win rang up. Decided to have flat! Whoopee! Didn't see Bert at all.
Wednesday 18th	Went to Winchmore Hill. Pub crawl and party. Oh dear. So tired. Bed 1.30am!
Thursday 19th	12.15 Curwen's *Bambi*! Lovely time. Lunch and tea with Maurice. Saw electric and gas man. Got my photos. Good. Up at 5am to see Bert off!!
Friday 20th	Came home 10am. Home 5ish. Grand. Phyl came up. Chatter, chatter!
Saturday 21st	8.30pm Hutchy. Home. Good lesson. On to Chester-le-Street. Stayed the night at Etheringtons.
Sunday 22nd	*Elijah*. Chester-le-Street. 2.30pm. Rehearsal 11.30. 6 gns. Empire Theatre. Went of very well. Home 9ish. Wrote lots of letters.
Tuesday 24th	Blackpool Tower Circus. 7pm £8.8.0 Rehearsal 2.30. Went off well. 'Softly awakes my heart', 'Swing low', 'Hark the echoing air', 'Arise O Sun' [J E Nicholson, conductor].
Wednesday 25th	Cockermouth. 'Art thou troubled', 'Pack clouds away', 'Go no more a-rushing', 'Deep in my heart', 'Arch denial', 'Love is a Bable', 'Fairy lough', 'Sigh no more', 'Go not happy day', 'By a bier side'.
Thursday 26th	Home from Cockermouth. Went to Wyn's and knitting bee. Frank Mullings nice.
Friday 27th	Phyl should have come but didn't. Cleaned up. Bed early.
Saturday 28th	Washed curtains, hair, self. Wrote letters. 1001 jobs.
Sunday 29th	Stanley. 'Softly awakes', 'I have a Bonnet', 'Steal away', 'Water Boy', 'My boy Willie', 'Merry month of May', 'Home to our mountains'. Stayed in damp bed. Morning at Newcastle. Brr!
Monday 30th	Secondary School, Crewe 7pm. 9.20am. Concert OK stayed at Dr's house nice.

December:	
Tuesday 1st	Holmes Chapel. Reformatory school. Lovely time. Concert good. Lovely hospitality.
Wednesday 2nd	Winsford. Good audience. Hospitality good. Stayed at H. Chapel till 4.30. Lovely easy time.
Thursday 3rd	Great Saughall. Dreadful kids in audience. Told 'em off! Good for me! Little brutes. Staying in Chester.
Friday 4th	Chester. Queen's School afternoon. Town Hall 7pm. Good concert. Left to catch train to Manchester. Bed at midnight. Bit weary!
Saturday 5th	Helen 5th to 12th. Up with the blooming lark 6am. Caught

train to Newcastle. Two concerts. Both went off well. Maurice couldn't come!!!

Sunday 6th — Up early again. Off to Malton near York. Bit of a dead audience, but seemed pleased. Quite tired. Bed early. Stayed at the *Green Man.*

Monday 7th — Got lost in blackout! Arrived in Hackness 50mins late! Just caught the audience! Got back to Scarborough alright.

Tuesday 8th — Runswick Bay. Wonderful people! Dreadful concert. Only 20 odd there! Ham and eggs! O boy! Lovely place.

Wednesday 9th — Crook, Durham. Nice audience. Stayed at *County*, Durham. Nice. Letter from Maurice.

Thursday 10th — Lunch hour Newcastle. Went off well. Had lesson with Hutchy. Stayed at the *County*. Bed early. Lovely. Flat OK!

Friday 11th — Dreadful weather. Wrote lots of letters. Good concert at night. Maurice came. All supped together and talked. Bed late. Date for National Gallery! Whoopee!!

Saturday 12th — Lovely concert at Sunderland. Just Maurice and me. Helen Munro went. Practised in morning. Arranged programme for Nat. Gallery. Went to Manchester on 6.50. Slow journey. Arrive mid-morning.

Sunday 13th — *Messiah* Bolton. Baillie, Greene, Easton. Went off very well. Bert there. Stayed in B.L.

Monday 14th — Millom. Good. Eve. Concert with John McKenna. Vi Carson.

Tuesday 15th — Came home. Lots of things packed for removal.

Wednesday 16th — Pop went to Withnell Fold. Got things ready. Busy day.

Thursday 17th — Moving. Poured all day. All packed by 3pm. Win and I went to Wyn's. Grand!

Friday 18th — Paid all bills. Said farewells. Went to Wyn's again. Helen rang up.

Saturday 19th — Off to Edinburgh. Win to London. Went to Peggie's. Out to Mrs Maitland's. Bed soonish. Lovely time.

Sunday 20th — Edinboro! Went to Jack's. Saw his Pop. Stayed in hotel in Glasgow.

Monday 21st — Saw Wilfred and his Pop off. Came to Wyn's. Bath, meal and bed. Lovely.

Tuesday 22nd — Took Peter to Carlisle. Phew! Bed early.

Wednesday 23rd — Runcorn. *Elijah* 7pm. Rehearsal 3.30. Roy Henderson very pleased and encouraging. Stayed with Spencer Hayes.

Thursday 24th — Up with the blinking lark for London. Whoopee! Bad cold. O dear! Furniture arrived. Hurrah!

Friday 25th — Worked all day. Black as a nigger. Staying at Mrs Mac's.

Saturday 26th — Went to Dreda [Boyd]'s *Messiah.* Jolly good. Spoke to Robert Easton and Heddle Nash.

Sunday 27th — Phyllis turned up! Staying at Mrs McArthur's. Worked all day on curtains etc. Friends in evening.

Monday 28th — National Gallery! Went off very well. Crowds there. Went to flix. 'May night', 'Love song', 'Gardener', 'Secrecy', 'Spring',

'Fairy Lough', 'Love is a Bable', 'Bier side' [accompanied by Maurice Jacobson].

Tuesday 29th	Worked again. *Messiah* from Tillett. Whoopee!
Wednesday 30th	Pop came. Nearly straight. Madge came too. Worked hard.
Thursday 31st	Phyl went home. Didn't wait up for the New Year. Too blooming weary.

Diary for 1943

January:

Friday 1st
Went to Madge's for curtains. Put curtain rails up. Music from Mark Raphael. Ironed and messed about generally

Saturday 2nd
Lunch 1 Maurice and Kathleen Moorhouse. Didn't get much rehearsal. Curtains up at last in lounge – posh!

Sunday 3rd
Good dinner. Lovely walk on Hampstead Heath with Win and Dreda. Ironed and sorted music.

Monday 4th
Stained floors – made curtains. All sorts of jobs. Mended thousands of stockings.

Tuesday 5th
Went to Midday Nat Gall. Jean S. MacKinlay and Maurice. Good. Had tea. Went to Curwen's. Met Win. Went to *Blithe Spirit*. V.G. Rang Wyn up.

Wednesday 6th
Shopped. Madge and Tom to tea. Lots of telephone calls. Lovely! Went to neighbours.

Thursday 7th
Rehearsal 3.30. Good one. Duets with Mark Raphael. Went on to *Blithe Spirit*. Very good. Letter from Tillett re audition in Albert Hall! Gosh.

Friday 8th
Went to Midday Myra Hess and Griller. Had audition [Carl Rosa Opera Company] with Mrs Phillips [wife of owner H.B. Phillips] and [Music Director Arthur] Hammond. King's, Belsize Pk Rd 2.30 [?Hammond's address]. Went to exhib[ition] of painting by [Jack] Bilbo. Dreadful. Tea with Eve and cousin. Full day!

Saturday 9th
Helen rang up. Had lunch with her and sister at the MM [Mainly Musicians] Club. Nice! Stained the last floor! Wrote lots of letters.

Sunday 10th
Cleaned up. Practised. Eve Game and Roy came. Maurice and Bert rang up. Dreadful day. Foggy and cold.

Monday 11th
Went to Edinburgh. Took 11½ hours! Stayed with Maitlands. Gorgeous. Spoilt to death! Bath and bed.

Tuesday 12th
Edinburgh. Stayed in all day. Rehearsed with Harold Thomson. Party at night. Ordeal but nice. Mrs Walter Elliot and others there. Maitlands grand.

Wednesday 13th
Air raid in train! Edinburgh Midday. Brr! May Night, Secrecy, Loughareema, Swallow, Vain Suit, Bier Side, Love Song, Spring, Gardener, Salley, Go not happy.

Thursday 14th
Thirsk with Maurice and Raphael. Most lovely concert. Had gorgeous pub. Grand day. *Dichterliebe* wonderful. Maurice's accompanying [a] revelation.

Friday 15th
West Wylam [Northumberland]. 7.30. Lousy audience. With Helen and Margot Wright. Bit tired. Stayed at Mrs Cook's.

Saturday 16th	Had lesson with Hutchy. Travelled to Colne. Rang Audrey. She came down and we ginned and limed. Her birthday. Clement Hardman turned up.
Sunday 17th	Saw Greenwoods. Colne £8.8.0 Duets. Treated us royally. Softly awakes, O lovely night, Loughareema, Voyagers.
Monday 18th	Terribly late train. 3 hours. Good rehearsal. Siren but no raids.
Tuesday 19th	Audition 2–5. Ring King's, Swiss Cottage. Dr Jacques and CEMA staff nice. Helen Pyke played for me. Nice.
Wednesday 20th	Audition 11.10. Not bad. Sir Henry Wood and Arthur Wynn there. Lunch with M.J. Helped him with catalogue. Went to local and had sausage roll and ale. Gorgeous.
Thursday 21st	Practised. Saw Miss Nixon of I & T. Very nice. M.J. rang up. Practised some more. Ideal boiler not living up to its name!
Friday 22nd	4pm Nat. Gallery. Brook's Club, St James St SW1. 3pm Feldman's. Wardour St. Lunch with Maurice. Tea and flix with Mr Maitland. Nice day.
Saturday 23rd	Shopped. Prices dreadful! Carpet £3 yard! Didn't get any! Had Dreda Mother and Lilias in for supper. Lunched at my club!!
Sunday 24th	Maurice and Susannah and Vi came to tea and to look over flats. Lovely weather. Practised. John Whittaker rang up.
Monday 25th	Lovely. Helped with catalogue. Had a jaunt to Kingsway and sausage rolls and beer. Being spoilt to death.
Tuesday 26th	10.15 photos. Chop Suey. 5pm Piccadilly Circus. Went to *Traviata* with Hardman. Joan Hammond in. V.G. Had lots of fun. Introduced to Ivor Newton. Francis Russell there.
Thursday 28th	*Rigoletto*. Did the shopping in the morning.
Friday 29th	Lunch 12.15 with M.J. Went to pub but crowded. Helped with catalogue. Beer and sausage rolls again. O boy!
Saturday 30th	*Faust*. Didn't go. Very wild weather. Blowing a gale.
Sunday 31st	Went to hear *Winterreise*. Victor came. Joan Taylor and Hardman came back for a meal. Awful weather.
February:	
Monday 1st	Ring Albert Hall. Washed. Didn't go out all day. Another date from I & T. Whoopee. M.J. rang up. Also Mrs Phillips again! Bert posted to Wales.
Tuesday 2nd	Ironed. Letter from Phyl. *Rigoletto* V.G. Gwen Catley splendid.
Thursday 4th	[Carl Rosa Opera Company] Audition 1pm. Bit rusty. Sang for Phillips and Walter Susskind. Lunched at Macks. *Barber* [*of Seville*]
Friday 5th	Dinner at Mrs Macs with Dreda and Joan. Nice. Played Schubert duets. Some funny noises! [*Madam*] Butterfly.
Saturday 6th	Went to hear Myra Hess. V.G. Had lunch at MM club. Went to News flick and our pub.
Sunday 7th	Concert. I & T. Rehearsal 10.30 Piccadilly Theatre 2.30. Not so bad but rusty. Harriet Cohen and Clement. Chop sueyed after with Win, Dreda, Reg and Clement.

Monday 8th	12pm Mr Phillips. *Faust*. Two free tickets so took Kathleen M. Pretty awful. Lunch with M.J. Lovely. Voice worrying. Rick [Davies] rang up from L'pool.
Tuesday 9th	Joiners came at last! Had easy day for a change. Bed at 9pm.
Wednesday 10th	3 more dates from Tillett. Whoopee. Another easy day. More joiners.
Thursday 11th	Ramsgate. Lunch and rehearsal with Maurice. Missed the train but caught another! Lovely concert. Voice better, thank Heaven. Lovely hotel. *Rowena Court* Hotel at Westgate-on-Sea. To Music, Spring, Love song, Gardener, Secrecy, Salley Gardens, Loughareema, By a bier side, Love is a bable
Friday 12th	Faversham. Walk in morning with Kathleen. Poor audience at night. Stayed at Canterbury.
Saturday 13th	Herne Bay. Looked at Canterbury Cathedral. Nice concert at convent with Eleanor Warren and Maurice. Home 10.30pm.
Sunday 14th	MM Club. 4pm Didn't go. Went through songs with Maurice. Met Clement. Flix and chop suey and walk. Home 9.30 and in McArthur's. Bed and bath late.
Monday 15th	Washed and ironed. Cold, blowy. Also cold in nose! Didn't go out.
Tuesday 16th	Walk, shopped, practised a lot. Clement rang up. Knitted and listened to Brains Trust.
Wednesday 17th	Lots of phone calls. Lovely! Saw Roy Henderson – nice. Another *Messiah* in Wales.
Thursday 18th	2.45 Norman Franklin, 19 Randolph Rd. Cunningham 3082 Warwick Avenue Tube Stn.
Friday 19th	Rehearsal with Clement. Tom and Madge coming.
Saturday 20th	Clement ringing. Playing for him at Masonic Club. Joan coming back to sleep.
Memoranda	29 bus from Camden Town. 1pm Rehearsal Rubenstein. 5 Coleridge Rd, Finsbury Park N4 (Seven Sisters Rd behind *Astoria*)
Sunday 21st	*Messiah* Cradleigh Heath. 10.10 Paddington. Rehearsal 3pm. Lovely *Messiah*. Mary Hamlin, Henry Wendon, Arthur Copley.
Monday 22nd	Staffs. Up at 4.30am. My goodness! Concerts at 10am and 5pm. Slept all afternoon. Bath and bed 8.30!
Wednesday 24th	Staffs. Miss Glasgow came. Very successful. Went to see *She stoops to conquer*.
Thursday 25th	Staffs. Three concerts today.
Friday 26th	Staffs. Last two concerts. Very nice. Stayed at Uncle B's.
Saturday 27th	Went to see Bert's new school. Very nice. Caught 5pm train. Home in good time. Dreda came in.
Sunday 28th	Mostyn Club. Leslie England. Helena Rubinstein. North 1957. Send groups.

March:

Tuesday 2nd	Seeing Madge. 12. Peter Jones China Dept. Lunched with Madge. Saw Maurice re Scotch programmes.
Wednesday 3rd	Lots of phone calls. Lovely. Noisy raid but no bombs near. Dreda and Mrs Mac came in. Up at 5am.
Thursday 4th	Lunch with Maurice and Susannah. Flix and tea with Clement. Home early. Mended and knitted.
Friday 5th	Going to *Two Brewers*, Chipperfield [Herts] 6.06 Euston to King's Langley [arr. 6.43].
Saturday 6th	Llanelly.[dep. London Paddington] 1.55 [arr. Llanelly] 7.38. *Thomas Arms.*
Sunday 7th	Llanelly. Laelia Finneberg and Heddle Nash. Riot of a concert. Great success.
Monday 8th	Home 2.30.
Tuesday 9th	12.15 Roy Henderson [her first singing lesson with him]. ¼ to 4 Piccadilly Circus. Harold Thomson.
Wednesday 10th	Crewe. [dep. London Euston] 11.55 [arr.] 3.20. *Crewe Arms* Hotel. Che faro, Pack clouds away, To Music, Erl King, Silent Noon, Salley Gardens, Swing low, Kitty my love.
Thursday 11th	[trains back] 9.20–12.58 [or] 10.24–1.40. Susannah's [Jacobson].
Friday 12th	11.30 Ruth Pearl. 20 Addison Gdns. Tube to Shepherds Bush. 2.30 Roy H.
Saturday 13th	*Dream of Gerontius* [scored through, reason unknown]. Wigmore Studios 10.30. 12.45 [London] Victoria to Lewes. Lewes with Pauline Juler and Gerald Moore. 3pm. [her first engagement accompanied by Moore]. Che faro. How changed. To Music. Erl King. Silent Noon. Go not happy day. Fairy lough. Spring. Salley Gardens. Lewes 4.55 [arr. London Victoria] 6.20 [Bradshaw's timetable says 4.54 arr. 6.23]. Kings Cross to York 7.0–11.12 [*The Aberdonian*].
Sunday 14th	Malton afternoon 3pm.
Monday 15th	Bury 7pm.
Tuesday 16th	Staying Newcastle.
Wednesday 17th	Consett. *Merrie England*. Rehearsal 2.30. Avenue Church.
Thursday 18th	Morpeth 10.30. Staying York.
Friday 19th	Altrincham 5pm. 5gns [plus] exps. [train dep.] Altrincham 11.10 [pm. dep. Manchester]. London Rd 12.5AM [arr. London Euston 5.46 am].
Saturday 20th	*Elijah* 2.30pm Stoll Theatre.
Sunday 21st	Woolwich Polytechnic.
Monday 22nd	Gladys 2. Dartmouth St 3.30. Maurice 5.
Thursday 25th	Roy 2.15. Afternoon frock for factory concerts £7.15.5.
Friday 26th	Rehearsal. Ring Ham[pstead] 5394 Peggie. 11. Mr Cook. Chenalls. 12.15 Weekes, Hanover St. Evening gown £9.12.5.
Saturday 27th	Two evening gowns £30.9. Galleries Lafayette.
Monday 29th	Ayr. Glasgow [dep.] St Enoch 5.10 [pm. arr. Ayr 6.00].
Tuesday 30th	Perth

Wednesday 31st   Dundee.

April:
Thursday 1st   **Montrose**
Friday 2nd   Aberdeen. Pneumonia. Ambulance 6s.3d. [Bedridden in a
nursing home until 20 April]
Saturday 3rd   **Dunblane.**
Sunday 4th   **Stonehaven Town Hall. 7.30.**
Monday 5th   **Montrose, St George's Church.**
Tuesday 6th   **Carnoustie.**
Wednesday 7th   **Stirling**.
Thursday 8th   **Falkirk**.
Friday 9th   **Killearn.**
Saturday 10th   **West Stirlingshire.**
Friday 16th   7pm Newcastle rehearsal.
Saturday 17th   *St John Passion*. King's College, Newcastle. 3pm. Rehearsal
10.30am King's Hall. Cancelled.
Sunday 18th   Helen? [Anderson?] Bowes Museum. Barnard Castle. Can-
celled. Out for first time.
Monday 19th   Helen? Travelling?
Tuesday 20th   Helen? Travelled to Carlisle. Stayed at Ena's. [Nursing home]
fees £26.2.1. 30/- tips. Taxi 5/- Nursing home to Aberdeen
station. 2/-. Carlisle station to hotel.
Wednesday 21st   Home to London.
Thursday 22nd   To Surrey [with her father and sister, convalescing at a hotel
in Blindley Heath for six days].
Good Friday 23rd *Messiah*. Cambridge. Guildhall. Cancelled. B. awful weather.
Saturday 24th   Mass. 4tet. Lunchtime. St Albans. [Cancelled].
Sunday 25th   Darlington. Evening concert. Regal Cinema. Miscellaneous.
Cancelled.
Tuesday 27th   Travelling to Aber[ystwyth]. [Cancelled]
Wednesday 28th   Aberystwyth. Cancelled. [She returned to London]
Thursday 29th   Aberystwyth. *Messiah*. 12 gns. Shiloh Chapel. Rehearsal
afternoon. Municipal Hall. Cancelled.
Friday 30th   Aberystwyth. *Messiah* evening. Cancelled.

May:
Saturday 1st   Mr Oppenheim 11am
Sunday 2nd   Aberayron CEMA. Cancelled.
Tuesday 4th   3.30 Kathleen M's. Saw Malcolm Sargent in flower shop.
Maurice rang up. Safe home from Dublin.
Wednesday 5th   Celebration. 3 Fitting. 4.30 Lesson.
Thursday 6th   Drs 2pm. Madge's 5.30. Bill from Dr £6.7.6.
Friday 7th   Sussex farm [till 10th] 5.00 Waterloo – Haslemere. Mrs
Russell. 10.45.
Saturday 8th   Blew a gale all day but out twice. Very nice farm.
Sunday 9th   Still blowing gale.

Monday 10th	Wind worse than ever. Theatre. *Love for love*. Lovely play. Very naughty.
Tuesday 11th	4.30 Lesson. Good one. Went chopsueying with Clement and Joan. Gorgeous.
Wednesday 12th	Saw Mr Tillett! Sole agent now. Mr Cook 11am.
Thursday 13th	Wonderful day at Kew. Boiling hot. Lovely.
Friday 14th	Rehearsal [*Messiah*]. 9am-1pm. Royal College. 5pm W. Abbey. Taxi to Royal Albert Hall 3/6d. Royal College to Westminster Abbey 5/-. Met Miss Evelyn!! Funny – peculiar.
Saturday 15th	Met Nina Barbone for lunch (11/6). Gorgeous weather. Wrote 8 letters.
Sunday 16th	Gorgeous weather. Out on Heath. Legs burnt. Air raid at night.
Monday 17th	Westminster Abbey. *Messiah*. 5pm. Bella Baillie, Peter Pears, William Parsons. Went off well. Annie Chadwick there! All sorts of folk there. M.J. rang up.
Tuesday 18th	Llanelly 7pm. [dep. Paddington] 8.55- [arr. Llanelly] 11.55. £3.4.2d. Father of Heaven. Nearer my God. To Music. Duets. Hark, hark.
Wednesday 19th	Home again. More bombs and terrific gunfire. Letter from Ronnie Hunt.
Thursday 20th	Went to collect bikes. Meal with Maurice. Home on bus. Only one alert. Still gorgeous weather.
Friday 21st	Nice run on bikes. Shopped, practised etc. John Francis rang up. Good reports of *Messiah*.
Saturday 22nd	Shopped. Mrs Mac to lunch. Win golfing. Washed and ironed smalls. No raids. Lovely.
Sunday 23rd	5.30 train to Manchester. Fare £1.17.8 Porters 1/0. Taxi 2/.6 (station to hotel).
Monday 24th	Manchester tour. Tilly Conneley. George Roth. Music case £2.2.0d.
Wednesday 26th	Liverpool Midday.
Friday 28th	Albert Hall *Messiah*! Whoopee!! Tips 1/- Frock £6.6.0d.
Sunday 30th	Manchester.
Monday 31st	Manchester.
June:	
Tuesday 1st	Manchester. Maurice's broadcast 1.30–2. Heard bits. Hair 3pm. (6s.6d.)
Wednesday 2nd	Shoe repairs (concert shoes) 5s.8d.
Thursday 3rd	Manchester.
Friday 4th	Manchester. Went to Flo's. George Roth. Went back to London. Wilsons.
Saturday 5th	Manchester. Garden party at Parks.
Sunday 6th	Ate, slept, walked and knitted. Saw Mr and Mrs Read.
Monday 7th	Back to M[anchester] with Tilly and Jan van der Gucht. Nice. Orchestral parts (Softly awakes) £2

Saturday 12th	End of Manchester tour.
Monday 14th	Chester. CEMA. 7.30. Nice concert. Mantle Childe. Sylvia Spencer. [Leon Goossens and Ivor Newton scored through]. Fairest Isle, Love is a bable, White lily grow, Hark the echoing air, Loughareema, Cupid's Garden, Boy Willie, Spring, Salley Gardens, Pretty ring time.
Tuesday 15th	Back home. Lots of phone calls and letters to answer.
Wednesday 16th	Nat. Gallery. Lesson 2.45. Sequins for evening frock 7s.od.
Thursday 17th	Maurice's broadcast. Chop suey with Clement and Betty Sagon. Evening shoes £1.10.9d.
Friday 18th	Hair washed. Awful weather.
Saturday 19th	Home Service. 10.50pm M[aurice's?] Trio broadcast.
Sunday 20th	Wednesbury CEMA. 11.10 train
Monday 21st	3pm rehearsal Ruth Pearl. Chop suey Joan and Clem, Pop and Win.
Tuesday 22nd	12.30 Lesson (£1.1.0d). Went to see *La Fin du Jour* and *Pygmalion*. Grand.
Wednesday 23rd	Staffs tour for a week. 8.25am [to Stoke-on-Trent]. Factories.
Thursday 24th	Uncle B. 4.45. Went to see *In Good King Charles' Golden Days*. V.G. Good report from [Eric] Blom.
Saturday 26th	Lovely concert at Stoke for Harry Vincent. Terrific enthusiasm.
Sunday 27th	Gorgeous weather. Lost my voice! No concerts fortunately.
Tuesday 29th	End of tour. Send music to Buxton. Concerts cancelled. Laryngitis.
Wednesday 30th	12.30 lesson.

July:

Saturday 3rd	Buxton, *Sandringham* Hotel. Rehearsal 4–5.30. Cancelled
Sunday 4th	Buxton. Cancelled.
Tuesday 6th	D[octo]r and injections 15/-.
Wednesday 7th	CEMA Broadcast. Art thou troubled, Hark the Echoing Air, Pretty ring time, Down by the salley gdns. OK I think.
Thursday 8th	Wrote a lot of letters. Coldish weather. Gladys Crook rang up.
Friday 9th	*Kingdom* rehearsal. Wigmore Galleries. Lunch with Clement at MM. Went to Prom (Janet Howe) 7/6d.
Sunday 11th	Lunch at Canuto's. Lovely one and flix at night.
Monday 12th	Golf. W.P. Too windy.
Wednesday 14th	Susannah rang up. Bert rang up.
Thursday 15th	Lunch with CEMA organiser (Helen A[nderson]) 12.45. Maurice dinner. 5.30. Lovely chop suey. Gorgeous! Bought new [black] coat! £16.15.2d.
Friday 16th	Lesson 3.30. Good one. Straight home. In MacArthur's. Duetting.
Saturday 17th	Helped Susannah. Madge, Hilda and Elsie came to tea. Madge stayed the night.
Sunday 18th	Practised. Stayed in all day. Cheque to China aid fund £1.
Monday 19th	Regents Park 7. *Lady Precious Stream* [1935 play by Hsiung

	Shih-I] – very good. Peggie Sampson rang up. Music (Augener) Volume and 2 songs £1.4.7d.
Tuesday 20th	Dentist 9.30. Helped Susannah in house. Looking better.
Wednesday 21st	10.27 Waterloo – Farnham. Helen's. Rained <u>all</u> day. Brought home lovely flowers and apples. Cosmetics 12/6d.
Thursday 22nd	Dentist 9.30.
Friday 23rd	1.00 concert Nat[ional] Gall[ery]. Lesson 3.30.
Saturday 24th	3.30 Weekes. Ring first thing. Practise. Studio 2/-. Accompanist 5/-.
Sunday 25th	Norwich. 10am train, arr. 2.10. Bell Hotel. 8pm concert.
Monday 26th	Cromer. Send 'Softly awakes'.
Tuesday 27th	Back home. Thousands of letters.
Wednesday 28th	Lunch 12.30 Maurice and lesson. Hat for Gloucester Cathedral £2.5.11d.
Thursday 29th	Leave at 7.45. Paddington 9.5am arr. 12.30. Gloucester Cathedral. *The Kingdom.* 6.30 evening. Rehearsal 2pm. Very good.
Friday 30th	9.20–12.45. Travelled in lavatory all the way to London! 2.30 Helen Pyke. Lesson 4pm. Weekes. 8 Pembroke Ct. Kensington Cinema.
Saturday 31st	Leicester. *Grand* Hotel. [London] St Pancras [dep.] 5.30pm, arr. 8.9pm.

August:	
Sunday 1st	Leicester aft and eve. George Gray. Organist Cath. Grand. Softly awakes, Art thou troubled?, Hark the echoing air, Che faro, Ave Maria, Over the mountains.
Tuesday 3rd	Swansea Pad[dington] 8.55 arr 1.39. Rehearsal 2.30. Brangwyn Hall. *Messiah* evening. *The Mackworth* Hotel.
Wednesday 4th	8.50 arr. 1.25 [or] 11.00 arr. 3.55. Phone M[aurice] on arrival.
Thursday 5th	2.30 Weekes. Norman Lumsden. 5.30 Maurice. Saw Harry Vincent.
Friday 6th	Euston 5.38 arr 9.47. *Grosvenor* [Hotel], Manchester.
Saturday 7th	Broadcast 1.30[-2pm. Two songs with viola by Brahms with Stanley Wootton]. Helen Munro's 7.30ish. Mrs Cook's. Travelling shocking. 8hrs Manchester to Newcastle.
Sunday 8th	Durham 8th-15th. 2.55 bus from Marlboro Cres to Annfield Plain. Concert at Consett. OK.
Monday 9th	Tantobie.
Tuesday 10th	Stanley
Wednesday 11th	Annfield Plain. Nice concert.
Thursday 12th	Tea at my digs. Supper at Norman's. Nice concert at Burnopfield.
Friday 13th	Whitby. <u>Hours</u> of travelling. Stayed at Sneaton Castle. Very dormitoryish!
Saturday 14th	Win home. Two concerts. Sunderland 3pm. Blackhill 7pm. What a rush! Rang Win.

Sunday 15th	Durham. Barnard Castle. All a bit off! Tired! Travelled in guard's van to Newcastle.
Monday 16th	Carlisle. 8.15 train. Bert met me. Two concerts at RAF MU. Wyn and Jack came. Went to theatre. Dreadful.
Wednesday 18th	Went to Ena's in evening. Another late night. Weary unto death.
Thursday 19th	Bert went back. Saw Mrs Graham and girls. They and Ena and Billie came round at night. Glad we're going tomorrow!
Friday 20th	Went to Cockermouth. <u>Wh</u>at a journey! Kids sick all over place. Two concerts at Workington. Bed early. Gorgeous.
Saturday 21st	Free day. Gorgeous. Wrote letters, washed hair, shopped. Walk at night.
Sunday 22nd	Walk in morning. Rained. Lovely country. Bed early.
Monday 23rd	Lakes tour. Scramble on bus again.
Wednesday 25th	Went to Wigton paper works. Tea and supper at Wyn's. Gorgeous seeing them all again. Peter big.
Thursday 26th	Went to Moyra Collins. Very nice.
Friday 27th	Concert at Cleator. Phil Byrne's sister there. Dreadful conditions. Taxi all the way home. Saw Dr Simpson in morning.
Saturday 28th	9.5 arrive 2.25 Crewe. One hour late.
Sunday 29th	Spent day at Harry's. Went to service hymn broadcast at night.
Monday 30th	Staffs. Nice lunch hour concert. Met the 4tette. Great hilarity. Concert at night at Uttoxeter.
Tuesday 31st	Only one lunch hour concert today. Went to flix at night.
September:	
Wednesday 1st	2 concerts. Gorgeous lunch and concert.
Friday 3rd	3.25 Stoke to Euston (6.20). Home again. Whoopee! 29 concerts in 28 days. Bert home for 24 hours
Saturday 4th	End of tour. Goldsmith's *Elijah*. Elijah good. Chop suey with Clem, Joan and Charles.
Sunday 5th	Stayed in. Lazy day. Lovely. Knitted gloves.
Tuesday 7th	Lesson 2.30. Good one.
Wednesday 8th	Lunch and Studio One with Clement. Rehearsal in morning with Helen Pyke.
Thursday 9th	Washed, ironed, baked, made jelly. Gorgeous. Cranberry and apple.
Saturday 11th	11.5 Paddington. Packed train. 9½ hrs to Aberystwyth.
Sunday 12th	Aberystwyth. King's Hall. Rehearsal 10.30am. Evening 8pm. *White Horse*. 4 solo app[earance]s. Gluck. Softly awakes. How lovely. Swing low. My boy Willie.
Monday 13th	Holidays 13–17? *Sleepy Hollow* Hotel, Storrington. Had to stand with 1st Class ticket. Mighty mad. 10am train to Pulborough 1.15.

Tuesday 14th	Biked and walked. Managed to loan bike. Memorable day. Gorgeous weather.
Wednesday 15th	Biked to Amberley. Picked brambles, back for dinner.
Thursday 16th	Biked to Steyning in morning. Easy afternoon. Walk and dinner.
Friday 17th	Uncle Codner came. Maurice and I off round Arundel Castle on bikes. Gorgeous day. Played cards.
Saturday 18th	3.30 Marylebone to Nottingham with Joan. Stayed at the *Stratford*. Early to bed.
Sunday 19th	Nottingham. Theatre Royal. *Elijah*. Good perf. afternoon. Joan [Taylor], Roy [Henderson], Trefor Jones and me. Joan stayed the night.
Monday 20th	Quiet day. Joan went about 11am. Wrote letters, washed smalls.
Tuesday 21st	Did the shopping. Slept in aft. Terrific headache. Wrote letters. Practised.
Wednesday 22nd	Shopped. Met Kati and Johnny. Lovely autumnal weather.
Thursday 23rd	10.30 Roy. Collect tickets for *Merrie Widow*. 3.30 Kensington Cinema. Theatre 6pm.
Friday 24th	10.45 Helen. 12.30 Lunch Maurice. 3 Rehearsal. Jan's.
Saturday 25th	Silsden. Miscellaneous. 4tet. 'Good night' (*Martha* Flotow) Evening. Kirkgate Methodist. 9.5 [train] to Keighley. Mrs Smith. *Clear View* Tel: Steeton 3227
Sunday 26th	Silsden aft and evening. He shall feed, Nearer my God, How lovely, Father of Heaven, Lord, we pray Thee, The Lord is my shepherd. Strike the lyre and Harvest [not sung].
Thursday 30th	Tea and supper Susannah's 4.30. Nice! Maurice saw me on tube.
October:	
Friday 1st	3pm Helen P[yke]. Lesson 4. Bert came home 24 hrs.
Saturday 2nd	4.00[pm] train to Crewe.
Sunday 3rd	Crewe. Afternoon and evening. Rehearsal 11.45.
Monday 4th	Ring Susannah on arrival.
Tuesday 5th	Peter Pears concert Wigmore Hall 6pm. 4.15 Roy.
Wednesday 6th	Padd[ington] 8.55-[arr.] 2.36. Tredegar. Workmens' Hall. Evening. 7pm. Castle Hotel. Softly awakes, He was despised.
Thursday 7th	11.20–3.55 Padd[ington].
Friday 8th	Rehearsal Grimsby. Kings X 1.10 – arr 5.34. Mrs Osborne.
Saturday 9th	Grimsby. Aft and evening. 2.30 and 6.30. Yarborough.
Sunday 10th	9.21–2.36 Kings X.
Monday 11th	Lunch Maurice 12.15.
Wednesday 13th	Laura coming. Helen 11. M[aurice]12.30.
Thursday 14th	Aberdare. *Coliseum* 6.30. Miscellaneous. *Black Lion* Hotel. Home to our mountains. It was a lover – Walthew. Fairest daughter of the Graces. Ave Maria. Steal away. Water boy. [Annie Webber: accompanist]

Friday 15th	Phyllis coming.
Saturday 16th	Southwark Cathedral. *Messiah.* 2.30. Rehearsal 11.
Monday 18th	Lesson 12.15 [Maurice Jacobson]. Lunch 1.45. Roy [lesson] 3.15 Tea. Two lessons £2.2.0d. (M.J. lieder and Roy H. opera)
Tuesday 19th	1.00[pm] Euston to Carlisle.
Memoranda	Mitchel 29 Howard Pl. Carlisle. Could you put me up for one night 19th.
Wednesday 20th	Stanley. *Merrie England.* Evening. Hutchy 11.30 lesson £1.1.0d.. Helen lunch 12.30.
Thursday 21st	Mrs Luke , Main St, Stanley.
Friday 22nd	Broadcast midnight. Love is a bable. Fairy lough. Cupid's garden. Silent Noon. Pretty ring time.
Saturday 23rd	Travel to Maesteg. Train 1.55–6.30 [or] 3.55–8.35
Sunday 24th	Maesteg. Joan Cross. Barcarolle. Accompanist ill. Played for Marie Wilson. Very badly I'm afraid.
Monday 25th	Up with the lark!
Friday 29th	Staffs. Rehearsal with Hallé. Miss Crook came.
Saturday 30th	Sheffield. *Grand* Hotel, Leicester. Che faro. Hark the echoing air. Adieu forets.
Sunday 31st	Hinckley Leic. *Elijah* afternoon. Rehearsal 12.30.Mrs Smallshaw, 21 Woodland Rd. Leicester 6.55pm – St Pancras 9.30 [or] 7.04 -9.40, 8.21–11.06
November:	
Monday 1st	Shopping. Wyn. Ring Roy 12pm.
Tuesday 2nd	Smethwick (Staffs) evening. Miscellaneous.
Wednesday 3rd	Maurice 2.30.
Thursday 4th	Lesson 2.30.
Friday 5th	Lesson 2.15.
Sunday 7th	Treharris (Glam) 8pm. The *Palace.* Laelia Finneberg. Joan d'Arc, Where'er you walk, Steal away, O lovely peace, The Lord is my shepherd.
Wednesday 10th	12.30 Laelia. Chop suey.
Friday 12th	*Frauenliebe.* 6ish. J.W.
Saturday 13th	Shaw (Oldham) evening. Miscellaneous. Co-op Hall. 8.30 train [arr.] 1.37. Softly awakes, Calm silent night (Goetze), Weary heart, Come, let's be merry, Merry month of May, Water boy, Sigh no more.
Sunday 14th	Barnoldswick. Mr A. Harper [organiser]. *Palace* Theatre. Miscellaneous. Evening. [Margaret Gott accompanist] Taxi Oldham to Barnoldswick shared with Henry Wendon £1.10.0d.
Monday 15th	Barnoldswick to Skipton (bus) 10d, Skipton to Leeds (train) 3/1d., Leeds to York 12/5d. York recital. Nice. Che faro, Lord we pray Thee, Echoing air, Art thou troubled?, Trout, Erl King, Ave Maria, Silent Noon, Happy Day, Steal away, Salley Gardens, P[retty] R[ing] T[ime]

Wednesday 17th	York to Liverpool (train) £1.5.2d. Liverpool recital 12.15–12.55.
Thursday 18th	L'pool recital 12.25–12.55. 1.25–1.55. Lime St – Euston 3[pm]–7.40, 5.25–9.40
Friday 19th	*Hansel and Gretel*. V.G.
Saturday 20th	*Bartered Bride* aft. Lovely. Peter Pears splendid!
Monday 22nd	Hungarian club. Nice.
Tuesday 23rd	Port Talbot. *Messiah*. *Walnut Tree* Hotel. Phew! Isobel B. Roderick Lloyd.
Thursday 25th	Photographs 11am. 2.10 Padd. Bromsgrove. *Grand*. B'ham.
Friday 26th	Bromsgrove Worcs. Aft *Messiah*. Hospitality.
Saturday 27	Rehearsal Maurice. Madge and Tom here.
Sunday 28th	Dover. Y.M.C.A. *Frauenliebe und Leben*. Two sirens not counting me!

December:

Wednesday 1st	Lesson 12.30. Call about gold bracelet. 4.30 rehearsal Ivor Newton.
Thursday 2nd	2.30 P[hyllis] Spurr 8s.0d.
Friday 3rd	11.45 Lesson. P. Spurr 2.15. Lesson £1.1.0d. Studio and pianist 9s.0d.
Saturday 4th	Alison's tea 4pm.
Sunday 5th	Bristol. Afternoon 2.45. Che faro, Hark the echoing, Art thou troubled?, Pack clouds away, Love is a bable, Loughareema, Salley gdns, Pretty ring time.
Monday 6th	Kathleen Moorhouse. Nat. Gallery.
Tuesday 7th	3–5 Studio IIIA Rehearsal BBC London.
Wednesday 8th	Dvorak Requiem. 10.30–1.30. Studio I Corn Exchange, Bedford.
Thursday 9th	Call for bag – Baker Street. 3.45 lesson.
Friday 10th	*Queen* Hotel, Huddersfield.
Saturday 11th	Huddersfield. *Messiah* afternoon. Rehearsal 10am. Town Hall. Fur coat £105.0.0.
Sunday 12th	Lytham aft. Rehearsal 11am. *Messiah*. *Ship and Royal* Hotel. [Samuel Broughton, conductor]
Wednesday 15th	Runcorn. *Messiah*. Evening. Reh 4pm. Bill Parsons.
Thursday 16th	Aberdare. *Judas Maccabeus*. Evening. *Black Lion* Hotel. Rehearsal 3pm. 9.38 Runcorn, 3.34 Aberdare.
Saturday 18th	Train to Ilford. Goodmayes. *Messiah* 2.30.
Sunday 19th	Dunstable *Messiah* afternoon. 5.45. Rehearsal 12 noon. 12 train. Luton 12.43. 11am Kings Cross Hotel lounge.
Tuesday 21st	Todmorden. *Messiah* evening. Town Hall. Rehearsal 3pm. [train] 8.15–2.18
Wednesday 22nd	[train] 8.6–2.10 change Manchester.
Thursday 23rd	Tonypandy (Glamorgan) Misc. oratorios. Central Hall, evening. *Pandy* Hotel. Mrs Page. Lord we pray Thee, He shall feed his flock, Prepare thyself Zion, Lord is my shepherd, O lovely peace. [Gwen Watkins accompanist].

Sunday 26th   [*Messiah*] Albert Hall, afternoon. Rehearsal 10am. [train]
                     7.20–10.40 Crewe.
Monday 27th   [train from Crewe] 9.25–10.54 Pr[eston] 11.40–12.9. Blackburn
                     Messiah evening.

Diary for 1944

January:

Saturday 1st	Train to Bournemouth.
Sunday 2nd	Bournemouth. *Messiah* 2.15 and 6.15. Rehearsal 10.30.
Tuesday 4th	Retford. Danes Hill Hostel. 8pm. [Recital] 1.10 Kings Cross arr. 4.30. Lunch *Casa Prada* Eve Kisch.
Wednesday 5th	Ring Roy Henderson 7.30ish.
Thursday 6th	Warrington. Evening. 7.30. [Recital]. *Norton Arms* Hotel.
Friday 7th	Electricity up to Nov[ember] '43 £1.15.4.
Saturday 8th	1.25 from Charing X, Sundridge Park or Bromley North. Rehearsal 2pm.
Sunday 9th	Bromley Scotch Presby[terian]. Church. Bach *Christmas Oratorio*. Afternoon.
Monday 10th	Maurice Codner portrait 10.30.
Wednesday 12th	Maurice Codner 10.15.
Thursday 13th	Photographs 2.30. Helen Pyke 3.45. MM Club 6.15. Went to *Boulestin* with Gerry Field Reid. Marvellous meal. Home with me after.
Friday 14th	2.30 Lesson. *The Little Humpbacked Horse* [ballet] and Chop Suey with Maurice. Leading a gay life. This must stop!
Sunday 16th	Portrait 11am. Getting on.
Monday 17th	Ballet 6.45. New Theatre. *Façade*, *Nutcracker* and *Job*. Lovely.
Thursday 20th	Neath (Glamorgan). *Messiah*. Evening. Norman Lumsden. Shocking pub and orchestra. 12gns.
Friday 21st	3.30 lesson. Win away for weekend. Two noisy raids.
Saturday 22nd	Still here! Quiet weekend. Drew and painted Win's frieze.
Sunday 23rd	Win back. Wrote 9 letters. Short walk on heath.
Monday 24th	Maurice Codner 10.30. Val Drewry [BBC] 35 Marylebone High Street.
Tuesday 25th	3pm lesson.
Friday 28th	3.30 lesson.
Saturday 29th	Train to Oxford. Rehearsal 5pm.
Sunday 30th	Oxford Bach Choir. W[illia]m P[arson]s [baritone]. Sheldonian Theatre. Aft. 15 gns. Rehearsal morning. Black woollie. Vaughan Williams Mass in G. Handel's *Samson*. Mrs Cross, 27 Linton Rd.

February:

Wednesday 2nd	Tredegar. Evening. Miscellaneous. Joan of Arc, Lord we pray Thee, Sigh no more, Bold unbiddable child.
Thursday 3rd	Maurice 3.30.

Friday 4th	Lunch with composer 12/6d. Mr Montague ENSA 2.30. Taxi from Drury Lane to [Royal] Academy [of Music] 3/-. Lesson 3.30 £1.1.0d
Saturday 5th	Uncle Codner 10.30
Sunday 6th	Cradley Heath [& District Choral Society]. *Messiah*. Evening. White pleated. 10.10 Paddington. 2.30 from Snow Hill, Birmingham. 12gns.
Monday 7th	Wednesbury. Black short-sleeved. [CEMA]
Tuesday 8th	Nuneaton [CEMA].
Wednesday 9th	Rugby [CEMA].
Thursday 10th	5pm. Uncle B[ert, Kathleen's maternal uncle]. Wolverhampton [CEMA].
Saturday 12th	Train to Colne.
Sunday 13th	Colne [Orpheus Glee Union] Municipal Hall. Evening. White pleated. 14gns. Che faro. Softly awakes. Turn ye to me. Flower Duet Act 2 *Butterfly*. [the soprano was Noel Eadie].
Monday 14th	Leigh Grammar School. Gerald Moore. White pleated. 13gns.
Tuesday 15th	Manchester Midday. [deputising for Astra Desmond at Houldsworth Hall. Gerald Moore accompanist]. Short-sleeved black. 10gns. 11am Kathleen Riddick.
Wednesday 16th	Aberdare. Bethania Chapel. Miscellaneous. Evening. Black short-sleeved. 18gns. Where'er you walk. Lord we pray Thee. Caro mio ben. Swing low. Come ma little darlin'.
Thursday 17th	Broadcast 3.30–4? Dr William Cole. Balance test 2pm. Studio 1, Delaware Studios. Maida Vale. 6gns.
Friday 18th	Horrid raid. Phew!! [possibly why the following is scored through: Alison. Lesson 2pm. Wigmore Galleries 2.30 Rehearsal Margaret Field Hyde].
Saturday 19th	Southwark Cathedral. *The Kingdom*. 2.30 Black woollie. 7gns.
Sunday 20th	10.45 Maurice, Hampstead. Mayfield. Recital. Black woollie. Another horrid raid. Nice but freezing.
Monday 21st	NE CEMA with London W[omen]'s S[tring] O[rchestra], conductor Kathleen Riddick]. Bishop Auckland. Red. [1.] Che faro, Hark the echoing air. [2.] Silent Noon, Pretty ring time, Willow song, Bold unbiddable child.
Tuesday 22nd	NE [CEMA] Newcastle City Hall. Red.
Wednesday 23rd	NE [CEMA] Stanley. Red.
Thursday 24th	*Midland* [Hotel] Manchester
Friday 25th	*Midland* Manchester
Saturday 26th	Broadcast. Stockport. Centenary Hall. 7–8.30. Rehearsal 2.30. Red. 10gns. [Home Service 'Our Northern Choirs'. Debussy *The Blessed Damozel* with Joan Cross, soprano, Maia Ladies' Choir, BBC Northern Orchestra, Charles Groves, conductor].
Sunday 27th	Hinckley. *Messiah*. Afternoon. Short. [Manchester] London Rd 10.10 arr. Nuneaton 12.35.
Tuesday 29th	Clyffe Pypard [an airbase in Wiltshire] 7.30. Black woollie.

1.55–3.40 *Great Western* Hotel, Swindon. With Harold Fairhurst [violinist] and Wendy Taunton [accompanist].

March:

Wednesday 1st	Gloucester. National Service Club. Black woollie.
Thursday 2nd	BBC Brahms Alto Rhapsody [scored through].
Saturday 4th	Pontypool. Tabernacle Baptist Church. Miscellaneous. Evening. Pink and gold. Che faro. Lord we pray Thee. Swing low. Kitty my love.
Sunday 5th	*Midland* [Hotel] Birmingham.
Monday 6th	Stourbridge. *Carmen* evening. Pink and gold. 6.30pm finishes 8.45. Reh 2.30. *Midland* [Hotel] Birmingham.
Tuesday 7th	9.10 [train] from Snow Hill. *Castle* Hotel Neath
Wednesday 8th	Glyn-Neath. *Welfare* Hotel. Miscellaneous. Evening. *Castle* Hotel, Neath. Short-sleeved black. Softly awakes my heart. O rest in the Lord. Silent Noon.
Thursday 9th	Oxford. Queen's College. *St John Passion.* 8pm. Rehearsal 2.30. Hospitality. Short-sleeved black.
Friday 10th	Train to Silsden 1.15 [Birmingham] New Street.
Saturday 11th	Silsden. Pink and gold. Joan of Arc. Art thou troubled? Come let's be merry. Sound the trumpet.
Sunday 12th	Silsden. Afternoon. Ave Maria. He was despised. Lord is my shepherd. Evening. Hear my prayer. Sing ye a joyful song. Abide with me. O lovely peace.
Monday 13th	Rehearsal Maurice Cole.
Tuesday 14th	Darlington. Friends' Meeting House, Skinnergate. 7.15pm. Recital. Pink and gold. Ada Alsop [Darlington-born soprano].
Thursday 16th	Dr Blair.
Sunday 19th	Burnley. *Merrie England.* Rehearsal 2pm. [Patricia Davies, soprano] Evening 6pm. Red. *Thorn* Hotel.,
Wednesday 22nd	Cleethorpes. Mill Road Hall. 7pm. 3 groups. Pink and gold. Che faro. Hark the echoing air. Constancy. Barefoot. Silent Noon. Pretty ring time.
Thursday 23rd	9am train. Rehearsal 3pm Wigmore Galleries. Tea with two violinists MM [Club].
Friday 24th	Lunch Maurice. Train 2.40.
Saturday 25th	Liverpool Phil. Bach B minor Mass. Afternoon 2.30. White accordion. [Kate Winter, Edward Reach, Victor Harding, Sir Malcolm Sargent].
Sunday 26th	Newcastle on Tyne. *Dream of Gerontius.* 7pm. White accordion. *Station* Hotel.
Monday 27th	Train Newcastle to Carlisle. Train to Wigton.
Tuesday 28th	*Central* Hotel Glasgow.
Wednesday 29th	Glasgow. St Andrew's Hall. *Elijah.* Rehearsal 10am. Red. Travelling overnight.
Friday 31st	Pre-recording. Rehearsal 2–3.30. Recording 3.30–4.45. 200 Oxford St Studio 4.

April:

Saturday 1st	Southwark. *St Matthew Passion*. 2.30. Rehearsal 11am. Short and squirrel. Tea with soprano and tenor.
Sunday 2nd	Leicester. *St Matthew Passion*. Afternoon. Rehearsal morning. Black woollie. Victor Harding. Mary Hamlin.
Tuesday 4th	Kathleen Moorhouse 8pm.
Wednesday 5th	Lesson. Maurice 5pm. Chopsueyed. Lovely.
Good Friday 7th	Albert Hall. *Messiah*. [Royal Choral Society afternoon]. Rehearsal 10am. New white, green and gold. 10gns. Archway Hall. *Messiah*. Evening same. 5gns.
Saturday 8th	Win away until 16th. Train to Aberdare. *Black Lion* [Hotel].
Sunday 9th	Aberaman, near Aberdare. Evening. Miscellaneous. Rehearsal 2.30. White accordion. 18gns. Softly awakes. Che faro. Sigh no more. It is the merry month. Bold unbiddable. Goodnight (*Martha*). *Black Lion* [Hotel].
Monday 10th	*Black Lion*.
Tuesday 11th	*Black Lion* Hotel 3 days £3.10.0d.
Wednesday 12th	Crynant (nr Neath) Boys Club evening. Miscellaneous with Joan Hammond. Red. Softly awakes. Art thou troubled? *Mackworth* [Hotel] Swansea.
Thursday 13th	Hanley. Victoria Hall. *Messiah*. White accordion. *North Stafford* Hotel, Stoke. Ask for letters.
Saturday 15th	Keighley. Wesley Place Methodist Church Musical Festival. 25 gns. Evening. Red. 25gns. Miss Driver (Keighley 4012). Che faro. Joan of Arc. Skye Boat Song.
Sunday 16th	Keighley. Afternoon and Evening. Lord we pray Thee (Mozart), Steal away, Swing low. Hear my prayer (Dvorak), I will lay me down (Greene), O praise the Lord.
Tuesday 18th	Rehearsal 6.30. Studio VIII B[roadcasting].H[ouse]. Broadcast 7.15–7.50 Alfredo Campoli. 10gns.
Wednesday 19th	Stocksbridge nr Sheffield. Miscellaneous. Eda Kersey. 9.50 Marylebone, [Sheffield] Victoria 2.19. *Grand* [Hotel] Sheffield. Che faro (orch), Water boy, Come, let's be merry.
Saturday 22nd	Morriston, Glamorgan. *Samson*. Evening. Rehearsal 2pm. Red. 8.55 train. Norman Lumsden. *Castle* Hotel, Neath.
Monday 24th	Liverpool for a fortnight.
Saturday 29th	Liverpool. Welsh Choral [Union]. *Messiah*. Rehearsal 10am. White, green, gold. [Ruth Naylor soprano, Parry Jones, tenor, Marian Nowakowski, bass. Liverpool Philharmonic Orchestra, conductor Dr Malcolm Sargent].

May:

Thursday 4th	Liverpool. Dinner dance with Rick Davies. Gorgeous time.
Saturday 6th	Port Talbot. Tabernacle Newydd Chapel. *Elijah*. Rehearsal 2.30. Red. 18gns.
Sunday 7th	Merthyr Tydfil. Theatre Royal. Miscellaneous. Joan Hammond and Norman Allin. Rehearsal 4pm. Red. Guest house accommo-

dation. 18gns. *Walnut Tree* Hotel. Che faro. Art thou troubled? Pack clouds away, Flower duet.

Monday 8th   Train to Chester. *Queen* Hotel, Chester.

Tuesday 9th   Chester. City Grammar School Hall. 11–12 for children [age] 14–17 Secondary School. Che faro, Trout, Loughareema, Whyte lily, Constancy, Salley, Pack clouds away, Barefoot, P.R.T. 2.45 for 45 minutes, [age] 10–14 Elementary School. Where'er you walk, Pack clouds, Trout, Water boy, Ave Maria, Barefoot, Little darling, Willie. Red. £21.

Thursday 11th   Train to Stoke. Hanley. Victoria Hall. [Recital]. Red. *Grand* Hotel. 15gns. Che faro, Sigh no more, Loughareema, P.R.T.

Saturday 13th   Maesteg. Town Hall. Evening. Miscellaneous. Mauve. 17 gns. Che faro, Steal away, Flower duet, Home to the mountains, *Rigoletto* 4 tette.

Monday 15th   *Barber of Seville*. Gorgeous. Sat next to Benjamin Britten!! R.D. [Rick Davies?]

Tuesday 16th   Train to Durham. Bad cold. Leon Goossens, Frank Phillips, Gladys Crook, Maurice Cole all staying at hotel. *County* Hotel, Durham.

Wednesday 17th   Durham Music Society. [Recital of three groups of four songs]. Black velvet. How changed, Caro mio ben, Trout, Erl King. Secrecy, The Gardener, May Night, Barefoot. Fairy lough, P.R.T., Star candles, Sigh no more.

Thursday 18th   Train to Manchester. Broadcast 7.20–8. Houldsworth Hall. Rehearsal 2.30. *Midland* [Hotel]. R.D.

Friday 19th   HMV 11.30–1 pm. Abbey Rd. Cancelled. Train to Swansea. *Civic* Hotel.

Saturday 20th   Swansea. Brangwyn Hall. *Elijah*. [Isobel Baillie, Peter Pears, Roy Henderson]. Rehearsal 12.30. Black velvet. 18gns. Sleeper [train].

Sunday 21st   Norman Lumsden coming to tea.

Monday 22nd   Gladys Ripley *Dream of Gerontius*. Fitting 12 noon Marshall and Snelgrove. Lunch Roy.

Tuesday 23rd   Wednesbury. CEMA. 9.10 from Paddington. Che faro, Water boy, I have a bonnet, My boy Willie.

Wednesday 24th   Wolverhampton. Red.

Thursday 25th   Tonypandy. Miscellaneous. Evening. Red. 18gns. Softly awakes, Art thou troubled?, Joan of Arc, Butterfly [Flower duet].

Friday 26th   5pm. Academy. Michael Head. Win breaks up. R.D.

Saturday 27th   Albert Hall. *Messiah*. Goldsmiths. Afternoon. Rehearsal 10.30am. White satin. 10gns.

Sunday 28th   12.30 Paddington to Lechlade, Gloucestershire. Americans [air base].

Monday 29th   Americans.

Tuesday 30th   Americans.

Wednesday 31st   Americans. R.D.

June:

Thursday 1st	Americans.
Friday 2nd	Dr Harold Darke's room, King's College [Cambridge]. Rehearsal 2.30.
Saturday 3rd	Cambridge. King's College Chapel. Bach. Mass in B minor. 2.30. Hospitality. Black, short-sleeved. £21.
Sunday 4th	Cambridge.
Monday 5th	Letter from Rick.
Tuesday 6th	Broadcast. Evening. 'Make your own Music'. Michael Head. 6.30–7. Rehearsal 4pm. Studio II, Delaware Rd, Maida Vale. 8gns.
Wednesday 7th	Wrote to Rick. Train to Blackburn.
Thursday 8th	Blackburn High School. Evening. Black. 14gns. [Sang ten songs].
Wednesday 14th	Rehearsal 8.30am. 10–10.30 Broadcast. 15 mins. 2 Groups. Lesson 12.15. Call for frock. *Monseigneur*, Marble Arch. To Music, Who is Sylvia, Trout. Steal away, Swing low, My boy Willie, I have a bonnet.
Thursday 15th	Ashford, Middlesex. 10.24 from Waterloo. William Parsons. Red.
Friday 16th	Parry Jones 1pm. *Casa Prada*, Warren Street. Roy Room 22 [Royal Academy]. 3pm or earlier.
Saturday 17th	Train to Newcastle.
Sunday 18th	Newcastle. City Hall. 3pm. Miscellaneous. Pink. 18gns. *Station* [Hotel].
Monday 19th	Bishop Auckland
Tuesday 20th	Whitby.
Wednesday 21st	Leadgate, Co. Durham. Front Street Methodist Church. Evening. Miscellaneous. Pink. 15gns. Hospitality. Mrs Howe, Redwell Hills, St Ives Rd. O Peaceful England. Two groups: [1] Softly awakes [2] Water boy, Little darlin', My boy Willie.
Thursday 22nd	Northallerton.
Friday 23rd	Nuneaton. Send songs to Violet Carson, 18 Fleetwood Rd, Bispham, Blackpool.
Saturday 24th	Rehearsal 7pm. *Bull* Hotel, Nuneaton.
Sunday 25th	Bedworth, Nuneaton, Warwick Parish Church. *Elijah*. Afternoon. Short black.
Monday 26th	Fitting frock 11.30.
Wednesday 28th	3pm train. Miss Morton. 90 Howard Rd, Leicester.
Thursday 29th	Leicester Art Gallery. 1pm. Black short-sleeved. [Two song groups]. Telemann [Cantata].
Friday 30th	HMV 10.30 (taxi 6/-) [Abbey Road, Studio 3, her first recording session of four between this date and 21st September 1945. These four test records with Gerald Moore were all she made for HMV and were not issued until 1978].

July:

Sunday 2nd	Todmorden *Hippodrome* Theatre afternoon and evening. Cancelled. 2.28 Victoria to Lewes. ENSA. *White Hart* [Hotel]. Telegram from Rick.
Monday 3rd	Lewes. Roy ringing up.
Tuesday 4th	Bury St Edmunds Cathedral. Evening. 8.30. Percy Hallam (organist). 10gns.
Wednesday 5th	Bury St Edmunds. 8.15. [Recital]. 10gns. Rehearsal 7.30 Red. Take taxi to *Angel* Hotel. Lord we pray Thee, Art thou troubled, I will lay me down, O praise the Lord, Agnus Dei
Sunday 9th	Luton Co-op. Central Hall. Evening. 7.30. 2 Groups. Short black. 15gns. 10 mins. Lord we pray Thee, I will lay me down, O Praise the Lord. Art thou troubled?, How lovely. Miss Bessie Burdekin [accompanist].
Thursday 13th	Gloucester Cathedral Choral Society. Alto Rhapsody and one group. Rehearsal afternoon. Short-sleeved black. 10gns. Expected to lunch. Mr & Mrs Sumsion 20 College Green.
Saturday 15th	Rick Davies turned up for lunch! Rehearsed with Helen Pyke. Roy Henderson to supper on way to train for Scotland. Whattaday.
Sunday 16th	Broadcast. 2–3.pm. Gustav Holst. Rehearsal 12.15. Concert Hall BH. Flowered. [This was a live broadcast entitled 'Chamber Music Concert' on the Home Service with piano accompanist Harry Isaacs. Holst's work was the 1st group of his Rig Veda Hymns]. Dr Jacques, Hampton Court 6.30. 5gns.
Monday 17th	Prom. *Sea Pictures*. Janet Howe. 11am Helen's.
Tuesday 18th	Rick rang up last time before going abroad. Sad, very sad. Alison and Gordon came up. Brought roses and red currants. Lovely.
Wednesday 19th	Walter Legge. 7pm.
Thursday 20th	Rick arrived on French soil. Prom? Nancy Evans Recit & Air de Lia [*L' enfant prodigue* by Debussy. This concert was cancelled by the authorities due to flying bombs].
Sunday 23rd	Aberystwyth. King's Hall. Evening. Rehearsal 10.30. Talbot Hotel. 18gns. Art thou troubled?, Joan of Arc, Steal away, Sweet chance, Come let's be merry. Let Tom Harrison know dates.
Wednesday 26th	Win goes away. Letter from Rick. OK. *Midland* Hotel [Manchester].
Thursday 27th	Broadcast Manchester. 9.45–10.15am. Rehearsal 8.45. *Midland* Hotel. I will go with my father a-ploughing, O men from the fields, Song to the seals, Boat song, Merry greenwood.
Friday 28th	Train to Durham.
Saturday 29th	Hetton le Hole [Durham]. Miscellaneous. Softly awakes, Trout, Erl King, Che faro, Swing low, Spanish lady.

Sunday 30th	Hetton le Hole. Afternoon. I will lay me down in peace, O praise the Lord, How lovely. And evening, Nearer my God
Monday 31st	Stephen [Wearing]'s Prom [This concert was cancelled by the authorities due to flying bombs]. To Durham *County* Hotel for seven days.

August:

Tuesday 1st	In bed with cold and stomach.
Thursday 3rd	Proms. 5 Tudor Portraits [Astra Desmond. This concert was cancelled by the authorities due to flying bombs].
Saturday 5th	Letter from Rick.
Thursday 10th	Concert Liverpool. Brahms Serious Songs. Rehearsal 2pm. Nancy Evans.
Friday 11th	Holidays. 1.45 to Tebay. Change at Preston.
Tuesday 22nd	To Bangor. *Castle* Hotel.
Wednesday 23rd	Bangor. Parry Jones. White, green and gold. *Castle* Hotel.
Thursday 24th	*Midland* [Hotel] Manchester.
Friday 25th	*Midland* Manchester.
Saturday 26th	End of holiday. Broadcast Four Serious Songs – Brahms. Dr M. Sargent. BBC Manchester 3.30–5. Rehearsal 10am. 10gns. [Sargent orchestrated the songs while keeping vigil at his daughter Pamela's bedside. She died on 25th August and Julius Harrison conducted instead]. *Mount* Hotel [Fleetwood].
Sunday 27th	Fleetwood. *Marine* Hall. Evening [recital]. Reh 5.30. Flame red. *Mount* Hotel. 18gns. Flowered.
Monday 28th	Back [home].
Tuesday 29th	Lunch and lesson [a guinea]. Roy.
Wednesday 30th	Lesson £1.1.
Thursday 31st	Lunch Jan v.d. Gucht 12.15 Café Royal.

September:

Saturday 2nd	Buxton. Rehearsal 4.30. Provide band parts. Flame. £21. Mrs Dobbie, The *Claremont*, Buxton. To music, Trout, Who is Sylvia?, Sigh no more, Star candles, Bold unbiddable child.
Sunday 3rd	Buxton. Afternoon – Art thou troubled?, Swing low. Mauve. Evening – Softly awakes, Water boy, Little darlin', Spanish lady. Flowered.
Friday 8th	*Park* Hotel, Preston.
Saturday 9th	Blackburn. Queen's Hall. Evening. Miscellaneous. Heddle Nash. Flowered. 15gns. Softly awakes or Joan of Arc, Sigh no more, Star candles, Bold unbiddable.
Sunday 10th	Preston 1.9, Euston 6.37.
Monday 11th	Cuppatea 4pm Mrs Mac's.
Tuesday 12th	Rehearsal Bedford. 12 noon train St Pancras.
Wednesday 13th	Bedford. BBC. Dvorak. *Stabat Mater*.
Thursday 14th	Bedford Midland Rd 1.40, 2.19 Hitchin, 2.36 from Hitchin,

	2.41 Letchworth. Letchworth, Herts. 7.30. *Judas Maccabeus.* Short-sleeved black. 10gns.
Friday 15th	Dentist 3.45. Mr Alan Thompson, 33 Harley Street.
Saturday 16th	Listen in 3.30.
Monday 18th	SW. [Stephen Wearing accompanist?] Americans 5 days. Leominster. *Talbot* Hotel. 9.45 Paddington-Leominster 3.47.
Wednesday 20th	11.40 for Newport. *King's Head.*
Saturday 23rd	College Hall, Worcester. Dr Jacques. Flame red. Che faro. Water boy, Cradle song, My boy Willie.
Sunday 24th	11.5 from Worcester – 3.50 [London Euston]. Ring Roy *Queen's* Hotel, Birmingham.
Monday 25th	Birmingham 8.40 – Euston 11.16. [Roy's train?] Roy lunch 12.30. Lesson. Recording [?test session] 3.15. *Gerontius.*
Tuesday 26th	Decca 2pm.
Wednesday 27th	Tylorstown, Rhondda. Ebenezer Chapel, Welfare Hall. Miscellaneous. Rehearsal 2.30. Elena Danieli. Floral. 18gns. Change at Cardiff and Porth. Hospitality. Mrs Williams, 23 East Rd, Tylorstown. *Butterfly* [duet], Softly awakes, Where'er, Pack clouds, Water boy, Spanish lady, Joan of Arc, Che faro.
Thursday 28th	Mountain Ash, Glamorgan. Evening. Miscellaneous. John Hargreaves, Ingrid Waxman, Tom Culbert. Duets with JH. 2 Quartets. Floral taffeta. 18gns. Che faro, To Music, The Trout, Ave Maria, O lovely Night, O lovely peace. Fairest daughter (*Rigoletto*).
Friday 29th	5.15 Dentist.
Saturday 30th	2.30 HMV [her first published 78rpm records, Columbia label, excerpts from anthems by Maurice Greene, accompanied by Gerald Moore, produced by Walter Legge]. 5.30 train [to Crewe].

October:

Sunday 1st	Crewe. Wedgwood Methodist Church. Afternoon and evening. Miscellaneous. Norman Lumsden. Black with velvet.
Monday 2nd	10.8 [train from] Crewe [to London]. Ivor Newton 3pm. Dentist 5.30.
Tuesday 3rd	Lunch Parry Jones – *Casa Prada* 1pm. Maurice reh. 11.30. 4.15 train Paddington. The *Rodney* Hotel, 4 Rodney Place, Clifton, Bristol.
Wednesday 4th	Bristol [recital]. Flame. £7.13.6d. [Two groups] Love song, May night, Barefoot. Whyte lily, Star candles, Come let's be merry, Bold unbiddable.
Thursday 5th	8.55 [a.m. train to] Aberdare. *Coliseum.* Reh. 3.30. Evening 6.30. Miscellaneous. Joan Fullerton, Hindley Taylor, Ronald Stear. White, green and gold. 18gns. Che faro, To Music, Spirituals, O rest in the Lord, Passing by, Love is meant to make us glad.

Friday 6th	11.40 [train from] Aberdare. Pontypool Rd 1.48 arr Manchester 6.39. *Midland* Hotel.
Saturday 7th	Huddersfield Music Club. St Patrick's Hall. Afternoon 2.30. Recital with Leon Goossens and Ivor Newton. 18gns. Flame. To Music, The Trout, Erl King, May night, Love song, Constancy, Barefoot, Sweet chance, Star candles, Silent Noon, P.R.T. Huddersfield 5.57 – Manchester 6.52. *Midland* Manchester.
Sunday 8th	Manchester London Road 10[am train to] Leicester 1.3pm. *Grand* Hotel.
Monday 9th	Leicester Philharmonic. Mass in B minor. Sir Adrian Boult. Rehearsal 2.45. Evening 6.30. White, green and gold. 18gns. *Grand* Hotel.
Tuesday 10th	Dentist 5.30.
Wednesday 11th	10am recording. Lunch – lesson Roy. Reh 4pm Daphne [Ibbott].
Thursday 12th	8.55 train. Abercrave, Swansea. Welfare Hall, Abercrave Miscellaneous. Evening. Joan Taylor, Ronald Hill. Flame. 18gns. Softly awakes, Wher'er you walk, Pack clouds away, Whyte lily, Come let's be merry, O lovely peace.
Friday 13th	Not do concert – 24th. November 9th recording. Is Louth hospitality 19th October? [these were probably questions to be asked of John Tillett].
Saturday 14th	11.15 Dentist. 1.5 Euston, 6.54 Blackpool Central. Mrs Oates.
Sunday 15th	Blackpool. Co-op Jubilee Theatre. Miscellaneous. Rehearsal 3pm. White, green and gold. 18gns. [Two groups]. To music, Erl king, Come let's be merry. *Carmen* – Over the hills and Gypsy song. Mr Nicholson [conductor], 18 Stanley Hill Avenue. Mrs Oates 110 Adelaide St, B'pool.
Monday 16th	[Trains] Blackpool Central 9.35. 10.33 & 10.44 from Preston, 3.15 & 3.25 in Glasgow. *Central* [Hotel] Glasgow.
Tuesday 17th	Stevenston, Ayrshire. Ardeer Recreation Club. Evening. Miscellaneous. Flame. 23 guineas. [Glasgow] St Enoch 1.45, arr. Ardrossan South Beach station 2.50. Accompanist Dr Traill. Rehearse at hotel 3.15. Hotel *Kilmeny*, Ardrossan. Mr Jamieson [organiser?]. House next door to hotel. Met on arrival. Che faro, Art thou troubled, Pack clouds away, Whyte lily, Come let's be merry, Merry month, Passing by.
Wednesday 18th	Ardrossan 8.36 or 9.27, Glasgow 9.30 or 10.16. Glasgow 10.0, Leeds 3.56. *Griffin* Hotel.
Thursday 19th	Leeds Central 10.15. Leeds to Grimsby Town arr. Doncaster 11.40, Grimsby 1.23. Grimsby 3.4 [arr.] Louth 3.36. Louth Music Club. King Edward VI Grammar School. Evening 7.30 with Colin Horsley. Provide accompanist out of fee £26.5. Flame. Che faro, Prepare thyself Zion, Caro mio ben, Pack clouds away, Whyte lily, Willow song, Cradle song – Byrd, Arch denial, *Sea Pictures*.
Friday 20th	Louth 9.17, Grimsby 9.51. Grimsby 10.30, Doncaster 12.22.

	Doncaster 12.27 Leeds Central 1.17. Leeds <u>City</u> 3.20, Huddersfield 3.40. *George* Hotel, Huddersfield.
Saturday 21st	Huddersfield. *Israel in Egypt*. Aft. 10am rehearsal. White, green, gold. 15gns. Go to Hebden Bridge with Mr Lingard.
Sunday 22nd	Hebden Bridge. Co-op Hall. Mr J.W. Lingard. Evening. Miscellaneous. Flame. Eva Turner. 15gns. Softly awakes, Swing low, Spanish lady, Barcarolle [duet].
Monday 23rd	Hebden Bridge 11.59, Burnley 12.56. *Thorn* Hotel.
Tuesday 24th	Burnley Masonic Charity Concert. Mechanics' Institute. 6.45. John Hargreaves. White, green gold. 18gns. Softly awakes, Whyte lily, Come let's be merry, Merry month of May, *Rigoletto* 4tet. *Thorn* Hotel.
Wednesday 25th	Burnley 9.44, Preston 10.40. Preston 11.6, Crewe 12.35. *Crewe Arms* Hotel.
Thursday 26th	10.38 Crewe. 1.18 Hereford [or] Crewe 10.35 Hereford 12.52. Hereford Shire Hall. Miscellaneous. Evening. Reh 4pm. Accompanist arranged. Michael Mullinar. 18gns. *Residence* Hotel, Broad St. Che faro, Art thou troubled, Pack clouds away, Whyte lily, Come let's be merry, Steal away, My boy Willie, Merry month of May.
Friday 27th	[Hereford] 9.10 am – look out for R[oy] H[enderson] – Crewe 12.36. Crewe 1.34, Glasgow 7.10. *More's* Hotel, India St., Glasgow.
Saturday 28th	Glasgow. St Andrew's Hall. *Dream of Gerontius*. Evening. Rehearsal 10am. White, green gold. 23gns. Roy H[enderson].
Sunday 29th	Train sleeper. Snow Hill [Birmingham] to Cradley 2.38. Rehearsal 3.15. Cradley Heath. *Majestic* Theatre. *Elijah*. Evening 7.30. Flame. 15gns.
Monday 30th	Win's half term.
Tuesday 31st	Mr Thompson [Dentist] 6pm.
November:	
Wednesday 1st	5.30 Mr Thompson.
Thursday 2nd	Merthyr Tydfil. Zoar Chapel. Miscellaneous. Evening. Pink and gold. 18gns. Pat[ricia] Davies [soprano], Herman Simberg [tenor]. *New Inn* Pontypridd.
Friday 3rd	Dr Sargent 3.30.
Sunday 5th	Liverpool Philharmonic. *Sea Pictures*. In Haven, Sabbath Morning, Where corals lie [not Sea Slumber Song or The Swimmer]. *Love the Magician* – de Falla. Afternoon 2.30. Rehearsal 10.15. Red £21.
Tuesday 7th	Pontypridd. Town Hall. Miscellaneous. Evening. Duet with Eva Turner. Reh 2.30. Mauve. 18gns. Barcarolle, Joan of Arc, Softly awakes, Che faro.
Wednesday 8th	4.30 Maurice.
Thursday 9th	H.M.V. 10.30.

Friday 10th   [Royal] Academy 11am. Lunch and lesson. 1.10 train to
                       Bradford. *Great Northern.*

Saturday 11th   Bradford. Eastbrook Hall. *Judas Maccabeus.* [Patricia Davies,
                       soprano]. Aft. Rehearsal 10.30. Red. 15gns.

Sunday 12th   Barnoldswick. *Palace* Theatre. John Hargreaves. Evening. Red.
                       18gns. Art thou troubled?, Pack clouds away, Come let's be
                       merry, It was a lover.

Tuesday 14th   Broadcast. Maurice. Reh 4.30. Studio IIIA BH.

Wednesday 15th   Hanley. Victoria Hall. Newcastle-under-Lyme String
                       Orchestra. Evening. Red. 18gns. Where'er you walk, Cradle
                       song, Arch denial ([these three with] string accompaniment).
                       Love is a bable, Sweet chance, Come let's be merry. *North
                       Stafford* [Hotel] Stoke.

Thursday 16th   Halifax. Victoria Hall. *Judas Maccabeus.* Rehearsal 2pm.
                       Concert 6.15. 18gns. 9.33 train. 1.40 Halifax [via] Stockport
                       and Stalybridge. *White Swan* [Hotel].

Friday 17th   *Queen's* Hotel Leeds.

Saturday 18th   Leeds Philharmonic. Town Hall. *Dream of Gerontius.* Aft.
                       Rehearsal 10am. 18gns. Bert's leave. *Queen's* Hotel Manchester.

Sunday 19th   Chorley. Plaza Cinema. *Messiah.* 2.30. White accordion.
                       12gns.

Wednesday 20th   To Carlisle.

Thursday 23rd   Carlisle. Central Hall. *Sea Pictures.* 2 groups. Evening.
                       Accordion pleated. 18gns. Pack clouds away, Whyte lily, Come
                       let's be merry, Love is a bable, Star candles, Spanish lady.

Saturday 25th   Hexham. *Messiah.* White accordion. 15gns.

Sunday 26th   Maryport Presbyterian Church. Evening. Miscellaneous.
                       20gns. 11.3 train from Hexham. 1pm bus to Maryport [arr.]
                       3pm.

Wednesday 29th   Crook, Co. Durham. Hope Street Wesleyan Church.
                       Miscellaneous. Evening. Red. Jan van der Gucht. 18gns.
                       Passing by (duet), Where'er you walk, Pack clouds away, Who
                       is Sylvia, Ave Maria, Steal away, Come let's be merry. Train
                       from Darlington arr. Crook 2.30. Mr W T Scales, 1 Milton St,
                       Crook.

December:

Saturday 2nd   Bradford. Eastbrook Hall. *Messiah.* Afternoon. Rehearsal
                       10.30am. White, green, gold. 15gns. Joan Taylor.

Sunday 3rd   Yeadon. Town Hall. *Messiah.* Aft. White, green, gold. 15gns.

Tuesday 5th   Rehearsal Henry Cummings. Watford 2355

Wednesday 6th   Blackpool Philharmonic Society. Tower Circus. *Messiah.*
                       Evening 7pm. Reh 3pm. White accordion pleated. 18gns.
                       [Dorothy Greene, soprano, Eric Greene, tenor] B[ill] P[arsons].
                       Clifton Hotel B'pool. Mr T. Donnelly. [Frank Rawes, cond.].

Thursday 7th   *Clifton*, B'pool.

Friday 8th   Sheffield Phil[harmonic Society]. City Hall. *Sea Pictures.* Hallé

	and John Barbirolli. Evening. White accordion. 20gns. *Grand*, Sheffield.
Saturday 9th	11.39 – 2.25 LNER *Midland* Hotel, Manchester.
Sunday 10th	Oldham. Co-op Hall, King Street. *Messiah*. Afternoon. Elena Danieli. 15 gns. White accordion. Rehearsal 11.30. [Train] Vic[toria] 9.55–10.20 [or] 11.20–11.46.
Monday 11th	3pm Helen Pyke.
Tuesday 12th	Lesson. Pick a room. 10.30 Wigmore Galleries.
Wednesday 13th	Darlington. Baths Hall. *Messiah*. Evening. Reh 3pm. White accordion. 9.40 Kings X, 2.41 [Darlington].
Thursday 14th	Darlington. Evening. Black velvet.
Friday 15th	*Grand* [Hotel] Sheffield.
Saturday 16th	Nottingham. Albert Hall. *Messiah*. Afternoon. 9am train. White accordion. 18gns. [Linda Parker, soprano, Bradbridge White, tenor, Nowakowski, bass]. Ena [Mitchell] with Parry [Jones, both met KF in Manchester that evening perhaps?]. Manchester *Midland* [Hotel].
Sunday 17th	Stockport. Carlton Cinema. *Messiah*. Afternoon. Reh. 11.15 Ella [Elena] Danieli. [Jan van der Gucht, tenor, Robert Easton, bass]. Black velvet. 15 gns.
Tuesday 19th	Lesson 11.30. 3pm. Parry [Jones] *Casa Prada* 1pm.
Wednesday 20th	Bishop Auckland. *Messiah*. Evening. Black woollie. 15gns. Mrs G Spanton, 12 Westfield Rd., Bishop Auckland.
Thursday 21st	Ferryhill, Co. Durham. Mainsforth Welfare Hall. *Messiah*. Evening. No rehearsal. Black woollie. 15gns. Miss Lazenby. Cragg House, Ferryhill.
Friday 22nd	Win breaks up.
Tuesday 26th	Blackburn. *Messiah*. Evening 15gns. White satin. *White Bull*, Blackburn.
Wednesday 27th	Huddersfield. *Messiah*. BBC Manchester broadcast 2pm [from] Huddersfield. White Satin. £14.7.4. [Joan Cross, soprano, Heddle Nash, tenor, George Pizzey, bass. The conductor was Malcolm Sargent whose initials she adds beside the circled date 27th].
Thursday 28th	Sheffield Philharmonic with Hallé. City Hall. *Messiah*. Evening. Reh 2.30. Malcolm Sargent. White satin. 18gns. B[ill] P[arsons]. *Grand* [Hotel] Sheffield.
Saturday 29th	1.30 Waterloo [train to Bournemouth].
Sunday 31st	Bournemouth. The Pavilion. *Messiah*. Afternoon and evening. White satin. 18gns. [Conducted by Roy Henderson. Mary Hamlin, soprano, Parry Jones, tenor, Roderick Lloyd, bass, Bournemouth Municipal Orchestra and Choir].

Diary for 1945

January:

Wednesday 3rd — Abertridwr. Glamorgan *Messiah*. Black woollie.

Friday 5th — Lesson

Saturday 6th — 4.5 St Pancras. Hotel *Portland* Chesterfield.

Sunday 7th — Chesterfield. Regal Cinema. *Messiah*. Short-sleeved black. 2pm. 15gns. Bill Parsons.

Monday 8th — *Queen's* [Hotel] Leeds.

Tuesday 9th — Dewsbury Town Hall. *Messiah*. Evening. Reh 3pm. Short-sleeved black. Hospitality Mrs Hurst, 51 Moorlands Rd. 1.15 from Leeds.

Thursday 11th — Merthyr Vale. Disgwylfa C[alvinistic]. M[ethodist] Ch[apel]. Evening. Miscellaneous. Hospitality. Red. Che faro, Sweet chance, Piper, Swing low, Darlin', Willie, Softly awakes, Ave Maria, Despised, Lover and lass, Barcarolle.

Friday 12th — Chiltern Court. Daphne [Ibbott] 3pm.

Saturday 13th — Croydon. Civic Hall. Listen to *Apostles*. Victoria to East Croydon.

Sunday 14th — Pontnewyndd, Pontypool. The *Pavilion*. Evening. Reh 5pm. Miscellaneous. Elena Danieli. Softly awakes, Che faro, O rest, Despised. *Clarence* Hotel.

Monday 15th — Roy 3pm. Daphne 4pm. Dentist ¼ to 6.

Wednesday 17th — Darlington. Recital with Henry Cummings. White flowered. May night, Gardener, Vain his pleading, Sweet chance, Star candles, Merry, Softly Awakes. Hospitality Mrs Hamilton, 11 Southend Avenue.

Friday 19th — Hospital concert for Norman Allin [St Mary's Paddington?] Car at 5.35.

Saturday 20th — Cambridge. Technical School Society. Recital afternoon Mr Bimrose. 18gns. Prepare thyself, Che faro, Pack clouds away, Whyte lily, Willow song, Arch denial, To Music, The Trout, Secrecy, Gardener, Barefoot, Silent noon, Happy day, Star candles, Sweet chance, Sigh no more.

Sunday 21st — East Twickenham. St Stephens. Alto Rhapsody. Maurice Greene. 3.30. Nearest station Richmond.

Monday 22nd — Lunch MM [Club] 12.30. Janet 2pm Wigmore. Lesson 3.30.

Tuesday 23rd — *Central* Hotel [Glasgow] and bath.

Wednesday 24th — Renfrew. Town Hall. Reh 5pm. Elliot Dobie's studio, 152 Buchanan Street. Duet with Norman Allin. Joan of Arc, Art thou troubled?, Pack clouds away, Sweet chance, A piper, Merry. *Central* Hotel [Glasgow].

Thursday 25th	Bert lunch *County* [Hotel], Carlisle. Wyn.
Friday 26th	Wyn.
Saturday 27th	Shaw, nr Oldham. Co-op. Reh 2.30. Hospitality. Che faro, Love song, Barefoot, Sweet chance, Bold unbiddable, It was a lover, 4 tette. Pat Davies [soprano], Roderick Lloyd [baritone], Henry Wendon [tenor].
Wednesday 31st	Janet [Hamilton-Smith] rehearsal. Daphne. Wigmore [Studios].

February:

Thursday 1st	2–3.30 Helen's with Janet [Hamilton-Smith].
Friday 2nd	*Central* Hotel [Glasgow].
Saturday 3rd	Glasgow. St Andrew's Hall. [Beethoven] Mass in D. Kodaly's *Te Deum*. 23gns. [Janet] Hamilton-Smith, [Eric] Greene, [William] Parsons. Black woolly. Sleeper.
Monday 5th	11–1 studio. Ena [Mitchell].
Tuesday 6th	12.30 Roy. Rehearsal 3pm. 9 Belgrave Square. Dr J[acques]. *St Matthew Passion.*
Wednesday 7th	Wigmore Studios Hilda Bertram. ¼ to 2 Dr Blair.
Thursday 8th	Llanelly. Tabernacle Choir. *Messiah*. Evening. Black woolly. *Thomas Arms* [Hotel].
Saturday 10th	Southwark Cathedral. *Messiah*. Short black and velvet. 10gns. Rehearsal 11am. *Park* [Hotel] Preston.
Sunday 11th	Burnley. *Empire* Theatre. Evening. Reh noon. A[lbert] Hardie. Flowered white. 18gns. Softly awakes, Love is a bable, Sweet chance, Sigh no more. *Thorn* Hotel.
Monday 12th	[Train] 7.35am-1.40.
Wednesday 14th	Gloucester. Guildhall. 3 and 7. Black woolly. Hospitality. To Music, Trout, Gardener, Barefoot, Merry, Darlin', Spanish lady, Willie. Prepare thyself Zion, Willow song, Pack clouds, Secrecy, Gardener, May night, Barefoot.
Thursday 15th	Rehearsal [with] Flora Kent [accompanist]. 5.30 Rick rang up from L'pool!! [Hotel in] Manchester.
Friday 16th	Frodsham. Music and Arts Comm[ittee]. Senior School. Evening Recital. Flora Kent Flowered white. Rowland Shelborne [organiser] Windover, Townfield Lane. *Grand* [Hotel]. Prepare thyself Zion, Che faro, Pack clouds away, To Music, The Trout, Erl King, 4 Serious Songs, Spring, Salley Gardens, Piper, Sweet chance. Rick came to concert.
Saturday 17th	Macclesfield. Friends of Music. King's School. 6.30. Black woolly. Freda Johnson, 57 Beech Lane. Pur dicesti, To Music, The Trout, 4 Serious Songs, Sweet chance, A piper, Ca' the yowes, My boy Willie.
Sunday 18th	Colne. Misc. Evening. [Recital]. Nowakowski. Flowered white. £16. Joan of Arc, Swing low, Kitty my love, Whyte lily, Merry.
Monday 19th	Win's holiday. *Queen's* [Hotel], Leeds.
Tuesday 20th	*Station* Hotel, Glasgow.

Wednesday 21st	Kirkcaldy. Adam Smith Hall. White flowered. *Station* Hotel. [Elsie] Suddaby, [Heddle] Nash, Gordon Clinton, Alie Cullen. Softly awakes, Joan of Arc, Art thou troubled?, Pack clouds away, Ca' the yowes, Willie, Spanish lady, Lovely peace, Turn ye to me, Home to the mountains, Passing by.
Thursday 22nd	Ring Hutchy. *Station* [Hotel] Newcastle.
Friday 23rd	Albert Hardie reh. Forsyths [Manchester]. Rick ringing 7.30ish. *Midland* [Hotel].
Saturday 24th	*Midland* Hotel, Manchester.
Sunday 25th	Uppermill, nr. Oldham. Recital with Edward Isaacs. 3pm. Black woolly. 18gns. *Midland* Hotel, Manchester. How changed, Willow song, Art thou troubled?, Hark the echoing air, 4 Serious Songs, Bable, Loughareema, Star candles, P.R.T.
Monday 26th	Ring up Tues morning Blackpool LMS 3405. *Midland* Hotel, Manchester.
Tuesday 27th	Manchester Midday. Albert Hardie. Black woolly. Ena [Mitchell] gave me lovely gold bangle. Can't think why! Piu dicesti, Verdant meadows, Prepare thyself Zion, Serious Songs, Spring, Silent noon, Sweet chance, Bold unbiddable. Blackpool Tower Circus. 7pm. Marjorie Blackburn [accompanist], Ceinwen Rowlands [soprano], Francis Russell [tenor]. Che faro, Art thou troubled?, Sigh no more, Ca' the yowes. Spanish lady, Merry month of May. [Train] Sleeper.
Wednesday 28th	R[ick] ringing. Ring Maurice.
March:	
Friday 2nd	Lesson 2.15. Ena 3–3.45.
Saturday 3rd	Crookhill, Ryton-on-Tyne. Methodist Church. Miscellaneous. 6.30. Red. Che faro, Whyte lily, Merry, Sweet chance, Piper, Swing low, Willie, It was a lover. Taken to and from concert by car. 3pm. *Station* Hotel, Newcastle.
Sunday 4th	Ashington, Northumberland. Central Hall. Miscellaneous. 7.30. Nowakowski. Red. Che faro, Sweet chance, Piper, Merry, Ca' the yowes, Swing low, Willie, O peaceful England. Normanton Barron, 12 Darnley Rd. *Grand* Hotel, Ashington. 2.20 [train] Manors North
Monday 5th	Rick ringing.
Tuesday 6th	Rehearsal Maurice 4.30.
Wednesday 7th	Witney, Oxfordshire. Social Centre, Market Place. 8pm. Leon Goossens. Ivor Newton. Che faro, Pack clouds away, Erl King, Love song, May night, Barefoot, Sweet chance, Piper, Salley Gardens, P.R.T. Hospitality Mrs Leigh, Witney. Red?
Thursday 8th	Cheslyn Hay [Staffs]. Salem School. 7.15. Red? Art thou troubled?, Softly awakes, Merry, Ca' the Yowes, Bold unbiddable. Tenor duets. Mr Hawkins, Grasmere.
Saturday 10th	Sherborne School with Maurice. 4.45. Black woolly. 18gns. Dr Rickett, Hill House. Che faro, Prepare thyself Zion, Verdant

meadows, Pack clouds away, To Music, The Trout, May Night, Gardener, Barefoot, Bable, Loughareema, Spanish lady, Ca' the yowes, Willie.

Monday 12th	Parry Jones 1pm *Casa Prada*.
Tuesday 13th	Lesson 10.30.
Wednesday 14th	4.30 Maurice. 6.30 Wigmore Hall.
Friday 16th	Reh 10am-1pm Royal College. [Reh] 4–7 Albert Hall. *St Matthew Passion*.
Saturday 17th	Southwark Cathedral. *St Matthew Passion*. Short black draped. [Margaret] Field-Hyde, [Eric] Greene, Roy [Henderson], [Henry] Cummings. [Conductor, Dr E. T. Cook]. Rick's last weekend before going back to Germany. Went to *The Circle*. Splendid. Yvonne Arnaud, Gielgud.
Sunday 18th	Royal Albert Hall. *St Matthew Passion*. Dr Jacques. Black velvet. 11 & 2.30. Field-Hyde, Greene, Pears, Parsons, Cummings. Lovely performance. Wonderful day.
Monday 19th	Rick went back. Lunched at *Casa Prada*.
Tuesday 20th	*Central* [Hotel], Glasgow.
Wednesday 21st	Larkhall, Lanarkshire. Trinity Church. *Elijah*. Reh 2.15. [Laelia] Finneberg, Brad [tenor Bradbridge White], Roy. New green. Marvellous hospitality two days. Mr T.B. Corbett, Avonholm, Strathavon.
Friday 23rd	Etruria. Opening of Harry Vincent's new hall. Great success presented with Royal Doulton lady. Maurice. Miss Glasgow. Short black.
Saturday 24th	Liverpool Philharmonic. Recital. Afternoon. Eileen Joyce. Albert Sammons. Green. Millicent came round. Win and Jane there. Wonderful letter from Rick. *Adelphi* [Hotel]. How changed, Caro mio ben, Pack clouds away, May Night, Gardener, Secrecy, Barefoot.
Sunday 25th	Went to Waterloo for day. Lovely. Greeted with gin and orange and lovely lunch. Murray's at night. *Adelphi*.
Monday 26th	Warrington Musical Society. Parr Hall. 6.45. *Messiah*. [Elsie] Suddaby, Cyril Hornby, tenor, George Allen, bass]. Reh 3pm. Green. Lunch David Webster. *Crewe*.
Tuesday 27th	Birmingham. Town Hall. *St Matthew Passion*. Reh 2pm. Black velvet. 18gns. Joan Taylor, Greene, Parsons, Cummings. *Queen's* Hotel.
Wednesday 28th	Win's holiday. 8.40 [train from Birmingham] New St.
Friday 30th	London, Highgate. *Messiah*. 7pm Suddaby, [Ronald] Bristol, Cummings. Black velvet.
Saturday 31st	African broadcast. 9.15–9.30pm. Reh 8pm. 200 Oxford St. Studio 4. Prepare thyself Zion, Margaret, Secret, Barefoot, Blacksmith.

April:	
Sunday 1st	Tea. Church Row. Mr Fussell. 4.15

Monday 2nd	*Central* [Hotel] Glasgow.
Tuesday 3rd	Dumbarton, Scotland. Burgh Hall. Miscellaneous. Evening. Black velvet. Che faro, Pack clouds away, Sigh no more, Star candles, Bold unbiddable, O lovely peace, Turn ye to me. [Ingrid] Hageman [soprano], Herman Simberg [tenor].
Thursday 5th	Hanley. Ceramic [Choir] Victoria Hall. *Messiah*. Black velvet. Evening. Ceinwen Rowlands, Trefor Jones, Henry Cummings. *North Stafford* [Hotel].
Friday 6th	Went with Roy to hear him recording.
Saturday 7th	Reading. Town Hall. *Messiah*. Dr Jacques. Reh 3pm. Black woolly. Field-Hyde, Greene, Cummings. Mrs Leese.
Sunday 8th	Bristol. *Ambassadors* Cinema, Kingswood. Aero Engines Choral Society. 7.45. Reh 3pm. Green. Softly awakes, Art thou troubled?, Pack clouds away, Bable, Silent noon, Star candles, Piper. Reg Denning [accompanist]. *Royal* [Hotel]. Dorothy Charles, 19 Downend Rd, Kingswood.
Monday 9th	[Train to London] 9.0–11.30.
Tuesday 10th	Euston 4.0. Colwyn Bay 9.53. *Cartmells* [Hotel].
Wednesday 11th	Colwyn Bay Ladies Choir. Norman Lumsden. Green. *Cartmells*. Have mercy Lord, Father of Heaven, Despised, *Inflammatus*.
Thursday 12th	Lovely day with Eileen. Heavenly weather. Eileen Dawes 6 Egerton Road. [Liverpool].
Friday 13th	Gown £25.11.9. *Adelphi* [Hotel].
Saturday 14th	Liverpool Philharmonic. Welsh Choral Union. *Messiah*. White satin. [Victoria] Sladen, [Edward] Reach, [Marian] Nowakowski. 15gns. Lunch with Jean. Dinner with Stephen [?Wearing] *Adelphi*.
Sunday 15th	Macclesfield. Aft and eve. Miscellaneous. Short pink. [Recital] Mrs Abraham, 'Invercraig', Langley – lovely. [Afternoon] Art thou troubled, Verdant meadows, Pack clouds away, Hear my prayer, God is my shepherd, Sing ye a joyful song, Lord we pray thee, I will lay me down in peace, O praise the Lord. [Evening] Ye men of Israel, Return O God of Hosts, O thou that tellest, He was despised, O rest in the Lord, How lovely, Abide with me with chorus.
Monday 16th	*Queen* Hotel, Huddersfield.
Tuesday 17th	Huddersfield Glee [Club]. Town Hall. Misc. Leslie Woodgate 7pm. Green. 15gns. Che faro, Prepare thyself Zion, Secrecy, Gardener, Barefoot, Bable, Loughareema, Bold unbiddable. Harold Syke, 1 Beaumont Park Road, Huddersfield. *Queen* [Hotel].
Wednesday 18th	Huddersfield 8.41, Cardiff 2.28. *Royal* Hotel Cardiff.
Thursday 19th	Landore, Swansea. New Siloh Chapel Choir. Evening. Green. Ruth Packer, Heddle Nash. Hymn of praise, Return O God of hosts, How lovely, O rest in the Lord, Verdant meadows.
Friday 20th	Recording 2.30. Spring, Come to me soothing sleep – Handel.

	Reh[earsal] Dineley [Studios] BBC. [accompanied by Gerald Moore, produced by Walter Legge]. Ring Roy.
Saturday 21st	Heard Verdi Requiem at Sheffield, Barbirolli conducting. *Red Lion* [Hotel], Market Place, Pontefract.
Sunday 22nd	Knottingley, nr Pontefract. Rope Walk Methodist Church. 2.15. *Messiah*. Short-sleeved black. Mary Hamlin, Trefor Jones, Henry Cummings. Party with Henry and Kate. Nice. *Queen's* [Hotel] Leeds.
Monday 23rd	Piano rehearsal Beethoven Mass [*Missa Solemnis*]. Sargent – Royal College.
Tuesday 24th	Margaret Parker's.
Wednesday 25th	Liverpool. Bibby's. 12.15–12.55. Black draped. Che faro, Prepare thyself Zion, Art thou troubled?, Pack clouds away, Willow song, Merry, Love song, Barefoot, Bable, Sweet chance, Piper, Yowes, Spanish lady, Willie. Margaret [Parker's].
Thursday 26th	Liverpool. St Nicholas. Black draped. Che faro, Prepare thyself, Verdant meadows, Pack clouds away, O praise the Lord, Willow song, Merry, To Music, Who is Sylvia?, Sweet chance, Star candles, Piper. *Bridge* Hotel, Bedford.
Friday 27th	Rehearsal BBC Corn Exchange. Cancelled.
Saturday 28th	Royal Albert Hall. Beethoven Mass [*Missa Solemnis*]. Reh 10am. Aft. 2.30 12 [guineas]. White accordion. Royal Choral Society. Joan Hammond, Trefor Jones, George Pizzey. Dr Sargent.
Sunday 29th	Ring Roy.
Monday 30th	To supper to Waterloo. Such pets. *Adelphi* [Hotel, Liverpool].

May:

Tuesday 1st	Liverpool Bachad Fellowship. Phil[harmonic Hall, accompanist Ronald Settle]. [Mark] Hambourg, [Alfredo] Campoli. White accordion. Jean and Millicent to dinner *Adelphi*. Bought lovely opal ring (£45). Maurice came later. Long chat. Che faro, Piu dicesti, Art thou troubled?, Bable, Loughareema, Piper, Bold unbiddable.
Wednesday 2nd	Spennymoor, Co. Durham. 6.30. Margot [Pacey née Wright, accompanist]. Walter Glynne [tenor]. Green.
Friday 4th	Dinner *Martinez* – Cecil McGivern (BBC producer).
Saturday 5th	Croydon. Civic Hall. *The Kingdom*. Aft. 3. Reh 10.30. Green. 10 [guineas]. Lovely performance, Mr [Alan] Kirby conducting. [Isobel] Baillie, [Eric] Greene, [William] Parsons. 7pm train arr 1.45am! *Station* Hotel, Newcastle.
Sunday 6th	Newcastle. City Hall. Broadcast. Brahms Serious Songs. Reh. 10am. Green chinese. Northern Orchestra. Clarence Raybould [conductor] £24.9.6d *Station* Hotel, Newcastle.
Monday 7th	Roy 3.30 Wigmore. End of the war in Europe. Thank goodness!
Tuesday 8th	VE day. St Mary's [Paddington] Hospital concert cancelled –

	hurrah. Went on Heath, saw all bonfires, fireworks, search-lights. Very sober crowds.
Wednesday 9th	Holiday again. Southwark recital cancelled. Win making evening frock – gorgeous.
Thursday 10th	Gloucester Cathedral. Recital from organ loft. Lovely. Short black draped. Prepare thyself, Zion, Slumber beloved, Have mercy Lord, *Inflammatus*, Brahms No.4, Cradle song, Angel's Farewell – *Gerontius*. John Sumsion, 20 College Green.
Friday 11th	Reh 5pm for Westminster Abbey *Messiah*.
Saturday 12th	Royal Albert Hall. *Gerontius*. Goldsmiths [Choral Union and Symphony Orchestra]. Heddle [Nash], Norman Walker. Died a 1000 deaths. Poor orchestra and conductor [Frederick Haggis]. Went to see *The Duchess of Malfi*. Excellent. Trouncer, Ashcroft, Gielgud, with Win and Norman. Good antidote.
Monday 14th	Westminster Abbey. *Messiah*. Dr Jacques. [Joan] Taylor, Brad[bridge White], Norman [Lumsden]. Short black draped. 12 gns. 3.30 Park Lane – Auntie May. Met Margaret *Casa Prada* 8pm.
Tuesday 15th	Whattaday! Bought new hat. Lunch at MM with Margaret. Tea with her uncle at *Grosvenor*. Theatre *Gay Rosalinda* with Win, Margaret, Auntie May and 9 others. Dinner dance at SAVOY!! Lovely day.
Wednesday 16th	Bournemouth with Pop. Gorgeous weather.
Friday 18th	Win came to Bournemouth. Weather going off.
Saturday 19th	Weather definitely gorn orf!
Sunday 20th	Weather broken – pouring down! Went to flix, saw *Quiet Wedding* again. Lovely film. Lovely in evening.
Monday 21st	Chilly but fine.
Wednesday 23rd	End of holiday. Bournemouth holiday £22.17s.9d.
Thursday 24th	*Hamlet?*
Friday 25th	Letchworth Free Church. Sacred [concert] with Roy. Evening 12gns. Plain blue. Lord we pray Thee, Ombra mai fu, Praise the Lord, *Inflammatus*, He was despised, Sound the trumpet. Phil. J. Wright, 18 Hillshott, [Letchworth].
Sunday 27th	Broadcast 10.15–10.30. 15 gns. Come my voice, Spring (Handel), Whyte lily, Nightingale, Flocks. *Station* Hotel, Newcastle.
Monday 28th	Haltwhistle. St Cecilia Choral [Society]. Westgate Methodist Church. Evening 25gns. Blue. Che faro, Pack clouds away, To Music, Sylvia, Willow song, Merry, Fidgety bairn, Bonnet. Mrs Lees, Oaklea, Hexham [Tel] 223.
Tuesday 29th	*Adelphi* [Hotel], Liverpool.
Wednesday 30th	Liverpool. Crane Hall. 12.10 and 1.10. [Two recitals]. £8.7s.5d. Blue. Fairest isle, Hark the ech'ing, Soothing sleep, Spring, Piu dicesti, Caro mio ben, Love song, Swallow, Vain suit, Star candles, Piper, Ca' the Yowes, Bonnet, Bold unbiddable. Ronald Settle [accompanist] Cranes Music Studios, Liverpool. *Angel* [Hotel], Cardiff.

Thursday 31st	Pontypridd. Town Hall. Ruth Packer, Norman Allin. Green chinese. 20gns. To Music, Who is Sylvia?, Barefoot, Sigh no more, Star candles, Bold unbiddable, Duets with both. *New Inn*.

June:

Saturday 2nd	Golf with Norman [Allin], Brad[bridge White].
Monday 4th	Week's CEMA. Harry Vincent with Douglas Cameron, Phyllis Spurr. Black draped. Pink with coatee. [No programme or other details known for this or the following two concerts].
Tuesday 5th	Stoke CEMA.
Wednesday 6th	Stoke CEMA.
Thursday 7th	Stoke CEMA. Liverpool. Evening. Bluey green gathered. Turquoise. 20 gns. [accompanist] Stephen [Wearing]. Spring, Troubled?, Whyte lily, Come let's be merry, Swing low, Water boy, Kitty, Spanish lady, Little darlin'.
Saturday 9th	Theatre. *Peter Grimes*. Magnificent. Ring Michael Head.
Sunday 10th	Stage door canteen 5pm. Lousy! Red.
Monday 11th	Manchester. Bachad. Houldsworth [Hall]. 7pm. Red. To Music, Who is Sylvia?, Barefoot, Whyte lily, Willow song, Merry. *Midland* [Hotel].
Tuesday 12th	Lesson 4.30.
Wednesday 13th	Kensington Palace. Dr Jacques. Laudamus Te, Prepare thyself Zion, Watts Cradle song, Bonnet. Cancelled.
Friday 15th	11.30 fitting D[ebenham] & F[reebody]. Send songs to Newcastle. John Francis between 2.30 and 3 with Ena. Rehearsal studio 3–6. Ena staying night.
Sunday 17th	Trix coming?
Tuesday 19th	M[ichael] Head 2.30.
Wednesday 20th	Newcastle-upon-Tyne. Methodist Church. Turquoise. 20gns. Softly awakes, Verdant meadows, Pack clouds away, Whyte lily, Come let's be merry, Merry month of May, O peaceful England. *Station* [Hotel]
Thursday 21st	Helen. Newcastle with Margot. Aycliffe 12.30. Car calling at hotel 10.45. Collect Margot – back to Durham after lunch. [Stayed with] Margot [?Wright]
Friday 22nd	[Stayed with] Margot [?Wright]
Saturday 23rd	Hetton le Hole. Turquoise. 30gns [two appearances]. Spring, Art thou troubled?, Whyte lily, Merry, Loughareema, Bold unbiddable. Duets with soprano including Mendelssohn.
Sunday 24th	Hetton le Hole. [Recital] duets with soprano. Turquoise. Come, come my voice, Ombra mai fu, Come to me soothing sleep, Lord we pray Thee, O lovely peace, Where'er you walk, Ave Maria. [Helen Anderson soprano, accompanist Margot Wright].
Monday 25th	Bedlington Station. CEMA. Methodist Church. 7pm. Helen

	with Michael Head. 6gns. Turquoise. *Station* [Hotel] Newcastle.
Tuesday 26th	Auntie May.
Wednesday 27th	Darlington. Victoria Rd Methodist Church. Reh 3pm. Turquoise. 25gns. Come to me sleep, Spring, Loughareema, Bold unbiddable, Ca' the Yowes, Fidgety bairn, Home to our mountains. Duets with J Wick [tenor]. [Stayed with] Auntie May.
Thursday 28th	Send photograph to Mrs Sharpe, 33 Market Street, Hetton le Hole, Co. Durham. Charlie Hutchinson, Maple House, Haltwhistle.
Saturday 30th	Rugby Musical Society. Chinese green. 1pm Euston. 2.30 Rugby. Jim Dickson (Hexham doctor). Kenneth Stubbs hospitality. Prepare thyself Zion, Come, come my voice, Spring, Soothing sleep, Piu dicesti, Caro mio ben, Four Serious Songs, Bable, Loughareema, P.R.T.

	July:
Sunday 1st	Rugby School. Evening. Red. Che faro, How changed the vision, Verdant meadows, Pack clouds away, To Music, Who is Sylvia?, The Erl King, May night, Swallow, Barefoot, Sweet chance, Star candles, Piper, Bonnet, Ca' the Yowes, Willie.
Tuesday 3rd	Lunch Mr and Mrs Lees, Hexham. Laurence Holmes [singer] Farewell [concert] with Ena.
Wednesday 4th	Lunch: Parry [Jones]. Rehearsal John Lowe [conductor]. *Gerontius* 11am at Roy's. Roy's with Ena 8pm.
Thursday 5th	Cambridge Guild Hall *Gerontius* Evening. Rehearsal 2.30. Polling Day. [Roy Henderson, Heddle Nash, postponed to 12th due to the Hall's requisition for the General Election]. Golf with Win, Norman, Bill Parsons. Ashford, Middlesex. Take camera. 9.44 Waterloo.
Saturday 7th	Golf. Haste Hill.
Sunday 8th	Golf. Haste Hill. Lovely. Rehearsal Laurence Ager 4.45.
Monday 9th	Lunch. W[alter] Legge. 12.30 *Pagani's*. Take diary.
Wednesday 11th	Mr Cornwell [either at] St Mary's Hospital. [or] Norfolk Place, Praed Street.
Thursday 12th	Cambridge. King's College Chapel. *Gerontius*. Evening. Reh 2.15. Dark blue.
Sunday 15th	Hampton Court. J[acques] S[tring] O[rchestra]. Reh 2.30. Turquoise. 7gns.
Monday 16th	Rehearsal Southwark. 6.30.
Tuesday 17th	*Peter Grimes* with Mr and Mrs Prof [Hendersons].
Wednesday 18th	Southwark Cathedral. Recital. Short black. Flix Swiss Cottage Mr and Mrs Prof.
Friday 20th	Golf.
Saturday 21st	Crowborough, Sussex. Christ Church Hall. 6pm. Chinese

green. 15gns. Victoria 1.45 – Groombridge 3.1, Groombridge 3.17 – Crowborough 3.29.

Thursday 26th	Fleetwood for fortnight. [curtailed to nine days].
Sunday 29th	Fleetwood. Marine Hall. Miscellaneous. 20gns. Chinese green. With orchestra: Che faro, Cradle song, Art thou troubled? [With piano] To Music, Who is Sylvia?, Fidgety bairn, Spanish lady, Willie [Tom Smith, conductor].

August:

Friday 3rd	Fleetwood ends. Went to Liverpool. Played golf. Lovely time.
Saturday 4th	Came home. Pop fine.
Sunday 5th	Auntie May coming.
Monday 6th	Bank holiday on Heath. *No Medals* at night. Marvellous but made me sob!
Tuesday 7th	*Private Lives.* Splendid.
Wednesday 8th	Theatre – *The Cure for Love*. Robert Donat magnificent. Send music to Wells. Canon T H Davis, The Liberty, Wells. Auntie May went. Send time of arrival – Dr Rickett, Hill House, Sherborne.
Thursday 9th	Golf and dined and danced at the *Savoy*.
Friday 10th	Golf. Ironed and did odd jobs.
Saturday 11th	Saw golf final at Richmond. *Savoy* at night.
Sunday 12th	Golf. Did an 87. Whoopee! Walk on Heath.
Monday 13th	Lunch at M.M. Saw Alison. Ena came.
Tuesday 14th	Win, Auntie May. Went to Sherborne.
Wednesday 15th	Wells Cathedral. 10gns. Ena and Maurice. Short black. Sound the trumpet, Lord we pray thee, Soothing sleep, Cradle song. Duet Brahms, To Music, Brahms No.4, Ears of Pan [Jacobson], Dirge for Fidele [Vaughan Williams].
Thursday 16th	Oxford. Town Hall. Recital with Roy. 6.30. Chinese green. 25gns. Willow song, Come let's be merry, Let us wander, Fairest isle, Hark, Sound the trumpet, To Music, Gretchen, Heidenröslein, Silent noon, Star candles, A piper, Folksong.
Saturday 18th	Buxton. Chinese green. Spring, Verdant meadows, Pack clouds away, Whyte lily, Willow song, Come let's be merry. Mrs Dobbie, *Claremont* [Hotel].
Sunday 19th	Buxton. Afternoon and evening. £31.10s od. [for 18th and 19th]. Red. Mrs Dobbie. Afternoon service: Come, come my voice, Hark the ech'ing air. Night: Che faro (Orch. parts), Ca' the yowes, Fidgety bairn, Bonnet.
Monday 20th	Ring Roy on arrival. Decca 3.30. [Tom Smith, conductor].
Tuesday 21st	Recording Latin America. Aldenham. Reh 2.30–3.30. Recording 3.30–4. 141 bus from Edgware Underground at 2pm to *The Plough*, Elstree. BBC car. Nightingale, Flocks, Willow song, Fairest isle, Hark the ech'ing air. Take another.
Thursday 23rd	Crewe Christ Church. (Rev. Young). Miscellaneous. Evening. Turquoise. 20gns. Come, come, Feed his flock, Soothing

	sleep, Lord we pray thee, O praise the Lord, Sweet chance, Star candles, Watts Cradle song. Mrs Lea.
Tuesday 28th	Birmingham. Town Hall. Evening. 6.30. Recital Roy and Trimbles. [piano duo, the sisters Joan and Valerie Trimble] Turquoise. 20gns. *Queen's* [Hotel].
Wednesday 29th	Lunch Maurice, Ben [Britten].

September:

Saturday 1st	Blackburn. Queen's Hall. Evening. Duets Trefor Jones. Good classical. Green. Che faro, Come, come my voice, Art thou troubled?, Who is Sylvia?, The Erl King, Tenor duets!
Sunday 2nd	[Home].
Monday 3rd	[Train to Glasgow]. [*Central* Hotel].
Tuesday 4th	Glasgow Cathedral. Evening. Meet Mr Wilfred Emery at gate of Cathedral at 5.30 for rehearsal. Short black. 30gns. Prepare thyself, Soothing sleep, O death, Though I speak, *Inflammatus*, O praise the Lord, Lay me down in peace. *Central* [Hotel] Glasgow or sleeper?
Friday 7th	Party.
Saturday 8th	10 am [train from] Kings X.
Sunday 9th	Bishop Auckland. Central Methodist Church. Afternoon and evening. Swathed black. 42gns. Let I & T [Ibbs and Tillett] know time of arrival.
Monday 10th	[Bishop Auckland]. Evening. Miscellaneous Concert. Green. Tenor duets. Donald Murday [entered for 9th but actually 10th]. Auntie May's.
Thursday 13th	Banbury. Town Hall. 7pm with Leon Goossens, accompanist Mary Barry. Cancelled.
Saturday 15th	PROM RAH 7pm. Reh morning 10am. Joan of Arc Farewell. £19.13.9d. Lamé. Taxi to rehearsal 12/6d. Taxi to lunch 4/-. Lunch: entertaining £1.2.6d. Taxi to and from concert £1.10/-. Taxi home and back for orchestral parts £1.
Monday 17th	Recording 2.30. [scored through].
Tuesday 18th	Glyndebourne. 10.28 Victoria. [This was an audition for John and Audrey Christie arranged through Rudolf Bing at the request of Roy Henderson – letters dated 27 August – 14 September 1945 in Glyndebourne Archive].
Wednesday 19th	Llandudno. Town Hall. Music Club. Recital. 7.30. Lamé. 20gns. 8.15 [Euston], arr. 1.27 Colwyn Bay. *North Western* Hotel. Meet Mr H B Johnson. Spring, Soothing sleep, Piu dicesti, Caro mio ben, Whyte lily, Willow song, Arch denial, Silent noon, Fairy lough, Bold unbiddable, Star candles, A piper, An die Musik, Gretchen, Röslein, Love song, Barefoot.
Thursday 20th	Hanley Ceramic [Choir]. Victoria Hall. Evening. Alto Rhapsody and Miscellaneous. Lamé. Spinning chorus [Kathleen sang Mary's interjections]. To Music, Erl King, Silent noon, P.R.T.
Friday 21st	2.30 Recording duets [with soprano Isobel Baillie, acc.

Gerald Moore, producer Walter Legge. Music by Purcell and Mendelssohn].

Saturday 22nd   10am Recording [scored through]. 4pm Colwyn Bay.

Sunday 23rd   Colwyn Bay. Pier Pavilion. 8pm. Reh 4.30. Lamé. 20gns. Two groups. [1] To Music, Sylvia, Erl King. [2] A piper, Star candles, P.R.T. Eileen's. Glenwood, 6 Egerton Rd.

Tuesday 25th   Llanelly. Zion Baptist [Church]. Evening. Miscellaneous. Hospital concert. 3 solos and duet. Churchy items. Chinese green. 25gns. [Janet] Hamilton-Smith. Peter Pears. Lord we pray thee, Art thou troubled?, Pack clouds away, Steal away, The fidgety bairn, Sound the trumpet(?), Come let's be merry. *Thomas Arms.*

Wednesday 26th   Glyn-Neath. Bethania. Evening. Miscellaneous. Chinese green. 25gns. Joan of Arc, Soothing sleep, Spring, Star candles, Piper. Merry month, Passing by, It was a lover, Voyagers, O lovely night. Tenor and baritone duets. *Castle Neath* [Hotel].

Friday 28th   CEMA party. 23 Knightsbridge, Hyde Park Corner. 6–8.

Saturday 29th   10.15 [Humphrey] Procter-Gregg – Maida Vale. Swindon. *Elijah.* Evening. Reh 2.30. Hospitality. Lamé. 20gns.

October:

Thursday 4th   Hereford. Baptist Church. Evening. Miscellaneous. Chinese green. 25gns. Nancy Ellis Bateman [soprano]. 9.45 Paddington – 2.40 [Hereford] Rehearsal 5.30 Mr A. Denham. Lord we pray Thee, Come, come my voice, Prepare thyself Zion, I will lay me down, O praise the Lord, Hear my prayer, Sing ye a joyful song, O lovely peace. [hospitality] Kathleen Llewellyn.

Friday 5th   Hereford 9.55, Cardiff 11.30.

Saturday 6th   Morriston, Swansea. Unitarian Male Voice Choir. Tabernacle Chapel. Miscellaneous. Orchestra. Evening. Chinese Green 25gns. Softly awakes, Che faro, Watts Cradle song, Water boy, Willie. My own parts. *Grand* [Hotel] Swansea.

Monday 8th   Hilda Bertram 11-ish. 6 Raymond Buildings, Grays Inn [studio]. Train to Birmingham. *Grand* Hotel.

Tuesday 9th   Birmingham. Town Hall. *Dream of Gerontius.* [Peter Pears, Roy Henderson, George Cunningham, conductor]. White satin. *Grand* Hotel.

Wednesday 10th   Birmingham. Town Hall. *Dream of Gerontius.* Accordion pleated. *Grand* Hotel.

Thursday 11th   Ystradgynlais nr Swansea. Welfare Hall. Miscellaneous. Victoria Sladen and Peter Pears. White satin. Art thou troubled?, Spring, Whyte lily, Merry, My heart is weary. Duets with soprano and tenor. Mendelssohn. Sound the trumpet. *Grand* Swansea.

Saturday 13th   Southwark Cathedral. *Dream of Gerontius.* [Jan van der Gucht, Roy Henderson, Dr E.T. Cook, conductor]. Morning reh. Short black swathed.

Monday 15th	Recording [scored through]. 11am Hilda Bertram. 4.15 Sing to [Carl] Ebert and Sir Thomas [Beecham]. Borgioli's Studio. Bought jewel case – lovely.
Tuesday 16th	St Helens. Grange Park Music Society. Miscellaneous. 3 or 4 groups. Evening. Green. Flora Kent. 10am taxi. 10.45 Euston, St Helens Junction 4.14. Spring, Art thou troubled?, Whyte lily, Come let's be merry, Sylvia, Erl King, Bable, Star candles, Piper. 9.24 Shaw St – Liverpool Lime St 9.58 [or] St Helens Junction 10.34 – Liverpool 11.07.
Wednesday 17th	Ring Hilda Bertram. Casals concert.
Thursday 18th	Broadcast CEMA [scored through]. Golf Roy afternoon. 10.30 Wigmore H[ilda B[ertram]. 12 noon Mr Rubinstein.
Friday 19th	Rehearsing 11am. Lunch Parry [both scored through]. R[utland] B[oughton] 3pm [see Kathleen's letter to Boughton 20th October 1945].
Saturday 20th	Nottingham. Albert Hall. *Elijah* [Edna] Hobson, [Bradbridge White], Roy [Henderson]. Evening. Reh aft. Green. 20gns. 9.50 Marylebone. *Victoria Station* Hotel.
Sunday 21st	Hebden Bridge. Co-op Hall. Evening. Miscellaneous. Green. 20gns. 10.48 Nottingham Midland, change Derby 11.28–11.35, being met at Leeds City Station at 1.48. Che faro, Spring, Soothing sleep, Sigh no more, Star candles, Come let's be merry, Tenor duets, Abide with me? With choir? Mrs Redman, Rockville, Hebden Bridge.
Monday 22nd	*Station* [Hotel] Newcastle.
Tuesday 23rd	Gateshead. Central Hall. Low Fell Oriana [Society]. Miscellaneous. 7pm. Reh 4.30. Hospitality. Green. David Lloyd [tenor]. Che faro, Art thou troubled?, Pack clouds away, Star candles, Come let's be merry, Tenor duets – Merry month, Passing by. Silent noon, Water boy – encores. Mrs Smith, 30 Denewell Ave, Low Fell. Train to Newcastle.
Wednesday 24th	South Shields. Glebe Methodist Church. Westoe Rd. Miscellaneous. Rehearsal 4pm. Green. Ada Alsop, Robert Easton. Che faro, Fairest isle, Hark the ech'ing air, Whyte lily, Come let's be merry, Silent noon, Sigh no more. Miss Dorothy Harley, 34 Central Ave.
Thursday 25th	South Shields. [Recital]. Blue. Joan of Arc, Soothing sleep, To music, Who is Sylvia?, Fidgety bairn, Bonnet, Willie.
Friday 26th	Elland. St Paul's School Room Recital. Evening. 7pm. Green. Eric Harrison. *Queen* [Hotel] Huddersfield. Prepare thyself Zion, How changed the vision, Verdant meadows, Whyte lily, Merry, Secrecy, Gardener, May night, Barefoot, Bable, Loughareema, Bold unbiddable, Fidgety bairn, Spanish lady.
Saturday 27th	Hotel £1.10/-. Taxi to station 5/-. Electric blanket for travelling £3.15?-. Train to Keighley 9/6d. Taxi to hotel 3/6. [Train] 5.55. Change Halifax and Queensborough. [Queensbury is meant].
Sunday 28th	Keighley. Temple St Methodist Church. *Messiah*. Afternoon

and evening. Plain blue. 20 gns. Taxis two perfs. 15/-. W Butterfield, 94 Mornington St, Keighley.

Tuesday 30th	Parry lunch. R.B. [?Rutland Boughton: both scored through]. Roy, golf.
Wednesday 31st	R.B? [scored through]. Afternoon frock 7gns.

November:

Thursday 1st	Llandeilo, Carmarthenshire. Tabernacle Chapel. Evening. Miscellaneous. Pink tailored. 25 gns. Janet Hamilton-Smith, David Lloyd, Tom Williams. Softly awakes, Lord we pray thee, Hence to our mountains, Merry month, Voyagers, Lovely night. *Thomas Arms* [Hotel].
Friday 2nd	Rutland Boughton? [scored through].
Saturday 3rd	Darlington. North Rd Methodist Choir. Reh 3pm. Flame. Let us wander, Hark the ech'ing air, Sound the trumpet, Art thou troubled, Pack clouds away, *Elijah*, Star candles, Sigh no more, Bonnet, Spanish lady, O no John. Roy [Henderson] – programme together.
Sunday 4th	Darlington. Short black. Lord we pray Thee, I will lay me down in peace, O praise the Lord, Come, come my voice, Fairest isle.
Monday 5th	Send music to Sunderland. Frock, stockings, gloves, undies £35.4.9d. Rehearsal [Albert] Coates (scored through).
Tuesday 6th	Piano reh 10–1. 35 Marylebone High St. Reh 2.30–5.30, 7–10. Studio 1, Delaware Rd.
Wednesday 7th	Albert Hall [scored through]. Albert Coates. *On the Field of Kukileva* [should be *Kolikovo* by Yury Shaporin]. Maida Vale Studio. 7.45–9. Reh 2.30–5.30. [recording for BBC. BBC Symphony Orchestra and Choral Society, Albert Coates, conductor, Laelia Finneberg, soprano, Frank Titterton, tenor, Roderick Jones, baritone].
Saturday 10th	Sunderland. Cleveland Rd Methodist Church. Evening. Miscellaneous. Flame. Joan of Arc, I would that my love, Art thou troubled?, Loughareema, Bold unbiddable, Water boy, Fidgety bairn, I have a bonnet.
Sunday 11th	Sunderland. Evening. [Recital] Dark blue. Mendelssohn 13th Psalm, Come, come my voice, O lovely peace, He was despised, Lord we pray Thee, Abide with me. Rev. Andrew Thornton, 12 Westlands, Sunderland.
Thursday 15th	Worcester. College Hall. Broadcast CEMA 3pm. Balance test 2pm. Turquoise. £17.19.8d. *Hopmarket* Hotel, Foregate Street. Che faro, Art thou troubled?, Where corals lie, In Haven, Sea Slumber Song? [Kathleen's question mark].
Saturday 17th	Bristol. Central Hall. *Messiah*. Evening. 6.30. Reh 2pm. Turquoise. 20gns. Paddington 11.45, Bristol 1.45. *Royal* [Hotel].
Sunday 18th	[Train] 8.55–12.25.
Monday 19th	Train to Glasgow £6.3.2d *Central* [Hotel] Glasgow.

Tuesday 20th	Stevenston. (Ardeer Recreation Club). Roy. Reh 3.30. Lamé. [Glasgow] St Enoch 1.45 to Ardrossan South Beach Station. Met at 2.45 [by] Betty Govan.
Wednesday 21st	Kirkcaldy. *Adam Smith* Hall. Miscellaneous. Lamé. Roy and Trimble [sisters]. *Station* Hotel. Let us wander, Fairest isle, Hark the ech'ing air, Sound the trumpet, Silent noon, Star candles, Piper, Bonnet, O no John. Mrs Torrance, Belhaven, Kinghorn, Fife.
Friday 23rd	Hilda Bertram 11am. Lunch Uncle Reg, *Norfolk* Hotel Surrey St, WC2 1pm. Studio and accompanist 12/6d, gramophone record 5/7½d, lesson £1.1/-, stamps 5/-.
Saturday 24th	Bromley. Boys County School. *Messiah*. 6pm. Reh 2.30. Turquoise. [Margaret] Field-Hyde, Brad[bridge White], [Henry] Cummings. 2.04 train Victoria. 2.31 Bromley South. Flowers for frock 12/6d.
Monday 26th	Hilda Bertram 11am.
Wednesday 28th	Brierley Hill, Staffordshire. Parish Church. Evening. *Messiah*. Dark blue. Taxi 8.30, 9.10 Paddington. Train to Birmingham, taxi to Brierley Hill. *Grand* [Hotel] Birmingham.
Thursday 29th	8.40 New Street, 11.24 Euston. 2.45 9 Manchester Square, Arnold Goldsbrough.
Friday 30th	Kings Cross 1.25 – Grimsby 5.38. Rehearsal for Grimsby. Mrs Osborne 22 The Park.
December:	
Saturday 1st	Grimsby. Central Hall. Aft and eve. *Messiah*. Turquoise. Flowers for frock 12/6d.
Sunday 2nd	Train to Liverpool. *Adelphi* [Hotel] Liverpool.
Monday 3rd	Warrington. Parr Hall. *Messiah*. Evening. White accordion. *Patten Arms* Hotel.
Tuesday 4th	Market Drayton, Shropshire. Parish Church. *Messiah*. Evening. Turquoise. Rehearsal Philharmonic Hall, Etruria. *Castle* Hotel, Newcastle-under-Lyme.
Thursday 6th	Hexham. *Forum* Cinema. *Elijah*. Turquoise.
Friday 7th	Car to Skipton. 3.30 [train] to Shipley 4.14, [then] 4.18 to Bradford 4.30. *Great Northern* [Hotel] Bradford.
Saturday 8th	Bradford. Old Choral [Society]. *Messiah*. Aft. Reh 10.30. White accordion. *Midland* [Hotel] Manchester.
Sunday 9th	Manchester. Belle Vue. Hallé. *Messiah*. Reh King's Hall 10–1. White accordion. 25gns. *Midland* [Hotel] Manchester.
Monday 10th	Photos 11 or 11.30. *Midland* [Hotel] Manchester.
Tuesday 11th	Manchester Midday. Marjorie Lawrence concert [for the polio-stricken soprano]. Turquoise. Spring, Soothing sleep, Pack clouds away, Dearest consort, Blacksmith, May night, Roses three, Swallow, Barefoot, Lover's curse, Men from the fields, B for Barney, Salley Gardens, I have a bonnet. *Midland* [Hotel] Manchester.

Wednesday 12th	Derby. Central Hall. Choral Union. *Messiah*. Reh 3.20. Ceinwen [Rowlands, soprano].
Thursday 13th	Blackpool Tower Circus. Phil. *Messiah*. Evening. Turquoise. *Palatine* [Hotel].
Saturday 15th	Pudsey, Yorks. Trinity Methodist Church. *Messiah*. Aft. reh 10.30. Lunch arranged. Turquoise. *Thorn* [Hotel] Burnley.
Sunday 16th	Burnley. *Odeon* Theatre. Afternoon and Evening Miscellaneous Concerts. Duets and 4tets. Gwen Catley, David Lloyd, Robert Easton, Gerald Moore. Turquoise and accordion white. Aft: Dearest consort, Salley Gardens, Men from the fields, Spanish lady. Eve: Silent noon, P.R.T. Whyte lily, Come let's be merry. *Thorn* [Hotel], Burnley.
Monday 17th	Train to Darlington. Auntie May.
Tuesday 18th	Bishop Auckland. Wesley Chapel. Evening. *Messiah*. Turquoise. Auntie May.
Wednesday 19th	Bradford. Festival Choral [Society]. Evening. *Messiah*. Turquoise. *Great Northern* [Hotel].
Thursday 20th	Halifax. Victoria Hall. *Messiah*. Evening. Reh 2.30. Turquoise. *Queen* [Hotel] Huddersfield.
Friday 21st	Huddersfield. Town Hall. *Messiah*. Evening 7pm. Reh 3pm. White accordion. *Queen* Huddersfield.
Saturday 22nd	Liverpool Phil. *Messiah*. Afternoon. White, green and gold.
Sunday 23rd	Liverpool Phil. Afternoon. *Messiah*. Velvet and muff.
Monday 24th	Train to London £2.10.7d
Wednesday 26th	Blackburn. *Messiah*. Evening. Reh 2.30. White, green and gold. *White Bull* [Hotel].
Thursday 27th	Hanley. Victoria Hall. Stoke Choral Society. *Messiah*. Evening. Reh 2.30. White, green and gold. [Elsie] Suddaby, [Tom] Culbert, [Henry] Cummings. *North Stafford* [Hotel], Stoke.
Friday 28th	Train to Liverpool. [No concert, so perhaps a visit to Rick Davies].
Saturday 29th	*City* [Hotel] Dunfermline.
Sunday 30th	Dunfermline Abbey. *Messiah*. Afternoon. *City* [Hotel] Dunfermline.
Monday 31st	Dunfermline. Carnegie Hall. Evening. Miscellaneous. *Central* Glasgow. Che faro, Silent noon, Star candles, Willie.

Diary for 1946

January:

Tuesday 1st   Glasgow. St Andrew's Hall. *Messiah*. Noon. Turquoise gathered. Evening concert, items with orchestra. Che faro. Art thou troubled? White accordion. First [class] sleeper.

Thursday 3rd   Auntie May – lunch *Casa Prada* 12.30. Theatre.

Friday 4th   Mr [Rudolf] Bing 10.15. 66 Gt. Cumberland Place. Rehearsal John Francis 11.30–1. Words for Derby.

Saturday 5th   Albert Hall. Royal Choral [Society]. *Messiah*. Turquoise velvet [afternoon]. 5.58 St Pancras, 7.30 Chesterfield. Hotel *Portland*.

Sunday 6th   Chesterfield. *Regal* Cinema. *Messiah*. Turquoise velvet. Hotel *Portland*.

Monday 7th   Marshall and Snelgrove. Two gowns. £96.1s.8d.

Tuesday 8th   Abertridwr. *Elijah*. Car 2pm. Reh 2.45. Pink lamé. *Angel* [Hotel] Cardiff.

Wednesday 9th   Abertridwr. *Judas* [*Maccabeus*]. D[avid] Lloyd. Pink lamé. *Angel* [Hotel] Cardiff.

Thursday 10th   Cardiff 9.20 Gloucester 11.17, dep. 11.40 (dining car), Burton 2.13. *Royal* Hotel.

Friday 11th   Ashby de la Zouche. CEMA. John Francis [flute]. Che faro, Prepare thyself Zion, Soothing sleep, Spring, Blacksmith, May night, Vain suit, Silent noon, Star candles, Piper. Eric Hardy, Sunnyside. *Royal* Hotel.

Saturday 12th   Nottingham. Albert Hall. Oriana. 6.30. Reh aft. Pink lamé. Che faro, Spring, Soothing sleep, Pack clouds away, Art thou troubled?, Silent noon, Bable, Star candles, Piper, Salley Gardens, Bonnet. *Victoria* [Hotel].

Sunday 13th   Michael Head?

Monday 14th   Madge 11am. Lunch Maurice 12.30. Tea Roy's.

Tuesday 15th   Cambridgeshire villages [recitals till 23rd]. Sawston Village College. 8pm. Dark blue all week. *Blue Boar*. Spring, Sleep, Fairest isle, Hark. Four Sea Songs, Bable, Salley gdns, Bonnet, Bold unbiddable, Blacksmith, Roses three, May night, Swallow, Barefoot.

Wednesday 16th   Cam: vill: Bottisham Village College. 7.45. Dark blue.

Thursday 17th   Cam: vill: Soham Grammar School. 7.15.

Friday 18th   Cam: vill: Linton Village College. 7.45. Sea songs.

Saturday 19th   Cambridge Technical School. Recital aft. 4.15. Prog. Sea songs, Brahms Ser[ious Songs], Handel. Eric Bimrose. *University Arms* [Hotel].

Sunday 20th   Peter Pears?

Monday 21st	Lunch Parry. Daphne 3pm Dineley.
Tuesday 22nd	6.15pm. Alison and Gordon.
Wednesday 23rd	Witney, Oxon. 8pm recital. Roy. Pink lamé. 1.45 Paddington, 4.10 Witney. Purcell, Spring, Sleep, Pack, Art thou troubled?, Bable, Silent noon, Bonnet, Willie. Mrs Leigh, Croftdown.
Thursday 24th	Derby. *Central* Hall. Albert Sammons. Gerald Moore. Supply words. Pink lamé. Pur dicesti, Caro mio ben, Musik, Gretchen, Röslein, Bable, Loughareema, Bold unbiddable, Fidgety bairn, Spanish lady. *Midland* Hotel.
Friday 25th	Reh. Maurice Cole 4pm.
Saturday 26th	Euston 1.10, Preston 6.7. *Park* Hotel.
Sunday 27th	Morecambe. *Empire* Theatre. 2.30. Roy. Pink lamé. An die Musik, Gretchen, Heidenröslein, Four Serious Songs, Let us wander, Fairest isle, Sound the trumpet. Preston 10.53, Morecambe 11.33am.
Tuesday 29th	*Central* [Hotel] Glasgow.
Wednesday 30th	Renfrew. Town Hall. Miscellaneous. 7.30. Pink lamé. Stephen Manton. *Central* [Hotel] Glasgow. Spring, Art thou troubled?, Blacksmith, The swallow, Barefoot, Salley gdns – Hughes, Bonnet, Bold unbiddable.

February:

Friday 1st	Send parts to Cleethorpes. Rowland Leafe, Leighton, 19 Cromwell Rd. Rehearsal. Maurice Cole travelling from Chester.
Saturday 2nd	Bournemouth. St Peter's Hall. 5pm. Maurice Cole. Black woollie. Prepare thyself, How changed, Verdant meadows, Whyte lily, Merry, Piu dicesti, Caro mio ben, An die Musik, Gretchen, Röslein, Sweet chance, Star candles, Piper, Salley Gardens, P.R.T., What the Minstrel told us – Bax. Can you play it encore.
Sunday 3rd	Overseas recital. BBC. 8.10–8.30. London Studio. Eric Warr. Reh 7.15 at Studio 3, 200 Oxford St. Dearest consort 7¼', Let me be wailing 3' [? Lascia ch'io pianga], Pack clouds away 2', Nightingale 3', Flocks 2'.
Monday 4th	Lunch Parry. Rehearsal Watson Forbes, 13 Haslemere Av.
Tuesday 5th	University College, London. Gower St WC1. 5.30. Brahms with viola [Watson Forbes], Serious Songs. Tea 4.45. Sherry afterwards. Black woollie.
Wednesday 6th	Recording 5.30. Kingsway Hall. National Symphony. Dr Sargent. 'Have mercy Lord [from Bach's *St Matthew Passion*, her first commercial recording with orchestra]. Laudamus Te [entry scored through, it was originally planned for the session].
Thursday 7th	Llanelly. Tabernacle. *Messiah*. Evening. Blue. *Thomas Arms* [Hotel].

Friday 8th   Malvern Girls' College. Recital. 5pm. Red. Pay Daphne. Che faro, Spring, Sleep, Pack clouds away, Caro mio ben, Piu dicesti, Musik, Gretchen, Heidenröslein, Bable, Loughareema, Bold unbiddable, Salley Gdns, Bonnet, Bonny lad, Bobby Shaftoe. *Grand* [Hotel] Birmingham.

Saturday 9th   Train to Burnley. *Thorn* Hotel.

Sunday 10th   Burnley. Empire Theatre. Evening. Red. [Irene] Kohler 2.30. Albert Hardie. Send piano copies to Grimsby, also time of arrival. *Thorn* Hotel. Che faro (orch.) To Music, Sylvia, Erl King.

Tuesday 12th   2.30 Phyllis. Tulse Hill 6132.

Wednesday 13th   Southwark Recital 12.30–1.45. Rehearsal 11.30. Have mercy Lord, Prepare thyself Zion, Agnus Dei, Father of Heaven, Despised. Cancelled. Kings X 4.11 [Grimsby] 8.11.

Thursday 14th   Grimsby. Cleethorpes *Central* Hall. [Recital]. Red. Che faro or Art thou troubled?, Whyte lily, Willow song, Come let's be merry, To daisies, Star candles, My bonnie lad, Bonnet.

Friday 15th   Lincoln. Hannah Memorial Church Choir. Evening. Recital – own accompanist (Phyllis Spurr). Red. Prepare thyself Zion, Come to me soothing sleep, Art thou troubled?, Pack clouds away, Lord we pray thee, I will lay me down in peace, O praise the Lord, To Music, Who is Sylvia?, Though I speak – Brahms, Watts Cradle song, Sweet chance, Star candles, A New Year carol. Mrs Nelson, White Bay, Grantham Rd, Bracebridge Heath.

Monday 18th   Maidstone Music Club. Grammar School. Recital. Phyllis Spurr. Flame. Ring Maurice Codner. 4.18 Victoria, 5.23 Maidstone.

Tuesday 19th   Maurice Codner 10.30. Lunch Maurice [?Jacobson] – Maurice's withoot a doot! duit or dwt?

Wednesday 20th   Melksham. Wiltshire Music Club. Melksham House. 7.30. Flame. Winifred M Kempster, 38 Caledonia Place, Bristol. *Kings Arms.* Paddington 9.15, Chippenham 11.48. Che faro, Spring, Sleep, Pack clouds away, Whyte lily, Willow song, Merry, Blacksmith, Roses three, Swallows, Barefoot, Bable, Salley Gdns, Bonnet, Silent noon, Star candles, Piper.

Friday 22nd   Theatre *The Rivals*. Win, Michael Head, his sister, Alan Bush. Golf Brad[bridge White].

Saturday 23rd   Southwark *Messiah*. Suit.

Sunday 24th   Cradley Heath. *Majestic* Theatre. *Elijah*. Evening. Reh 3.30. Chinese green. Snow Hill 2.40 to Cradley Heath.

Monday 25th   Etruria. Recital. Green Chinese. *North Stafford* [Hotel]. Spring, Sleep, Dearest consort, Pack clouds away, Blacksmith, Roses 3, May night, Swallow, Vain suit, Lover's curse, B for Barney, Salley Gdns, Men from the fields, Bonnet.

Tuesday 26th   Call for records at Rugby? 8.43am Stoke. 10.50 Rugby. Lunch with Mr Salmons.

Wednesday 27th	Recording Kingsway Hall. 6pm. Che faro, Art thou troubled? LSO. [conducted by Malcolm Sargent]. Evening meal Roy and Bo [Henderson].
Thursday 28th	York British Music Society. Tempest Anderson Hall. Museum Gardens. 7pm. Gwendolyn Mason (harp) Margot. [as] Bournemouth programme Feb 2nd. *Station* Hotel.

March:	
Friday 1st	Concert frock £27.6/-. *Queen* [Hotel] Huddersfield.
Saturday 2nd	Brighouse, Yorkshire. Parish Hall. Miscellaneous. Evening. Green. Che faro, Pack clouds away, Prepare thyself Zion, Come, come my voice, Whyte lily, Merry, Love is a bable, Salley gdns, Bold unbiddable. *Queen* [Hotel] Huddersfield.
Sunday 3rd	Sheffield. City Hall. Evening. Chinese Green. *Sea Pictures*: In Haven, Where corals lie (with band). 'Dearest Consort', 'Art thou troubled' (piano). *Grand* [Hotel].
Monday 4th	Ask about nighties, pants. Mrs Prof [Bo Henderson]. See Roy *Victoria* Hotel. Auntie May.
Tuesday 5th	Auntie May.
Wednesday 6th	Auntie May. Ferryhill. Mainsforth Welfare Hall. Miscellaneous. [Laelia] Finneberg, [Jan] van der Gucht, [Robert] Easton. Softly awakes, Brightly dawns, Fidgety bairn, Boy Willie. Duets – It was a lover, Until.
Friday 8th	Blackpool. *Jubilee* Theatre. Evening Recital. Marjorie Blackburn. Leon Goossens. Chinese Green.
Saturday 9th	Crookhill Methodist Church. 10am reh. Chinese green. Spring, Troubled, To Music, Sylvia, Star candles, Bold unbiddable, Ma Bonny Lad, Bobby Shaftoe. *Station* Hotel Newcastle.
Sunday 10th	*Midland* [Hotel] Manchester.
Monday 11th	Manchester broadcast. Reh 5pm. Dearest consort, Where corals lie, Four Serious Songs. *Midland* [Hotel].
Tuesday 12th	Stocksbridge. *Victory* Club. Miscellaneous. Chinese green. Che faro, Come, come, Art thou troubled?, To Sylvia, Erl King. Fur cape etc. £240. *Grand* [Hotel Sheffield].
Friday 15th	Send parts to Bromley.
Saturday 16th	Liverpool Phil. Recital afternoon [2.30]. Rehearsal 11 and 11.30. Roy Henderson, Clifford Curzon, Albert Hardie. Green and red. Purcell [songs and duets], German [Schubert], Silent noon, Star candles, Piper.
Sunday 17th	Chester *Gaumont* Cinema. Recital. Roy Henderson, Clifford Curzon. Green and red.
Tuesday 19th	Wallasey Music Club. 1½hr recital. 7.30. Green and red. Ronald Settle. Reh 4pm at Nora Reynolds, 20 Torrington Rd, Wallasey. Prepare Thyself Zion, Come, come my voice, Fairest isle, Hark the ech'ing air, Dearest consort, Pack clouds away, Pur dicesti, Caro mio ben, Musik, Gretchen, Röslein, Whyte

	lily, Willow song, Merry, Silent noon, Star candles, Piper, My bonny lad, Bobby Shaftoe.
Wednesday 20th	Liverpool. Central Hall. *Elijah.* Evening 7pm. Reh 3pm. Green and red.
Saturday 23rd	Bromley Boys County School. Orchestral concert. Reh 4pm. Chinese green. Che faro, *Largo*, Hark the ech'ing air, Watts Cradle song, Water boy, Bonnet. Victoria 4.54 – Bromley South 5.23.
Sunday 24th	Bournemouth. *The Apostles.* Evening 7.30. Reh 2.30. Turquoise velvet. Car Brad[bridge White]. *Westover Gardens* [Hotel].
Monday 25th	Lunch Ena M.M. 1pm.
Tuesday 26th	Trowbridge. Nelson Haden School. [Recital] 7.30. Chinese green. Prepare thyself, Come, come, How changed, Art thou troubled?, Pur dicesti, Caro mio ben, 3 German Schubert, Sweet chance, Star candles, Piper, Salley gdns, P.R.T. Paddington 9.15 – Trowbridge 12.30. *George* Hotel.
Wednesday 27th	Bridgwater Town Hall. [Recital] Herbert Sumsion.7.30. Chinese green. Spring, Sleep, How changed, Pack clouds away, Viola songs – Brahms, Love is a bable, Silent noon, Men from the fields, Bonnet. *Royal Clarence.*
Thursday 28th	Stroud High School. Afternoon and evening 6.45. Herbert Sumsion. Chinese green. Spring, Art thou troubled?, Pack, Blacksmith, Swallow, Barefoot, Spanish lady, Bonnet, Willie, Bobbie. (Back to Gloucester).
Friday 29th	Rehearsal Edgar Knight 3.30.
Saturday 30th	*Station* Newcastle.
Sunday 31st	Newcastle-on-Tyne. Bach Mass [in B minor]. 2.30. Reh 10am. Olive green. Mrs Lees, Hexham.

April:

Monday 1st	Auntie May.
Tuesday 2nd	Menston. Leeds Council Schools. 7.30pm recital. Edgar Knight. Reh 6pm. Olive green. Che faro, Spring, Sleep, Pack clouds away, Fairest isle, Hark the ech'ing air, Music, The Trout, Erl King, Blacksmith, Roses three, Barefoot, Bable, Loughareema, Bold unbiddable. *Queen* [Hotel] Leeds.
Wednesday 3rd	Spennymoor. New Town Hall. 6.30. David Lloyd. Olive green. Joan of Arc, Che faro, Art thou troubled?, Spring, Silent noon, Merry. [Hotel in] Darlington.
Friday 5th	Royal College of Music Reh 10–1. Albert Hall 6–9.
Sunday 7th	Albert Hall. *St Matthew Passion.* 11 and 2.30. Black woollie.
Monday 8th	*Royal Clarence* [Exeter] (Nice).
Tuesday 9th	Exeter. St Michael's Church. *St Matthew Passion* (abridged Novello) Evening. Reh Boyd Neel 4pm. Choir reh 5pm. Black woollie. *Royal Clarence* [Hotel]. Remember Mr Davies to Dr. Wilcox.
Wednesday 10th	Minehead. *Regal* Ballroom. *Music Makers* and group. Rehearsal

4.30. Evening 8pm. Chinese green. Che faro, Pack clouds, Art thou troubled? W J Amherst (conductor). *York House* Hotel. Room reserved.

Saturday 13th   Rugby [School]. Temple Speech Room. *Apostles*. Evening. Reh 2pm. Turquoise velvet. *Crescent* Hotel (terrible!)

Sunday 14th   Broadcast 11.3–11.25[pm]. Reh 10pm. Studio VIII BH. [Broadcasting House]. Handel: How changed, Sleep, Sweet rose and lily. Mozart: Adieu, Evening thoughts.

Monday 15th   Twickenham. St Stephen's Church. 7.30. Reh 4.30. *St Matthew Passion*. Brown two-piece.

Wednesday 17th   Albert Hall. Goldsmiths. *Dream of Gerontius*. Evening. Reh 11. White silver. Peter Pears. Norman Walker. Evening meal Roger.

Thursday 18th   Taxi to and from Benj[amin] Britten 10/-.

Friday 19th   Cardiff. Wood St Church. *Messiah*. 6.45. [Edna Hobson, Trefor Anthony], D[avid] Lloyd. Reh *Capitol* Cinema, Queen St. 2.30. *Park* Hotel end of street.

Saturday 20th   Train to Aberdare. *Black Lion*.

Sunday 21st   Aberaman. *Grand* Theatre. Miscellaneous Evening. Reh 3pm. Helen Hill, Tom Culbert, [Kenneth] Ellis. Dearest consort, Pack clouds, Sigh no more, Star candles, Bobby Shaftoe, Duets with tenor: Sound the trumpet, Regular Royal Queen, Brightly dawns. *Black Lion*.

Thursday 25th   Hanley. Ceramic. *Messiah*. White silver. *North Stafford*.

Friday 26th   Sheffield. *Gerontius*. Barbirolli. Evening. Reh 2pm. White silver. *Grand* [Hotel].

Saturday 27th   Liverpool. Welsh Choral. *Messiah*. Reh 10am. White silver.

Sunday 28th   Macclesfield. Park Street. Aft and eve. Miscellaneous. Brown two-piece. Soothing sleep, Art thou troubled?, Come, come my voice, Sweet chance, Star candles, Ombra mai fu, Fairest isle, Despised, Watts Cradle song, New Year carol.

May:

Wednesday 1st   Liverpool. Bachad. Phil 6.30. Reh 3–4. [Cyril] Smith and [Phyllis] Sellick. Red. Ronald Settle [accompanist]. Dearest consort, Sleep, *Largo*, Pack clouds away, Blacksmith, Roses 3, Barefoot, Swallow.

Friday 3rd   To Hull.

Saturday 4th   Hull. *Queens* Hall. Roy. Miscellaneous. White silver. Let us wander, Fairest isle, Hark the ech'ing air, Sound the trumpet.

Sunday 5th   Oldham. Aft and eve. Misc. Brown two-piece. Car meeting at Guide Bridge 12.46. Aft: Art thou troubled?, Lord we pray Thee, I will lay me down, O praise the Lord. Eve: Come, come, Ombra mai fu, He was despised, O rest in the Lord.

Wednesday 8th   Recording [Decca Studios, Broadhurst Gardens] and South-wark [rehearsal at 10.15am]. Pergolesi *Stabat Mater*. Short

	black. [with Nottingham Oriana Choir, conducted by Roy Henderson, Joan Taylor, soprano].
Friday 10th	6.15 Mr [E.J.] Moeran. 8 Phyllis Rehearsal.
Saturday 11th	Croydon. Civic Hall. *Gerontius*. Evening. Reh 10am. White satin.
Monday 13th	Rehearsal Mr Salmons. Geoffrey Tankard 2pm.
Tuesday 14th	Blackburn. Madge. No fee. Pink lamé. Dearest consort, Pack clouds, Art thou troubled?, To Music, Sylvia, Erl King, Silent noon, Sigh no more, Star candles, Bobbie Shaftoe. *White Bull* [Hotel].
Wednesday 15th	*Queen* [Hotel] Huddersfield.
Thursday 16th	Leeds. Great Hall, University. Concert Society. Recital. 7pm. Phyllis. Pink lamé. Prepare thyself Zion, Fairest isle, Hark, Dearest consort, Pack clouds, Four Serious, Silent noon, Star candles, Piper, Salley Gardens, P.R.T. [*Queen* Hotel, Huddersfield].
Friday 17th	Send solos to Idwal Kinsey, 8 Court St, Maesteg and to Miss Tetley, 29 Shire Oak Rd, Leeds 6.
Saturday 18th	Banbury CWS. Marlborough Rd Hall. Evening. Miscellaneous. Chinese green. Taxi 1.30. 2.10 Paddington – 3.38 Banbury. Met by car UD 5891. *Whately Hall* [Hotel]. How changed, Art thou troubled?, Ombra mai fu, Pack clouds. Love is a bable, Silent noon, Sweet chance, Star candles, Bold unbiddable.
Sunday 19th	Rugby School. [Recital]. Chinese green. Taxi from Banbury to Woodford 11.37. Rugby 12 noon. Dearest consort, Soothing sleep, Fairest isle, Ech'ing air, Willow song, Whyte lily, Merry, An die Musik, Gretchen, Röslein, Blacksmith, Roses 3, Vain suit, Bable, Loughareema, Bold unbiddable, Salley gdns, B for Barney, Spanish lady.
Monday 20th	Phyllis 2.30.
Tuesday 21st	Reh Oxford *Gerontius*. 11am Royal College. Dr [Thomas] Armstrong. Mr Rubinstein 2.30.
Wednesday 22nd	Maesteg. Bethel English Church. Evening. Miscellaneous. Green chinese. Spring, Art thou troubled. Whyte lily, Merry. Sigh no more, Star candles, Bobby Shaftoe. Encores: My boy Willie, Swing low, Pack clouds away. Ena [Mitchell] duets: I know a bank, In Springtime.
Friday 24th	Golf. Roy. 3.30.
Saturday 25th	Leeds. Brunswick Methodist Church. Evening 8.30. 4 sacred solos. Dark blue. Art thou troubled?, Lord we pray Thee, Ombra mai fu, Come, come my voice, I will lay me down, O Praise the Lord. To Music, Though I speak. Sweet chance, Star candles, Watts Cradle song, Salley Gardens. Gurney encore. Accomp. Miss Tetley. *Queen* [Hotel].
Monday 27th	Rehearsal Dr [Thornton] Lofthouse 10.30. No.19 or 22 [bus] to Carlisle Sq, Chelsea Town Hall.
Tuesday 28th	Recording 10am. [Decca Studios, Broadhurst Gardens, Pergolesi

Stabat Mater solos and duets with Joan Taylor, soprano, conducted by Roy Henderson, completing session begun on 8 May]. Mr [Hans] Oppenheim 4.30 5 Bina Gdns., Gloucester Rd 10 mins.

Wednesday 29th	Reading. Town Hall. Bach Mass in B minor. Evening 6.45. Reh 4pm. Royal blue. 1.55 [train from Paddington].
Thursday 30th	Oxford. *Sheldonian* Theatre. *Gerontius*. Dr Armstrong. Evening. Reh 2.30. Royal blue. *Kings Arms*.
Friday 31st	11am Mr Schneider. 2.30 Schorr's wigs, 14 or 96 from Hyde Park to *Forum* Cinema, Fulham. Roy 3.45 3 Bolton Studios, Gilston Rd SW10. Reh 5pm *St John Passion*. Central Hall [Westminster].

June:

Saturday 1st	London University Choir. Evening. *St John Passion*. Central Hall Westminster. Turquoise gathered.
Sunday 2nd	Cardiff. *Elijah*. *Capitol* Cinema, Queen St., Afternoon. [Elsie Suddaby, Haydn Adams, William Parsons] *Park* [Hotel]. Cancelled.
Tuesday 4th	10.30 Phyllis. 3.15 Hair Miss Rosalie. 4.30 Mr Oppenheim.
Wednesday 5th	10.30 Mr Schneider. 6.30–8 Phyllis. Ring *Canuto's* [restaurant].
Thursday 6th	Dr. morning, [again] 5–6.
Friday 7th	11 Madame Huntley. Lunch with Win and Alison, *Canuto's* 12.30. Rehearsal Boris Ord 1.30 Mary Hamlin's flat, 163b Sutherland Ave, W9. Ring Rudi Bing re train. 2.45 Mr Schorr. 3–3.15 Mr Oppenheim. [KF then writes a summary] 11 frock, 12.30 lunch, 1.30 rehearsal, 2.45 wig, 3.15 Oppenheim [for coaching on *Rape of Lucretia*].
Saturday 8th	Cambridge. Kings College. Beethoven Mass. Evening. Reh aft. Liverpool St 10- 11.32
Sunday 9th	Cambridge. [train] 8.16, arr 9.53 Liv. St.
Monday 10th	Rehearsals Glyndebourne [for Britten's *Rape of Lucretia*. [Now under contract, her weekly salary is entered].
Saturday 15th	Earned £6.
Thursday 20th	London Albert Hall. Bach Choir. B minor Mass. Evening. Reh 10am. [conductor Dr Reginald] Jacques.
Saturday 22nd	Earned £6.
Saturday 29th	Earned £6.

July:

Friday 5th	Earned £6.
Wednesday 10th	Reh[earsal] [Joan] Cross, [Anna] Pollak, [Margaret] Ritchie, [Peter] Pears.
Friday 12th	[Opening night of *Rape of Lucretia*]. Cross, Pears, [Owen] Brann[igan], [Otakar] Kraus.
Saturday 13th	Earned £20.
Monday 15th	[Performance of *Rape*]. Pears, Cross, Brann[igan], Kraus.

Wednesday 17th	[Performance of *Rape*]. [Flora] Nielsen, Pollak, Pears, [Norman] Walker.
Saturday 20th	[Performance of *Rape*]. Nielsen, [Aksel] Schiøtz, [Frank] Rogier, Walker. Earned £40.
Monday 22nd	[Performance of *Rape*]. Nielsen, S[chiøtz], Rogier, Walker.
Thursday 25th	[Performance of *Rape*]. Nielsen, Pears, Kraus, Walker.
Friday 26th	[Performance of *Rape*]. Cross, Pears, Kraus, Brann[igan].
Saturday 27th	Glyndebourne ends. Earned £40.
Monday 29th	Tour. Manchester Opera House.
Tuesday 30th	[Performance of *Rape*]. [Kathleen writes] On.

August:

Friday 2nd	On. [Performance of *Rape*].
Saturday 3rd	Night. [Performance of *Rape*]. Earned £40.
Monday 5th	Liverpool Royal Court. [Performance of *Rape*].
Tuesday 6th	[Performance of *Rape*].
Friday 9th	[Performance of *Rape*].
Saturday 10th	Matinée [performance of *Rape*]. Earned £40.
Sunday 11th	*Caledonian* [Hotel, Edinburgh].
Monday 12th	Edinburgh *Lyceum*. Rug for music room £4.
Tuesday 13th	[Performance of *Rape*].
Friday 16th	[Performance of *Rape*].
Saturday 17th	Night [performance of *Rape*]. Earned £40.
Sunday18th	*Central*, Glasgow.
Monday 19th	Glasgow *Royal*. [Performance of] *Rape*.
Tuesday 20th	[Performance of *Rape*].
Friday 23rd	[Performance of *Rape*].
Saturday 24th	Matinée [performance of *Rape*]. Earned £40.
Wednesday 28th	London.
Thursday 29th	[Performance of *Rape*].
Friday 30th	[Performance of *Rape*]. Earned £28.15/-. ½ week!
Saturday 31st	[Performance of *Rape*].

September:

Sunday 1st	MAHLER – ICH BIN DER WELT ABHANDEN GEKOMMEN.
Monday 2nd	Recording *Elijah*. 3.30. [two arias 'O rest in the Lord' and 'Woe unto them'. ?Decca Studios, Broadhurst Gardens with the Boyd Neel Orchestra, Boyd Neel, conductor].
Tuesday 3rd	[Performance of *Rape*].
Friday 6th	[Performance of *Rape*]. Auntie May – meet 1.30 train Kings X.
Saturday 7th	[Performance of *Rape*]. Earned £40.
Monday 9th	[Performance of *Rape*]. Baroness Ravensdale.
Tuesday 10th	[Performance of *Rape*]. Joan [Cross?] 12 noon.
Wednesday 11th	Mr Schubler 11am. Basil Douglas 12.15. Hans Schneider 2.30.
Friday 13th	[Performance of *Rape*].

Saturday 14th	Matinée [performance of *Rape*]. Rick and Jean coming. Call Euston re sleeper. Earned £40.
Tuesday 17th	[Performance of *Rape*].
Thursday 19th	8.30 Roy.
Friday 20th	[Performance of *Rape*].
Saturday 21st	[Performance of *Rape*]. End [of] London. Sales coming round (Hull).
Monday 23rd	Oxford [Performance of *Rape*]. *Eastgate* [Hotel].
Tuesday 24th	[Performance of *Rape*].
Friday 27th	[Performance of *Rape*].
Saturday 28th	Matinée [performance of *Rape*].
Monday 30th	Holland [for performances of *Rape of Lucretia* beginning on 2nd October at Amsterdam and The Hague. The one on 4th October from the Stadsschouwburg and conducted by Hans Oppenheim, was probably the one which was broadcast by Hilversum II and later issued commercially].

October:	
Sunday 6th	End Holland.
Wednesday 9th	Home. Send programme to Canterbury.
Friday 11th	Broadcast of *Lucretia*. 20gns. [from Camden *Hippodrome*, London. Rehearsal 10.30–1.30. Act one 7.15pm. Act two 9.15–10.25pm].
Tuesday 15th	[To] Denmark [on holiday].
Saturday 26th	End [of holiday].
Sunday 27th	Keighley. Temple Street. *Messiah*. Afternoon and evening. [scored through].
Monday 28th	Flora [Nielsen] 8pm.
Tuesday 29th	Ring Rudi [Bing]. ¼ to 6 Mr Thompson, 40 Harley St. [dentist].
Wednesday 30th	Oppy [Hans Oppenheim] 2pm. Flora 8pm. Call at Chappell's for 'Mad Bess'. Ask about recital Knottingley.
Thursday 31st	2pm Mr Thompson. Book March 17th and April 28th Broadcasts [1947].

November:	
Friday 1st	Concert Hall BH. 11.15. reh 10am. Mr Thompson 12.30 and 5.15.
Saturday 2nd	11am Roy. John Turner coming morning. Roy to supper. Broadcast. Reh 4.45. Studio II, Delaware Rd, Maida Vale. Gretchen, Erster Verlust, Musensohn, Erl König.
Sunday 3rd	Bach Cantatas No.6 Bide with us and No.11 [*Ascension* Oratorio]. Dr Jacques. Reh 2.30–7. Broadcast 8.10 -9.15. 20gns.
Monday 4th	[BBC] Latin America. 15mins [13½]. 7pm Maida Vale, Studio 5. Reh 6pm. 20gns. Mad Bess, Airy violin [Purcell], Fairest isle, Evening hymn. Dentist 2.45. Studio 3.30. Maurice Miles P.O.4, Borehamwood, Herts. Bruno Walter 4.30. [This was their first encounter and it took place at the home of his friend Yvonne

Hamilton. Her name and address are also listed in Kathleen's diary for this crowded day as Mrs Hamish Hamilton, 34 Hereford House, North Row, W1 off Park Lane.]

Tuesday 5th   Hans Schneider 12 noon. Joan 2.45. Ben 3.45. Rubbra 5.30. ½ year's coal £4.

Wednesday 6th   Bedwas nr Newport. Workmens' Hall. Evening. Miscellaneous. Chinese Green. Train leaves Newport 1pm [arr.] 1.25. Mr Tom Jones. Hospitality. Che faro, Art thou troubled?, Pack clouds away, Sigh no more, Star candles, Bold unbiddable. Tenor duets James Johnston.

Thursday 7th   Newport. Grand Central Hall. Civil Defence Choir. Miscellaneous. Green Chinese. Redvers Llewellyn. Adrian Holland [accompanist]. Che faro, To Music, The Erl King, It was a lover – duet. *Talbot* [Hotel].

Friday 8th   Brecon. Aberrhonddu Male Voice Choir. Bethel Chapel. Evening. Miscellaneous. Green chinese. Air de Lia, Che faro, Who is Sylvia, Erl King. Home to our mountains. Gerald Davies [tenor]. *Castle* Hotel, Brecon.

Monday 11th   Canterbury. King's School. (Boys 14–18) Recital 8pm. Black woollie. 12gns. How changed, Soothing sleep, Sweet rose (learn), Whyte lily, Willow, Flocks (learn), 4 [Serious Songs] Brahms, Silent noon, Loughareema, Salley gardens, Sweet chance. *County* [Hotel].

Tuesday 12th   Lunch 12–12.30 Alison.

Wednesday 13th   4pm 96 Harley St. 7pm dinner Joan.

Saturday 16th   Clitheroe. *Messiah*. Evening 7pm. Black jersey. Euston 8.30 to Preston 1.43, Clitheroe 3.14. Ernest Allen [car reg.] CJP 281. Mr Foster, Low Mill Lane Cottage, Addingham, Ilkley.

Sunday 17th   Skipton. Town Hall. Music Club. Evening recital. Black jersey. Mr Foster, Low Mill Lane Cottage, Addingham, Ilkley. [How] Changed, Soothing sleep, Sweet rose (Learn!), Whyte lily, Merry, Blacksmith, Roses 3, Vain suit, Swallow, Barefoot, Loughareema, Bold unbiddable, O men from the fields, Spanish lady, Salley gdns., Bonnet.

Tuesday 19th   Chester. Schools Music Society. City Grammar School. Morning 11–12. Aft 2.45–3.30. Mantle Childe. Black jersey. 21gns. Morning: Spring, Sleep. Music, Gretchen, Röslein. Salley gdns, Barney, Bonnet. Afternoon: Troubled, Byrd Cradle, Hark ech'ing, Blacksmith, Roses 3, Barefoot, Spanish lady, Ca' the yowes, Bobby Shaftoe.

Wednesday 20th   Chester. Town Hall. Music Society. Recital with Mantle Childe 7pm. Black jersey. Dearest consort, Changed vision, Verdant meadows, 4 Brahms, Bable, Fairy lough, Bold unbiddable, Sleep, P.R.T.

Friday 22nd   Warrington. YMCA. Winmarleigh St. Music Club. Recital. 7.30. Black jersey. Train arrives about 3pm Warrington. Paid Marjorie [Blackburn] 8gns. Che faro, Sweet Rose, Fairest isle,

Hark, Lily, Willow, Merry, Blacksmith, Roses 3, Vain suit, Swallow, Barefoot, Bable, Lough, Unbiddable, Yowes, Bonnet, Bobbie.

Saturday 23rd   10am [train] arr. [London] 2.12. Meet Peter Diamand 5.15 Buffet entrance Waterloo [Station]. Waterloo 6.30 arr. [Bournemouth] Central 9pm.

Sunday 24th   Bournemouth. Pavilion. Two perfs *Elijah*. Aft 3 and eve 8. Reh 10.30. Chinese green.

Monday 25th   Send photo to Peter D.

Tuesday 26th   Huddersfield. Town Hall. Glee and Madrigal [Club] Evening [Recital]. Reh 4pm. Frederick Chadwick. Blue carnation. *Queen* [Hotel]. Vision, Sleep, Sweet rose. Lily, Willow, Arch denial. Silent noon, Star candles, Piper, P.R.T.

Thursday 28th   Halifax. Victoria Hall. *Dream of Gerontius*. Evening. Reh 2.30. White silver. *Queen* [Hotel].

December:

Sunday 1st   Knottingley. Pontefract (Horsefair) Methodist Church. *Messiah*. Aft. Reh 10.30 Town Hall. Four songs in evening, Art thou troubled?, Lord we pray Thee, I will lay me down, O praise. *Red Lion*, Market Place, Pontefract. Mrs Poulson. Knottingley 169.

Monday 2nd   Bedford. Corn Exchange. *Messiah*. 7pm. Reh 2.30. Isobel [Baillie], Heddle, Bill Parsons, Boyd Neel. *Bridge* [Hotel].

Tuesday 3rd   Dentist 11am. Interview 12 noon Decca. Lunch Aksel, Pollak, Joan, Hans Schneider *Casa Prada* 1pm [cancelled].

Wednesday 4th   Prudhoe-on-Tyne. *Rio* Cinema. Evening. Miscellaneous. Taxi 8.45. Kings X 9.15 What is life? [first mention in the diaries of Che faro in its English translation but also see Letter No.10], How changed, Whyte lily, Merry, Sigh no more, Ma bonny lad, Bobby Shaftoe. *County* [Hotel] Newcastle.

Thursday 5th   Grimsby. Central Hall. Philharmonic Society. *Messiah*. 8.10am York, Doncaster, Retford Mrs Osborne, 22 The Park.

Friday 6th   Grimsby. Central Hall. *Messiah*. Evening.

Saturday 7th   *Midland* [Hotel Manchester]. Book room for Peter. 20th.

Sunday 8th   Manchester. King's Hall, Belle Vue. Hallé. *Messiah*. Aft. Reh 11am. *Midland* [Hotel].

Monday 9th   Huddersfield.

Tuesday 10th   Dewsbury. Town Hall. *Messiah*. Evening. Reh 2.30. Black velvet. Huddersfield.

Wednesday 11th   Swinton. *Messiah*. St Paul's Methodist Church. Evening. Reh 3.45. Black velvet *Midland* [Hotel].

Thursday 12th   Hanley. Victoria Hall. Stoke Choral Society. *Messiah*. Evening 6.45. White and silver. *North Stafford* [Hotel].

Friday 13th   Bradford. Eastbrook Hall. Festival Choral. *Messiah*. Evening 6pm. Reh 2.30. Black velvet. P[eter] P[ears]. *Great Northern* [Hotel].

Saturday 14th   Pudsey. Trinity Methodist Church. *Messiah. Great Northern* [Hotel].
Sunday 15th   Burnley. Aft and eve. Helen Hill, [Henry] Wendon, [Redvers] Llewellyn, G[erald] Moore. Train from Bradford 10.30, arr. 1.45. *Thorn* [Hotel]. Aft: 1. Art thou troubled, Pack clouds away. 2. Who is Sylvia?, Erl King. Eve: 1. Che faro. 2. Bable, Star candles, Bold unbiddable. With Helen Hill: Barcarolle, The Voyagers. 4tettes: Come everyone that thirsteth [*Elijah*], Good night beloved (Pinsuti).
Monday 16th   *Queen* [Hotel, Leeds]
Tuesday 17th   Leeds. Town Hall. Philharmonic Society. Evening. *Messiah.* P[eter] P[ears]. *Queen* [Hotel].
Wednesday 18th   Bolton. Choral Union. Victoria Hall. *Messiah.* Evening. Reh 2pm. P[eter] P[ears]. *Swan* [Hotel].
Thursday 19th   Blackburn. King George's Hall. *Messiah.* Evening 7pm. Reh 2.30. *White Bull* [Hotel].
Friday 20th   [Bolton] 9.42, [Liverpool] Ex[change] 10.39.
Saturday 21st   Liverpool Phil. *Messiah.* 6.45. Reh 2–5. P[eter] P[ears]. Supper for six afterwards at *Adelphi* [Hotel].
Sunday 22nd   Liverpool Phil. *Messiah.* Cancelled. (Rev. Levi Dawson, 1 Dewey Ave., Liverpool 9. Refused to sing at Methodist Church – engagement in London). Broadcast. Bach *Christmas Oratorio.* Parts I & II. 6.45. Aft reh.
Monday 23rd   Broadcast. Part III [*Christmas Oratorio*]. Brahms Alto Rhapsody.
Tuesday 24th   Broadcast. Music Anthology: Oratorio. 6–7.
Wednesday 25th   Joan Cross 7pm.
Thursday 26th   Bo's [Henderson].
Saturday 28th   Liverpool. Philharmonic Society. *Messiah.* 6.45. Reh 2–5.
Sunday 29th   Blackpool. Tower Circus. Liverpool Phil[harmonic Orchestra]. *Messiah.* Evening. [According to the programme, the performance took place in the Opera House]. *Palatine* [Hotel]. [Isobel Baillie, soprano, Peter Pears, tenor, Norman Walker, bass, Sir Malcolm Sargent, conductor]
Tuesday 31st   Sleeper [to Glasgow].

Diary for 1947

January:

Wednesday 1st	Glasgow. *Messiah*. Noon. Turquoise silver. Miscellaneous 7pm. Sleeveless green. How changed, Watts, Hark, New Year carol, Star candles, Piper, P.R.T. *Central* [Hotel].
Thursday 2nd	*Central* [Hotel].
Friday 3rd	Milngavie. Music Club. Recital. 7.30. Ailie Cullen [accompanist]. Emerald green. 10.35 sleeper. Consort, How changed, Verdant, Pack clouds, Willow, Whyte lily, Nightingale, Flocks, May night, Blacksmith, Roses 3, Swallow, Barefoot, Bable, Loughareema, Sigh, Salley, P.R.T.
Sunday 5th	Rick's birthday.
Monday 6th	Oppy [opera coach Hans Oppenheim]: *Fairy Queen*. Phew! Facial £1.10. German lesson. £1.10. Bus fare 2s. Seats for opera £1.1. Taxi to and fro £1.15.
Wednesday 8th	5pm Oppy. German lesson £1.10.
Thursday 9th	*Tosca*. Sadlers Wells. Good.
Friday 10th	*Antony and Cleopatra*. Magnificent.
Saturday 11th	Oppy 11. Rubbra 2pm.
Monday 13th	Oppy 11.
Tuesday 14th	Ralph [Hawkes] Boosey 12 noon.
Wednesday 15th	*Tosca* B10 B11 [seat numbers].
Friday 17th	Oppy 11am. Roy 4.30.
Saturday 18th	Rehearse [Eric] Bimrose morning. Taxi 12.45. Kings X 1.25. Leeds 5.59. Mrs Poulson.
Sunday 19th	Castleford. *Messiah*. Afternoon 2.30. Reh 1pm. Chinese green. New Picture House, Station Road. No food.
Monday 20th	*Figaro*. Mr Rubbra morning rehearsal. Oppy 2.30.
Tuesday 21st	Rubbra 11.30. Flora 8.15.
Wednesday 22nd	Harpenden. Public Hall. Hertfordshire Music Club. Recital. 745. Roy and Gerald Moore. Chinese green. Purcell, Brahms Four Serious, Silent Noon, Sleep, P.R.T. Five eyes – duet.
Thursday 23rd	St Bartholomew's, Holborn. 6.15. Brahms Four Serious. [Premiere of Three Psalms by] Rubbra [who accompanied her]. [William] Pleeth. Black woolly.
Friday 24th	Dinner. Rubbra, Margaret Good, Pleeth.
Saturday 25th	Cambridge Technical School. Recital. 4.15. Daphne [Ibbott]. Chinese green. Vision, Dearest consort, Sweet rose, Caro mio ben, Pur dicesti, An die Musik, Gretchen, Röslein, Lough, Bold, Star candles, Piper, Sleep, P.R.T.
Sunday 26th	BBC. Concert Hall BH. Schubert. 6.20–7.30. reh 4pm.

[Frederick Stone accompanist]. 1. Kennst du das Land?, Heiss mich nicht reden, So lasst mich scheinen, Nur wer die Sehnsucht kennt. 2. An den Mond, In Haine, Schlummerlied, Die junge Nonne.

Tuesday 28th	Lunch Parry. To Gloucester 6.35 [train].
Wednesday 29th	Gloucester. Guildhall. Two recitals. 3 and 7pm. Chinese green. Troubled?, Cradle song, Flocks, Pack clouds, Yowes, Kitty my love, Bonnet, Bobby. Evening like Melksham [30th] except German Schubert.
Thursday 30th	Melksham Music Club, Wiltshire. Melksham House. Recital. 7.30. Take accompanist. Herbert Sumsion 10 gns. Chinese green. Ring Rick 6.15. How changed, Verdant meadows, Sweet rose and lily, Nightingale, Flocks, Cradle song, Arch denial, To Music, Who is Sylvia?, Erl King, Watts, Loughareema, Bold unbiddable, New Year carol, Sleep, P.R.T.
Friday 31st	Rudi [Rudolf Bing] 3pm. Phyllis 7pm.

February:

Saturday 1st	Sherborne. Recital. 4.45. Take accompanist. Phyllis Spurr. <u>Cancelled</u>.
Monday 3rd	Rehearse. Daphne. Kings X 3.30 Train to Hartlepool.
Tuesday 4th	West Hartlepool Music Society. St George's Hall. Miscellaneous. Evening. Reh 3pm [accompanist] Ella Pounder. Chinese green. Che faro, How changed the vision, O praise the Lord. Blacksmith, Roses 3, Swallow, Barefoot. To Music, Who is Sylvia?, Erl King. Bable, Lough, Bold unbiddable, Spanish, Kitty. [Stay with] Auntie May.
Wednesday 5th	Haltwhistle. Westgate Methodist Church. Evening. Miscellaneous. Chinese green. 12.20 from Newcastle. Mrs Lees. Vision, Soothing sleep, Hark, Blacksmith, Roses 3, Barefoot, Silent noon, Star candles, Sigh no more.
Thursday 6th	*Queen* [Hotel] Leeds.
Friday 7th	Leeds. University. 1.20–2. Green chinese. Changed vision, Lascia ch'io pianga, Whyte lily, Willow, Flocks, Brahms, Bable, Lough, Bold, Salley, Spanish Lady – arr. Hughes. Daphne 10 gns. John Turner ringing. *Midland* [Hotel] Manchester.
Saturday 8th	Bolton. Albert Hall. Recital. Evening. Morning reh. Green. Sleeper. How changed, Lascia, Whyte lily, Willow, Flocks, Blacksmith, Roses 3, Swallow, Barefoot, Bable, Lough, Bold, Salley gdns – arr. Gurney, Spanish lady.
Tuesday 11th	BBC 7–8pm. Bach Cantata No.86. Reh 2.30–5.30. Studio 1, People's Palace, Mile End Rd. £500 Bonds 2½%.
Wednesday 12th	Ipswich. Public Hall, Westgate Street. *Elijah*. Evening. Reh 2.45. Cuts: 23, 24, 36, 40, 41. Sing Trio and 'Holy, holy'. Chinese green. *Gt White House* [Hotel].
Thursday 13th	Orpington. Civic Hall. 5pm and 8pm. Roy. [Irene] Kohler. Chinese green. Daphne Ibbott [accompanist] 10gns. Let us

wander, Fairest isle, Ech'ing air, Art thou troubled?, Pack clouds, Sound the trumpet, Bonnet, Salley Gardens, Shaftoe, Five eyes, Silent, Star candles, P.R.T.

Friday 14th   *Casa Prada* 1pm. Lunch Anna and Rose.

Saturday 15th   Walsall. Central Hall. Miscellaneous. Evening. Reh 4pm. Chinese green. Che faro, Ombra mai fu, Soothing sleep, Softly awakes, Merrie month. Paddington 10.30. *Victoria* [Hotel] Wolverhampton.

Sunday 16th   Wrexham. Odeon Cinema. 7.45. Norman Walker and Harriet Cohen. Silent noon, Star candles, Sigh no more, Troubled, Che faro, Pack clouds, Schubert or Folksongs. Chinese green. W'hampton GWR Low Level 10.33 am. *Wynnstay Arms* [Hotel].

Monday   17th   *North Staffs* [Hotel].

Tuesday 18th   Market Drayton. St Mary's Church. Evening. Miscellaneous. Reh 3–4. Black woolly. I waited for the Lord [with] Isobel [Baillie]. Lay me down, O praise the Lord. Lord we pray thee – Mozart, Soothing sleep, Star candles, Sweet chance. *North Staffs* [Hotel].

Wednesday 19th Manchester. CWS. Albert Hall. Evening. Miscellaneous. Reh 3.30. Albert Hardie. Chinese green. Che faro, Spring, Sigh no more, Star candles, Bold unbiddable. Alto Rhapsody. Sound the trumpet. Tenor duets. *Midland* [Hotel].

Thursday 20th   Train [from Manchester] to Liverpool. Belfast.[boat] 10 pm.

Friday 21st   *Grand Central* [Hotel].

Saturday 22nd   Belfast. Queen's University. Great Hall. Afternoon 3pm Chinese green. Where corals lie (request), 4 Schubert (German), Blacksmith, Roses 3, Swallow, Barefoot, Dearest consort, Spring, Verdant meadows, Fairest isle, Hark, Star candles, Piper, W[here] C[orals] L[ie], Sigh no more. 7 pm. Black woolly. Che faro, Sweet rose, Soothing sleep, Pack clouds, Whyte lily, Willow song, Byrd, Flocks, Brahms, Bable, Loughareema, Bold unbiddable, Sleep, P.R.T. Gerald Moore 50gns. *Grand Central* [Hotel].

Sunday 23rd   *Grand Central* [Hotel].

Monday 24th   Return. Gerald [in] cabin 67. Euston arriving 3pm.

Wednesday 26th Ilkley. King's Hall. Players Concert Club. 8pm. Gerald Moore. Chinese green. Changed, Soothing sleep, Sweet rose, Cradle song – Byrd, Whyte lily, Willow, Flocks, Brahms, Loughareema, Star candles, Piper, Sleep, P.R.T. Dr Gott, Hampton House, Ilkley.

Thursday 27th   Leeds 9.58, 2pm Kings X.

Friday 28th   Fayer photo 4pm. 66 Grosvenor St., W1.

March:

Saturday 1st   Leicester. Whitwick Methodist Church. Evening. Green Chinese. Che faro, Troubled, Pack clouds, Whyte lily, Cradle

	song, Merry, Sigh no more, Star candles, Bobby S. 11.50 Train to Leicester, car to Whitwick.
Sunday 2nd	Leicester. Whitwick Methodist Church. Afternoon: To Music, Lord we pray Thee, Lay me down, O praise the Lord. Evening: He was despised, Come, come my voice, O rest in the Lord. Mrs Stelling, 94 Hall Lane.
Monday 3rd	Wycombe Abbey School, Bucks. 8pm. Phyllis [Spurr] 8 gns. Che faro, How changed, Sweet rose, Pack clouds, Whyte lily, Cradle song, Willow, Musik, Gretchen, Röslein, Swallow, Barefoot, Loughareema, Star candles, Piper, Sleep, P.R.T.
Tuesday 4th	Dentist 12pm. 3.15 taxi. 3.55 train to Huddersfield.
Wednesday 5th	Huddersfield. Town Hall. Colne Valley. Pink lame. 1. Alto Rhapsody. Che faro, Fairest isle, Hark. 2. To Music, Sylvia, Erl King. *Queens* [Hotel].
Thursday 6th	Stourbridge. Town Hall. Evening. Reh 3.45. Pink lamé. Leeds City 10.50 train, then to Birmingham. Car to Stourbridge. Alto Rhapsody. How changed, Sleep, Hark, Silent noon, Star candles, Sigh no more.
Friday 7th	Car to Birmingham, train to London. Dentist 5.15.
Saturday 8th	Rehearsal 2.30 *St Matthew Passion*. Cuts: 9, 10, 61 from D to end. Elgar/Atkins ed. *Station* [Hotel].
Sunday 9th	Newcastle. 2.30. *St Matthew Passion*.
Monday 10th	Train to Manchester. Ring Cheadle – John Turner. *Midland* [Hotel].
Tuesday 11th	Manchester Midday. How changed, Verdant meadows, Sweet Rose and Lily, Nightingale, Flocks, Schubert 4 [songs], Bable, Loughareema, Sleep, P.R.T., Star candles, A piper.
Wednesday 12th	North Shields Memorial Methodist Church. Albion Rd. Miscellaneous. Evening. Troubled, Ech'ing air, Blacksmith, Swallow, Barefoot, Sigh no more, Bold unbiddable, Ca' the yowes, Bobby, It was a lover, Merry month. [Train] sleeper.
Friday 14th	Recording 2.30 [Decca studios, Broadhurst Gardens]. Tea Phyll. Facial and hair £2.5. Taxis to Decca 15/-. Lesson £1.1. Studio and accompanist £1.1. [two Schubert songs, Gretchen am Spinnrade, and Die junge Nonne, accompanied by Phyllis Spurr].
Saturday 15th	Albert Hall. Royal Choral Society. *Gerontius*. Aft. Reh 10am.
Sunday 16th	BBC. Brahms Four Serious Songs. 10.20–10.35. Reh 9.15. Studio 5, Delaware Rd. Mr [Basil] Lam – supper. [All] Cancelled.
Monday 17th	BBC. Bach. 8.45–9.30. Reh 6.45. Studio 1 Delaware Rd.. Lunch Mr Barnes [scored through and replaced by] Mr Tillett 1pm. Ring [Harry] Sarton [Decca]. [All were cancelled].
Wednesday 19th	Lincoln. Hannah Memorial Church. Evening recital. Phyllis. Fairest Isle, Hark, Cradle song, Verdant meadows, Flocks. 4 Serious Songs. Road to Bethlehem, Men from fields, Loughareema, New Year Carol. Cancelled [postponed to April 23rd then again to 25th]. 3.45 Basil Lam.

Thursday 20th	Lunch Mr Tillett 12.30.
Friday 21st	Rehearsals. Royal College. 10–1 [and] 6pm.
Saturday 22nd	Southwark *St Matthew Passion*. Afternoon.
Sunday 23rd	Albert Hall. *St Matthew Passion*. 11 and 2.30.
Wednesday 26th	Derby. Central Hall. Choral Union. *St Matthew Passion*. Evening. Reh 2.30. *Midland* [Hotel].
Thursday 27th	Hanley. Victoria Hall. 9.15 [from Manchester] arr. Stoke 10.30. Concert 12 noon. Bring dress and music. Consort, Sweet rose, Pack clouds, Flocks, Willow, Whyte, Sigh no more, Star candles, Bold. *North Stafford* [Hotel].
Friday 28th	[Train to] Manchester 9.20. John Turner 11.30 Forsyths.
Saturday 29th	Liverpool. Welsh Choral Union. *Apostles*. 6.30.
Monday 31st	Basil Lam 4pm.Rehearse Wimbledon. Mr [Hubert] Greenwood 8pm. [Draft telegram] *Gresham* [Hotel, Nottingham], Have you single room tomorrow Tuesday?

April:

Tuesday 1st	Nottingham. St Mary's Church. Pergolesi *Stabat Mater*. Evening. Black woolly.
Wednesday 2nd	Wimbledon. Christ Church Hall, Cottenham Park Rd., West Wimbledon. 8pm. Hubert Greenwood [accompanist]. What is life?, Sweet rose, Sleep, Pack, Whyte lily, Willow, Cradle song, Flocks, Caro, Piu dicesti, Music, Gretchen, Röslein, Bable, Lough, Bold, Sleep, P.R.T.
Thursday 3rd	Parry lunch. Leave Daphne's [Ibbott] music [at] MM [club].
Good Friday 4th	Croydon. Phil[harmonic Society]. Davis Theatre. *Messiah*.
Saturday 5th	Bournemouth. St Peter's Hall. Recital. 5pm. Roy. Purcell duets. Fairest isle, Hark, Four Serious Songs, Silent noon, Sleep, P.R.T. Five eyes [duet].
Monday 7th	Recording [scored through] 11am. *Song of Norway*.
Tuesday 8th	Recording [scored through]. Jean [Cocteau]. *Eagle has two heads*. Wonderful Eileen Herlie.
Wednesday 9th	Recording [scored through].
Thursday 10th	Hanley. Ceramic. Victoria Hall. *Messiah*. Evening. Reh 2.15. *North Staffs* [Hotel].
Friday 11th	Elland. St Paul's Church. Recital. 7.30. Roy and Eric H[arrison]. Changed vision, Soothing sleep, Sweet rose, Silent noon, Piper, Sleep, P.R.T. Purcell group. Five eyes duet. Fear no more.
Saturday 12th	Manchester Cathedral. *Gerontius*. Evening. Reh 2.30. *Midland* [Hotel]. Sleeper.
Monday 14th	Recording 2.30, West Hampstead [scored through]. BBC Brahms Four Serious [Songs]. 6–6.40.
Tuesday 15th	London, Chelsea Town Hall. Recital 7.30. John Francis.
Wednesday 16th	Kidderminster. Town Hall. *Gerontius*. Evening.
Thursday 17th	12.30 Maurice. 2.30 Rubinstein. 3.30 Wigmore [Studios] Gib[ilaro].
Saturday 19th	Liverpool. [Welsh Choral Union]. *Messiah*. 6.30.

Monday 21st   Stourbridge. Town Hall. *Gerontius*. Evening 7.30. Reh 3pm.
Tuesday 22nd   Parry lunch.
Wednesday 23rd   Lincoln [postponed from March 19th and again scored
                      through].
Thursday 24th   Grimsby. Central Hall. Cleethorpes Orchestra. Miscellaneous.
                      Evening. Soothing sleep, Pack clouds away, Sylvia, Erl King,
                      Silent noon, Sigh no more.
Friday 25th   Lincoln. Phyllis Spurr 12 gns. [programme listed on original
                      date of March 19th].
Saturday 26th   Hull. Queen's Hall. Male Voice Choir. Heddle Nash. Alto
                      Rhapsody. Merry month of May. Che faro, Cradle song,
                      Spring. Bable, Star candles, Sigh no more, Bold unbiddable.
Monday 28th   BBC [Broadcast] Bach Cantatas Nos.170 and 53. Concert Hall
                      BH. 7.30–8.30, 8.50–9.30. Reh 5pm.
Tuesday 29th   Italian 10.30–12. Lunch John Bull.
Wednesday 30th   Ebbw Vale. Libanus Church. Misc. Evening. Troubled, Pack.
                      To Music, Sylvia. Sigh no more, Star candles, Willie. Soprano
                      duets, Mendelssohn. O Lovely peace. Mrs Harris, 13 Garden St.

May:
Thursday 1st   Mr Gib[ilaro] 3.30. Phyllis 7.30.
Friday 2nd   Lunch Café Royal 12.30 Mr Gibbs.
Saturday 3rd   Southwark Cathedral. *The Kingdom*. Afternoon.
Tuesday 6th   Birkdale. Lulworth Rd. St James [Church]. Recital. Wilfred
                      Clayton. 8pm. Che faro, Changed, Sweet rose, Cradle song,
                      Willow, Flocks, Four Serious, Lough, Star, Sweet Chance,
                      Piper.
Thursday 8th   Broadcast. BBC Music in Miniature. 8.30–9[pm]. Reh 3.30.
                      Studio 5, Delaware Rd. 12.30 Mantle Childe, *Casa Prada*.
Friday 9th   Mr Gibilaro 10–12 here.
Saturday 10th   Brighton. The Dome. *Sea Pictures*. 7.45. Reh afternoon.
                      Cancelled.
Sunday 11th   Taxi 3pm. Victoria 3.45. [Lewes] 4.48.
Monday 12th   Glyndebourne rehearsals.
Tuesday 13th   BBC Schubert broadcast (scored through).
Wednesday 21st   [?rehearsals for Glyndebourne] 10.30–1.30, 2.30–5.30.
Thursday 22nd   BBC. *St Matthew Passion*. 6.30–8, 9–11. Reh 10.30. Studio 1,
                      Delaware Rd. Lunch Peter Diamand?
Saturday 24th   Romford Girls County High School. Brentwood Rd. 7pm.
                      Recital. Blech String Quartet [scored through].

June:
Wednesday 4th   [Rio Tinto concert 10.30pm at Glyndebourne, fee 20gns.
                      She sang an aria and trio from *Orfeo* accompanied by John
                      Pritchard, and the Flower song from *Lucretia* accompanied
                      by James Iliff].
Thursday 19th   First night *Orfeo*.

Saturday 21st	*Orfeo.*
Sunday 22nd	Recording 10–2. [Kingsway Hall, London. *Orfeo* with Ann Ayars (Euridice) soprano, Zoë Vlachopoulos (Amor) soprano, Southern Philharmonic Orchestra, Glyndebourne Festival Chorus, Fritz Stiedry, conductor].
Monday 23rd	Recording 10am [as 22nd].
Tuesday 24th	*Orfeo.*
Thursday 26th	*Orfeo.*
Friday 27th	*Orfeo.*
Sunday 29th	[Recording] 10–2 [as 22nd].
Monday 30th	*Orfeo.*

July:

Wednesday 2nd	*Orfeo.*
Thursday 3rd	*Orfeo.*
Friday 4th	*Vogue* 12.30. 37 Golden Square, Piccadilly. Recording *St Matthew Passion.* 2–5, 6–9. [Kingsway Hall. Jacques Orchestra, Reginald Jacques (conductor)].
Saturday 5th	*Orfeo.* End.
Monday 7th	*Rape* [of *Lucretia*].
Friday 11th	*Rape* [of *Lucretia*].
Saturday 12th	Holiday. Ireland.
Saturday 26th	End [of holiday].
Tuesday 29th	Devon. 10.50 Waterloo – Braunton.

August:

Wednesday 13th	12.30 Photo. 6 Old Bond St. 4.15 Hair. Café Royal Parry 1pm.
Thursday 14th	Covent Garden 7pm. [Ballet Russes mixed bill].
Monday 18th	9.45 Terence Gibbs.
Tuesday 19th	Ring Mr Stein. Gib[ilaro] 11 Bluthner.
Thursday 21st	11am fitting.
Friday 22nd	Mary Young 10.30. Rehearsal from 2.30. Maida Vale, Studio 1. I[bbs] and T[illett] 4.30.
Saturday 23rd	Mary Young 8pm.
Monday 25th	Mary Young 11am. Roy and Phyllis 2.30.
Tuesday 26th	11am fitting. Reh 2.30. Mozart [recitative Ombra felice and aria Io ti lascio K.255 for Prom].
Wednesday 27th	Albert Hall. Prom. 7.30. Brahms Alto Rhapsody. Reh 12 noon.
Friday 29th	Pearl Freeman 11.30.
Saturday 30th	Bruno Walter arrives. *Hyde Park* Hotel. Ring evening. Taxi for Bruno Walter 15/-. *Etoile*, Charlotte Street.

September:

Tuesday 2nd	Chenalls 2.30. Sleeper [to Edinburgh].
Wednesday 3rd	*Figaro* Mr [John] Christie.
Thursday 4th	Rehearsal afternoon.
Friday 5th	Edinburgh. Bach morning. Freemasons' Hall. 11am. Prepare

	thyself Zion, Schlage doch. Lunch Elliots. Tea 5pm. Evening rehearsal.
Saturday 6th	Reh morning. Lunch Moran [Caplat]. [Elisabeth] Schumann afternoon.
Sunday 7th	Party 5pm. Mrs Maitland's.
Monday 8th	12.45 King's Theatre [Renato] Cellini. 4 'Sally' Club. *Macbeth* [Glyndebourne's performance of Verdi's opera].
Tuesday 9th	[Patricia ('Paddy')] Jewett. Whoopee! [appointed secretary to Kathleen and companion to her father William, recommended by Roy Henderson].
Wednesday 10th	11am. Roy with Lady Alice. Afternoon rehearsal.
Thursday 11th	Edinburgh. Usher Hall. Evening Mahler's *Song of the Earth*. [Vienna Philharmonic Orchestra, conductor] Bruno Walter. Reh morning.
Friday 12th	Edinburgh. Afternoon. [as 11th].
Saturday 13th	Vienna [Philharmonic Orchestra] afternoon. Sleeper.
Monday 15th	Ring Basil Douglas. Fitting John Turner. Phyllis 8pm.
Wednesday 17th	*Fidelio*. Basil Douglas.
Thursday 18th	Lent Cellini £10.
Friday 19th	Dentist 11am 40 Harley St. *Fidelio*.
Saturday 20th	Lunch Mr Tillett 1pm.
Monday 22nd	Norwich. St Andrew's Hall. 9pm. Reh Dineley [Studios] 10–1, 2–5. *Royal* [Hotel].
Tuesday 23rd	Reh 11.30 *Royal* [Hotel].
Wednesday 24th	Norwich Musical Festival. St Andrew's Hall. *Gerontius*. Evening. 30gns. *Royal* [Hotel].
Friday 26th	Lunch *Etoile* Hans 1pm. Roy 6.45.
Saturday 27th	Overseas BBC. Leonard Isaacs. Bush House Studio 1. 10–10.30. Reh 8.30. Song of songs [Jacobson]. Rubbra. Rahoon, Merry greenwood, Britten's folksongs.
Monday 29th	Mr Thompson [dentist] 5pm.
Tuesday 30th	10. Paddy for Roy. *Central* [Hotel] Newcastle.

October:

Wednesday 1st	Newcastle. *Lucretia*.
Saturday 4th	Newcastle. (Matinée). *Lucretia*. Mrs Lees – dinner? Sleeper 10.35.
Sunday 5th	Mr Alec 7.45 *Ritz*. Win coming in morning.
Monday 6th	Lunch Mr [John] Culshaw. Decca [scored through].
Tuesday 7th	Recording 2.30. [Decca Studios, Broadhurst Gardens. Brahms' Four Serious Songs Phyllis Spurr, piano].
Wednesday 8th	Recording 2.30. [as 7th October]. Hotel *Metropole* Leeds.
Thursday 9th	Rehearsal 11.30. *Queen* [Hotel]. Leeds.
Friday 10th	Leeds Festival. Town Hall. Bach Mass [in B minor]. Malcolm [Sargent] 11.30am. Lunch 1.45 Civic Hall. *Queen* [Hotel] Leeds.
Saturday 11th	Newcastle. Brunswick [Methodist Church]. *Messiah*. 6.30. Reh 2.30. *Station* [Hotel].

Sunday 12th	Newcastle [Recital] Morning 10.45: Lord we pray Thee, Sweet chance, Maurice Greene. Watts Cradle song. Evening 6.30: Art thou troubled, Cradle song, Star candles, Bethlehem, To Music, O death – Brahms.
Tuesday 14th	Covent Garden [*Rape of Lucretia*]. Win [and] 2 friends. 4.45.
Wednesday 15th	Liverpool. Phil. (Rushworth) Recital with [George] Thalben-Ball. 6.45. Bach Cantata and 2 or 3 groups with organ and piano. Schlage doch: Deh placatevi con me, Che faro, Bable, Silent noon, Spanish lady. *Adelphi* [Hotel].
Thursday 16th	BBC Music in Miniature. Studio II, Maida Vale. Reh 3pm. [Broadcast] 8.30–9. Ombra ma fu, All praise to the Lord.
Friday 17th	Covent Garden. [*Rape of Lucretia*]. Win, Ena and Paddy.
Saturday 18th	Hair 9.30. Southwark [Cathedral]. *Gerontius*. 2.30. Tea FLUFFY'S! [scored through]. *Albert Herring* (4) to book.
Sunday 19th	Send money to Augener, Mr Hawkes, Ibbs and Tillett. (6gns.) Brahms Records 30 gns.
Monday 20th	12.30 MM Club Basil Lam. Lunch with BBC £2. Train to Bournemouth. *Westover Gardens* [Hotel].
Tuesday 21st	Bournemouth. [*Rape of Lucretia*]. *Westover Gardens*.
Wednesday 22nd	Bournemouth. [*Rape of Lucretia*]. *Westover Gardens*.
Thursday 23rd	Fitting 11am.
Friday 24th	2.30 Donald Brook (Life story). 6pm Gunnersbury station (Charlotte).
Saturday 25th	Train to Keighley. St Pancras 3.20, Leeds 7.53, Keighley 8.37.
Sunday 26th	Keighley. Temple St. *Messiah*. Aft and evening.
Monday 27th	Dinner 7.15 Tilletts.
Tuesday 28th	Oxford. [*Rape of Lucretia*]. 15gns. [Train] 1.45, [arr.] 3.15. *Eastgate* [Hotel].
Thursday 30th	Oxford. [*Rape of Lucretia*]. *Eastgate*.
Friday 31st	Rehearsal. Frederick Stone [accompanist] 10.30–12.30. Hair 2pm.
November:	
Saturday 1st	Darlington. North Rd Methodist Church. Recital. Evening. Phyllis [Spurr]. 35gns. Che faro, Vision, Come to me, Pack clouds, Brahms, Whyte lily, Cradle song, Flocks, To Music, Sylvia, Erl King, Star candles, Piper, Sleep, P.R.T.
Monday 3rd	BBC. Studio V, Delaware Rd. 10.35–11pm. Reh 9.30. Holst – Dawn [or Ushas, first song in the Vedic Hymns cycle], Rubbra [Three Psalms], Jacobson [Song of Songs], [which replaced the Flower song from Britten's *Rape of Lucretia*], and Moeran (Rahoon and Greenwood).
Tuesday 4th	Norman 3pm. 7.30–9.30 Rehearsal? [perhaps for 6th but scored through].
Wednesday 5th	Albert Hall. *Israel in Egypt*. Evening. 25gns.
Thursday 6th	Albert Hall *Song of the Earth* London Phil. Rehearsal morning.

	[all scored through]. [*Peter*] *Grimes* C[ovent] G[arden]. 1.10 Kings X [to Huddersfield].
Friday 7th	Huddersfield Choral Society. *Music Makers*. 7.30. Reh 2pm.
Saturday 8th	Tea 5pm Mosco Carner. *Kindertotenlieder*.
Monday 10th	BBC. Schubert. Brahms. 6–6.30. Junge Nonne (D minor), Erster Verlust C minor, Frühlingsglaube F major, Sehnsucht E minor, Musensohn E major, Sapphic Ode, Liebestreu, Minnelied.
Tuesday 11th	London. Albert Hall. Goldsmiths. *Gerontius*. Evening. Reh 2.30.
Wednesday 12th	Reh 10.30–12.30 Studio 5a Dineley. Reh 6.30. Westminster Cathedral Hall.
Thursday 13th	Albert Hall. Bruno Walter. *Choral* Symphony, Beethoven. *Te Deum*, Bruckner. Reh 10am. [performance 7.30. London Philharmonic Orchestra. Isobel Baillie, Heddle Nash, William Parsons]. Party: Win, Michael, Maitlands, Lady Alice, Terence, Roy and Bo, Lottie.
Friday 14th	Julius Harrison. Tea 3.30.
Saturday 15th	Romford Girls County High School, Brentwood Rd. 7.30pm. Phyllis. Lunch with Ruth Draper. How to travel? Let Ibbs know. Not paid. Deh placatevi, Che Faro, How changed, Verdant meadows, Pack clouds away, 4 Serious Songs, An die Musik, Gretchen, Heidenröslein, Love is a bable, Loughareema, Bold unbiddable, Sleep, P.R.T.
Monday 17th	Lunch Terence and Hans. *Coq d'or* 1pm. Take frock 12 noon.
Tuesday 18th	Train to Liverpool.
Wednesday 19th	Liverpool. Central Hall. *Messiah*. Evening. Reh 3pm.
Thursday 20th	Hanley. Ceramic. [Victoria Hall]. *Music Makers*.
Friday 21st	4.30 Mosco Carner.
Saturday 22nd	1.10 to Doncaster. Train to Knottingley.
Sunday 23rd	Knottingley. *Messiah*. Afternoon.
Monday 24th	Lunch *Café Royal* Terence Gibbs. Rehearsal 6.30. Studio 1.
Tuesday 25th	BBC. *Kindertotenlieder*. 7.10–7.50. [conductor] Mosco Carner.
Wednesday 26th	10.30. Sir Adrian [Boult]. Norman [Allin] 2.30.
Thursday 27th	Swansea. Brangwyn Hall. Mass in B minor. Evening.
Friday 28th	Maurice Codner 2.30. Reh Studio 1 Delaware Road, 6.30–9.30. [Mahler Symphony No.3].
Saturday 29th	Maurice Codner 10.30. BBC. Mahler's 3rd [Symphony]. 8.35–9.45, Reh 4.30–6.30. [BBC Studios Maida Vale. BBC Symphony Orchestra, Chesham Ladies Choir, 20 boys from London Choir School, Sir Adrian Boult, conductor].
Sunday 30th	Bournemouth. Winter Gardens. *Gerontius*. Evening 7.30. Reh 3pm.

December:

Monday 1st	Lunch Hans 12.30. 5pm Mosco Carner.
Tuesday 2nd	10am Basil D[ouglas]. 2pm Max Gilbert, Phyllis [Spurr].

Wednesday 3rd	Grimsby. *Messiah*. Ev[ening] [cancelled]. BBC Manchester. 6.30 -7 (Mr [Arthur] Spencer [BBC producer]). Reh 5pm. Evening Hymn, Lovelorn turtle, Laura smiles, Rest sweet nymphs, Sleep, P.R.T., Two songs by MJ [Hush and At night by Maurice Johnstone], Piper, Slumber [both by Michael Head]. [Beryl Dallen, accompanist]. *Midland* [Hotel].
Thursday 4th	Grimsby [*Messiah*].
Friday 5th	Grimsby [*Messiah*].
Saturday 6th	John [Turner] and Leon [Fontaine] 5.30. *Midland* [Hotel].
Sunday 7th	Manchester. Hallé. King's Hall, Belle Vue. *Messiah*. 2.30. Reh 10. *Midland* [Hotel].
Monday 8th	3pm Doctor vaccination. 5.30 Reception British Council, 74 Brook Street. Recording rehearsal [for December 18th first at Guildhall School of Music then changed to the West London Synagogue at 5.45pm. Scored through].
Tuesday 9th	Recording. 6pm. Brahms [Two songs with] viola. Max Gilbert. [Phyllis Spurr, piano, Decca Studios, Broadhurst Gardens. Successful takes finally made in February 1949].
Wednesday 10th	Westminster Cathedral Hall. 6pm. Brahms. 1pm Maurice *Ritz*. Maurice 8.15 *Casa Prada*.
Thursday 11th	Blackpool. Tower Circus Ballroom. Phil. *Messiah*. 7pm. Reh 2.30. [Albert Tysoe conducted the Blackpool Symphony Orchestra and Blackpool Philharmonic Choir. Reginald Dixon was the organist, the trumpeter was Enoch Jackson from the Liverpool Philharmonic Orchestra]. *Palatine* [Hotel].
Saturday 13th	Liverpool Phil. *Messiah*. 6.45.
Monday 15th	Wolverhampton. Civic Hall. *Messiah*. 7pm. Reh 2.30. Lime St 10.25, W'hampton 12.37. [He was] Despised – all of it. 18th century score. 52–55 omitted. Mrs Griffith.
Tuesday 16th	Leeds. Town Hall. *Messiah*. Evening. *Queens* [Hotel].
Wednesday 17th	Swinton. St Paul's Methodist Church. Station Rd. *Messiah*. Evening. Reh 3.45. *Midland*.
Thursday 18th	Recording. 6.30 Kingsway Hall. [Brahms] Alto Rhapsody. Clemens Krauss 5.30 [London Philharmonic Orchestra and Choir].
Friday 19th	Recording. Brahms Alto Rhapsody. 10am [as 18th December]. London RAH. 7.30. Ernest Read Concerts. *Messiah*. Part 1 and Carols: Slumber beloved, Lullay my liking. Reh 2–5. [Concert of Christmas music with Elsie Suddaby, Eric Greene and Roy Henderson. London Senior Orchestra, conductor Ernest Read].
Saturday 20th	Sheffield. City Hall. Philharmonic Society. *Messiah*. Evening. *Grand* [Hotel].
Sunday 21st	*Grand* [Hotel, Sheffield].
Monday 22nd	Birmingham. Town Hall. *Messiah*. Evening. *Grand* [Hotel, Birmingham].

Tuesday 23rd	Parry [Jones] lunch *Casa Prada* 1pm. Portrait 3pm. Elsie, Jean, Eric 4pm for records.
Wednesday 24th	BBC 9–9.30. Reh 6–8? London Studio. Schlage doch.
Saturday 27th	Liverpool. Phil. *Messiah.* 6.45.
Sunday 28th	Blackpool. Opera House. *Messiah.* Evening. *Palatine* [Hotel]. [Liverpool Philharmonic Choir and Orchestra, Isobel Baillie, soprano, Peter Pears, tenor, Norman Walker, bass, Sir Malcolm Sargent, conductor].
Monday 29th	Birmingham. Town Hall. *Messiah.* Evening. *Grand* [Hotel].
Tuesday 30th	America [recital repertoire]. Ombra mai fu, Dearest consort, Deh placatevi, Che faro, An die Musik, Gretchen, Erster Verlust, Erl King. Four Serious Songs. Silent noon, Fairy lough, Salley gdns – Britten, Bonnet, Spanish lady.

Diary for 1948

January:

Thursday 1st	Sailed on *Mauretania* to New York. Strike at Southampton! Taxis £1.10/-, Train £1.18.6d, Fare £102, Tips £1.
Friday 2nd	Hair, facial, manicure £3. Deck chair £1.
Saturday 3rd	North of the Azores. Sun shining – wonderful.
Sunday 4th	Storms, but still intact.
Tuesday 6th	Wines etc £10. Tips £6.
Wednesday 7th	A marvellous voyage. Arrived 3pm. Staying *Weylin* Hotel E 54th. Ann [Ayars] and Dottie [Tete] came – lovely.
Thursday 8th	10.30 Andre Mertens. Columbia Concerts Inc. 113 West 57th St, NYC. Lunch Mary Townsend. 3.15 Hair – André. 6.30 Andre Mertens.
Friday 9th	4pm Arpad Sandor. Towels, Hanks, Make up 20 dollars.
Saturday 10th	1.30 Lunch Ann and Dottie. Boots 20 dollars, shoes 22 dollars, Repairs $6.
Sunday 11th	5pm Piano rehearsal.
Monday 12th	4.45 Rehearsal Bruno Walter.
Tuesday 13th	Reh 10–1.
Wednesday 14th	Reh 10–1. Doctor's fees $40, Medicines $10, Evening slippers and rubbers $14.05.
Thursday 15th	Carnegie Hall. Mahler *Das Lied*. N.Y. Phil. B. Walter. Reh 10–1. Taxis $2.
Friday 16th	Carnegie Hall. Tea Mrs Scherman.
Saturday 17th	12.15 Sandor reh. 7.15 Ruth Draper dinner.
Sunday 18th	Carnegie Hall. Mahler. [*Das Lied von der Erde*. 3pm broadcast on WCBS/CBS. Set Svanholm, tenor, New York Philharmonic Orchestra, Bruno Walter, conductor].
Monday 19th	9.45 Sandor. 10.45 *Vogue*. 1pm lunch Mary Townsend – $750 in advance.
Tuesday 20th	Ottawa [Illinois].
Wednesday 21st	Des Plaines [South Chicago, Illinois].
Thursday 22nd	Dinner Dickie Leach, Mr Cardelli. NCAC Chicago. Wonderful evening.
Friday 23rd	Chicago. Snowing! Snowing!! Snowing!!! Art gallery and lunch Mr Anderson. Very nice.
Saturday 24th	11.30 Mr Wisner and lunch Mr Mertens. 3.30 Mrs Smith – *Musical Journal*. 4pm Tea Mrs Martin.
Sunday 25th	Dickie – dinner 7.30.
Monday 26th	East Chicago, Indiana.

Tuesday 27th	Ring Mr Wisner. Collect syrup. 12pm Mr Anderson, University Club.
Thursday 29th	10.15 Frick Museum on 70th St off 5th Avenue. 3pm Anita – shopping. Ring Arpad and Mary Townsend. Brown dress $27, Slip $8.11, Girdle & bra $23.97, Afternoon frock 52. Arpad 7.15
Friday 30th	11.15 Lunch Mr Mertens. Lunch 12.30 [Artur] Schnabel. Miss Jarmel 3pm publicity. Dinner Bruno Walter.
Saturday 31st	10 Mrs Tuck. 12.30 Photies. Mr Felix, Accounts. 1.30 Mary Townsend lunch. 4.30 Mrs Fonaroff. Dinner Willie – Records.

February:

Sunday 1st	Afternoon perf. Ruth Draper. Mrs Stiedry 7pm.
Monday 2nd	Expect call from Mr Felix. Mrs Hunt Colony Club 1pm. 3pm Dickie's wife. 4.30 Prof Walter. 6.45 Dinner Schermans. Concert Scherman. Party? Rickie's 42 W. 53rd St.
Tuesday 3rd	Photies 11am. Mr Mertens 11.30. 12.45 Lotte Walter at *Weylin* [Hotel]. Franz 5.30 cocktails. 7pm Elisabeth Schumann. 520 E-90th St. NYC.
Wednesday 4th	*Queen Mary*. [Cabin] B/27 Bed and Bath. Ticket No. E892043. Prof Walter has no time. 5 pm Dr Weissman. 6.15 Dottie, Ann, Willie, Dennis, Arpad and wife. *Queen Mary* 10pm.
Thursday 5th	Sailed 6am.
Tuesday 10th	Home again! Taxi home 17/6d. American doctor's bill £10.
Wednesday 11th	Albert Hall. Royal Choral Society. *Gerontius*. Evening.
Thursday 12th	Bristol Philharmonic Society. Cathedral. Evening. Items with organ accompaniment. Reh 4.30. Troubled, Ombra mai fu, Lord we pray Thee, Watts Cradle song, Road to Bethlehem, Knight of Bethlehem. *Royal* [Hotel].
Friday 13th	Phyllis 3pm.
Saturday 14th	Archway Hall, Highgate. Recital. Phyllis. Evening. Fee to include accompanist.
Monday 16th	BBC [music by] Stanford. 6.20–6.55. Reh 5.30. Studio V, Maida Vale. La belle dame, Heraclitus, The Monkey's Carol, Loughareema. [accompanist Frederick Stone].
Thursday 19th	Lunch Hans. BBC Music in Miniature. 8.30–9. Reh 3.45 Studio II Maida Vale. [*Radio Times* states: A musical entertainment given by Kathleen Ferrier (contralto), Phyllis Sellick (piano), Alfred Cave, Leonard Dight (violins), Watson Forbes (viola), John Moore (cello), J Edward Merrett (double bass). Programme arranged by Basil Douglas.] [It is possible that she sang Blow the wind southerly for the first time. See Introduction to the Diaries].
Friday 20th	Welwyn Garden [City]. Music Club. Parkway Restaurant. 7.45. Recital. Phyllis. Dearest consort, How changed, Evening Hymn, Hark the ech'ing, Musik, Gretchen, Erster Verlust, Junge Nonne, Brahms Four, Silent noon, Loughareema, Sleep, P.R.T.

Saturday 21st	Farnham [and Bourne Music Club]. Surrey. Girls' Grammar School. 3pm. Fee to include accompanist [Phyllis Spurr]. Same [programme] as Welwyn. Waterloo 12.57 or 1.17. Arr. 2.3 or 2.15. [Kathleen's encore was Blow the wind southerly. See Introduction to the Diaries pp. 273–4].
Monday 23rd	Phyllis 11.30.
Tuesday 24th	Stockport. Centenary Hall. Maia Ladies Choir. Evening. Blue silver. O peaceful England, Turtle, Pack clouds away, Sylvia, Erl King, Silent noon, Merry greenwood, Spanish lady. Harold Dawber [conductor, Beryl Dallen accompanist]. Train 10.20 Euston.
Wednesday 25th	Crewe. Corn Exchange. Industrial Music Club. Recital. 7.30. Blue and silver. Prepare thyself Zion, Turtle, Verdant meadows, Pack clouds, Musik, Gretchen, Erster Verlust, Nonne, Brahms, P.R.T., Sleep, Rahoon, Merry greenwood. A.E. Roberts. Auntie May in London.
Thursday 26th	Flora [Kent] 3pm cuppachar.
Friday 27th	Oxford. Musical Festival. Evening Recital. Include accompanist Phyllis. 10gns. Same [programme] as Crewe. *Eastgate* [Hotel].
Saturday 28th	Lunch Alec. 1pm *Ritz*. 4.15 [train] Paddington [to Cardiff]. *Royal* [Hotel].
Sunday 29th	Cardiff. [Celebrity Concert] *Empire* Theatre. Philharmonic Society [Franz Osborn, piano]. 3pm. Reh 11.30. With [Cardiff Philharmonic] Orchestra: Che faro, Ombra mai fu. Watts Cradle song, Softy awakes. Take orch. encores. *Royal* [Hotel].
March:	
Monday 1st	Phyllis 3pm.
Tuesday 2nd	Elland. St Paul's Schoolroom. 7.30. Pergolesi. *Stabat Mater*.
Wednesday 3rd	Huddersfield. Town Hall. Colne Valley Male Voice Choir. Evening. Blue silver. Turtle, Pack clouds, Evening hymn, Gretchen, Erster Verlust, Junge Nonne, Bable, Loughareema, Merry greenwood.
Thursday 4th	Hull. Queen's Hall. Choral Union. *Music Makers*. Four Serious Songs. Evening. Blue silver. Send music Mrs L. Williams.
Saturday 6th	Sherborne. 4.45 Recital. Phyllis. 12.30 Waterloo [arr.] 3.34. Che faro, Changed, Sweet rose, 4 Serious Songs, Musik, Gretchen, Erster Verlust, Sweet chance, Star candles, A piper, Sleep, P.R.T. [return train] 6.45.
Sunday 7th	3pm Flora cuppachar.
Monday 8th	12 noon Hans frock. Order lunch *Casa Prada*. 5.50 Covent Garden, *Valkyrie*. Basil.
Tuesday 9th	11am X-ray Dept, Hampstead General Hospital. Take letter. X-ray 2gns. Basil Lam 3pm.
Wednesday 10th	London RAH. Bach Choir Festival. *St John Passion* 7.30. Reh 10–1. Parry [Jones] lunch *Casa Prada*, 1.15. Lunch 2gns.
Thursday 11th	10 Flora. *Tristan*

Friday 12th	11.30 L.B. [?Leslie Boosey], 8 Warwick Ave. 3.30 Muriel Gale [contralto]. 5.30 Hans.
Saturday 13th	Southwark [Cathedral] *St Matthew Passion* afternoon. Reh for 14th 10–1, 6–9pm. Royal College of Music. Alison's birthday.
Sunday 14th	London RAH. *St Matthew Passion.* 11am and 2.30pm.
Monday 15th	[Theatre] *The Relapse.*
Tuesday 16th	Flora afternoon, supper 8pm?
Wednesday 17th	BBC Overseas. 8–10. *St Matthew Passion.* Reh 6.
Thursday 18th	BBC 2–3.30, St Marks, Nth Audley St.
Saturday 20th	Birmingham. Town Hall. *St Matthew Passion.* 7pm. Reh 2pm. [Hospitality] Mr Bean.
Sunday 21st	Manchester. Hallé. Belle Vue. *Gerontius* 3pm. Reh 10–1. [Telegram to T E Bean, Hallé Concerts: Travel to Liverpool Sunday night but grateful for hospitality on Sat.].
Tuesday 23rd	Birmingham. Town Hall. *St Matthew Passion.* Evening. *Grand* [Hotel].
Wednesday 24th	Nottingham. Albert Hall. Mass in B minor. Evening. *County* [Hotel].
Thursday 25th	Mr Miller 5.30.
Friday 26th	RAH. Royal Choral Society. *Messiah.* Afternoon. Reh 10.30. Wembley Philharmonic Society. Town Hall. *Messiah.* Evening.
Saturday 27th	Ring [Sadie] Lereculey. 11.30 Mosco [Carner]. Sleeper [to Edinburgh to stay with the Maitlands].
Tuesday 30th	Rosalind's [Maitland?] party [gave a recital]. Vision, Turtle, Deh placatevi, Che faro, Musik, Gretchen, Erster Verlust, Nonne, Erl King, Liebestreu, Sapphic Ode, Minnelied, Folksongs.
Wednesday 31st	Sleeper 10.20pm.
April:	
Thursday 1st	Send music to Holland. 3.30 Mosco. 5 Mr Miller. Sadlers Wells 6.45.
Friday 2nd	Ring Auntie May. See about tickets to Holland. 12.15 Kathleen Moorhouse. 5.15 Simpson's. Cambridge Theatre 2.
Saturday 3rd	11am Gerald [Moore]. Reh 4.30–5.30 Studio I, Delaware Rd.
Sunday 4th	BBC Lennox Berkeley. Jacques Strings [in fact Goldsbrough String Orchestra, conductor Arnold Goldsbrough]. Bond St recording. 30gns. Reh 4.15 Studio 2, Delaware Rd. Supper L. Berkeley. Recording of broadcast £3.15s.
Monday 5th	[Projected annual costs entered here] Secretary-Housekeeper allowance £104, from New Year, taxis [nothing entered], Stamps 10/- per week, piano tuning £3.3s., Hair and facials £52, Massage £26, Rent, £35.15., Tips for taxis per journey [nothing entered], Makeup £12, Stockings £15, Underclothes £20. 5pm taxi. 6pm train. *Midland* [Hotel].
Tuesday 6th	Manchester Midday. Balance test noon. Gerald. Junge Nonne, Erl König, Erster Verlust, Sappische Ode, Minnelied, Rubbra [Three Psalms], Rahoon, M[erry] Green W[ood], Flower, Ash

grove, O[liver] C[romwell]. Evening Stoke[-on-Trent]. Gerald. Nonne, Erster, Erl König, Liebestreu, Sapphische, Minnelied, M.G.W., Flower, Ash, O.C.

Wednesday 7th	*Casa Prada* 1.30.
Thursday 8th	Holland. Air and sea trip.
Friday 9th	10.20 Amsterdam. *American* Hotel.
Sunday 11th	Amsterdam. British House. Recital afternoon. [Isja] Rossican [accompanist] 50 minutes. [Telegram to Peter Diamond: Post office will not insure music parcel or guarantee delivery. Feel risk is too great and will bring it all with me.] Spring, Come to me soothing sleep, Whyte lily, Flocks are sporting, Love is a bable, Loughareema, Sleep, P.R.T., Rahoon, M.G.W.
Monday 12th	The Hague. Recital. 8pm. Dearest consort, Vision, Evening hymn, Hark. Musik, Gretchen, Erster Verlust or Erl König. Rubbra, Silent Noon, Bable, Loughareema, Sleep, P.R.T., Rahoon, M.G.W.
Tuesday 13th	Paddy's audition.
Thursday 15th	Hilversum. Broadcast. *Kindertotenlieder.*
Friday 16th	Rotterdam. Recital. Hague programme [12th]..
Saturday 17th	Amsterdamsche Bank 11am. Otto [Otakar Kraus] 12.15 Drink!! 3–3.30 Bulbs.
Sunday 18th	Hilversum. Recital broadcast. 2pm. Peter's [Diamond].
Monday 19th	12pm. [Marius] Flothuis.
Wednesday 21st	Terence 10. 3.30 Tea with pianist. 4 Mr Rossican.
Thursday 22nd	Amsterdam. Recital. Prepare thyself, Turtle, Soothing sleep, Pack clouds away, Sapphische Ode, Junge Nonne, Erste Verlust, Gretchen, Erl König, Minnelied, S.N. [Silent noon], Piper, Star candles, Flower song, Salley gdns, Oliver Cromwell.
Friday 23rd	11.30 Mr Flothuis. Overnight [travel home].
Saturday 24th	Croydon. Philharmonic Society. Civic Hall. *Apostles.* Evening. Reh afternoon. Taxi 1.30, 9.30 back.
Sunday 25th	Uncle Bert lunch and tea.
Monday 26th	BBC. Brahms with viola. Musensohn, Erl König, Romance, Wandrers Nachtlied, Du bist die Ruh. Car 6.45.
Tuesday 27th	8.30 car. 9am Sloane St. Take off 10.30.
Wednesday 28th	Utrecht.
Thursday 29th	Utrecht.
Friday 30th	Dinner Peter, Maria, Hazel, Dick. [Recitals in Kings Lynn scored through and postponed until 7th May].

May:

Saturday 1st	11.30 Mr Flothuis.
Sunday 2nd	2pm Hilversum (415m) me! Recital Amsterdam.
Monday 3rd	11.30 Airport. Nett earnings in Holland less air and sea travel £52.14.0d. Recording 6–9. [Kingsway Hall. *St Matthew Passion.* Jacques Orchestra, Reginald Jacques (conductor)].
Thursday 6th	Anglo-Austrian [Music Society] 12.30. [possibly a meeting to

discuss 11 June] Silent, Star, Piper, Ash grove, O.C. [reason for listing these songs is unclear] 3pm Phyllis.

Friday 7th   Kings Lynn. Town Hall. Recitals. 1–1.45, 3.30–4.15. How changed the vision, Whyte lily, Pack clouds. Gretchen, Heidenröslein, Erl König. Roses 3, The swallow, Why go barefoot?. Piper, Star candles, Spanish lady, Bonnet, Bobby S. [Hospitality] Lady Fermoy.

Saturday 8th   Recording 6–9. [as 3rd May]. Rose 1.15 *Casa Prada*.

Sunday 9th   12.30 from home to our Win's. Taxi.

Monday 10th   Oxford. Sheldonian Theatre. Bach Choir. *Gerontius*. 6.15. Reh 2pm. *Eastgate* [Hotel].

Tuesday 11th   *Coq d'or* 1pm Terence. 3.30 Phyllis. 7pm HMV. Abbey Rd. Rehearsal. Sir T. Beecham, 39 Circus Rd, NW8 at 8.30pm [scored through].

Wednesday 12th   London RAH. Royal Philharmonic. Sir T Beecham. 8pm. Beethoven 9th. Rev. Southward's translation. Cancelled. Dinner 6.45 *South Kensington* Hotel, 47 Queens Gate Tce. SW7 Dr Thomas Wood

Thursday 13th   Bromley. Ripley Choir. Boys County Grammar School, Hayes Lane. Brahms Alto Rhapsody. Evening. 15gns. Taxis.

Friday 14th   Recording 2.30. Kingsway Hall. Handel *Largo*. [Ombra mai fu, London Symphony Orchestra, Sir Malcolm Sargent, conductor]. 8pm Athlone [Irish radio transmitter] *Kindertotenlieder*. Listen.

Tuesday 18th   Birmingham. Barber Institute. 7pm. 52gns. Phyllis 12 gns [with Gerald scored through]. Junge Nonne, Erster Verlust, Erlkönig, Brahms Lullabys (viola). Bable, Loughareema, Bold unbiddable, Rahoon, Merry greenwood, Ash grove, O.C.

Wednesday 19th   5.15 Roy. Maria [Curcio, pianist wife of Peter Diamand] 9–10.

Thursday 20th   BBC. Thursday Concert. 7.30–8.30. Reh 3–4. Concert Hall BH. Evening dress. [Kathleen sang 15 minutes of music] An die Musik, Gretchen, Wandrers Nachtlied, Junge Nonne, Tod und das Mädchen. Hans dinner. Ask about blue and white cheque ['que' scored through, 'k' added].

Friday 21st   Send American programmes. Wigmore Hall tickets Win 3. Max Gilbert 2. Miss Hawkins 3. Hampton Court 4.

Saturday 22nd   Train to Newmarket Liverpool Street 11.50, [arr.] 2.16.

Monday 24th   Ring Decca.

Tuesday 25th   BBC [America]. BH Concert Hall. 2–3pm. Come let's be merry. Phyllis 7.30.

Wednesday 26th   Maria [Curcio] Evening. Mozart concerto. Peter Stadlen 6.30.

Thursday 27th   Uppingham School, Oakham. 8.15. Recital – send programme to include Schubert. Hotel booked. Vision, Soothing sleep, Whyte lily, Pack clouds away. Du bist die Ruh, Tod, Heidenröslein, Wandrers Nachtlied, Musensohn. Bable, Loughareema, Bold unbiddable, Ash grove, O.C.

Friday 28th	Luncheon Mrs Partridge? Allies Club, 6 Hamilton Place (Piccadilly). Madge tea. Win. Auntie May's birthday.
Saturday 29th	Meriel St Clair 10.30. BBC Music in Miniature. Recording. 2.30–3.30.. Reh 11.30. B.H. Concert Hall. A poor soul sat sighing, Romance from *Rosamunde*. 6.30 Mr Tillett.
Sunday 30th	Peter and Maria [Diamand].
Monday 31st	6.30 Gerald and Enid [Moore].

June:

Tuesday 1st	9.30 Belmont School, Belmont Road [Erith, Kent?] Blue check. 11.30 Peter Stadlen [scored through]. 12.30 lunch Hans Schneider.
Friday 4th	Phyllis 11am.
Saturday 5th	Phyllis 10.30. Max [Gilbert] rehearsal. 11am Brahms. Flora 8pm.
Wednesday 9th	11.30 hair. Recording 6–9. [Kingsway Hall. *St Matthew Passion*. Jacques Orchestra, Reginald Jacques (conductor)].
Thursday 10th	Recording 2–5, 6–9 [as 9th June].
Friday 11th	Wigmore Hall. Gerald. 12 noon. [Anglo-Austrian Music Society]. Junge Nonne, An die Musik, Tod und das Mädchen, Du bist die Ruh, Musensohn. Gretchen, Wandrers Nachtlied, Haiden Röslein, Erster Verlust, Erlkönig.
Monday 14th	Fitting 12. Oppi 5.30. [Hans Oppenheim].
Wednesday 16th	BBC Manchester. 10.15–10.45. On Wings of Song. Milton Hall, Deansgate. Reh 3pm. Balance 9pm.
Thursday 17th	Music in Miniature on radio 8.30–9. Taxi home 10/-.
Saturday 19th	Max [Gilbert]: rehearsal 11am. Oppi 3pm.
Sunday 20th	Lunch 1pm Meriel St Clair.
Monday 21st	Fitting 12 o'clock. Oppi 3pm.
Tuesday 22nd	11am new hat – Hans. 2.30 Recording Brahms Lullaby [this was a second attempt, the first was on 9 December 1947, to record the Two songs with viola Op.91 with Max Gilbert, viola, and Phyllis Spurr, piano]. Supper Ben and Peter 6.45.
Wednesday 23rd	Mr Tillett's funeral.
Thursday 24th	Memorial Service [for John Tillett]. 2.30 Recording. Brahms.
Friday 25th	Freddie 11–12.30. Lunch Sir John Keane. 1.30 46 Pall Mall [Army & Navy Club]. Parry 6pm MM [Club]. 6–9 Mr Rubinstein's 24 St Mary Abbots Court W14.
Saturday 26th	BBC Schubert and Beethoven. 6–6.40. Studio II, Delaware Rd. 4pm Balance test. [The songs by Beethoven were Andenken, Wonne der Wehmuth, Ich liebe dich and Neue Liebe, neues Leben. Frederick Stone accompanied].
Monday 28th	Boat tickets. Sail to Holland.
Tuesday 29th	Rehearsal 11am.
Wednesday 30th	Rehearsal 9.30.

July:

Thursday 1st	Holland. Amsterdam. *Das Lied*. Szell. Reh 10.30.
Friday 2nd	Reh. Hair 3pm. Ballet.
Saturday 3rd	Holland. Scheveningen. *Das Lied*.
Sunday 4th	Recital. Hilversum. Ombra mai fu, Che faro (own parts), Laudamus Te.
Monday 5th	Sail back.
Tuesday 6th	Taxi home 15/-.
Wednesday 7th	John Turner 2.30. Win tea.
Monday 12th	Holiday £40. Sail to Ireland.
Friday 23rd	Return.
Tuesday 27th	10.30 Mr [John] Culshaw, Decca. Mr Flothuis 8.30.
Wednesday 28th	11am Mr Wilson. House warming John [Turner], 4 o'clock for tea and fitting gowns, 4c Observatory Gardens, Kensington W8. Housewarming to follow.
Thursday 29th	Hair 10.30. Roy 12 noon. 4.30 Miss Bass. Maurice – supper.
Friday 30th	Victoria 9.53am train to Lewes.
Saturday 31st	Paddy's birthday.

August:

Sunday 1st	Drinks Susannah's [wife of Maurice Jacobson] 8pm.
Tuesday 3rd	10.45 Glyndebourne.
Thursday 5th	Music – *Blessed Damozel* [Debussy]. New ed. United Publishers Monteverdi *Lamento d' Ariana*. Music 15/-.
Friday 6th	Received Decca £63. *St Matthew Passion*. 2.30 Recording. [Two Christmas Carols Silent Night, O Come all ye faithful, Boyd Neel String Orchestra, Boyd Neel, conductor].
Friday 13th	Lesson Prof 4.45–6. Reh Prom. 6.30. Maida Vale.
Saturday 14th	Lesson.
Monday 16th	11.30 Grunwald. Lunch Hans. Prof 5pm Schubert.
Tuesday 17th	Prom. BBC. Alto Rhapsody. Reh 11.40. Tickets for Sherman and Marjorie Ewing, Dick and Kay Leach, Paddy and Pop, Dr Cope, John and Leon.
Wednesday 18th	1pm train to Edinburgh. Sleeper £1.17.6d.
Monday 23rd	Arrive [Edinburgh]. *Don Giovanni*. [Ann Ayars was singing Zerlina].
Tuesday 24th	Boyd Neel. Lunch Ann, Dottie, Win, Basil D., Neville W., Moran *Medea*.
Wednesday 25th	10.15 *Daily Express*. Kathleen Long 11am. *Don Giovanni*.
Thursday 26th	Win 11am. Edinburgh Recital. Freemason's Hall. Evening [accompanist Gerald Moore]. Junge Nonne, Brahms, Musensohn, Erster Verlust, Tod und das Mädchen, Du bist die Ruh, Erlkönig. Bable, Loughareema, Sleep, P.R.T., Rahoon, M.G.W. Meal – *Albyn* Rooms.
Friday 27th	11am Leon Goossens. Lunch Mr and Mrs Dickie Leach. Tea. Mr and Mrs Goldsmidt. Liverpool Phil Sargent.
Saturday 28th	Party Rosalind [Maitland]'s 5–6.15. *Belshazzar's Feast*.

Sunday 29th	Edinburgh Festival. Usher Hall. Reh morning. Sir Malcolm. Afternoon. Bach B minor Mass. Night – Menuhin. Win.
Monday 30th	Maggie Teyte. *Cosi fan tutte*. Sleeper.
Tuesday 31st	Worcester rehearsal. 2–5 [at the Royal College of Music].

September:

Wednesday 1st	Reh 11.55 and 4pm. Lunch Maria and Peter [Diamand].
Thursday 2nd	10.30 Rehearsal *Gerontius*. 12 noon Roy. Lunch Remo's.
Sunday 5th	Train to Worcester [Three Choirs Festival]. Rehearsal 10am. Tea – Guildhall, Mayor. 6.20 train.
Monday 6th	11.45 [*St Matthew*] *Passion*. 3pm *Gerontius*.
Tuesday 7th	Sir Ivor Atkins – At Home. Tea. Guildhall.
Wednesday 8th	Worcester. *St Matthew Passion*. Morning 11.15 and afternoon. 4pm Dean of Worcester – At Home.
Thursday 9th	Worcester. 8pm. *Dream of Gerontius*. Lunch with Mayor, Guildhall 1pm.
Friday 10th	Worcester 11.15. Morning and afternoon. *Blessed Damozel*. *Messiah* Parts II and III.
Saturday 11th	*Beggars Opera*.
Monday 13th	11 Betty Clare. Hair. Lunch Hans *Quo Vadis*.
Tuesday 14th	Phyllis 10.30. Lunch Mary Townsend.
Wednesday 15th	Phyllis 11am. Joan Cross 7.45.
Thursday 16th	Phyllis 11am.
Friday 17th	Flight to and from Copenhagen £39.3s.0d.
Monday 20th	Copenhagen. Prepare Thyself Zion, Che faro, Cradle song, Art Thou troubled?, Hark. An die Musik, Romance (*Rosamunde*), Tod, Erl king. [Royal Orchestra conducted by Egisto Tango].
Thursday 23rd	Odense. With Kjell Ollson [accompanist]. Dearest consort, Lovelorn turtle, Ev. Hymn, Schubert, Four Serious, Silent noon, Loughareema, Sleep, P.R.T., Rahoon, M.G.W.
Sunday 26th	Swedish Church. Memorial Service [for Count] Bernadotte. [Bach] Schlage doch.
Monday 27th	Copenhagen: Dearest consort, Lily, Ev. Hymn, Junge Nonne, Erster Verlust, Musensohn, Gretchen, Erlkönig, 4 Serious, Silent noon, Loughareema, Salley gdns, Bonnet, Spanish lady.
Tuesday 28th	Næstved.
Wednesday 29th	Holbæck.
Thursday 30th	Plane 10.05am. Home 2.30!

October:

| Friday 1st | John Turner. Walter Goehr 2.30. Mary Townsend and Lady Upcott Tea 4pm. |
| Saturday 2nd | Hereford. Shire Hall. Recital. 7pm. Phyllis. Vision, Whyte lily, Soothing sleep, Flocks, Gretchen, Haidenröslein, Musensohn, Wandrers Nachtlied, Erlkönig, Roses 3, Swallow, Barefoot, Bable, Rahoon, M.G.W., Ash grove, O.C. Sir Percy [Hull]. Broomy Hill. Hereford. |

Sunday 3rd	[Train from Hereford] 10.35, [Paddington] 2.55.
Monday 4th	John Turner. Lunch Jean? 6pm Phyllis.
Tuesday 5th	Sunderland. Grange Congregational Church. Evening. Phyllis. Vision, Whyte lily, Flocks are sporting, Soothing sleep, Pack clouds away. To Music, Who is Sylvia?, Hark, hark, The swallow, Barefoot, Knight of Beth[lehem], Star candles, [Road to] Bethlehem, Loughareema, A piper. Hotel (request).
Wednesday 6th	Ilkley. Town Hall. 8pm. Recital. Accompanist in fee. Phyllis 12 gns. Piango, Che faro, Lasciatemi, Piu dicesti, Evening hymn, Willow song – Warlock, Hark the ech'ing air, Arch denial. Gretchen, Haidenröslein, Musensohn, Wandrers Nachtlied, Erlkönig, M.G.W., Rahoon, Bable, Ash grove, O.C.
Thursday 7th	Recording 'Ombra mai fu'. 7.30pm. [Kingsway Hall. London Symphony Orchestra, Sir Malcolm Sargent (conductor)].
Friday 8th	Phyllis. [Richard] Arnell 5.15 M.M. [Club].
Saturday 9th	Train to Skipton. Plumbing £1.7.6.
Sunday 10th	Skipton. Town Hall. Music Club. Recital. 7.30. 52gns with accompanist. Phyllis 12gns. Gluck – Piango, Che faro. Monteverdi, Lotti. Hark, Willow, Arch denial, Gretchen, Haiden, Musensohn, Wandrers, Erlkönig, Moeran, Bable, Britten.
Monday 11th	Joan Pomfret [journalist] 3pm *Lancashire Life* [the interview with Kathleen appeared in the January 1949 edition of this monthly magazine]. Train to Manchester. *Midland* [Hotel].
Tuesday 12th	Manchester. Reh 2pm. *Midland* [Hotel].
Wednesday 13th	Manchester. Hallé. *Kindertotenlieder*. [conductor, Barbirolli]. Broadcast 6.30–7.35. Reh 10–1. 11.15.
Thursday 14th	Manchester. Hallé. *Kindertotenlieder*. 5.45.
Friday 15th	Sheffield. City Hall. Hallé. *Kindertotenlieder*. 7pm. Reh 4–5. *Grand* [Hotel].
Saturday 16th	Home. John T[urner] 2-ish.
Monday 18th	Train to Huddersfield.
Tuesday 19th	Brighouse. Parish Hall, Church Lane. 7.30. Alan Loveday [violin]. Accompanist provided. How changed, Dearest consort, Whyte lily, Flocks. An die Musik, Gretchen, Tod, Musensohn. Salley Gardens – Britten, P.R.T., Ash grove, O.C. Ask about 4 tickets H[udders]field recital Mr Paddy. Sleeper.
Wednesday 20th	Lady Margaret's wedding 2.15! [Lady Margaret Egerton married Sir John Colville].
Thursday 21st	Lunch – Emmie [Tillett], Wigmore Hall. 1.20. Write to Oppi.
Friday 22nd	Bradford. Eastbrook Hall. Hallé. *Kindertotenlieder*. 7.15. Reh 2–5. *Midland* [Hotel] Bradford.
Saturday 23rd	*Midland* [Hotel] Manchester.
Sunday 24th	Uppermill. Saddleworth Music Club. Mechanics' Hall. Recital. 52gns. [pay] Phyllis 12gns. Same as Woking [11th January 1949] except last group: Silent Noon, Pretty Ring Time, Flower, Ash grove, O.C. Phyllis lunch. *Midland* [Hotel].

Monday 25th	[Liverpool] Ruth Lever. Recital. 7.30. Vision, Soothing sleep, Lily, Pack. Gretchen, Du bist die Ruh, Musensohn, Erlkönig. Bable, Loughareema, P.R.T., Ash grove, O.C., *Adelphi* [Hotel] Liverpool.
Tuesday 26th	Whitchurch [Shropshire]. Music Club. Broughall Modern School. 7.30. Recital in conj[unction with] Wigmore Ensemble (Korchinska, Gilbert, Riddle). Vision, Lily, Willow song, Merry. (Interval). Gretchen, Musensohn, Heidenröslein, Erlkönig, Bable, Fairy lough, P.R.T., Ash grove, O.C. *Swan* Hotel.
Wednesday 27th	9.26 [train], 1.20 Euston. Ring Lereculey re Edinburgh. Look up Uppingham contract 27th May [1948]. Time in Colchester. Danish concert – Albert Hall.
Thursday 28th	Colchester. Moot Hall. Recital. 7pm. 52gns to include 12gns for accompanist Phyllis. Same as Harpenden [24th September 1948].
Friday 29th	12.30 Lunch Hans *Coq d'or*. Phyllis 3.30.
Saturday 30th	St Pancras 3.15, Keighley 9.01.
Sunday 31st	Keighley. Temple Street [Methodist Church]. Afternoon and evening. *Messiah*.

November:	
Monday 1st	Phyllis 3.30.
Tuesday 2nd	John, fitting coat. Lunch Mr [Anthony] Derville 12.30 *Akropolis*, Percy St., Tott[enham] Ct. Rd. 2pm. Camden *Hippodrome* Theatre. Walter Goehr [Rehearsal for Vaughan Williams' opera *Riders to the Sea*, see also November 18th and 26th].
Wednesday 3rd	Albert Hall. *Messiah*. Evening. Rehearsal morning.
Thursday 4th	10.30–12.30. Reh *Kingdom* and *Frauenliebe*. Phyllis 4pm.
Friday 5th	Huddersfield. Choral Society. *Kingdom*. Evening. Reh 2.15. Ring Auntie May.
Saturday 6th	Spennymoor. Rosa Street Methodist Church. Recital. Evening. Phyllis. Che faro, Vision, Whyte lily, Pack, Gretchen, Musensohn, Heidenröslein, Erlkönig, 4 Serious, Bable, Star candles, P.R.T., Ash grove, O.C. or To Music, Who is Sylvia?, Hark, hark, Swallow, Barefoot.
Sunday 7th	[Train] 10.53–3.30.
Monday 8th	Freddie [Frederick Stone] 11am. Positive party 5–7.30. Prof 8.15.
Tuesday 9th	Albert Hall. Goldsmiths. *Gerontius*. 7.30. Reh afternoon.
Wednesday 10th	Musicians' Benevolent Fund. 7 Carlos Place, Grosvenor Square, W1. 3.30. [Recital]. How changed the vision, Whyte lily, Willow song. Love is a bable, Silent noon, P.R.T., Ash grove, O.C.
Thursday 11th	BBC Third [Programme] Freddie [Frederick Stone] 11am. *Frauenliebe*. Studio II, Delaware Rd. Balance test 8–9pm. 10.15–11.30.

Friday 12th	Welwyn Garden City. Recital. Gerald 12 noon. 2 from *Orfeo*, Lasciatemi morire, Piu dicesti, Hugo Wolf: Verborgenheit, Gärtner, Auf ein altes Bild, Auf einer Wanderung. Schubert: all Goethe. Gretchen, Haiden, Musensohn, Wandrers, Erlkönig. Modern English and folksongs: Rahoon, M.G.W., Bable, Ash grove, O.C.
Sunday 14th	Southend-on-Sea. *Palace* Hotel Ballroom. 3.15. 50 gns to include accompanist 10gns Phyllis. 3 groups. Gretchen, Musensohn, Heidenröslein, Erlkönig. Vision, Whyte lily, Willow song, Come let's be merry. Bable, Loughareema, P.R.T., Ash grove, O.C., *Frauenliebe* recording 6pm.
Monday 15th	11.20 Mr Miller. Lunch Hans *Casa Prada*. 12.30. Roy 4.30. Morley College 6pm rehearsal.
Tuesday 16th	Mr Anthony Bernard 12. Collect fur coat. Lady Jowitt 6–7.
Wednesday 17th	Chester. Town Hall. Recital. 7pm. 52gns to include accomp. Phyll. Piango il mio ben cosi, Che faro, Lasciatemi morire, Piu dicesti. Verborgenheit, Gärtner, Auf ein altes Bild, Auf einer Wanderung. Gretchen, Heidenröslein, Musensohn, Wandrers Nachtlied, Erlkönig. M.G.W. Rahoon, Bable, Ash grove, O.C. *Blossoms* Hotel.
Thursday 18th	[Train] 9.32–1.20. Paddy 5pm. Reh V[aughan].W[illiams]. 6–9 *Camden* Theatre [see also November 2nd and 26th].
Friday 19th	Private view 10–5 (Royal Institute Galleries) 195 Piccadilly. Mr Miller 12.30. Collect silver pencil. Phyllis 6-ish. Max, Barbara, Phyllis, Win, Scottie 7.30.
Saturday 20th	1.45 West Hampstead Mr Olof. 3.30 Fluffie. Dinner Gramophone Federation, *St Ermin's* Hotel, Caxton St, SW1 (Westminster).
Sunday 21st	London. His Majesty's. Recital. Cancelled. John, Leon tea?
Monday 22nd	Worcester. Alice Ottley School. 2.45 recital. 52 gns with accompanist. Taxi 9.10, call for Phyllis 9.15, Paddington 9.45, arr 12.51. Vision, Whyte lily, Lovelorn turtle, Pack clouds. Musensohn, Tod und das Mädchen, Heidenröslein, Erlkönig. Blacksmith, Roses 3, Swallow, Barefoot, Fairy lough, A piper, Ash grove, O.C. [Train back] 6.5–9.5.
Tuesday 23rd	Parry lunch 12.30 *Casa Prada*. 5pm Roy H. Dinner Eva Turner 7pm. Cocktails. £100 for Bruno [Walter] recital 6th September. Work at Salzburg 18, 19, 20 August [1949]. Ask about *B[ournemouth] Belle*. [4 December 1948].
Wednesday 24th	Harpenden. Music Club. Public Hall. 8pm. Gerald. 40gns. Like Welwyn. 2 from *Orfeo*, Lasciatemi morire, Piu dicesti, Hugo Wolf: Verborgenheit, Gärtner, Auf ein altes Bild, Auf einer Wanderung. Schubert: all Goethe. Gretchen, Haiden, Musensohn, Wandrers, Erlkönig. Modern English and folksongs: Rahoon, M.G.W., Bable, Ash grove, O.C.
Thursday 25th	Hanley. Ceramic. Victoria Hall. *Kingdom*. Evening. Reh 2pm. *North Staffs* [Hotel].

Friday 26th	London. Central Hall, Westminster. 7pm. [Morley College Concert series]. Reh 4.30. 10gns. [Concert performance of Vaughan Williams' opera *Riders to the Sea* in which she sang the role of Maurya].
Saturday 27th	Matinee – Phyllis, Scottie. Phyllis rehearse.
Sunday 28th	Sutton Coldfield. Highbury Little Theatre. 3 and 6pm with Stanley Mason. Phyllis. 11.10 Paddington 1.40 [Birmingham] Snow Hill. Mr Baker under clock on arrival. How changed, Mad Bess, Ev. Hymn, Musensohn, Du liebst mich nicht, Heidenröslein, Erlkönig. Silent noon, P.R.T., Soft day, Bold unbiddable. *Grand* [Hotel].
Monday 29th	Haslingden. Arts Club. Modern School Hall. 7.30 with Iris Loveridge. [Hospitality] arranged Mrs Landless. Prepare thyself, Soothing sleep, Whyte lily, Pack clouds away. Gretchen, Musensohn, Erster Verlust, Erlkönig, Loughareema, P.R.T., Ash grove, O.C.
December:	
Wednesday 1st	Huddersfield. St Patrick's Hall. 7.30. Phyllis (12gns). Prepare thyself, Soothing sleep, Whyte lily, Pack clouds away. Gretchen, Wandrers N., Musensohn, Erster Verlust, Erlkönig, Liebsetreu, Sapphische Ode, Gärtner, Auf ein altes Bild, Auf einer Wanderung. Fairy lough, P.R.T. *Rape* [Flower Song]. Ash grove and O.C.
Thursday 2nd	10.17 from Wakefield Westgate, 1.55 Kings X. Find out about Woking accompanist. 4pm Mr Miller.
Friday 3rd	Ask for 3 tickets *Kindertotenlieder* [RAH 7th December]. Emmie 12.30. John Michael 3. Phyllis 6 o'clock.
Saturday 4th	Bournemouth. St Peter's Hall. Recital. 5pm. 50gns to include accompanist. Phyll 10gns. *Bournemouth Belle*, Waterloo 12.30, [arr] 2.30. [return] 7.50 [arr] 11.15. Train £2.5s.9d. Vision, Turtle, Evening Hymn, Hark. Junge Nonne, Wandrers Nachtlied, Romanze, Erlkönig. Liebstreu, Sapphische Ode, Minnelied. Rahoon, M.G.W., *Lucretia*, Ash grove, O.C.
Sunday 5th	Lunch 1pm Emmie.
Monday 6th	Has Phyllis got Southend money? 1.15 B[roadcasting] H[ouse] Mr Derville. Woman's Hour talk 2pm. Roy 4.30 (Phyl). Win ringing. 6pm Mr Cripps [Josef Krips].
Tuesday 7th	Albert Hall. *Kindertotenlieder*. London Symphony. Joseph [Josef] Krips. [Sir Malcolm is scored through].
Wednesday 8th	Leeds. Town Hall. Choral Society. *Messiah*. 35gns. *Queens* [Hotel].
Thursday 9th	Blackpool. Tower Ballroom. Philharmonic Society. *Messiah*. Evening. Reh 2pm. Tower Pavilion. *Palatine* [Hotel].
Friday 10th	[Train home] 8.20–1.50. Phyllis 6pm.
Saturday 11th	Flora's recital (Nielsen) Wigmore [Hall] 3pm. *Midland* [Hotel].
Sunday 12th	Manchester. King's Hall. Belle Vue. Hallé. *Messiah*. 2.30pm.

	Reh 10.30. [Telegram to] Maitland, 6 Heriot Row, Edinburgh: No trains north Sunday night from Manchester. Must travel 9.30 Monday morning arriving 3.31.
Monday 13th	Edinburgh. Freemasons Hall. Recital. 8pm. Phyllis. Manchester Victoria 9.30, arr. 3.31. Like as the lovelorn turtle, Soothing sleep, Pack clouds away, Evening hymn, Mad Bess. Brahms. Wolf 4 [Auf einer Wanderung, Auf ein altes Bild, Gärtner, Verborgenheit]. Britten 4 (Flower, Cushion, Ash grove, O.C.). Stay the night [at] Mrs Maitland's.
Wednesday 15th	West Hartlepool. Town Hall. Evening. *Messiah.*
Thursday 16th	Auntie May.
Friday 17th	Bradford. Eastbrook Hall. Festival Choral Society. *Messiah.* Evening. Reh 3pm. *Great Northern* [Hotel].
Saturday 18th	Liverpool. Phil. *Messiah.* 7pm. 11 Oxford Drive [Home of Rick Davies].
Sunday 19th	Liverpool. Phil. *Messiah.* 3pm.
Monday 20th	Stephen Vaughan, American Consulate, Cunard Building.
Wednesday 22nd	Bolton. Victoria Hall. Choral Society. Evening. *Messiah.* Reh 2.15.
Thursday 23rd	*Cambridge* Theatre 7pm. *Cage me a peacock.*
Friday 24th	BBC Serenade programme. 9.20–10.20. Reh 6–9 Concert Hall BH. 25gns. Geistliches Wiegenlied, Slumber beloved, O my dear heart (Warlock).
Tuesday 28th	John 3pm. Sleeper [to Edinburgh].
Wednesday 29th	Edinburgh. *Kindertotenlieder*, Hark the echoing air, Evening hymn. Reh 2.30.

Diary for 1949

January:

Saturday 1st Glasgow. *Messiah*. Noon. Evening *Kindertotenlieder* ([Walter] Susskind).

Sunday 2nd Glasgow. Recital. Reh 10am, Greens Playhouse, Renfield St. Two groups: Prepare thyself Zion, Have mercy Lord. Ombra mai fu, Che faro.

Monday 3rd John. Hair 11am. Ring Emmie. Dinner evening? Parry/Phyllis. 4 tickets for 12th. Salzburg dates for hotel. 7.15 Emmie.

Tuesday 4th Phyllis 5pm.

Wednesday 5th Golf. Bill and Norman. 10am from Baker Street. Green Line 718 to Windsor. Fordbridge Rd, Ashford. Ask for Ashford Manor G[olf] C[lub]. Phyllis morning 10.45. Peter – lunch, check restaurant Edgware Rd. Hair 3pm. Win 5-ish party.

Thursday 6th Nottingham. Blue Triangle Hall. Recital 7.30. Phyllis. Get two tickets for Dorothy. Mad Bess, There's not a swain, Ev. Hymn, Hark. Junge Nonne, Tod, Musensohn, Liebst mich nicht, Erlkönig. Four [by] Wolf. Bable, Soft day, La belle dame, Ash grove, O.C. *Black Boy* [Hotel].

Friday 7th [Train back] 9.25, arr. 12.35. Mrs Ostrer *Casa Prada* 1.15. Freddie 5–6 Reh room Maida Vale.

Saturday 8th Albert Hall. *Messiah*. Royal Choral Society. Aft. Bobbie and Eddie coming round. Dinner Victor Olof.

Sunday 9th Reh 10.30. Recording 11.30–12.15. Studio 5, Maida Vale. Zwerg, Erster Verlust, Schiffer, An den Mond, Schlummerlied, Du liebst mich nicht, Der Kreuzzug, Wiegenlied. 12.45 Lunch Ivor Newton, Garrick Club. Ruth D[raper].

Monday 10th 10 Phyllis. 12–1 Mr Gibilaro, 14 Dineley. Sir M[alcolm Sargent]. 9 Albert Hall Mansions 3pm. Aft. 4pm John. Final fitting.

Tuesday 11th Woking Music Club. County School for Boys. Christ Church Hall 8.15. 50gns. Including 10 [for] Phyllis. 11.30 train. Prepare, Soothing sleep, Whyte lily, Pack. Junge Nonne, Tod, Musensohn, Du bist die Ruh, Erlkönig. Blacksmith, Roses 3, Swallow, Barefoot. Bable, Lough, *Rape* [Flower song], Ash grove, O.C.

Wednesday 12th Albert Hall. Four Serious. 7.30. Sir Malcolm. [BBC Symphony Orchestra] Reh 10.30. John tickets (2).

Saturday 15th Laren [Holland] 7pm. Dearest consort, Art thou troubled?, Lasciatemi, Piu diceste, Che faro, *Frauenliebe*, Stanford. *Magnificat*. Reh 11.30. Dr Mengelberg.

Sunday 16th Hilversum. AVRO [Algemene Vereniging Radio Omroep or

	General Association of Radio Broadcasting]. Alto Rhapsody. Mengelberg. 10 mins on a boat. Where'er you walk, Sigh no more, Bobby Shaftoe.
Monday 17th	Lunch 12.30 Raphael [*sic*] Kubelik. 10.30–11.30 [BBC] Home Service Schubert.
Tuesday 18th	Bussum.
Wednesday 19th	The Hague. Like 25th except Prepare thyself Zion, Soothing sleep, Junge Nonne.
Thursday 20th	Mr Kubelik concert.
Friday 21st	Amsterdam (University) Dearest consort, Art thou troubled? Lasciatemi morire, Piu dicesti, Che faro. *Frauenliebe*. La belle dame, Fairy lough, Soft day, Bold unbiddable.
Saturday 22nd	Mr Cronheim 8.30.
Sunday 23rd	Amsterdam. British Council. Vision, Art thou troubled? Willow, willow, Mad Bess, The lover's curse, Salley Gardens, Blow the wind southerly [first mention in a diary].
Monday 24th	Amstel 228 Donemus 11.30. Lunch 12.30.
Tuesday 25th	Amsterdam [Concertgebouw]. Hark the ech'ing, Evening hymn, There's not a swain, Mad Bess. An die Musik, Du liebst mich nicht, Haidenröslein, Tod, Musensohn. Verborgenheit, Gärtner, Auf ein altes Bild, Auf einer Wanderung. Flower song, Salley Gardens, Cushions, Ash grove, O.C.
Wednesday 26th	Middelburg
Friday 28th	Rotterdam same as Hague [19th].
Saturday 29th	Delft [scored through]. Amsterdam. 2.30 Peter [Diamand]. Tea Mr Welvaars 4pm.
Sunday 30th	Amsterdam aft. Tea – Mr Hon. Sec. Peter's party.
February:	
Wednesday 2nd	Kirkaldy. How changed, Soothing sleep, Hark ech'ing, There's not a swain, Mad Bess, Bable, O soft day, P.R.T., Cushions, Ash grove, O.C. Green Chinese. *Station* Hotel.
Thursday 3rd	[Travel to Belfast]. *Grand Central* [Hotel].
Friday 4th	Belfast. Queen's University. Hark, Evening hymn, There's not a swain, Mad Bess. *Frauenliebe*. Salley gdns, Cushions, Ash grove, O.C. *Grand Central* [Hotel]. £26.10.
Monday 7th	Dublin. 3 and 8pm. £31.10. [Aft.] Vision, Turtle, Ev. Hymn, Mad Bess, Gretchen, Haiden R., Wandrers, Erlkönig, 4 Serious, S. Noon, P.R.T., Sleep, Ash G, O.C. [Eve.] Che faro, Pur dicesti, Soothing sleep, Spring is coming, Junge Nonne, Ruh, Tod, Musensohn,. Wolf group. Bable, Lough, A soft day, Sigh no more, M.G.W.
Wednesday 9th	London, Kensington. Not paid. With Roy. John supper. 8gns. As Emmie about Kirkaldy, Nov & Dec.
Thursday 10th	Recording 2.30. Maida Vale No.4. [seven folksongs, unaccompanied or with Phyllis Spurr, piano]. Photographs. Kubelik 5.30pm. Norman with paints! Win [with paints!]

Friday 11th	Recording 10am [as 10th]. Nancy [Evans] lunch? 1.15 *Casa Prada*. Reh 3.30–5 Maida Vale, 7–10 Albert Hall.
Saturday 12th	London Albert Hall. Dvorak *Stabat Mater*. Kubelik. Evening 8pm. Reh 10–1.
Sunday 13th	BBC. Dvorak *Stabat Mater*. Balance 2pm. Studio 1, Maida Vale. 3–5. Ena?
Monday 14th	Call for *Orfeo* parts, Novellos. Recording 2.30pm. [Schubert songs, with Phyllis Spurr] Christopher. 6pm 12 Onslow Gdns., SW7.
Tuesday 15th	Recording 2pm. Max Gilbert. [final, and successful, attempt at Brahms Op.91]. Win, tea. Dr Cope ringing.
Wednesday 16th	Hans 6 Windmill St 2.45. 10.30–12.30 Mr Gib. Lunch Dr Cope. Tea Mr Howes. 6.30 Roy.
Friday 18th	Sail *Queen Mary*. Wonderful day, sun shining. At Purser's table with 2 American girls – one tea taster! – and nice business man. Lovely cabin to myself!
Friday 25th	Arrived 10.30-ish. 36 hours late. Roger Hall met me – went to *Weylin* [Hotel] then rehearsal with Tommy Scherman. Lovely dinner with Dottie. Ann away on tour. Reh. Apt. 11E 130 W57th St. 5pm Mr Scherman. Dottie dinner 7pm.
Saturday 26th	Hair 3pm. Dottie dinner 7pm.
Sunday 27th	Reh. Apt. 11E 130 W57th. 5.30 Lotte Lehmann. Supper Dickie Leach. Lovely day. Owe Mr Scherman 12 dollars.
Monday 28th	Town Hall 1–4ish. Mr Mertens/Miss Jarmel 4.45. Dinner Ann and Dottie.

March:	
Tuesday 1st	Reh [for *Orfeo*] 1.15. Fisher Concert Hall, 57th St. Soloists. Tea afterwards at Mrs Scherman's. Lovely. Call for photie. [A Community Concert recital at Holyoke, Mass. was cancelled].
Wednesday 2nd	New York Town Hall. *Orfeo*. 8.30 Ann Ayars. Mr Scherman. 1pm reh Town Hall. Reception, Willie's [Griffis], lovely. Concert riotous success.
Thursday 3rd	Room 1620 Roger Hall 10.30. Lunch Weissman 1pm. Mr Meyer 2.45, Arpad 3.30.
Friday 4th	Arpad 11. 4pm Oliver, *Sunday Times*, Lounge, *Weylin*. *Götterdämmerung* 7.30.
Saturday 5th	Ring Prof Walter (Butterfield 8–3289) Mrs Lindt [Walter's daughter Lottie]. 12 Arpad. Bruno Walter 4. Take Brahms. Mr Mertens 7pm.
Sunday 6th	Breakfast 38 W53rd!!!! Willie's 3.30.
Monday 7th	10.30 ears Dr Allan, 11 Miss Wilson, 12 Arpad. Night train to Granville.
Tuesday 8th	Granville, Ohio. Arrive 8.50. Paid Arpad. Lots of audience knitting! Lovely hospitality on farm. Mrs James Sexton, Bryn Du Farm, Granville. Left after midnight for train to New York.
Wednesday 9th	Arrived in New York 4.30. Caught 11pm for Montreal. Terrible

night in train – nearly dead. Arpad about as helpful as a can of beans. How I loathe his playing.

Thursday 10th   Montreal 3pm. Arrived 8am. Breakfast – then bed till 1pm. Concert at 3pm. Phew! But lovely audience – renewed my faith in myself. Dinner at Mrs Russell Smith's. Made two friends in her and President, Mrs Langdon. Another night journey to Detroit.

Friday 11th   Arrived in Detroit after lunch, went to flix and caught night train to Indianapolis.

Saturday 12th   Indianapolis. Arrived at 8am. Good lunch with secretary. Sleep and concert went well including sight-reading the *Angelus*! Dance and dinner afterwards. *Angelus*! Prepare, Soothing sleep, Spring, Lily, Pack, Bable, Lough, P.R.T., Soft day, Ash grove, O.C.

Sunday 13th   Had mad driver who didn't know the way to the station and only just caught the train for Pittsburgh. Engine broke down and arrived 2.15am instead of 10.15!!

Monday 14th   Cold, snowy weather. Hair washed and wandered round. Interview and taken for ride by Mrs Gallup and to her home for supper. Very nice.

Tuesday 15th   Broadcast 9.30. Lunch 12.30.

Wednesday 16th   Pittsburgh. Prepare, Bist du bei mir?, Four Serious, Junge Nonne, Wandrers, Musensohn, Du liebst mich nicht, Erlkönig. *Frauenliebe*. Concert a great success. Just caught the train and lost Arpad but found him later.

Thursday 17th   Back in New York. Captain Johnson 5.45. Lovely dinner. Nice white-bearded pet!

Friday 18th   Morriston, New Jersey. Reh 12. Thick snowstorm, not very exciting concert. Went on bus, came home on train 1am.

Saturday 19th   Ann and Dottie.

Sunday 20th   Capt Johnson 5.45.

Monday 21st   Newark, Delaware. Wonderful audience, very thrilled.

Tuesday 22nd   Ring Bruno Walter. Mary Townsend, lovely lunch.

Wednesday 23rd   11.30 Bruno Walter. Mr Oliver 4.30.

Thursday 24th   12.45 Town Hall. 7pm Mr and Mrs Brownlee.

Friday 25th   12.30 Dr Weissman. 1pm Miss Dispeker. 2.45 rehearsal. 7pm Dottie and Ann.

Saturday 26th   10.45 Arpad. Rev. Pugh Luncheon 12 noon. 5.30 B.W. 8pm Dinner Mr Oliver. Lovely.

Sunday 27th   Demonstrations in New York against Mr Churchill. Shostakovich. Lunch Mrs Berman 12.30?

Monday 28th   New York. Recital. A riot! Made some money! Packed, standing and sitting on stage! What an ordeal! Prepare, Soothing sleep, Whyte lily, Pack clouds. Junge Nonne, Erster Verlust, Musensohn, Tod, Du bist die Ruhe, Erlkönig. Four Serious. Bable, Lough, P.R.T., *Rape*, Ash grove, O.C.

Tuesday 29th   Thea [Dispeker] 12. Train to Ottawa [Canada] 11pm.

Wednesday 30th	Ottawa. Arrived bad-tempered and tired. No hotel room available! Concert all right, but [hall] too big - 3000. Nice Montreal friends came. Contacted John Newmark.

April:

Friday 1st	Train was four hours late, staggered to Highland Park [Illinois] – still very bad-tempered. Arpad tearful, depressed and no joke.
Saturday 2nd	Mr Anderson calling lunchtime.
Monday 4th	La Crosse, Wisconsin. Lovely concert and hospitality.
Wednesday 6th	St Paul, Minnesota.
Friday 8th	Northfield, Minnesota.
Monday 11th	Evanston, Illinois. Concert of 3000 in the gymnasium. No proper lighting, green room mirror and all rather miserable. Anne and David [sister-in-law and nephew] turned up!! 'O rest in the Lord' Mrs Ross [?by special request].
Wednesday 13th	Evanston, Illinois.
Thursday 14th	11.30 Miss Young. 12.30 Mr Anderson. 4pm Mrs Cress and Mrs Jackson, La Crosse.
Good Friday 15th	Christian Science 10.30. 11.30 Lake Shore Drive. Lunch Mrs Cardelli. 12.30.
Monday 18th	Battle Creek, Michigan. Party after. Arrived on wrong train so Committee missed us. Hotel with convention, My God! Grocers' convention – rolling cans of grapefruit downstairs all night!! Didn't sleep a wink.
Tuesday 19th	Photographer at station. Arrived in Flint [Michigan] – met by two tired, stony women. No porters available – everybody rude, including electrician backstage. Went to flix.
Wednesday 20th	Flint, Michigan. Walked miles in morning. Bed in aft. Interview on radio 5pm. Concert 8.30.
Thursday 21st	Lousy train 3.12. No porters and 7 bags. What a to-do. Went to Miss Young's. Lovely!
Friday 22nd	Lunch Mr Anderson 12. Johnny 4pm. Rehearsing 6 dollars, Studio 1 dollar. Roger Ballard 6pm.
Saturday 23rd	Johnny [Newmark] 4pm. Mrs Cardelli 7pm.
Sunday 24th	Luncheon Dorin Anderson. Left 11.59 – mistook the hour because of summer time. Very bilious after luncheon, feeling lousy.
Monday 25th	Cape Girardeau, Missouri. Arrived St Louis 7.43am. Left on slowest train 8.48. Arrived Girardeau 12.24. Could have travelled direct from Chicago without change. Heigh-ho! Met at station. Nice concert but many children picking noses. Wanted Wagnerian arias! Feeble party afterwards.
Tuesday 26th	Taken for lovely run in morning. Caught train – no porters again on same train to St Louis 3.40 arrival. Had drunken porter. Left luggage in five lockers. Went to flix. Phoned

	Danville frantically re travelling on bus but without success. Caught train to Louisville 10.30.
Wednesday 27th	Danville, Kentucky. Arrived Louisville 7.10. Telephoned again but no luck. Left for Danville 8.45. arr noon. Nobody to meet us. Took taxi last 4 miles. Funny peculiar hotel with drugstore restaurant, but kind. Concert in flick – filthy dirty, no dressing room, noisy audience but calmed down. Turner-over cried all night!! Rush for train. Just time for sandwich in milkbar. No reception and no departure.
Thursday 28th	Arrived Columbia 4.45pm. Another train to Sumter arr. 7pm. Had to change again – no redcaps [porters] – in desperation had expensive taxi! 40 miles. Committee missed us tho' secretary advised of arrival. Had southern fried chicken – <u>very</u> delicious.
Friday 29th	Florence, South Carolina. Looked around shops – bed in afternoon – concert in nicest hall yet, acoustically. More children. Road house supper with two of the silliest twerps ever, ignorant and malicious. Home very late.
Saturday 30th	Walked round in the morning. Early lunch. Left for Savannah 1.20. Lost very beautiful watch!! Arrived Savannah 5.55. Stayed in hotel 8 miles out – wonderful location. Drink, dinner, walk, and bed.

May:

Sunday 1st	Up 6.30 for early train to Macon. Met by nice secretary and reporter. Really hot weather – lovely!
Monday 2nd	Macon, Georgia. Lovely concert. Substituted 4 Serious Songs and most appreciative. Very happy here. Party afterwards – very nice too.
Friday 6th	Havana, Cuba. Concert a great success. Shocking piano but good hall.
Saturday 7th	Cocktail party at Mary McArthur's in wonderful garden. Very nice. Taken for meal and sight-seeing. Home 1-ish.
Sunday 8th	Walked to hotel and watched the bathing – gorgeous day. Luncheon at Yacht Club – whattanoise – coffee with Mrs Hoyt – Musical to-do – Mozart 4tet and I tried out some Brahms. Dinner with British Minister and spouse – very nice.
Monday 9th	Flew to Miami. 10.45. Rotten, bumpy. Met by Mrs Volpe – interview with paper and late lunch. No air ticket for me, but fortunately plane fairly empty. Came out to *Coronado* Hotel. Fifteen miles from Miami – in the middle of nowhere! Lots of letters waiting at last. Bought new frock and swimsuit.
Tuesday 10th	Went into Miami Beach on bus. Bought new pen – took shoes to be mended, films etc. Had lunch there – came back on bus and bathed. Heavenly water, warm as toast, cold wind and later thunderstorm. Dinner and bed earlyish.
Wednesday 11th	Bathed in morning. Gorgeous. Getting very pink! Shopped a

bit, lunch and dinner in Miami Beach. Mrs Volpe calling 3pm. Large tea, photies and all! Wrote letters.

Thursday 12th   Bathed again – wonderful. Meal at Pickin' Chicken and flick – not very good flick.

Friday 13th   12 Hair. 4pm Miami Music Sorority. Made a sister in Sigma Alpha Iota!

Saturday 14th   Rehearsal 2.30. Went well. Very hot. Had ice cream soda and rehearsed with pianist. V.G. Broadcast 6.45.

Sunday 15th   Miami, Florida 4.30. Elgar *Sea Pictures*. Staggered through them, but encores went better. Party afterwards. Pianist – Mr Stoll – took me home.

Monday 16th   Concert went well again but row between Mrs Volpe and Dr Allos in which I played the part of Samson (?) No – Solomon! Jeffrey Stoll played well – nice pet and took me out to supper and home 2am! Bathed in perspiration at concert – frock wet through.

Tuesday 17th   Flight EAL 610 to New York – 8.15am! Up at 6.15! Seat cancelled and had excess fare of $28.41 to pay. Sorry to leave Miami. Car banged into another on way, but no damage done – very lucky! Back to *Weylin* [Hotel] – 50 odd letters waiting, 2 months old!

Wednesday 18th   Slept until 12 noon! Lunch with Andre [Mertens] – pleasant but some straight shooting! Klever Kaff! Shopped summer girdles – stockings, bag and shoes. Phew! Dinner Mr French and Andre. Very nice but more straight shootin'! Klever Kaff. Got fees up another $50 a concert. A drop in the ocean, but better than nowt!

Thursday 19th   1pm Mr Majeski. 3pm Andre. Mr Meyer.

Friday 20th   Income Tax – alien papers etc all settled! My God! Lunch with Mr Homburger and concert arranged in Toronto for next year. 9.45 Roger Hall.

Saturday 21st   12 Mr Van Klooster Phew! 1.45. Andre. Mr Pease. Went to Andre's house in country – large noisy party – very nice.

Sunday 22nd   Fly to Louisville through tornado!! Not at all nice begorra! Glad to get on terra-cotta! Frightful party.

Monday 23rd   Louisville, Kentucky.

Tuesday 24th   Louisville, Kentucky.

Thursday 26th   Neenah Menasha, Wisconsin.

Friday 27th   Caught the 'Lizzie' 9pm! Phew! Whattarush!

Saturday 28th   Return *Queen Elizabeth*. Shared table with Mr and Mrs Moiseiwitsch, Mr and Mrs Heifetz and Mr [Emanuel] Bay – good fun.

June:

Sunday 5th   Heifetz Concert. Dinner Mrs Tillett.

Monday 6th   Dinner Mr Bay.

Wednesday 8th   Adrian Beecham 9pm.

Friday 10th	Flew to Holland.
Thursday 23rd	Dress rehearsal [*Orfeo*].
Friday 24th	*Orfeo* 1st night. Win, Rick, Rosalind and Alec there.
Monday 27th	The Hague. Koninklijke Schouwburg. *Orfeo*.
Tuesday 28th	Amsterdam. *Orfeo*.

July:

Friday 1st	3pm Mr Bruck. 5pm Flot [Marius Flothuis]. *Il Seraglio*.
Saturday 2nd	*Rosenkavalier*.
Sunday 3rd	11.30 Flot 1pm Lunch Mrs Welvaar. Tea Hazel. *Don Giovanni*.
Monday 4th	Reh 9.30 *Orfeo*. 10.30 Bach Concertgebouw. Lunch Maria. Tea Basil Cameron.
Tuesday 5th	10.30 Mr Bruck. Reh 7.30.
Wednesday 6th	Concertgebouw. Bach *Magnificat*, [Cantata] 169, Purcell *Te Deum*.
Thursday 7th	Flot 4pm.
Friday 8th	Amsterdam. *Orfeo*.
Saturday 9th	Flot 11.30 [and] 3.30. Luncheon Desi Halban. Dinner Roth's 6pm.
Sunday 10th	Flot 11am. Annie 4.30. Julia Culp 7–7.30.
Monday 11th	9.30 Concertgebouw. B[ritish] Council 5–7. Reh 7–10pm.
Tuesday 12th	*Orfeo*. Kurhaus – Scheveningen. Rehearsal 9.30.
Wednesday 13th	Rehearsal 9.30. Tea 5–5.30 Mrs Schill. Rehearsal 7.
Thursday 14th	Amsterdam Concertgebouw. Reh 9.30. *Spring* Symphony [world premiere with Jo Vincent, soprano, Peter Pears, tenor, Concertgebouw Orchestra, Eduard van Beinum, conductor].
Friday 15th	Scheveningen Kurhaus. *Spring* Symphony. Reception after.
Saturday 16th	Party 11pm.
Sunday 17th	Home again!
Monday 18th	Address in Salzburg. Money at bank (Swiss).
Tuesday 19th	Win tea 4.30.
Wednesday 20th	John.3.30.
Thursday 21st	Phyll 4pm.
Friday 22nd	Ena coming. Prof 3.15.
Saturday 23rd	11am Freddie. Jean 4. Roy 6.
Monday 25th	4pm Hair. BBC Concert Hall 7.30–8. Gretchen, Erster Verlust, Suleika, Nur wer die Sehnsucht, Heidenröslein, Rastlose Liebe, Wandrers Nachtlied, Meeresstille, Erlkönig.
Tuesday 26th	Prof 2. Phyll.
Wednesday 27th	John 4-ish. Susannah's dinner.
Thursday 28th	London. Prom. 7.30. Four Serious Songs. Reh morning 12.
Friday 29th	10.30 Mr Montague. 11.30 Fluffie. Lunch Eva. 12.45 *Kempinski*, Swallow St. Mr Sholto.
Saturday 30th	Off to Switzerland. Splendid journey.

August:

Wednesday 17th	Arrived Salzburg.

Thursday 18th	Reh. Salzburg.
Friday 19th	Reh. Salzburg.
Saturday 20th	Reh 10am. Radio 4pm.
Sunday 21st	Salzburg 11am.
Monday 22nd	Salzburg [*Das Lied von der Erde*. Bruno Walter].
Thursday 25th	Home again – grand.
Saturday 27th	Phyll 2.30.
Sunday 28th	Phyll 10.30.
Monday 29th	Phyll 11am. John 5.30.
Tuesday 30th	Prof 3–4.30
Wednesday 31st	John 2.30. [To Edinburgh]. D3 [sleeper berth] 10.30[pm].

September:

Thursday 1st	Collect return journey sleeper 10pm 11th Sept.
Friday 2nd	Ailie lunch.
Saturday 3rd	Morning concert. Afternoon party. Lunch Cowans – Alice
Sunday 4th	Rehearsal *Kindertotenlieder* morning. Reh 6pm Dr Jacques.
Monday 5th	Edinburgh. Freemasons. *Laudamus Te*. *St Teresa*. Lunch Peter. Dr Reininck. 4pm Festival Club. Mr Morton.
Tuesday 6th	Aksel [Schiøtz] – morning, Moran 1pm *Albion* [Hotel]. Call for music. Ailie 4pm. Turner-over!
Wednesday 7th	Edinburgh. Usher Hall. Evening [7.30–9pm]. Recital with Bruno Walter. Junge Nonne, Du bist die Ruh, Du liebst mich nicht, Tod und das Mädchen, Suleika, Romance. *Frauenliebe und Leben*. Immer leiser, Der Tod, Sonntag Morgen, Wir wandelten, Von ewiger Liebe, Botschaft. Supper *Albion* [Hotel].
Thursday 8th	Edinburgh. *Kindertotenlieder*. B. Walter. Evening. Reh 12 noon. [Orchestre de la Société des Concerts du Conservatoire (Paris)].
Friday 9th	Lunch Roy. Beethoven programme 1st Symphony and 3rd (*Eroica*). Wunderbar!
Saturday 10th	Edinburgh. *Kindertotenlieder*. B. Walter. (Paris Orchestra). Evening. Luncheon French Ambassador. Dinner Aksel and Gerd [Schiøtz].
Sunday 11th	11.15 Moran [at] Festival Club. 12 Broadcast ['What the Edinburgh Festival has meant to me']. 2.30 Mr [Ian] Whyte.
Tuesday 13th	John 4pm mit frocks. Theatre John.
Friday 16th	Winnie Theatre 7.
Monday 19th	11–12. St Hilda's, Maida Vale, Shirland Rd. Canadian broadcast. 3 Harriet Cohen's friend. 4 Mr Moore.
Tuesday 20th	John 4pm. Emmie 7.15 Allies Club.
Wednesday 21st	2.30 Phyl. 7 Nigel Spottiswoode. 8pm dinner Dr Scholte.
Thursday 22nd	11 Phyllis.
Friday 23rd	Phyl. John, fitting!
Sunday 25th	Phyl 3pm.
Monday 26th	Phyl 11am.

Tuesday 27th	Ring Bruno Walter 9am *Hyde Park* Hotel. 2.45 Hair. Reh 6.30 *Criterion* Studio, 24–26 Lower Regent Street.
Wednesday 28th	London. Central Hall, Westminster. Bruno Walter. Evening. Recital! 9am balance test. Reh 10–1 Maida Vale.
Thursday 29th	Wedding 2.30 Lord Harewood [to pianist Marion Stein. According to her letter to Benita Cress of 10th October, Kathleen attended the premiere of *The Olympians* by Arthur Bliss at Covent Garden that evening].
Friday 30th	Reh 10–1. 6.30 Maida Vale.

October:

Saturday 1st	London. Albert Hall. Evening. Mahler 2nd (*Resurrection*). *Kindertotenlieder*. Bruno Walter. Reh 10 RAH. Dinner Alec and Alice.
Sunday 2nd	Broadcast 3–5. Bal Test. 2pm. Reception Austrian Society 6–8, 27 Pembroke Gdns, W8.
Monday 3rd	Boyd Neel 12.45. Mr Notcutt [dress fitting] 5.30.
Tuesday 4th	Recording [2.30pm Kingsway Hall, Mahler *Kindertotenlieder*. Vienna Philharmonic Orchestra, Bruno Walter, conductor, Walter Legge, producer]. Tower Hill Station – collect visas.
Wednesday 5th	[To Copenhagen, flight delayed by an hour] Reh 1–3. Brahms Alto. Che faro.
Thursday 6th	Copenhagen 8pm. Reh12. [Denmark Radio, Studio 1, Brahms Alto Rhapsody, Danish Radio Symphony Orchestra and Male Voice Chorus, Fritz Busch, conductor. Two Lieder: Von ewiger Liebe, Wir wandelten were encores accompanied by Phyllis Spurr]. 1800kr[oner].
Friday 7th	Stockholm.
Saturday 8th	Stockholm. Swedish broadcast. Suleika, Erster Verlust, Gretchen, Musensohn, Heidenröslein, Nur wer die Sehnsucht, Rastlose Liebe, Wandrers Nachtlied, Erlkönig.
Wednesday 12th	Oslo. Alto Rhapsody. 12 minute group. Lennox Berkeley.
Thursday 13th	Oslo.
Friday 14th	Oslo. [Alto Rhapsody. Studio of Norwegian Radio, Oslo Philharmonic Orchestra and Male Voice Chorus, Eric Tuxen, conductor].
Sunday 16th	[Studio of Norwegian Radio, song recital with Phyllis Spurr, piano. Songs and arias by Purcell, Handel, Wolf, Jensen].
Friday 21st	Copenhagen. Recital.
Sunday 23rd	Aarlborg.
Monday 24th	Aarhus.
Tuesday 25th	Copenhagen.
Wednesday 26th	Odense.
Friday 28th	Copenhagen. Edinburgh programme and: Vision, Turtle, Hark, Mad Bess, Piu dicesti, Lasciatemi morire, Che faro. Verborgenheit, Der Gärtner, Auf ein altes Bild, Wanderung

	and Musensohn. Bable, Soft day, Flower song, Ash grove, O.C.
Saturday 29th	[Arrives home 4.30–5].
Monday 31st	Infra-Ray Lamp £9.6.3.

November:

Tuesday 1st	Recording 6.30. Bach [Cantatas] 11 and 67. [Kingsway Hall, Cantata No.11. Ena Mitchell, William Herbert, William Parsons, Jacques Orchestra, Reginald Jacques, conductor].
Wednesday 2nd	RAH *Messiah*. Reh 10–1.
Thursday 3rd	Recording. Kingsway Hall. 6.30. [Cantata No.67. William Herbert, William Parsons, Jacques Orchestra, Reginald Jacques, conductor].
Friday 4th	Worcester Grammar School. Recital. Evening 7pm. Phyll. 11.45 Paddington. Spring, Soothing sleep, There's not a swain, Ech'ing air, Mad Bess. Gretchen, Wandrers Nachtlied, Suleika, Sonntag, Wir wandelten, Von ewiger Liebe. Ca' the yowes, Spanish lady, Shenandoah, Blow the wind, Keel row.
Saturday 5th	Dinner Peter Heyworth. *Eastgate* [Hotel, Oxford].
Sunday 6th	Oxford Town Hall. Aft recital 2.30 or 3. £52.10. Phyl. Caught train to Paris! Spring, Soothing sleep, Ech'ing air, Mad Bess. Suleika, Wandrers Nachtlied, Musensohn, Erlkönig. Modern English. Silent noon, M.G.W., Rahoon, A soft day, Bold unbiddable.
Monday 7th	Arrived Paris 9.30. Rehearsed 11. Lunch Lady Alexandra-Johnston. Sleep. Interview. Cocktail party. Rehearsal after good dinner.
Tuesday 8th	Paris Société Philharmonique. 20,000fr. Salle Gaveau. Hotel *Newton*. Mr André Collard [accompanist]. Rained hard but gazed at wondrous shops – rehearsed, lunched and slept.
Friday 11th	Edinburgh. Usher Hall. *Gerontius*. Reh 2.30.
Saturday 12th	Glasgow. St Andrew's Hall. *Dream [of Gerontius]*. *Central* [Hotel].
Monday 14th	Haslingden Arts Club. Assembly Hall. 7.30. Recital. Phyllis. *Midland* [Hotel]. 3pm. Spring, Turtle, Ech'ing air, Mad Bess. Che faro, Piu dicesti, Junge Nonne, Heidenröslein, Wir wandelten, Botschaft. Folk songs.
Wednesday 16th	Hull Music Club. University College. 7.45pm. Recital. Phyll. Spring, Lovelorn turtle, Ech'ing air, Mad Bess. Gretchen, Musensohn, Tod und das Mädchen, Heidenröslein, Erlkönig. Wir wandelten, Botschaft, Sonntag, Von ewiger Liebe. Ash grove, Ca' the yowes, Spanish lady, Shenandoah, Bobby Shaftoe.
Thursday 17th	York. British Music Society. Tempest Anderson Hall. 7.30. Recital. Phyll. Ditto [as Hull].
Sunday 20th	Bournemouth. Winter Gardens. Evening. Alto Rhapsody. Schlage doch. 9.45 Waterloo. [arr.] 12.30.

Monday 21st   Gerald 2pm. John tea.

Tuesday 22nd   Reh 6pm Hewitt St. *Midland* [Hotel].

Wednesday 23rd   Manchester. Albert Hall Reh 10–1. 12 noon. Lennox B[erkeley
                   Four Poems of St Teresa of Avila]. Brahms Alto [Rhapsody].
                   Broadcast 6.30. *Midland* [Hotel].

Thursday 24th   Manchester. Hallé. Albert Hall. 6pm. Lunch 12.45 Mr [Arthur]
                   Spencer. BBC. *Midland* [Hotel].

Friday 25th   Sheffield [as Manchester]. *Grand* [Hotel].

Sunday 27th   Cambridge Arts Theatre. 2.30. Recital – Gerald. Lady Whitby,
                   The Master's Lodge, Downing College. Spring, Soothing sleep,
                   Ech'ing air, Mad Bess. Junge Nonne, Suleika I, Musensohn,
                   Romance, Erlkönig. Wir wandelten, Botschaft, Am Sonntag
                   Morgen, Von ewiger Liebe. Sleep, P.R.T., Rahoon, M.G.W.,
                   Ash grove, O.C.

Monday 28th   Ring Basil – timings Bach. Ring tickets [for] Sat.

Tuesday 29th   Reading Town Hall. 7.30. [Recital] Gerald. Home same night.
                   Spring, Soothing sleep, Ech'ing air, Mad Bess. Junge Nonne,
                   Du bist die Ruh, Romance, Musensohn. Brahms (Cambridge).
                   Folksongs.

Wednesday 30th   London. Ministry of Supply. Thames House, North Canteen,
                   Millbank. 8.15. [reh] 6.30 Phyll. Spring, Soothing sleep,
                   Ech'ing air, Mad Bess. Whyte lily, Willow, Pur dicesti, Che
                   faro. Gretchen, Romance, Musensohn, Wandelten, Botschaft.
                   Ash grove, Spanish lady, Yowes, Bobby Shaftoe.

December:

Thursday 1st   Doncaster. Nether Hall Rd Church. Evening. *Messiah*. Reh
                   3pm. *Danum* [Hotel].

Friday 2nd   John tea.

Saturday 3rd   Lunch 12.45 Hans. 3.30 Phyll.

Sunday 4th   Poole, Dorset. Great Hall, Parkstone. Aft. 2.15. Phyll. Reading
                   programme [29 November].

Monday 5th   2.30 [train to Liverpool] 8pm Mr [Hugo] Rignold. 25 Sefton
                   Park Rd, L'pool 8.

Tuesday 6th   Liverpool Phil. 7pm. *Das Lied*. Reh 2pm.

Wednesday 7th   Dinner Mrs Tillett.

Thursday 8th   BBC 7.30–8.30. Reh 2.15. [25 mins]. B[roadcasting] H[ouse] LG
                   140. [Frederick Stone]. Wolf: Gesang Weylas, [Auf ein altes]
                   Bild, Auf einer Wanderung, Selbstgeständnis. Brahms: Die
                   Mainacht, Sapphische Ode, Botschaft, Nachtigall, Sonntag.

Friday 9th   Lunch Emmie 12.30.

Saturday 10th   Sheffield. Phil Society. City Hall. *Messiah* 7pm. (City of
                   Birmingham Orchestra). *Grand* [Hotel].

Sunday 11th   Manchester. Hallé. King's Hall. 2.30. *Messiah*. *Midland*
                   [Hotel].

Monday 12th   Gerald 2.30. John 5.30.

Tuesday 13th   Chelsea Music Club. Town Hall. 8pm. Recital. Gerald. Lady

	Piggott. Vision, Turtle, Hark, Swain on plain, Bess. *Frauenliebe.* Wir wandelten, Sonntag, Botschaft, Liebestreu.

Wednesday 14th   Lunch Mr Boosey. 12.45. Telemann Reh 11–12.

Thursday 15th   BBC Studio 5, Delaware Rd. Reh 4–6. [6–7]. Telemann. Bach. Dinner Basil (on me). [Bach: Vergiss mein nicht and Ach, dass nicht die letzte Stunde, Telemann: *Kleine Kantate von Wald und Au*. Millicent Silver, harpsichord, John Francis, flute, George Roth, cello]. 10.30 Mr Huggins.

Friday 16th   Roger Musgrave. Interview. 12.30 Hans M&S 82 Baker St.

Saturday 17th   Johnnie mit boy friend, Kensington 4pm. *Let's make an opera* 5.30. *She stoops to conquer.*

Monday 19th   10.5 Medical Dr Parsons. Recording [Schubert] Musensohn – Brahms [Botschaft, Sapphische Ode] 2.30 [Decca Studios, Broadhurst Gardens. Phyllis Spurr, piano].

Wednesday 21st   *Queen Eliz.* A58. £159!

Tuesday 27th   Mr McLean 11.30. Mr Mertens 12.30.

Wednesday 28th   Supper Willie's.

Thursday 29th   Dinner 7.30 Mr Hawkes 710 Park Ave.

Friday 30th   11 Mr Hermann C.B.S. 12.30 Paul Moor. Mary Townsend 7pm.

Saturday 31st   Page Edwards 11am. Dickie 12.30. Party Ann's.

Diary for 1950

January:

Sunday 1st   Breakfast – Johnny [Newmark]. Willie 5.30. Party – Ruth Draper's 7.15. Lovely, sang lots of songs. Johnny played beautifully. Arrived in New York after terrible difficulty of Immigration – only just made it after contacting embassies and lawyers – and at great expense. What a to-do!

Monday 2nd   Mr McLean 11.30. Luncheon Rudi [Bing]. Very nice. The Stiedrys came in. Train 5.25 to Tennessee.

Tuesday 3rd   Arrived 4. Met by Alice Sumsion's sister! Very warm weather.

Wednesday 4th   Nashville – Tennessee Community. Lovely concert – very appreciative. Caught train for Cincinnatti 11.45pm. Lost my beautiful brolly.

Thursday 5th   Arrived Cincinnatti, slept a lot, saw a good flick, *The Heiress* and had lovely dinner in most modern hotel in the world! Caught night train to Lancaster.

Friday 6th   Lancaster, Pennsylvania. Arrive 1.50pm. No one to meet us. Full audience but bad-tempered at casual treatment.

Saturday 7th   Left for New York 9am. Rehearsed for tomorrow.

Sunday 8th   New Friends [of Music]. New York. [Town Hall] 3 Bach. Brahms Serious. Very nervous but staggered through. Party – Ralph Hawkes, very nice then on to Simon Goldberg's. Late to bed 2am.

Monday 9th   11 Hair. Mrs Lit lunch 1pm. Hotel *Regis*, Oak Room. 6 Dinner with Andre. Tommy Scherman concert 8.30. Quite a day! Had lesson with Clytie Mundy, wonderful help!

Tuesday 10th   Packed, caught 12.55 train for Columbia.

Wednesday 11th   Columbia, Missouri. Straight sales. How changed, Turtle, Hark, Bess. *Frauenliebe*. Botschaft, Wandelten, Von ewiger Liebe, S.N. [Silent noon], M.G.W., Soft day, Bold unbidd. Train late. Missed all connections. Four hours on Greyhound bus. Met with bouquet and many students and Benita [Cress] and Stella from La X! Lovely concert.

Thursday 12th   Fulton. Went by car – another lovely concert, but tired. Reception after, nothing to eat much, so repaired to dive and had bacon and eggs at midnight! Lovely!

Friday 13th   Car to Mexico Mo. [Montana] and pleasant train ride to Kansas City. Saw *The Fallen Idol* – magnificent and good dinner afterwards. Washed 1000 of smalls.

Saturday 14th   Shopped. Rehearsed two hours and saw *Adam's Rib*. Very amusing. Grand dinner – the best yet.

Sunday 15th	Arrived Omaha. Went to see *Quartet* [film] – very fine.
Monday 16th	Omaha, Nebraska. Lovely concert – very cold and icy. Caught train for Chicago after concert.
Tuesday 17th	Met Ann on the station!! Lovely surprise. Shared a room at the *Steven* [Hotel]. Saw Danny Kaye in *The Inspector General* and had dinner with John Brakebill. Lovely day.
Wednesday 18th	Went to Freeport. Saw Bob Hope in *The Great Lover*. Very amusing.
Thursday 19th	Freeport, Ill. Five of Johnny's pals turned up. Concert a bit difficult but everybody pleased. Sang *Frauenliebe* afterwards in private house.
Friday 20th	Arrived 7.28. Benita and Bill [Cress] to meet me and cameraman. Such a welcome! Wonderful dinner and bed.
Saturday 21st	La Crosse. Alto Rhap and Pergolesi *Stabat Mater*. Rehearsal 1.45. Concert went well – did extra group and Johnny came speshully. Everybody thrilled. Two bouquets of roses!
Sunday 22nd	Visited and had dinner at Stella's. Saw Mr Hood's jade – wonderful collection. Caught midnight train to Chicago.
Monday 23rd	Arrived 6am! Went to Dr Reynolds for sleep and bath. Caught 1.39 *The Chief* for Santa Fe.
Tuesday 24th	Arrived Lamy 1pm. Met by Mrs Sitz and driven to Santa Fe. 7000 feet high and very short of breath – but interesting and sun shining.
Wednesday 25th	Santa Fe. Bought earrings, bracelet and ring of silver and turquoise. All Indian work – also pinafore. Snow and hot sunshine. Concert went well but oh! so short of breath!
Thursday 26th	Caught 1pm train for Phoenix – wonderful day.
Friday 27th	Phoenix, Ariz. Arizona Ranch House. Wonderful weather.
Saturday 28th	Left for Los Angeles.
Sunday 29th	Met by Ann's Momma and Poppa [Mr and Mrs Pelliciotti] 7.25am. Delightful. Had dinner with Ann's cousin and family. Lovely – early to bed.
Tuesday 31st	Went to Bruno Walter's house – wonderful. Just Fanny and Adolph there to look after me. Lovely dinner and early to bed.
February:	
Thursday 2nd	Los Angeles. Concert went with a bang – all my pals there! Very casual man in charge. Lovely party afterwards at the Pellis [Pelliciotti family], bless them.
Saturday 4th	Went to Dottie's Mammy's for weekend. Lovely house and orchard and Siamese –Yum-yum.
Sunday 5th	Went to Santa Barbara for lunch and ride. Raining a bit but no matter. Lovely dinner in evening with friends of the Tetes [parents of Dottie Tete].
Monday 6th	Back home at 608 N. Bedford Dr. Bought new frock – grey jersey. Dinner Brazilians.
Tuesday 7th	11am Bullocks store. Pictures. Evening theatre *Turnabout*.

Fascinating, puppets and live show with Elsa Lanchester. Lovely day with Pellis.

Wednesday 8th	Fritzi Massary [Kathleen writes Massari]. 1pm luncheon. Gorgeous.
Friday 10th	9.45 20th Century Fox. Mrs Reinhardt 2pm Topanga Canyon. Mrs Hadow British Consul 7.30. 835 N. Orlando Ave.
Saturday 11th	10.45 Pellis. Wonderful day at Laguna Beach, San Juan de Capistramo and Knotts Berry Farm. Sunshine all the time – gorgeous.
Sunday 12th	Saw Ed. G. Robinson's collection of French paintings – wonderful. 8.30 musical evening. Slight hiatus about uninvited guest but otherwise lovely.
Monday 13th	Lunch Mrs Tete 12. Caught train for Sacramento. Mrs Pelli saw us off. Sad to go. Been just wonderful!
Tuesday 14th	Sacramento. Had hair done – good concert. Mr Skinner came for us, drove us 90 miles back to San Francisco. Had bacon and egg sandwich in fist on the way. Oh! so good. Bed 3am.
Wednesday 15th	Rehearsal 10. Fine. Bed, then drink at the *Top of the Mark* – wonderful and *Stromboli* – lousy!
Thursday 16th	San Francisco. *Orfeo*. Pierre Monteux. Went beautifully. Mrs Monteux gave me lovely pearl ring! Lucky Kaff. Flowers and flowers – real p.d. [prima donna].
Friday 17th	San Francisco – aft[ernoon]. Went well again. Reception at Yacht Club and lovely Chinese dinner over the longest bridge in the world. Mrs Monteux very amusing. Told Johnny to wipe the grease off his chin – I nearly choked!
Saturday 18th	San Francisco. Amusing lunch with the Monteuxs and another present of fox stole – beautiful. Concert went even better. So happy. Sweet Howard Skinner gave me lovely necklace of Peking glass and Mr Monteux extra cheque!! Spoiled to death.
Sunday 19th	Had lovely run in morning with Howard Skinner to see the giant Sequoia trees and lovely lunch at the Fisherman's Wharf. Caught afternoon train for Portland, Oregon.
Monday 20th	Arrived Portland. Anne Ferrier there to meet me! Dinner with friends. David big boy. Tired out! Johnny went on to Aberdeen – don't blame him!
Tuesday 21st	Aberdeen, Washington. Train and car to Aberdeen. Difficult hall and still worn out with wun thing and another! Nice party afterwards with Dr and wife.
Wednesday 22nd	Had extravagant taxi 60 miles to Tacoma. Can't bear changing with 8 pieces of luggage from locals to buses to trains. Non posso! Worth every dime! Met Anne and David on station and had dinner all together. Saw them off at 10pm!
Thursday 23rd	On train all day – lovely. Did a lot of work on Chausson [*Poème de l'amour et de la mer*].
Friday 24th	Arrived 9.30 La X. Met by Benita and Bill, bless 'em. Johnny

went on to Chicago. Went out for dinner and dance – good fun, but another very late night. My BAGS!

Saturday 25th — Tried fur coats on but none nice enough! Lovely dinner at Benita's.

Sunday 26th — Cocktail with Doc, then caught afternoon train to Chicago. Johnny met me – two presents from him, necklace, earrings etc, lovely. Gorgeous dinner and floor show at hotel. Lovely evening, but late again!

Monday 27th — Wheaton, Ill[inois]. Lunch with sweet Bruno after hearing rehearsal. Dr Evans drove us out. Concert only just took place, owing to coal strike. Icy cold but lovely audience and nice party afterwards. Drinks at Dr Evans afterwards.

Tuesday 28th — Luncheon with Mr Anderson. Went to Bruno's concert and saw him afterwards. Dinner again with Mr Anderson, also Johnny, and party at Drs Evans and Reynolds, both pets. Home early – K.K. – without supper!

March:

Wednesday 1st — Downers Grove. Dr Reynolds took us – Benita turned up! – still icy cold. Concert all right. Martinis in car, dinner afterwards in Pump Room. Nice.

Thursday 2nd — Johnny chose two new hats for me! Luncheon 1pm Ginette Young and Mrs Cardelli – nice. Tea 4pm Wolfgang Stresemann. Left for St Catherines.

Friday 3rd — St Catherines. Good concert and party at high-pitched laugh lady's. Nice pet just the same!

Saturday 4th — Taken to Niagara Falls! Very fine, nice luncheon overlooking them – icy cold weather. Caught train for Toronto.

Sunday 5th — Saw Terence Gibbs for dinner and Mr and Mrs Woods for cocktails. Radio show and supper at conductor's house. Lovely day. Rehearsed in aft[ernoon] at Grannie's. Johnny's girl friend!

Monday 6th — Peterborough. Went well – a thrilled audience. Still icy cold! Nice pet of a Gwen Brown, thrilled to bits. Party afterwards. Very nice. Bacon and eggs in coffee house after!!

Tuesday 7th — Train all day – met by Stella and Ethelwyn and all had gorgeous dinner, great enthusiasm all round. Flowers to greet me and everything beautiful. Bless their hearts!

Wednesday 8th — All day at Johnny's – shopping – met Eric McLean and sweet Frenchie [Paul] Roussel. Luncheon cooked by J. – dinner at French place and party after. We rehearsed. Bed by 11pm.

Thursday 9th — Montreal. Vision, Turtle, Hark, Bess. *Frauenliebe*. Immer leiser, Am Sonntag Morgen, Botschaft, Wandelten, Von ewiger Liebe. S.N., M.G.W., Soft day, Bold unbiddable. Went beautifully and everybody thrilled. Party after, then dinner at Stella's. Home late.

Friday 10th — Luncheon with Ethelwyn at University Club with others – tea

	alone with her – two recorded interviews [CBC Radio with Eric McLean] and train to St John, N[ew] B[runswick].
Saturday 11th	St John N.B. Arrived at 11.40. Good rest in afternoon, needed it! Concert went well – nice party.
Sunday 12th	Went out to Rolf's – Johnny's pal – had walk in icy snow, fell four times!
Monday 13th	Moncton. Bit hard work but very nice. Tired out – not sleeping very well. Couldn't have bath – water icy cold. Not true! Cold water marked hot and hot, cold! Didn't discover it for a long time.
Tuesday 14th	Left for New York, going to have a hellova rush when I get there, but can relax for a bit now. Have developed a tickling throat, hope it's only morning dryness from this overheating. Discovered water's hot in cold tap! Ha! Clean again.
Wednesday 15th	Town Hall rehearsal 3pm. Two rehearsals. Off train and dinner with Ann and Dottie. Lovely!
Thursday 16th	Newark N.J. *Orfeo*. Rehearsal afternoon – went very well, but barn of a place and had fuss with spotlights – won at the interval! Home very late.
Friday 17th	New York. *Orfeo*. [Ann Ayars (Euridice), soprano, Louise Kinloch (Amor), soprano, The Little Orchestra Society, Thomas Scherman, conductor]. Ring Johnny. Went to see Walt Disney's *Cinderella*. <u>Lovely</u>. Slept, then wonderful reception. Supper at Mrs Scherman's. Nice.
Saturday 18th	Century Club 3pm. Lunch Paul Moor 12.1.5. 3pm reh. Didn't go, had headache. Rehearsal 6 Bruno. 9.30 Rudi. Essex House. Slightly dull!
Sunday 19th	Hunter College. Recital with Bruno Walter. Junge Nonne, Romance, Musensohn, Wandrers N., Du liebst mich nicht, Suleika. *Frauenliebe*. Immer leiser, Der Tod, Am Sonntag Morgen, Wir wandelten, Botschaft, Von ewiger Liebe. Lovely concert, full house. Bruno pleased. Party at Ann's afterwards, lovely.
Monday 20th	11am Judy Holliday. Luncheon Andre. 3.30 Mrs Mundy. Dinner *Majeski*. Horowitz wonderful! What a day!
Tuesday 21st	Butler, Pa. Arrived with stiffest neck after night in train – couldn't bow – and thought I sang like a cochon, but audience didn't seem to mind. Left after concert for Chicago.
Wednesday 22nd	Arrived Chicago 8am. Stayed with Mrs Cardelli – lovely. 2pm rehearsal. Wasted time for 2½ hrs, but rehearsed finally with Reiner. Party afterwards with President's wife. Slept 12 hours - wonderful.
Thursday 23rd	Chicago. *Kindertotenlieder*. Fritz Reiner. Went well – everybody thrilled. Had sandwiches at Cardelli's after with Dickie Leach, sweet Dr Reynolds, Evans and Jack Burton. Sweet poppets!
Friday 24th	Chicago. Afternoon. Wonderful notices – concert went even

	better. Lovely dinner with Mrs Cardelli for the Andersons. Great success.
Saturday 25th	Went to see Anderson baby. Lunch with Reynolds fan club – one too many Martinis – think I saw *Mad Woman of Chaillot*! Not impressed, but probably me! Cocktails with fan club and caught train for Toronto.
Sunday 26th	Johnny met me, bless him. All well. Rehearsed, slept, cocktail party and dinner with John Polwarth – late Newcastle BBC.
Monday 27th	Toronto. Bist du bei mir, Turtle, Hark, Mad Bess. Wandrers N., Du liebst mich nicht, Suleika, Musensohn, Four Serious Songs. Salley gdns., Spanish, Southerly, Keel row. Bought new frock. Wonderful last concert – everybody stamping and shouting! Party afterwards at Mrs Woods – lovely – she's a poppet!
Tuesday 28th	Had strange telephone call!! Lunch with Woods – nice. Dinner (last) with Johnny. Caught train for N.Y.
April:	
Tuesday 4th	Home again! All well.
Friday 7th	Glyndebourne. Lewes Musical Festival. *St Matthew Passion* (Black gown). Reh 10.30. 8.45 Vic[toria]. 8.50 [return] Lewes to Brighton.
Wednesday 12th	To theatre with J.T. [? John Turner]
Thursday 13th	Auntie May 2.30.
Friday 14th	Ring about Zurich hotel. Mr Krips 11.30. Anglo Austria 5.45.
Saturday 15th	Reading Town Hall 7pm. Mass in B minor. Soprano sing *Laudamus te*. Reh 3pm. (Black)
Sunday 16th	Lunch Sir George Fran[c]kenstein. 12 ock. Paddington-Taplow. *Devere* Hotel.
Monday 17th	Gerald 2.30. Norman supper.
Tuesday 18th	Newcastle-u-Lyme Municipal Hall. Evening recital. Gerald. (Blue chiffon) Highgate programme [see April 29th]. Taxi 11.40. Train 12.15 – 3.07. Ring about hotel, Switzerland.
Wednesday 19th	Reh 4.30.
Thursday 20th	Bournemouth. Winter Gardens. 7.30pm. *Das Lied von der Erde*. Reh morning. (Red gown). 50gns.
Friday 21st	Lunch with Dudley 1.15. *Kempinski*. Fittings before. Ena – Tea – Win.
Saturday 22nd	Reh 3–6pm.
Sunday 23rd	London RAH aft. *Das Lied von der Erde*. Josef Krips. Reh morning. (White satin) Balance 7pm EMI Studios Abbey Rd. 7.55 - 9.05. 45gns.
Monday 24th	Phyll 4.30.
Tuesday 25th	Wimbledon Town Hall 7.30 Phyll. Spring, Soothing, Hark, Mad Bess. Suleika, Wandrers N., Musensohn, Erlkönig. Wandelten, Botschaft, Sonntag Morgen, Von ewiger Liebe. Ash G., Ca', Shenandoah, Spanish, Bobby. Lovely supper after. Emmie,

	Jimmie Smith and Hamiltons. Taxi 6pm. Take Shenandoah. Rehearsal [morning] Freddie [for Thursday concert].
Wednesday 26th	12.30 Victor – *Casa Prada*. Order table!
Thursday 27th	Andre Mertens – lunch. Balance 6.15. Thursday concert *Frauenliebe*. [Frederick Stone]. Ticket for Alec. Meet him ¼ hour before broadcast.
Friday 28th	Kings Lynn. Town Hall 1 and 3.30. Two 45 minute recitals. 3.30 for children. 50gns. Bist du bei mir?, Turtle, Hark. Suleika, Wandrers N., Musensohn, Sonntag, Botschaft. [or] Sylvia, Haiden R., Musensohn, Sonntag, Vain suit. Salley Gdns., Spanish, Blow, Keel. Taxi 9[am].
Saturday 29th	Highgate. Central Hall. 7pm Recital. Phyll. 50gns. Bist du bei mir?, Turtle, Hark, Che faro. An die Musik, Du liebst m.n., Suleika, Musensohn. Botschaft. Wir wandelten, Sonntag, Von ewiger Liebe, Salley gdns., Spanish lady, Southerly, Keel row.
Sunday 30th	Uncle Bert.

May:

Monday 1st	Michael H[ead] and our Winnie 4.30.
Tuesday 2nd	Mr Carpenter 11am. Lunch John. *Fête du jour*. Fittings afternoon. 7.30 Emmie – Moiseiwitsch's.
Wednesday 3rd	Reh *Kindertotenlieder*, Albert Hall 11.30. 5.30 42 Malvern Court. Londonderry House 8pm. Park Lane. Lecture – Holland Festival.
Thursday 4th	Reh *Kindertotenlieder* 12pm. Lunch Boyd Neel 1pm Allies Club.
Friday 5th	Dorchester. Corn Exchange. 7.15. Recital. Phyll. 50gns. (as Bideford) [May 7th].
Sunday 7th	Bideford Grammar School. Recital. 3.15. Phyll. 50gns. Bist du bei mir, Turtle, Hark, Che faro. *Frauenliebe*. Wandelten, Sonntag, Botschaft. Bable, Soft day, Blow, Keel row.
Monday 8th	Birmingham. Barber Institute. 7pm. Phyll. Supper Anthony Lewis. Bist du bei mir? Lovelorn turtle, Whyte lily, Swain, Mad Bess. *Frauenliebe and Leben*. S.N., Piper, Salley gdns., Sleep, P.R.T.
Tuesday 9th	8.40 New St, Euston 11 [or] 9 Snow Hill, Paddington 11.20. 12.45 Miss Scott, Forum Club luncheon, 6 Grosvenor Place, Hyde Park Corner. John 3pm.
Wednesday 10th	Ring Emmie about Nov 7th. Dep[ar]t Kensington Air Station 13.13. Take off 14.28. Arrive 16.00 BEA.
Friday 12th	Amsterdam Reh 4.15. *Kindertotenlieder*. LPO. Van Beinum.
Saturday 13th	Dep[ar]t 13.45 KLM 14.45. Arrive Northolt 15.20.
Sunday 14th	Brighton. Dome. 2.45. 40gns. Herbert Menges. Che faro, Erbarme dich, Hark the echoing air. Encores. 11am Vic Southern [*Brighton*] *Belle*. Reh 12.15.
Monday 15th	Basil – lunch. St Mary's [Hospital, Paddington?]. 8.30pm. Derek Harvey [accompanist]. Turtle, Hark, Mad Bess. Suleika,

Musensohn, Wandelten, Sonntag, Von ewiger Liebe. Soft day, M.G.W., Salley, Spanish, Bonnet.

Wednesday 17th	Mrs Hamish Hamilton 43 Hamilton Terrace. 8pm dressed. Lovely.
Thursday 18th	Albert Hall *Kindertotenlieder*. van Beinum. Reh 10am.
Friday 19th	To Scotland.
Tuesday 30th	Salzburg Festival Society: 17 Hyde Pk Gardens, W2. 5.45. *Isola Bella*, Frith St. 7.30 Ann.
Wednesday 31st	6.30 Italian Institute. 39 Belgrave Square. Dinner Ann.

June:

Thursday 1st	[Else] Mayer-Lismann 6pm.
Friday 2nd	Alison's 12. Lunch H[amish] H[amilton] [at his] home 1pm.
Saturday 3rd	7.15. Ann *Venus Observed*. Wonderful. Met Sir Laurence.
Sunday 4th	Leave London 2pm.
Monday 5th	Arrive Zurich 8.57, leave 4.10. Arrive Vienna 6.20 Airport. *Astoria* Hotel.
Wednesday 7th	Photies 9.45. Reh *St Matthew Passion* 6pm.
Thursday 8th	Proben [Rehearsal] 10am *St Matt*.
Friday 9th	Vienna. *St Matthew Passion* 6pm. 9.30 *Magnificat* Grosser Musikvereinsaal. [Irmgard Seefried, soprano, Walther Ludwig, tenor, Paul Schoeffler, baritone, Walter Berry, bass-baritone, Otto Edelmann, bass, Wiener Singverein, Vienna Symphony Orchestra, Herbert von Karajan, conductor].
Saturday 10th	*Magnificat* 8pm.
Tuesday 13th	Reh 9.30. [Musikvereinsaal]. Lotte 4.30. Mrs Samuels 8.45. B-cks!
Wednesday 14th	Reh 9.30. [Musikvereinsaal]. 6pm Mr Hartmann. Krips – dinner.
Thursday 15th	Vienna. Reuter 12. [Bach] Mass in B minor 6pm. [Elisabeth Schwarzkopf, soprano, Walther Ludwig, tenor, Alfred Poell, baritone, Paul Schoeffler, bass. Wiener Singverein, Vienna Symphony Orchestra, Herbert von Karajan, conductor].
Saturday 17th	[Travel from Vienna to Zurich].
Monday 26th	Reh 7pm.
Tuesday 27th	Zurich. Tonhalle. *Kindertotenlieder*. Erich Kleiber. 1000 Swiss.
Thursday 29th	Arrived Milan. Met by Hans S. and Gamsjäger!
Friday 30th	Lovely day with Hans. Heard *Missa Solemnis* – Schwarzkopf esp. fine.

July:

Saturday 1st	Hans recalled because of international situation.
Sunday 2nd	Milan. *Scala*. Bach Mass [in B minor]. 9.15. Reh 11.30. [Performance] 9.15.
Monday 3rd	Milan. *Scala*. [another performance] 9.15. Miss Della Chiesa 11.30. Prue's birthday.
Tuesday 4th	Leave for Zurich. Zurich to Calais 10.5.

Wednesday 5th	Home 4–5.
Thursday 6th	Glyndebourne first night with Roy and family. Nice evening. Opera [*Die Entführung aus dem Serail* – Mozart] not bad.
Wednesday 12th	Johnny [Newmark] arrives. 2.30 recording. [Decca Studios, Broadhurst Gardens. Schumann Lieder, Brahms Four Serious Songs, Two traditional folksongs].
Thursday 13th	[Recording] 6.30 [but was probably cancelled].
Friday 14th	[Recording] 6.30 [as 12th].
Monday 17th	[Recording] 2.30 [as 12th]. Ethelwyn. 6.30 *Casa Prada*, Warren St.
Tuesday 18th	[Recording] 6.30 [but was probably cancelled]. Hans M&S 12.45.
Wednesday 19th	*Cosi* [*fan tutte*] with Stanleys – wonderful. [Glyndebourne].
Friday 21st	Joan Cross 2.30.
Saturday 22nd	Win's with Pop. 3pm.
Monday 24th	Lunch John – Allies [Club] 12.45. 6pm Phyll.
Tuesday 25th	Lesson 12. Tommy Scherman. *Beggars* [*Opera*] 7pm.
Wednesday 26th	10.45 Mr Dunston. 12. Prof. Phyl 6.30. Helen 8pm. Welcome to all pleasures *St Cecilia's Ode* – Novello.
Thursday 27th	11.45 Prof. Hans 6pm M&S.
Friday 28th	Dunstan 11am. 12 Prof. 1.15 John. Allies [Club].
Saturday 29th	Win 12.30 *Casa Prada*. Music for Oppi.
Monday 31st	Ring Phyll. Paddy's birthday. Oppi aft 3.30–5.30. Ice skating 7pm Manor House
August:	
Tuesday 1st	10.30 Mr Barnet. 12.30 Nancy's [Evans]. 3.30 Oppi.
Wednesday 2nd	Prof 11.45. Oppi. Dinner Parry 6.30.
Thursday 3rd	John 11.30. Oppi. Supper Victor.
Friday 4th	Prof 12.30. Oppi 2–4. Jamie 7.30.
Saturday 5th	3pm Oppi. Rick 96 Club.
Tuesday 8th	John 1pm Club. Fitting. Tate 5.10 Terence and Hans. Emmie dinner 7.15-ish.
Wednesday 9th	11.30 Prof. Ring Glyndebourne. Biddy Angus tea.
Thursday 10th	Reh. Glyndebourne. 11.45 Victoria [to Lewes] 12.48.
Friday 11th	3pm Prof. Jamie 7.30 Prom, dinner and dance. Gorgeous evening.
Saturday 12th	Fitting 5.30. John and Leon dinner on me.
Wednesday 16th	Alice lunch 1pm.
Thursday 17th	12.30 Emmie. Eva's [Turner] 7.30. 26 Palace Court W2.
Monday 21st	11.45 Prof. 7pm *Seagulls*. Emmie Apollo.
Thursday 24th	Send Stoke prog, also Manchester Midday. Edinburgh 10.15. [Telegram draft] See you for breakfast tomorrow Fri - much love.
Friday 25th	6 Heriot Row. *Ariadne*.
Saturday 26th	Ena lunch? Round after concert.
Sunday 27th	Reh 9.30. Victoria de los Angeles.

Monday 28th	Edinburgh. Usher Hall. Evening. Brahms Alto Rhapsody.
Tuesday 29th	Jennie Tourel – recital. Fine.
Wednesday 30th	11 Grillers. Lunch 12.30 Jennie Tourel. 7pm Theatre. *Figaro* with Alice.
Thursday 31st	Mr and Mrs Cowan lunch.

September:

Friday 1st	Lunch – home 12.
Saturday 2nd	Lunch. George London 12.15 here.
Sunday 3rd	Peter D[iamand].
Monday 4th	10.30 Press conference. Peter 12.30.
Tuesday 5th	George London 1pm *Union* Grill. Ailie [Cullen] 4.30.
Wednesday 6th	1pm Rhona.
Thursday 7th	Portrait 2.30. Audrey Christie 4pm.
Saturday 9th	Gerald 10am, Ben and Peter 11am. Send Cambridge prog. Lunch Jamie and Jack Jones. Win and Jane Tea. Rick Supper.
Sunday 10th	Rick lunch. Dinner Ann, Fluffy, Win, Robert.
Monday 11th	Hanley. Recital with Gerald. Spring, Soothing sleep, Whyte lily, Che faro. An die Musik, Lachen und Weinen, Musensohn, Wandrers Nachtlied, Erlkönig. Brahms Serious. Ca' the yowes, Fidgety B., Spanish lady, Southerly, Keel row.
Tuesday 12th	Marx Bros.
Thursday 14th	London Prom. Brahms Serious Songs. [Sir Malcolm Sargent, conductor]. Reh 11.30. Dinner Malcolm and Hamiltons. Monologue from Malcolm!
Friday 15th	Reh Rudolf Steiner Hall, NW1. 11am for Swansea.
Saturday 16th	BBC. Orchestral. *Kindertotenlieder.* 2.30 Camden Theatre. Taxi 8pm.
Monday 18th	BBC. 11am Freddie [Stone]. 7.45 reh Maida 3. 8.50–9.25. Brahms: O komme holde Sommernacht, Scheiden und meiden, In der Ferne, Blinde Kuh, Jungfräulein, Die Sonne scheint nicht mehr. Cornelius: *Brautlieder.*
Tuesday 19th	Pre-recording Music in Miniature. Studio 2 Delaware Rd, Maida Vale 10–1. Memorial service Suggia – Brahms. Win supper. Mrs Russell Smith 6.45.
Wednesday 20th	*Vogue* 12 noon. Irving Penn. 7 Rossetti Studios, Flood St. Kings Rd. Paul Moor 1.30 *Isola Bella* Frith St.
Thursday 21st	Swansea Brangwyn Hall. *Kindertotenlieder.* Possibly *Spring Symphony* [scored through] Che faro. Reh 5pm. *Grand* [Hotel].
Friday 22nd	2.30 Ben and Peter 22a Melbury Rd. 5pm Sir Thomas. *Ritz* Room 206.
Saturday 23rd	Reh: Arthur Wayne – accompanist [for Worthing next day]. Ann dinner.
Sunday 24th	Worthing. Pier Pavilion. 7.45. Rhapsody in English – Herbert Lodge. Love is a bable, A soft day, Fidgety bairn, The Spanish lady, Ca' the yowes. 4.30 [rehearsal].

Monday 25th   United Nations. Central Hall Westminster 6.45. Ben and Peter. Mad Bess, Lovelorn turtle. Duets (3). Lachen und Weinen, Suleika, Wandrers Nachtlied. I saw a ship, Ash grove, Ca' the yowes.

Tuesday 26th   10.45 Fleischmann. Parry lunch Casa 1pm.

Wednesday 27th   11.30 Gibson-Moore. 2pm John Wills. 4pm Phyll.

Thursday 28th   Thursday Concert BBC. 3.15. Reh 2.30–3.30. Wo die schönen Trompeten blasen, Urlicht, Ich ging mit Lust, Starke Einbildungskraft. Bable, Soft day, Twilight fancies, Homeward way, Go not happy day.

Friday 29th   Dr Fleischmann. Lunch 1pm Dudley *Kempinski's*. John and Leon dinner.

Saturday 30th   Mr Fleischmann 5pm. John 7pm. Decca contract renewed until September 1951.

October:

Monday 2nd   [Leeds] 5.30 Kings X. *Queen's* [Hotel]. Take *Spring* Symphony.

Tuesday 3rd   Leeds Town Hall 7.30. Reh 2pm. Dvorak – *Stabat Mater*. [Sir Thomas Beecham, conductor] Luncheon 12.15 Lord Mayor.

Wednesday 4th   Reh Manchester *Gerontius* 2–5 Hewitt St. Call at Hallé office first. Rosalind arriving.

Thursday 5th   Leeds Town Hall. Alto Rhapsody. 7.30pm. Reh 2pm. Emmie and Clem Roebuck.

Saturday 7th   Leeds Town Hall. *Gerontius*. 7.30. Reh 2pm. *Queens* [Hotel].

Monday 9th   2.45 Fleischmann.

Tuesday 10th   Lunch Maurice – *Isola Bella*. 6.30 Sadlers Wells *School for Fathers* with Hamiltons. Excellent. Met Compton Mackenzie.

Wednesday 11th   6pm Fleischmann. Reh 8pm Westminster Cathedral Hall.

Thursday 12th   RAH London Phil. *Gerontius*. 7.30. Sir Adrian. Dull in the extreme.

Friday 13th   Bath Abbey. 7pm. 2.35 train. *St Matthew Passion* Reh 6.30 - 9.30. *Fernley* [Hotel].

Saturday 14th   [Bath] Abbey Reh 10.30am. 2.30–4 Part 1 performance, 5–7 Part 2 performance. Elgar-Atkins [edition]. 8.30 Reception Banqueting Rm Guildhall.

Sunday 15th   Lunch Dorothy. Dinner Elsie. Party Cuthbert Bates.

Monday 16th   Bath. Pump Room. 3pm 'Schlage doch'. Shopping evening. Shoes £9. Dinner Elsie and Jean.

Tuesday 17th   Lunch – Mayor.

Wednesday 18th   Lunch – Lord Methuen.

Thursday 19th   [Bath] Abbey. *St John* [*Passion*]. Atkins [edition]. Rehearsal 10.30am. 4.30–6. Perf. 7.30.

Friday 20th   Lunch Mrs Ostrer 1.15pm. *Speranza*. Photie.

Sunday 22nd   Rhyl Music Club. Pavilion. 3pm. Gerald. Spring is coming, Soothing sleep, Hark, Mad Bess. An die Musik, Lachen und Weinen, Du liebst mich nicht, Musensohn. Wir wandelten,

	Botschaft, Sonntag, Von ewiger Liebe. Bable, Loughareema, Soft day. What is life – request. *Merville* Hotel. 11.35 sleeper.
Monday 23rd	Reh Phyll.
Tuesday 24th	Woking Music Club. Christchurch Hall. 8pm. Recital – take own pianist. Phyll. Car. Spring, Nightingale, Piu dicesti, Che faro, An die Musik, Gretchen, Lachen, Sylvia. Four Serious. Silent noon, Little Road to Beth[lehem], Piper, Blow, Bobby.
Wednesday 25th	London RAH Henry Wood [Concerts Society]. *Messiah*. 7.30. Reh 10–1.
Thursday 26th	12 Emmie and lunch. 3pm Mr Meadmore. 4pm Phyl.
Friday 27th	Shopping. 11.45 *Ritz* Rosalind. Maitlands ordered wonderful new gown for me. Oh boy! Rosalind, Alice and Alec *Second Mrs Tanqueray*. V.G.
Saturday 28th	11am Mr Fleischmann. 4 Phyl. 6.30 Jamie. Drinks. Nice.
Sunday 29th	Edinburgh. 10.15 Kings X.
Monday 30th	Bridge of Allan. Gerald. *Royal* Hotel. Rosalind's. Lovely concert. Also Wir wandelten, Botschaft, Sonntag, Von ewiger Liebe.
Tuesday 31st	Rosalind's.
November:	
Wednesday 1st	Perth. City Hall.3 groups, 12 mins each. Spring, Soothing sleep, Whyte lily, Che faro. An die Musik, Musensohn, Lachen und Weinen, Erl King. Ca' the yowes, Fidgety bairn, Southerly, Spanish lady, Keel row. *Salutation* [Hotel].
Thursday 2nd	Dundee. Chamber Music Club. Training College Hall. 7.30. *Royal British* [Hotel].
Friday 3rd	7.55 Pullman [train home].
Saturday 4th	Gerald 2pm. Victor. Short recital for gram[ophone] clubs.
Sunday 5th	Cambridge. Arts Theatre. Guildhall 2.45. Recital. Gerald. Supper 9.30 Emmie. Bist du bei mir, Turtle, Dido's lament, Hark. *Frauenliebe*. An die Musik, Du liebst mich nicht, Lachen und Weinen, Wandrers Nachtlied. Bable, A soft day, Twilight fancies, Go not happy day.
Tuesday 7th	Manchester Midday. 1.15–2pm. 36 mins singing. Edward Isaacs evening. *Grand* [Hotel]. Suleika, Lachen und Weinen, Musensohn. *Frauenliebe*. Wandelten, Sonntag, Botschaft. Ethelwyn's sister, Mrs Moon, lunch.
Wednesday 8th	Hanley. Victoria Hall. *Apostles*. Staggered thro' – don't like *Apostles*. Supper with Harry and Madge [Vincent]. *North Stafford* [Hotel].
Thursday 9th	Reh 7pm. *Gerontius*. Allan Brown. Central Hall.
Saturday 11th	London Central Hall. Westminster Choral. *Gerontius*.
Sunday 12th	Lunch Allies [Club] 12.30–1pm John and Leon.
Monday 13th	Dinner Hans. 6.30 Listened to broadcast of Scala Mass – v.g.
Tuesday 14th	Bolton. Victoria Hall. Evening recital. 7.15. Get accompanist.

	Phyl. Spring, Soothing sleep, Turtle, Che faro. Rest same as G[rims]by. *Grand* [Hotel].

Phyl. Spring, Soothing sleep, Turtle, Che faro. Rest same as G[rims]by. *Grand* [Hotel].

Wednesday 15th   Jamie's birthday. *Queen* [Hotel] Huddersfield.

Thursday 16th   Grimsby. Cleethorpes String [Orchestra]. Central Hall. 7.30. Phyll. Recital mit accomp. Spring. Nightingale, Turtle, Che faro. An die Musik, Musensohn, Lachen und Weinen, Erl King. Bable, A soft day, Twilight fancies, Go not happy day, Ca' the yowes, Fidgety bairn, Ash grove, Spanish lady.

Friday 17th   [draft telegram to Peter Diamand's Artists' Management] Diamanaging Amsterdam. Suggest Lennox Berkeley *Hymns of St Theresa*. 12 mins. Have my own orchestral parts.

Saturday 18th   Fly. Rehearsal – Bach.

Monday 20th   Haarlem Bach cantatas.

Tuesday 21st   Leiden. Recital

Wednesday 22nd   Arnhem. Recital.

Saturday 25th   Amsterdam. Small Hall. Bist du bei mir, Art thou troubled?, Dido's lament, Mad Bess. Suleika, Lachen und Weinen, [Romance from] *Rosamunde*, Wandrers Nachtlied, Musensohn. Wir wandelten, Botschaft, Sonntag, Von ewiger Liebe. Ca' the yowes – Britten, Fidgety bairn, I once loved a boy, Kitty my love.

Sunday 26th   Peter 3pm. 5 Dinner Otakar.

Monday 27th   Rotterdam. Recital.

Tuesday 28th   Rehs 4 and 7.30.

Wednesday 29th   Amsterdam. Gluck. Alto Rhapsody.

Thursday 30th   Amsterdam. Orch.

December:

Saturday 2nd   Hague. Gluck. Alto Rhap.

Monday 4th   Delft. Recital.

Wednesday 6th   Hague. Recital

Friday 8th   Amsterdam. Alma Musica. Big Hall. Where'er, Lovelorn. Gretchen, Jüngling an der Quelle, Du liebst mich nicht, Erl King. 4 Serious. Twilight fancies, Happy day, Salley – Gurney, Sigh no more.

Sunday 10th   Amsterdam. *Das Lied von der Erde*.

Tuesday 12th   Hengelo. Recital.

Thursday 14th   Kathleen Long reh. Gerald – lecture 7pm.

Friday 15th   Oxford. Private party given by Mrs Atkinson. Boars Hill House, Boars Hill. Recital with K. Long. *Frauenliebe*. Schubert: Suleika, Gretchen, Lachen und Weinen, Musensohn.

Saturday 16th   Lunch Emmie at Jamie's. Nice!

Sunday 17th   Rick 4pm.

Monday 18th   Fitting 12 o'clock. Phone Arthur Spencer 11–4 o'clock.

Tuesday 19th   10.30 Phyl. 9pm. Gerald. 20 gns. Lady Norman, Thorpe Lodge, Campden Hill.W8.

Wednesday 20th   Ruth – Jamie lunch. John 7 o/c.

Thursday 21st	Win 11 MM [Club]. Emmie lunch 1pm at office.
Friday 22nd	Peter P[ears] 1pm *Quo Vadis* 26 Dean St. Emmie dinner 7.30.
Saturday 23rd	Maurice 6pm.
Wednesday 27th	11am Sir Arthur Bliss. 1pm Norman. 7pm Michael.
Thursday 28th	Lunch Krips 1pm De Vere. 3pm BBC Yalding House. Bable, Stanford. Bliss.
Friday 29th	BBC North Region. 8.30 [recorded Studio 2 Maida Vale]. Gerald. Lunch 1pm Hamiltons. Where'er, Turtle. Gretchen, Lachen, Musensohn. Silent noon, Bethlehem, Sigh no more.
Saturday 30th	Madge tea.
Sunday 31st	11 Emmie – paints. Tea – John's.

Diary for 1951

January:

Monday 1st — Hans and Terence to supper. Pop not well at all – in bed with flu.

Tuesday 2nd — Flew in snowstorm to Amsterdam. Peter [Diamand] waiting with red tulips. Rehearsal 4pm, 8–10. Bed early.

Wednesday 3rd — Massage 9. Reh. 10.30–1. 2.30 -4. Dinner Mr Bruck.

Thursday 4th — Massage 8.45. Reh. 10–2, 3–6. Very tired. Dinner with Roderick Jones.

Friday 5th — Overslept. Reh 10–1. Slept all afternoon, mended and wrote letters. Rang Paddy. All well.

Saturday 6th — Mr Bruck dinner.

Sunday 7th — Dinner Cronheims 7pm.

Tuesday 9th — *Orfeo*. Amsterdam. [Greet Koeman (Euridice), Nel Duval (Amor), Netherlands Opera Chorus and Orchestra, conductor Charles Bruck].

Thursday 11th — *Orfeo*.

Sunday 14th — Opera matinée. Coffee Mr Bruck.

Monday 15th — 4.45 Flot.

Tuesday 16th — *Orfeo*.

[Pages for 17th, 18th, 19th and 20th January are missing but letters to Win and to Stella mention 17th as the day she travelled by train at 12.30 to Paris while the forward planner mentions P.B. Lesson, Paris on the five consecutive days 18th to 22nd January. P.B. was the singer Pierre Bernac].

Sunday 21st — Lunch Charles Bruck. *Orfeo* 9pm.

Monday 22nd — RASOLINE Molinard of Grasse [shaving cream] for John. Party Madame Gélis-Didot 6–8.

Tuesday 23rd — Paris. Recital. Popular. Gerald. Where'er, Turtle, Hark, Mad Bess. Gretchen, Lachen und Weinen, Wandrers N., Erl King. Pur dicesti, Lasciatemi, Che faro. Bable, Loughareema, Ca' the yowes, Spanish lady, Ash grove.

Wednesday 24th — Train 7.30! Arrive Zurich 2.56. Leave 4.2, St Gallen 5.13. Reh 8pm Tonhallesalle. Hotel *Hecht* St Gallen.

Thursday 25th — St Gallen Switz. 1,000 Swiss francs. *Kindertotenlieder*. Reh 11am.

Friday 26th — 9.53am. arr 11.35. Rehearse aft. Walter Lang 5pm. Bluidy awful. *Dolder Grand*.

Saturday 27th — Zurich radio. Aft 5–6. Where'er, Turtle, Gretchen, Lachen, Musensohn, Silent Noon, Bethlehem, Sigh no more. Rosalind [Maitland was staying in Rome], Via Principessa Clotilde 2, Rome. Capn. N[igel] Henderson.

Sunday 28th	Zurich recital. Tonhalle 8.15. Kleine Saal. As Paris [see January 23rd]. Oh! so depressed. Kennedy Cook. British Council.
Monday 29th	Leave for Rome. 14.08.
Tuesday 30th	My pappy died peacefully after flu and slight stroke. Rang up home and decided to carry on with tour. Had all my Swiss francs stolen £40. Rather bleak day. Hotel *Savoia*.
Wednesday 31st	Take music. 3 tickets. Mr Favoretto 12 noon. Klemperer 2 tickets. *Flora* Hotel. Cocktail party. Dine 9pm.

February:
Thursday 1st	Morning Sistine Chapel. Lunch 1pm. Kennedy Cook. Rehearsal 3pm Favoretto.
Friday 2nd	Rome. Recital. Rehearsal and lunch. Giorgio Favoretto. Supper party. Where'er, Turtle, Hark, Mad Bess. Pur dicesti, Lascia, Che faro. Gretchen, Lachen, Musensohn, Sonntag, Botschaft. Bable, Lough, Ca' the y, Spanish.
Saturday 3rd	12pm. 5pm rehearsal.
Sunday 4th	Florence. Cara sposa, Ombra mai fu. *Kindertotenlieder*. 5pm. Take orchestral material. *Anglo-Americano* Hotel.

[Pages for February 6th to 9th inclusive (Milan and Turin) are missing from the diary but Italian Radio lists a recording session at RAI Studios on Tuesday 6th February with Giorgio Favoretto accompanying Kathleen in the programme she had sung with him in Rome four days earlier].

Saturday 10th	Caught 6.45am train. Arrived Perugia 8.45pm. Tired out. Dinner party at end of it!
Sunday 11th	Perouse. Recital. Stayed with Count Ranieri Sorbello. Very nice.
Monday 12th	Caught 9.40 train.
Tuesday 13th	Paris. Hurrah! Arrived 10.30. 5pm lesson [one of three with Pierre Bernac].
Wednesday 14th	4.30 Lesson.
Thursday 15th	7pm *Roblin*. Mr Harvey Wood. Lesson.
Friday 16th	Lunch 1pm Madame Gélis-Didot. Rehearsal 4.30pm Piano. Emmie coming 5pm. 6.30pm rehearsal. 4 tickets!!!!
Saturday 17th	10am rehearsal. Drink. 12.30 Mr H. Wood. Win and Emmie. Dinner Mamselle Gélis-Didot 7.30.
Sunday 18th	Paris. Orch aft. Carl Schuricht. Dinner Mme Boulanger.
Monday 19th	Home again – Emmie and Win came for supper. Auch John and Leon.
Wednesday 21st	12pm Fitting. Phyll. 3pm. Hans and Terence 6pm.
Thursday 22nd	Dinner Imperial College. Women's Assoc. Sir Roderic Hill. I made a shocking red-faced speech, sat down quick!
Friday 23rd	1.15 *Savoy Grill*. Noel Sullivan. Very nice San Francisco pet.
Monday 26th	Sold a lot of furniture for £70. Bernie [Hammond] came for tea – decided to try us out. Am delighted.
Tuesday 27th	Train to Manchester 12.5. Reh 5pm.

Wednesday 28th   Manchester. Hallé. 6.30. Chausson. Albert Hall. Reh. 11.30. Supper Sir John – lovely! Concert great success.

March:

Thursday 1st   Manchester. Albert Hall. 6pm. Supper – Sir John.

Friday 2nd   Piano reh 11am. Hewitt Street.

Saturday 3rd   Reh 10–1, 2–5 Manchester Town Hall. [Broadcast 8–8.50pm Milton Hall, Deansgate Chausson *Poème de l'amour et de la mer*, Hallé Orchestra, Sir John Barbirolli (JB), conductor].

Sunday 4th   Manchester. Belle Vue. *Orfeo*. 3pm. Reh King's Hall 10–1. Went without a slip. JB thrilled, orchestra magnificent. Audience wonderful. Great reception mit flowers for us all. <u>Very</u> nice too. Stay [*Midland* Hotel erased]. Went back to JB's.

Monday 5th   Stayed at JB's. Easy day. Had walk and saw Whitworth Museum and another. Bed afternoon. Easy evening and lamb and garlick. Oh boy!

Tuesday 6th   Rode to Hanley in Daimler with JB – very grand. Went to rehearsal and had merry supper with him and Ena. <u>Am</u> enjoying this. Went to solicitor, swearing affidavit my Pappy's will – one more job done.

Wednesday 7th   Hanley. Victoria Hall. Hallé. 7pm. *Orfeo*. Reh 2–5. Went beautifully. JB <u>so</u> pleased. 50gns.

Thursday 8th   Caught train to Manchester. Stayed at *Grand*. Bed early.

Friday 9th   BBC Manchester. Chausson. 8–8.50. Milton Hall, Deansgate. Reh 2.30–5.3 Stayed at JB's. Saw his meat balls!! mit garlick.

Saturday 10th   Sheffield. *Orfeo*. 7pm. Reh 2–5. [City Hall. Sheffield Philharmonic Society, Hallé Orchestra, Ena Mitchell – Euridice, Fulvia Trevisani – Amor]. Went well. Lovely dinner afterwards. Rode back with JB to Manchester. Heavenly day – memorable 10 days!

Sunday 11th   Rick came for me – miserable day, snowing and blowing.

Tuesday 13th   Liverpool Phil. 7pm. *Kindertotenlieder*. Hugo Rignold. Reh 2–5. 75gns. Bit nosey but not so bad. JB lost his appendix bless him! Caught night train.

Wednesday 14th   One day home. Did a 1,000,000 jobs. Bernie doing wonders – everything fine!! Letters straight!! Great heavens!

Thursday 15th   Arrive 11.20 Cologne. Met by Maikie [Schill] and Mr Fineman. Very tired. Up at 5.15 this am. Told Bernie my worries.

Friday 16th   Cologne [radio]. *Dom* Hotel. Where'er, Turtle, Sleep, Spring. *Frauenliebe*. Gretchen, Lachen, Wandrers, Musensohn. Silent Noon, Pretty ring time, Ash grove, Spanish lady [according to KF's overview of 1951 prefacing this diary, these two days were spent recording a broadcast at Cologne Radio].

Saturday 17th   [Amsterdam scored through and the overview states] Cologne afternoon radio.

Sunday 18th   Amsterdam. Vierhouten or same as A'dam kleine Zaal. Spring,

Soothing sleep, Piu dicesti, Lasciatemi, Hark. *Frauenliebe.* S.N., Flower Song (*Rape*), Loughareema, P.R.T.

Tuesday 20th	Rotterdam. *St Matthew Passion.*
Wednesday 21st	Amsterdam. *St Matthew Passion.*
Good Friday 23rd	Glyndebourne. *St Matthew Passion.* Reh. 10.30. Cuts: 24–29, 38–41, 48–52, 62–69, 76. 50gns.
Saturday 24th	11am Interview Oslo. 12 Dr [Gwen] Hilton. All work cancelled.
Sunday 25th	**Albert Hall.** Painting.
Monday 26th	Painting.
Tuesday 27th	Roy's party. Jamie dinner.
Wednesday 28th	Medical? Roy and Bo. 6–8.
Thursday 29th	**Fly** [to Silkeborg]. Jamie. 7.45. Take Brahms Alto records.
Friday 30th	**Silkeborg.** 7.30 *Ritz* Alec.
Saturday 31st	Dinner Emmie.

April:

Monday 2nd	**Odense Recital** [forward planner says Aarhus].
Tuesday 3rd	Lunch with JB. Tea at home. Lovely day. Dinner at Jamie's.
Wednesday 4th	**Aarhus. Recital** [forward planner says Odense]. Lodovico on his knees. Flattered but non posso!
Friday 6th	**Copenhagen with chamber orchestra. 3 or 4 arias, 2 folksongs.** Wonderful dinner with JB. *Rules.* Memorable.
Saturday 7th	Lunch – Bernard [Burnet] Pavitt and Hamiltons.
Monday 9th	**Swedish broadcast Malmo 30 mins Lieder.** Hospital UCH.
Tuesday 10th	**Gothenburg. Orch.** *Kindertotenlieder.* Operated 5.30. OK.
Thursday 12th	**Copenhagen. Recital.**
Sunday 15th	**Stockholm. Recital £75.**
Monday 16th	**Stockholm. Radio.**
Tuesday 17th	**Reh.**
Wednesday 18th	**Oslo. Orchestra.**
Friday 20th	**Sarpsborg. Recital.**
Saturday 21st	**Oslo. Recital. Same as Stockholm.**
Monday 23rd	**Copenhagen. Recital. Same as Stockholm.**
Tuesday 24th	**Copenhagen. Radio. 10 mins with piano.**
Saturday 28th	**Send string parts to Marjorie Whyte, Ripley, Bromley, Kent** [for 26th May].
Sunday 29th	Uncle B.

May:

Friday 4th	**London.** [The English Opera Group had a Festival Season of operas by Britten at the Lyric Theatre, Hammersmith. Kathleen was scheduled to sing *Lucretia* on 11th, 12th and 19th and, as at the premiere in 1947, it was double cast with Nancy Evans on 16th and 17th. It seems most likely that Evans stood in for her].
Monday 7th	**Reh 3–6?**
Tuesday 8th	**London.**

Wednesday 9th	**Reh 10–1, 3–6.**
Thursday 10th	**Dress reh. 10–1.**
Friday 11th	*Lucretia.*
Saturday 12th	*Lucretia.*
Tuesday 15th	**Dorchester. Corn Exchange. Phyl. 7.15 Recital.**
Thursday 17th	**Cambridge. Guildhall. 8.30. Recital. Gerald. Brahms viola. 75gns.**
Saturday 19th	*Lucretia.*
Monday 21st	**Dorchester.**
Tuesday 22nd	**Peterborough Cathedral. Evening. *Gerontius*. 50gns.**
Thursday 24th	**London. Royal Choral Society. Albert Hall. Evening. *Gerontius*. Reh. 10am. 40gns.**
Saturday 26th	**Bromley. Ripley Choir. County School for Boys. 8pm. 50gns.**
Monday 28th	**Albert Hall. *Sea Pictures*. Malcolm.**
Wednesday 30th	**Croydon.**
Thursday 31st	**Hanley. Victoria Hall. *Gerontius*. Malcolm. 50gns.**

June:

Saturday 2nd	**Reh. am. Reh? pm.**
Sunday 3rd	**RAH. London Bach Choir. *St Matthew Passion*. 11am. 2.30. 50gns.**
Monday 4th	**Jennie Tourel. New Hall.**
Thursday 7th	**Newcastle-on-Tyne Assembly Rooms, Westgate. Recital. Gerald.**
Saturday 9th	**York Minster. *Gerontius*. Sir J.B. Reh 2pm.**
Sunday 10th	**Reh. pm.**
Monday 11th	**Wigmore Hall. 8pm. Reh 10.**
Thursday 14th	**Bournemouth Winter Gardens. *Das Lied* 8pm. 50gns.**
Friday 15th	**Pierre Bernac – Bournemouth**
Saturday 16th	**Dorchester. Corn Exchange. 7.15. Recital. Phyl. 87gns incl.**
Tuesday 19th	London RAH 7.30. Bach Choir. Mass in B minor. Reh 10–1. 50gns.
Thursday 21st	Winchester Music Club. Guildhall. Recital. Phyl. 75gns.
Friday 22nd	Reh. 3pm. Studio 1 M[aida] V[ale].
Saturday 23rd	BBC Third. Brahms Alto. 8–9.55 (9.05). Reh. 3.30.
Friday 29th	Norwich. City Hall. *Gerontius*. Evening. (Reh 10.30 *Messiah*, 11 The Close). 2.30 (Reh) *Gerontius*. St Andrew's Hall. 100gns.
Saturday 30th	Norwich. *Messiah*. Mng and aft. 6.25 train? [London Symphony Orchestra, Leader: George Stratton. Soloists: Margaret Ritchie, Kathleen Ferrier, Eric Greene, Richard Standen. Harpsichord: Boris Ord. Organ: Cyril Pearce. Conductor: Dr Heathcote Statham. This concert was part of the Norwich Festival and the Festival of Britain].

July:

Sunday 1st	Holland. [Flew to Schiphol Airport, Amsterdam to sing at the Holland Festival].

Monday 2nd	Holland [four-hour rehearsal].
Tuesday 3rd	*Orfeo*, Haag.
Wednesday 4th	*Orfeo*, Amsterdam.
Friday 6th	Bach Mass in B minor. [Georges Enesco, conductor]
Saturday 7th	Bach Mass in B minor.
Monday 9th	**Harrogate. Royal Hall. JB.** [morning rehearsal with Klemperer for Mahler 2].
Tuesday 10th	*Orfeo*, Amsterdam. [8.30pm Stadsschouwburg. Greet Koeman (Euridice), Nel Duval (Amor), Netherlands Opera Chorus and Orchestra, conductor Charles Bruck].
Thursday 12th	Concertgebouw, Amsterdam. Klemperer. Mahler 2nd. Kath and Jo Vincent [soprano]. Also *Kindertotenlieder*. [8.15pm. Concertgebouw Orchestra, Amsterdam Tonkunstkoor].
Friday 13th	Concertgebouw [Orchestra], Scheveningen [programme as the 12th].
Monday 16th	Reh 10–1, 6–9.
Tuesday 17th	BBC Bach Mass in B minor. [7.55–10.35pm. Concert Hall, Broadcasting House, London. Suzanne Danco (soprano), Peter Pears (tenor), Bruce Boyce (bass), Boyd Neel Orchestra, BBC Chorus, George Malcolm, harpsichord, Georges Enesco, conductor].
Wednesday 18th	Bach Mass in B minor.
Thursday 19th	Josef Krips 11.30. R. Garden Party. Jamie's 6pm.
Friday 20th	Hosp. 11.30. Lunch Ruth [Draper?] *Connaught*. Gerald 3pm.
Sunday 22nd	Brighton. Dome. 7. Alto Rhap. 50gns.
Wednesday 25th	To Liverpool.
Thursday 26th	Liverpool Phil. 4 Serious. Car to *Buxton Palace* Hotel.
Friday 27th	Kings Lynn. Evening. *Nelson* Mass. Bach [Cantata] 102. With Krips. [Boyd Neel scored through]. Lady Fermoy, Park House, Sandringham.
Saturday 28th	Kings Lynn. Recital afternoon. Gerald. Where'er, Turtle, Dido, Mad Bess. Piu dicesti, Lascia, Che faro. Ganymed, Ich ging mit Lust, Dein blaues Auge, Botschaft. Salley – Gurney, Go not happy day, Sleep, P.R.T., Folksongs: Ca' the yowes, Bairn, Spanish, Shaftoe.
Sunday 29th	BBC Birmingham 8–10. Reh 3–6 Nuffield Hall. Bach Cantata 102 and Haydn *Nelson* Mass.
Monday 30th	Hospital.
Tuesday 31st	Paddy's birthday.
August:	
Friday 3rd	Dr [Reginald] Hilton took me to Barbirollis at Seaford.
Saturday 4th	Lovely day out.
Sunday 5th	Another lovely day – Dr H to supper and brought me home.
Friday 17th	Myra [Hess] to tea.
Saturday 18th	Reh Bruno Walter aft. Very pleased.

Monday 20th   Paddy married. John and Evelyn came for me. Off to Seaford for five days. Pouring down.

Wednesday 22nd   Went to Rye and Winchelsea – feeling like death.

Friday 31st   To Scotland.

September:

Monday 3rd   Edinburgh. BBC. 7.30–10. [Song Recital] 12.30 at Queen St. Rehearse 12.45–2.30. 7–7.30 Balance. Ganymed, Lachen und Weinen, Suleika I and II, Wir wandelten, Ruhe Süssliebchen, Botschaft. *Frauenliebe.*

Tuesday 4th   **Recording. BBC. Frauenliebe. Brahms.**

Wednesday 5th   4.30 Bruno to 6.

Thursday 6th   Edinburgh Recital. Bruno Walter. 12.15pm rehearsal. An die Leyer, Ganymed, Lachen und Weinen, Wandrers N., Suleika I and II. Liebestreu, Auf dem See, Ruhe Süssliebchen, Dein blaues Auge, Mainacht, Heimkehr. Trompeten, Ich ging mit Lust, Ich bin der Welt, Ich atmet' einen Lindenduft, Um Mitternacht.

Friday 7th   Edinburgh. Chausson. Hallé. Sir John.

Sunday 9th   Marple. Regent Cinema. 8pm. Gerald. 75gns incl: accomp: Where'er, Turtle, Dido, Hark. *Frauen.* Bable, Lough, Salley-Gurney, P.R.T., Yowes, Kitty.

Wednesday 12th   Ilkley. King's Hall, Town Hall. Phyl. Incl: fee. Recital. 87gns incl: Dr Gott, Hampstead House, Ilkley. Where'er, Soothing, Hark, Bess. *Frauenliebe.* Après un rêve, Lydia, Nell. S.N., Go not, happy day, Little Rd., P.R.T.

Friday 14th   University College [Hospital] 11.30. Send p.c. to Dorchester.

Saturday 15th   Bournemouth. Winter Gardens. *Gerontius.* Evening 8pm. Reh 3pm.

Tuesday 18th   Dorchester. Corn Exchange. 7.15. Phyl. Inclusive fee. Where'er, Turtle, Dido, Bess. Junge N., Lachen & W., Suleika II, Ganymed, Musensohn. S.N., P.R.T., Salley, Yowes, Kitty, Bobby. Mrs Higginson, Stinsford House.

Wednesday 26th   Lord and Lady Methuen 6–8. 6 Primrose Hill Studios, Fitzroy Rd, NW1.

Thursday 27th   Nottingham. Albert Hall. 7pm. Hallé. Chausson – Tita [John Barbirolli]. Reh 3.30. *Victoria Station* [Hotel].

Friday 28th   John – tea.

Sunday 30th   [Decca] Gramo[phone] contract [renewed] until Sep 1953.

October:

Monday 1st   Milton Hall, Deansgate [Manchester]. Reh 2.30. *Midland* [Hotel].

Tuesday 2nd   BBC Manchester. 7.50–8.45. Reh 2.30. *The Enchantress* – Bliss. Meet Miss Pullen, friend [of] Millicent [Silver]. *Midland* [Hotel].

Wednesday 3rd   *Midland* [Hotel].

Thursday 4th	Hanley. Victoria Hall. 7pm. Recital. Phyl. Ring Harry. *North Staffs*. Where'er, Bess, Hark, Che faro. Junge Nonne, Musensohn, Mainacht, Botschaft, Ich ging mit Lust, Mitternacht. Silent Noon, P.R.T., Salley, Go not happy day, I once loved, Kitty.
Friday 5th	**Pittsburgh, Pennsylvania.**
Monday 8th	**Newark, Delaware.** Tita Supper? Ena Lunch. Emmie. Bun. Take Chausson.
Tuesday 9th	Basil C[ameron] 11am. Ruth [Draper?] *Connaught* 1pm. Win coming. Take *Das Lied*.
Wednesday 10th	**Ithaca, New York.**
Thursday 11th	Reh RAH 4pm.
Friday 12th	**Rehearsals, New York.** RAH 7.30. *Das Lied*. [conductor] Basil Cameron. Reh 10.45 [Richard Lewis, tenor].
Saturday 13th	**Rehearsals, New York.** John 7pm. J v der Gucht tea. [Jimmie] Smith 3.30.
Sunday 14th	**Rehearsals, New York.**
Monday 15th	**New York City.** Tita. Supper train? *Manetta*, Clarges St 1.15.
Tuesday 16th	***Queen Mary.***
Wednesday 17th	Hazel Pullen 3pm.
Thursday 18th	**Winona, Minnesota.** Maurice 12.30. Mr Carpenter 4.
Friday 19th	Yvonne lunch 1.15 Stephen Spender. Win – supper.
Saturday 20th	**St Paul's, Minnesota.** Dress rehearsal *Turandot*. Tita train. Supper? 10.45 stage door.
Monday 22nd	**Winnipeg, Canada.** *Turandot* first night.
Tuesday 23rd	Dentist 5pm. Sir JB 3pm.
Thursday 25th	**Montreal, Canada.** Dress Reh. *Aida* 5.45. 9.30 Mr Thompson.
Friday 26th	Basil – 50 St Martin's Lane 1pm. Dinner Rosalind 7.30. Bernie and me.
Saturday 27th	**Ottawa, Canada.** *Aida* 1st night. Dr Reg. Party Harewood's.
Sunday 28th	Painting!
Monday 29th	**Mount Royal, Canada.** *Aida*. Jimmy Smith. Lunch – Peter, Maria, *Isola Bella*, Frith St.
Tuesday 30th	Tita
Wednesday 31st	**Toronto.** Norman 6.30.
November:	
Thursday 1st	Hazel Pullen 3pm. Michael 4pm. *Magic Flute* 7pm. Basil.
Friday 2nd	**East Lansing, Michigan.** Intnl. Music Assoc. Elisabeth Schumann. 6pm 14 South Audley St, W1. Hospl. 11am. Parry 12.30 *Casa Prada*.
Saturday 3rd	Rick and Norman.
Tuesday 6th	**Louisville, Kentucky.** Maida Vale. Reh 10–1. Lunch Tita.
Wednesday 7th	11.45 Miss Heath [Marjorie or 'Binks']. 2pm John. 4pm Howard Ferguson. 6.15 *Bolivar* Dr Reg [Hilton]. Albert Hall Sir J. 8pm. Supper John, Evelyn, Reg, Mammy [Barbirolli's mother Mémé?].

Thursday 8th	**Cincinnatti.** Mateneé – Ruth. Evening Maida Vale? Sibelius. Isaac Stern. 8ish Dr Reg.
Friday 9th	Emmie dinner.
Saturday 10th	**New York City.** Hiltons. Tea Ruth 5pm.
Sunday 11th	Painting. Tita 7.45 Maida Vale.
Monday 12th	*Turandot.*
Tuesday 13th	**London, Ontario.** Jamie's.
Wednesday 14th	**Hamilton, Ontario.**
Friday 16th	[Manchester] Opening of the Free Trade Hall. Sang Land of Hope and Glory. The Queen there. Memorable day.
Saturday 17th	**Rehearsal, Coral Gables [Florida].** Manchester. Emmie and I to concert in new Hall – dinner afterwards. Very nice.
Sunday 18th	**Coral Gables.**
Monday 19th	**Coral Gables.** Clem's. [She stayed for three days with Clem Roebuck at Star Botton, near Skipton in Yorkshire].
Thursday 22nd	Home – lovely.
Sunday 25th	Gerald and Enid [Moore].
Monday 26th	**Carmel, California.** Hans and Terence, Emmie and Win. Ring Mr Carpenter.
Thursday 29th	**San Francisco.** Mr and Mrs Hamilton – evening.
Friday 30th	**San Francisco.** Phyl 3.30.
December:	
Saturday 1st	**San Francisco.** *Billy Budd.*
Monday 3rd	**Broadcast ?SF.** Gerald 11. 3.30 Hair.
Friday 4th	**Los Angeles, California.** [Recital]. Gerald. Lady Norman. Where'er, Hark the ech'ing air, Lasciatemi, Piu dicesti, Che faro. Bist du bei mir. Junge Nonne, Suleika I, Lachen und Weinen, Mainacht, Sonntag, Botschaft. Ca' the yowes, Ash grove, Blow, Bonnet, Kitty.
Wednesday 5th	Lunch 12.30 Café Royal. Terence G.
Thursday 6th	**Date near L.A.** Alice E. dinner.
Friday 7th	Neville Cardus – lunch *Ivy*. Emmie [and] Pierre Bernac dinner.
Saturday 8th	Win lunch. Phyl 3. [Ebe] Stignani.
Sunday 9th	Painting. Whacko!
Monday 10th	**Rehearsal, Chicago.** Recdg. 2–5. [Decca Studios, Broadhurst Gardens. Phyllis Spurr, piano. O waly, waly, I have a bonnet, My boy Willie, I will walk with my love, The stuttering lovers, Now Sleeps the crimson petal].
Tuesday 11th	**Rehearsal, Chicago.** Recdg. 2–5. [Decca Studios, Broadhurst Gardens. Phyllis Spurr, piano. Quilter songs: I know where I'm going, Fair house of joy, To daisies].
Wednesday 12th	Recdg. 2–5. [Decca Studios, Broadhurst Gardens. Phyllis Spurr, piano. Over the mountains, Ye banks and braes, Drink to me only]. Gerald 7.30.
Thursday 13th	**Chicago, Illinois.** 10.30 X-ray. 12.45 Rhona [Phillips] Aperitif, Jermyn St.

Friday 14th   **Chicago, Illinois.** Dr. 7 Wimpole St 4.15pm. Jamie's dinner.
Saturday 15th   Kathleen M[oorhouse] 4pm. To meet Neville Cardus' wife.
Sunday 16th   Painting.
Monday 17th   **Milwaukee, Wisconsin.** 1.30pm Hair. Myra 4.30.
Tuesday 18th   Norman [Allin].
Wednesday 19th   John. 20 Brunswick Gdns. 7.30.
Thursday 20th   Maikie 4pm. Gerald and Enid 6pm.
Friday 21st   Emmie's!
Saturday 22nd   Sir John 5.30.
Monday 24th   JB. Hair 3.15. Susannah's. Alison's.
Wednesday 26th   Gerald, Enid, Emmie, Roy, Bo, Win, Reg, JB, Yvonne, Jamie,
                    Norman A, Mrs Norman A, Hans, Terence, Bern[ie], me.
Thursday 27th   Sir John?
Friday 28th   Lunch – *Frears*? Sazzy [Myra Hess' companion, Anita 'Saz'
                    Gunn] 3pm.
Saturday 29th   Robert Masters – dinner. Tea – Vincents. Rick.
Monday 31st   Auntie May tea?

Diary for 1952

January:

Wednesday 2nd	Luncheon R.A.C. Pall Mall 12.45. Decca.
Thursday 3rd	12 John. 4 Elsie S. [Suddaby].
Friday 4th	Hair 10.30. Jamie 6pm.
Saturday 5th	Kathleen M. tea. Dinner out.
Monday 7th	London. Prom RAH 7.30. Reh mng. 12 noon. [Brahms Four Serious Songs, conductor Sir Malcolm Sargent].
Tuesday 8th	Ben's rehearsing. Train Ald[eburgh]. £2.15.9. Taxis £1. Taxi 10 miles £1.10. Porters 5/.
Wednesday 9th	Ben.
Thursday 10th	Home.
Friday 11th	John. 4. J.B.
Saturday 12th	Gerald 2.15. Emmie dinner. Rehearsal.
Sunday 13th	London – Festival Hall. 7.30 Chausson. Gaston Poulet [conductor]. Reh mng. Gerald Played. [Because orchestral parts for the soprano version had been erroneously sent, Gerald Moore agreed to accompany Kathleen in the *Poème*].
Monday 14th	Grimsby. Gerald. 7.30. Where'er, Soothing, Hark, Bess. Gretchen, Haiden Röslein, Suleika, Musensohn. Four Serious. S.N., Little Rd., P.R.T., Kitty. Mrs Osborne.
Tuesday 15th	Ring Mr Robson. *Pavilion* [Hotel, Scarborough].
Wednesday 16th	Scarborough. Central Hall. 7.30 Gerald. Where'er, Soothing, Hark, Bess. Piu dicesti, Lasciatemi morire, Che faro. Four Serious Songs. Silent noon, Go not happy day [G.N.H.D.], Little Rd., P.R.T.
Thursday 17th	Newcastle. 7.30. Old Assembly Rooms, Westgate Rd. Gerald. Junge Nonne, L & W [Lachen und Weinen], Suleika II, Ganymed, Musensohn. *Frauenliebe*. Four Serious Songs. S.N., G.N.H.Day, Salley, P.R.T.
Friday 18th	Lunch Dr Hutch?
Saturday 17th	Carlisle County High School Hall. Lismore Place 7.30. Gerald. Bist du bei mir, Turtle, Hark, Mad Bess. *Frauenliebe*. Gretchen, Lachen & W., Musensohn, Sonntag, Botschaft. Ca' the yowes, Blow, Keel row, Kitty.
Monday 21st	Nottingham. Reh 2.30. [Peter Pears, tenor, Benjamin Britten, piano] Che faro, Sweet nymph I go before my darling. Purcell: Corydon and Mopsa, Gretchen, Suleika II, Lachen und Weinen, Du liebst mich nicht. Cantata *Abraham and Isaac*. [premiere of Britten's Canticle II]. Ash grove, Waly, waly, Ca' the yowes, O[liver] Cromwell. *Victoria Station* [Hotel]. [Encore: 'The deaf woman's courtship' which Britten wrote especially for this tour].

Tuesday 22nd	Birmingham. [as Nottingham 21st]. *Grand* [Hotel].
Wednesday 23rd	Dinner Rick. *Adelphi* [Hotel].
Thursday 24th	Liverpool. [as Nottingham 21st]. *Adelphi.*
Friday 25th	Manchester. [stayed with] J.B. [as Nottingham 21st].
Sunday 27th	Skipton Town Hall. Gerald. 7.30. Where'er, Turtle, Dido, Mad Bess. Ganymed, L&W., Suleika II, Musensohn. *Frauenliebe*, S.N., Loughareema, Bable, Kitty.
Tuesday 29th	Lunch. Tita 1pm *Casa Prada*. John tea 4.30.
Wednesday 30th	Southall. King's Hall. 7.45. Gerald. Where'er, Turtle, Dido, Hark. *Frauenliebe*. Bable, Lough, Salley, P.R.T., Yowes, Kitty.
Thursday 31st	Ev[ening] dresses. Tita.

February:

Saturday 2nd	Reh 11am. Ben and Peter. Tita 5pm.
Sunday 3rd	Vic[toria] and Albert [Museum]. Ben and Peter. 11am reh. [first London performance of *Abraham and Isaac*], Suelika I and II.
Monday 4th	BBC Reh 2–3.30. Recdg. 3.30–5 Studio 2 Delaware Rd. Ganymed, Liebst mich nicht, Lachen & Weinen. Pur dicesti,. Sweet Nymph duets. Dialogue. Canticle [*Abraham and Isaac*, Peter Pears, tenor, Benjamin Britten, piano].
Tuesday 5th	Bristol. *Royal* [Hotel]. [as Nottingham 21st].
Wednesday 6th	Transmission 8.20–9.20. The King died. [broadcast postponed to 13th May].
Thursday 7th	Flying. BEA Kensington Air Stn. Coach 8.39. Take off 9.34 [to Belfast]. *Grand Central* [Hotel].
Friday 8th	Belfast Whitla Hall, Queen's University. 7.30. Gerald. Junge Nonne, L & Weinen, Suleika II, Ganymed, Musensohn. Chausson. Four Serious. *Grand Central* [Hotel].
Saturday 9th	Coach 8.15. Flight 9.10.
Sunday 10th	Tea John's. 4ish.
Monday 11th	Broadcast from B'ham. X-Ray 11.30am (perfect) Taxi hospital £1.
Tuesday 12th	4pm John. Bun.
Wednesday 13th	*Daily Dispatch* 3.30. Doc.
Thursday 14th	John – tea.
Friday 15th	**Paris.** King's funeral.
Saturday 16th	Lunch Mrs Ormerod. 12 Old Square, WC2. Taxis £1.5.
Sunday 17th	Rick coming.
Monday 18th	**Basle. Alto Rhap. An die Hoffnung. Reh mng.** Broadcast from B'ham. Taxis hosp. £1.
Tuesday 19th	**Basle.** Broadcast.
Wednesday 20th	Taxis hosp. £1.
Thursday 21st	**Fribourg.** Bet your life 7.30. Taxis £1.5.
Friday 22nd	**Reh. Berne 3pm piano.** Tita – lunch. Jamie – Sadlers Wells. Taxis hosp. £1.
Saturday 23rd	**Berne.** Saz 3pm. [Anita Gunn].

Monday 25th   **Reh Zurich**. Yvonne. Taxis hosp £1.
Tuesday 26th   **Zurich**. Reh am.
Wednesday 27th   **Winterthur**. June Osborne 3pm. Taxis hosp £1. Taxis £1.5.
Friday 29th   **La Chaux de Fonds.** Taxis hosp.£1.

March:
Saturday 1st   Taxis £1. Christopher's birthday. Alison. Lincoln's Inn and Mémé's for chicken. Lovely.
Sunday 2nd   **Zurich. Recital**. Ena [Mitchell] and Nancy E[vans] – supper. Taxis £1.
Monday 3rd   *King Lear*. Taxis hosp. £1.
Wednesday 5th   **Geneva Alt Rhap**. Ev. and Reg. Taxis hosp. £1.
Thursday 6th   **Lausanne**.
Friday 7th   **Neuchatel**. Ev. John Turner. Emmie's dinner 7.30 Taxis hosp. £1.
Monday 10th   **Düsseldorf**. Madge. Tea. Carpet. Taxis hosp. £1.
Tuesday 11th   **Leverkusen Kasino**. Phyl 3.30. Flix. Accomp £1. Studio 10/-
Wednesday 12th   *Much ado*. Wonderful. Taxis hosp. £1. Taxis. Play £1.
Thursday 13th   **Cologne – Recital**. Tita!
Friday 14th   **Reh. Köln**. Tita. Supper. Gerald? Taxis hosp. £1.
Saturday 15th   Alison and Gordon – tea. Win.
Sunday 16th   **Cologne.** *Orfeo*.
Monday 17th   **Cologne.** Taxis hosp. Tita.
Tuesday 18th   Lady Norman 7.45. John 5.30–6pm. Taxis £1.
Wednesday 19th   **Baden-Baden. Recital broadcast**. Taxis hosp. £1.
Thursday 20th   **Baden-Baden**. Listen? Jamie and Yvonne to lunch.
Friday 21st   **Reh. *Das Lied***. Taxis hosp. £1. Mrs Ian Hunter at home 6–8. Lennox Berkeley.
Saturday 22nd   **Reh. *Das Lied***. Robert Wallenborn. 7pm.
Sunday 23rd   **Baden-Baden. *Das Lied von der Erde***.
Monday 24th   **Frankfurt. Alto Rhap. Where'er, Cradle song, Hark, Che faro.**
Tuesday 25th   Festival Hall London Phil [Boult]. Alto Rhap. Schlage doch, Che faro. Reh. 12 noon
Wednesday 26th   Tita lunch. Haydn, Ravel concert. Lovely. Taxis £1.
Friday 28th   G. M. [?Gerald Moore] afternoon. Rehearsal pianist £1.10.
Saturday 29th   Reh morning and evening. Kingsway Hall. Taxis £3.
Sunday 30th   RAH, London. *St Matthew Passion* 11am. 2.30. Taxis £2.10.

April:
Tuesday 1st   Middle Benchers. 5pm Where'er, Turtle, Hark, Che faro. Gretchen, Lachen und Weinen, Musensohn, Sonntag, Botschaft. S.N., Loughareema, Bable, Blow, Kitty.
Wednesday 2nd   BBC Third [Programme]. Brahms songs 9.55–11.20. Reh 8–9 BBC Concert Hall. Taxis £1.10. [Frederick Stone, piano]. Ruhe Süss, Auf dem See, Der Tod, Wir wandelten, Es schauen, Der Jäger.

Thursday 3rd	Theatre. *Call me Madam*. Taxis £1.5, Theatre £1.10, Dinner £4.10.
Friday 4th	Reh 12. Tita. Taxis £1.10.
Saturday 5th	Reh? 2.30. Taxis £1.10. Papers and periodicals for year £12.18.
Sunday 6th	Festival Hall. Evening. *St Theresa*. *Enchantress* [Arthur Bliss]. (1st London perf.) Hugo Rignold.
Monday 7th	BBC Third [Programme]. 9.10–10.5. 10.25–10.55. *St Theresa*. Bliss. Reh 6–8.30. Studio 1, Maida Vale. Taxis £1.
Wednesday 9th	To Manchester 6pm [arr.] 9.40.
Thursday 10th	Manchester. Free Trade Hall. Hallé. *Gerontius* 7pm. Reh 3pm FTH. Taxis £1.10. Flowers 15/-. Throat sweets 3/9d, Telephone 5/6d.
Good Friday 11th	Doctor £3.3. Medicine 15/-.
Saturday 12th	Reh 2–5. Hewitt St. Taxis 15/-.
Sunday 13th	Manchester Free Trade Hall. *Messiah*. 2.30. Reh 11 FTH. Taxis £1.10.
Monday 14th	Tita. *Aida*.
Tuesday 15th	Emmie's. X-Ray 3pm. Taxi £1.10.
Wednesday 16th	Hair 2pm. Biddy Tea. Win Row!
Thursday 17th	Yvonne's [Hamilton].
Friday 18th	Hendersons – tea. Theatre.
Saturday 19th	To Manchester. Mr and Mrs Douglas.
Monday 21st	Reh 10–1, 2–5 FTH [Free Trade Hall].
Tuesday 22nd	Heavenly birthday party mit cake! Studio broadcast *Das Lied*. BBC Third. Manchester 7.30–8.45. Reh 11am. Milton Hall. [Richard Lewis, tenor, Hallé Orchestra, Sir John Barbirolli, conductor]
Wednesday 23rd	Wolverhampton Civic Hall. Hallé. *Das Lied* 7pm. *Victoria Hotel*.
Thursday 24th	Manchester Free Trade Hall. Hallé. *Das Lied* 7pm. Ethelwyn 2pm.
Friday 25th	Hosp. 3pm.
Saturday 26th	Jamie and Yvonne 3pm. Bed all day.
Sunday 27th	Bed.
Monday 28th	Hosp. 10.45. 4pm Snakes. Roy? 8.45pm.
Tuesday 29th	Hosp. 10.45. Hair 4.45. Ena. Yvonne 6pm.
Wednesday 30th	Party! Queen Elizabeth and Princess Margaret – Eldon S[quare] – Lord Salisbury. Bonham Carter, Hamiltons etc etc. Marvellous – sang and sang with Gerald. Princess M. sang – <u>very</u> good! Memorable evening.

May:	
Thursday 1st	Hosp. 10.45. Fitting 12.15. Jamie's 6pm.
Friday 2nd	Sheffield City Hall. Hallé. *Das Lied* 7pm. Reh 2–5. 9.40 St Pan[cras]. *Grand* [Hotel].
Saturday 3rd	[Sheffield] Midland 10.58. [St Pancras] 2.39. Hans 6.30. Party Win's.

Sunday 4th   Uncle Bert – lunch. Sir Benj[amin] Ormerod.

Monday 5th   **Paris. Bruno Walter.** *Das Lied von der Erde.* **Theatre Champs Elysées**. 11.30am Hospital. Perry [Hart] 4pm.

Tuesday 6th   Hosp. 11.15. Lady Clark 1pm.

Wednesday 7th   10am Sir Stanford Cade. 11.45 Euston [Hanley] 2.54. Victoria Hall. Hallé. *Das Lied* 4pm.

Thursday 8th   Manchester. Reh 4tet. 4pm.

Friday 9th   **Wimborne**. Hans. Lovely dinner.

Saturday 10th   **Wimborne**.

Sunday 11th   Manchester – Hallé Pension [Fund Concert]. Alto Rhapsody. Art thou troubled, Cradle song, Hark.

Monday 12th   Hospl. 2. Hair 3.

Tuesday 13th   Fly 9.20 arr 2.20. BE 622. Hotel *Ambassador* Vienna. Fares to Vienna £106.

Wednesday 14th   [?Balance tests at Musikvereinsaal for recording sessions of *Das Lied von der Erde*]

Thursday 15th   [?Recording sessions for *Das Lied von der Erde*, Julius Patzak, tenor, Vienna Philharmonic Orchestra, Bruno Walter, conductor].

Friday 16th   [?as 15th].

Saturday 17th   Vienna [*Das Lied von der Erde*, Grosser Musikvereinsaal] 3pm. (7,000 shgs = £100).

Sunday 18th   Vienna [*Das Lied von der Erde*, Grosser Musikvereinsaal] 11am.

Monday 19th   [?Playback sessions of *Das Lied von der Erde*]. Lady Caccia 6 Metternichgasse Vienna.

Tuesday 20th   [?Recording sessions for three of Mahler's *Rückert* Lieder, Grosser Musikvereinsaal, Vienna Philharmonic Orchestra, Bruno Walter, conductor].

Wednesday 21st   Home. Taxi from airport £2.15.

Friday 23rd   Jamie lunch.

Saturday 24th   Train to Newcastle.

Sunday 25th   Newcastle-on-Tyne City Hall. Hallé. Aft 3pm. Reh 10am. [Chausson's *Poème*].

Monday 26th   Tita – supper.

Tuesday 27th   Reh 11.30 [at] 9 Hanover T[erra]ce, NW1. Reh Maida Vale 6.30.

Wednesday 28th   Royal Festival Hall 8. *Spring* Symphony. Sir M[alcolm] S[argent]. Reh mng 10am. Taxis £2.10.

Thursday 29th   Cambridge Guildhall. Recital. Gerald. Die junge Nonne, Suleika I, Gretchen, Ganymed, Musensohn. Brahms with viola. Nightingale – [Henry] Carey, Cradle song, Swain, Mad Bess, Silent noon, Loughareema, Salley gdns – Gurney, G.N.H. Day. Gordon Jacob [Songs of Innocence].

Saturday 31st   Wimborne. Bryanston School 4.30. Cranborne Chase School 8pm Bist du bei mir, Turtle, Hark, Piu dicesti, Che faro. An die Musik, Lachen und Weinen, Gretchen, Wandrers N.,

Musensohn. Loughareema, Go not H.D., Salley, P.R.T., Waly waly, O.C. Taxi home 12/6d.

June:

Tuesday 3rd	Festival Hall. Hallé. Sir J. *Gerontius* 8pm. Reh 3pm. Taxis £2.
Wednesday 4th	Tita – morning. 12.30 hospl. 4pm Frederick Stone.
Thursday 5th	Concert. BBC Home Service. Recital 7.30–8. 6.30 Concert hall. 8.45 Paris friends. [Frederick Stone, piano]. Loughareema, Soft day, Bable, Silent noon, Go not H.D., Sleep, P.R.T., Waly waly, Newcastle and another [Kitty my love].
Friday 6th	Win? 11am Angus McBean. 12.30 Hospl. Taxis £1.10.
Monday 9th	11.45 *Vogue*. 2 Hospl. Taxis £1.
Tuesday 10th	12.30 Hospl. Flo tea 4pm. Dinner Denis 7.30 9 Upper Killimore Gdns, W8.
Wednesday 11th	12.30 Hospl. Tita – aft. Theatre – Ruth.
Thursday 12th	Jamie dining 12.30. Tita aft. Taxis £1.
Friday 13th	Lunch. Pierre Bernac. Train to Aldeburgh. Taxi 12 miles. £1.10.
Thursday 19th	Canticle [*Abraham and Isaac*] with Peter.
Friday 20th	Tita dinner. Hotel.
Saturday 21st	Cornwall [with Emmie, Bernie and Win].
Monday 30th	K.M.V. birthday [Kathleen Mary Vincent – goddaughter].

July:

Thursday 3rd	Prue's birthday.
Saturday 12th	[Returned to London] Dinner on train £1.2s, Taxi home 12/6d, Hotel/Tips £4.
Monday 14th	12.30 Peter D[iamand] *Isola Bella*.
Tuesday 15th	Glyndebourne – *Macbeth*.
Wednesday 16th	Yvonne.
Thursday 17th	Bernie and I went to Burnet's – <u>so</u> comfortable.
Saturday 19th	Alan Jarvis arrived. Sang for the young Queen at Hon. David Bowes-Lyon. Burnet played – chatted for ½ hr. – lovely. Celebrated in champagne after till 2.30.
Tuesday 22nd	Gardened and wrote 21 letters. Lovely weather.
Wednesday 23rd	Free. Tita came – listened to *Tristan*.
Friday 25th	Hair 4.30. Yvonne 8.15.
Sunday 27th	Denis 1pm.
Monday 28th	John 12 noon. Willetts. Dick[in]s & Jones. Virginia Mather 4pm.
Tuesday 29th	Emmie dinner with Clive and Vera Robinson.
Wednesday 30th	Lovely day at Hatfield House. Evelyn, Mémé and John for supper afterwards. Burnet called in with photies.
Thursday 31st	Worked on *Orfeo* translation with JB. Wonderful dinner at Mémé's.

August:

Friday 1st	Lady Lamington 7.45. 26 Maitland Court.
Sunday 3rd	Ormerods.
Tuesday 5th	*Millionairess* matinée.
Wednesday 6th	*South Pacific* matinée.
Thursday 7th	Lunch. Mrs Spachner. Here 12.30. Ring for table *Isola Bella*. Entertaining £3.10.
Friday 8th	Rehearsal [for Hereford *Gerontius* 11 September] 3pm. Mr Meredith Davies. Emmie's.
Monday 11th	Gerald ringing. Willetts 11am. Hilda G-D friend.
Tuesday 12th	Back. Free till 25th. Parry – lunch. *Casa Prada* 1pm.
Wednesday 13th	2.30 John at Darnleys.
Thursday 14th	Tita. *Orfeo*.
Friday 15th	Noon. Helen Latham. Tita. Day out to Hughenden etc. lovely.
Saturday 16th	Emmie. Dinner. Miss Ormerod 3.30 Tube.
Sunday 17th	Burnet's all day! Whoopee.
Monday 18th	Tita 1pm. Frenchie 6.30.
Tuesday 19th	John 4pm. Hans and Terence supper.
Wednesday 20th	Lovely day in Suffolk [?at Emmie Tillett's house in Bungay].
Friday 22nd	Hair 12.
Saturday 23rd	Margaret Britton aft and ev.
Sunday 24th	Edinburgh 10.15 [train from] Kings X.
Tuesday 26th	Degas with Burnet and Alec. 3.30 Dr [Hans] Gal.
Wednesday 27th	Maria [Curcio]'s birthday. 3.30 Usher Hall Reh.
Thursday 28th	Edinburgh. *Das Lied*. Van Beinum. Patzak. Concertgebouw. Reh 10am. Lunch Richard.
Friday 29th	Basil – lunch. **Tea – Laura Cooper.** Peter and Maria *Mathis* [*der Maler*. British stage premiere of Hindemith's opera given by Hamburg Opera conducted by Leopold Ludwig].
Saturday 30th	Youth concert. **12.15 Laura Cooper** *Albyn*. **Lunch – John Pritchard? Rhona.**
Sunday 31st	Afternoon. Fischer-Dieskau. Rehearsal 5pm.

September:

Monday 1st	Cowans lunch. 10.30 Press Bureau. **12.15 Laura Cooper.**
Tuesday 2nd	Edinburgh. Usher Hall. 10am reh. Lunch Alice and Rhona. Brahms: *Liebeslieder* Waltzes Op.52 and Finale (zum Schluss), *Neue Liebeslieder Waltzes* Op.65. Three vocal 4tets Op.64. [8–8.55 and 9.10–9.40pm. Irmgard Seefried, soprano, Julius Patzak, tenor, Horst Günther, baritone, Hans Gal and Clifford Curzon, piano duet].
Wednesday 3rd	Luncheon. Mr Creswell Scott: Music Merchants Assoc., Royal British, 20 Princes St. 12.15–12.45. Hair 2.30. [Edinburgh] Tattoo.
Thursday 4th	*Messiah*. Reh 12–1 Usher Hall. Lunch – Tita. Miss Speedy *Scotsman* 3pm [?interview].
Friday 5th	Edinburgh. *Gerontius*. Hallé. Reh 2–5.

Saturday 6th	Edinburgh. *Messiah*. 7.30. Hallé. Reh 10–1.
Sunday 7th	12.30 *Albyn* Laura Cooper. 10.40[pm] train.
Monday 8th	Home. Hospl. 3.45. .
Tuesday 9th	Hospl.12.15. 7 Last songs of Mahler.
Wednesday 10th	11.30 Hair. Train Padd[ington] 4.45, [Hereford] 8.30 *Green Dragon* [Hotel].
Thursday 11th	Hereford. *Gerontius*. Laura Jones coming round. *Green Dragon* [Hotel].
Saturday 13th	11.45 Euston, Manchester 3.40.
Sunday 14th	Sale. Odeon Cinema. Hallé. 2.30. 75gns. Art thou troubled, Che faro, Hark, Alto Rhap. Reh 10–1.
Monday 15th	Carnforth. Leighton Hall. 8.30 Gerald. [programme] as for Croydon [see 23rd]. [Hospitality] Mrs Reynolds.
Wednesday 17th	Hospl. 2pm Bought new chest of drawers – adorable!
Thursday 18th	Prom. 7.30 Reh 11.30. Serious Songs and Myra.
Friday 19th	In bed – <u>very</u> [underlined three times] poorly mit cold.
Saturday 20th	1pm *Etoile*, Burnet. Emmie's dinner 7.30.
Sunday 21st	Lunch Jamie and Yvonne. Sir Arthur [Bliss] 6pm 15 Cottesmore Gdns., W8.
Tuesday 23rd	Croydon. Civic Hall. Lunch hour 1.5–1.55. Gerald. Lunch Mr Callender. Prepare, Turtle, Hark. *Frauenliebe*. Thro' the fair, I once loved a boy, Spanish lady. Draft of telegram to Hilda Gélis-Didot: Thank you for wonderful parcel. Look forward with great pleasure to your visit. With love. Kathleen.
Wednesday 24th	11.30 Miss Heath. 1pm lunch Harewood's. Hilda G-D arrives. *Savoy*. Bernie out pm. Epstein Tate Gallery. Draft of telegram: My best wishes and deep regret at unavoidable absence.
Thursday 25th	*Mermaid* Theatre 6.30. Bach cantatas. Bernie. German.
Friday 26th	Reh. Freddy?
Saturday 27th	Gerald 3pm. *Mermaid* Theatre *Dido* 6.30.
Monday 29th	BBC 3rd programme. Lieder Schubert 10.25–11.15pm [BBC Maida Vale, Studio 2, Frederick Stone, piano. Reh 8.15pm]. 18 [mins.] Suleika [I], Romanze [from *Rosamunde*], Rastlose Liebe, Junge Nonne, Wasserflut. [Myra Hess played solo items by Schubert and Schumann].
Tuesday 30th	St Sepulchre. [Recital in aid of the] Mus[icians'] Benev[olent Fund]. 1 hour. 5.30pm Bist du bei mir, Art thou troubled, Praise the Lord. Four Serious. Soft day, Little Rd, Close thine eyes, Song of pilgrims. Decca contract renewed 30th Sept. Supper Sir Ben's.
October:	
Wednesday 1st	Westminster Abbey 11.30am. Rehearse 3pm. Peter. Gerald.
Thursday 2nd	Peterborough. Recital with Gerald. 6.30pm rehearsal. Bist du bei mir, Art thou troubled, O praise the Lord. Brahms: Alto Rhapsody. Four Serious Songs. Soft day, Little Rd, Close thine eyes, Pilgrims Song. *Great Northern* Hotel.

Friday 3rd	Bernie's burfday. Reh 3.
Saturday 4th	Reh 3.
Sunday 5th	London Vic[toria] and Albert [Museum] 8pm. Peter and Gerald morning. Ena coming. Monteverdi duet, Bist du bei mir, [duet with] Peter [by] Morley, [Purcell] *Corydon. Abraham and Isaac.* Schumann duet. Von ewiger Liebe, Auf dem See, Vergebliches Ständchen. Folksongs.
Monday 6th	ISM [Incorporated Society of Musicians] dinner. Roy and Bo. 2.30 X-Ray. Hurseal [a portable radiator advertised at the time for £13.17.11d].
Tuesday 7th	Recdg. Kingsway Hall 2–5, 6–9. [Arias by Bach. London Philharmonic Orchestra, Sir Adrian Boult, conductor]. Qui sedes, Agnus Dei, Grief for sin, It is finished.
Wednesday 8th	Rcdg. 10–1, 2–5. [Kingsway Hall. Arias by Handel. London Philharmonic Orchestra, Sir Adrian Boult, conductor]. Father of Heaven, O thou that tellest, Despised, Return O God of hosts. Tita dinner. Sleeper.
Thursday 9th	Bridge of Allan. Museum Hall. Recital. 8pm. Gerald. Prepare, Turtle, Hark. *Frauenliebe.* Liebestreu, Mainacht, Auf dem See. Fair, Bonnet, Yowes, N'castle. *Royal* [Hotel].
Friday 10th	Sleeper.
Sunday 12th	Paddy. Lady Jarratt 2.30.
Tuesday 14th	Hair 10am.
Wednesday 15th	1.15 *Mirabelle*, Curzon St downstairs.
Thursday 16th	*Café Royal* 12.45. Mr Boosey. Peter.
Saturday 18th	RAH *Messiah*. Sir M.S. 7.30. Reh [no time entered].
Sunday 19th	Mary Gillow, *Flemings* Hotel, Half Moon St 6.30.
Monday 20th	Passport! Tita 2pm.
Wednesday 22nd	Hospl. Tea Auntie May [scored through].
Thursday 23rd	Fly [to Dublin]. *Gresham* Hotel. Fare £7.15.
Friday 24th	Reh evening 6pm. Phoenix Hall (Radio Eireann Orchestral Studio).
Saturday 25th	Dublin. *Theatre Royal.* Hallé. Orchestral concert. 3pm. [Art thou troubled, Che faro, Hark the ech'ing air].
Sunday 26th	Dublin *Theatre Royal. Gerontius.* 3pm. Reh 10.30.
Wednesday 29th	Manchester FTH. Hallé. Four Serious Songs. Gold sandals £5.16.9.
Thursday 30th	Manchester FTH. Hallé. Sleeper.
Friday 31st	Theatre – Alec. *Ritz* 7pm.
November:	
Saturday 1st	Lunch Emmie's. Maitlands.
Sunday 2nd	Windsor. Little Chapel, Windsor Park. *Messiah* Lunch 12.30. Reh 1.30. Perf. 3.30. [attended by H.M. the Queen, the performance was conducted by Lionel Dakers, the other soloists were Isobel Baillie, William Herbert and Owen Brannigan].

Monday 3rd	Gerald 4pm.
Tuesday 4th	Philharmonia Concert Society. Recital. Festival Hall. Gerald. Evening. Prepare thyself Zion, Turtle, Hark, Bess. *Frauenliebe*. Liebestreu, Blaues Auge, Mainacht, Sonntag, Botschaft. She walked thro' the fair, Bonnet, I once loved a boy, Spanish lady. Alec and Rosalind, Alice, Jamie [and] Yvonne – meal.
Wednesday 5th	Lady Lamington 9.
Thursday 6th	Maria lunch.
Friday 7th	Tita supper.
Saturday 8th	Lunch *Savoy* Grill 1.15. Fitzgeralds.Win.
Sunday 9th	Burnet's.
Monday 10th	Prof Krips 3pm at home. 4pm Richard Lewis. Covent Garden 5pm? Flix. Dinner.
Tuesday 11th	Tita 1.15.
Thursday 13th	Hair 10am. Monarch 8833 Lord Moore 6.15.
Friday 14th	Maurice 12.30. Gerald – lecture.
Saturday 15th	Highgate Archway. Recital Gerald. 7pm. Reh 11am. Where'er, Soothing, Hark, Bess. *Frauenliebe*. Après un rêve, Lydia, Nell. Bable, October Valley, Go not, P.R.T.
Sunday 16th	Piano reh. Krauss 5pm.
Monday 17th	Albert Hall. Vienna Phil[harmonic Orchestra] *Kindertotenlieder*. 8pm. Reh 10am – earlier piano reh. **Furtwängler.** Clemens Krauss.
Tuesday 18th	Huddersfield Glee and Mad[rigal Society]. Town Hall. 3 groups. Gerald. Where'er, Hark, Piu dicesti, Che faro. Junge Nonne, Gretchen, Lachen, Musensohn. Go not, Little Rd., Bonnet, Ca' the yowes, Bobby Shaftoe.
Wednesday 19th	6pm Derek. *Boheme*. Tita drink after.
Thursday 20th	Hospl. 11.30 Taxi hospl. £1. Ena afternoon.
Friday 21st	Oxford. Kathleen Long. Mrs Atkinson, Boar's Hill House. *Frauenliebe*. Junge Nonne, Wandrers N., Gärtner, Auf ein altes Bild, Sonntag, Botschaft.
Sunday 23rd	London. Festival Hall. *Das Lied [von der Erde]* 7.30. Reh am. [Richard Lewis, tenor]. Josef Krips [conductor].
Monday 24th	Connaught Rooms 12.15 for 12.45 lunch – cancelled. [Went to the] Royal Concert. Royal Festival Hall 8pm. Baroness Ravensdale after [at] 9 the Vale, Chelsea SW3.
Tuesday 25th	Flemings 7pm.
Wednesday 26th	2.45 Hospl. Taxis £1. Emmie, Roy and Bo, Myra.
Friday 28th	Hospl. Ballet – Yvonne.
Sunday 30th	**Leigh. Recital. Gerald.**
December:	
Monday 1st	Letter from the Prime Minister!! [an arrow to the right-hand page implies that it arrived on Wednesday 3rd].
Tuesday 2nd	K[athleen] Long.

Wednesday 3rd	Lunch 12.30 Neville Cardus, *Ivy* and Brumas. John 4.30. Win and Fluffie.
Thursday 4th	Burnet and Yvonne.
Friday 5th	Hospl. 10.45.
Saturday 6th	Sheffield City Hall 7pm. *Messiah*. Reh 2–5. Morning train. Tita.
Sunday 7th	Manchester Belle Vue. *Messiah* 2.30pm.
Monday 8th	Train to Carlisle. Wyn.
Tuesday 9th	Wyn Heth[erington].
Wednesday 10th	Ena's. Dinner – Phyl. 7pm Ena's.
Thursday 11th	Carlisle. Central Hall. 7.30. Gerald. Mrs Don. *Red Lion* [Hotel]. Prepare, Soothing sleep, Piu dicesti, Che faro. An die Musik, Junge Nonne, W. Nachtlied, Erlkönig. Serious Songs. Bable, Go not H.D., Lt Rd to Beth., P.R.T.
Friday 12th	Freddie [Stone]. 11.30. Lunch Francis Stonor. Ena.
Sunday 14th	Gerald 11.30. Blech concert. [Harry Blech Quartet?]
Monday 15th	Kathleen 4.30.
Tuesday 16th	Ernest Lush 11.30.
Wednesday 17th	Reh 8.30–9.30. Recdg. 9.30–10.30. Studio 2 Maida Vale. Brahms [see 24th].
Thursday 18th	Reh 7–8. Pre-recording 8–9. Studio 2, Maida Vale. Ernest Lush. Alleluia, 3 Mummers, Oct. Valley, G.N.H.D., Pilgrim's song [?No.2 from *Pilgrim's Progress* by Vaughan Williams]. Howard Ferguson [*Discovery*] [All scored through].
Friday 19th	Gerald.
Saturday 20th	Gerald.
Monday 22nd	2pm. Charles Groves BBC Maida Vale. Tita 2.30ish. .
Tuesday 23rd	BBC *Messiah*. 7.15–9, 9.15–10. Reh 10.30–1.30. Studio 1 Maida Vale.
Wednesday 24th	BBC recording Third [Programme] 8.30. Tita aft. Auf dem See, Ruhe Süss., Blinde Kuh, Mainacht. *Zigeunerlieder*.[see 17th]. Lunch Hamiltons, Alison's dinner.
Thursday 25th	Myra – tea. Emmie's – dinner.
Friday 26th	Mémé's.
Saturday 27th	Mr Boosey 6pm. 7.45 Lady Lamington with Win.
Sunday 28th	Emmie, Lady Wood, Myra.
Wednesday 31st	11am Covent Garden. [draft of a telegram to] Dr Vaughan Williams O.M., Dorking: Sincere and affectionate greetings and all good wishes.

Diary for 1953

January:

Thursday 1st — Awarded C.B.E.!! Lovely party. 100s messages. Very spoiled. Ormerods (3). Moores (2). J.B. (2). Us (3). Norman Allin (2).

Friday 2nd — 11am Reh – ballet. Hammersmith. 12.30 Hospl. 4. Tita. Win stayed.

Saturday 3rd — Party Ormerod's. Telegrams and letters pouring in.

Sunday 4th — In bed with cold. Wrote letters.

Monday 5th — Photies 10. X-ray 11. Recdg. Kingsway Hall Brahms Alto cancelled. Snotty cold. Letters pouring in! Sophie [Fedorovitch] 5pm.

Tuesday 6th — Recdg 2–5. 4 Serious. Cancelled.

Wednesday 7th — Recdg. 2–5, 6–9. Alto. Serious. Cancelled. Yvonne – JB cancelled. Bloody backache.

Thursday 8th — 12.30 Binks. Room A. Freddie 2.30. *Tristan* rehearsal.

Friday 9th — 10.30 Freddie Ashton. Full rehearsals. Grand. Ben 3. *Tristan* 1st performance marvellous. Supper Tita's.

Saturday 10th — Ernest Lush. 3.30.

Sunday 11th — Nannie Jamieson.

Monday 12th — BBC Ernest Lush [piano. Songs by] Howard Ferguson, Rubbra, [and William Wordsworth]. Reh 2–3. Recdg 3–4. Studio 5 Delaware Rd. [Broadcast on 4th April]. Burnet, Theatre.

Tuesday 13th — Hospl. 10.15. C.G. 10.30. [Covent Garden]

Wednesday 14th — Scarborough Central Hall Recital. Gerald. 8pm Cancelled.

Thursday 15th — 12.30 Hospital.

Friday 16th — 10–1 C.G.

Saturday 17th — Room A 3pm Reh. Tita – supper.

Sunday 18th — Arthur Spencer [BBC] 3pm.

Monday 19th — Hospl. Hardy Amies 2.30.

Tuesday 20th — Reh 2.30.

Wednesday 21st — Hospl. 12. Lunch Yvonne 1pm. Reh 2.30.

Friday 23rd — 12.45 Hospl. 2pm Foyer. Jamie and Yvonne fly to USA.

Saturday 24th — Tita aft. late lunch.

Sunday 25th — Rehs. 10.30. Tita, Ben, K and J. *Mizzen Mast.*

Monday 26th — Reh am. 12, 2–5.

Tuesday 27th — 10.30, 2–5. Piano dress. Dinner Peter, Basil.

Wednesday 28th — 10.30 stage orch. Hospl. 3pm. 7.30 home.

Thursday 29th — 10.30 Act II. Broadcast Third [Programme] records 10.35pm.

Friday 30th — 10.30 Costume etc. 2.30 Hospital.

Saturday 31st — 11.30 Charles Creed.

February:
Monday 2nd   *Orfeo* Dress rehearsal. 10.30.
Tuesday 3rd   *Orfeo* - first night. Bernie. Win. [Frederick Ashton, director, Veronica Dunne (Euridice) soprano, Adèle Leigh (Amor), soprano].
Wednesday 4th   Photos.
Thursday 5th   Douglas Glass 2.30.
Friday 6th   *Orfeo*. Win. Bern. Michael. Binks.
Saturday 7th   **Stage. 11.30.**
Monday 9th   **Phyll[is] Sellick.** 2pm Hospital.
Tuesday 10th   **3.30 [BBC] Manchester. Home [Service] re life story.**
Wednesday 11th   ***Orfeo*. Win, Bernie, Elsie [Suddaby] and Jean [Allen].**
Saturday 14th   ***Orfeo*. Win, Bernie, Paddy, Tony, Uncle B.** Tita.
Monday 16th   **Manchester.**
Tuesday 17th   **Cardiff.** Installation. [CBE investiture. Unable to attend].
Wednesday 18th   **RAH Gerontius. Reh 10am. Wolverhampton**
Thursday 19th   **Hanley.** (Home tonight).
Friday 20th   **Festival Hall. 8pm. Brahms Alto. LPO. Van Beinum. Bradford.**
Saturday 21st   **Leave 9.45am. FH London 2–5, 6.30–9.30 RFH.**
Sunday 22nd   **London F.H.**
Monday 23rd   **Edinboro.**
Tuesday 24th   **Edinboro.**
Wednesday 25th   **Edinboro.**
Thursday 26th   **London.**

March:
Sunday 1st   **Leigh Hippodrome 7pm.**
Monday 2nd   **Glasgow.**
Thursday 5th   **Birmingham Town Hall. 7pm.** *Das Lied.* **Reh 11.30. Rudolf Schwarz.**
Sunday 8th   **Southend-on-Sea. Odeon Theatre** *Messiah.* **3.15. Reh 11am. Mdme. Freda Parry.**
Tuesday 10th   **Broadcast BBC.**
Thursday 12th   **York. Phyl. Tempest Anderson Hall. 7.30 Recital.**
Sunday 15th   **aft. Festival Hall [London]. Sale Choir [Cheshire], fee to include accomp.**
Tuesday 17th   **BBC 10.30–10.45 Home S[ervi]ce.**
Friday 20th   Removal to 40 Hamilton Tce.
Saturday 21st   **Royal College of Music. Rehs. 2–5, 6–9.**
Sunday 22nd   **RAH** *St Matthew Passion.* **11 and 2.30.**
Tuesday 24th   Jean Moore 3.45.
Thursday 26th   Megan Foster 4.
Friday 27th   **BBC Home Service Friday recital.** Norman Allin.
Saturday 28th   **Royal College of Music. Rehs. 2–5 Rehearsals.**
Sunday 29th   **RAH** *St Matthew Passion.* **11 and 2.30**
Monday 30th   Ann [Ayars?] 4pm.

April:

Thursday 2nd	**Manchester FTH 7pm** *Gerontius*. Temperature 101 – couldn't go home!
Good Friday 3rd	No papers. Cold as charity. Longer day than usual.
Saturday 4th	**Sheffield. Gerontius. 7pm. City Hall**. HOME! HEAVEN. With Win, Bern, Mollie [Turner] and Rhona. Surrounded by flowers. [Broadcast 6.50–7.20pm of recording session of 12th January].
Sunday 5th	**Manchester FTH** *Messiah* **Hallé**. Jamie and Yvonne and John Gielgud came in, also June and Franz [Osborn].
Tuesday 7th	**Liverpool. Phil.** *Enchantress* **[Bliss] and group. 7pm. Reh 2pm.**
Monday 13th	**Devizes Corn Ex. 7pm. Alto Rhap. Art thou troubled, Cradle song, Hark with strings and encores ditto. Send strings F. V. Weaver, Homerfield, Devizes.**
Wednesday 15th	**Bristol. Colston Hall**. Enid and sister. Mollie.
Thursday 16th	Locks am. Ben aft. Rhona. Ernest Lush.
Friday 17th	**Manchester FTH. Recdg?**
Saturday 18th	Out in garden on seat. Heaven. Burnet to lunch. June in.
Sunday 19th	Fluffie 7.30.
Monday 20th	**Leeds Town Hall**. [overview lists **Glasgow** with **Leeds** entered on 23rd].
Tuesday 21st	Heavenly day – hot sun. JB aft lunch.
Wednesday 22nd	**Newcastle City Hall**. Gorgeous birthday. Win, Evelyn and Enid to supper.
Thursday 23rd	Sir Raymond Evershed and Ben tea. Binks dinner.
Friday 24th	Ben and Peter. Corset fitting 4.30. Mrs Hilton, Moll 4.45.
Saturday 25th	**Edinburgh Music Hall**. Win, Gerald and Enid, Jamie.
Monday 27th	**Leicester. De Montfort Hall**. Molly and Win.
Tuesday 28th	Rhona tea. Bun theatre. Win.
Wednesday 29th	Anita Moiseiwitsch. Seefried. Molly. Yvonne. Tita. Veronica Dunne.
Thursday 30th	**London. Festival Hall**. Party – Hamiltons. Sicked up mi dinner!

May:

Friday 1st	Ben 4.30. Molly. Rhona. Tina staying [Barbirolli's niece Maria Concetta Gibilaro].
Saturday 2nd	**Liverpool Phil 7pm.** *Gerontius*. **Reh 2–5**. Jamie.
Sunday 3rd	Photie in *Times* – lovely. Uncle Bert. Gladys Parr. Nancy. Emmie. Bill and Meg Douglas Gerald and Enid.
Monday 4th	Molly. Tina.
Tuesday 5th	12pm Arthur Spencer. Ben 4.30.
Wednesday 6th	**Manchester FTH. Mahler 2**. Moll dinner.
Thursday 7th	**Manchester**. Nurse Yaegers 5.30.
Saturday 9th	*Orfeo*
Sunday 10th	Easy day for a change!

Monday 11th　　　　**BBC.** John and Leon 6.30.

Tuesday 12th　　　　*Orfeo?* Tita and Ev[elyn] lunch. Gerald and Enid. Mr Haddy and Lee – Decca [sound engineers].

Wednesday 13th　　*Orfeo?* John Mallet. Lady Esher. Ben and K. Ormerod. Pat Davies. Moll.

Thursday 14th　　　Dr Eccles. Derek. Tina.

Friday 15th　　　　　Moll.

Saturday 16th　　　Miss Hurst 3.30. Win home. Filthy weather.

Sunday 17th　　　　Quiet day. Rain, wind and a ha'porth of sun. Jamie. Hans and Terence.

Monday 18th　　　　*Orfeo* **BBC.** Victor [Olof] – lunch. Binks. Mollie.

Tuesday 19th　　　　*Orfeo* **BBC.** Mrs Gordon. 3pm X-ray.

Wednesday 20th　　**Yvonne Arnaud 4.30. Rhona – dinner.** Win.

Thursday 21st　　　**Bath. Gerald and Enid. Sir Ben. Rhona.** Doc.

Friday 22nd　　　　**Bath.** Veronica 4. Win and Moll. Dr Eccles – must have mi ovaries removed.

Saturday 23rd　　　**Bath Abbey Mass in B minor. 4.15–5.30, 5.45–7. Reh 11.30.**

Monday 25th　　　　**BBC** *Orfeo.* **Festival Hall. Coronation Concert LSO.**

Tuesday 26th　　　Hospital again. JB.

Wednesday 27th　　**Harrogate. Royal Hall. Hallé.**

Thursday 28th　　　**Recdg.** *Orfeo.*

Friday 29th　　　　**Recdg.** 4.30 Yvonne Arnaud.

June:

Monday 1st　　　　**Rehs.** *Spring* **Symphony.**

Tuesday 2nd　　　　**Reh evening Maida Vale.** Coronation. Enid.

Wednesday 3rd　　**London. Festival Hall.** *Spring* **Symphony. 8pm.**

Thursday 4th　　　**London 3rd programme. Cancelled.**

Wednesday 17th　　Enid.

Thursday 18th　　　Bun.

Tuesday 29th　　　K.M.V.'s birthday [god-daughter Kathleen Mary Vincent, whose birthday is actually on June 30th].

July:

Thursday 2nd　　　Prue's birthday.

August:

Monday 31st　　　　**Prom [rehearsal].**

September:

Tuesday 1st　　　　**Prom. RAH.** *Kindertotenlieder.* **7.30.**

Thursday 3rd　　　**Edinburgh [the period 3rd to Sunday 13th is bracketed].**

Monday 28th　　　　**Rehs?**

October:

Monday 5th	**Leeds Town Hall.** *Coronation* **Mass – Mozart. Krips. Mahler 2.**
Tuesday 6th	**Leeds.** *Apostles* [Elgar]. **Sargent.**
Thursday 8th	**Leeds.** *Mass of Life.* **Delius.** [Kathleen died this day].
Saturday 10th	**Leeds Festival.** [scored through in diary but not in the overview].

[There are no further entries in Kathleen's diary for 1953].

OCTOBER 1953   OCTOBER 1953

Mon. 5 Leeds. Town Hall. *Coronation Mass. Mozart* Krips

Fri. 9

Tues. 6 Leeds *Apostles - Sargent.*

~~Leeds Festival.~~   Sat. 10

Wed. 7

19th after Trinity Sun. 11

Thur. 8 Leeds *Mass of Life Delius*

Memo.

Selected Tributes

Bishop Cuthbert Bardsley's Address spoken at the Memorial Service held at Southwark Cathedral on Tuesday 24th November 1953.

Wisdom of Solomon Chapter 4 vv.13 and 14: 'He being made perfect in a short time, fulfilled a long time: for his soul pleased the Lord'.

Substitute the words 'she' and 'her' for 'he' and 'him' and this verse exactly fits Kathleen Ferrier.

From time to time the news of a person's death shocks a nation. One can recall the death of the late Archbishop William Temple or the death of Dick Sheppard. Millions mourned the loss of somebody they had come to love.

Few deaths have caused such a widespread sense of bereavement as that of Kathleen Ferrier.

In less than ten years her voice had become known and valued throughout the length and breadth of Britain and indeed the world. People stood in queues for her concerts. Millions listened to her voice over the wireless.

Wherein lay the secret of her success? Hard work? Seldom has anyone devoted herself with greater abandonment to her craft.

Joie de vivre? Her exuberant love of life communicated itself through everything she sang.

Artistry? Her innate musicianship brought to perfection through training and intelligence made her one of the greatest singers of all time.

But over and above hard work, joy in life and artistry there was something else – an indefinable other worldliness. She seemed to bring into this dull, drab world of time and space a radiance from another world. She was as one exalted. Her face shone. Her character proclaimed an inner harmony with the Divine Source of beauty and truth. She was at times transfigured. A shining radiance not of this world came forth from her.

And yet she was no recluse. With both feet planted firmly on the ground she noticed and loved her fellow men. Her work revealed a deep humanity.

Born among the warm hearts of the North country, her mysticism found expression in a genuine compassionate caring for her fellow men. She wore herself out on their behalf. Travelling long hours in crowded railway carriages, sleeping in badly heated hotels, endeavouring to answer every human appeal for help.

She knew that she was a steward of a great and glorious possession and was determined to use it to bring happiness into the lives of millions.

Wherever she went she brought gaiety and fun to people whose lives were difficult and dreary. Her sense of humour was irrepressible, her gaiety infectious, the dullest party would come alive under the magic of her charm, the saddest life would find fresh hope because of her overflowing gaiety.

Her life was no easy progress to fame. Brought up in a schoolmaster's home in Blackburn, she worked for nine years as a telephonist in a Lancashire post office. Till 1937 prosaic progress through local music festivals. Then, following the discovery of the unique quality of her voice, the hard, relentless, grinding work that inevitably lies behind the headlines and highlights of a famous name.

No, not an easy life. A life of constant setbacks, sorrows and disappointments that led to her final suffering and premature death.

But through it all her character was fashioned – the character that shined like a beacon of hope in this grey and groping world.

To meet her was to meet one who called you from the cloying consolation of a dull mediocrity. For you discovered instantly that here was a being whom nothing less than the best could satisfy. She evoked from people ideals and aspirations that once had shined bright but which had in the course of years been allowed to become dim. She challenged the jaded to fresh efforts. She encouraged the despondent to new attempts.

The incomparable beauty of her voice will ever remain among the most cherished possessions of our memory.

All of us will have different memories. For some the loveliness of her singing of the Angel's music in Elgars *Dream of Gerontius*. Some will remember her singing of Bach's 'Have mercy Lord' – others again will ever see before them her face as she sang 'He was despised and rejected of men'.

We meet today under the shadow of a great loss. These grey walls in which but a few years ago her voice brought joy and gratitude into the lives of hundreds, will never hear her voice again.

And yet she would not have us mourn as they who have no hope. In Kathleen Ferrier the walls of time and space seem very fragile.

She was, if I may dare say so, a celestial spirit with one foot in eternity and the other in time.

She calls us onward to fresh endeavour. Her arms surround us. Her presence is with us. She is, I feel sure, singing in other spheres and some echo of that voice will come to comfort us in moments of depression.

She could not have sung as she did had she not been possessed by a living faith in God, the source of all beauty and truth. That faith was communicated to us during her lifetime. We felt the better for meeting her. She longs to communicate her faith to us now.

As I was writing this tribute to her memory, I seemed to sense her presence bidding me bring you the assurance that she is alive. Her vibrant presence still lives – she, though dead, yet speaks. She bids me remind you that death is not the end – rather is it the passing from one room to another in God's great household of life.

For 42 years God lent us Kathleen Ferrier. She brought to us (as Mr Gerald Moore so vividly expressed it) a spiritual beauty, an unearthly nobility, an all-embracing humanity that seared our souls.

For that precious gift we praise our God. And we believe that in the halls of eternity once again we shall be privileged to hear that voice we loved long since and lost awhile.

Till then we shall go forward strengthened by our memories, fortified by our faith in Jesus Christ who taught us that death is but the gateway to eternal life and encouraged by the presence and prayers of one whose character and artistry will ever evoke from our lips a psalm of gratitude and a song of praise.

[Letter from Benjamin Britten to Winifred Ferrier]
11th October 1953   4 Crabbe St., Aldeburgh, Suffolk
My dear Wynn.

Our thoughts are very much with you, as indeed they have been these last terrible months. May I send my deepest sympathy?

There is no need to say how much we loved and admired darling Kath, how we treasured her friendship, and were honoured and proud to work with her and for her. It is unbelievable that she is no longer with us, and that we shall never hear that glorious voice again. But it will be a very long time before the memory of countless lovely concerts fades, and I myself will never forget, selfishly, her incomparable *Lucretia* or *Abraham and Isaac*. They were written for her, and in future one will only hear pale copies.

If there is anything we can do please let us know, but I know that Kath's innumerable friends will be ready to help.
With deepest sympathy
Benjamin Britten

[Letter from Peter Pears to Winifred Ferrier]
[11th October 1953]   4 Crabbe St., Aldeburgh, Suffolk
My dear Win.

It was such dreadfully sad news – although of course not unexpected – but one always hopes for miracles, and at one time a miracle seemed to have happened. I am so dreadfully sorry and want to send you my very warmest thoughts of sympathy for the loss of such an adorable sister and friend. You know very well how much she was loved by every single person who had the privilege of knowing her. What a brave, creative, loving creature she was. We shall all miss her terribly. There's no one like Kath.
Much love to you my dear
Yours ever
Peter Pears

[Letter from John Barbirolli to Winifred Ferrier]
8.X.53   8 St Peter's Square, Manchester 2
My dear Win

Helpless and utterly at a loss as I feel to say anything, I still want to send you a word, even an inarticulate one. She was a wondrous being and I feel very humbly privileged to have known and loved her. Only those of us near to her in these last few months can have known her true greatness, and the miracle of her sublime courage, and the exquisite dignity with which it was borne, will live with me and be an inspiration for ever. I shall be eternally grateful that I was with her a little last Sunday, Monday and Tuesday. On Tuesday [two days before she died] I somehow sensed she was saying goodbye to me, and that the merciful sleep of eternity would not long be denied her, for she was already beginning to acquire a radiance and loveliness not of this earth. The kind of radiance she suffused us with when she sang the Angel in *Gerontius*, a radiance and comfort she will continue to give to this troubled world, through her Blessed Art, as long as this poor world remains civilised.

My love to you ever

John

Appendix

Judging by Kathleen's regular purchases of stamps ('Stamps 5/-' is frequently part of a diary entry), there must have been many more letters than the 409 gathered within this book and hopefully more will come to light. Here are four late arrivals. The first letter mentions a concert given in London by Marian Anderson, the black American contralto. The two singers had met some three months earlier during Kathleen's American tour. According to Win's biography, Anderson attended the rehearsal for *Orfeo* conducted by Pierre Monteux at San Francisco on February 15th 1950 and her immediate response to hearing Kathleen's voice was 'My God, what a voice and what a face!' The 'Doc' mentioned could be Dr John (surname unknown), recipient of Letter No.197.

No.397 [Letter to Bill and Benita Cress]
29th May [1950]   2 Frognal Mansions, NW3
Dearest Bill and Benita

Another grand letter waiting from you when I arrived home from a week's holiday in Scotland yesterday. It is lovely to hear from you and I love all the bits and bobs you put inside. Thank you so much for sending us the parcel – it hasn't arrived yet – they take about six or seven weeks – but oh! we will bless you for all the trouble you have taken, and the contents will be just wonderful. Things are looking up here a bit now – petrol has just come off the ration, the first time for ten years – so perhaps butter, meat and sugar will soon follow. I love the two stories in your latest letter and 'our father' nearly dropped his teeth larfing.

I am so relieved to hear Doc has got a new maid – what a joy – long may she last to fatten him up!

The bath is still reposing in the hall, but the lav's back in its usual place – heaven be praised. But we're going to look awfie smart when we're all through, so I guess it's worth it.

Now I go to Vienna on the 4th June and stay at the *Astoria* Hotel there until the 17th – then on to *Grand Dolder* Hotel, Zurich until 3rd July – oh boy – that looks a lovely place.

Ann Ayars is here and with two friends of mine we went to hear Marian Anderson last night in the Albert Hall – 7000 seats and every one taken including platform ones. It is rare to see such a capacity house in this barn of a place. She looks a lovely person and she had a great reception – her spirituals were very beautiful and moving – the many negroes in the audience (I've never seen so many – didn't know there were so many in all England!) must have been proud of her.

Ann is here to do Antonia in [*Tales of*] *Hoffman* (film) with Sir Thomas Beecham, but so far has just been held up because of words copyright – and is she fed up after flying all the way in a hurry. She's a honey of a girl and would give you a lovely concert if you wanted her anytime – she's NCAC.

I had a lovely rest in Scotland but it <u>was</u> cold and no central heating – I'm getting soft since my American trips! We painted and viewed the amazing scenery and it was all very peaceful and nice.

Many, many happy returns to you both for another 50 anniversaries – may they all be as good as last year's – that was a good party wasn't it? I still have my cork in pride of place – on mi mantelpiece, not where <u>you</u> think despite the dry rot!! you bad girl!

Much love to you both and thank you for everything – look after yourselves and I'll look forward to hearing from you in Vienna!

God bless, much love

Kaff

The other three letters are to another contralto, this time Nancy Evans, Kathleen's fellow-Lucretia in 1946. Although the word 'divorce' is never mentioned in the first letter ('the very sound of the word is horrid'), Kathleen's own marriage had just been annulled in 1947 and Nancy Evans would divorce Walter Legge and marry Eric Crozier within a year. By this time Kathleen's view of her own twelve-year non-marriage was of 'a millstone round my neck' and, having gone through the process, she is offering Nancy her support. The second letter was written the day after the premiere of Britten's opera *Albert Herring* at Glyndebourne. Kathleen's phrase 'everybody's sore eyes' is probably a reference to the song in Act 2 Scene 1, 'That's a fine sight for sore eyes', sung to the character and singer called Nancy.

No.398 [Letter to Nancy Evans]

Thurs[day April 17th 1947]   In train

Bless you, dear Nancy, for lovely letter knowing the stacks of letters you must have to reply to, it was all the more precious. I have kept meaning to ring you up to say 'Come and celebrate' but the tempus has fugited and new songs and works have raised their ugly heads and my smalls have cried out for a whiter wash – so the celebrations have been postponed.

I am so glad for you that something satisfactory is happening – it is such a plunge to take and the very sound of the word is horrid, but the feeling to me now is as the releasing of a millstone round my neck and I'm sure it will be to you too. Bless you, love – if there's anything I can do to help at any time, I'm all yours.

I wonder if you are free for lunch on any of these days? (this is the joggliest train ever) Wed. 23rd April, Tues. 29th, Fri. May 2nd? It would be gorgeous if you were and we could giggle together – say at *Casa Prada* (Warren St.) at 1pm. <u>Do</u> look in book, darlint! Leave flat tomorrow (Fri.) at 10am until 22nd so four words on p.c. 'Can Cum on –' will do beautifully.

Loads of love.

Kathleen

No.399 [Letter to Nancy Evans]

Sat. morning [June 21st 1947]   2 Frognal Mansions, London NW3

Dear Beau'ful Nancy

  We came round and said inadequate words of praise to everybody last night but missed you, love. You must have shot off to room and I wondered if you were feeling like I always do on these occasions – with relief and excitement – wanting to cry on everybody's bosom?! Isn't it daft? I had to make a quick exit on Wed[nesday] night and it looks so potty when you're happy and thrilled to bits.

  Bless you, dear Nancy, for a most lovely performance – you looked ravishing, completely confident, sympathetic and a joy to everybody's sore eyes and ears. I heard nothing but praise and my ears were pinned back.

  I <u>did</u> want you to know how proud, pleased and very moved we all were for your success and all the Herrings too.

My love

Kathleen

The final letter was probably written in the summer of 1953. We know that a television set was hired so that Kathleen could watch the Coronation. The Club was her hospital room, transformed at six o'clock into an 'illicit' bar which provided drinks for visiting family and friends.

No.400 [Letter from Bernadine Hammond to Nancy Evans]

Tuesday [June or July 1953]   [University College Hospital]

Dear Nancy

  Kath says to please thank you very much for the narcs and exotic water lilies. They have been a joy, especially the latter. Kath is a little better, getting on slowly but we think more surely now. She is taking a great interest in the cricket and tennis on the television, keeping us all well informed.

Much, much love

Bernie

[P.S.] Will let you know when the Club reopens – we'll blow our heads off with champagne corks!

On the very day that I was editing the final proofs of this book I received a telephone call offering me a further nine letters. They were found in a copy of Winifred's biography owned by Jerry Field Reid and his wife Mary Carter, and I am grateful to their niece Rowan Denyer for contacting me. Field Reid's Christian name was actually Eric, but he called himself Jerry and to confuse matters further Kathleen addressed him as Gerry. Born in 1903, he was a music lover, amateur flautist and by profession a water engineer. The letters, sent to his Westminster home, were written in the space of a year between 18th January 1944 and 14th January 1945. Field Reid is mentioned just once in her diary, on Thursday 13th January 1944, the occasion which prompted Kathleen to write the first of these letters. Field Reid married his second wife Mary Carter in October 1946. She was a professional violinist, who led the Carter String Trio, with Anatole Mines and Peggie Sampson as her colleagues. Towards the end of her life Kathleen sang Gordon Jacob's *Songs of Innocence* with the Trio at the Guildhall in Cambridge (see diary entry for 29th May 1952). As an oratorio soloist under conductors Boyd Neel and Reginald Jacques, Kathleen frequently encountered Mary who was also a front desk player in their respective orchestras.

No.401 [Letter to Gerry Field Reid]
Tuesday [January 18th 1944]   2 Frognal Mansions, Hampstead NW3
Dear Gerry

This seems to me like 'repayment a thousand fold'. Good Heavens – I didn't want any coffee back! I only gave you about a tablespoonful. Thank you very much indeed. It smelt so good when I opened it. Pop and I had a cup each even though it was almost lunchtime.

By the way, after you left on Thurs[day] I found two bottles both half full of coffee. (Shows the state of my cupboards!) They were hiding behind multitudinous (?) sundries.

I don't know any hymns except 'There is a Tavern' and 'Little Brown Jug'.

You weren't unkind re photos – only one of many who think they're frightful. Had them 'done' again – will see result tomorrow.

I enjoyed Thursday too very much, only I didn't notice you were tongue tied! I'm afraid I make noises through mouth and nose and am unaware of same – you should have nipped me – it's a bad habit I've got – one of many!

Thank you again very much indeed for a lovely time on Thurs and <u>pounds</u> of coffee in return for a spoonful!
Lots of luck.
Yours etc
Kathleen

No.402 [Letter to Gerry Field Reid]
Saturday [February 12th 1944]   In train [to Colne]
My dear Gerry

I have been an age replying but I have had a terrific ruddy blush this week and am feeling slightly numb as a result!

We have had a week of late concerts [CEMA tour of Staffordshire], plenty of travelling and intermittent food. I was looking forward to a rest on Monday and Tuesday, but at the last moment have to deputise for Astra Desmond who is ill. Which gives me eleven concerts in as many days. These two extra ones are recitals with Gerald Moore, which makes life easier but they are something of a strain. So when I eventually get home I am going to bed for two days and disconnecting phone!

I love the photograph of Jean Layton – I think it's a beauty. I enclose same here, and hope it's no worse. Have been with Olive Zorian this week – I think she's grand. She said she had met you. We got on like a house on fire – two Lancashire lassies let loose (allitteration [*sic*] begorra!)

This is writing under difficulties, so forgive the brevity and the scribble.

Kind greetings. Keep the write-up. I may be glad of it one day! Was it bribery and corruption that you managed two tickets for Southwark? Amazing I call it!
Sincerely
Kathleen

No.403 [Letter to Gerry Field Reid]
[Tuesday February 22nd 1944]   2 Frognal Mansions, Hampstead NW3
                                       In train [from Bishop Auckland to Newcastle]
Dear Gerry
Thank you so much for nice letter. It was a dull do, wasn't it? But then they always are. I looked all over audience [Elgar's *The Kingdom* on 19th February at Southwark Cathedral] but couldn't see you anywhere. Wasn't it a shiverer too? My goodness, it was cold, after sitting for about 6 hours – rehearsal and performance.

I'll have to see what I can do about the hat, though probably with fur to match coat, it would take at least a year's savings!

Am just on my way to Newcastle for CEMA. Am in a non-smoker with 3 blokes smoking me out, so I'm going to go 'off the handle' any minute – mi blud's up!

Thank you again for writing. I hope 'The Passion' is a bit better and the atmosphere not quite so cold. Hope it didn't bring your flu on again.
Cheerio
Yours
Kathleen

No.404 [Letter to Gerry Field Reid]
Tuesday 21st March [1944]   2 Frognal Mansions, Hampstead NW3
Dear Gerry
I am terribly sorry to have been such an age replying. Your letter followed me round for a while and I have been 'on the trot' ever since I recd. it.

How good of you to write letters blowing my trumpet to the Anglo Austrian Soc[iet]y.

My next concerts in London are April 1st (*St Matthew*), April 7th *Messiah* in Albert Hall and the evening of same day *Messiah* at Archway Hall. Then I am away almost continuously until the middle of May, but not appearing in London.

March 22nd I'm in Cleethorpes. I am going there today actually at 4pm. I am terribly sorry to have left it so long – I would have loved to have come if I'd been free.

Forgive me for being a bad correspondent – only came home yesterday after weeks away. Hope you are very fit – what a narrow squeak Eve [Kisch] had – whattalife!

Yours

Kathleen

No.405 [Letter to Gerry Field Reid]

Saturday [1st April 1944]   2 Frognal Mansions, Hampstead NW3

                                                                In train to Leicester

Dear Gerry

You made me feel like a <u>real</u> prima donna today! Thank you so very much for the wondrous orchids – they are simply lovely. You are very observant – I didn't even notice Isobel [Baillie] was wearing flowers last time.

I have worn them all day – my 'Professor' (!) said I had better not wear them for the performance – it being a funereal sort of 'do' [*St Matthew Passion* at Southwark Cathedral] but I donned them again as soon as it was over. I am sorry I didn't see you. Win said she had a few words with you.

It was terribly cold again, wasn't it? I wish they would do these things in the summer.

Eve stayed with us last night but we hadn't time for much chatter, as I had been travelling all night from Glasgow the night before and was ready for bed when she arrived at 11pm and I had to shoot off for rehearsal this morning, besides having a husband at home too, to cook a breakfast for (sorry! for whom to cook a breakfast).

This <u>is</u> a whirling train – I hope you can read this.

Thank you again, Gerry, very much indeed for the wonderful orchids – the first I have ever had. Hope you are very fit.

Yours etc

Kathleen

No.406 [Letter to Gerry Field Reid]

[24th May 1944]   2 Frognal Mansions, Hampstead NW3

Dear Gerry

I think it's Wed. but I'm not sure! Have been doing 2 concerts a day with Dr Jacques and haven't had time to think. Am at this moment waiting to go on to do my stuff to hundreds of schoolchildren [in Wolverhampton]. Sufficeth it to say that I am in Welsh Wales on the 25th to my sorrow – that's tomorrow – I have to start off on an 8am train [to Tonypandy].

Loads of love to Eve and say I am looking forward to doing the Telemann again at Leicester [29th June].

My sister said the broadcast was very badly balanced. – I had a streaming cold and nearly gave it up, but staggered thro' at the last minute.

Must shoot – Dr Jacques is just about to announce me.

Best wishes

Yours

Kathleen

No.407 [Letter to Gerry Field Reid]
[Envelope postmarked Hampstead, Monday 17th July 1944]

                                        2 Frognal Mansions, Hampstead NW3
Dear Gerry

Still all in one piece (crossing fingers) despite doodlebugs.

Sorry you weren't at Hampton Court [16th July] – it was all a terrific rush as I had broadcast in the aft[ernoon] and I hardly saw anyone to speak to. Rushed off after singing as old friend turned up from Aldershot and had to get back there, so we had to do a rush for buses and trains.

The siren went in the middle of my Gluck but by swelling out veins and achieving a rich puce in colour – managed to drown it – nearly!

This is my 13th letter and I'm getting writer's cramp so forgive the brevity thereof.

Best wishes
Kathleen

No.408 [Letter to Gerry Field Reid]
23.9.[19]44   In train [to Worcester]
Dear Gerry

Thank you very much for letter. So glad you enjoyed the 'Stabat Mater' [by Dvorak broadcast on 13th September]. It is lovely to sing and I thought probably t'was more exciting to take part in it than to be a member of audience. (This train is <u>leaping</u> about – making this very difficult).

For the next 2 months I am hardly at home at all, and I have so much to learn, that when I am, I must 'burrow' deep into the large stacks which await me. All my jobs at the moment seem to be new works or songs – when *Messiah* time comes along, life will be busy but not so hectic.

I have just finished an American hospital tour, which, but for one concert has been an utter fiasco and a waste of time, so I have been in a tearing temper all week and am only just now recovering.

So glad for Eve and her success at Durham – I hope she is a terrific success. Glad to hear too that you are still in one piece despite front line activity.

Best wishes
Sincerely
Kathleen Ferrier

No.409 [Letter to Gerry Field Reid]
Sunday [14th January 1945]   2 Frognal Mansions, Hampstead NW3
                                                        In train [to Pontypool]
Dear Gerry

Thank you very much for two lovely cards. I am so terribly sorry to hear Eve is ill. I don't know her address, so could you forward the enclosed for me? I heard she wasn't well just before Xmas in Durham area, but didn't know it was so serious. I <u>do</u> hope she is improving now.

For the last 3 months I have hardly been at home and life has been fairly hectic, and I have so much to learn in the way of new works etc., that for the moment it is all bed and work, especially as we are entirely without help at home.

I hope you are thriving and successfully avoiding these beastly rockets – life is complex isn't it?

Am just on my way to S. Wales – very early – Sunday morning and very cold – on these occasions I dream enviously of a normal 9–5pm office job!

Best wishes for 1945.

Sincerely

Kathleen

Bibliography

Books directly relating to the life and career of Kathleen Ferrier:

Campion, Paul: *Ferrier. A career recorded* (Julia Macrae, London 1992, Thames rev. 2005)

Cardus, Neville ed.: *Kathleen Ferrier. A memoir* (Hamish Hamilton, London 1954)

Ferrier, Winifred: *The Life of Kathleen Ferrier* (Hamish Hamilton, London 1955)

Leonard, Maurice: *Kathleen. The Life of Kathleen Ferrier (1912–1953)* (Hutchinson, London 1988)

Lethbridge, Peter: *Kathleen Ferrier* ('Red Lion Lives') (Cassell, London 1959)

Rigby, Charles: *Kathleen Ferrier. A biography* (Robert Hale, London 1955)

Spycket, Jérôme: *Kathleen Ferrier* (Payot Lausanne, Lausanne 1990) (in French)

Further reading:

Baillie, Isobel: *Never sing louder than lovely* (Hutchinson, London 1982)

Blunt, Wilfred: *John Christie of Glyndebourne* (Bles, London 1968)

Brook, Donald: *Singers of today* (Rockliff, London 1949)

Carpenter, Humphrey: *Benjamin Britten, a biography* (Faber, London 1992)

Douglas, Nigel: *More legendary voices* (Andre Deutsch, London 1994)

Hammond, Joan: *A voice, a life* (Gollancz, London 1970)

Hughes, Spike: *Glyndebourne* (Methuen, London 1965)

Kennedy, Michael: *Barbirolli, Conductor Laureate* (MacGibbon & Kee, London 1971; Barbirolli Society, rev. 2003)

Moore, Gerald: *Am I too loud?* (Hamish Hamilton, London 1962)

Moore, Gerald: *Furthermoore. Interludes in an accompanist's life* (Hamish Hamilton, London 1983)

Reid, Charles: *John Barbirolli, a biography* (Hamish Hamilton, London 1971)

Ryding, Erik and Pechefsky, Rebecca: *Bruno Walter, a world elsewhere* (Yale University Press, New Haven and London, 2001)

Smith, Cyril: *Duet for three hands* (Angus & Robertson, London 1958)

Steane, John: *Singers of the century* (Duckworth, London 1996)

Personalia

Adams, Haydn: singer.

Ager, Laurence: composer.

Allen, George: singer

Allin, Norman: singer.

Alsop, Ada: singer.

Anderson, Helen: singer, CEMA
organiser for the north east.

Anderson, Marian: singer.

Angeles, Victoria de los: singer.

Ansermet, Ernest: conductor.

Armstrong, Thomas: conductor,
organist at Christ Church, Oxford.

Arnaud, Yvonne: actress, musician.

Arnell, Richard: composer.

Ashcroft, Peggy: actress.

Ashton, Frederick: choreographer,
Orpheus at Covent Garden, 1953.

Atkins, Sir Ivor: conductor, organist of
Worcester Cathedral.

Atkinson, Dorothy (née Ferrier): cousin.

Austria, Maria: photographer.

Ayars, Ann: Kathleen called her
'Euridice', the part she sang in
Gluck's *Orfeo* at Glyndebourne in
1947 and in New York, 1950.

Baillie, Isobel: singer.

Baker, George: singer, by 1953 Chairman
of the Royal Philharmonic Society.

Ball, Beryl: member of staff at Ibbs
and Tillett, and later Emmie Tillett's
secretary.

Barbirolli, Lady Evelyn: oboist, wife of
Sir John.

Barbirolli, Sir John: conductor.

Barbirolli, 'Mémé': mother of Sir John.

Barbone, Nina: singer.

Bardsley, Dr Cuthbert: Bishop of
Croydon, gave the address at
Kathleen's Memorial Service.

Barker, Alfred: conductor and orchestral
leader.

Barker (née Chadwick), Annie:
singer and friend from Blackburn.
Kathleen's first singing teacher.

Barker, Tom: singer, husband of Annie
Chadwick.

Barnard, Anthony: conductor, organist,
pianist and composer.

Barnes, George: Head of BBC Third
Programme.

Barry, Mary: accompanist.

Bartlett, Ethel: pianist.

Bateman, Nancy Ellis: singer.

Bates, Cuthbert: conductor, founder of
City of Bath Bach Choir.

Bay, Emanuel: accompanist.

Beecham, Adrian: composer and eldest
son of Sir Thomas Beecham.

Beecham, Sir Thomas: conductor.

Beinum, Eduard van: conductor.

Benjamin, Arthur: composer.

Berkeley, Lennox: composer.

Berman, Rita: friend in America, cousin
of Edward Isaacs.

Bernac, Pierre: singer, Kathleen's coach
for French when learning Chausson's
Poème.

Bernadotte, Count Folke: diplomat

Bertram, Hilda: pianist.

Bilbo, Jack: painter and founder of the
Modern Art Gallery.

Bimrose, Eric: organist

Bing, Rudolf: General Manager at
Glyndebourne, Director of the
Edinburgh Festival 1947–1949.

Bliss, Sir Arthur: composer.

Blackburn, Marjorie: accompanist.

Blom, Eric: writer on music.

Boosey, Leslie: co-proprietor of

publishers Boosey & Hawkes, lessee of Covent Garden 1944 - 1949.

Booth, Webster: singer

Boughton, Rutland: composer.

Boulanger, Nadia: composer.

Boult, Sir Adrian: conductor.

Bowes-Lyon, David: brother of Queen Elizabeth, neighbour of Kathleen's friend Burnet Pavitt.

Boyce, Bruce: singer.

Boyd, Dreda: friend and neighbour in Frognal Mansions.

Bradfield, Jane: Winifred Ferrier's companion and friend.

Bragg, Frances: friend from Silloth.

Braithwaite, Warwick: conductor.

Brannigan, Owen: singer.

Bristol, Ronald: singer.

Britten, Benjamin: composer.

Brook, Donald: writer on music.

Brownlee, John: singer

Bruck, Charles: conductor.

Brunskill, Muriel: singer.

Busch, Fritz: conductor.

Bush, Alan: composer.

Butt, Clara: singer.

Caccia, Lady Anne: wife of Sir Harold Caccia, British Ambassador to Austria 1951–1954.

Cade, Sir Stanford: surgeon at Westminster Hospital.

Callender T.E.: chief librarian and General Manager Civic Hall, Croydon.

Cameron, Basil: conductor.

Cameron, Douglas: cellist.

Campoli, Alfredo: violinist.

Caplat, Moran: assistant General Manager at Glyndebourne.

Cardus, Neville: music critic.

Carner, Mosco: conductor, writer on music, married to Helen Pyke.

Carson, Vi[olet]: accompanist, later TV actress famed for the role of Ena Sharples in *Coronation Street.*

Carter, Mary: violinist.

Casals, Pablo: cellist.

Cassidy, Claudia: music, drama and dance critic for Chicago newspapers.

Catley, Gwen: singer.

Cebotari, Maria: singer

Chadwick, Annie: see Barker, Annie.

Cheselden, Kathleen: member of staff at Ibbs and Tillett, wife of tenor Eric Greene.

Childe, Mantle: pianist.

Choveaux, Nicholas: organist of St Bartholomew-the-Great and organiser of concerts.

Christie (née Mildmay), Audrey: former singer and wife of John.

Christie, John: founder of Glyndebourne Festival Opera.

Clayton, Wilfred: accompanist.

Clinton, Gordon: singer.

Coates, Albert: conductor.

Codner, Maurice ('Uncle'): painted portrait of Kathleen Ferrier.

Cohen, Harriet: pianist.

Cole, Maurice: pianist.

Cole, William: organist, conductor and pedagogue.

Collard, André: accompanist.

Cook, Dr Edgar Thomas: organist of Southwark Cathedral.

Copley, Arthur: singer.

Coyd, Eleanor and Bill: friends living in Cumbria.

Creed, Charles: couturier.

Crellin, Herbert G.: conductor of Archway Choral Society.

Cress, Benita (Bonnie) and Bill: friends living in La Crosse, Wisconsin, USA.

Crewdson, Henry: Clerk to the Worshipful Company of Musicians.

Cronheim, Paul: Director of Netherlands Opera

Crook, Gladys: CEMA official in London.

Cross, Joan: singer.

Crozier, Eric: producer of *Rape of Lucretia.*

Cruickshank, Miss: school teacher at Blackburn High School.

Culbert, Tom: singer.

Cullen, Ailie: accompanist.

Culp, Julia: singer.

Culshaw, John: record producer at Decca.

Cummings, Henry: singer.

Cunningham, George (G.D.): conductor

and organist at Birmingham Town Hall.

Curcio, Maria: pianist, wife of Peter Diamand.

Curzon, Clifford: pianist.

Dakers, Lionel: organist.

Dallen, Beryl: accompanist.

Danco, Suzanne: singer

Danieli, Elena: singer.

Darke, Harold: organist and conductor.

Davies, Gerald: singer.

Davies, Meredith: conductor.

Davies, Pat: singer.

Davies, Rick: antiques dealer from Liverpool and Kathleen's partner for some years.

Dawber, Dr Harold: conductor and Music Director of the Maia Choir, Stockport.

Derville, Anthony: producer Home Talks Department, BBC.

Desmond, Astra: singer.

Diamand, Peter: Director of the Holland Festival.

Dispeker, Thea: American agent and member of the Music Committee of Casals' Prades Music Festival.

Dobrowen, Issay: conductor.

Douglas, Basil: member of staff at the BBC music department, later an agent.

Douglas, Billy: surgeon in Manchester.

Dowling, Eddie: American actor, producer, composer, song and screen writer.

Draper, Ruth: entertainer and diseuse.

Duerden, Margaret (née Ferrier): cousin, married to Thomas Duerden.

Duerden, Thomas: organist of St John's Church, Blackburn, Kathleen's second singing teacher

Dunlop, Yvonne: amateur composer.

Dunne, Victoria: singer, Euridice in *Orpheus* at Covent Garden, 1953.

Duval, Nel: singer, Amor in *Orfeo* at Holland Festival, 1951.

Eadie, Noel: singer.

Easton, Robert: singer.

Ebert, Carl: opera producer at Glyndebourne.

Eccles, Dr C Yarrow: homeopath and family doctor to Myra Hess.

Edelmann, Otto: singer

Egerton, Lady Margaret: Lady-in-waiting to Princess Elizabeth.

Ellis, Kenneth: singer.

Emery, Wilfred: organist and Master of Music at Glasgow Cathedral.

Enesco, Georges: conductor.

England, Leslie: pianist.

Evans, Nancy: sang the title role of Lucretia in the alternate cast at Glyndebourne, 1947.

Evershed, Sir Raymond: Master of the Rolls 1942–1962.

Ewing, Sherman: American producer.

Falkner, Keith: singer, British Council Music Officer in Italy.

Favoretto, Giorgio: accompanist for her visit to Italy, 1951.

Fedorovitch, Sophie: scenery and costume designer for *Orpheus*, Royal Opera House, Covent Garden 1953

Ferguson, Howard: composer.

Fermoy, Lady Ruth: founder of the Kings Lynn Festival.

Ferrier, Anne: sister-in-law.

Ferrier, David: nephew.

Ferrier, George: brother.

Ferrier, George: uncle.

Ferrier, Maud: aunt.

Ferrier, William: father ('Pop' or 'Pappy').

Ferrier, Winifred: sister.

Field-Hyde, Margaret: singer.

Fineman, Gustaf: German agent based in Cologne.

Finneberg, Laelia: singer.

Fischer-Dieskau, Dietrich: singer.

Fleischmann, Ernest: impresario and orchestra manager.

Flothuis, Marius: Dutch composer.

Fonaroff, Nina: dancer and choreographer.

Fontaine, Leon: pianist and administrator.

Forbes, Watson: violist.

Foster, Megan: singer

Foster, Muriel: singer.

Francis, John: flautist and founder of the London Harpsichord Ensemble.

Franckenstein, Sir George: former Austrian ambassador, domiciled in UK during WW2.

Freeman, Pearl: photographer.

Fullerton, Joan: singer.

Furtwängler, Wilhelm: conductor.

Gal, Hans: composer and pianist.

Gale, Muriel: singer.

Gardner, Margaret: headmistress of Blackburn High School.

Gélis-Didot, Hilda: patron of Parisian music salons.

Gibbs, Terence: employed at Decca, then music producer at CBC in Canada.

Gibilaro, Alfonso: Sicilian pianist and language coach for *Orfeo* at Glyndebourne 1947. Barbirolli's brother-in-law.

Gibilaro, Maria Concetta (Tina): daughter of Alfonso and Barbirolli's niece

Giddy, Reginald: cellist and writer.

Gilbert, Geoffrey: flautist.

Gilbert, Max: violist.

Glasgow, Mary: head of CEMA.

Glass, Douglas: *Sunday Times* photographer.

Glynne, Walter: singer.

Goehr, Walter: conductor.

Goldberg, Simon (later Szymon): violinist.

Goldsbrough, Arnold: conductor.

Good, Margaret: pianist wife of cellist William Pleeth.

Goossens, Leon: oboist.

Greene, Eric: singer.

Greenwood, Hubert: accompanist.

Griffis, William: American actor and New York friend.

Griller, Sidney: leader of Griller String Quartet.

Groves, Charles: conductor.

Gucht, Jan van der: singer.

Günther, Horst: singer.

Gylling, Einer: Dutch agent, who she also called 'Einer Kleine'.

Haddy, Arthur: Decca sound engineer.

Hageman, Ingrid: singer.

Halban, Desi: singer.

Hambourg, Mark: pianist.

Hamilton, Hamish ('Jamie'): publisher and friend.

Hamilton, Yvonne: wife of Hamish.

Hamilton-Smith, Janet: singer.

Hamlin, Mary: singer.

Hammond, Arthur: Musical Director of the Carl Rosa Opera Company.

Hammond, Bernadine: nurse, companion and secretary to Kathleen from March 1951.

Hammond, Joan: singer.

Hardie, Albert: accompanist.

Harding, Victor: singer

Hardman, Clement: singer.

Hargreaves, John: singer.

Harrison, Eric: accompanist.

Harrison, Julius: conductor.

Harrison, Rex: actor.

Harrison, Tom: CEMA organiser in the Midlands.

Hawkes, Ralph: co-proprietor of music publishers Boosey and Hawkes.

Head, Michael: singer and composer.

Heath, Marjorie 'Binks': radiographer at University College Hospital.

Heifetz, Jascha: violinist.

Henderson, Captain Nigel: Naval Attaché in Rome.

Henderson, Roy ('Prof'): singer and Kathleen's fourth teacher.

Henie, Sonja: ice skater and actress.

Herbert, William: singer.

Herlie, Eileen: actress.

Hess, Myra: pianist.

Hessen-Kattenburg, Mrs van: friend and correspondent in Holland.

Hetherington, Wyn: friend.

Heyworth, Peter: music critic and writer.

Hill, Helen: singer.

Hill, Sir Roderic: Air Chief Marshal, Rector of Imperial College.

Hilton, Dr Gwen: consultant radiotherapist (clinical oncologist) at University College Hospital.

Hilton, Dr Reginald: Kathleen's doctor and consultant physician at St Thomas' Hospital, amateur violinist.

Hobson, Edna: singer.

Holland, Adrian: accompanist.

Holliday, Judy: actress.

Hollweg, Ilse: singer.

Holmes, Laurence: singer.

Holst, Henry: violinist.

Homburger, Walter: Canadian agent.

Hopkins, John: conductor.

Hornby, Cyril: singer.

Horowitz, Vladimir: pianist.

Horsley, Colin: pianist.

Howard-Johnston, Lady Alexandra: daughter of Earl Haig, wife of historian Hugh Trevor-Roper.

Howe, Janet: singer.

Hull, Sir Percy: organist of Hereford Cathedral.

Humby, Betty (Lady Beecham): pianist and wife of Sir Thomas Beecham.

Hunter, Ian: Director of the Edinburgh Festival, 1950 – 1955.

Hurst, Audrey: in charge of BBC engagements at Ibbs and Tillett.

Hutchinson, Dr John Ernest ('Hutchy'): teacher, adjudicator and Kathleen's third singing teacher.

Ibbott, Daphne: accompanist.

Iliff, James: accompanist.

Isaacs, Edward: pianist and composer, founder/director of the Tuesday Manchester Midday Concerts.

Isaacs, Harry: pianist.

Isaacs. Leonard: Music Supervisor, BBC European Service.

Jacobson, Ena: journalist.

Jacobson, Maurice: accompanist, adjudicator, chairman of the music publishers J Curwen.

Jacques, Dr Reginald: conductor of the Jacques Orchestra and the Bach Choir, Director of CEMA.

Jamieson, Kathleen: school friend from Blackburn High School.

Jamieson, Nannie: violist.

Jarratt, Lady: wife of Sir Arthur Jarratt, a director on the board of the English Opera Group.

Jarvis, Alan: fine arts and furniture expert.

Jewitt, Patricia (Paddy): until 1951 Kathleen's secretary and companion to her father William Ferrier.

Johnston, James: singer.

Johnstone, Maurice: Head of Music at the BBC in Manchester.

Jones, Parry: singer.

Jones, Roderick: singer.

Jones, Trefor: singer.

Joyce, Eileen: pianist.

Juler, Pauline: clarinettist.

Karajan, Herbert von: conductor.

Kaye, Danny: comic actor.

Keane, Sir John: Irish barrister and politician.

Kent, Flora: accompanist.

Kersey, Eda: violinist.

Kinloch, Louise: sang the role of Amor in *Orfeo* in New York, 1950.

Kirby, Alan: Croydon businessman, amateur choral conductor, friend of Elgar.

Kisch, Eve: CEMA organiser in the north west. Flautist.

Kleiber, Erich: conductor.

Klemperer, Otto: conductor.

Koeman, Greet: singer, Euridice in *Orfeo* at Holland Festival, 1951.

Kohler, Irene: pianist.

Korchinska, Maria: harpist.

Kraus, Otakar: singer.

Krauss, Clemens: conductor.

Krips, Josef: conductor.

Kubelik, Rafael: conductor.

Kyasht, Lydia: ballet dancer.

Lam, Basil: BBC producer.

Layton, Jean: violinist

Leafe, Rowland: conductor.

Legge, Walter: record producer.

Lehmann, Lotte: singer.

Leigh, Adèle: sang Amor in *Orpheus* at Covent Garden, 1953.

Lereculey, Sadie: member of staff at Ibbs and Tillett.

Lewis, Anthony: conductor and musicologist.

Lewis, Richard: singer.

Llewellyn, Redvers: singer.

Lloyd, David: singer.

Lloyd, Roderick: singer.
Lofthouse, Thornton: harpsichordist.
London, George: singer.
Long, Kathleen: pianist.
Long, Norman: entertainer.
Loveday, Alan: violinist.
Loveridge, Iris: pianist.
Lowe, John: conductor.
Lumsden, Norman: singer.
Lunn, Louise Kirkby: singer.
Lush, Ernest: accompanist.

Mackenzie, Compton: writer.
MacKinlay, Jean Sterling: Scottish
  folksinger and lecture-recitalist.
Mahler, Alma: widow of the composer
  Gustav Mahler.
Mahler, Anna: daughter of the
  composer Gustav Mahler.
Maitland, Alexander and Rosalind:
  friends with whom Kathleen stayed
  when in Edinburgh.
Malcolm, George: harpsichordist.
Mallet, John: fine art expert.
Manton, Stephen: singer.
Marsden, Harold: conductor.
Mason, Gwendolyn: harpist.
Mason, Stanley: singer.
Massary, Fritzi: singer, actress.
Masters, Robert: violinist.
Mayer-Lismann, Else: music lecturer
  and opera workshop director.
McBean, Angus: photographer.
McKenna, John: singer on CEMA
  tours, recommended Kathleen to Eve
  Kisch.
McLean, Eric: Canadian broadcaster.
Menges, Herbert: conductor.
Menges, Isolde: violinst wife of Herbert.
Mertens, Andre: Kathleen's New York
  manager at Columbia Artists.
Mildmay, Audrey: see Christie, Audrey.
Miles, Bernard: actor, theatre and
  festival director.
Miles, Maurice: conductor.
Milne, Alison: violist and mother of
  Kathleen's son Christopher.
Mines, Anatole: violist.
Mitchell, Ena: singer and friend in
  Carlisle.
Moeran, E.J.: composer.

Moiseiwitsch, Benno: pianist.
Monteux, Pierre: conductor.
Moore, Gerald: accompanist.
Moorhouse, Kathleen: cellist.
Morel, John: singer.
Mukle, May: cellist, owner of the MM
  (Mainly Musicians) Club.
Mullinar, Michael: accompanist.
Mullings, Frank: singer.
Mundy, Clytie: American singing coach.
Murday, Donald: singer.
Murray, Albert: Kathleen's maternal
  uncle Bert.

Nash, Heddle: singer.
Neel, Boyd: founder/conductor of the
  Boyd Neel Orchestra.
Neveu, Ginette: violinist.
Newmark, John: accompanist.
Newton, Ivor: accompanist.
Nielsen, Flora: singer.
Nikolaidi, Elena: Greek-American
  singer.
Nixon, Monica: a Director of Ibbs and
  Tillett.
Norman, Lady: born Florence Priscilla
  McLaren, socialite and former
  suffragette.
Nowakowski, Marian: singer.

Olivier, Sir Laurence: actor.
Ollson, Kjell: accompanist.
Olof, Victor: recording manager at
  Decca.
Oppenheim, Hans ('Oppy'/'Oppi'):
  associate conductor and coach at
  Glyndebourne.
Ord, Boris: conductor, Director of
  Music at Kings College, Cambridge.
Ormerod, Sir Benjamin: judge, friend
  from Blackburn.
Osborn, Franz: pianist.
Otterloo, Willem van: conductor.

Packer, Ruth: singer.
Parr, Gladys: singer.
Parry, Freda: founder of Southend-
  on-Sea Music Club orchestra.
Parsons, William: singer.
Patzak, Julius: singer.
Pavitt, Burnet: friend.

Pearl, Ruth: violinist and leader of a string quartet.

Pears, Peter: tenor, sang Male Chorus in the first cast of *Rape of Lucretia*, Glyndebourne, 1947.

Peasgood, Osborne: organist.

Penn, Irving: American fashion photographer who photographed Kathleen Ferrier for *Vogue*.

Phillips, Frank: singer, later a BBC radio newsreader.

Phillips, H.B. and Mrs: owners of the Carl Rosa Opera Company.

Phillips, Rhona: nursing sister at University College Hospital.

Piper, John: opera set designer.

Pizzey, George: singer.

Pleeth, William: cellist, married to pianist Margaret Good.

Pollak, Anna: singer.

Poulet, Gaston: conductor.

Pounder, Ella: accompanist.

Primrose, William: violist.

Pritchard, John: accompanist, conductor.

Procter-Gregg, Humphrey: pianist, composer and conductor.

Pyke, Helen: accompanist and composer, wife of Mosco Carner.

Pynn, Norris: composer

Raphael, Mark: singer.

Ravensdale, Baroness: Mary Curzon, music lover and socialite.

Raybould, Clarence: conductor.

Reach, Edward: singer.

Read, Ernest: conductor.

Reiner, Fritz: conductor.

Riddick, Kathleen: conductor of the London Women's Symphony Orchestra.

Riddle, Frederick: violist.

Rignold, Hugo: conductor.

Ripley, Gladys: singer.

Ritchie, Margaret (Mabel): singer.

Robertson, Rae: pianist.

Robinson, Clive and Vera: Oslo friends of Emmie Tillett with whom Kathleen stayed in October 1949.

Robinson, Edward G.: actor.

Robinson, Stanford: conductor.

Rodzinski, Artur: conductor.

Rofe, Miss: PT teacher at Blackburn High School.

Rogier, Frank: singer.

Rossican, Isja: accompanist in Holland for Kathleen's visit in April 1948.

Roth, George: cellist.

Rowlands, Ceinwen: singer.

Rubbra, Edmund: composer.

Russell, Francis: singer.

Sabata, Victor de: conductor.

Sammons, Albert: violinist.

Sampson, Peggie: cellist.

Sandor, Arpad: accompanist.

Sargent, Sir Malcolm: conductor.

Sarton, Harry: Manager of Artists' Department at Decca records.

Saul, Eileen: a friend in Carlisle.

Scherman, Thomas: conductor.

Schiøtz, Aksel: singer.

Schnabel, Artur: pianist.

Schneider, Hans: costume designer for *Rape of Lucretia*.

Schoeffler, Paul: singer.

Schumann, Elisabeth: singer.

Schuricht, Carl: conductor.

Schwarz, Rudolf: conductor.

Schwarzkopf, Elisabeth: singer, wife of Walter Legge.

Seefried, Irmgard: singer.

Sellick, Phyllis: pianist.

Serkin, Rudolf: pianist.

Settle, Ronald: accompanist.

Shacklock, Constance: singer.

Shawe-Taylor, Desmond: music critic.

Silver, Millicent: harpsichordist, wife of John Francis.

Simberg, Herman: singer.

Simpson, Phyllis: music mistress at Carlisle High School.

Sladen, Victoria: singer.

Smith, Cyril: pianist.

Spencer, Arthur: BBC music producer.

Spender, Stephen: poet.

Spottiswoode, Nigel: cinematographer.

Spurr, Phyllis: accompanist.

Stadlen, Peter: composer, pianist, musicologist and critic.

Stanelli (Edward Stanley de Groot): entertainer.

Statham, Heathcote: conductor, composer and organist.

St Clair, Meriel: singer and teacher.

Stear, Ronald: singer.

Stern, Isaac: violinist.

Stiedry, Fritz: conductor of *Orfeo* at Glyndebourne, 1947.

Stignani, Ebe: singer.

Stoll, Jeffrey: accompanist.

Stone, Frederick: accompanist.

Stratton, George: violinist.

Stravinsky, Igor: composer.

Stresemann, Wolfgang: conductor, composer.

Suddaby, Elsie: singer.

Suggia, Guilhermina: cellist.

Sumsion, Herbert ('John'): organist and conductor.

Sutton, Joyce: singer.

Susskind, Walter: conductor.

Svanholm, Set: singer.

Szell, Georg: conductor.

Tango, Egisto: conductor.

Tankard, Geoffrey: pianist.

Taylor, Hindley: singer.

Taylor, Joan: singer, pupil of Roy Henderson.

Tete, Dottie: writer and editor, friend of Ann Ayars.

Teyte, Maggie: singer.

Thalben-Ball, George: organist.

Theuveny, Franck: pianist

Theuveny, Marie-Claude: violinist.

Thomas, Marjorie: singer.

Thomson, Harold: accompanist.

Thompson, Alan: Kathleen's dentist.

Thorndike, Sybil: actress.

Thorne, Gordon: BBC Music producer in Manchester, composer and pianist.

Tidboald, David: conductor and composer.

Tillett (née Bass), Emmie: Joint Managing Director of Ibbs & Tillett.

Tillett, John: Joint Managing Director of Ibbs & Tillett.

Titterton, Frank: singer.

Toscanini, Arturo: conductor.

Tourel, Jennie: singer.

Trevisani, Fulvia: singer.

Trimble, Joan and Valerie: piano duettists and sisters.

Turner, Eva: singer.

Turner, John: dress designer.

Turner, Mollie: Kathleen's physiotherapist at University College Hospital.

Tuxen, Eric: conductor.

Tysoe, Albert: conductor.

Vincent, Harry: CEMA organiser for the Potteries and conductor.

Vincent, Kathleen Mary: Kathleen's goddaughter.

Vincent, Jo: singer, (Britten's *Spring Symphony* in 1949 and Mahler's Symphony No.2 in 1951).

Vlachopoulos, Zoë: singer, Amor in *Orfeo* at Glyndebourne, 1947.

Wadely, Frederick: organist and composer.

Walker, Frances: Kathleen's piano teacher.

Walker, Norman: singer.

Wallenborn, Robert: pianist.

Walter, Bruno: conductor.

Walter-Lindt, Lotte: Bruno Walter's daughter.

Walters, Leslie: composer

Ward, Beatrice (Trixie) (née Ferrier): cousin.

Warren, Eleanor: cellist and wife of conductor Walter Susskind.

Wearing, Stephen: pianist.

Webber, Annie: accompanist.

Webster, David: General Administrator, Royal Opera House Covent Garden 1945–1970.

Wendon, Henry: singer.

Weylitsch, Ljuba: singer.

White, Bradbridge: singer.

Whyte, Ian: conductor

Whyte, Marjorie: conductor Bromley and Chislehurst Orchestra.

Williams, Ralph Vaughan: composer.

Williams, Tom: singer.

Wilson, Bert: Kathleen's husband from 1935 to 1947.

Wilson, Marie: violinist.

Wilson, Steuart: Director of Music at

the Arts Council 1945–1948, then Head of BBC Music.

Wood, Anne: singer, manager of the English Opera Group.

Wood, Harry Harvey: founder of the Edinburgh Festival.

Wood, Sir Henry: conductor.

Wood, Dr Thomas: composer.

Woodgate, Leslie: choral conductor.

Wordsworth, William: composer.

Wright, Kenneth: BBC producer.

Wright, Margot: accompanist.

Wynn, Arthur: BBC Music Department, London.

Yacamini, David: composer, organist and CEMA organiser in Scotland.

Zorian, Olive: violinist.

Kathleen Ferrier on Composers

Kathleen Ferrier on Conductors

Kathleen Ferrier on Kathleen Ferrier

1940:
I <u>shall</u> need a lot of pennies that day!

1942:
Malcolm Sargent. O boy!

Audition went off well. Decided to live in London. Phew!

Washed a bit, ironed a bit and made a posh vest out of skirt and pants!

Miserable weather. Practised. Washed and ironed.

Washed and ironed. Poured all the ruddy day. Never knew such weather!

Down to earth with a wallop. No letters.

Washed curtains, hair, self. Wrote letters. 1001 jobs.

Date for National Gallery! Whoopee!!

Dreadful kids in audience. Told 'em off! Good for me! Little brutes.

1943:
Oh boy! did my knees knock!

I've even negotiated the bedpan and haven't done anything over the edge!

1944:
Here's a naughty limerick ... I don't improve, thank God!

I hope you can read it – I am in a train.

I would be grateful if I didn't have to go to Pontypridd.

I have so much to learn and very little time for learning.

I do need some time off for learning all the things I don't know!

1945:
I must learn the *Apostles* sometime!

1946:
I'm a cautious Lancastrian!

I am getting more work than I can cope with.

I'm a very good washer-upper!

Am still enjoying being raped three or four times a week!

I have been very worried by my automaton-like extremities!

If I can keep my engagements down to about ten a month.

I haven't had time to wash my smalls!!

I don't think I'm a very good *Sea Pictures*-ite.

Having just done seven concerts in six days in six different towns, am feeling more than usually weary.

1947:
This is the joggliest train ever.

One of these days he won't know what's hit him!

I wish I didn't cry so easily 'cos I can shout too.

Last night I went to the local with the stage manager and had a dirty big pint.

Come, if only to see me singing my way thro' Hell fire wiv me 'arp in mi 'and!!

From Carlisle to Covent Garden in five years! Lucky Kaff!'

Have been being 'raped' twice a week in the Provinces and I find it very tiring!!

I stabbed myself and fell like a hard-baked dinner roll.

Have been shouting my head off in Huddersfield!

Oh for a peaceful *Messiah*.

[Orfeo] The one part I have always dreamed of doing.

1948:
Whattalife!!

Feeling the complete diva!

Please excuse my writing, – this train is more than usually buoyant!

I'll have to wear my barbed wire drawers – golly is he forthcoming.

1949:

I'LL NEVER PAY MI BILL!!!!

Some of the audience were knitting!! I could have spat on them.

Nice concert but many children picking noses.

Turner-over cried all night!!

Am going to have a bath and leave a tidemark just to get mi moneysworth.

Fly through tornado!! Not at all nice begorra! Glad to be back on terra cotta!

Last *Orfeo* tonight.I think I am very good now in it.

I do wonder why I do it sometimes but wouldn't miss it!

Must go and put mi Tampax in!! T.T.F.N.

He talks about not working me too hard - bollocks!

I've only six weeks in England this year. No ironing!

Better than a kick in mi new nylon pants!

Had some unexpected debauchery!! It did me good!

Well! Well!! WELL!!!

I'm <u>lousy</u> on the stage. I fall over my own feet and wave my arms like a broken down windmill!

Out of a gross $17,500 I had $2,500 left.

Makes you ashamed of being such a lazy linguist.

I can get my 'oo' but I'm buddered if I can get mi 'cuck'!

I am in my element in this sort of music [Bach].

And now for Ben and his beastly augmented 9ths!!

Our father which art in Hampstead.

Jars, bottle and buckets of love.

If the <u>orchestra</u> thinks you are good, then you really <u>are</u> good.

They had to be content with superior nods of the cranium!

1950:

Santa Fe 7000 feet up. Concert went well but oh! so short of breath.

Thought I sang like a cochon, but audience didn't seem to mind.

Wonderful last concert – everybody stamping and shouting!

I am as happy as a lark.

I <u>am</u> a lucky twerp!

Voulez-vous coucher avec moi? – oh no, that's the rude one.

Heigh-ho, ain't I a lucky ole budder!

Sliding innocent-eyed through the Customs.

I'm pickled tink!

'Our father' nearly dropped his teeth larfing.

Shall enjoy having dearmaria with me own lav!

I guess I'm meant to be a lone she-wolf.

I don't like broadcasting – always dither and get frogs!

The more I see of opera the less I want to take part in it, except *Orfeo*.

I'm glad he's interested in my passage.

Gerontius. Sir Adrian. Dull in the extreme.

Roll on 1951.

Inahellovarush!

1951:

Stayed at JB's, saw his meatballs!! Mit garlick.

You're bound to come down once you're up, as the actress said to the bishop!!

Oh! I <u>shall</u> miss him and his good temper and ear-to-ear grin.

God bless all doctors.

It's something about frying mi lover in hot oil.

Told Bernie my worries.

Oh! so depressed.

I had discovered a bump on my 'busto'.

I haven't had a bath for over six weeks! – I don't arf pong!

I'm very lop-sided at the top but am

camouflaging with great taste and delicacy!!

I hope the audience took my groans for passion!!

[Opera] is a lot of play-acting, [whereas] I live and love and die in a song.

What the heck, as long as I feel well and can sing a bit, eh?

I am full of bounce and perkier than ever.

The trouble is on a knob of the spine.

Bernie's a jewel, a jewel, a jewel.

My cup is very full!

I am having a rest, the like of which I haven't had for ten years!

I am playing Mozart violin sonatas with the Doc – not singing a note.

I am feeling very happy.

At this moment I'm jes full o' beans!

I have been frightened of television. My diaphragm would pant from fright.

Played Lexicon and the first word I achieved was 'urine'.

1952:

I am feeling fine and very perky, and am fair, fat and forty (nearly!).

Being a lady of leisure instead of a busy 'low singer'!

Rhyl was a wow; a boarding house with the last meal at five and a plug that wouldn't pull!

Apart from rheumatiz in my back, feel okeydoke.

I'm very lazy at heart!

Concerts with Barbirolli which I always adore. Lucky Kaff.

It's not the singing that's wearying, it's the travelling and social side.

Even got mi nose brown! See you soon – whoopee!

I'm fine – fingers crossed.

Chatted with the young Queen on all subjects – sweet poppet she is.

Turned down Bayreuth, Scala, New York, Stravinsky in Germany – must get my bulbs in!!!!

I am still rheumaticky from the neck down – makes me feel my age ducks!!

Would I receive the honour of Commander of the British Empire? Can a duck swim?

1953:

Awarded CBE!! Lovely party. 100 messages. Very spoiled.

Bloody backache.

In the next week's post I had 300 letters and telegrams!

I will try and rush them at Covent Garden, but it's a bit like moving the Pennines!

The slightest cold sets off my 'screwmatics'.

Hope I can manage to curtsey!!

I snipped a bit of bone off in my leg, so here I am once again reposing in UCH.

Your wonderful, amazing, delicious, heavenly, gorgeous chocolates arrived.

My leg is a bit wonky and I can't negotiate 48 steps.

It's heaven to be in my own bed again, virgin couch though it be!!

I'm fine. Farting freely.

I accept with a very full heart the Gold Medal of the R.P.S.

The telephone has been removed from my room.

With love and oh! such deep gratitude for so much care and kindness.

Wouldn't it be lovely if I could just go to sleep and not wake up again?

See you soon – whoopee !

Index of Letters

(Listed alphabetically by recipient followed by Letter No.)

Index of Works

Repertoire as it appears in lists at the back of Kathleen Ferrier's diary for 1943
Where'er you walk
Hark the echoing air
Deep in my heart
Art thou troubled
Cradle song – Byrd
Arch denial
Water Boy 4tet
O England my country
Down by the Salley Gardens
Spanish lady
My boy Willie
Come ma little darlin'
I have a bonnet
Come, let's be merry
Orchestral pieces
Ave Maria
Softly awakes
To music
Caro mio ben
Che faro
How changed the vision
Art thou troubled
With strings
Che faro – Gluck
Hark the echoing air

Full orchestra
Dove sei
Softly awakes
Strings
Five eyes
Ballads etc
Softly awakes
Caro mio ben
How lovely are thy dwellings
Down in the forest
Arch denial – Arne
O peaceful England
Che faro – Gluck 5½'
Willow Song
None but the weary heart
Come, let's be merry
Ave Maria
Over the mountains
On wings of song
Handel
Where'er you walk
Art thou troubled
How changed the vision
Pack, clouds, away
Lascio ch'io pianga
Spring
Come to me soothing sleep
Purcell
Fairest isle
Hark the echoing air
When I am laid in earth
Bach
Lord, what thou wilt
God is aye our sun and shield
Prepare thyself Zion
Giordano
Caro mio ben
Lotti
Pur dicesti
Schubert
To Music
Erl King
Fishermaiden
Secret
The Trout
Hark, hark the lark
Who is Sylvia?
Ave Maria
Brahms
Four Serious Songs
Constancy
Why go barefoot
Love song
May night
Vain suit
Swallow from over the sea

Index of Places, Venues and Festivals

General Index